IN THE MIDDLE

THIRD EDITION

Nancie Atwell

IN THE MIDDLE

A Lifetime of Learning About
Writing, Reading, and Adolescents

HEINEMANN
PORTSMOUTH, NH

Heinemann
361 Hanover Street
Portsmouth, NH 03801–3912
www.heinemann.com

Offices and agents throughout the world

The author and publisher wish to thank those who have generously given permission to reprint borrowed material:

Excerpt from "An Horatian Notion" in *Split Horizon* by Thomas Lux. Copyright © 1995 by Thomas Lux. Published by Houghton Mifflin Harcourt. Reprinted by permission of the publisher.

"Ten Conditions for Engaged School Reading" from *The Reading Zone* by Nancie Atwell. Copyright © 2007 by Nancie Atwell. Published by Scholastic, Inc. Reprinted by permission of the publisher.

"How to Read History and Science for Understanding and Retention" adapted from *Comprehension and Collaboration: Inquiry Circles in Action* by Stephanie Harvey and Harvey Daniels. Copyright © 2009 by Stephanie Harvey and Harvey Daniels. Published by Heinemann, Portsmouth, NH. All rights reserved.

"Girl Help" from *Poems Old and New, 1918–1978* by Janet Lewis. Copyright © 1981 by Janet Lewis. This material is used by permission of Ohio University Press, www.ohioswallow.com.

Library of Congress Cataloging-in-Publication Data
Atwell, Nancie.
    In the middle : a lifetime of learning about writing, reading, and adolescents / Nancie Atwell. — Third edition.
        pages   cm
    Includes bibliographical references and index.
    ISBN 978-0-325-02813-2
    1. Language arts (Secondary)—United States. 2. English language—Study and teaching (Secondary)—United States. 3. English language—United States—Composition and exercises. I. Title.
    LB1631.A72 2014
    428.0071'2—dc23   2014026845

Editor: Maureen Barbieri
Production: Patty Adams
Cover and interior designs: Lisa Fowler
Typesetter: Kim Arney
Manufacturing: Steve Bernier

Printed in the United States of America on acid-free paper
18 17   EBM   2 3 4 5

DEDICATION

This one is for Anne,
with love and admiration
and in anticipation

CONTENTS

ACKNOWLEDGMENTS

My career and this book owe everything to the friends and associates who ushered in a golden age of research, pedagogy, and professional development in the language arts. How lucky was I to be in the classroom just as the old paradigms of English instruction were being fractured by article after speech after book reporting on real kids and teachers, real classrooms, and the real processes of writers and readers.

A large measure of my good fortune was to be a student of Dixie Goswami's at the Bread Loaf School of English. At the vanguard of the teacher-as-researcher movement, Dixie urged me to observe my students and make sense of my observations by writing about them. She also told me I could write—perhaps her greatest gift and, because of its effect on me, one I made sure to pass along to countless kids.

At Bread Loaf I met Peter Stillman and Bob Boynton of the publishing house Boynton/Cook. They gambled on a book by a middle school English teacher from Maine, and when Boynton/Cook became a part of Heinemann, I did, too. I've been privileged to work with extraordinary executives and editors, people who respect teachers and put what's good for children above all else: Phillipa Stratton and Tom Seavey, Toby Gordon, Mike Gibbons, Lesa Scott, Lisa Fowler, Vicki Boyd, Lois Bridges, Leigh Peake, videographer Kevin Carlson, and Maureen Barbieri, the editor of this third edition. Maureen's readings of a book-in-progress are a writer's dream: careful, specific, insightful, and heartening. She made me want to go back to work, which is no small thing.

I'm the teacher I've become because of the writer and researcher Donald Graves. His influence is that direct and essential. Don's most significant leap of imagination, writing workshop, gave teachers and our students a scaffold—a structure to support authentic self-expression in the classroom. Thirty-five years down the road, it is still strong and essential.

Graves and the writer Donald Murray, in residence together at the University of New Hampshire in the 1980s and '90s, created a mecca for a new breed of teachers and researchers. The curiosity and generosity of the Dons encouraged my work and that of many others. Through them I met and learned from Susan Sowers and Lucy Calkins, Jane Hansen, Brenda Powers, Ruth Hubbard, Linda Rief, Maureen Barbieri, my boon companion Mary Ellen Giacobbe, and the genius of us all, Tom Newkirk, whose friendship and support are unstinting.

Glenda Bissex and Janet Emig introduced me to the concept of children as intentional writers engaged in a process of making meaning, whether preschooler or twelfth grader. The sure instincts of the teacher and humanist Shelley Harwayne have been a touchstone, as have Frank Smith's insights about, well, everything. I learned from Ken Macrorie, Georgia Heard and Ron Padgett, Toby Fulwiler and Art Young, and Alice

Trillin about, respectively, plain style, poetry, writing as a mode of learning, and how to help teachers understand writers and writing.

Closer to home, I'm grateful to decades of seventh and eighth graders, whose prose and poetry are the heart of this book, and to my K–6 colleagues at the Center for Teaching and Learning, who nurture and transform our students as writers and readers. I thank Helene Coffin, Caroline Bond, Ted DeMille, Jill Cotta, and Glenn Powers for their smart work with children, professionalism, and easy laughter.

My daughter, Anne Atwell-McLeod, is a new member of the crew. When I retired at the end of my fortieth year as an educator, the faculty hired her as CTL's teacher of grades 7–8 writing, reading, and history. Her previous experiences as a student in and a teacher of writing–reading workshop, combined with her appreciation of teaching as an intellectual enterprise and her responsiveness to kids, give me hope for the future of the profession. In the words of Walt Whitman, no pressure, Anne, but I'm "Leaving it to you to prove and define it, / Expecting the main things from you."

I thank Anne for typing this manuscript, since I still write everything in longhand. I'm indebted to Patty Adams, my production editor, who is beyond helpful and conscientious; to Lisa Fowler for yet another clean, elegant design as well as her photographs that reveal both my students and the pleasure Lisa takes in kids and classrooms; to editorial coordinator Anthony Marvullo for his work behind the scenes; and to Eric Chalek and Rachel Small for getting the word out with thoughtfulness and enthusiasm.

Finally, I am luckiest to be married to Toby McLeod, the most literate person I know. From him I learned how to read literature, love it, and share my passion for poems and books with my students. He teaches me always, and he makes sure our house is a place I can write and get the job done.

PART I

WORKSHOP ESSENTIALS

ALWAYS BEGINNING

If the angel deigns to come, it will be because you have convinced her,
not by your tears, but by your humble resolve to be always beginning.
—RAINER MARIA RILKE

CHAPTER 1

LEARNING HOW TO TEACH

*The logic by which we teach is not always the logic
by which children learn.*

—GLENDA BISSEX

Forty years into my life as an English teacher, I'm convinced it is one of the great careers—demanding of time and energy but meaning-filled, worthwhile, and *interesting*. Every morning that I step into a classroom I know I'll be surprised—mostly in a good way—by something a student says or does as a writer or reader. I'll experience the sense of literary communion that led me to declare a major in English all those years ago. I'll show or tell something about writing or reading that gets put to good use by my students. And I'll enjoy the kinds of relationships with adolescents that drew me to teaching in the first place.

I'm confident of these outcomes because I teach English as a writing–reading workshop. Students choose the subjects they write about and the books they read. Because they decide, they engage. Because they engage, they experience the volume of sustained, committed practice that leads to growth, stamina, and excellence. Each year my students read, on average, forty books representing fourteen genres. They finish an average of twenty-one pieces of writing across thirteen genres. They win regional and national writing competitions, get published, and earn money. Most importantly, they discover what writing and reading are good for, here and now and in their literate lives to come.

The benefits for me, as the grown-up writer and reader in the workshop, are a teacher's dream. I get to demonstrate what's possible, teach what's useful, establish the conditions that invite engagement, and support the hard work of *literary* reading and writing. The workshop impels me and compels them because here the work of "doing English" is real. Students of every ability are encouraged, hooked, and transformed. In turn, their growth as readers and writers is such a source of satisfaction to me that, for forty years, I've kept coming back for more.

The third edition of *In the Middle* is my invitation to English teachers, veterans and novices, to understand writing and reading from the inside and recognize our potential to influence our students' literacy for a lifetime. Like the two that preceded it, this edition represents my current best set of blueprints for how I build and maintain a writing–reading workshop—the expectations, demonstrations, models, choices, resources, rules and rituals, pieces of advice, words of caution, and ways of thinking, planning, looking, and talking that make it possible for every student to read with understanding and pleasure and aspire to and produce effective writing. But *In the Middle* also tells the story of my teaching life.

I didn't start out as a workshop teacher. A confluence of experiences drew me out from behind the teacher desk at the front of the classroom and helped me shift focus, from a static curriculum, annual calendar of assignments, and one-size-had-better-fit-all perspective, to the development of methods that uncover and build on each student's intentions, strengths, and challenges. My particular methods grew from my particular experiences in the classroom but also from what I've learned along the way as a writer, reader, researcher, and parent.

One of my essential teachers is Glenda Bissex. Her brilliant book GNYS AT WRK (1980) is a study of her son Paul's early literacy learning, especially the spellings he invented as a preschooler. Until then, the received wisdom was that reading came first. But Paul wrote all kinds of messages before he learned how to read. Glenda's observation about the disjunctures between how children learn and how teachers try to teach them is a quote I have come to live by—and the epigraph to this chapter. It reminds me to observe kids, question the teaching status quo, and try to make sense of what's going on in the classroom.

My teaching story begins when the gap between the reality of my students and the logic of my methods yawned its widest. It starts with an eighth-grade boy who challenged me to stop making assumptions and assignments and start learning in my classroom.

MY TEACHING STORY

I moved to Maine in 1975, when I was hired to be the middle school English department at Boothbay Harbor Grammar School. I'd just finished my second year of teaching seventh-grade English in a suburb of Buffalo, where I'd grown up. I moved to Maine because of Maine.

That summer my husband, Toby, and I wended our way north up Route 1, then south down a twelve-mile peninsula to the village of Boothbay Harbor. We were looking for a small, beautiful place to vacation; instead we found a small, beautiful place to live. The year-round population of the communities nestled along the peninsula is just over four thousand, and water is everywhere—coves and crashing waves, salt pond marshes and mud flats, tidal rivers and freshwater lakes—and everywhere surrounded by towers of pines, firs, and birches.

On the last day of our vacation, we took a final drive around Southport Island. Toby parked at Hendricks Head beach, where we sat and stared at our Triple-A maps, the lighthouse, the islands, and each other. I asked, "What do you suppose you could do if you wanted to live here? You know, as a job?" Toby said, "Well, you're a teacher."

I was a teacher. There was an opening. I got the job. We put a new tailpipe on our old Valiant, rented a truck, loaded our furniture, tranquilized our dog, and returned to Boothbay Harbor on Labor Day weekend.

The first time I saw my new classroom was the day before I was to teach in it. The building for grades 7 and 8 was a two-story, two-room brick bunker, separated from the grammar school proper—a classic, clapboard schoolhouse—by ledge, playground, and tradition. I walked up a dark stairwell and found my room, its linoleum floor half gone, bare lightbulbs hanging from a falling-tile ceiling, and walls peeling green paint. One wall consisted of massive sheets of plywood that divided into halves what had once been a normal-sized classroom. Terry, the science and social studies departments, taught next door. The next morning, when our students arrived, I discovered that every word said in either room was perfectly audible in the other.

The principal handed me "the curriculum," which turned out to be a copy of my schedule: six periods each day of reading and English. Then he scurried back across the blacktop to the safety of K–6 and white clapboard. I took a good look around.

No books sat on the dusty shelves. No papers filled the rattletrap file cabinet. But there were twenty-seven desks to somehow squeeze into position in my half of the room. On Tuesday morning, when my first class of twenty-seven eighth graders chose their seats, one of them was Jeff. He was hard to miss.

He was almost sixteen and *big*. His parents traveled because of their work, and they withdrew him from school over the years to take him with them. Because he hadn't grown up with his classmates and had missed so much school, Jeff was a loner. He stood out academically, too. All these years and kids later, I've still to encounter a student with so many challenges.

Jeff could barely read the primary-level basal readers the school's reading coordinator provided. He had trouble distinguishing some letters from others: *m* from *n* and *d* from *b*. He could spell his name, the names of his brothers and sisters, and maybe two dozen other words. I talked with his previous years' teachers and heard six versions of the same report: they'd done what they could in the limited time they had him, tried to assign appropriate remedial work, and either kept him back or, because of his size, promoted him. Jeff's mother told me he was learning disabled and that nothing could be done for him.

That fall I banished memories of my suburban New York classroom, colleagues, and students. I began to learn about life in rural Maine from kids whose families mostly made a hard living from the sea—small-boat building, fishing, lobstering, and the seasonal tourist industry. I covered the peeling walls with posters, begged funds for a set of textbooks, spent my own money on folders for writing, and tried to figure out what to do about Jeff.

At recess he stayed in most days to talk to me or Terry, whichever of us didn't have playground duty. I liked him. Because of his family's travels, he knew about things I didn't—boats, sailing and navigation, and the American Southwest. But I did know something about books on those subjects. I raided our home library, and *Dove, Kon-Tiki, Ram, Survive the Savage Sea*, and *The Teachings of Don Juan* became the texts for Jeff's personalized remedial reading program. I wanted to inundate him with reading experience, and I figured the best way was to endow his reading with huge measures of personal meaning. All that fall and winter, while the other kids suffered the Scott, Foresman anthology I'd ordered, I gave Jeff time, books, and recess conversations, and he took my breath away. I watched him teach himself to read. First he moved his lips and a finger as he traced words, and then he abandoned pointing when it got in the way of his new fluency. It was my first act of discovery, of *research*, as a classroom teacher—a rewarding experience, but one that was overshadowed when it came time for Jeff to write.

I brought with me to Maine a writing curriculum that I'd developed with my colleagues in New York. It drew on James Moffett's hierarchy of discourse (Moffett and Wagner 1976), and its underlying theory was that students learn to write by working systematically through a sequence of modes and genres, from dramatic writing to narrative to exposition. My former colleagues and I had coauthored an article about the program, which appeared in *English Journal*. It was my first professional publication. I was wedded to this curriculum.

I had a writing assignment, accessorized with a prewriting and postwriting activity, for every week of the school year. On a Monday in September, my students might role-play a handful of scenarios and then choose one to draft as a dramatic monologue. Midyear, I'd start a school week by assigning them to read stories from the literature anthology; then they wrote fictional vignettes in response. In the spring, they read other selections from the anthology and wrote essays about them.

On Wednesday of every week, I took home class sets of first drafts and wrote comments all over them, directing students to revise. On Friday, I collected the final drafts. On Saturday, at home, I groaned whenever I passed the room where I'd stashed them. On Sunday, I wrote comments all over them again, recorrected the same mistakes, and then created a ditto master for the next writing assignment.

Week in and out, my students' compositions broke into three categories. Five or six writers were able to make my task their own and do something wonderful with it, a dozen kids more or less fulfilled the requirements, and the rest threw me into a state of despair. Yet I persevered.

Teaching this way fit my assumptions. I assigned the topics for kids to write about because I thought they were intimidated by expressing themselves on paper and couldn't write without a prompt from me. I believed that teacher directions were necessary for students to write well. And I assumed my ideas for writing were more valid and worthwhile than any my students might entertain. From my vantage, from behind the big teacher desk at the front of the classroom, it looked as if I were teaching writing, even if many of my kids weren't learning writing. Then came Jeff.

One of my assignments for narrative writing asked students to draw a chain and make each link represent a personal experience. They were supposed to talk about their experiences with a partner, choose one link, and write about it. While the other eighth graders worked through the prescribed steps, Jeff whispered, hummed, and sketched a picture of a boy on a beach, kneeling in front of a pitched tent. At the end of class he folded up his drawing and took it home. The next day he came to school with a one-page rough draft—an account of his baby brother's death on a beach in Mexico. Although I wrote questions all over it that pushed him to elaborate, Jeff just copied the story over, one excruciating letter at a time.

This became his pattern. At school he drew a becalmed sailboat; at home he wrote a *Dove*-like short story. He sketched a desert scene in class, and at night he wrote about peyote, witch doctors, and Don Juan. My raised voice penetrated the plywood wall as I ordered Jeff to *stop drawing and get to work*.

I made assumptions about Jeff and tested them. When they didn't hold water, I made new ones. Since his drafts featured surprisingly few misspellings, I asked him about it. He said, "My sister helps me when I get stuck." I assumed he drew during class instead of writing because he was embarrassed to ask for help in front of the other kids. I told him not to worry about spelling on drafts—he and I could work on correctness later on. Jeff agreed not to worry. Then he drew all through the next writing class.

I assumed he was distracted by the noisy classroom, that he didn't want peers to see how slowly he wrote, that he was frustrated by the absence of an art program. My theories and attempts at remedies accumulated, and Jeff continued to draw in class and write at home. I never asked him why. My focus was on the curriculum. I didn't know how to focus on a writer or his writing.

After suffering my remonstrations for half a school year, Jeff ran out of patience. One morning during recess, he let me have it: "Listen, Ms. Atwell. This is the way I do it, the way I write. As long as I get it done, what do you care?" He was so vehement I backed off, finally conceding his right to use whatever process worked for him, just as long as I got the requisite number of products to file away in his writing folder.

By the end of the year, Jeff's folder was as fat as some of the others. And although he continued to draw in his spare time, he seldom drew during the writing classes of late spring. He wrote. Maybe something in Jeff changed. Maybe persevering in the face of his teacher's stony disapproval became too much for him. Whatever the reason, once again, I didn't ask. I just held my breath every Monday and hoped he'd go along with the prewriting activity.

Jeff moved on to high school. New kids moved in. I dug out my folder of September writing assignments, cut fresh ditto masters, and began to teach the curriculum again.

Two years after Jeff, I had reason to be grateful for his perseverance. A friend sent me a volume of papers presented at a conference at S.U.N.Y. Buffalo; among them was Donald Graves' "The Child, the Writing Process, and the Role of the Professional" (1975). Graves, who had yet to conduct his breakthrough research at Atkinson Academy in New Hampshire, described his early observations of seven-year-old writers. One, John, wrote slowly, spoke as he wrote, proofread at the single-word level, and, most significantly, rehearsed his writing through drawing. Graves concluded by suggesting that teachers pay attention to the behaviors of beginning writers and learn how to accommodate and build on them.

His words rang in my head for days. Seven-year-old John called up too many images of sixteen-year-old Jeff. I cringed as I remembered how hard I had worked to overcome the evidence that my curriculum had thwarted him. In Jeff's case, the evidence was blatant—all that talking to himself and all those drawings. What about the other students who had faced my big desk, the hundreds of writers of whom I knew nothing except the degree to which they satisfied the requirements of the Monday assignment?

As for Jeff, I felt lucky he had insisted I let him go his own way. Although I had missed the opportunity to understand what he was doing and talk with him about it, even if I'd had the background of Graves' article about John, how might I have helped? What should I have said? I didn't know.

This was the moment I understood that students can't be the only learners in a classroom. Teachers have to learn in our classrooms, too. Credentials and certification, good intentions, a clever curriculum, and adherence to standards are not enough. As Graves observed in the conclusion to his 1975 paper:

> It is entirely possible to read about children, review research and textbooks about writing, "teach" them, yet still be completely unaware of their processes of learning and writing. Unless we actually structure our environments to free ourselves for effective observation and participation in all phases of the writing process, we are doomed to repeat the same teaching mistakes again and again.

I didn't want to be doomed as a teacher, and I didn't want students to be victims of my mistakes. Two years after Jeff, I was teaching in the new, consolidated Boothbay Region Elementary School. My sparkling classroom in the middle school wing featured carpeting, books and bookshelves, banks of fluorescent lights, wall-to-wall posters, heat, and plenty of room for desks to arrange however I chose. I had a smart, supportive principal. I even had colleagues; now I was one of three middle-level English teachers. Yet I felt anxious and uneasy. How could I learn about kids' writing development? How could I learn to look at their processes as writers and make sense of my observations? How could I learn *anything* at the end of a long peninsula in rural Maine?

The next summer I left Boothbay Harbor for seven weeks to try to start learning. The Bread Loaf School of English Program in Writing was then in its second year. Bread Loaf had secured full-tuition grants for English teachers from rural schools, and I applied. My qualifying essay was the story of Jeff and me.

I chose Bread Loaf because its catalog seemed to offer professional resources that Boothbay Harbor couldn't provide. But when I got there, my teacher persisted in nudging me to become *my own resource*, to learn firsthand by acting as a writer and researcher of my writing. Dixie Goswami asked her grad school students to examine and describe how we wrote and to think about what out discoveries might mean for our middle and high school students. It was a summer of contradictions.

I saw that the choices I made as a writer—deciding how, when, what, and for whom I wrote—weren't options for the writers I taught. But I continued to perceive an unbridgeable gap between us. As an adult writer, I knew my intentions, and I had the skills to act on them. As an English teacher, I clung to my belief that students needed explicit direction from an experienced grown-up.

When Bread Loaf ended and school started, I went back to my curriculum, but with a few twists. I implemented a daily freewrite in journals. I gave kids more options for how they might respond to the weekly assignments. And I started to write with them. I took on a journal and the Monday assignments, and I shared my responses with the kids. It was not an illuminating experience.

My assigned poetry was formulaic and cute. Because the scenarios didn't engage me, the assigned monologues and dialogues never went beyond a first draft; I wrote them at the breakfast table the morning they were due. My assigned essays consisted of well-organized, earnest clichés. The worst was the daily freewrite. We started every English class with ten minutes in our journals, and I either had nothing to say or so much that ten minutes was an exercise in frustration.

All the while I was writing with my students, I was trying to conduct a classroom research project. As part of my Bread Loaf course work, I'd proposed to Dixie that I'd show the effects on students' writing when they viewed the teacher as a writer. But this wasn't writing; it was performance. I did my real writing, mostly poetry and letters, at home. I wasn't even conducting research. I was method testing. In January I abandoned the research project, buried my embarrassing writing portfolio in the back of a file drawer, and rationalized hard.

Maybe I needed assignments that were *even more* creative and prewriting activities that were *even more* hands-on. And maybe it was time to look at what was going on down in K–6. Why weren't entering seventh graders being prepared by the other teachers to make my assignments sing?

In the winter of 1980, mostly, I'm ashamed to say, because I wanted a hand in shaping what happened in the younger grades, I volunteered to serve on a K–8 writing curriculum committee. The teacher in charge suggested that the committee begin by posing questions we could investigate together—a smart move, as it turned out. We brainstormed and settled on a modest little inquiry: *How do human beings acquire written language?*

Our question was so ambitious it was ridiculous, but it had a remarkable effect. It sent us into unexplored—and stimulating—territory. We couldn't exchange writing assignments, borrow philosophies or curricula, adopt someone's standards, or patch together a grade-level skills list. Instead, we began to search for resources to help us pursue answers to our question. Remembering Jeff, I wrote to Donald Graves, by then a professor at the University of New Hampshire (UNH). He responded by sending us Susan Sowers.

Graves, Sowers, and Lucy Calkins were then nearing the end of their second year as researchers-in-residence at Atkinson Academy, a public elementary school in rural New Hampshire. Under a grant from the National Institutes of Education, they spent two years following sixteen first- and third-grade writers and their teachers (Graves 1983; 2003). They observed students in the classroom *in the act of writing* in order to discover how children develop as writers and how teachers can help.

Susan Sowers came to Boothbay Region Elementary School with copies of what was known at UNH as The Packet: a collection of in-progress reports of their research. She also brought her authority as a teacher and researcher, a wealth of knowledge, and patience. What she had to say was not what I was ready to hear.

Children in the Atkinson study learned how to write by exploring the options available to real authors. These included daily time for writing, conferences with the teacher and peers during writing, pace set by individual writers, and opportunities for publication—for their writing to be read. Most significantly, Atkinson students decided what they would write about.

The Atkinson children developed their own topics. They produced an astonishing range of genres. They revised, edited, and grew as writers because they cared about their subjects. And their teachers had come out from behind their big desks to circulate among, listen to, learn from, and write with young writers.

Atkinson Academy sounded a lot like Camelot. As Susan Sowers extolled its merits, I rolled my eyes and jotted snide comments to the teacher sitting next to me. At the end of the committee meeting, I stayed behind to argue.

"But, Susan, what if my writing assignments are *individualized?* Like, what if I give kids a choice of four really funny scenarios, and they get to role-play these and then choose the one they want to write up as a dramatic monologue?"

"Well, that sounds nice," she answered politely. "But it's an exercise."

"Wait, wait. What if, for a prewriting activity, I tell kids to . . ."

It was an exercise. They were all exercises.

My learning isn't pretty. I'm a resister. For the next week, I fumed about how the implications of the Graves team's research did not and could not apply to me and my students—how everything in my background as a secondary English teacher argued against the anarchy being advocated by crazy people from New Hampshire. But during free periods at school and evenings at home, I read and reread The Packet. The evidence was so compelling that eventually I saw through my defenses to the truth.

I didn't know how to give students responsibility for their writing. Worse, I was reluctant to give up control. I liked my big desk. I liked being the creative one who came up with the ideas. I liked the authority I derived from establishing deadlines and orchestrating *the* writing process. Besides, I was an English teacher, and this was my job. If responsibility for their writing shifted to my students, what did that leave for me to do?

After a long weekend of reading, fuming, and soul searching, I decided to talk to my students. On a Monday in March, instead of distributing dittoed copies of the assignment of the week, I closed my classroom door and told my students about this elementary school in New Hampshire where kids developed their own ideas for writing, worked at their own paces, produced texts that were read by all kinds of real audiences, and received responses from their classmates and the teacher *while* they were drafting. I asked, "Could you do this? Would you like to?"

Yes. Some said it tentatively, some resoundingly, but every kid in every class voted *yes*. Then, together, we made an amazing discovery: they did have ideas to write about. Even more amazing, given the nonsense I'd been assigning since September, they had interesting, worthwhile ideas. We discovered that school writing could be good for something—could help kids explore and capture what's important to them, ask questions, solve problems, make sense of experiences, express feelings, and move, entertain, and persuade readers. This was not Camelot. It was genuine, it was happening in my classroom, and it was thrilling.

Brooke wrote a short story about the slaughter of baby seals. Doug wrote about duck hunting, and Greg remembered a day of deep-sea fishing. Shani described the night her big brother died in an automobile accident. Evie wrote letters of inquiry to private high schools, and Ernie wrote a parody of Stephen King. One of my Sarahs told about learning to drive a junked Oldsmobile in her parents' driveway; another Sarah took us on a bus trip through Harlem that had shaken her rural complacency. Eben's short story about the aftermath of a nuclear holocaust went through such extensive revisions it became a letter to the editor of the *Portland Press Herald* objecting to the threat of the reinstitution of selective service. Melissa's letter to the Society for Animal Protective Legislation was forwarded as evidence to a Congressional subcommittee. Lauren's letter to the local YMCA resulted in expanded gym hours for middle school students. Erin's letter to author Louis L'Amour questioning the credibility of the plot of one of his Westerns brought a letter from L'Amour outlining his historical source.

Ted wrote an angry essay about the effects of time on his life, Kim wrote a loving essay about the impact of her mother's life on hers, and Joey wrote an essay about himself as a writer. When a Maine dairy announced a Down East story-writing contest, a group of eighth graders decided to enter. They listened to and researched Marshall Dodge's *Bert and I* albums, taking notes about dialect and story structure, and then wrote draft after draft. Roy won the contest and a $250 scholarship; five of his classmates were runners-up.

There were no longer five or six top writers per class. Now every student could seek help from me and peers in conferences, spend sustained time crafting pieces of writing, and discover that the ability to produce effective writing isn't a gift or a talent. Their commitment to their ideas and purposes made them work hard; their hard work made significant writing happen. Writing took its rightful place in the curriculum, not as an exercise, performance, or regurgitation, but as *self-expression*.

After the novelty of self-selected topics faded, the writing didn't always come easily. By April some students begged, "Just tell me what to write. Anything, I'll write it." Instead I questioned and insisted. "What do you care about? What do you *love?* What have you experienced that make you *you?* What do you know? What do you know about that other kids don't?"

The teaching didn't come easily, either. But despite "blocked" writers, my uncertainty about how to talk with kids about drafts of their writing, and big, administrative questions about grading, record keeping, and classroom management, I couldn't wait to get to school in the morning to see what my students would do next.

I saw them take chances as writers as they tried new subjects, styles, and genres. I saw them take responsibility: sometimes a writer judged a single draft sufficient, while the next time it might take five drafts to meet his or her intentions. I saw them take care as they edited and proofread, so their real readers would attend to their meanings and not be distracted by their mistakes. I saw them take time, as they wrote and planned their writing outside of school as well as in. I watched my English classroom become a writer's workshop.

Here was an approach to teaching writing that allowed me to observe individuals in action, support them, and learn in my classroom. The first thing I learned was that freedom of choice does not undercut discipline or rigor. Instead, students become accountable to learn about and use—and I become accountable to learn about and teach—the structures that serve their diverse purposes as writers. Everyone sits at a big desk in writing workshop, and everyone plans what will happen there.

As I navigated a classroom filled with big desks, I talked with students about their ideas and options. Then I taught the whole class about what I had gleaned from these conversations, so they could speak writer to writer with one another. I expected that every student would write every day and that none of it would be an exercise. From Mary Ellen Giacobbe and Lucy Calkins, I learned about the power of the *minilesson*, and I began to provide brief explanations and demonstrations at the start of each workshop about topic development, techniques of craft, genre features, and conventions of usage. I organized the room so that students had access to essential supplies and resources, publication opportunities, and a physical layout that supported independent work and the hard thinking of writing. And I started taking notes.

FINDING A BALANCE

The first edition of *In the Middle*, published in 1987, describes my initial understandings of writing workshop and the teacher's role. Afterward, I continued to learn in my classroom. I wrote and spoke about my discoveries, and I read about the teaching of writing, especially the work of Donald Graves and his UNH colleague Donald Murray. I gave birth to a daughter. In 1990, funded in part by the royalties I earned from the first edition of *In the Middle*, I built a school, a place where I could teach kids and teachers at the same time.

The Center for Teaching and Learning (CTL) is a nonprofit, K–8 demonstration school in Edgecomb, Maine. Its mission is to develop and disseminate authentic, rigorous, joyful methods across the curriculum—to teach and influence a heterogeneous cross section of children of midcoast Maine, along with classroom teachers from everywhere. Teachers come to CTL for a week at a time as "interns," and we conduct workshops and write about our work. My book *Systems to Transform Your Classroom and School* (2014) describes the methods, innovations, and traditions that define our school community and lead to engagement and excellence for every child. CTL began as a K–3 school in a prefab Cape designed to my specifications. We added wings as we added grades, and in 1994, when we reached grade 7, I became CTL's teacher of middle school writing, reading, and history.

My understanding of writing as a process of discovering meaning and refining it has given me permission to view teaching as a process, too. I gained the courage to change my mind and the humility to revise my practice when experience shows me there's something else I can do to help students grow. I came to appreciate how teaching can be a *life's work*, how my methods are a screen on which my professional and personal identities play themselves out.

When I look back at the 1980s, I'm not surprised by my ecstatic response to the egalitarian community of writing workshop. I was still in my twenties when I transformed myself from *English teacher as ultimate authority* into a *writing coach* and a *facilitator of writing process*. It was a revolution, and I needed its broad strokes to break free from the old English teacher paradigm of assignments and deadlines.

As my kids began to choose their own topics, genres, and audiences, as they wrote and wrote and wrote, I watched and listened. I had to learn how to stop performing, slow down, pay attention, and become quiet. The 1980s were heady times for many English teachers as, under the influence of Graves and Murray, we cleared the way for our kids' voices and abandoned the "old orthodoxies," Graves' term for the so-called *right* ways to teach English, which he argued had become "substitutes for thinking" about effective instruction (Newkirk and Kittle 2013).

But something happened to me, as an English teacher, that's typical of revolutions. As part of my transformation, I embraced a whole new set of orthodoxies. And as child-centered as the new "rules" for teaching writing seemed to me at the time, they had an effect similar to the old paradigm: they put limits on my students' potential as writers and mine as their teacher.

The first edition of *In the Middle* is filled with the new orthodoxies, in the form of *nevers*. *Never* praise students' writing, or they'll become hooked on your approval and won't develop their own criteria for effective writing. *Never* read students' drafts; instead, insist that they read their writing aloud to you, so you can listen to their voices and not be distracted by their errors. *Never* suggest to writers what to do or try next, or they'll rely on you to solve their writing problems for them. *Never* ask kids to attend to spelling or punctuation while they're drafting, because, as writers, they can only think about one thing at a time, and that should be content. *Never* teach a minilesson longer than seven minutes because . . . I can't even remember the rationale for that one.

Above all, teachers should never, ever usurp students' *ownership* of their writing. That means don't write on it, tell them what to do, or require anything. I learned how to orchestrate "conferences" in which my role was to lead writers to guess what was on my mind about how to improve a piece of writing and then to convince them they "owned" the improvement.

The problem with any orthodoxy, however well intentioned, is that it takes away someone's initiative. Instead of engaging in direct, grown-up-to-child conversations and demonstrations—instead of *teaching* my students based on my knowledge of writing, my previous experiences with students, and the needs and intentions of each writer—I allowed the *nevers* to curb my effectiveness as a teacher and my students' growth as writers.

I don't believe that teachers have to be parents to be effective in the classroom, but I've learned we do need to act there as the most thoughtful parents we can imagine. When I became a parent for real, the shift in my identity helped me focus on the nature of the relationship between a nurturing adult and an intentional child. My role as a grown-up in Anne's life opened a window on how a writing teacher could guide students and still respect their intentions. Because of her, I had to rethink the *nevers*.

I remember when Anne was five and told me she wanted to learn how to tie her shoes. I didn't offer hints or make her guess. I showed her how. She watched and listened as I invented a shoe-tying story and made a bow. Then I molded her fingers into position and recited the story with her, until she felt ready to take over. When she did, I cheered like mad. Later, when I thought she was old enough to set the dinner table, I showed her the conventions, set it with her a few times, and helped her if she missed anything. Then she took over, chose the placemats, put the cutlery where it belonged, created a cool way to fold the napkins, and got plenty of praise from Toby and me.

Jerome Bruner (1986) refers to this phenomenon—when an adult intervenes, demonstrates, and gradually provides less assistance—as the *handover phase* of learning. In handover, understandings and strategies that emerge during an interaction between a more competent grown-up and a less competent child get internalized by the child.

I like the term *handover* because it connotes the fluidity and purposefulness of a productive adult–child interaction. It's not hands-off: the adult is active, directive, and involved in the task. It's not a handout: the child is active, intentional, and involved in the task. And neither one is distanced from the work at hand. The adult and child aren't having a philosophical discussion of principles of shoe tying or table setting—not to mention corn-on-the-cob eating, teeth brushing, or long division. We're both engaged. When I taught Anne, she watched me, I watched her, I did it, she tried it, we talked, and I lent a hand when I saw she needed help, until she got it and didn't need me anymore.

In handover, the teacher is acting like an adult, like someone who is competent, knows some things, and wants to make a new task easy, efficient, and meaningful. The adult gives over control when the child seems ready, because the goal is for the child to act independently. There isn't an orthodoxy or a *never* in sight; there is plenty of child intention and adult intervention. And it feels like a human interaction, not the facilitation-by-formula of my early years of teaching writing in a workshop.

The key to handover is that it draws on an adult's *knowledge*. The assistance I gave Anne was selective. It was informed by my knowledge of the skill I was teaching her, my knowledge of children of Anne's age, and my specific knowledge of Anne. When it came to shoe tying, I had been tying my own for forty years; I knew that five was an appropriate age to learn how to make a bow; my daughter wanted to abandon Velcro and tie real laces; and, since processing physical sequences was hard for her, I figured I'd make up a story to accompany the steps.

In thinking about the implications for teaching adolescents—for handover in writing workshop—I realized I could bring my knowledge of writing to my classroom in a similar way. I started with what I've learned about good writing across the genres. This includes information I glean from my own successes *and* failures as a writer, from a lifetime of reading other people's writing, good and bad, and from the advice of other writers and teachers. I also bring the developmental knowledge I've acquired of what seventh and eighth graders are like. And I work hard, from the first day of school every year, to learn about the individual writers I teach—to understand their challenges, strengths, intentions, interests, and processes.

Handover is the word that characterizes my approach in today's writing workshop. I present myself to my students as an experienced writer and reader, someone who shows them how things are done, gives useful advice, knows what she's talking about, and responds with praise to smart problem solving and effective writing. This doesn't mean I've reverted to playing God and making all the decisions from behind a big desk. It does mean that I don't withhold ideas, directions, or alternatives when something I know can help students solve problems, try something they've never done before, produce stunning writing, and, over time, become independent of me.

What I strive for now is a fluid, subtle balance. I want to serve students as a listener *and* a teller, an observer *and* an actor, a collaborator *and* a critic *and* a cheerleader. Writers learn what they can expect from me. Sometimes they're even grateful—a thank-you after I've conferred with a kid about a draft moves me like nothing else in my teaching life.

Handover manifests itself when I sit shoulder to shoulder with students, help them identify their writing problems, demonstrate solutions, explain my confusions as a reader, and teach the techniques of craft and the conventions of usage that will strengthen their texts. When I show drafts of my poems, stories, and essays and describe the problems I encountered and the solutions I attempted, that's handover. And handover is at work when I illustrate minilessons with relevant writing samples, invent terms and metaphors that make something difficult doable for my kids, and conduct genre studies that help them focus on the attributes of different kinds of writing.

Teacher knowledge and student initiative are *counterweights* in writing workshop. I'm on a quest every day to maintain the balance—to value the choices, intentions, and needs of the writers I teach *and* to respond to them, lead them, and show them how to grow. The persona I present to kids in September is of someone who is serious—passionate—about writing, someone who works hard at writing well, understands writing to be life-changing work, knows techniques that will help young writers craft literary texts, loves literature, and is at the service of her students.

Tess, a student on the receiving end of all this persona, painted a word picture of her vision of handover—of me at work in the workshop and her, changed as a writer and reader because of it.

TEACHER

I.
She perches in her rocking chair at the front of the room,
shows us little pieces of her heart—
Collins, Salinger, Dickinson, Cummings,
Dessen, Draper, O'Brien, Shakespeare—
and invites us to take them into ours.

II.

She leans over my shoulder,
tweaks a verb, rights an adjective,
and suddenly my lopsided poem
shakily returns to its feet.

III.

She quietly confers with me
about my latest journey between the pages.
She shares my love of the new worlds I've visited
and always knows the novel I should devour next.

IV.

She stands in front of the class
compelling us to think for ourselves,
to form our own opinions about the world
even when they're different from hers.

V.

I watch her as she gently steers us onto our paths
and maybe—just maybe—
catch a glimpse of who I want to become.

—*Tess Hinchman*

What About Reading?

At Boothbay Region Elementary School, the same students who took breathtaking initiative in each day's writing workshop reappeared in my classroom when it came time for reading, scheduled as a separate class, to find me barricaded back behind my big desk. While writing had become something students did, literature remained something I did to students. I passed out class sets of anthologies or novels, wrote vocabulary words on the blackboard, lectured about background information, assigned pages, spoon-fed interpretations, and gave tests to make sure students read the assigned readings and got what they were supposed to get. In the mid-1980s, my friend Tom Newkirk drove up from UNH for a visit and, at the end of a day of observation of my classes, wondered aloud about whether my writing workshop wasn't a kind of "writing ghetto": the one period in their day when students made choices, took responsibility, and found meaning and purpose as learners.

While admitting that problems with my old writing program had been painful, acknowledging problems with my reading program threatened a pedagogical heart attack. Literature was my field. I became an English major because I love literature; I became an English teacher in order to teach literature. Choosing and teaching works of literature was a huge, satisfying chunk of my teaching identity. But then came Tom's nudge, the first in a series of personal and professional circumstances that challenged my role as a teacher of literature and led to the creation of a second workshop, this one for readers.

The next clue came on the heels of research I read that showed that sustained silent reading boosted students' fluency and comprehension. I began to permit my kids to read books they chose one day a week, and my kids began to drive me crazy: "Are we having reading today? Is this the day we read?"

We had reading every day—at least that was my take on it. Although I felt pinpricks of conscience whenever students voiced a desire for more time with books they chose, there were too many class sets of novels I loved, too many worthwhile selections in the literature anthology, and too many lesson plans I'd invested years in to waste time dallying with the unformed tastes of seventh and eighth graders. I continued to cling to four days of curriculum and one day of reading.

Then some Bread Loaf friends came to Maine for a weekend, and over dinner my anglophile husband discovered that one of our guests read and loved his favorite obscure author. Long after the table had been cleared, the dishes washed and dried, and everyone else had taken a walk down to the beach and back, Toby and Nancy Martin, the pioneering theorist and researcher of children's writing, remained at our dining room table to gossip by candlelight about the characters in Anthony Powell's sequence of novels, *A Dance to the Music of Time*. While their conversation didn't help me appreciate Powell, it did open my eyes to the wonders of our dining room table.

It is a literate environment. Around it, we talk the way literate people do. We don't need prompts, lesson plans, teacher's manuals, Post-it notes, or discussion questions. We need only another literate person. And the talk is never grudging or perfunctory. It's filled with arguments, anecdotes, observations, jokes, exchanges of information, and accounts of what we loved, what we didn't, and why. It's a place and time to enter literature together. My next teaching question became, how can I get that table into my classroom and invite every student to pull up a chair?

I considered how I'd found my own seat at the dining room table. I remembered a conversation with a teacher friend who sold encyclopedias on the side. He mentioned how surprised he was when customers told him they'd never owned a book before. I replied, "Well, I get it. The only books in my house when I was growing up were a set of encyclopedias. They represented a major investment for my parents. When each volume of the World Book arrived in the mail, my brother and I read it cover to cover like a novel." My friend, surprised again, said, "From the way you talk about books, I guess I assumed your parents must have been English teachers or something."

My father was a postal carrier, and my mother waitressed. Although my brother, sister, and I had library cards, the turning point in my life as a reader came in fifth grade, when I contracted rheumatic fever. I spent most of that school year off my feet and se-cluded in my bedroom. Books, the library, and my mother saved me.

She began to scour the shelves of the local library, looking for anything she could imagine I might like. At first I read out of boredom: no child in 1961 had a television, let alone a computer or telephone in his or her bedroom. But then I began to fall in love—with Ellen Tibbetts, Henry Huggins, Beezus and Ramona, the March sisters, and the heroes and heroines in the Landmark biography series. I escaped my room in the company of Lotta Crabtree, Jenny Lind, Annie Oakley, Clara Barton, and Francis Marion the Swamp Fox.

The day my mother brought home *The Secret Garden*, I wrinkled my nose at its musty cover and put it at the bottom of the pile. When, out of books and desperate, I gave in and cracked it open, I read it straight through. It was my story but not my story. I was Mary; I was Colin. I remember calling downstairs to my mother and thanking her over and over again for the best book I ever read. "Can you get me some more like this one?" I begged.

My poor mother tried, but there is only one *Secret Garden*. She renewed it four times for me that winter and spring. All that quiet time, reading stories chosen for me by an adult who loved me, changed me forever—granted me a passion for stories and the ability to read fast and with feeling. The novelist Graham Greene wrote, "There is always one moment in childhood when a door opens and lets the future in" (1940). This was my moment.

When I recovered from rheumatic fever, I continued to love reading in the company of two teachers. In sixth grade, Jack Edwards read books to our class long after his colleagues had abandoned read-alouds as childish. We talked about the characters in the books and the authors who created them. He loved novels, and through Mr. Edwards, I met E. B. White and understood, for the first time, how reading could be a communal experience. Playground enemies forgot about the playground when Mr. Edwards' voice took us to the Blue Hill fair, when Wilbur's broken heart broke all of ours. Remembering this, as a teacher now myself, I wondered: had my students ever laughed or cried together over a piece of literature? I couldn't remember one time.

The second teacher is Toby. In my sophomore year of college, I was a student in his Survey of World Literature course—yes, reader, I married my teacher. Toby McLeod lives at the dining room table. I had never met—I still haven't—anyone as knowledge-able about literature or who finds more satisfaction in reading. I know that some of my passion for literature comes from my admiration for Toby, from wanting to *be like him*. Did my students know or admire me as a reader? Would anyone remember me as a teacher who helped them love literature and take it into their lives forever?

Finally, I took a cue from Dixie Goswami. She had asked me to study my writing process and consider the implications. Now I tried to match my habits as a reader against the reading process I enforced in my classroom. It was not a close fit.

Mostly, I decide what I'll read. When my reading isn't up to me—when an application has to be filled out the right way or I want dinner to be edible—at least I decide *how* I'll read. My students never decided. They read selections I assigned at a pace I set and a fragment at a time—a chapter or bunch of pages instead of a coherent literary whole.

I read a lot, and I have routines, times I count on, like before I fall asleep at night and in the early morning on weekends. My students told me that beyond the weekly silent reading period, they seldom read independently. As their teacher, I did nothing to encourage or accommodate the development of reading habits.

Most significantly, there was that dining room table, where my family and friends talk about books, authors, and writing as a natural extension of our literate lives. My students had zero opportunities for congenial chats about books. They were the passive recipients of literature I selected and interpretations I devised. Four days a week I dosed them with my English teacher notions of good literature, and on Fridays, for fifty minutes, they got to be readers.

In response to their pleas for more days like Friday, I began a slow dismantling of the wall around the writing ghetto. One fall, I scheduled a second day of independent reading. In January I added a third and the following September another, until the literature curriculum languished in the drawers of my file cabinet. Students became readers full-time, and I began to learn about authentic reading and response to literature. Here, my students were my best teachers.

They taught me about young adult literature, a field that didn't exist when I was their age, when the rare book for teenagers asked one of two questions: *Will the mystery be solved before it's too late? Will she get to go to the prom?* Other readers of my generation may also recall Trixie Belden, Nancy Drew, the Hardy Boys, *Jean and Johnny*, and *Seventeenth Summer.*

My students introduced me to contemporary authors of juvenile fiction who write as brilliantly for adolescents as my favorite contemporary novelists write for me. Today, young readers with access to books and opportunities to read them can live vicariously alongside three-dimensional boys and girls who inhabit compelling stories about growing up in every time, place, and circumstance, with crafted language, inspiring character development, and themes that resonate in the lives of contemporary adolescents—identity, conscience, peer pressure, social divisions, prejudice, first love, political strife, loneliness, friendship, family, change. It is a remarkable body of literature.

My students taught me to fill the classroom with irresistible books—novels and also memoirs, journalism, humor, short story anthologies, and volumes of poetry. They showed me that if I provided opportunities, they would devour young adult and transitional literature. The year I scheduled reading workshop for three days a week, my students read an average of twenty-four books. The next year, with four reading workshops a week, they averaged thirty-five titles. I never had enough books.

I learned that the context of books that students choose is ripe for rich dining room table talk. We went deeper than I'd thought possible into such traditional literary features as theme, genre, tone, and character development. We moved beyond teacher's manual questions to new issues—reading processes, the myriad relationships among books and authors, and analyses of writers' choices, styles, techniques, and diction. Our reader-to-reader conversation was a far cry from lesson-plan questions and book-report answers: it was specific, personal, and *critical* in all the best senses of the word.

I am embarrassed to admit it took me so long to discover an essential truth. Everyone, and that includes every student we teach, loves a good story. The lure of stories is an English teacher's superhero power.

My students showed me that in-school reading, like in-school writing, could *do something* for them—that reading for meaning and pleasure has nothing to do with gender, class, family background, or prior experience. It develops through the power to choose, great stories to choose among, time set aside to read, and a teacher who knows the literature and his or her kids. I learned it's not a luxury for students to select their own books, that choice is the wellspring of literacy and literary appreciation. As Virginia Woolf put it, "Literature is no one's private ground, literature is common ground . . . let us trespass freely and fearlessly and find our own way for ourselves" (1947). I flung open the gates so that none of my students would have to trespass, so that every one of them could find the books, authors, and characters they love.

Inviting my students to select their own books is still the most controversial of my practices as an English teacher. But for me, student choice is synonymous with student *engagement*, in both writing and reading. It's my responsibility as an English teacher to invite, nurture, and sustain every student's engagement with literature. This means finding and stocking the classroom library with books that tell stories that kids will find interesting and worthwhile. My students become avid, skilled readers because they decide what they will read.

Reading workshop is not a study hall, where students "Drop Everything And Read," while I sit back and watch the clock. Here, the English teacher is a reader, a critic, and a guide. In my daily, whispered conversations with readers I say, "Tell me about your book. Who's the main character? What are the conflicts? What are you noticing about the author's writing? Are you happy?" And I'm an enthusiastic reviewer. In frequent booktalks (Lesesne 2003), students or I announce to the group, "Here's the next good story. Here's who and what it's about. Here's why I think you'll love it as much as I did." Reading workshop is a deliberate environment, one that supports immersion in stories, characters, themes, and writing. It points kids, always, to the next great book.

Take Heidi. She entered CTL as a seventh grader with limited experience in choosing or reading books. She *ate* Stephenie Meyer's Twilight series—as far as I'm concerned, not the next great books—like candy. I let her. Stories like these can help an inexperienced reader learn how to manage the experience of a big, fat book. They're a means to an end, not an end in themselves.

Across the school year, I booktalked, nudged, and challenged Heidi and her classmates. In June, she named *The Poisonwood Bible* by Barbara Kingsolver and *A Tree Grows in Brooklyn* by Betty Smith as her favorites of the forty books she finished. She said, "You know, I went back to try to reread one of the Twilight books, and I just couldn't get into it, I was so surprised by the writing. She's not really a very good writer."

A realization like Heidi's isn't an accident. It's a response to the power of choice, purposeful teaching about literature, and the dozens of good stories I'd purchased for the classroom library that had spoken to her as a reader. Along the way, Heidi learned to tell the difference between literary novels and popular fiction, which is something many adults never do, as evidenced by any Sunday's *New York Times* best-seller list.

Frequent, voluminous book reading builds fluency, stamina, vocabulary, confidence, and comprehension. It sharpens tastes and preferences, critical abilities, and knowledge of genres and authors. Even the cultural knowledge that E. D. Hirsch espouses is a function of habitual reading and a carefully selected classroom library. My students leave our tiny school in rural Maine as skilled, literary readers, but also as people who are *smart* about the world they'll meet out there—about ideas, words, history, current events, human experiences, and places they've encountered only in the pages of the hundreds of stories they've read.

Malcolm Gladwell writes in his book *Outliers* (2008) about the ten thousand hours of committed practice required for an expert to acquire his or her expertise. Students at CTL get that practice. The year Heidi was a seventh grader, my kids finished an average of fifty-three books. Many were prepared to be able to love *Pride and Prejudice, The White Tiger, To Kill a Mockingbird, The Poisonwood Bible, Lord of the Flies, Brave New World, All Quiet on the Western Front, The Adventures of Huckleberry Finn, The Iliad, The Road, The Scarlet Letter, Catch-22, Life of Pi*, and titles by Russell Banks, Michael Chabon, Dave Eggers, Tobias Wolff, Margaret Atwood, and Kurt Vonnegut, Jr., when they picked them up on their own. Access to and awareness of good stories, free choice of books, conversations about them, and *practice* create literary readers. A nonreader confronted by the assignment of a novel by Dickens, Twain, or Hawthorne doesn't stand a chance.

Some critics of reading workshop argue that the English classroom is a place for the classics, and the classics only—that, left to their own devices, kids will pick junk, which they can read in their free time. But the evidence is overwhelming: U.S. adolescents *don't* read in their free time. The National Endowment for the Arts reports that only 27 percent of eleven- to fourteen-year-olds read books outside of school. The NEA described "a calamitous, universal falling off of reading" around age thirteen, which continues throughout a student's life (2007).

We know that independent reading declines after the elementary grades. So do reading scores. In 2007, fully 70 percent of our eighth graders read *below the proficient level* on the National Assessment of Educational Progress. The results of every major assessment of reading ability—NAEP, SAT, PISA, you name it—show that the most proficient student readers are those who are habitual independent readers. Beatrice Cullinan's study "Independent Reading and School Achievement," funded by the U.S. Department of Education, marshals the compelling evidence (1998-2000) for students to select their own books and read them.

English teachers can engage in magical thinking and assign a strict diet of classics or other whole-class novels, and then watch as students read *maybe* six books a year—if they actually read them, of course. The dirty little secret of secondary English is how many students fake assigned readings through SparkNotes, Wikipedia, listening to discussions, or selective skimming. I know. It's what I did.

Or English teachers can decide to teach the students we've got. The kids I've got choose their own books, and they read for twenty minutes each day at school and at least half an hour at home, seven nights a week. Assigning students to read books they love is the most important homework I can give, as well as a high-priority use of class time. My students range from children with dyslexia to inexperienced readers to sophisticated literary critics. The common denominator is that they know what it feels like to be in what they call "the reading zone," and they want to be there. Instructional fads come, and they go. Human needs and desires remain constant. Our students—*all* of them—want the same sense, satisfaction, and meaning that adult readers of stories seek. Worthwhile, interesting, appropriate books have the power to sustain every student's interest.

In the end, it's handover that distinguishes reading workshop from a pleasant study hall. While good books, free choice, practice, and time are essentials, it's how I structure my teaching that determines whether compelling stories and voluminous reading will become the beating hearts of my program. As with writing workshop, it's the responsibility of a reading workshop teacher to *know* three big things: the books, adolescent readers in general, and each reader in particular.

Handover is at work when I wax enthusiastic about stories written by authors who dedicate themselves to a young adult audience. It's handover when I've read enough young adult titles that I can put the right one in a student's hands at the right moment. It's handover when I present booktalks about transitional, adult, and classic titles and authors: books that are great for some kids now, and for others in their literary lives to come.

It's handover when I describe my criteria for choosing or abandoning books and invite kids to develop and articulate their own; when I show how and when I skim or scan a novel; when I nudge readers to shelve titles they're not enjoying; and when I lead a discussion of ways a reader can investigate a book before deciding whether to read it. When I ask students to maintain "someday pages" of the books they might want to read, I'm helping them plan as intentional, independent readers do. And when I give them forms to keep track of titles and authors they finish or abandon, I'm enabling them to consider and develop reading preferences.

Each day we begin our writing–reading workshop by reading a poem or two (Atwell 2006). Here, it's handover when I show students how I unpack a poem, teach them to identify and name literary techniques, and introduce poets who have the potential to engage, inform, and provoke them for a lifetime, from Gwendolyn Brooks, E. E. Cummings, Emily Dickinson, Robert Frost, Langston Hughes, William Shakespeare, Walt Whitman, and William Carlos Williams to Billy Collins, Rita Dove, Allen Ginsberg, Jim Harrison, Tony Hoagland, Ted Kooser, Pablo Neruda, Naomi Shihab Nye, Mary Oliver, Marge Piercy, William Stafford, and Wallace Stevens.

Handover is at work when I show students examples of insightful literary criticism, ask them to tease out and discuss the features, and assign them to reflect on books in *letter-essays* to me and their friends. These are informal reviews that readers write to each other about their observations of craft, character, and theme—skills of critical analysis students will put to work in high school and beyond.

Finally, it's handover when I teach students how and where to find good books beyond CTL—when each June we discuss bookstores, libraries, periodicals and websites, literary awards, and the school's website pages, and when I help them select books from the classroom library to borrow to read over the summer.

Years ago, when I started to speak and write about writing–reading workshop, teachers sometimes told me, "Your approach is such common sense, I can't believe I didn't think of it myself." At first I was miffed. Little of what I do or ask kids to do is a function of common sense—or intuition or chance. The workshop is an accumulation of my knowledge of writing, reading, and teaching them, of young adolescents, and, every year, of each writer and reader who enters my classroom.

I think a better term than *common sense* is Glenda Bissex's *logic*. The logic of my teaching stands on a foundation of knowledge, a base that workshop methods are built on *and* build upon. Workshop teachers garner information and give it. We observe learning and participate as learners. We endeavor every day to uncover the logic by which our students learn and support it. The third edition of *In the Middle* is everything I've learned over the past three decades that makes writing–reading workshop the only logical way to teach English.

CHAPTER 2

GETTING READY

You make the thing because you love the thing
and you love the thing because someone else loves it
enough to make you love it.
And with that your heart like a tent peg pounded
toward the earth's core.
And with that your heart on a beam burns
through the ionosphere.
And with that you go to work.

—THOMAS LUX, "AN HORATIAN NOTION"

On a spring day in 1982, Donald Graves and Mary Ellen Giacobbe, then a first-grade teacher at Atkinson Academy and already an inspiration to educators striving to transform their writing instruction, drove up together from New Hampshire to visit Boothbay Region Elementary School. Since my students had been hearing about them a lot, their appearance at the school was an occasion. Bert happened to be passing through the front lobby when Don and Mary Ellen arrived. He took the stairs to the middle school wing three at a time, then whipped down the corridor like an eighth-grade Paul Revere, shouting as he passed each room: "The world's most famous writing teachers are here! The world's most famous writing teachers are here!"

With Donald Graves in attendance during writing workshop, no one moved off into a peer conference area. My kids planted themselves at their desks and wrote, heads down, in eerie, absolute silence. Every now and then one of them chanced a glance to locate Graves as he moved among the others, each of them dying for him to drop by and whisper his magical entrée, "Tell me about your writing." Bert's anticipation was rewarded. Don knelt by his desk for a long chat about Bert's passion for science fiction and Stephen King.

It was a good day. At the end of it, Graves stood in my classroom doorway with his raincoat on, beaming. "What are you smiling about?" I asked.

"I'm smiling at you," he said. "You know what makes you such a good writing teacher?"

Oh, God, I thought. Here it comes: validation from one of the world's most famous writing teachers. In a split second I flipped through the possibilities. Was he going to remark on my piercing insights in conferences? Spot-on minilessons? Passionate commitment to literacy?

"What?" I asked.

"You're so damned organized," he answered.

In response to the way my face must have crumpled, Don stopped smiling. "Look," he explained, "you can't teach writing this way if you're not organized. This isn't an open-classroom approach, and you know it. It's people like you and Mary Ellen who make the best writing and reading teachers. You two always ran a tight ship, and you still do, but now it's a different kind of ship."

A workshop *is* a different kind of ship. Traditional methods for teaching English put the teacher and the assignment at center stage: as an organizational structure, it's familiar and obvious. In a workshop, teachers have to structure the space and their instruction to support both a whole-group lesson and the independent activity of two dozen or more individuals. Here, being organized means figuring out what writers and readers will need to grow and providing plenty of it in a setting that's predictable and reliable.

Before any student comes anywhere near my classroom in September, my job is to ready it as a place for impelled, voluminous writing and reading. This means determining what I expect will happen, how, where, and when. I organize myself and the environment in August so that when students arrive, they'll find everything they need: time for independent writing and reading, tools, materials, resources, folders and forms, lots of good books, and a space dedicated to the work of real writers and readers, along with systems to organize themselves, monitor their activity, and experiment with approaches that will lead to effective writing and engaged reading.

MAKING TIME

I pulled my chair up next to Amanda's and read the lead of a memoir about a Neil Diamond concert she attended with her parents and sister. It began:

> "Okay, you're here. Do you want Mrs. Cook's binoculars? If you do,
> there are three caps you can't lose. Be careful not to let anything happen to

them because they're not ours. If you have to go to the bathroom, go now, not during the intermission, so you won't get lost and it won't be crowded. At the end, meet us by the place where the hockey players go in. Okay?"

I recognized Amanda's father's voice, smiled, and read on. She had filled two pages with close descriptions and verbatim dialogue—her family's, as well as the chatter of the people in the seats around them. I laughed and shook my head. "Amanda, however did you remember all this?"

"Oh, I didn't," she answered. She pulled out a tiny spiral-bound notebook and flipped through its pages. "I knew before we went that I'd want to write about it, so I brought this along and took notes all night on what was going on."

Robbie was at home watching television, with school the farthest thing from his mind, when "out of nowhere," he said, came the perfect ending for his short story. He grabbed the only paper he could find and scribbled away. In the morning he showed up at writing workshop with a shopping bag bearing the perfect conclusion.

In a status-of-the-class conference, Anne told me she was putting aside the review she'd been working on to continue the first draft of a new poem. "When did you start this one?" I asked. "Standing by my locker this morning," she answered. "I saw this frozen mist in the meadow on the way to school, and I got an idea I didn't want to lose."

Amanda, Robbie, and Anne thought about their writing when they weren't writing because they write day in and day out. Writers need regular, frequent chunks of time that they can count on, anticipate, and plan for. When teachers make time for writing—when we designate it a high-priority activity of English class—students take on the habits of mind of writers. In his research, Donald Graves (1983, 1994) found that teachers need to allot at least three class periods a week to writing if students are to develop significant topics, sustain projects, and plan, think, act, produce, and grow.

Without at least three writing classes a week, students will not—cannot—learn to write well. Writers of any age build quality on a foundation of quantity. Without sufficient time to produce drafts and consider and reconsider what they have written, most kids won't achieve clarity, meaning, or conventionality of usage. The same is true of most adults—it's certainly true of me.

After thirty years of serious attempts at writing, I still produce clumsy first drafts—strident, overwritten, glib, or vague. But when I carve out time to think, plan my writing off-the-page, scrawl sheets of double-spaced draft, read and reread what I've written, think some more, generate new options off-the-page, add, take a break, refine, delete, and polish, chances are I can solve the problems I've created as a writer and produce a coherent text. I am not alone.

Ernest Hemingway revised the conclusion to *A Farewell to Arms* thirty-nine times. He took the time he needed to solve any writer's greatest problem: "Getting the words right" (Plimpton 1963). Kurt Vonnegut Jr. considered time to be the great leveler when it came to writing. He claimed that anyone who was willing to put in the plodding hours could make a go of it:

> Our power is patience. We have discovered that writing allows even a stupid person to seem halfway intelligent, if only that person will write the same thought over and over again, improving it just a little bit each time. It is a lot like inflating a blimp with a bicycle pump. Anybody can do it. All it takes is time. (1984)

Katherine Paterson, author of the Newbery Award–winning *Bridge to Terabithia*, described the way a habitual writer's plodding days can set the stage for the amazing ones:

> Those are the days you love. The days when somebody has to wake you up and tell you where you are. But there are a lot of days when you're just slogging along. And you're very conscious of your stuff and the typewriter is a machine and the paper is blank. You've got to be willing to put in those days in order to get the days when it's flowing like magic. (1981)

Writing is a craft, and, as with any craft, doing it well takes time. Too many accounts of the practices of literary writers are available to us—*Writers at Work: The Paris Review Interviews* is the best-known series—for any English teacher to cling to such myths as first-draft finals, timed writing assignments, or whole-class deadlines.

Even when students do write every day, writing development is a slow growth process, more like math than any other subject in terms of learning and reviewing conventions and concepts, failing and succeeding, and practicing, practicing, practicing. This is where English teachers come in. Regular, frequent time for students to write means regular, frequent occasions for us to teach students how to write.

My students have a writing–reading workshop four days a week. Each day I teach a minilesson to the whole class about either writing or reading. Then I meet with every writer at least every other day as I circulate among students during independent writing time. After kids finish a piece of writing, they copyedit it and submit it to me for final editing. The following day I meet with these writers individually and introduce one or two conventions of standard American English that showed up as problems in their pieces. This means that in a typical school year, when my students finish twenty or more pieces of writing, I meet twenty or more times with individual writers to address, in context, the issues of usage that each needs to master.

I don't believe English teaching can get more efficient, productive, or logical than this. Nor can English learning. Regular time for writing gives my students opportunities to think on paper, experiment with techniques of craft and process, work in new genres, struggle with writing problems, conquer them, get help in context as they need it, apply minilessons, grow as writers, and grow up, period.

And their writing gives adolescents a canvas on which to capture and consider their lives so far—a place to inhabit their childhoods again, measure themselves against who they used to be, and reflect on the changes they find. Every year I watch as seventh and eighth graders compose poems, memoirs, and essays that explore what they believe, care about, desire, regret, and remember. This reflective writing is *useful* to them as human beings. It is a reason for adolescents to write.

Hope, a seventh grader, used the genre of memoir as an opportunity to reflect on the passage of time, her fleeting childhood, and the changes to come.

THE LAST COOKIE

At the deli counter, under the bright lights of Hannaford, I flip open the plastic box marked "12 and under only take one please thank you." I snatch a perfectly round sugar cookie. The deli guy asks me if I'm still twelve. His words are accusing, but his smile shows he's only teasing. I grin. "Yup, just barely." And then I hustle off to the meat section to find Mom.

As I munch on my golden treat, I remember when Hannaford was Shop 'n Save and the plastic box seemed sky high. I ran through the produce section then and stretched for the cookies with pudgy fingers. I strained to grasp my dessert-before-dinner until, with a flourish of triumph, I claimed my prize and ran off to catch up to my mother, crumbs clinging to my shirt. I measure the distance between now and then, when the bribe was so urgent, the cookie sweeter, the wait to grasp it in my hand seeming to last forever.

Now I long for the days when a cookie was that important, when happiness was so easily found. And I think of the Children's Museum in Portland. When I was seven, I crawled through the tunnel of a glassed-in ant farm. I was impressed with the wonder of the ants, their homes all around me. I stared in awe. How did they make so many tunnels? What a team they were! Exhilarated, I carried on from one bright room of the museum to the next. After hours, when it was time to leave, I was so enthralled with the place, so eager to come back, I asked the lady at the door, "How old, till I can't come here anymore?"

"Oh . . . I think the age limit is thirteen," she replied with a knowing smile. Then Dad took my hand and led me out under the gray skies of the city. Thirteen seemed a lifetime away. But still I shuddered at the thought of a day when the doors of the Children's Museum would be closed to me.

My cookie is almost devoured when I recall another sweet moment—a Halloween night after trick-or-treating. Grampa was alive then, and I was at his house, sitting around the fireplace with him, Dad, and my cousin Annie. Annie and I had already sorted our candy into neat piles of Reese's, Snickers, and Smarties on the thick, red rug. Lights flickered, making the gems on my cowgirl costume sparkle and wink. I gazed at Annie's enormous stash and promised myself that next year mine would be bigger than hers.

Then, from the corner of my vision, I noticed a hand reach down and snatch a Reese's. I whirled around. "Grampa!" I screamed. "Give it back!" I jumped to my feet and reached for the orange packet. Grampa just grinned and held the Reese's out of reach. Now Dad snatched a Milky Way from my pile. "Dad!" I whined.

"Oh, did you want this?" He and Grampa laughed. "Sorry, I didn't realize."

"Come on, Hope, you need to learn how to share a little." Annie smiled maliciously. "Stop being such an only child." They all laughed as they unwrapped their candies.

Defeated, I huffed back down on the rug. "Well, just one," and I picked a Hershey's kiss, smiling to myself as we gulped down our chocolates together. Now Grampa is gone. His house is empty; that moment is a memory. Last Halloween I went shaving-creaming.

I lick the cookie crumbs from my fingers. I peer down the bread and cereal aisle, where I spy Mom. She looks up. "Honey Nut Cheerios okay?"

"Yeah, sure," I answer. The taste of the cookie lingers. It's just a few weeks until my thirteenth birthday. I won't be able to go to the Children's Museum. Or taste the sweetness of a free cookie each time I pass the deli counter. Or ever go trick-or-treating again.

But it's not the little luxuries of cookies, bright plastic exhibits, or free candy that I'll miss. It's the title I'll lose and the one I'll gain—not a child anymore: innocent, easily pleased, curious. I will be thir*teen:* too on-the-verge of becoming a grown-up. A thing I thought was far away is now . . . close. My future is coming at me like a train with one speed: hard and fast. Often I long for it to speed up. But sometimes, like at the deli counter, I scream at the conductor to stop, maybe because I don't want my free-cookie pass to expire. Or maybe I'm just not sure I'm ready.

My mother and I head for the checkout lanes, then emerge from the bright lights of Hannaford to the cloud-filled skies of the small town I will leave behind me all too soon.

—*Hope Logan*

Since I began teaching middle schoolers forty years ago, their lives outside of school have been brimful—of sports, music and dance lessons, babysitting and other first jobs, homework, pop culture obsessions, and killer social agendas. In the new millennium, some kids' bedrooms became entertainment centers equipped with high-speed Internet access, computers and televisions, DVD collections of games and movies, iPods, iPads, and iPhones. It's even harder today to make time in an adolescent's day for the most essential schoolwork of all, the single activity that's the most significant predictor of a child's academic success. That is the amount of time he or she spends *reading books*. The National Assessment of Educational Progress reports that the top 5 percent of students in the United States read up to 144 times more than the kids in the bottom 5 percent.

Although I'm a technological Luddite—I still handwrite everything—I have re-sisted being drawn into the Internet-vs.-books debate because it misses the point. It's not either/or. It's *both*. If they get the right kind of encouragement, kids can text *and* read and love stories. Göran, a seventh grader under the spell of poet William Stafford, borrowed from Stafford a title for a poem that captures his adolescent identity. Among his high- and low-tech adventures and obsessions, he cherishes a ritual reinforced by all his teachers at CTL, starting in kindergarten. Göran reads himself to sleep.

WHAT'S IN MY JOURNAL

Dirt-bike crashes,
picking potatoes hand down,
hand over, hand open.
Sports:
soggy cleats stained with grass,
dirty shirts caked with mud,
swimming trunks hanging on a clothesline,
and balls with toothmarks in them.
Home videos
and card games:
Yu-Gi-Oh, Pokemon, Magic Cards.
Duct tape, gorilla tape, wire-man's tape, Scotch tape—
tape.
Deimos Rising,
an iPod,
anything electronic,
and a bed + a book = the reading zone.
Band-aids
and scars that tell
stories.

—*Göran Johanson*

My students who have access to e-books have brought them to school and tried them out in reading workshop. So far, every one of them has reverted to paper books They said they miss the geography of reading—of holding a book in their hands and being conscious of how far they've read into a story and how much longer it has to un-spool and resolve. They find it hard with an e-book to flip back to clarify a confusion or reread a favorite passage. Most significantly, e-books feel isolating to my kids. They find identity and camaraderie in the physicality of books—covers and titles are like badges they wear as they make connections with one another through the stories and authors they're reading.

The Internet culture is here to stay. English teachers need to accept it *and* make sure that our students are reading books. We do this by inviting them to choose their own, carving out time for independent reading, and insisting that students take books home and continue to read them there. Reading will get pushed into the background only if schools allow it—if teachers don't expect and support frequent, voluminous reading. My students' bedrooms may be wired for the twenty-first century, but they're also filled with books they borrowed from the classroom library.

My schedule gives me and my students generous time each day for reading and writing at school. On Monday through Thursday, I have eighty-five-minute blocks with combined groups of seventh and eighth graders. Because of what I know about the attention spans of young adolescents, and because I want them to be able to anticipate and plan for their engagement as writers and readers, I break the block into predictable, discrete segments.

MY WRITING–READING WORKSHOP SCHEDULE:
Eighty-five-Minute Block

- reading and unpacking a poem, many from *Naming the World: A Year of Poems and Lessons* (Atwell 2006): ten or fifteen minutes
- a minilesson about writing or reading, with notes either recorded by students or distributed by me and then taped into their writing–reading handbooks: five to twenty minutes
- my status-of-the-class check-in with each writer about his or her plan for the day: two to three minutes
- independent writing time, when I meet and talk with as many writers as possible: twenty-five to thirty minutes
- booktalks by me or students about new or recommended titles, or a reading from the genre we're studying in writing: ten to fifteen minutes
- independent reading, when I check in with each reader: twenty minutes

On Tuesdays and Thursdays, at the start of class, my kids also spend five minutes on individualized spelling studies. The standing homework assignments are for everyone to read for at least half an hour every night of the week and, over the weekend, to write for an hour: I've found that Thursday to Monday is too long for them to go without losing their momentum as writers. I want them to keep their juices flowing.

If my teaching schedule were more typical—if it consisted of daily, fifty-minute periods instead of blocks—I'd still devote all class time to writing and reading. So that students could experience the sense of continuity and routine that writers and readers need, I'd carve out a firm schedule: specific days they write, and specific days they read. I'd devote more in-class time to writing because, in my experience, kids need more one-to-one help, teacher demonstrations, and structured time in support of their work as writers. Here's what that schedule would look like.

A PROPOSED LANGUAGE ARTS SCHEDULE:
Daily Fifty-Minute Periods

- **writing workshop** on the same three or four days each week (e.g., Monday, Tuesday, and Wednesday, or Tuesday, Wednesday, Thursday, and Friday)
  - a five-minute spelling study at the start of writing workshop on two of the writing days
  - a writing minilesson each day, followed by time for independent writing and individual conferences with the teacher
  - a standing homework assignment of an hour's worth of writing every weekend

- **reading workshop** on the other one or two days of the week (e.g., Thursday and Friday, or every Monday)
  - at the start of reading workshop, the reading and unpacking of a poem, and then either a reading minilesson or booktalks, followed by independent reading time and individual conferences with the teacher
  - a standing homework assignment of half an hour's worth of independent reading, seven nights a week, at least twenty pages per day

If I were assigned a teaching schedule of fifty-minute periods, I'd at least attempt to negotiate a block schedule—to shake some extended chunks of time out of the system by approaching the colleagues who teach my students and asking if they'd be willing to experiment with the shape of the day. For example, an English teacher might trade off shorter, single-period classes with a math teacher, in order to create double periods twice a week for math and writing–reading workshop for the students they have in common.

And if class novels were a strict requirement at my school, I'd pass out copies of a book, introduce it so kids could enter it with ease and purpose, and then give them two weeks or so to read the whole thing independently. If I felt I needed to, I'd give a just-the-facts quiz on the day of the deadline to make sure that students had read it. Then we'd discuss the book for a few days as the whole work of art the author intended, thus freeing up class time for independent writing and reading, and also avoiding the ubiquitous chapter-at-a-time assignments and discussions that shatter the integrity of a literary work and the vision of its author. Just imagine how much anyone would appreciate another narrative art form—movies—if every fifteen minutes an authority figure threw on the houselights, gave a quiz, and called on the audience to discuss their responses to the film so far.

When I sit down with my planbook in August, I write *Writing–Reading Workshop* every place where it would otherwise say *English*. The workshop isn't an add-on; it is the English program. Here, I'll teach everything that counts with logic and power, in the context of whole pieces of student writing, whole-group lessons about pertinent information, whole-group discussions of poems and short prose works that exemplify the genre they're studying as writers, and whole books selected by individual readers.

This means no commercial programs or textbooks, memorization of vocabulary lists, grammar lessons, book reports, public speaking or oral reports, art projects, double-entry journals, graded class notes, or, except for a week or so of practice with the format of standardized tests, no redesign of instruction or curriculum to align with state or national standards. Engaged writing and reading, practical minilessons, close readings of poems, a diversity of genre studies, letter-essay critiques of books, editing protocols, and individual editorial conferences more than satisfy, for example, the Common Core State Standards (2010).

As for the rest of the practices I've banished, as far as I can determine, there is no correlation between any of them and achievement in writing, reading, or speaking. For example, more than a hundred years of research have shown that grammar study has a *detrimental* impact on student ability because of the time it takes away from practice in writing, speaking, and reading. *Writing Next* (Graham and Perin 2007), a report from the Carnegie Foundation, reviewed numerous quantitative studies of the effects of different methods on student achievement in writing. The authors found a *negative* impact from teaching parts of speech and kinds of sentences. They concluded, "Such findings raise serious questions about some educators' enthusiasm for traditional grammar instruction as a focus of writing instruction for adolescents."

A team of British researchers at York University (Andrews et al. 2004) looked specifically at the effects of grammar instruction on the accuracy and quality of the writing of five- to sixteen-year-olds. They reviewed and synthesized the soundest of the studies conducted since 1966, most of these experimental, with similar findings and implications: "There is no high quality evidence that the teaching of grammar, whether traditional or generative/transformational, is worth the time if the aim is the improvement of the quality and/or accuracy of written composition."

In college I was an English major with a 4.0 grade average. Of course I wrote and spoke grammatically. Yet when I decided to become an English teacher, I was required to take a course in grammar so I could teach the names of syntactical structures. I was struck then by the absurdity of grammar instruction, of teaching native speakers to describe what our brains are programmed to do. Today I'm appalled by the sheer waste of time, not to mention the damage done to the kids who will never be able to identify adjectival phrases, auxiliary verbs, predicate nouns, reciprocal pronouns, or compound-complex structures, yet desperately need information about *usage*—about spelling, punctuation, and diction—so they can write and speak with accuracy and without embarrassment. I do use the terms that writers use—*noun, verb, adjective, adverb*—in writerly contexts, but I don't teach grammar.

However we achieve it, time for independent writing and reading in school isn't the icing on the cake, a reward we grant the senior honors students who survived the curriculum. Independent writing and reading *are* the cake. When we fight for time and choice, we demonstrate to students that our priority is their growth as *writers* and *readers*. We make a space in the chaos of adolescence for kids to slow down, focus on their intentions, practice and produce writing, love books, develop reading habits and proficiency, notice and name the features of literature, and grow up healthy and whole.

The Room

It is an education to watch Mary Beth Owens, CTL's art teacher and a children's book illustrator and author, as she spends August dismantling the art room and putting it back together again, her arrangement is that thoughtful and deliberate: cups of pencils organized by hue and grade, paper sorted by weight and purpose, paint brushes gathered by size and type. She makes sure that a child will find, with ease, everything he or she needs to act as an artist. The organization and display of materials invite creativity and productivity. It makes my fingers itch.

When students enter my classroom in September, I want the environment to make their brains itch. My own experience as a writer, along with years of working with young writers, has taught me a lot about the kinds of materials, resources, and systems that make a difference. So I'm at school in August, too, cleaning, gathering, organizing, writing, photocopying, and setting up systems to support kids so they can begin to act as authors and readers right away. This process starts in July, with the CTL faculty's annual letter to parents about the supplies children should bring to school in September.

I ask that every student I teach purchase three dozen no. 2 pencils with eraser heads, three red pens to be used for self-editing writing, a box of paper clips, a marble composition notebook to serve as the journal where they'll write letter-essays about books, and an 8½ × 11–inch spiral-bound notebook of at least a hundred pages, which will become their writing–reading handbook.

The last item, the writing–reading handbook, is not a writer's notebook or daybook—kids will do their writing elsewhere. Instead, it's a class notebook and individualized reference, divided into sections, in which students record five kinds of data across a school year: ideas for writing topics, titles of books they might want to read someday, information presented or created in minilessons, literary vocabulary that emerges in our discussions, and, during genre studies, analyses of relevant readings.

I don't use writer's notebooks in my teaching. My students' sense of purpose when they bite off a topic or project that intrigues them, bull it through to completion, and experience a whole and satisfying writing process, time after time, genre after genre, is too powerful to sacrifice. As their teacher, I get to provide direct assistance to intentional writers during daily conferences. And I'm able to engage with each of them at least twenty times a year about the editorial issues they need to resolve to ready their drafts for the eyes of their readers. The focus I've chosen as a writing teacher is on sustained experiences of writing process that end in publishable products.

On the first day of school in September, I collect the kids' pencils, red pens, and paper clips and create a communal storehouse in a file drawer. For the remainder of the school year, I make sure that the writing materials center features at least two dozen sharp pencils, a cup of red pens, and a dish filled with paper clips, along with resources I supply: pads of lined paper, an electric pencil sharpener, staplers, scissors, five desk-type tape dispensers, and lots of rolls of half-inch transparent tape. The last are necessary because many of the notes that students add to their writing–reading handbooks will be handouts from me: photocopies I've trimmed with a paper cutter (since spiral notebook pages are slightly smaller than standard copy paper), which kids tape onto the pages of their handbooks.

Optional items for a writing materials center include narrow-tipped highlighters, decorated printer paper, formal bond, stationery and envelopes, glue sticks, packs of Post-it notes, index cards of different sizes and colors, and a class set of clipboards, so students can write outdoors and on field trips.

The materials center is also where I stack the plastic trays I've labeled for each class to submit writing that's ready for my copyediting, along with numerous copies of the forms students will use for self-editing, weekly homework assignments, spelling studies, and peer writing conferences.

My school purchases student folders for writing, reading, spelling, and other subjects because teachers want them to be identifiable by color. It helps me and the kids if I can cast an eye around the minilesson circle during the first weeks of school and check that, yes, everyone has his or her blue writing-in-process folder, yellow homework folder, teal poetry folder, and so on.

A file cabinet in the classroom has drawers enough for all my students to store folders of their finished writing. I dedicate another file drawer—or a crate with hanging files—to reading folders, which contain records of the books students finish or abandon. The only student work that stays in the classroom are these two folders. I require kids to bring their writing–reading handbooks, books for independent reading, and other folders to class with them each day as good training for the responsibilities they'll shoulder as ninth graders.

Another set of shelves contains standard references and useful books about craft, publication, conventions of usage, and literature. The basics include *The New Roget's Thesaurus* (1986), *Writer's Inc.* from the Write Source (2001), college dictionaries, three or four handheld spellcheckers, Kate Turabian's classic *The Student's Guide for Writing College Papers* (1976), *Bartlett's Familiar Quotations* (2004), *The Scholastic Rhyming Dictionary* by Sue Young (1997), *The Synonym Finder* by J. I. Rodale (1986), *Write to Learn* by Donald M. Murray (1998), the most recent edition of the brilliant *On Writing Well* by William Zinsser (2006), *Benet's Reader's Encyclopedia* (1996), and four essential books about writing poetry: *An Introduction to Poetry* by X. J. Kennedy (1993), *The Teacher's and Writer's Handbook of Poetic Forms* by Ron Padgett (1987), *A Kick in the Head* by Paul Janeczko (2009), and *Writing Poems* by Robert Wallace (1996).

I also collect and shelve back issues of CTL's eighth-grade yearbook and *Acorns*, the school literary magazine, along with the ad hoc anthologies of student poems, memoirs, reviews, short short stories, and essays that I cut, paste, and duplicate for class readings at the end of genre studies. There's a file of information about magazines and journals that publish middle school writers, and a bulletin board display of announcements of writing contests, where I also post student writing that has won prizes or been accepted for publication. Appendix J includes contests and publication options that my students and I have deemed reliable.

Today, more and more classrooms are equipped with computers networked to a printer. I started out with a handful of computers, along with a schedule that allowed each student one day a week at a keyboard. Through grants, school expenditures, and donations of aging machines adequate for word processing, over the next decade I accumulated a motley assortment of mostly credible computers, enough so that I can assign every student to a word processor for the duration of the school year.

A few of my students choose to draft everything they write on a computer. Others draft their poems in longhand but their prose on the keyboard. Still others prefer to first-draft everything by hand. Individuals need to experiment and discover what works best for them, in terms of productivity and craft. But all students type their final copies, to achieve instant publication and to prepare for high school, where most teachers will no longer accept handwritten text. And everyone revises by hand.

I've learned that young writers have a hard time revising on a computer. The bits of text they view as they scroll along seem just fine. So I teach them to print a double-spaced copy, walk away from the computer, pick up a pen, and read and revise their drafts as potential whole works of literature, not discrete chunks of text on a screen. Then they go back and type in the changes.

Word processing helps kids produce more pages of draft, finish more pieces of writing, and mess around more—save, rearrange, add, delete, experiment with form, and make corrections. Computers help all my students, but especially those with learning disabilities, to create conventional, legible copy that can go straight out into the world beyond the classroom and make a difference there.

In terms of teacher equipment, it takes three seats to support me in the workshop. The first is a pine footstool, where I sit sometimes during minilessons, with kids gathered around me on their beanbags. It puts me at their level but not on the floor, where I can no longer go if I'm reliably to get up again. I carry the footstool with me when I confer with individual readers, so I have a place to perch as I approach them in the throes of the reading zone.

When I conduct booktalks, read aloud, or present minilessons, I roost in a big pine rocker I bought at a secondhand furniture store. My third seat is a small, lightweight folding chair that's easy to lift when I circulate among students during independent writing time and stop alongside their computers or tables to talk with them about their drafts.

Although my younger CTL colleagues, savvy citizens of the twenty-first century, use an LCD projector to present some of their minilessons, my audiovisual equipment still consists of an overhead projector and screen and a low-to-the-ground wooden easel (Figure 2.1). The last, constructed from scrap one-by-three and plywood, holds 27 × 33–inch pads of lined paper that I use like a blackboard, except that these notes are permanent, so students and I can flip back through them for reference or revision. I copy poems or quotes onto the easel pad, record notes before I present a minilesson or during a class discussion, gather data from kids, and write instructions and homework assignments. When a pad is filled, I remove it from the easel rings and replace it, but I store it in a corner of the classroom so we can refer to it if we need to. At the end of the year, I page through the pads and save the sheets that contain ideas and examples I don't want to lose.

I love teaching from an easel. While I appreciate the permanent record it grants me and the kids, I prize the intimacy it creates. It puts us into the minilesson circle together. And about that overhead projector: I know it's old-fashioned. I know I am mocked by my friends in the professional community. But I've attended too many presentations that relied on computer imagery and devolved into technological disasters. My overhead projector has never let me down.

Writing workshop teachers need to develop systems for saving and filing lessons, examples, and successful pieces of student writing to use in subsequent years. I store most of my teaching materials in a crate I keep near the school photocopier. It contains a folder of quotations I've collected for the walls of my classroom and my own edification (see Appendix A), a copy of my teaching anthology *Naming the World: A Year of Poems and Lessons* (2006), and five three-ring binders, four of which expand on materials I included in *Lessons That Change Writers* (2002).

After *Lessons That Change Writers* was published, I continued to develop minilessons and collect writing. I added these to the original *Lessons* binder until it split at the seams. Then I divided its contents into quarters: one binder dedicated to minilessons that address conventions of spelling and usage; one for lessons about topic development and craft; one for features of different genres and minilessons for teaching them; and one to hold examples of good prose across the genres—the memoirs, micro and flash fiction, essays, profiles, advocacy journalism, humor and parodies, thank-you notes, letters of condolence, gifts of writing, and letter-essays about literature that I'll give students to read, critique, and learn from.

The fifth binder is for poems I've found since *Naming the World* was published. I inserted tabs that duplicate the anthology's thematic headings—*What Poetry Can Do, Your Life, Ideas in Things,* and so on. As I find new poems that I love and think my students will, I three-hole-punch them and add them to the appropriate section.

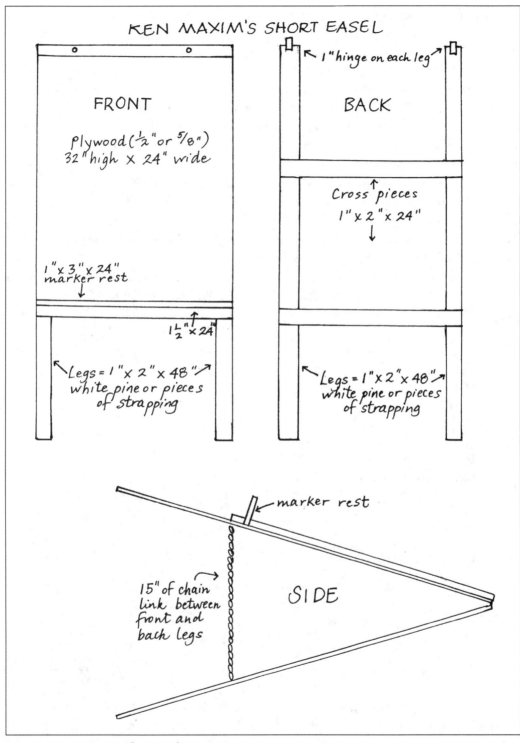

Figure 2.1 *Ken Maxim's Short Easel*

The crate is my most precious possession as a teacher. It puts what I need for mini-lessons at my fingertips, and it provides the inspiration for fresh lessons, which I especially need because I teach my students for two years, in a grades 7 and 8 combination. On Friday afternoons I select poems for the following week and photocopy class sets. I plan my minilessons for Monday and Tuesday and reproduce the quotations and over-head transparencies I'll use and the notes students will tape into their writing–reading handbooks. I seldom plan in detail beyond Tuesday. Although I have a clear direction in mind—the next steps in a genre study, for example—I need to wait and see where the first two days of the workshop will take us.

I use a calligraphy pen to create poster-size versions of pertinent quotations and display them everywhere in my classroom, but especially on the wall behind my rocker, so I can refer to them as I teach. On the first day of school, when my students walk through the door, they enter an inspiring environment, one that I hope will motivate them to assume the affect of writers, readers, and critics.

Göran drew inspiration from the classroom quotations when he crafted a found poem that combined fragments of his favorites. His "Advice from the Walls" is a wise, witty philosophy of writing and life.

ADVICE FROM THE WALLS

No tears
if the top of my head
doesn't get taken off
trying to find
where poems hide
but if you don't see
the sun rise be patient
because the poem will come
if you have a minimum
of talent
and one sacred memory
from childhood
for if there is no struggle

you
must be the change
you wish to see in the world.

—*Göran Johanson*

There is no teacher desk in my classroom. Instead, the easel, overhead projector, footstool, and rocking chair are front and center, along with the minilesson space—an area rug or a circle of carpet samples, pillows, or beanbags that defines the arch where students will gather when we huddle at the start of class, like a coach and the team before a game. Two low sets of shelves are packed with supplies and resources, and computer stations line parts of three walls. Beyond the minilesson circle, the rest of the room is filled with small tables, separated to ease my way as I navigate among them and meet with individual writers, and also to discourage peer conversations and distractions.

While one student may ask another for response to a piece of his or her writing, their conversation does not take place at a table or computer. The hard thinking of writing requires concentration; concentration requires quiet. Figuring out how to accommodate a writer's need to think *and* have access to responses from classmates presented one of my biggest headaches as a workshop teacher. At first, my students wrote and conferred at their desks, and I found myself standing up half a dozen times during class to announce, "It's too noisy in here. Knock it off."

The solution is to give writers places to go to talk about their drafts. Today a student who wants a peer's help picks up his or her draft, along with a clipboard that contains a peer conference record form (Appendix F), and moves off with an amenable classmate to one of just two places I've identified as a conference area. Over the years I've carved out spaces under tables, in corners and closets, and between lockers and coatracks, all sites I passed as I circulated during independent writing time, so I could keep an ear on the volume and nature of the talk. In an early September minilesson, I teach my students how to use the peer conference form, and I ask for volunteers to help me role-play unhelpful and helpful conversations about writing.

Peer conferences focus on style and content only, not conventions of spelling or usage. Expecting middle school students to be able to edit one another's drafts proved beyond problematic for me. Peer editors *added* errors and misspellings to pieces of their friends' writing, and I found I was spending as much time editing editors as I was writers. At grades 7 and 8 and below, the teacher is the rightful copy editor.

In terms of readying the room for the other half of the curriculum, reading workshop, books are the obvious necessity. Following a recommendation from the American Library Association, back at Boothbay Region Elementary School I started by shooting for twenty titles per student. I borrowed many of these en masse from the school library and then signed out books to individual students. I persuaded the principal to give me a budget for a classroom library, since I wasn't asking for expensive sets of textbooks, and I spent my own money—it was, and still is, that important to me that students have books to read. I sent home a letter to parents before the winter holidays telling them that anyone inclined to purchase a teacher present couldn't do better by me and their children than a gift certificate to the local bookstore. Today, if I taught in a public or charter school, I'd be sure to sign on to a website like DonorsChoose and make a case for donations to establish and sustain a classroom library.

I shelve titles alphabetically by authors' last names, in bookcases I label with categories that prove inviting and useful to my students. Today these include memoirs, biographies, journalism, humor, science fiction and fantasy, dystopian fiction, paranormal affairs, adult thrillers and horror, classics, sports fiction, historical fiction, war and antiwar, free-verse narratives, graphic narratives, adult and transitional fiction, short story anthologies and collections, Shakespeare, poetry anthologies by theme, poetry collections, essay anthologies and collections, drama, and—the largest grouping—contemporary realistic fiction for young adults.

Books I don't purchase for my classroom library include sports statistics, *The Guinness Book of World Records*, most of the formulaic series churned out for teen readers, comic books, repair manuals, computer gaming guides, celebrity biographies, and novelizations based on television shows or movies. I want every volume I put into their hands to compel my kids, through the strength of its narrative threads, to enter the reading zone and stay there.

I purchase books based on reviews, teacher friends' recommendations, and visits to bookstores. A couple of times a month I drop in at a local bookstore with a decent collection of young adult literature, and I graze. I pick up any title that looks plausible in terms of an author, genre, or theme that proved popular in the past, and I keep in mind particular students and their tastes as readers. I sit with the stack, skim initial chapters, and feel fortunate when I find three or four titles I can imagine booktalking with enthusiasm.

I read reviews of young adult titles in *Booklist*, the *ALAN Review*, *VOYA*, *Voices from the Middle*, and *English Journal*, and on book blogs and websites. I also pay attention to reliable awards and citations. On the back or inside the front cover of a paperback I look for:

ALA (American Library Association) Top Ten Best Books for Young Adults

ALA Quick Pick for Reluctant Young Adult Readers

ALA Alex Award Winner

New York Public Library Books for the Teen Age

National Book Award Winner or Finalist

Coretta Scott King Award Winner

Michael Printz Award for Excellence in Young Adult Literature

School Library Journal Best Books of the Year

A reference to a *starred* review in *Kirkus Reviews*, *Publishers Weekly*, *Booklist*, *The Horn Book*, or *School Library Journal*

Two additional sources that I recommend to teachers are Kids Recommend and You've Gotta Read This, pages on www.c-t-l.org, our school website. The first lists books that our K–8 students have nominated in response to this question: "If you knew a girl or boy who was just like you in every way, except that he or she doesn't love to read, what stories are so good that you'd give them to your friend, so he or she could love books, too?" CTL teachers ask our students to review their reading records at the end of each trimester and give us the titles of any new books that answer the question. We update the lists so often because the fields of children's and young adult literature change quickly. And we divide the grade-level lists into girls' choices and boys' because their tastes in books aren't reliably the same; in grades 7 and 8, the overlap in favorites is only about 20 percent.

Middle school teachers who consult Kids Recommend might be surprised by the relative sophistication of some of the titles. One of the many good things that happen when all the children in a school choose books and read them in daily workshops is a significant bump in their fluency and tastes. Some of my students age out of young adult literature, while some of our fifth and sixth graders choose and love books that had once been my kids' domain, while the third and fourth graders begin to inhale intermediate titles. I invite teachers to check out the books our students recommend and, as necessary, adjust to the appropriate level of interest or difficulty. When I initiated reading workshop, I never dreamed that someday seventh and eighth graders would choose, read, and love Shakespeare, Homer, Dostoevsky, Austen, Orwell, or Twain, alongside titles by the latest and greatest young adult authors.

CTL's other website page related to books, You've Gotta Read This, is a blog of reviews by students in grades 5–8. Each student adds at least one review every year. This has become another go-to resource for teachers from other schools seeking information about surefire titles to purchase for their classroom libraries.

I continue to read a ton of young adult literature, and I continue to love it, but I don't and can't read every book I add to the classroom library: I will never have that much time. I read as many new titles as I can, as fast as I can. On a quiet weekend morning, I can skim-read at least two.

To be honest, I can no longer bring myself to read some of the books. These include science fiction, where Vonnegut is my limit, quest fantasies, paranormal romances, and techno-thrillers. But I do have students who love—or might love—these genres, and it's my responsibility to give them advice and direction. So I pay attention to the experts in my classroom and ask them to teach me and their peers about their genre specialties. When Cole, a seventh-grade boy new to CTL, was ready to go beyond Christopher Paolini, I was ready with Nancy Farmer, Philip Pullman, David Eddings, and Patrick Ness, thanks to the fantasy-obsessed readers who had preceded him. I often hand off new titles to students who I think might like them, ask if they'd be willing to preview them, and, if they're any good, booktalk them to the group.

I'm being realistic as a teacher in a workshop. I can't read every book and also plan minilessons, prepare daily poems, edit writing, answer letter-essays, publish class magazines, and write evaluations. But I can become intimate enough with the literature to introduce titles and converse with authority about books and authors. *Intimacy* with the literature on the shelves of my classroom is the goal.

By the second week of every school year, a battered display case I bought when a local bookstore closed is transformed into the heart of my classroom. It houses the books-we-love collection, and it holds about seventy-five titles with their covers facing front. On the first day of school, it is empty—it has to be. Students will spend the year packing, unpacking, and repacking it with the books they love and want to recommend to other readers. In combination with the several hundred booktalks each class of readers and I conduct every year, kids select a lot of the books they read from the books-we-love display.

Forms and Folders

In August I devote serious hours to the folders and forms students use to collect and keep records of their writing and reading. I spend time in the summer so we can save it later—so that right from the start we'll have systems in place for managing the flow of paper and range of activities. Once the school year begins, I'll be up to my ears in kids, pieces of their writing, books they're reading, and plans for teaching them. I'll want to be in easy, thorough touch with every student's activity and progress. And, come the end of the first trimester, I don't want anyone—me, students, or their parents—to be surprised. So August means I'll refine old forms, sometimes create new ones, and, no matter what, think about how systems can help me stay on top of students' work and make them responsible for managing and recording what they're doing as writers and readers.

For years I maintained a "Stuff to Do or Make" checklist on a couple of ratty index cards. For the purposes of this book, my typist transformed it into the elegant version that appears as Figure 2.2. Everything on the list, except for the handful of items with asterisks, is included here in figures or appendices and permitted to be duplicated for classroom use.

This is a lot of paper. All of it is significant. The systems I've devised for the workshop make it predictable and productive. It's essential for any workshop teacher, but especially those with large classes, to invest in ways that students can maintain their own records and, once school starts, to teach and reteach kids how to use the systems. When students select their own books for reading and develop their own ideas for writing, when some days it seems as if every student is doing something different, following the paper trail could become a teacher's full-time nightmare. At CTL, even our kindergarten teacher turns over record-keeping responsibilities to young writers just as soon as they have a good enough sense of consonant sounds to start inventing spellings.

The ultimate responsibility for what happens with kids during our year together is mine. This means I keep some records, too. For thirty years I've been trying to streamline the information I chronicle by asking myself, again and again, *what do I really need to know?*

COPIES AND MATERIALS NEEDED FOR THE FIRST WEEKS OF WORKSHOP★

(One Per Student Unless Otherwise Noted)

- (W)   Writing status-of-the-class form: one for every week of the school year for each class
- (R)   Reading status-of-the-class form: a dozen for each class
- (W)   Writing Record form, two for each student
- (R)   Reading Record form, four for each student
- (W)   Expectations for Writing (hole-punched)
- (W)   Rules for Writing Workshop (hole-punched)
- (W)   Individual Proofreading List (hole-punched), two for each student
- (W)   Editing Checksheet: enough blank forms to attach to every piece of finished writing, September–June
- (W)   Sample Editing Checksheet (from a student from a previous year)
- (W)   Peer Writing Conference form: many
- (W)   A lined writing pad for each student to pocket in his of her writing-in-process folder★
- (R)   Expectations for Reading
- (R)   Rules for Reading Workshop
- (R)   "Genres So Far" list
- (R)   Book-borrow cards: a stapled packet of four 4 × 6 cards for each student★
- (R)   In a Good Letter-Essay, a Critic *Always* . . .
- (R)   In a Good Letter-Essay, a Critic *Might* Comment On . . .
- (W)   Personal Spelling List (hole-punched): two for each student
- (W)   Procedure for Independent Word Study
- (W)   Procedure for Partner Tests
- (W)   Weekly Word Study Slips: one for each student for every week of the school year
- (W)   Lists I compiled from the Internet of frequently misspelled words★
- (B)   Folders for each student for writing (two), spelling, poetry, prose, reading, and homework★
- (B)   Homework Assignment Sheet: one for every student for each week of the school year
- (B)   Team assignments (four small groups) for a classroom-resources scavenger hunt on the first day of school★
- (B)   "Mapping the Room" scavenger hunt list: one for each small group
- (B)   Blank maps of my classroom attached to clipboards: one for each small group★
- (B)   Icebreaker activity: Peer Bingo OR Beach Ball Questions OR Human Treasure Hunt OR Find Someone Who . . .
- (R)   Daily poems for the first week of school★
- (W)   September Student Writing Survey
- (R)   September Student Reading Survey
- (W)   My most recent list of writing territories, reproduced on overhead transparencies
- (B)   Quotations on the walls that focus on poetry and identity
- (W)   A computer password for each student (I use the last names of poets)★
- (R)   New titles for me to booktalk and add to the classroom library★
- (W)   A poem I wrote, along with all its pages of drafts and notes, for students to study as researchers of writing process
- (W)   The Rule of *So What?*

(W) = needed for writing workshop
(R) = needed for reading workshop
(B) = needed for both or either

★*not* reproduced as a figure in Chapter 2 or 3 or included in the appendices

Figure 2.2 *Copies and Materials Needed for the First Weeks of Workshop★*

I need to know, on a daily basis, what each student is writing and reading. I need to know if they're finishing books, homework, and pieces of writing. I need to know what they need help with and where I might nudge them next. For me, simple status-of-the-class records in writing and reading accomplish much of this.

Status-of-the-Class Records

After juggling record-keeping systems that involved folders, notebooks, Post-it notes, self-adhesive labels, and three-ring binders, I settled on two clipboards of notes for each class. One clipboard holds my notes of the weekly status-of-the-class record for writing workshop (Figure 2.3). The other holds status-of-the-class records for about a month of reading workshop (Figure 2.4).

On the writing record, I capture students' plans for the workshop: what they tell me they're going to do, following each day's minilesson, when I call the roll. As fast as I can, I record the topic, genre, and writer's intentions. I do it out loud for three reasons. The first is to create a contract: via his or her response, a student is making a commitment to a plan of action. If a writer deviates from the plan—goes off-task or starts fooling around—I can say, "You said you were doing X today. Please settle down and follow through."

I also want kids to hear what other students are writing about. Status-of-the-class responses are important sources of inspiration for new topics and genres: poems about vicious pets spread like wildfire after Heidi said she was writing one about her cat killing a blue jay, and Maura's abecedaria inspired a rash of them. Finally, this whole-group conference is an essential opportunity to teach and reinforce the language of writing process. When a writer tells me, "I'm starting this poem over" or "I'm typing the poem I wrote last night," I paraphrase with the appropriate terminology: "So, you're beginning draft two" or "You're typing a second draft."

Figure 2.3 is an early September status-of-the-class record. It shows writers who are starting a new poem, revising a poem, handwriting or typing a second or third draft, brainstorming titles, editing, meeting with me for an editing conference after I've copyedited a piece of their writing, typing a final copy, proofreading, taking a hiatus from one project to pursue a more compelling one, and abandoning a topic that didn't prove worthwhile. All of these are valid activities of writers in a workshop.

I carry the status clipboard with me when I circulate during independent writing time. At the start of the school year, I make a check mark whenever I meet with a writer, so I can be sure I've talked with every student every other day in the crucial first weeks, when I want everyone to get off to a successful start. I also make notes on the status form to remind myself that the next day I need to go first to students who seemed to be struggling, stuck, or not compelled by their topics. Sometimes I make a note of a nudge—when I've asked a student to brainstorm titles or experiment off-the-page with

NATALIE	Reread + revise—beach poem	D.3—beach	2-Day W.A. / D.1—my room	Revise room poem
SOPHIA	Revise—van. i.c. w/ m. syrup	Type D.2	" / D.1—field hockey	D.1—cont: f.h.
TRISTAN	Type D.2—old Legos	Revise D.2	D.3	2-Day W.A. / D.1—wings at Applebee's
ABBIE	Type D.2—g'moth. + sneeze	Cont. to type + revise—D.2	Cont. to revise / 2-Day W.A. / W.O.P.—Room poem	D.1—my room
TESS	Revise D.1—little things	Revise D.2	2-Day W.A. / Terr. list	Revise poem abt. March 15
PATRICK	Aban. hot balls—terr. list	Type D.2—1st fly-fishing	Finish D.2	2-Day W.A. / D.1—Duke
MAX	Cont. D.1—bookstore	Revise D.1	Type D.2	W.O.P. conclusions
GRAYDON	Type D.2—The wave	Revise D.2	W.O.P. conclusions + title / T. list	D.1—religion + me
COLE	Type D.2—tubing	2-Day W.A. / Terr. list	Revise—Risk w/ bro. Edit tubing	Ed Con Final
JOSIE	Revise—artichoke	D.2	Revise + type revisions	2-Day W.A. / Persona poem—frog princess
MORGANNE	Revise—grandmoth. + lake	Type revisions + 2-Day W.A.	W.O.P. abt. stuffie	Edit g'moth. + lake poem
AVERY	Abandon dogs—terr. list	Type D.2—my back yard	Revise D.2 + type changes	Revise D.3 W.O.P.—conclusions
SAMANTHA	Cont. D.1—neighbor	Type D.2—neighbor	Revise Title brainstorm	Play w/ form / Terr. list
ELOISE	Revise D.1—barking at strangers	Type revisions	Print D.2 + revise	Type revisions
BRIAN	Cont. D.1—Maid of the Mist	Type D.2—M.O.M.	Print + revise	Type revisions
GABRIELLE	Revise—sock puppet	2-Day W.A. / W.O.P.—India	Cont. D.1—India	Edit sock puppet Cont. D.1 India
LILLY	Cont. D.1—imag. friends	Type revisions	2-Day W.A. / terr. list	ab
CATHERINE	Revise—stargazing	D.1—my room	Edit—stargazing	Ed Con Final
ABE	Revise—snorkeling	Type D.2	Print + revise	W.O.P. conclusions—so what?

Figure 2.3 *Sample Teacher Status-of-the-Class Record of Student Writing*

Figure 2.4 *Sample Teacher Status-of-the-Class Record of Student Reading*

conclusions—so I can check in later. When I think a writer needs to bull through a piece of writing that's taking too long, I'll set a deadline with him or her, note it on the status record, and help the writer follow up. After I copyedit a piece of writing, which I do at home, I write *ED CON* in the next day's status column: tomorrow I'll return the piece to the writer and, in an editing conference, teach about a couple of the errors I found. And I often cast my eyes back across the days and weeks of writing workshop in search of patterns of activity and productivity.

When I move around the room during independent writing time, I also carry a pen and a pad of Post-it notes to demonstrate solutions to writing problems or jot reminders of our conversations to leave behind with kids. All the status-of-the-class records for a trimester stay stacked on the clipboard, arranged chronologically. At the end of a trimester, some of my evaluation comments about students' work habits will be based on these data.

To keep track in reading workshop, I divide each class in half and write their names across the tops of two grids. Figure 2.4 represents half the readers in one class on a page that captures eighteen days of reading workshop. Instead of calling the roll from my rocking chair, I slip among readers while they're reading, record the titles of their books, and note the page numbers they're open to. I'm following up on the half an hour of assigned homework reading by expecting students to be at least twenty pages beyond yesterday. I don't conduct the reading update out loud because it's obvious to kids, from the covers of their books and their conversations before and after class, what their friends are reading.

In addition to titles and page numbers, I make notes about readers who are abandoning too many books, students who should be abandoning their books, patterns of authors and genres, new developments in tastes, rereads, or the literary obsessions that build a reader's identity.

I fill out the reading status every time my students read. If a student is deep in the reading zone and happy, I'm likely to just look over his or her shoulder and record the page number. More often I stop, ask what the reader thinks so far, share an enthusiasm, extend one, or troubleshoot. Students know I'm coming, they know I'm interested in their choices and responses, and they know I'll check in to make sure they did the most important homework any English teacher can assign.

Over a career of experiments with writing and reading records, I understand how personal a decision it is when a teacher settles on a system. We need to ask ourselves: What's useful to me as the teacher of these children? What's manageable and convenient? What won't eat up my face time with kids? What will help me get to know them as writers and readers and be accountable to them and their parents? *What do I really need to know?*

Student Writing Record

I staple two blank writing records (see Appendix B) inside each student's finished writing folder—the one that stays in the classroom for the duration of the school year—and teach the kids to clip together all the components of a piece of writing with the final copy on top, file it, and record the title, genre, and date it was finished. This information gives a student and me a shorthand way to assess productivity, experiments, and patterns. After a frustrating first week of school when I turned the task over to students, I learned it's better for me to pre-staple the writing records into the folders. Among the more pathetic sights of my teaching career was a bunch of twelve- and thirteen-year-olds attempting to staple something to something else.

Student Reading Record

For the same reason, I staple four record sheets (Appendix C) inside each student's reading folder. I ask kids not to write down a title until they either finish or abandon it, and to use the "#" column to count completed books only. Here, again, the focus is on essentials: the number of books read; their titles, genres, and authors; the date finished or abandoned; and a rating. My kids and I rate everything—I mean everything: pizza, movies, my shoes—on a 1–10 basis, with 10 high and *bella* highest—more about that in Chapter 3. Especially when it comes to communitywide conversations about books, our rating system is a shorthand that everyone gets.

Expectations for Writing Workshop

When I launched my first writing workshop, on that March morning in 1980, I didn't know what to expect—of the workshop, myself, or my students. I invented ground rules as we went along, and the following September I came up with a short list of expectations: Writers in a workshop should develop their own topics, bring their writing-in-process folders to class every day, read over their drafts as critics before asking for someone else's response, write a lot, and experiment with writing as a process.

Since then, every year that I teach writing in a workshop, I learn more about what I can expect from seventh- and eighth-grade writers. Today I can barely squeeze my Expectations for Writing Workshop on one page (Figure 2.5). I am asking a lot. But there's a shadow document to this one, which kids can't see but soon infer. It tells them what they can anticipate from me so that they'll be able to meet my expectations, engage, produce, and grow.

When I say that I expect kids to find topics for writing "that matter to who you are, who you used to be, and who you might become," it means I've committed myself to minilessons that invite students to generate significant ideas across genres. When I

EXPECTATIONS FOR WRITING WORKSHOP

- Find topics and purposes that matter to who you are now, who you once were, and who you might become.
- Create and maintain your *territories* as a writer in your writing–reading handbook: the ideas, topics, purposes, genres, and poetic forms you'd like to explore.
- Make your own decisions about what's working and what needs more work in your drafts. Learn how to step back and read yourself with a critical, literary eye and ear.
- Attend to, ask questions about, and comment on your classmates' drafts in ways that help them move their writing toward literature.
- Take notes on minilessons in your writing–reading handbook. Record them chronologically, and create and maintain a table of contents (Rief 1992).
- Produce *at least 3–5 pages of rough draft each week* (Rief 1992). Recognize that good writers build quality upon a foundation of quantity.
- Work on your writing for at least an hour every weekend.
- Bear in mind that each year seventh and eighth graders complete about twenty pieces of writing. You're expected to finish writing in at least these genres:
  - poetry (3–5)
  - memoir
  - short short fiction
  - review (2)
  - essay
  - advocacy journalism
- Attempt publication beyond our classroom and school.
- Recognize that readers' eyes and minds need writing to be correct and predictable in terms of spelling, punctuation, capitalization, and paragraphing. Work toward conventionality—toward making your writing look like the writing you see in books.
- When you're stuck or uncertain, use the resources available to you, including the notes in your writing–reading handbook and your lists of territories. Experiment with the approaches and techniques that I show you in minilessons and I introduce in our conferences and that you glean from reading other writers' poetry and prose.
- Take care of the materials, resources, and equipment I've provided for you, as well as your two writing folders. Uphold your commitment to CTL's computer policy.
- Each trimester, work toward significant, relevant goals for yourself as a writer.
- In every writing workshop, take a *deliberate stance* (Harwayne 1992) toward writing well. Try to make your writing literature, and use what you've been shown to help you get there.
- *Work hard* as writer. Recreate happy times, reconcile to sad ones, discover what you know about a subject and learn more, convey information and request it, parody, petition, play, explore, entertain, argue, apologize, advise, analyze, sympathize, criticize, interview, observe, imagine, remember, reflect, celebrate, express love, show gratitude, and make money.

Figure 2.5 *Expectations for Writing Workshop*

require three to five pages of rough draft from every writer every week, I've obligated myself to ensure that the classroom is a place conducive to the contemplation that productivity and craft require; it also nudges me to teach strategies that student writers can use when they get stuck. I'm comfortable expecting that everyone will produce at least three to five poems, a memoir, a short short story, a review, an essay, and either a profile or a piece of advocacy journalism because these are genres I'll teach in depth.

The more I learn about good writing and how to teach it, the more I'm able to ask of students. The rigor and specificity of my expectations are underpinned by knowledge of writing and adolescents and by the confidence I gain from kids' successes as writers.

Rules for Writing Workshop

In the beginning there were four rules, which I adapted from Mary Ellen Giacobbe's first-grade classroom at Atkinson Academy: save everything; date, label, and put your name on it; write on one side of the paper only; and always skip lines. Over thirty years I've learned a lot about the conditions that support effective writing. My list of rules expanded in response to evolving circumstances, including the introduction of computers (Figure 2.6). But two of Mary Ellen's rules—write on one side of the paper and skip lines—are still the most important on this list.

Writing is thinking and rethinking on paper. If students don't skip lines when they handwrite drafts, if they don't print word-processed texts double-spaced, they *cannot revise*, cannot reconsider a draft because there's no physical space on the page to change their minds or develop an idea. Kids need to know that the writing of professional authors isn't single-spaced until it's published. My students fight me on this rule like mad. "It's wasting paper," they argue. "It's killing trees." I tell them, "God would kill a few trees if She thought you were going to learn how to revise your writing this year; it's that important."

I three-hole-punch copies of the expectations and rules so they're ready for kids to attach within the brass fasteners of their writing-in-process folders on the first day of writing workshop. I find that if we take it slow, they can handle brass fasteners.

Individual Proofreading List

After I've edited pieces of their writing, students copy onto their individual proofreading lists (Appendix D) the conventions of usage and technique that I teach them in individual editing conferences. I hole-punch two copies of this form for each writer. It's the third and final document students fasten inside their writing-in-process folders, and it goes on top, for easy access and reference when it comes time for them to edit a draft or me to teach a writer a new convention.

RULES FOR WRITING WORKSHOP

- Save everything. It's all part of the history of a piece and your history as its author. On the computer, **either** label and save multiple versions on your hard drive, **or** print a copy of each labeled draft and file it in your permanent folder when the piece is finished.
- Date, label, and put your name on everything. Keep track of what you've done, e.g., *writing-off-the-page, draft #1, title brainstorm*. On the computer, label multiple versions as D.1, D.2, etc., and be sure to type your name and the date on everything **before you print it**.
- Write on one side of the paper only. Always skip lines if writing by hand. On the computer always *print* double-spaced. Make revision and editing easier, more productive, and *possible* because you've left room on the page to think and change your mind. Be aware that professional writers always double- or triple-space until their work is published. On the computer, you may want to draft single-spaced, so you can glimpse more of the text at a time, and then shift to double-space before you print and prepare to revise.
- When you compose on the computer, **print a double-spaced version every two days**. Then read your draft away from the computer, with a pencil in hand. Write your revisions, and then return to the computer and type them in. Consider and work with *whole texts*, rather than the glimpses you get on a computer screen. Understand that while it's possible and productive for kids to draft on computers, it's difficult for you to revise there.
- Draft your prose in sentences and paragraphs. Draft your poems in lines and stanzas. Don't go back into a mess of text and try to impose form. Format as you go: this is what real writers do.
- Get into the habit of punctuating and spelling as correctly as you can *while* you're writing. This is something else professional writers do.
- When writing on the computer, **spellcheck once, at the end**, when it's time to edit. Record any misspellings—vs. typos—on your master spelling list.
- Understand that writing is thinking on paper. Do nothing to distract other writers. Don't impose your words on their brains as they're working to find words of their own.
- When you talk with me about your writing, use as soft a voice as I do: *whisper*.
- Talk with a peer about your writing when you have a reason to: when there's a specific problem that could benefit from a specific friend's response. Complete a peer conference form, and then move together to one of the conference areas. If you're a peer responder, record your reactions on the form, so the writer leaves the conversation with a reminder of what happened and a plan.
- Use the two-day walk-away as a strategy to gain distance on and rethink a draft. Put aside a piece that's close to completion, and tackle another project. Then come back—when you're two days older and smarter—and read and revise the text from a fresh perspective.
- Self-edit with purpose. Complete an editing checksheet to indicate the conventions you're focusing on. Use a red pen when you edit, so you and I can see the errors you were able to find on your own. Then put the piece *and* all of its drafts in the stack tray for your class.
- After I've followed up with a teacher-edit, produce a final copy in which you've corrected every indicated error. Proofread it against your edits and mine. Then put it in my chair for me to proofread—or *eyeball*—one last time.
- Maintain your proofreading list by adding the *exact* conventions and examples that I record in the *teacher's comments* column of your editing checksheets. Refer to your proofreading list when you edit your writing, and try to master these conventions this year.
- When a piece of writing is finished, clip together your final, writing-off-the-page, drafts, peer-conference form, editing checksheet, etc. and file them in your permanent writing folder, with the final on top. Record the piece on the form inside your folder. Collect data about yourself as a writer, look for patterns, and take satisfaction in your accomplishments.
- Write as well and as much as you can: work hard, and make literature.

Figure 2.6 *Rules for Writing Workshop*

Editing Checksheet

Editing should be a discrete, formal step for student writers. They should take pens in hand—red ones in my workshop, so I can see the changes they make—and correct every error they can identify in punctuation, capitalization, word usage, format, style, and spelling. The editing checksheet (Appendix E) makes editing a deliberate act. Students draw the conventions they list here from their individual proofreading lists.

Each time the content of a piece of writing is set—that is, when revision and polishing are finished and it's time to get the piece ready for the eyes of a reader—writers grab a fresh editing checksheet from the materials center and copy onto it the relevant items from their individual proofreading lists. Then, red pens in hand, they read their drafts in search of these and any other errors. When they're finished, they paperclip the editing checksheet to the top of the edited piece and place it in the class stack tray.

At the end of a school day, I grab the contents of the stack tray and take the writing home for a final edit. In black pen, I correct every error that a student missed. I note any misspellings I find in the "Spelling" box on the editing checksheet. Then I choose one or two errors to teach the writer about in an editorial conference in the next day's workshop. So I'll remember the specific conventions I want to teach, I note them in the "Teacher's Comments" column on the editing checksheet. When I meet with the student the next day, I explain the new conventions or techniques in the context of how they work in this piece of writing. Then students copy my notes from the "Teacher's Comments" column as the next items on their individual proofreading lists. Finally, a writer uses my black corrections, plus his or her red ones, to create—we hope—an error-free final copy.

Approaching conventions of writing in this deliberate way gives my students opportunities to learn from me one-to-one and in context about the standards of written American English and the techniques that literary writers use. Every time they edit a piece of writing, they reinforce my previous instruction and take growing responsibility for producing texts that others can read with ease and pleasure.

Peer Writing Conference Record

When I introduced peer writing conferences as "another fun thing you can do in the workshop," I reaped what I sowed. Their conferences with one another were 80 percent social and 20 percent on task. I had to step back to consider what practical benefits there might be to student discussions of drafts of their writing and how I could help kids realize them.

The obvious benefit to a writer is the opportunity for the eyes and ears of more readers. There's only so much teacher to go around, and I think that in classes with more than two dozen students, kids will need more response to their drafts-in-progress than one adult can provide. It just makes sense to show students how to ask a peer for help and how to give it when it comes to problems of information, clarity, organization, diction, imagery, or theme development.

In addition, the knowledge of particular students is a resource that needs to be tapped, since kids have expertise in areas that teachers don't. When Kyle was working on a short story that featured a skateboarding accident, Michael, an expert in the sport, helped him with the technical vocabulary. When Morgan recognized that the verbs in her poem weren't sensory yet, she tapped Carolyn, known for her sensory diction, for assistance (Figure 2.7).

Peer writing conferences should be worthwhile. To make this more likely, each fall, in a long minilesson, students and I agree on the purpose of a peer meeting and define each partner's roles and responsibilities. We review the form and the procedure: when one writer wants another's response, the student heads to the materials center, grabs a clipboard with a peer conference form already attached, fills out the top, and grabs the peer. Together they huddle in one of two designated areas: in the closet where the bean-bags are stored at night, or right behind my rocker. (See Appendix F for a blank copy of the Peer Writing Conference Record.)

Expectations for Reading Workshop

This list defines a time and place for students to behave as independent, habitual, engaged, critical readers (Figure 2.8). The guidelines promote immersion, combat distractions, reduce frustration, and ease my kids' entry into the reading zone. Just as there's a shadow document to my list of expectations for writing workshop, there's another about the teacher's role in reading workshop—except this time, students brought it out of the shadows.

In *The Reading Zone* (2007), I summarized research my students conducted about what teachers can do to encourage engaged reading. In an open-ended survey, they gathered data from classmates and the younger children at CTL about conditions that invite them to enter the reading zone. In the process, they created a healthy list of expectations for a teacher of reading workshop.

TEN CONDITIONS FOR ENGAGED READING, AKA THE ZONE

1. many booktalks—brief raves to the group about great books—along with minilessons about literary topics: recommended young adult authors, elements of fiction, how to unpack a poem, what efficient readers do, when to abandon a book, who won the Newbery Award this year
2. a big, diverse classroom library with continuous additions of new books
3. daily, quiet, in-class time to read

PEER WRITING CONFERENCE RECORD

Writer's Name ___Morgan___ Date ___10/2___

Responder ___Carolyn___ Topic/Genre ___Free Verse Poem___

Writer, when you've identified something you want help with in a draft of your writing, consider *who* in your group might be most effective in supplying it.

· For example, are you looking for a response to your title, lead, conclusion, dialogue, descriptions of thoughts and feelings, descriptions of individuals in action or other visuals, theme or *so what?*, logic, structure, flow, information, specifics, verbs, choice of narrative voice or verb tense, diction, sensory imagery, or use of such poetic techniques as line breaks, stanza breaks, compression, repetition, metaphor, simile, or personification?

· Next, given what you've learned about your classmates as writers, readers, and people, who might have expertise in this area? Approach that person because you think he or she knows about ___good verbs___

and ask for a response to ___help with sensory verb choice___.

Responder, when you agree to confer with a classmate, your job is to help the writer think and make decisions about his or her draft. To do that, you'll need to:

· Ask any questions to clarify what the writer wants help with, until you're sure you understand.

· Either read the draft, or listen as the writer reads it. Then give the writer the help he or she asked for.

· In addition, if there are any parts that confuse you, that you don't understand, that you'd like to know more about, or that don't draw you into the piece or keep you there, ask the writer about them.

· Jot down these reactions and questions on the lines below, for the writer's reference.

· Ask the writer what he or she plans to do next.

· Give this record of the conference to the writer.

___walk → stride___

___stood nervously → petrified___

___see → contemplate___

___sit → perch___

___have → put up___

___look → watch___

___see → spot?___

___Sit down → slouch___

Writer, at the end of the conference, jot down your plans so you don't forget them:

___revise my verbs___

Figure 2.7 *Sample Peer Writing Conference Record*

4. free choice of books, genres, and authors

5. a bookcase in the classroom dedicated to titles that individual readers love and want to recommend to other kids, along with personal recommendations of beloved books from friends and the teacher

6. comfort during reading: in beanbags, on pillows, stretched out on the floor, feet up on chairs, heads down on tables

7. literary correspondence with the teacher and friends about books and authors

8. conversations with the teacher about books students are reading as he or she circulates during the daily check-in

9. individual lists, maintained in readers' writing–reading handbooks, of the titles they want to read someday

10. a homework assignment of at least half an hour of book reading, seven nights a week

Rules for Reading Workshop

Students keep copies of the Expectations for Reading Workshop (Figure 2.8) and Rules for Reading Workshop (Figure 2.9) in a pocket of their reading folders, which, again, stay in the classroom. I based the rules on what I've learned about what habitual, literary readers do. Some of them contradict what I was taught by my own teachers: for example, that rereading a book is cheating; skimming, skipping, and looking ahead are blasphemy; and abandoning a book is an indication of a character defect. This is misinformation and bad advice.

In an essay I love, the novelist Robertson Davies characterizes reading as "a personal art." He writes that the goal of the reader-as-personal-artist is "to read for pleasure, but not for idleness; for pastime but not to kill time; to seek, and find, delight and enlargement of life in books" (1959). This sounds to me like language for a job description: *Wanted: An English teacher who can invite students to seek, and find, delight and enlargement of life in books.* My rules for reading workshop level with kids: good readers are personal artists who find and read a lot of books they love and that matter.

Genres So Far

When I ask students to note on their reading records the genre of each book they finish, my goal is to help them develop a sense of their tastes and accomplishments—to see themselves as readers who like dystopian fiction or contemporary realism, or to notice they've sampled fifteen genres. To help readers determine a book's genre, a group of my students compiled the list in Figure 2.10. My classes and I update it annually, and students store it in a pocket of their reading folders for easy reference.

EXPECTATIONS FOR READING WORKSHOP

- Read as much as you can as joyfully as you can. Practice with pleasure. Remember Malcolm Gladwell's ten thousand hours as the route to expertise.

- Read at home for at least a half an hour every day, seven days a week, all year long.

- Find books, authors, subjects, genres, and themes that matter to who you are now, who you once were, and who you might become.

- Try new books, authors, subjects, genres, and themes. Expand your literary experience, knowledge, and appreciation.

- On the *someday* pages in your writing–reading handbook, keep a running list of titles and authors you'd like to try, especially in response to booktalks and other recommendations.

- Recognize that a book represents a writer's ideas and the choices he or she made. Understand that you can step back from a story after you've finished living inside it and notice and discuss how the author decided to write it.

- Use the critical vocabulary you already know and the terms I teach you to talk and write about literature.

- Write a letter-essay every three weeks about what you noticed and appreciated about *one book you recently finished*. Go back into the book as a critic and consider how the book made you think and feel, what the author did to evoke this response, what worked, what needs more work, and the *themes*—the ideas about life you took away from the book.

- Recognize there are different approaches to reading. Readers take different stances in relation to different kinds of texts. Reading a novel is different from a poem, is different from a chapter in a history book, a graph of data, a newspaper editorial, a word problem in math, or the instructions for assembling a new bike.

- Develop and articulate your own criteria for selecting and abandoning books.

- Each trimester, work toward significant, relevant goals for yourself as a reader.

- In every reading workshop take a *deliberate stance* (Harwayne 1992) toward engaging and responding with your whole mind and heart. Take advantage of the workshop. *Use it* to find sources of satisfaction and inspiration. Enter the reading zone, stretch your imagination, find prose and poetry so well-written it knocks you out, understand experiences you might never know otherwise, find stories that make you happy or feed your soul, consider how other writers have written and why, acquire their knowledge and insights, wonder, escape, think, travel, ponder, empathize, laugh, cry, love, and grow up.

Figure 2.8 *Expectations for Reading Workshop*

1. You must read a book. Magazines and newspapers can't provide the sustained chunks of text you need to practice reading and develop fluency. More importantly, they won't help you discover who you are as a reader of books.

2. Don't continue to read a book you're not enjoying. Don't waste time with a title you don't like when there are so many great stories waiting for you—*unless* you decide to finish a bad book so you can criticize it in a letter-essay. Do develop your own criteria for abandoning books, e.g., *how many pages* will you give an author to intrigue or involve you?

3. If you don't like your book, find another. Check out the books-we-love display. Look at your list of someday titles. Browse our shelves and interview books. Ask me or a friend for a recommendation.

4. It's more than all right to reread a book you love. This is something good readers do.

5. It's okay to skim or skip parts of a story if you get bored or stuck: good readers do this, too.

6. On the form inside your reading folder, record the **title** of every book you finish or abandon, its specific **genre**, the **author**, the **date**, and your **rating** of the writing, 1–10. Use the number column on the left to keep track of the books you finish. Collect data about your reading, look for patterns, and take satisfaction in your accomplishments and discoveries.

7. Understand that reading is thinking. Do nothing that distracts your friends from the reading zone: don't put your words into their brains as they're trying to escape into literary worlds. When you talk with me about your book, *whisper*.

8. Take care of our books. Sign out every one you borrow, then sign it back in *with me*—I'll draw a line through the title and initial it. Reshelve the book in its section in the library, alphabetically by the author's last name, or, if it's a book you loved, add it to the books-we-love collection. Then return your card packet to the appropriate box.

9. Read the whole time.

10. Read as well, as much, and as happily as you can.

Figure 2.9 *Rules for Reading Workshop*

Book-Borrow Cards

Over the years I lost a lot of books. While one part of me was delighted that students were loving books so much they were borrowing them forever, another part fumed at the cost—both the price of replacing a title and its lack of availability to other readers. I went back and forth between elaborate checkout systems, which ate up my time, and freedom from systems, which ate up my books.

Action-adventure	legend
anti-war	magic realism
autobiography	manga
biography	memoir
classic	micro fiction anthology
comic novel	mystery: plot
contemporary realistic fiction	mystery: psychological
diary	mythology
dystopian fiction	new journalism
epic poem	paranormal romance
epistolary novel	parody
espionage	philosophy
essay anthology or collection	play script
family saga	poetry anthology or collection
fantasy	post-apocalypse
flash fiction anthology	retelling/recasting
free-verse memoir or novel	romance
gothic novel	science
graphic memoir or novel	science fiction
graphic narrative	series novel
historical fiction	short story anthology or collection
history	sports novel
horror	techno-thriller
humor	thriller
journalism	Western
law novel	zombie fiction

Figure 2.10 *Genres . . . So Far*

What works best is the simplest approach of all. I staple together packets of 4 × 6–inch index cards and print each student's name on the top card in a different bold color. I file the card packets in unlidded shoe boxes, one box per class, and throw in a couple of pencils. When a reader borrows a book, he finds his packet of cards in the class box and writes down the title—that's all the information we need. When a reader returns a book, she hands me her card packet and shows me the book—the ocular proof, as I like to say—and I draw a line through the title and write my initials next to it. Then the reader shelves the book or adds it to the books-we-love collection. Most often I initial titles back into the classroom library as I circulate among individuals during reading workshop check-ins. Now, instead of a third or more of the volumes in the classroom library disappearing, only a handful go missing each year.

Folders

I recognize that folders vs. a three-ring binder is a teacher's personal choice. Both have advantages and disadvantages. When my kids tried binders, the rings broke, they spent a *lot* of time reinforcing torn holes in their papers, and they still needed three folders anyway, for writing-in-process, finished writing, and reading. Today each of my students receives seven folders from me: one each for homework, poems, writing-in-process, reading, spelling, finished writing, and prose examples. Again, the school orders and purchases these because uniformity of type and color is important, but also because I want to be sure I have folders for every student, ready to be put to use, in the first days of school.

The *homework* folder has pockets. It travels between school and home every day and contains each week's homework assignment sheet, any ad hoc assignments, and any forms and notes for parents. At CTL, the homework folder is always yellow, so parents can identify it if they're inclined to monitor their children's work.

The *poetry* folder has pockets. It travels with students to the workshop each day. This is where they file the poems we unpack at the start of class. Because it gets fat, kids clean it out at the end of a trimester—they move the contents to a manila folder they keep in their lockers, and then start filing poems anew. Students collect the poems because at the end of each trimester, I'll ask them to decide which three are the best and then describe what makes them effective. In the process, students articulate their poetic criteria and demonstrate their knowledge of critical vocabulary. They also save the poems so they're available as models when a student decides to imitate the style of E. E. Cummings, the odes of Pablo Neruda, or the thirteen ways of Wallace Stevens.

The *writing-in-process* folder has pockets and brass fasteners. It travels with students to the workshop each day and goes home with them when they have writing homework, that is, every weekend. Inside it they keep the drafts of pieces of writing-in-process and a pad of paper. Two blank copies of the Individual Proofreading List, Expectations for Writing Workshop, and Rules for Writing Workshop are attached in the brass fasteners.

Reading folders have pockets only. They're stored in the classroom all year because they contain essential information about students as readers of books. Each contains four blank copies of the student reading record, stapled inside, along with Expectations for Reading Workshop, Rules for Reading Workshop, and Genres So Far, which kids tuck into one of the pockets during the first week of school.

The *spelling* folder has pockets and brass fasteners. It travels with students to all their classes, not just mine, so they can record misspellings and spelling uncertainties whenever and wherever they occur. Students attach two blank copies of the personal spelling list form in the fasteners. Procedure for Independent Word Study (Figure 4.22) and Procedures for Partner Tests (Figure 4.24) are filed in a pocket, along with a half dozen weekly word study slips (Appendix G) and a compilation of lists of frequently misspelled words that I download each fall from the Internet.

Finished writing folders have pockets and are stored in the classroom all year. They contain two blank copies of the student writing record, stapled inside, along with every piece of writing a student completes, filed chronologically, with drafts, notes, plans, peer conference record, and editing checksheet paper-clipped beneath the final copy. Finished writing stays at school so students and teachers can observe growth and set goals: it's the essential *evidence* on which evaluation is based at the end of a trimester.

The *prose* folder has pockets. It begins to see use when we move from poetry, our first genre study, to memoir, our second, usually around Columbus Day. Here, students file readings I give them: photocopies of strong memoirs, short fiction, parodies, reviews, essays, profiles, advocacy journalism, scripts, thank-you notes, and so on. Students save these so they can consult them when composing their own.

It's important not to lose sight of the reasons for all the forms and folders. They invite students to act as writers and readers, and they help them develop habits of mind and action that will support them as they go out on limbs. This is a lot of prep work and a lot of paper. While I appreciate that in the business world a high-tech company might decide to go paperless, this isn't an option for students in a writing workshop.

Starting from the first week of school, I plan rich, authentic experiences for my students. As writers I want them to learn about themselves and the world around them, understand the importance of practice, work from quantity, develop a repertoire of techniques of craft, finish pieces of writing, bring sufficient text to final copy so I can teach them how to edit and proofread and they can experience the satisfaction of completed work, be considerate of other writers, take care of materials and equipment, try to make literature every time they write, and discover what writing is good for.

I want student readers to learn about themselves and the people and world around them, understand they need to read a lot, develop preferences and criteria as readers, read poems and books and reflect on them as critics, be considerate of other readers, take care of our library, have an engaged, literary experience every time they read, and discover what reading is good for.

On August 1, like clockwork, I start to suffer the wacky dreams and outright nightmares familiar to any veteran returning to the classroom. Their meaning isn't subtle. It's time for me to get to work and make the workshop, the thing I love because my students love it so much they make me love it, too.

CHAPTER 3

GETTING STARTED

Children grow into the intellectual life around them.

—L. S. VYGOTSKY

The first week sets the tone. If students leave school at the end of it feeling ambitious and excited about themselves as writers and readers, and me as their teacher, we're halfway there.

I plan the first days in more detail than any others. A lot happens—it has to. Kids begin to know one another and come together as a corps of writers and readers. They explore the space, learn how it's organized, and glimpse what it offers them in terms of materials, resources, options, and inspirations. Many of the routines and procedures of the workshop are established during the first week, and so are my roles as teacher, writer, reader of books, responder to literature, and lover and unpacker of poems.

I begin to learn who my new kids are—about their lives outside of school and how they perceive themselves as writers and readers. I communicate the expectations and rules of the workshop. Students organize themselves—put their names on folders and insert forms. And I try to give all of them a taste of the satisfactions of writing and reading so authentic that they leave for the weekend believing this class is the real deal.

On the first day of school, CTL runs a shortened schedule. I use this class to initiate a few routines, get kids talking to one another, invite them to check out the room and its resources, and distribute surveys for students to complete about their backgrounds as writers and readers. The very first routine, a poem, is the way I start every workshop.

THE DAILY POEM

Since my students choose and read different books, the daily poems provide our common experience as readers of literature, in addition to the short prose readings that illuminate genre studies in writing workshop. Because it is a poem, it takes about ten minutes to read and talk about it. The compactness of the genre makes it possible for kids to enjoy a shared encounter with literature—to develop critical eyes and ears, criteria, and a vocabulary for talking about literary features—without robbing them of the time and practice they need to grow as independent writers and readers.

For students who aren't yet confident responders to literature, the daily poem is their entrée to literary discussion. Each morning I introduce a poem, distribute copies, and ask the group to follow along as I read it aloud. Many of my poems and introductions are included in *Naming the World: A Year of Poems and Lessons* (2006) and permitted to be reproduced for classroom use. In each lesson I describe some of the critical features that students might notice in a poem, suggest an appropriate response stance, and provide a benediction—closing remarks that point kids toward what might come next for them as poets, observers of their world, and thoughtful human beings alive on the planet.

I perform each poem with as much nuance as I can bring, and I rehearse my readings. I want kids to be able to ride on my voice into the world of the poem, hear its meaning, and observe how an experienced reader makes sense of verse forms.

Then I ask students to go back into the poem independently, read it, and mark it up. Depending on the poem, I might ask them to attend to the stanza breaks, metaphors, or verbs; to underline lines they wish they'd written, lines they don't understand yet, lines they can see, lines that surprise them, lines they think are the most important, lines that resonate, or the line where the poem changes; and, always, to mark anything they notice that a poet has done well. I annotate my copy, too. In the discussion that follows, volunteers read and talk about what they marked.

This means that I—and any students who already know some critical vocabulary—will teach less experienced critics about such features as diction, imagery, form, theme, tone, turns, figurative language, cadence, and sound patterns, in the context of shared poems. But students who aren't critical readers yet can still participate in the conversation. They can point to language that struck them or lines they could see as they lean on the security of their marked-up copies to cue their comments. Anyone can have something to say about the daily poem and, eventually, everyone does. It can even get a bit competitive. Here's Josie's account of one of our discussions.

IF AT FIRST YOU DON'T SUCCEED

So, there you are
on a typical morning—
a Monday if you must know.
Mondays are bad enough.
You're given a poem to read. Nancie's voice
echoes in the silence of the room.
You smile
at each *s* in a sentence,

the soothing sound of each line
cascading into another.
She finishes,
and, after a breathtaking pause,
everyone exhales.
You sit back
with a foolish grin.
Nancie assigns the task:
so, mark the lines and language you wanna talk about.

You feel a rush of excitement
as you ramble on and on, a page worth
of notes, critiquing and exploring the wonders
of the beautiful poem before you.
But one word, one line, one part
outshines the rest. The poem would die
without it. It gives the poem air to breathe.
This poem
was imagined, written,
and published for you and you alone.

But

you get so caught up in the revelation
of your genius
that you are half a second too late
to shoot your arm towards the sky
as a peer casually lifts a non-committal hand.
He's called on, naturally,
and asked to articulate
his contemplation
of the masterpiece.
He takes a few moments to react,
gathers his thoughts,
and finally speaks.

And

oh my God. You were going to say that
Exact. Same. Thing.
He reads the line. The few lines.
The whole stanza. With greed.
The poem is demolished
by a stolen response.
You are devastated.

Your life is ruined. Never
will you feel such satisfaction
ever
again.

Now

you realize, again too late,
that you've been called on,
your hand still waving pointlessly
in the air. You
utter a dumbfounded response
to some mediocre verb.
You feel tears prick your eyes
as you sit openmouthed,
trying to stabilize
your chaotic mind,
until Nancie asks the class
to turn the paper over
to another poem,
its theme the same.
You flip it, suspicious,
and read.
Hm. This is . . . good. Wow.
Actually . . .

On a Monday morning,
at 9:00, you
are asked to react to a poem
you've just read. Your hand
rockets
into the air.

This time
you get it.

—*Josephine Cotton*

If poetry has become a workhorse of my curriculum because of its brevity, I also count on the opportunities it affords me as a teacher of prose genres to explore issues of craft. There's no genre that can match it in terms of teaching writers about diction—about precise, vivid choices of words. In fact, apart from paragraphing, *every* lesson I want to demonstrate about effective writing begins with the daily poem: the need for a writer to find subjects that matter, the importance of first-person voice and reflection, how most adverbs and some adjectives are clutter, the value of tangible nouns and sensory verbs, how to use a thesaurus to find sensory verbs and adjectives, why and how to revise, how to polish writing at the single-word level, how repetition can create cadence and move a piece of writing, what titles do, why readers want concrete specifics, how a conclusion should resonate, how writers develop and support their themes, and how periods, commas, dashes, semicolons, and colons give voice to writing. Lessons they learn from poetry about diction, specificity, imagery, intentionality, meaning, voice, audience, organization, conclusions, and punctuation show up in my students' writing across the genres.

And if poetry has become the most effective way I know to teach about craft, I also appreciate its versatility. Poetry appeals and matters to my kids because they or I can find—or write—a poem about any subject that appeals and matters to them: growing up, every sport, childhood, siblings, gender, race, history, comic book heroes, friendship, food, war, peace, toys, nature, God, parents, chocolate, identity, dogs, death, computer games, school, prejudice, and poetry itself.

To find poems that middle school kids will like and want to talk about, I check out online poetry resources such as poets.org, poetryfoundation.org, and writersalmanac .publicradio.org. I also read and Post-it note my way through the collections, anthologies, and poetry journals that I purchase for the classroom library. Sometimes a whole book yields only one poem that meets my criteria: it's a poem I like, so I can demonstrate enthusiasm when I share it; it's a poem I found memorable, so there's a chance it might make an impression on my kids; it's a poem I think adolescents will like or at least be intrigued by; and it's a poem that shows something about poetry's range, so students will be helped to understand what their own poems can be about and do. I also save poetry by my kids—brave or funny poems, sensory ones, first attempts, interesting experiments, prizewinners, gifts for loved ones, and noble failures. Many of the authors of the daily poems are my students, current and former.

My students learn that I've taken poetry into my life because it's useful to me. On the first short day of school, I pass out copies of, read aloud, and talk from my heart about a useful poem—"To Be of Use" by Marge Piercy, "The Ponds" or "Wild Geese" by Mary Oliver, "How to See Deer" by Phillip Booth, or "Ode to an Apple" by Pablo Neruda. I distribute poetry folders and black Sharpies, and students write their names on the folders and file their first poem of the year. Then, on subsequent mornings, we read and discuss one of the first themed sequences in *Naming the World*, either poems that show "What Poetry Can Do" or poems about identity, gathered under the heading "Your Life."

ICEBREAKING

Every veteran teacher has a grab bag of September icebreakers. Two that do the trick for me and the workshop are a team scavenger hunt and a game of toss.

The night before school starts, I divide each class into four teams. These are the only groups I assign all year. I've found that small groups are more engaged and productive when their composition is congenial. On occasion I will ask a class to make sure there are boys *and* girls in their groups, or seventh *and* eighth graders, and I always intervene to help a lost soul find a place. On this first day I assign the teams because I want to be sure that students new to CTL have veterans to guide them, mix kids from the two grades I teach, and ask returning eighth graders to take the lead.

When students enter the classroom for the first time, they find the minilesson circle already defined by beanbags and pillows I arranged that morning before school. I announce the team assignments and the task: "Find everything on the scavenger hunt list headed 'Mapping the Humanities Room' (Figure 3.1). That means put your hands on it and site it on a map of the classroom by its corresponding number." Each team gets a clipboard with a map attached and a copy of the list, and off they go. I circulate and help with the clues as they discover how the room is organized or reorganized, where their reading and finished writing folders are stored, some of the systems and resources, and, especially, the books. Every team wins, and everyone earns a Tootsie Roll Pop as a prize.

For the second icebreaker, I bought the biggest beach ball I could find and covered it with nonthreatening personal questions I hope will get kids talking and laughing (Figure 3.2). After they return to the circle, I give the directions: "Play toss, be sure to include everyone, and, when you catch the ball, answer the question closest to your right thumb." We find out a lot of silly stuff about one another, and I begin to build my knowledge of my new students.

Then it's time for the first homework assignment of the school year: completion of writing and reading surveys. I designed the survey questions, which appear as Figures 3.3 and 3.4, to get at students' self-perceptions, histories, preferences, processes, strengths, and plans as readers and writers, plus their working knowledge of basic conventions of usage.

I tell the class, "We started our time together with you learning something about me, poetry, and a poem I've taken into my life. Then you learned about this space and what's in it for you as writers and readers. Finally, all of us learned deep, soul-baring information about one another from a beach ball. Tonight for homework, help me learn about you as a writer and reader. Teach me what you like, what you need, what you do, and what you know. The more you can tell me, the better I'll be able to teach you and make sure you're satisfied and successful as a writer and reader this year."

At this juncture, students will need their yellow homework folders and copies of the weekly homework assignment sheet (Figure 3.5). They label and write their names on the yellow folders, put Monday's date at the top of the homework sheet, and copy the assignment, which I've written on the easel pad, in the space for work due the following day: *Complete my writing and reading surveys as well as I can.* Then they file the two surveys and the assignment sheet in a pocket of their homework folders.

MAPPING THE HUMANITIES ROOM

1. The drawer you'll open when you've finished a book and need to record its title
2. The shelf where you'd look for books by Carl Deuker, John Coy, David Klass, and others who write great novels about sports
3. The place where you'll find collections by Langston Hughes, Wallace Stevens, and E. E. Cummings
4. A group of novels about the lives of kids during the Salem witch trials, War for Independence, Civil War, Holocaust, and Civil Rights movement
5. The tray where you'll place a piece of your writing after you've self-edited it in red, so Nancie can take it home and copyedit it in black
6. The place where you'll put a piece of your writing so Nancie may give it a quick read, i.e., *eyeball* it vs. copyedit it
7. The bookcases and shelves in this room that are off limits to kids because they contain Glenn's and Nancie's teaching materials
8. The place you'll put a book you want to rave about in a booktalk
9. When you've finished a piece of writing, the place where you'll record its title and genre and file it, together with all its drafts, notes, etc.
10. Where you'll head if Taboo, Mad Gab, or juggling are your cups of recess tea
11. The shelf where you'll find the five subjects of this instruction: "Will you please just take four pieces and *pass it on already?*"
12. The drawer you'll open for a new folder when one of yours self-destructs
13. The bookcase that houses a hero who wonders, "To be or not to be?"
14. The shelves you'll browse for a great true story
15. The center of the reading universe: the place where the best books in the room will soon be found
16. The cards on which you'll sign out, and Nancie will sign back in, every single book you ever borrow from this room from now until June or else
17. The place to look for stories told in the form of free-verse poems
18. The resource you'll crack open when you're seeking an alternative to a weak verb, such as *have*, *go*, *do*, *get*, or *make*
19. The utensils Nancie provides to you to *edit* your writing and *only* to edit your writing
20. The shelf where you'll find stories in which the future is bleak
21. The shelves to head to if you want to sample an adult or transitional title
22. The shelf where you'll find extra spelling study slips and blank homework assignment sheets
23. The place you'll find Ted L. Nancy acting like a nut, David Sedaris talking pretty, and white people being pale
24. The resource you'll consult if you're drafting a sonnet and need a word that rhymes with *elbow*
25. The place you'll go to satisfy an interest in paranormal affairs
26. The shelf that's home to anti-war and war stories
27. The premier pens on the face of the earth and a reviser's dream utensil

Figure 3.1 *Mapping the Humanities Room*

BEACH BALL ICEBREAKER QUESTIONS

Directions: Answer the question your right thumb is closest to when you catch the ball.

The story behind your first name?
A favorite flavor of ice cream?
A good movie you saw this summer?
Your middle name?
Right or left-handed?
Favorite sport to play? To watch?
Favorite TV show when you were little? Now?
Your pet's personality?
Your current favorite song?
Coffee, tea, cocoa, or chai?
Dark, milk, or white chocolate?
Last book you read—and would you recommend it?
Favorite Disney movie?
Favorite junk food?
Favorite and least favorite vegetables?
Favorite pizza topping(s)?
Favorite toy when you were little?
Ideal birthday cake?
Do you believe in ghosts?
Worst movie you saw in the last year?
Favorite Crayola color when you were little? Now?
A pet peeve?
Dream car?
Worst injury so far?
Most famous person you've met or seen?
Favorite kind of gum?
Coke or Pepsi?
Did you have an imaginary friend when you were little?
Favorite color M&M?
Someone you admire?
Would you consider a tattoo?
Favorite potatoes: mashed, baked, fries, chips?
Cats or dogs?
Time travel choice: future or past?
Favorite local restaurant and meal?
Comfort food?
Dream job?

Figure 3.2 *Beach Ball Icebreaker Questions*

SEPTEMBER WRITING SURVEY

NAME _____ DATE _____

1. Are you a writer? _____
   (If your answer is YES, answer question 2a. If your answer is NO, go on to 2b.)

2a. How did **you** learn to write?

OR

2b. How did other people learn to write?

3. What does someone have to do or know in order to write well? List as many of a good writer's abilities, habits, techniques, processes, kinds of knowledge, or approaches as you can think of.

4. What are your favorite genres—or kinds—of writing, and why?

5. What kinds of responses from others help you improve your writing?

6. What makes writing easier for you?

Figure 3.3 *September Writing Survey*   *(continues)*

7. What makes writing harder?

8. What do you think are your three greatest strengths as a writer?

  •

  •

  •

9. What would you like to get better at as a writer? Try to think of three goals.

  •

  •

  •

10. So far, what's the best thing that ever happened to you as a writer?

11. In general, how do you feel about writing and yourself as a writer?

12. Writers use the rules or *conventions* of written English to show readers what to *do* or *understand*. To the best of your knowledge, what are all the reasons a writer might use a . . .

Period?

Comma?

Apostrophe?

Colon?

Semicolon?

Dash?

Capital letter?

New Paragraph?

Figure 3.3 *Continued*

SEPTEMBER READING SURVEY

NAME _____ DATE _____

1. If you had to guess . . .

    How many books would you say you owned? _____

    How many books would you say there are in your house? _____

    How many books did you read during the last school year, September–June? _____

    And how many of those books did you choose for yourself? _____

    How many books have you read since school let out in June? _____

    Do you think you read a lot, about average, or less than average, compared with other American kids your age? _____

2. What are the best three books you've read in the past couple of years?

3. In your ideal novel, what would the main character be like?

4. What are your favorite genres—or kinds—of books to read?

5. Who are your favorite authors these days? List as many as you'd like.

6. Which poets are your favorites?

7. When and where do you like to read—what's your best time and place?

Figure 3.4 *September Reading Survey*   *(continues)*

8. What are some of the ways you decide whether you'll read a particular book?

9. Have you ever liked a book so much that you reread it? _____ If so, what's the title? Can you think of any others?

10. Do you know the title or author of the book(s) you'd like to read next? _____ If so, please tell me.

11. What makes reading easier for you?

12. What makes reading harder?

13. What do you think are your three greatest strengths as a reader of books?

   •

   •

   •

14. What would you like to get better at as a reader of books? Try to think of three goals.

   •

   •

   •

15. On a scale of 1–10, how do you rate reading as a free-time activity?

16. In general, how do you feel about books and yourself as a reader?

Figure 3.4 *Continued*

Gr. 7-8 HOMEWORK FOR THE WEEK OF _Sept. 6th_

[THIS FORM SHOULD APPEAR IN THE FRONT, RIGHT POCKET OF YOUR YELLOW FOLDER.]

DUE MONDAY
· If you received a letter last week, respond to a friend's reading journal
· Read a book for $^1/_2$ hour
· Writing: one hour's worth
  (My weekend writing plan: _____)
· Science: complete assigned lab write-up *and/or* assigned reading, highlighted, with big ideas
· Math: work on current assignment for $^1/_2$ hour *

Labor Day

DUE TUESDAY
· Read a book for $^1/_2$ hour
· Spelling: select five new words to study
· Science: science in the news clippings
· Math: work on current assignment for $^1/_2$ hour *

DUE WEDNESDAY
· Read a book for $^1/_2$ hour
· Math: work on current assignment for $^1/_2$ hour *
· Drama: _____
· Read and highlight science-in-the-news article

My writing and Reading Surveys, as much as I can tell Nancie

DUE THURSDAY
· Every third week, write a letter-essay in your reading journal to Nancie or a friend
· Read a book for $^1/_2$ hour
· Spelling: complete the word study
· Science: review mini-lesson notes and prompt response
· Math: work on current assignment for $^1/_2$ hour *

Pre-Lab due —
Read Timeline of Earth Packet

Deconstruct Political cartoons w/ Mom or Dad

1/2 hour of writing, free verse, about a territory that calls my name

DUE FRIDAY
· Read a book for $^1/_2$ hour
· Math: work on current assignment for $^1/_2$ hour, plus five additional words defined and referenced on your math word wall*
· Science: three-paragraph science-in-the-news reflection

•Homework Slip Signed by Mom or Dad

•Computer agreement Signed by M. or D. + ME

* Also see the separate math homework log: the first page in the student's math binder.

Figure 3.5 *Weekly Homework Assignment Sheet*

The homework assignment sheet is an attempt by my middle school colleagues and me to organize our students to do schoolwork at home. As a K–8 faculty, our homework policy is straightforward: no busywork and no assignment that won't be acted on in a significant way the next day. As the typed entries on the homework assignment sheet indicate, seventh and eighth graders have at least an hour's worth of homework every night: half an hour of math and half an hour of independent reading. Students record ad hoc assignments, like the writing and reading surveys, in the blank spaces.

In a joint letter home and in personal contacts we make with every parent in the first two weeks of school, the math and science teachers and I ask parents to look for the yellow folder and the assignment sheet inside it and help their children follow through, to ensure kids will be able to participate in class the next day, when activity will build on the homework. We also encourage parents and students to call or e-mail us at home if they have any question, ever, about a child's assignment.

Each of our students begins the year with one pass in every subject: one opportunity for a teacher to excuse an incomplete or missing assignment. After that, teachers mail home a form letter that indicates what wasn't completed for which class and asks parents for their involvement and oversight. After three homework letters for one subject, the teacher schedules a meeting with the student and his or her parents to discuss what needs to happen at home so the child can come to school ready to engage. In my classes, when a student is unprepared, I won't let him or her participate in the activity. Since most of my assignments are the bases for small-group discussions and activities, a student who didn't do the homework has to sit out and miss the fun. Worse, he or she has to sit in with me during noon recess and complete the assignment.

I am fierce about homework, but I'm careful to assign only what matters. The nightly half hour of reading is a prime example. Regular reading is essential. When reading isn't happening at home, the focus of my meeting with the student and parents is *why:* Is there no obvious time or place to read at home? Is the child forgetting to take home his or her book? Does the family not understand the importance of voluminous reading to the child's future? Then we negotiate an arrangement for when and where regular reading will happen in their household. I am not hoping that every kid will read every night; I am doing everything I can to make certain they do.

At the end of our first class, I remind students they'll need to bring their two new folders, for poetry and homework, to class with them tomorrow. I ask that they also bring the hundred-page spiral notebooks that will become their writing–reading handbooks. I collect the supplies they brought in—the pencils, red pens, and paper clips—which I store away and add to the materials center as necessary. Then I meet briefly with returning eighth graders to sign back in the books they borrowed from me over the summer and to start lining up veterans to present booktalks about favorite titles in the classroom library.

The other middle school teachers and I meet with all the kids later that day for forty-five minutes to discuss housekeeping issues: the Monday–Friday schedule, homework policy, behavior guidelines, social considerations, lunchtime procedures, recess possibilities, and computer rules.

The Launch: Writing Workshop

Students enter the minilesson circle on the second day of school with their writing–reading handbooks, poetry folders, homework folders, and writing and reading surveys, which I collect. At home that night I'll create a chart for each student and record shorthand notes about their habits and preferences as writers and readers and any emerging themes. I start with the writing surveys.

Yes or *no:* does a student perceive him- or herself as a writer? Is the individual's knowledge of the craft of writing *deep, fair,* or *superficial?* Which genres are favorites? What support is the student looking for as a writer? *Yes* or *no:* can he or she self-assess beyond spelling and handwriting? *Yes* or *no:* has the student had any positive experiences as a writer? Is the student's overall attitude toward writing *positive, neutral,* or *negative? Which* of the eight conventions doesn't he or she have a firm grasp of yet?

In terms of reading, my shorthand observations include a student's access to books in the home (*good, fair,* or *poor*); prior experience as an independent reader (*high, medium, low,* or *none*); range of genres (*wide, medium,* or *narrow*); knowledge of authors and poets (*deep, fair,* or *superficial*—the last means J. K. Rowling and Shel Silverstein); independent reading habits (*strong, medium,* or *limited*); the kind of support the student is looking for as a reader; the ability to self-assess beyond decoding (*yes* or *no*); and overall attitude (the rating-scale number and either *strong, fair,* or *negative*).

Students' responses to the surveys and my summary notes become the foundation for a year of their self-assessment as writers and readers, my assessment of them, and my plans as their teacher. Kids who own no books or don't read at home, can't name favorites, think reading is boring, don't perceive themselves as writers, demonstrate minimal knowledge of writing process, and can't name any strengths as writers will need my attention right away. I'll focus on getting books with great stories and characters into their hands, encourage them to find and raise their voices as writers, and celebrate their initial efforts like mad. In June, I ask students to complete the surveys again, compare their September and June answers, and, when they complete their final self-assessment of the school year, cite the changes they notice as part of their responses.

Back in the minilesson circle, after our first poetry discussion, I ask kids to label and put names on their writing–reading handbooks. I always buy a half dozen spiral notebooks in case any students weren't able to follow through and I give these to kids as necessary. Then I launch the workshop with a minilesson about finding topics for writing.

All year long I show my students different ways to uncover, capture, and act on their intentions as writers, and I make sure the classroom is a fertile environment for writing ideas. I read aloud, and we read together, poems, memoirs, short short fiction, essays, parodies, profiles, reviews, and advocacy journalism. I conduct the status-of-the-class survey out loud so they can hear one another's ideas for topics. I schedule class readings of cut-and-paste anthologies of their writing. I provide information about publication options—the school literary magazine, national and regional contests, websites and journals that feature teen writing, guidelines for letters to the editor and guest editorials in local papers, places to submit reviews, and the power of gifts of writing for people they love. I also conduct a lot of minilessons about topic development: each is an invitation to students to generate and record ideas they might explore in a different genre. And at every step I remind students: "You could do this."

I launch the year by demonstrating the range of my interests as a writer and inviting students to begin to name and lay claim to theirs. I call these ideas our *writing territories:* the ground each of us might cover as a writer. In August I update my own list of territories (Figure 3.6). Because I use it both to show kids what writing can be good for and to inspire topics, I make my territories specific, personal, unpretentious, and inviting: ideas of mine that might spark theirs. I reproduce my list on overhead transparencies and use it as the basis for my first minilesson.

> Will you please open your writing–reading handbooks and turn the first three pages? We'll set these aside, so later they can become a table of contents for the hundred-page handbook we'll write together this year. Your handbook is where you'll gather ideas for writing, keep track of books you want to read someday, take notes about minilesson information or tape in notes I give you, create a lexicon of literary terms, and, later in the year, respond to prose readings. Right now, please write the number *1* in the upper right-hand corner on the front of the *fourth* page in your handbook. We'll use the front sides of pages only. Title your page 1 as I did the overhead transparency: *My Writing Territories*.
>
> Today the most important thing for you to know about me is that I write, and for lots of different reasons. I call the ideas I'd like to pursue my *territories*. The ground I might cover as a writer includes topics I want to write about and the kinds of writing or *genres* that might fit them.
>
> My territories list is a window on who I am as a citizen, woman, teacher, learner, mother, wife, daughter, gardener, dog owner, food lover, and exercise hater. It's the place I go when I'm trying to decide what to write next. It's the bank where I deposit my ideas. It's a reminder: "Oh, yeah, I remember—I wanted to do *that* as a writer." And when I get a new idea, which I know I'll lose if I don't write it down, this is where I capture it. Keeping a list like this helps me be more organized, productive, and satisfied. It's a memo to myself—what I know and care about as a person who writes.

NANCIE'S WRITING TERRITORIES

- Almond M&Ms—my favorites: sugar *and* protein—an ode? a humorous essay?
- My love of flip flops—a poem that plays with their sound and rhythm?
- The heron on our pond: his F-R-R-R-A-A-H-H-H-N-N-K-K call when he arrives each June; how we know it's low tide when he comes to wade and fish . . . until this summer, when an oyster farmer took over the pond. Now it may never be low tide or summer again; cormorants have started to perch on the oyster pontoons, and they look like vultures to me—a memoir? a persuasive essay?
- Mashed potatoes: the ultimate comfort food—a personal essay?
- Bacon and O.J.: the ultimate combo—an ode?
- Rosie spitting out a four-leaf clover on the kitchen floor—a poem?
- Rosie then (a puppy) and now (aged eleven)—contrast her morning kisses, ball catching, walking and talking the garden together—a parallel stanzas poem?
- Ben & Jerry's New York Super Fudge Chunk has *everything*: it's salty, sweet, creamy, bitter, smooth, and chunky—an ode?
- Why exercise is stupid and boring—an essay?
- Dangerous stuff my parents let me do/didn't bother to check out: shooting a B-B gun, throwing snowballs with stones in them, dam-building and catching crayfish in a polluted creek, setting off fireworks, building go-carts with lawnmower engines, races and crashes, backyard dumps, midnight hide 'n' go seek, bike jumps, shed jumping, no-helmet-no-hands-no-feet bike riding, scabs, scars—a personal essay?
- An ode to the acorn—Cody's joke—à la Neruda's ode to an apple?
- The *need* for kids to choose their books—a speech or essay?
- Kids' bedrooms: Anne's and how she's long gone, but all the layers remain and create a shrine to her childhood and adolescence—an essay? a poem?
- Wild turkeys: prehistoric beasts that stroll past our screened-in porch and prove that birds did, in fact, evolve from dinosaurs—a poem?
- *In the Middle*, third edition—a professional book for teachers
- A lifetime of bad eyesight—20/500; I need glasses to find my glasses—a memoir?
- Blue—an ode to my favorite color
- Reading ritual: in my favorite chair with a great novel and Rosie in its mate beside me and upside down—a poem?
- Candy corn, Mary Janes, fireballs, candy cigarettes, and Canada mints: the gourmet foods of my childhood, plus memories of making sparks in the dark with wintergreen Lifesavers—a personal essay or a memoir?
- Shopping for shoes as one of my favorite acts of meditation—a poem or an essay?
- Writing by hand: my favorite, hard-to-find Liquid Expresso pens—their glide so easy it feels as if I'm thinking with my fingers—a personal essay? a poem?
- Connections between obsessive gardening and Anne growing up and leaving home—a memoir? an essay?
- Toby's and my all-occasion toast: "To Anne." A gift of writing for her?
- Why everyone in America should read *The New York Times* every day—a rant/essay?
- The sausage and egg McMuffin = my American guilty pleasure #1—a poem? a personal essay?

Figure 3.6 *Nancie's Writing Territories*

I'm going to talk from my territories list for ten minutes. If something I say rings a bell—makes you think of a topic you might like to try some-day—please jot it down on your territories list. When I'm done, you'll have ten minutes to continue your list, and then a chance to talk with others and glean even more ideas from them. That's not copying; it's being inspired. The goal is for you to gather as many topics as you can before you leave here today. Don't lose any germ of an idea that comes to you while I'm talking. Listen and write at the same time. Ready?

I've got to start my territories with the candy I can't see without buying it, the sweet treat I know *has* to be good for me, because, well, there's an al-mond in the middle, and that's a source of protein. Right? *Right?* I'm thinking I could write an ode to almond M&M's, like one of Pablo Neruda's odes to common things. Or maybe a humorous essay about my obsession with it. What's the candy you have trouble walking past without drooling and beg-ging your mom to buy it? Jot it down. . . . [And so on, down the list. My DVD project *Writing in the Middle: Workshop Essentials* (2011) features a complete riff on my territories.]

These are my writing ideas for the year—my obsessions, memories, re-sponsibilities, itches, rituals, and frustrations. My writing about these topics will take different forms—poems, memoirs, essays or articles, gifts of writing, even a book.

Now it's your turn. Please take ten minutes to continue your list of ter-ritories. It's fine for you not to consider genres today. It's more important to concentrate on topics. Go for quantity, and try not to censor yourself. See how many ideas you can capture, and anticipate that new ideas will piggyback on previous ones if you let them. The goal is to fill the page.

If you get stuck, you might want to consider this list of categories [Figure 3.7], plus two other writers' territories, generated on another first day of school by eighth graders Tristan and Sophia [Figures 3.8 and 3.9]. The check marks on Tristan's list indicate that these are topics he wrote about that school year.

I circulate among the kids, look over their shoulders, whisper questions, and point out categories of topics they haven't considered yet. After ten minutes, I ask them to partner up with two or three other writers and take turns reading aloud ideas from their lists, with inspiration as the goal: "When a classmate's idea rings a bell, add it to your own territories, because this is the reason your group is meeting." I tell them I'm confi-dent everyone will generate at least a half dozen additions. Again, I circulate and nudge.

When the small groups return to the minilesson circle, I celebrate quantity: "How many people found six new ideas? Ten? More than that?" And I issue an invitation. "Please add to your territories list *whenever* an idea for a piece of writing occurs to

IN COLLECTING YOUR WRITING TERRITORIES, REMEMBER AND CONSIDER . . .	
obsessions	clothing and shoes
idiosyncrasies	hairdos and haircuts
problems	pets, now and then
dreams	teachers, now and then
itches	places: school, camp, trips, a beach, times away with friends and relatives
confusions	
passions	hobbies
pet peeves	collections
sorrows	first times doing something
scars	holidays and family rituals
risks	sports
accomplishments	games: computers, board, team
fears	music
worries	books
fantasies	poems
memories of:	songs
grandparents	movies
mom and dad	writers and artists
cousins	food you love or hate or used to
friends, now and when you were little	beloved stuffies and other possessions
fads	all the loves of your life
favorites, now and when you were little	

Figure 3.7 *In Collecting Your Writing Territories, Remember and Consider . . .*

My Writing Territories   1.

Target Store   My desk
Reese's   My room
Hersheys   Gettysburg
Lindts   Board games
Buffalo wings from Applebee's with honey sauce
All pork
Life
Feebee my dog
Legos — used to play with them
My laptop
My video games— Sid Meiers Civilization IV and Blitzkreig 2
Family — Mom ⟩ sister — Saturday nights & dinner & movies
          Pop
          Grammy + Grampy
          3 aunts + uncles
No sports, though I like to watch baseball and hear about it
Going to learn how to play drums and guitar
Led Zeppelin, The Rolling Stones, etc.
Driving — tractors & cars
Black — favorite color
I love art
I hate flip flops
2 hobbies — Diorama making and card making
Camp Good News every year
Book stores
Meet the Fockers
House building
Mac and cheese — Kraft
Eating 2 packets of raw Domino's sugar
Good n' Plenty
Soda Jerk
Dunkin Donuts — chocolate frosted
Eggs

Figure 3.8 *Tristan's Writing Territories*

Writing Territories

putting make-up on when I was little
needing noise to fall asleep
Little Enstien's videos
Crying when I read The giving Tree
taste of Christmas (candy caine)
lamb chops – B-day dinner
picking out the perfect Christmas tree
Barbies
Worried I wouldn't fit in because I didn't have A&F or Aero
fudge from Perries nuthouse
School shopping
Star gazing
Getting my first American Girl doll
The smell of the plastic food in my grandmother's house
Love sagas w/ Barbies and w/ Josie
Sitting around the campfire
Snow forts
throwing wood in the basement
Riding bikes in dark
My room
Putting down Lilly
Going to the Red Sox
Chocolate lollie-pops
Building the camp fire w̄ my dad
how my cat presses his forehead to mine
Going to Treats w̄ Eloise alone
Jumping waves w̄ my dad
Thursday nights
Making fun of newspeople & TODAY w̄ my mom
3 dolphins in a arch
Eating in a cafe in NYC
Grand Canyon
Car rides w̄ mom

Figure 3.9 *Sophia's Writing Territories*

you—don't count on remembering it if you haven't written it down, and do take responsibility for developing projects that matter to you as a writer."

Finally, I assign homework: "Please draft for half an hour tonight, in the form of a free-verse poem, about a topic on your territories list that *calls your name*—one it would be intriguing and enjoyable for you to explore. We've already read two free-verse poems together. Here's a working definition: a free-verse poem doesn't rhyme and relies on the natural rhythms of speech." And I explain why we're starting with poetry.

"It is the mother genre—the literary foundation upon which you'll build excellence as a writer. Because its form is more compact than prose, you'll be able to finish pieces of writing right away, experience a whole writing process, and feel the satisfaction of finished work. Through writing poetry, you'll also learn how to pay attention, figure out what matters, make sense of it, give shape to it, consider diction or word choices, build themes, craft literature, and, more so than with any other genre, help yourselves lead lives of worth."

Since students don't compose in their writing–reading handbooks, I give each of them a pad of lined writing paper. Then I pass out the writing-in-process folders and demonstrate how to assemble the contents: the pad in a pocket and, inserted in the brass fasteners, the rules and expectations for writing workshop on the bottom and the two copies of the individual proofreading list on top. I circulate a cup of highlighting pens, and together we review and highlight the expectations for a year of writing workshop, with my copy projected on an overhead transparency.

I don't expect students to highlight based on my underlining. The point is for them to decide what's important enough to underline and to engage—eyes *and* ears *and* small motor. My kids agree that highlighting helps them focus, and, because they're twelve and thirteen, they like the bright colors—some so much that certain markers become preadolescent status symbols. Go figure. Anyone who's not convinced it's possible to write a poem about anything might consider Abbey's about blue highlighters.

LEGEND OF THE HIGHLIGHTER

Every weekday morning from 8:50 until 10:15,
my seventh-grade life revolved around one thing:
nabbing one of the two blue highlighters.

Yes—
those highlighters shone bright,
summer and winter
a soft reminder that vibrant orange
and lemony yellow would forever be
second bests.

The competition was tough.
The cup was stuffed with oranges

and filled with all the yellows
I could never want.
They didn't carry the winter sky
or summer ocean.

The two blues
vanished
into the same hands
every time.

The Rule of SO WHAT? OR THEME
was ruined for me.

Two
blue
highlighters.
Whenever the cup rounded our circle,
my face was a hundred-page book that read
disappointment.

But with a fresh year come fresh traditions.
The cup was passed counter-clockwise,
and my hand became a skill crane:
it was the first time I won
the prize.

It was
summer and winter
at once,
and I was an eighth grader.

               —*Abbey Hutchins*

The launch of writing workshop is the last day all my kids are doing the same thing. Starting tomorrow, when they bring in the drafts of the poems they started at home, each student will have a different agenda to pursue. This can be a daunting proposition for a teacher to get his or her mind around—it was for me. But because of workshop routines and rules, I know now not to panic. I've learned to look forward to whatever they show up with the next morning—to the diversity of their styles, perceptions, and topic choices, and to getting down to an approach to teaching that will make a difference for every one of them.

The third day of school brings a full-blown writing workshop with all its components in place: daily poem, minilesson, status-of-the class survey, independent writing time, and individual conferences with me. As the minilesson, we read and highlight the rules for writing workshop, and I point them toward the guidelines that make the biggest difference: "Write on one side of the paper, double-space, and, when word processing, always print double-spaced, so you'll get in the habit of creating the breathing space that makes revision possible." I also stress the need to understand that *writing is thinking.* Conversations and other distractions prevent deep thinking and literary writing. I read to them an essential quotation for the wall of any writing workshop, Kafka's observation, "One can never be alone enough when one writes . . . there can never be enough silence when one writes . . . even *night* is not *night* enough."

I'm responsible to create the potential of night, of solitude and quiet, for every writer. Right from the start I enforce the rule against talking at the tables or computers. As soon as I hear chat, I zoom over to the chatters and get stern: "This space and time is for the hard thinking of writing. When you talk, you're distracting the brains of writers who are working hard to craft literature. *Be quiet.*"

I help keep the volume low by keeping my own voice low as I circulate and meet with writers. I whisper, and I remind anyone who responds to me at a conversational level to whisper, too. If I'm loud, the room becomes loud; it never fails. I try not to be a distraction to the other writers when I settle my chair next to a student's and whisper, "How's it coming?" When there is a disturbance during independent writing time, I've learned to get up and travel to the source, instead of remonstrating across the room and raising the heads of the whole class.

After today's minilesson about workshop rules, I teach kids how to look at a piece of their writing, make plans for it, and then respond to the status-of-the-class survey:

> Each day, before you go your own way as writers, I'll ask you to tell me what you'll be doing: your topic, the genre, and where you are in the piece. I'll write down what you tell me. This is called a *status-of-the-class survey.* It's how I'll keep track of your activity and progress, since every writer in the workshop is doing something different.
>
> So, what's your plan for today? Let's consider the options. You might be continuing the first draft of the poem you started last night. Maybe you're starting a second draft: either typing or handwriting a new version of your poem. You might be reading it over and revising it—considering what you've written and making changes on the first draft. You may realize, in the cold light of a new day, that you chose a topic that doesn't call your name. Maybe you made a safe choice. If that's the case, it's more than okay to abandon it. Look at your territories list again, choose a topic that *yells* your name, and begin a new first draft. Everyone, take the next thirty seconds to look at what you have on paper and decide what you'll do today as a writer.
>
> Now, when I call your name, tell me the topic of your poem—not the title, because titles usually come at the end, but what your poem is *about.* Then tell me what you intend to do with it in today's workshop.
>
> Please don't talk while others are reporting their topics and plans. I want to do this quickly, so you can get down to work as writers, but I also want you to hear other writers' topics, because their ideas may inspire yours.

I use the vocabulary of writing process right from the start and teach it in context—*topic, first draft, second draft, revise, genre, abandon*. The last is a crucial concept, especially for students who haven't had experience developing their own ideas. They can settle on tired subjects that offer little potential for developing a theme or topics so broad it would take a book to do them justice. Instead of expecting kids to pursue weak choices to the bitter end, it just makes sense to give them permission to abandon an idea that isn't working and move on to one they can embrace.

Another reason I teach the vocabulary of writing process is to speed up the status-of-the-class survey. Giving kids the words means they can cut to the chase. But I need to cut to the chase, too. This isn't a time to confer with individual writers, since my purpose is to make a record. If status takes longer than a few minutes, I'm wasting the whole group's writing time. If a student hesitates, or if I have questions or qualms, I leave the space blank and come back to the writer once the minilesson circle has disbanded.

By the end of the status-of-the-class, each writer has made a contract with me, one I can hold kids to if they veer into misbehavior. Their responses aren't carved in stone—they can change their plans—but they recognize I'm holding them accountable for working and producing. Before they leave the circle, I offer the benediction I'll pronounce all year long at this juncture: "Off you go. Work hard, and make literature."

And then I'm on the move as I try to meet with every writer in this workshop or the next one, make sure everyone has an intriguing topic, and check that they're producing text and on track. It's a busy time. It passes so quickly I can never believe it when I look at the clock and see we're about to encroach on reading workshop.

In my first conference with seventh grader Carl about his first piece of writing, I encountered a writer who had gone off track. When I stopped at his desk, I found a rhyming poem about a general subject, without a first-person presence or the hint of a theme, and with a last line I could only regard as the act of a desperate rhymer (Figure 3.10).

"Carl," I said, after I skimmed the draft, "why are you writing about this?"

"'Cause, you know, it's my rep," he explained. "I'm in a lot of plays—everybody knows that."

"So, if you and everyone else already knows this, why are you writing about it?" Carl shrugged. I continued. "Do you think maybe you chose this topic *because* it's obvious? The problem with a list of things about school plays is that it doesn't let you see or feel anything. As a reader, I can't see or feel anything either. I'm wondering if maybe this was a safe choice, you know, for the first week of school. Would you consider abandoning it and moving on to a topic you do have strong feelings about?"

By the end of this nudge, Carl was ready. Together we looked at his territories list for an idea that yelled his name, and he jumped at a subject he did love and find compelling: Hans, his dog. But I had another question for him.

"Can you tell me why you rhymed this? The assignment was to write free verse."

9/8 School Plays Draft 1

School plays are Different—
not the same.
They Drive me right
out of my my Brain.
getting ready is a Big fuss.
Even if making them perfect
is not a must.
The Directer actually
knows your Name.
wich is a very
Big gain.
unlike the Big productions
you see
on Broadway and at MSMT.
These little plays are more
for the heart
wich means that they
can Be more of a fart.

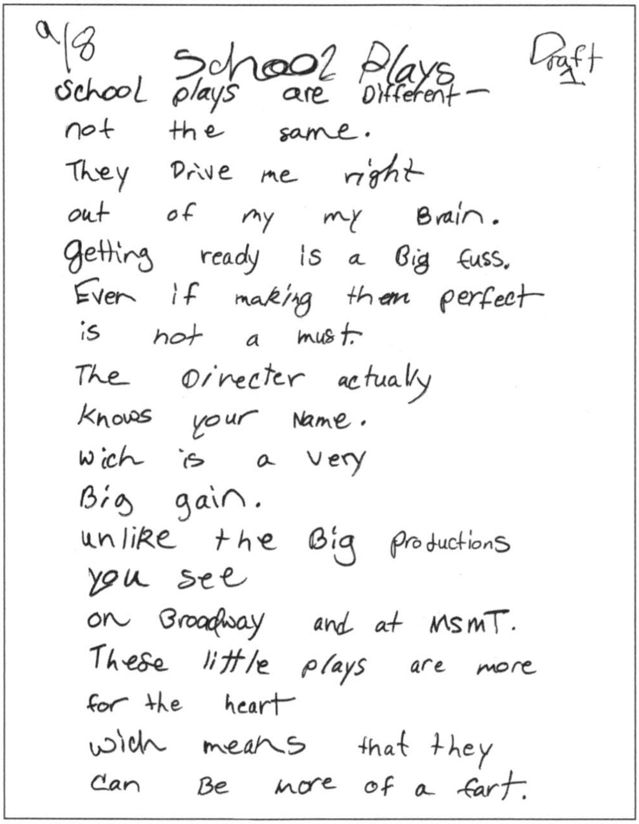

Figure 3.10 *First Draft of Carl's First Poem*

"Oh, my poems always rhyme," he said. "I've tried to write some free-verse ones, but all my poems come out rhyming."

"Carl, are you trying to tell me you have, like, rhymer's Tourette's syndrome? Look, free-verse poetry is based on the way people talk. If you can speak without rhyming, you can write a poem without rhyming. Talk to me about Hans—tell me something you love about him or like doing with him, and I'll start drafting a free-verse poem from what you tell me."

I scribed two or three lines from Carl's dictation, just enough to get him started. Then I made him a promise. "I know so many great things a poet can do besides rhyme. I'll teach your class all of them in minilessons. I promise you'll have a toolkit of free-verse techniques to bring to your poem about Hans."

Although longer than usual, this conference eliminated the need for the many subsequent meetings Carl and I would otherwise have devoted to attempts to salvage "School Plays." That poem did not have good bones. I could see it, and I helped Carl see it, learn from the experience of a poor topic choice, and move on. This is an example of teacher knowledge that makes handover possible in writing workshop. Yes, I've read a lot of good poetry and can bring what I've noticed to the advice I give kids. But I've read at least as many bad poems, and I recognize ways a student poem can go south. I wasn't willing to let Carl muddle along and produce mediocre work.

"Treasure," the poem about Hans, was Carl's first-ever work of free verse. I recognize in it techniques he drew from the poetry toolkit we built in minilessons. These include a first-person voice and presence that give readers someone to be with, simple color words and sensory verbs that create imagery, a title that's not a label, figurative language, repetition that creates a bit of cadence, a conclusion that resonates, and even some embedded rhyme. Here is a poem that captures Carl, the dog of his boyhood, and the shared treasure of a ritual they love.

TREASURE

I head outside
to where Hans
sits with an old,
worn tennis ball
in his jaws.

His green eyes
capture mine.
They beg me
to fling that ball
into the air
so far up
that only his keen
dog eyes can spy
the yellow sphere.

"Sit," I say.
I try to pry
the tennis ball
from his jaws.
He turns his head,
reluctant to surrender
his worn-out treasure.

Finally I get a hand
on the ball.
I yank it away,
then toss it
to my throwing arm.
Hans stares at the yellow
in my hand.
He wants it.
He needs it.
So I pull my arm back
and let it fly.

—Carl Johanson

My first meeting with another seventh-grade boy, Patrick, about his first piece of writing illustrates a different kind of handover. Here, the draft I encountered didn't look like a poem (Figure 3.11). In addition, Patrick had preceded every *s* at the end of any word with an apostrophe, except for the single possessive noun that requires one. Some sentences didn't make sense, there were lots of misspellings, and random words had gone missing.

9/9   PATRICK

        D 1

As I leap off the pier/Wich is
cracked and bumby from weather/
time slows down as the familar/
feeling of wneghtless ness/come
bac to me. with all the
other memories/of jumping the off
the pier come back to me/
For a split second wallaces
happy eyes meet mine
before the warm sea water
swallows me and chills
my whole body as emerge
the sun heats my head,
as tradition that has been
when my grandfather was a kid
is done.

Figure 3.11 *First Draft of Patrick's First Poem*

That night at home, when I read Patrick's responses to the September writing survey, I learned he didn't believe he was a writer. Thirty years ago I wouldn't have known where to begin with Patrick because of the severity of editorial issues in his draft. I'm afraid I might have just red-penned the apostrophes and told him to copy it over.

But look again: Patrick is already such a writer. Notice the strength and life of his verbs, nouns, and adjectives: *leap, pier, cracked, bumpy, familiar feeling of weightlessness, Wallace's happy eyes, warm sea water, swallows, chills, emerge, tradition, my grandfather.* The voice is first person and immediate, the tense is active, and as a reader I'm with Patrick in the moment. I can infer *why* this topic might matter to him.

I recognized in Patrick a writer who will need help with *parts* of the process, specifically legibility, editing, and proofreading. My priority today was to help him present his meaning as powerfully as possible and take pride in his accomplishment as a writer. This is the conversation that unfolded when I sat down next to him for our first conference.

"Hi. How's it coming?"

"Okay. I'm not sure. I can't really get a *so what?*" He paused. "The slashes are for line breaks."

I realized that Patrick had overheard me in conversation with his classmate Graydon, who had also drafted his first poem in prose form. I was appreciative of Patrick's slash marks, which indicate line breaks. "Can I just say, thank you for understanding, even though I wasn't having that conversation with you? That was smart—thanks for picking up on it."

"Yeah," he acknowledged, as he ducked his head.

Then I scanned his draft. "Oh, gee . . . this is nice . . . 'Wallace's happy eyes' . . . nice verb . . . nice verb . . . oh, this is lovely." A smile stretched across my face.

"Maybe I need to get more verbs?" Patrick mumbled.

"Oh, I don't know," I answered. "What you may want to do is go on to a second draft and see this as a poem. Hmm, I don't know if a tradition is 'done.' Do you know what I mean?"

"Completed?" Patrick offered.

"Fulfilled?" I suggested.

I had known Patrick's grandfather Eldon, who died the year before. "Is this one of the Eldon family traditions?" It was. "Want to make your mother cry?" I asked. Patrick laughed. "Can you end with a line about Eldon, say, *Eldon would have loved it?* Bring it back to your family, and find your *so what?* there?"

"Yeah," he agreed, ducking his head again.

"This has the bones of a great poem," I enthused, "the bones of a poem you can read in twenty years, and it will all come back to you. So, want to try a second draft, in lines, as a poem with a conclusion about Eldon?"

"Yeah," he agreed.

A few days later, after an editing conference with me, Patrick recorded two items on his individual proofreading list: "Apostrophes only on two kinds of words: possessive nouns (Patrick's dog) and contractions (don't)" and "Slow down and proofread for the missing words that readers need." In the meantime, he had typed and revised a second draft and edited it in red, and I had edited it in black and chosen what conventions to teach him. Then he typed a final copy of a poem I think he'll read with pleasure and nostalgia in the years to come.

WEATHERED

As I leap,
time slows,
and the familiar feeling of weightlessness
comes back to me,
along with all the memories
of jumping off the weathered pier
for the first time
summer after summer.
For a split second
Wallace's happy eyes meet mine.
The sea
cools my whole body.
I emerge,
the sun heats my head,
and the tradition that's been ours
since my grandpa was a kid
is fulfilled.
Eldon would have loved
to be here.

—*Patrick Jackson*

In handing over, I focused on Patrick's meaning and intentions, helped him realize them, and taught, in context, the conventions he needed to learn. He did not master these errors in his next piece of writing—apostrophes on plurals were a longtime bad habit—but I reviewed them with him and handed off responsibility to Patrick to find and fix them the next time around. By the end of the school year, his drafts were transformed in terms of their adherence to the conventions of standard written English.

THE LAUNCH: READING WORKSHOP

When I wrote CTL's faculty handbook, I opened the section about teaching reading with an epigraph from Frank Smith: "Children learn to read by reading. Therefore, the only way to facilitate their learning to read is to make reading easy for them" (1988). I would also add *inviting to them*. A big goal in the first days of school is to help every student find and enter a story he or she enjoys, no strings attached. This means lots of good books, intriguing booktalks, and time for kids to browse and read, along with teaching them how the reading workshop should sound and feel and why we have it in the first place.

Students should know the gist of the relevant research. Reading makes readers, and frequent, sustained, voluminous experience with books is the single activity that correlates with high levels of reading proficiency. I tell my new students the average number of books read by kids the previous year and that I anticipate more of the same. Then I distribute the highlighters and my lists of expectations and rules for reading workshop, and we review them together, with particular emphasis on the requirement to read books only, abandon a title if it isn't making the reader happy, be silent, and, when I come along to chat, whisper to me, so that no one is jarred out of the worlds created by the authors of stories they love. The overarching goal is for everyone to be able to enter and stay in the reading zone every day.

I acknowledge to kids, "It can take a little while to feel comfortable reading silently in a group, even a quiet, thoughtful one—this is something we'll talk about when we debrief at the end." Students pocket the highlighted expectations and rules in their reading folders and file the folders, and I start booktalking—enthusing about 9s and 10s I read over the summer.

I learned about the power of booktalks from young adult literature expert Teri Lesense. In sessions at NCTE conventions, she introduced great titles to middle school teachers with such delight, enthusiasm, and specificity that I bought every book she recommended. I recognized that I wanted to excite kids about books the way Teri does their teachers.

Efficiency was another consideration in introducing booktalks to the workshop. I found that in my daily check-ins during independent reading time I was synopsizing the plot of the same latest young adult novel a dozen times to different kids. In addition to these one-to-one recommendations, I needed a forum to inform the whole group about worthwhile titles.

So I started booktalking, and it does save time, but the most pronounced effect is on kids' book choices. At the end of any school year, around 90 percent of the titles my students name as favorites were the subjects of enthusiastic booktalks, either mine or a classmate's—spiels that brought life and color to the spines that line the shelves of the classroom library.

There's no prescribed format for a booktalk, no props, posters, reports, or notes, although I do keep track of my summer reading of y.a. titles on index cards, to jog my memory in September about books I finished in July. A booktalk is informal. In tone and content, it resembles the way adult readers talk to our friends about titles we love and think they might: tell how the book made us feel, describe main characters and conflicts, sketch the plot without giving away the surprises, mention theme, style, or genre, describe our encounter with the book—how we reacted to or read it. At the end of a booktalk, the booktalker takes questions. When a questioner pushes for plot resolution, I jump in, give a minilecture about the need to learn to tolerate ambiguity, and point out that the book itself is the answer.

My kids put an index card with their name on it inside a book they loved and want to recommend to the group, and then put the book on a shelf next to my rocking chair. A booktalked title must be one they rated at least a 9. A rating any lower is the kiss of death for a book for the rest of the school year. It should also be a title that hasn't already been booktalked by a classmate. The goal is to inform the rest of the kids about a great read, not for students to booktalk every title they loved.

The only exception to the no-repeat rule occurs when I am the initial booktalker. Some students regard my 9s and 10s with a healthy dose of skepticism. But when a peer rates the same book a 9 or 10, that title has been kid-tested, and the recommendation carries a different weight.

With a new book that I haven't had a chance to read yet, sometimes I explain what led me to order it—an award, good review, or previous encounter with the author—and read aloud the jacket flap and Library of Congress summary. Then I ask who wants to give it a shot and, if it's any good, booktalk it. I also introduce titles from my I-can't-go-there genres, science fiction and fantasy, and pass them along to fans to preview.

On rare occasions I break the no-lower-than-9 rating rule when a young adult novel has puzzled, disappointed, or even enraged me. I tell my kids, "This recommended book surprised/angered/flummoxed me, for these reasons. I'm not sure what to make of it. Will someone else try it and see what you think?"

When a competition breaks out about who'll get a booktalked title first, I do the time-honored, fair thing and ask everyone who's interested to raise his or her hand. The booktalker thinks of a number and asks for guesses. The closest guess gets the book, and, if a lot of hands are raised, I try to purchase another copy.

Before I give my first booktalks of the school year, I ask students to open their writing–reading handbooks and continue to number the right-hand pages in the upper-right-hand corner, through page 19. Then I explain:

> What you've just done, on pages 1 to 17, is create the skeleton for the *writing territories section* of your handbooks. All year long I'll issue invitations to you to come up with ideas for pieces of writing in different genres. This is where you'll capture them. Pages 1 to 17 are your ideas bank and, trust me, you will all be rich by June.
>
> Please turn now to pages 18 and 19 and copy this heading at the top of each: *My Someday Books.* These pages are the place to keep track of the titles you think you might want to read someday. I ask that you take responsibility for planning your reading. Open your handbook to your someday pages whenever I or a classmate conducts a booktalk and, if it's a title you'd like to check out, jot it down here. If a friend of yours is reading a book so enthusiastically that you want to remember the title, record it here so you don't forget it. [Figure 3.12 is the table of contents page from a student's writing–reading handbook, to show how it's organized, and Figure 3.13 represents a page of an eighth-grade girl's list of someday books.]
>
> It's important for you to become independent, intentional readers: readers with *plans.* Here's an easy, convenient way to plan a diet of great reads *and* feel a sense of security as someone who chooses and reads books—a way to relax and say, "Look at all the great stories still waiting for me when I finish this one."
>
> So, let the booktalking begin.

I booktalk several titles at a time. Sometimes I group them by author or genre—free-verse novels, antiwar fiction, dystopian fiction, humor, memoirs—and other times by theme: peer pressure, censorship, friendship, first love, sports. I try to strike a balance between new titles and proven reliables. I began a recent year of booktalking with an old favorite and a new one.

> *Neverwhere* by Neil Gaiman was published back in 1996. His *The Graveyard Book* was the first book ever to win both the U.S. Newbery Medal and the English Carnegie Medal. I have to say, I rated it an 8. I liked it, but I didn't love it. I love *Neverwhere.* I think it's Gaiman's best book. I rated it a 10.
>
> The main character is Richard Mayhew, a young man who leaves his village in Scotland to head to the big city. In London he works at an office, makes friends, gets engaged, and gets caught up in the routines of a nine-to-five grown-up life. Then, one night on the street, he rescues a battered, bleeding girl named Door, and Richard encounters the *other* London.

TABLE OF CONTENTS

TERRITORIES SECTION	
Writing Territories	1-2
Inspirations and Ideas from Other Poets	3
My Heart Map	4
Potential Subjects to Personify	5
Where poems Hide for Me	6
My Parody Ideas	7
Memoir-Worthy Experiences	8
Books, Movies, and TV Shows I might Review	9
What If'S? for my Micro fiction	10
potential Subjects for an Ode	11
Approaches to Holiday Gifts of Writing	12
Itches to Scratch in an Essay	13
Places I might set My Vision of America as a Poem	14
Approaches to Mother's Day Gifts of Writing	15
Local Women I might profile	16
Subjects I Might Praise in a Sonnet	17
MY SOMEDAY BOOKS	18-19
NOTES SECTION	
What Do writers Do?	20
The Rule of "So what?"	21
My Free-verse Tool Box – A definition of Free Verse	22
Tap the power of I	22
Break lines and Stanzas	22
Cut to the Bone	23
Conclude with Purpose	23
Use Repetition	23
Search for Sensory Diction	24
Compare	24-25
Experiment with Form	25
The Rule of Thoughts and Feelings	26
Why do we Have Reading Workshop?	27
A glossary of some poetic Terms	28-29

Figure 3.12 *Table of Contents of a Writing–Reading Handbook: First Page*

My Someday List (Cont'd)

One flew over the Cuckoo's Nest   Homeland ✓
If I stay ✓   Sex on the Moon
Boy's Life ✓   The Wonderus life of Oscar Wild
This Boy's Life ✓   city of theives
Beautiful Boy ✓   Game
No Country for Old Men   B/ack Ice ✓
The Good Theif
A Heartbreaking Work of Staggering Geinus ✓
My Left Foot
Rocket Boys
Where the Heart is ✓   Diary of a Young Girl ✓
The Dog Stars ✓   The Girl in the Green Sweater ✓
I Capture the Castle   Night
What is the What   Bringing Down the House ✓
I Hunt Killers ✓
The Art of Feilding
Stern Men ✓
Say Goodnight Gracie
Flight Behavior
The Round House ✓
The Chocolatre
Prep
Never Let Me Go ✓
What I Was
Between the Lines ✓
Override ✓
Schooled
Into the Wild ✓
Strange Piece of Paradise
Goldengrove
The Lock Artist ✓
The Sun Also Rises

Figure 3.13 *Helena's List of Someday Books, Second Page*

The system of subway trains in London is called the *Underground*. Gaiman uses it to imagine a mythological London Underneath. It's a parallel universe to the city Richard is living in, a place where people who fall through the cracks live, and it's filled with unforgettable characters. Some have magical powers, including the most horrific villains I have ever encountered in fiction, Mr. Croup and Mr. Vandemar. They terrified me.

This is a scary book. It's also suspenseful, funny, and surprising. I thought of *Alice in Wonderland* when Richard went underneath and lost himself. Except Richard isn't Alice—his experiences change him. He starts out a conformist who wants a safe, predictable life. And then he goes below, and he finds himself.

The themes of *Neverwhere* are big: compassion for others, loyalty, trust, and, especially, good vs. evil. Plus, it's a rollicking good adventure story. As I said, it's a 10. Any questions or comments?

Of all the new releases I read this summer, I loved this one best. It's by E. Lockhart, who wrote the trilogy of novels about Ruby Oliver. I rated *The Disreputable History of Frankie Landau-Banks* a *bella*. First I'd better explain what a *bella* is.

One year an eighth-grade girl asked, "How do I rate a book that's higher than a 10, it's that good?" The girl's name is Bella; *bella* in Italian means beautiful and good. In her honor, I decreed that a beautiful, good, beyond-10 book would forever more be known in these parts as a *bella*.

E. Lockhart has written a bella. Frankie, her main character, is smart, brave, independent-minded, and funny. She attends an elite prep school that Lockhart calls Alabaster Academy—think Exeter or Andover. Something amazing happens to Frankie in the summer between her freshman and sophomore years: she becomes beautiful—as Lockhart puts it, she goes from "a homely child to a loaded potato." As a result, Frankie becomes the girlfriend of her crush, Matthew Livingston, a senior, the acknowledged hottest boy at Alabaster, and the leader of a posse of rich, privileged guys. But Frankie discovers it's more than a posse. It's an all-male secret society, the Loyal Order of the Bassets, which her dad belonged to when he was a student at Alabaster. She's intrigued, and then she's angry. Frankie isn't content to be Matthew's arm candy. Her guts, intelligence, and imagination won't let her accept her diminished role as a female in Alabaster's power structure. And the plot thickens.

I can't tell you what she does. I can tell you it's cool, convincing, and I was with her every step of the way, because Lockhart describes Frankie's thoughts, feelings, and motivations so well. Lockhart writes like a dream—funny dialogue, convincing and memorable specifics, and great character development: not just Frankie's, but also tons of secondary characters who are believable, stand-alone people *and* who help us get to know Frankie better.

In my next life, I'd like to be as brave as Frankie. A *bella* for *The Disreputable History* was a no-brainer for me. Questions? Comments? Takers?

Each class of students and I conduct around 250 booktalks a year about titles we think are too good to miss. These are sales pitches, pure and simple. I liken them to the movie trailers that advertise coming attractions. They're the number one motivator for students to enter the reading zone, because they solve the number-one problem U.S. kids cite in explaining why they don't read more: they can't find books they want to read (Scholastic 2007). By creating frequent occasions to brief students about the great stories still waiting for them, booktalks make books visible, intriguing, and available. If a student hasn't yet given one by the end of the first trimester, I'll nudge him or her to make that a goal for the second trimester—to break the ice and take responsibility for helping peers, just as other kids pointed the reader to great stories.

After my first couple of booktalks, I show the class where their packets of book-borrow cards are stored, explain how to sign books out and in, warn them that they *may never* take a book from the classroom without signing it out, and turn them loose to browse among the titles in my library, chat about them, and make choices. Since I want everyone to have a book by the end of class, I hang out at the shelves and offer assistance—pull previously loved titles, introduce characters and summarize plots, explain genres, and encourage students to recommend to others the good books they're already familiar with.

Then students sign out their selections on their book-borrow cards and curl up on the floor, in beanbags, heads down on tables, it's their choice. The goal is comfort. A former principal of mine was irritated no end by the sight of adolescent readers sprawling, so I learned to spare him by taping a sign over the window in my classroom door: DO NOT DISTURB. READERS AT WORK.

Once kids are settled, I grab the clipboard to which I've attached their group's reading status chart, perch alongside or behind each reader, and note titles. "What did you find?" I whisper. "Why this one?" My essential responsibility, today and every day, is to make sure nobody is reading a book he or she doesn't like. A dissatisfied reader will learn the one lesson I never want to teach: reading is boring. Students need more than permission to abandon books that aren't pleasing them. They need strong encouragement—even the occasional cease-and-desist order. So I escort a reader who isn't happy back to the bookshelves and pull three or four acknowledged great stories for boys or girls. I tell a little about each one and ask the student to read the flaps, back jackets, and leads to see if one of them strikes a chord.

This has always worked. In the event it didn't, I'd pull another three or four books, tell their stories, and put those in the student's hands. The most important *should* in reading workshop is that every reader should be happy. Once kids develop a reading habit, the books themselves will form their tastes. Readers, like writers, need to begin the year feeling engaged and productive. I devote a lot of energy to choices and plans in the first week so individuals can find their seats at the dining room table as soon as possible, understand and trust the pleasure to be found in books, practice reading, and start growing as readers. This is the essence of handover in the reading workshop. The DVD *Reading in the Middle: Workshop Essentials* (2011) brings the day of the launch to life.

Everyone has homework tonight: to read for half an hour and remember to bring his or her book to school in the morning. Of course, someone will forget. When it happens, I growl, say, "That's your homework pass for reading class," and refer the student to my collection of short story anthologies from which to select a story or two to read during that day's workshop. I don't want the student to begin another book or for anyone to be reading two books at once. They should be enjoying, sustaining, and gleaning the benefits of one whole, literary experience at a time.

In the next day's workshop, after booktalks by me or a couple of eighth graders, I circulate with my clipboard again, this time recording page numbers. If they did their homework, readers should be around twenty pages beyond yesterday. If not, they've just used their pass for reading workshop; next time, it's a letter home. If my teaching schedule didn't allow for a reading workshop every day, I'd multiply twenty pages by the number of days since I'd last taken the reading status-of-the-class. Each student should be at least that far ahead.

Then I continue the whispered conversations we started yesterday. Some days, after I've checked in with every reader, I have a little time to return to my rocking chair, read my own book, or watch them reading theirs. Here are the same adolescents who at recess yesterday argued during a raucous game of horse as they exchanged iPods, sang, screamed, and teased. And now here they are, silent and *gone*—each one lost in the reading zone and living inside a story. It never fails to move me.

I hate to interrupt them, but it's time. "Boys and girls, please come up for air and segue out of the reading zone. Let's review: tomorrow you'll need your book, writing–reading handbook, yellow homework folder, teal poetry folder, and blue writing-in-process folder. I have loved our first three days together. I can't wait for all the days to come—to see what you'll do next, then next, then next, as real writers and readers. I'm already impressed and excited. It's already a privilege to be your teacher."

CHAPTER 4

Essential Lessons for Writers

It is not enough to be busy; the question is, what are we busy about?
—Henry David Thoreau

I'm a collector. I especially love Victorian antiques—Staffordshire dogs, carved shells, souvenir ruby flash glass, porcelain fairing boxes—and seafood cookbooks. The last is a function of living on the coast of Maine and trying to figure out what to do with the shrimp local fisherman haul in March.

They're tiny—the size of the tip of my baby finger—and cook in a minute. Other than boiling up a few pounds, shelling them at the table, and dunking them in melted butter, the ubiquitous recipe is a casserole that calls for two pounds of shelled shrimp, a can of cream of mushroom soup, one diced green pepper, and a cup of mayonnaise. Combine, top with crushed Ritz crackers, and bake for half an hour in a 325-degree oven. Voilà.

So I haunt flea markets in search of my favorite collectibles *and* appetizing Maine shrimp recipes. At some point, I paid a dollar for a battered seafood cookbook published by a local Grange, not because it broke with the mushroom-soup-mayonnaise-Ritz tradition, but because I was charmed by its epigraph:

> Good cooks are born, not made, they say.
> The saying is untrue.
> Hard trying and these recipes
> Will make a good cook of you.
> —*Anonymous*

As a basic cook at best, but also as a writer who didn't start writing until I was almost thirty, I appreciated the sentiment. Good cooks and good writers are too often lumped in the same category: people who are born with "it." When I started teaching, I wondered about this. Did strong student writers have "it"—a natural aptitude, a giftedness with language? Or could anyone learn to write well? As I accumulated experience teaching writing in a workshop, I stopped wondering. My answer is *yes:* every child can learn to write well.

As the cookbook poem observes, it's *hard trying*—practice—and *these recipes*—seasoned advice—that will make of someone a good cook or a good writer. Cooks and writers thrive when they're motivated, have time to work and reflect on the results, and benefit from the experience of mentors who can show them how. In writing workshop, the minilesson is an essential forum for a grown-up to show students *how*.

When it comes to influential methods, the minilesson that kicks off each writing workshop is at least an equal partner to my conferences with individual writers. A good minilesson is practical, relevant, accessible, and far-reaching. It's a whole-group conversation about writing problems, proven solutions, and productive directions. As an English teacher who knew a lot about English before transforming my class into a workshop, I welcomed minilessons as an opportunity to impart my knowledge while still providing a context for kids to discover and act on their intentions. As a teacher-researcher, I'm interested in the role of whole-group instruction in the workshop and how to make it maximally productive and worthwhile, given my own and every teacher's sense of urgency. We have just 180 days to try to make a difference for a lifetime.

In the beginning, my minilessons were responsive. Each night I reflected on the developments of the day and planned a lesson to address what I'd seen students doing or not doing. But over time, patterns emerged—lessons that make a difference in September and October, in midwinter, and in the spring, in terms of students' needs, advice that helps them move their writing toward literature and conventionality, and work in genres. My minilessons became a forgiving course of study—not a scope and sequence but a balance between worthwhile information about writing and teachable moments.

At the same time that I work to identify what's valuable to teach in minilessons, I search for vocabulary that will help students understand it. The brains of twelve- and thirteen-year-olds have frozen before my eyes when I talked at them about concepts like coherence, concrete specificity, sensory imagery, cadence, transitions, tricolons, reflection, compression, redundancy, and, the chilliest mind Popsicle of them all, theme. So I invented a lexicon, one that evokes the nuances of literary essentials for less-than-sophisticated writers: the Rule of *So What?*, the Rule of Write About *a* Pebble, Make a Movie Behind Your Eyelids, Cut to the Bone, the Rule of Thoughts and Feelings, the Power of Three, and others. As evidenced in students' writing—and their responses to the literature they read—these lessons stick.

The lexicon we build transforms what happens *after* the minilesson, when I meet and talk with individual writers and readers. It gives my students a prism for looking at drafts of their own writing, as well as the writing they're reading. Conversations about both become richer and more efficient. Kids and I aren't beginning at the beginning with every piece of writing because we have a shorthand language for observing features of text, requesting help, and giving advice.

This means that when I perch alongside a writer and ask, "How's it coming?" he or she might reply, "I'm not sure there's a *so what?* yet." "Can you make the movie here?" "I think this lead is a grabber." "I'm still writing off-the-page." "Do you think I have enough *T* and *F*?" "I'm experimenting with effective repetition." "I need to cut to the bone." "This is feeling like pebbles instead of *a* pebble. What can I do?" The vocabulary may be odd, but the criteria are not: these are features of literary writing that can be taught to young kids.

And they can be learned by teachers—when we begin to plan, draft, revise, polish, and edit pieces of our own writing, when we reject canned rubrics, when we read and consider the features of many kinds of crafted writing, and when we turn to writers and critics we can count on for accurate, generative insights. For me, that means Ralph Fletcher, Donald Graves, Georgia Heard, X. J. Kennedy, Ken Macrorie, Donald Murray, Mary Oliver, Ron Padgett, Kate Turabian, Robert Wallace, E. B. White, William Carlos Williams, and William Zinsser. Their advice for finding subjects and crafting clear, voiced poetry and prose has taught me techniques and criteria to draw on in my writing, responses to literature, and teaching of both.

At the end of each trimester, I look back through my plans and create a chronological list of the minilessons of the previous thirteen weeks. As part of our assessment procedure at CTL, parents receive a copy that their child has annotated, along with my notes about the child. They learn the big picture of what the class did, their child's take on it, and my take on the child's accomplishments and goals. Since I teach combined groups of seventh and eighth graders, I've developed a two-year cycle of minilessons. Each year I repeat the essential craft, topic, and convention lessons, illustrating them with fresh examples, and I teach new ones. Appendix K provides a brief summary of my teaching emphases in the two years. My students and I cover a lot of ground. I think all of it is worthwhile—relevant, interesting, useful, even inspirational.

My new favorite cookbook is another flea market find, *Martha Stewart's Quick Cook* (1983). This is early Martha—not the whole-hog incarnation that came later, but a collection of straightforward, elegant recipes. Following Stewart's advice, I can make sole with black butter and capers, sea scallops sautéed with scallions, and saffron-broiled chicken. My repertoire of ingredients and menus is enriched without the—for me—tensions of haute cuisine. And the results are wonderful because of the tweaks Martha suggests. She makes me want to cook again *and* develop recipes of my own. See the end of this chapter for my most successful experiment so far with Maine shrimp.

As teachers of writing, we need to be on the lookout for the tweaks that make a difference—for advice and models that make the intangible tangible and the difficult doable. Thoughtful, informed demonstrations and conversations with the group, followed by thoughtful, informed conversations with individual writers, give students knowledge, strategies, self-confidence, and opportunities for excellence.

PROCEDURES

In September and early October, two overarching goals are on my mind as I plan minilessons: to teach or review the procedures of writing workshop and to introduce or review the big-guns craft lessons that lead to powerful writing. I approach both in the context of a genre study of free-verse poems.

Although every year I teach newly enrolled CTL students who are inexperienced writers, the majority of my kids already have some experience of writing workshop. As I work one-to-one with the newbies, to help them get on top of procedures, I also remind veterans about how and why we do things in the workshop, and I ask them to serve as consultants to the novice writers.

When I started teaching writing this way, I was the only workshop teacher at Boothbay Region Elementary School. Later I became part of a group of K–8 colleagues who called ourselves the Boothbay Writing Project. But even then I couldn't count on every student knowing the ropes, because the workshop model wasn't used schoolwide. I learned that every fall I needed to devote serious energy to minilessons about procedures.

Writing workshop doesn't come naturally to kids. They need to be taught and re-taught its routines until they internalize the rhythms, until it becomes second nature for them to remember to fetch a pencil before they plunk down in the minilesson circle, take *four pieces of tape* when I distribute notes for them to add to their handbooks and then pass the dispenser along, use red pens for editing only, fill out an editing checksheet for every piece, assemble and file all the components of finished pieces of writing, and come to class each day with the right folders and notebook.

Routines are an essential emphasis in the first month of writing workshop. Once students have a sense of what to do next, they can regulate how to use their time, and I can concentrate on showing them how to improve their writing instead of answering the question "What should I do now?" twelve times a class. I cover many of the lessons listed below in the first few days of school; the rest unfold during the subsequent two weeks.

MINILESSONS ABOUT PROCEDURES OF WRITING WORKSHOP
- expectations for writing workshop
- rules for writing workshop
- how the room is organized and where supplies and materials are stored
- how to create, maintain, and use an individualized list of writing territories

- the daily routine: poem, minilesson, status-of-the-class survey, and independent writing
- how to respond to the status-of-the-class survey
- what to bring to class each day and have ready in the minilesson circle
- the writing-in-process folder and its purpose and organization
- the finished writing folder and its purpose, organization, and storage location
- the homework folder and the weekly homework assignment sheet
- the one hundred-page writing–reading handbook and its five sections and purposes: writing territories, someday books, class notes, literary terms, and responses to prose readings
- how to take four pieces of tape from a desk-type dispenser, stick them to the back of your hand, pass the dispenser to the next person in the circle, and then tape a page of minilesson data to the front of the next clean page in the class notes section of your handbook
- passwords for accessing the hard drives of computers (I use poets' last names)
- why the room needs to be silent during independent writing time
- how to talk with the teacher and peers about writing-in-process, including how to whisper: whispering happens in the front of your mouth, not the back
- what happens in a worthwhile peer writing conference
- what writers do and what they call these activities
- what to do when a piece of writing is finished
- where to submit a piece of writing that's ready for teacher editing
- where to submit a piece of writing that's ready for the teacher to "eyeball"—proofread for remaining errors or, if it's a lengthy prose piece, take home and skim
- guidelines for producing a perfect final copy

In a September minilesson about procedures, students and I explore what writing process is and what authors do. I've learned not to talk about *the* writing process, because it implies a lockstep routine. As a writer, I'm aware that my every act of first-drafting also involves making additions, substitutions, and deletions, rereading, making notes, reordering, and editing.

Accurate, generous guidelines give beginning writers direction and, at the start of a school year, lead everyone to the essential conclusion: writing is thinking and rethinking on paper. I begin the lesson by printing the heading "What Do Writers Do?" on an overhead transparency.

> Please copy this question at the top of page 20 in your writing–reading handbook. This will be the first entry in the *class notes* section of your handbooks. That question—what do writers do?—is one we'll answer in collaboration.

I'll start the answer with my definition of writing. Please copy it, and all the answers you and I come up with together, as I transcribe them. You can assume that my spelling and punctuation are correct, so try to make your notes look like mine. Here goes:

> Writing is thinking and rethinking on paper, which involves lots of different activities. What do writers do? They:

As a writer, I've learned that writing is thinking on paper. I put down my first thoughts, read and reflect on what's on the page, change my mind a little or a lot, and think and write some more. Writers don't copy down a smooth stream of ideas that flows out of our brainpans. Rather, we use writing to *discover* our ideas. We *make* meaning. What authors do is messy, complicated, and pretty wonderful, because anyone who can *think*, and has enough time can do it, can write. Let's brainstorm as richly as we can. You talk, I'll talk, I'll record, and you take notes, too: what are all the things you can think of that a writer does?

Figure 4.1 shows one class' response. When we finished, I told the kids, "This is a thorough, realistic list. Writing is playful, demanding, *and* nonlinear. Authors circle among all of these activities until, at some point, we *have* to stop—we have to let go

---

SAMPLE RESPONSE: WHAT DO WRITERS DO?

Writing is thinking and rethinking on paper, which involves lots of different activities. What do writers do? They . . .

brainstorm ideas	listen to the writing	polish the language
decide on a topic	skip lines	check the verbs
plan	cut and tape	consult a thesaurus
write off the page	add words with carets	write by hand
decide on a genre	take words away with cross-outs	type
experiment with leads	cut clutter	spell
take a tone	change their minds	punctuate
draft	substitute better words	capitalize
revise	get other people's reactions	paragraph
edit	organize their ideas and information	break lines
research	with numbers, arrows, etc.	break stanzas
take notes	think about a reader	brainstorm titles
make choices	take a break to let a draft settle	proofread
come up with new options	return with fresh insights and	make a final copy
read and reread what they've	perspectives	go public
written	experiment with conclusions	

Figure 4.1 *Sample Response: What Do Writers Do?*

of a piece of writing and send it off into the world. It's my job to teach you how to get better at everything on the list and give you the time you need to do it. To paraphrase Kurt Vonnegut, Jr., writers aren't necessarily smart people, but they have learned how to think on paper, how to use time, and how to be patient."

Procedural minilessons are brief, apart from this theory-building lesson and the first-week review of workshop rules and expectations. They serve as introductions. A student who is ready for the information on the day I present it—for example, a writer who's ready to edit his or her first poem on the day I teach about editing—will hear it best. I understand that I'll be reminding individuals how we do things in the workshop straight through until Columbus Day. The investment of time is worth it. It frees us to devote the other eight months to genres, conventions, and the craft of writing.

Craft

Good writing has voice. Students entering writing workshop have voices as speakers, but a strong writing voice isn't a transcription of the way someone talks. It's a combination of all the choices individual writers make about how they'll express themselves.

A writing voice starts with diction: are the word choices fresh and is each word the best one? Do tangible nouns, sensory verbs, and evocative adjectives bring the writing to life? Do concrete specifics make the writing memorable? Are there personal reflections that take a reader inside the writer's head and heart? What's the point of view? What's the tone—the writer's attitude toward his or her subject? Does the phrasing flow? Is it rhythmic? Is the meaning emphatic? Subtle? Is the description spare? Embellished?

Good writing is not a happy accident. It's the result of thinking on paper *in particular ways*—selecting, rejecting, substituting, clarifying. As William Zinsser put it, sweet and clutter-free, "Writing is a craft, not an art" (2006).

No matter how discouraged I am in September about misspellings, punctuation errors, and unconventional capitalization, I postpone whole-group teaching about usage and front-load the minilesson curriculum with techniques of craft. I remind myself that individual editing conferences will provide lots of opportunities for me to address students' errors in a context more powerful than any whole-group lecture. September craft lessons help students begin to develop voices and produce literary texts ASAP. When students feel the satisfaction of having written well, they're motivated to continue to work hard as writers. Plus they begin to care about the readability of this good writing and to apply themselves as editors of their texts.

Sometimes in craft minilessons I ask the class to collaborate with me to define a technique or approach. Other times I present a principle and show examples of writing that illustrate it. Some craft lessons demonstrate my own thinking and choices as a writer. For example, I might draft on overhead transparencies in front of the group and talk about what I'm thinking or, more often, reproduce a draft I worked on at home and distribute copies for students to study and discuss. Still other craft lessons are presented by students, with my assistance. When students take my advice and solve a writing problem or come up with solutions of their own, I ask them to show the class, via overhead transparencies, what they did. Every lesson about craft fulfills one of two agendas: it shows kids how to use writing to generate writing, or it highlights the choices that lead to voice and literature.

ESSENTIAL MINILESSONS ABOUT CRAFT

- some things a poet does when trying to write a good poem
- titles come last
- the Rule of *So What?* or theme
- the Rule of Thoughts and Feelings
- the Rule of Write About *a* Pebble
- writing off-the-page
- why writers draft and print double-spaced
- can a reader see it, hear it, feel it?
- make a movie behind your eyelids
- why smart writers think twice about adverbs
- sensory verbs and how to use a thesaurus
- essential revision techniques (carets, arrows, asterisks, numbers, spider legs, cut and tape)
- the two-day walk-away
- the Power of Three
- and lessons related to genre studies, for example, techniques for polishing or fine-tuning poems, stories, and exposition; kinds of narrative leads; time transitions in narratives; figurative language and sound patterns in poetry; leads and conclusions for essays; how to conduct an interview for a profile; ways to organize and present information in exposition; the uses of epigraphs, epilogues, and prologues

By the end of any first week of school, I have a mental list of the craft minilessons I want to present *right away*. A note I found in an old planbook reads *Where start? Draft double-spaced? So what? Rule of Pebble? Breaking lines and stanzas? First-person in poems? Writing off-the-page???* I wanted to teach every technique at once because each is so powerful. But one lesson will touch on and pave the way for all of them.

The most efficient, convincing invitation to students to think and act as writers is to show them how an adult tries to think and act as a writer. Observing an adult at work opens a window on what is possible. A teacher doesn't have to be the next great

American novelist to teach lessons of value. We only have to write a *little bit better than they do* for our students to learn from our demonstrations and build on them.

When I began to teach writing in a workshop, the National Writing Project was encouraging English teachers to write so our students would perceive writing as a worthwhile activity. I found stray moments in class to pull up a chair at an empty student desk and act like a role model: Look, kids, here's an adult who's writing . . . something. For all they knew, it was a grocery list. This was performance, not demonstration.

Then, as I attended professional conferences for English teachers, I began to make a point of signing up for any presentation by Donald Murray. A Pulitzer Prize–winning journalist, writing teacher, and author of books and articles that transformed the field of composition, Murray often drafted out loud while capturing his emerging text on overhead transparencies. His demonstrations pierced the mystique of "creativity" and challenged such orthodoxies as formal outlines and first-draft finals. I always learned from his presentations. The biggest lesson was how much of Murray's writing process was ordinary hard work. I never saw anything come to Don on the wings of a dove. As a novice writer, I found this encouraging.

Back at school I took a deep breath, turned on an overhead projector, took off the top of my head, and invited students to watch and hear the thinking of an adult who was trying to write well. They witnessed a messy process of pushing to get something—anything—down on the page, generating ideas, deleting ideas, choosing, moving, experimenting with leads and conclusions, listing, fleshing out skeleton ideas, trying alternative punctuation, fiddling at the single-word level, and continuous rereading: going back into the text again and again to regain a sense of it so far and try to jump-start the next part. In the process, I discovered things I hadn't realized—chief among them is that I spend more time reading my drafts than I do writing them.

This range of activity is what students can't see when a teacher perches at a student desk and writes: the disorderly reality of writing-as-process that remains hidden from students and teachers unless we write and make it explicit. I don't know how English teachers can ask students to undertake the essential work of revision if kids have never seen or heard it.

Today I bull through pieces of writing at home, save everything, photocopy class sets of it, and ask kids to study my drafts as researchers of writing. This way they get a sense of a whole process, start to finish. The discussion that follows, about what I did as a writer and why, is specific, revealing, and useful to my students.

Teachers who haven't written much and don't yet have a sense of their own writing process can tell kids this is the case, experiment with techniques I recommend, like double-spacing and writing off-the-page, and then show students the results of their experimentation. The point is for young writers to see how someone even slightly more experienced thinks on paper, changes his or her mind, considers what he or she understands about good writing, and pushes for voice and meaning.

Since poetry is our first genre study, every Labor Day weekend I write a poem about an idea from my latest territories list. The example below is about my English springer spaniel Rosie and the day she picked a four-leaf clover. She had trotted into our kitchen after a ball-throwing session with Toby, and, when I offered her a biscuit, dropped the two tennis balls she'd crammed in her greedy mouth. Stuck with spit to one of them was a four-leaf clover. It set me thinking about Rosie and luck—ours and hers. Over the course of five days, I drafted, revised, and edited a poem.

CHARMED

The dog pranced into the kitchen
and spat her hoard
onto red linoleum:
two tennis balls
and a four-leaf clover.
I picked it up in wonder,

and a hundred hours came back to me.
On my stomach and elbows
I combed the lawns of my childhood
for a clover like this one.
My fingers never did manage
to pluck that prize.

Our greedy trickster spaniel
captured the treasure I couldn't.
I laughed and sighed—
a lucky dog—
and I remembered the season
we lived with her in the kitchen,

the hundred hours we cuddled her on a carpet
thrown down to cover the red floor.
Six months old,
her hips were splayed.
Without surgery, a life of brevity and pain.
With it—maybe years of tennis balls.

So the braces for our child's teeth waited
while we paid for titanium bones.
The vet said we were her good luck—
the family that could afford to heal her.
When spring came, we rolled up the rug
and rolled with Rosie on a lawn of new clover.

And she has been the best dog,
full of kisses, jokes, and plots.
Grey muzzled and rheumy-eyed now,
she sleeps in the keyhole of my desk when I write.
I reach down and scratch a freckle
for luck.

It took me twelve pages of notes and drafts to get to this version of the poem. I assembled them chronologically, photocopied a set for each student, and assigned the class to take the packet home, study its pages as researchers, look for at least five specific *changes* and *choices* I made as a writer that they were curious about, and jot their questions on the photocopy next to the relevant choice or change.

At the minilesson the next day, the class interviewed me. I answered their questions by explaining my thoughts and motivations as the writer of "Charmed." The goal was for students to notice some of the things a grown-up considers and does when trying to write a good poem.

Figure 4.2 shows three of the pages: my writing-off-the-page, the start of the first draft, and a title brainstorm. Questions students asked me included:

- In the first line, why did you add "pranced into the kitchen?"
- Why did you cut "under hot sun and blue sky" from the second stanza?
- Why did you put "like this one?" in parentheses in the second stanza?
- Why did you write both "a dog with good luck" and "a lucky dog"?
- Why did you cut out the part about carrying Rosie's rump in a sling?
- Why do you say the linoleum is red and the carpet is brown—does it matter?
- Why did you change *daughter* to *child*? *Parts* to *bones*? *Save* to *heal*?
- Why did you cut "the chance to be a dog" and change it to "years of tennis balls, kisses, jokes, and tricks" and then change it again, later on, to "years of tennis balls"?
- No offense, but your first conclusion is pretty bad. What were you thinking?
- Why does each stanza have six lines?

At the end of the interview, I passed out index cards and asked students to write for five minutes: based on the text and my answers to their questions, exactly what had I done or considered as someone trying to write a good poem? How many specific activities or ways of thinking could they name, from writing-off-the-page to get started to brainstorming to find the best title?

I collected the index cards, created a master list of the kids' observations, and added a final one of my own. In the next day's minilesson, students taped photocopies of the list onto page 21 of their writing–reading handbooks, as the second entry in the class

Writing off the Page   9/2

                              kitchen   (red)
↱ clover on the ⌃linoleum

hours I spent on my stomach &
    elbows under a blue sky

We lived in the kitchen that winter —
↳ carpet on the linoleum   (brown)

                                              good
Dean said, "You were her ⌃
luck — family that could
   ⌃afford surgery."

Anne's braces — another year
    b/c of $

old now — sleeps when I write, like Justine said
grey muzzle
  rheumy eyes   You make your own
    & freckles   luck

              She's been our
              good luck   Her personality —
                                            greedy
                                            wild
                                        full of tricks

Figure 4.2 *Pages from a Minilesson: My Writing off-the-Page, First Draft, and Title Brainstorm*   *(continues)*

Title Brainstorm

Luck
Our Luck
Lucky
Our Lucky Charm
Good Luck
My Good Luck Charm
Good Luck Charm
Charmed Life
(Charmed)

D.1
9/2

The ?   pranced into the kitchen
My dog ∧spat out her horde
~~on the kitchen~~ onto the red linoleum:
two moldy tennis balls
and a four-leaf clover.
I picked it up in wonder
                                    (thousand?)
and flashed back to a hundred hours
on my elbows and stomach on ~~someone's~~
~~summer lawn~~
[under hot sun and blue sky,]
                                            neighborhood
combing the lawns of my childhood
                (like this one?)
for a clover with more than three leaves.
                            manage?
My fingers never did ∧pluck that prize.
                    (managed?)

And ~~now~~ my wild, greedy spaniel
~~has captured the treasure~~
∧found the prize   I never (could/did?)
I sigh^ed and laugh^ed —
a dog ∧with good luck
a lucky dog

Figure 4.2 Continued

notes section. Then, highlighters in hand, they took turns around the circle reading the list they created.

SOME THINGS A POET DOES WHEN TRYING TO WRITE A GOOD POEM

- finds a topic that matters—that calls his or her name
- writes off-the-page to generate ideas, details, a form, sensory verbs, a *so what?*, etc., plus to create enough momentum to start drafting in the first place
- writes off-the-page on the poem itself—in the margins—to capture words and ideas that otherwise would get lost and to brainstorm new possibilities
- drafts double-spaced, so there's room to change her mind and write off-the-page
- drafts in lines and stanzas
- experiments with form—the number of lines in each stanza, or how stanzas will begin or end
- focuses on verbs: are they sensory? especially: are they visual?
- draws a line when stuck during drafting, keeps going, and comes back later to fill it in
- consults a thesaurus to find a sensory word or one that will create alliteration or assonance
- tries to avoid adverbs and stick with strong verbs
- envisions sensory images and tries to find the words for them
- uses repetition to move the poem and create cadence
- listens for and deletes ineffective repetition
- rereads *a lot*—the whole poem and individual lines and stanzas—while drafting
- experiments with punctuation and the voice/tone/mood it can convey
- hunts for weak words
- brainstorms lists of strong words to replace a weak one
- draws a wavy line under "clunky" words or phrases
- indicates spelling uncertainties along the way by circling them
- uses ═ to create new stanzas and / to create new lines
- starts a new stanza when writing about a new idea
- *listens* to the poem and revises it in pursuit of rhythm, a good sound
- pushes for a *so what?* while drafting and revising
- cuts language to the bone: deletes anything that a smart reader doesn't need, doesn't make the poem stronger, or isn't specific
- gut-checks at the single-word level: is each word the right one?
- sweats the conclusion: generates different ways to end a poem because this is the most important part, where the deepest meaning or *so what?* is found

- thinks about the poem when not working on it—walks away for two days and lets the draft simmer
- comes back after the break with a fresh perspective
- brainstorms potential titles when the poem is done or close to it, in search of one that's not a label and that intrigues, invites, *and* fits the whole poem
- understands that a good poem isn't an accident. Writing is thinking and rethinking on paper: generating options, making choices, and being open to the surprises that happen along the way

I cannot begin to account for the positive effects of this lesson. In September and throughout the rest of the year, I'll see students refer to "Some Things a Poet Does . . ." when they're drafting and revising poems. In November, most kids name it as one of the three most significant lessons of the first trimester.

The list is packed with implications for teaching and learning writing. First, it's efficient: it gives students techniques to try right away, on the sixth day of school, while minilessons about discrete techniques of craft and free-verse poetry will continue to unfold. It creates a foundation for a year of teaching students how to be deliberate as writers. It demonstrates the practical benefits of the rule about drafting double-spaced. It builds a frame of reference for minilessons and conversations to come. And it establishes the teacher's authority. I'm not just lecturing students about what they should do as writers. I'm using the approaches, and they're working for me. In writing workshop, this is the ultimate version of handover—when English teachers reveal ourselves as people to whom students wish to apprentice themselves.

I have no illusions about "Charmed." It will never be accepted for publication anywhere but here. But I'm satisfied with it and happy I wrote it—that I described how we loved our Rosie. As a teacher of writing, I look for critical junctures to write for my students, moments when I can illuminate and exemplify a genre or technique. This doesn't always require whole pieces of writing. Sometimes a page or paragraph is enough to show a problem or a solution. And I have no compunctions about reusing a piece of writing another year.

While it's true that I've written articles and books, in my classroom any authority I have as a writer is a result of work like the poem about my dog. My kids are seventh and eighth graders, with all the self-absorption that implies. I could hold up a copy of *In the Middle* every day of the school year, announce it had sold half a million copies and won awards, and predict their reaction every time: "My uncle wrote a book." "I met Stephen King once." "Your hair looks weird in that picture." Observing me tackle projects I care about gives them perspective on how an adult values writing and thinks on paper.

The title of another big-gun craft lesson was coined by a student, Joe Powning, back in the 1990s. I was attempting to teach his class about theme and coming up against the usual brain freeze. With her permission, I used a memoir by another student to try to clarify the concept.

"Okay," I said, "Laurel has written the story of the day her father told her there was no Santa Claus. The question is, what does she make of it? How does she feel? Betrayed? Lied to? Let down? Will she be protective of the Santa myth from now on, on behalf of littler kids? Laurel's response—how she makes sense of the news—will become the *theme* of this memoir."

Joe piped up. "Oh, okay. So, now Laurel knows there's no Santa, it's *so what?*" And *so what?* became shorthand for the literary terms—*theme, purpose, central idea, motivation*—that didn't yet resonate with middle schoolers. Kids and I learned to ask of ourselves and other writers, "Okay, this happened. *So what?*" Ever since, each second week of September I pass out copies of the rule for my students to tape into their handbooks.

The Rule of So What? or Theme

Good writing in every genre answers the question *so what?* Good writing has a purpose, a point, a reason it was written.

The good writer looks for the meanings, the significances, the implications in the subject he or she has chosen.

Sometimes a *so what?* is subtle and implicit. Sometimes it's explicitly stated. But always a good reader finds something to think about because a good writer found something to think about.

Robert Frost wrote, "No tears in the writer, no tears in the reader" (1939). If you don't discover meaning in your life, your readers won't be able to discover meaning in theirs. Your *thoughts and feelings* about something are the best source of a *so what?*

A writer often finds a *so what?* through the hard thinking of writing. But even with hard thinking, some topics may not have a *so what?* These pieces can be abandoned or put on hold.

Two poems by Zephyr, an eighth grader new to CTL, demonstrate the impact of this lesson. The first, written prior to my teaching the Rule of *So What?*, is a classic example of the school genre "I'm writing this because I have to write something but I will reveal nothing." This was despite the question I asked multiple times: "Zephyr, why are you writing about a dead plant?"

It's Probably Thirsty

There is a dead plant in my room.

It didn't look thirsty, so I never watered it.
It wasn't really mine; it just ended up in my room.

Soon it became dusty, brown, and dry.
The vines snap off when I touch them.

Why do I want to write about this plant?

My failure to feed it?
It was my mom's?

I don't know.

At least if it has seeds,
I can start over next year.

When I taught the Rule of *So What?* to Zephyr's class, I illustrated it with two versions of a poem about my new puppy, one that I crafted on purpose without a *so what?* and another that took me multiple drafts to figure out the *so what?*, to capture what she was like, sort out my feelings, and convey what I discovered about her and me. Through revision, my litany of complaints became a love poem. Zephyr's next piece of writing was a poem about his dog. He used it to capture what she's like, sort out his feelings, and convey what he discovered about Athena and himself. It is a love poem, too.

QUEEN ATHENA IN ALL HER GLORY

She's a pug
with two separate moods:
crazed when somebody annoys her,
slothing in the heat as though she's boneless.

When another dog confronts her
over a sock or a partially skinned baseball,
her only hope is to clamp herself
onto the jowls of her attacker.

When she sits in the window
on a hazy summer day, she melts
until her wrinkles turn into
soft blankets in which she sleeps.

She's a pug.
She looks so low
but feels so high
above everyone else.

When she's feeling tired,
her tail hangs limp,
and she snores woefully
when someone disturbs her.

But if a dog barks,
she's gone,

howling at the door.
She sits in chairs like a sphinx

or a model with too much money—
until something comes up,
a dog needs reprimanding,
or the counter needs to be relieved of food.

She's (not just) a pug.

—*Zephyr Weatherbee*

The Rule of *So What?* issues a challenge that students are intrigued to take up: as they choose topics—as they feel a pull or itch inside of them that says a subject *matters*—to push below the surface and use writing to find out why. My students cite the Rule of *So What?* as the craft lesson that changes them more than any other. It helps them get to their feet as intentional, deliberate writers and stay there.

The Rule of Thoughts and Feelings is a partner to the Rule of *So What?* When writers mine their heads and hearts, when they describe their own reflections or, in works of fiction, those of their main characters, they create conditions for the mother lode, theme.

For years I read poems and memoirs about kids' experiences that should have resulted in compelling writing: climbing a mountain at sunrise, saying good-bye to a childhood best friend, welcoming a new sibling, switching schools. But as stories they were dead on the page. Because I couldn't figure out *why* they were boring, I gave bad advice and told students to add more description and embroider new details. What they produced in response were longer boring poems and memoirs about climbing a *really tall* mountain during a *bright pink* sunrise, bidding farewell to a *really, really* good friend, seeing the new *pink* baby, and moving from a *one-story* school to a *two-story* school. I'm embarrassed to admit it took me a *really, really long* time to understand that the problem with these stories and poems was that writers hadn't given readers someone to be with.

Because student writers hadn't revealed what they were thinking and feeling, I couldn't enter their experiences or empathize with them. Once I began to nudge them to weave in personal reflections, their poems, memoirs, and short stories took on lives of their own. Themes emerged as a matter of course through what was going on in their heads and hearts. The Rule of Thoughts and Feelings was born.

The Rule of Thoughts and Feelings

In a piece of writing that tells a story, the reader needs *someone to be with.* If the narrative is a lyric poem or a memoir, the someone is you. If it's a work of fiction, the someone is the main character.

Knowing your—or a main character's—thoughts and feelings is crucial to a reader if he or she is going to be able to enter your story. Personal reflections help make a story engaging, interesting, and possible for a reader to experience. And personal reflections are the source of the best *so what?*s or themes.

From now on, try to include thoughts and feelings as you draft. But if you discover that you needed your first draft to get the details of plot right, you can revise for thoughts and feelings by going back into the draft to capture your responses, or your main character's, to unfolding events.

When you revise for thoughts and feelings, you might insert asterisks at the points where you realize that readers will wonder what's going on inside you. Or use a numbered list to create notes of thoughts and feelings on a separate sheet of paper. Or tape on spider legs: strips of paper on which you've drafted thoughts and feelings.

The important thing to remember is this: thoughts and feelings bring a story to life and give it meaning. They invite a reader to enter the scene, experience it, understand it, and care about it.

Cody, another student new to CTL and writing workshop, wrote his first poem ever about a baseball game. Sports are a topic with the potential to make any writing teacher groan: *then they scored, then it was tied, then he passed, then I scored,* ad nauseam. When I stopped at Cody's desk and skimmed his first draft, I found, true to form, a play-by-play without the personal reflections to involve a reader or suggest a theme (Figure 4.3).

"Cody," I said, "I'm *guessing* this must have been a cool moment for you."

"Yeah, it was pretty cool," he confirmed.

"My problem as a reader is I can't understand why." I drew an asterisk between the third and fourth lines of the first stanza. "For example, here, when you're up to bat and the score is tied, I'm wondering what you're feeling."

He said, "I'm feeling sick. My stomach is all tied up in knots."

"That's sensory. Can you write that here—attach it to the asterisk?"

"Okay."

"Keep going. Read the rest of the poem and put an asterisk wherever you think a reader might wonder what you're thinking and feeling. Then go back and add your reflections next to each asterisk. Let your reader *be there* with you."

He did. The final version, titled "Base Hit" and his first-ever poem, is a solid start to two years of writing workshop and a portrait of Cody at the bat.

BASE HIT

I am waiting in the on-deck circle
with a runner on third with one out.
The score is 11 to 11.
I want to untie all the knots in my stomach—
the knots that make me feel sick.
The batter in front of me goes out on a called strike *three*.

I step up and call time to see the signals
from the third-base coach.
"Swing away!" he orders.
I only faintly hear him,
my ears are pounding so hard.
With my foot I dig a spot in the batter's box.

I let the first pitch go by.
"Strike!" the umpire bellows.
I clench my bat tighter.
The next pitch goes in the dirt for a ball.
I foul off the pitch, which is too low to make good contact.

I am down in the count: one ball and two strikes.
My heart races as if it is about to explode.
"Swing at anything close!" the third-base coach yells.
The next pitch goes right over the heart of the plate—
and that was the pitcher's mistake.

Ping!

The sound of aluminum striking leather echoes around the field.
The ball leaps off my bat,
a screaming line drive between first and second.
It rolls out into right field, a base hit.
The runner advances home, and we win the game.

The knots in my stomach untie themselves,
the joy of victory overtakes me,
and our team celebrates—briefly.
The next game starts
in ten minutes.

—*Cody Graves*

The Rule of Write About *a* Pebble is rooted in a conversation I had with Nathan, a seventh grader. When I sat alongside him one day and read his draft of a poem, I experienced a familiar, sinking feeling. His "Pebbles" (Figure 4.4) reminded me of decades of student poems with titles like "Dogs," "Cats," "Friends," "Basketball," "Snow," "Summer," and "Chocolate." The poems didn't work because the poets had written about general subjects instead of specific observations and experiences.

"Nathan, *why* are you writing about this?" I nudged. He had a good answer.

"Because I think pebbles and blades of grass and small things we don't think much about, that we take for granted, are cool."

"That's an interesting theme," I agreed. "My problem as a reader is that this draft doesn't convince me. I can't see, hear, or feel a bunch of pebbles. Do me a favor. Go out

Draft 2

I am waiting in the on deck circle

With a runner on third with one out

It's tied up 11 to 11

The batter in front of me strikes out on a called strike three

I *want* to untie all the knots in my stomach that make me feel sick the knots

I step up to bat and call time to see the signals

From the third base coach

"Swing away!" the third base coach calls down to me

I dig a spot in the batters box with my foot, ready to hit

My ears are pounding and I faintly hear him

I let the first pitch go by

"Strike!" The umpire bellows

The next pitch goes in the dirt for a ball

I foul off the a pitch, which was a little to low

I clench my bat even tighter

I am down in the count one ball and two strikes

"Swing away at anything close" the third base coach yells

The next pitch goes right over the heart of the plate

That was the pitchers mistake

Ping!

I swing at and send a screaming line drive between first and second

It rolls out into right field, a base hit

The runner advances home and we win the ball game

I had the game winning RBI that meant almost everything to the game

The knots in my stomach untie themselves as joy overtakes me.

Our team celebrates very briefly

Our next game starts in ten minutes

Figure 4.3 *Cody's Addition of Thoughts and Feelings*

to the parking lot, choose a pebble, bring it in, and write about it."

Off he went, spending *way* too much time in his search for the perfect pebble. It was worth it. Nathan's final version of his poem, the singular "Pebble," is a small miracle.

PEBBLE

Now I'm not talking
about any
pebble—
this one I mean—

that's polygon-shaped
and has
a rough
yet gentle
surface,

that I
can roll
around in
my palm,

that I
can
throw
up
in midair
and
catch
in my hand,

the one
that dropped
on the
table
makes a
click,
rattle,
click,

that's
so light

Pebbles
A minniral
a rock
a quiet inocent little thing
that comes in all shapes and sizes.

That you find on the beach
outdoors or on your floor

you think its just another ordinary thing
but if you think hard its something thats
special.

Where would all the beaches, sand, and
gravel driveways be if it weren't
for that one tiny quiet inocent
ordinary pebble.

Figure 4.4 *Nathan's First Draft: "Pebbles"*

I can
balance it
on my
thumb.

Now,
I hope
I'm
not
asking
too
much
but
can
you
look
closely,
like I did
at this
pebble,
then
find
your
own
special
thing
in
the
world?

—Nathan Bonyun

I could have called it the Rule of Concrete Specificity, or quoted William Carlos Williams and titled it the Rule of "No Ideas but in Things," but the Rule of Write About *a* Pebble is concrete and evocative: it shows kids *how* the rule means.

The Rule of Write About *a* Pebble

Don't write about a general idea or topic. Write about a specific, observable person, place, occasion, time, object, animal, or experience. Its essence will lie in the sensory images you evoke: observed details of sight, sound, smell, touch, and taste and the strong verbs that will bring the details to life.

Don't write about _____. Write about *a* _____.
    (pebbles)   (pebble)

Don't write about *fall*. Write about *this fall day*. Go to the window; go outside with a clipboard.

Don't write about *sunsets* or *rainbows*. Write about the *amazing sunset you saw last night* or *the rainbow that appeared when you needed one*.

Don't write about *dogs* or *kittens*. Observe and write about *your dog, your kitten*.

Don't write about *friendship*. Write about *your friend and what you do together* and bring your friendship to life.

Don't write about *soccer*. Remember and write about *a time you played that means something to you*.

Don't write about *reading*. Write about *an experience reading a book*.

Don't write about *pumpkins*. Write about *the pumpkin you carved last night, the pumpkin you grew from seeds, your family's jack-o'-lantern that the bad high school boys smashed on your road*.

Sarah took up the final challenge. Her singular pumpkin even has a name.

Twila the Pumpkin

My darling Twila,
oh, you sweet orange orb—
I am so sorry
I painted on your smile,
applied mascara to your delicate eyelashes,
and carved you out a button nose
so early.

Now you bide your time in the cold.
Little fuzzy fungi
attracted to your crisp fall scent
cling to your insides.

I'm afraid for you, Twila.
Will the mold overtake you?
I hope you live
to see your holiday,
to watch as the monsters,
fairies, and goblins
gawk at your glowing radiance.

But now you sit
with a blank expression,
your smiling not as dazzling
as when you were fresh.
You watch each leaf fall,

your Bambi eyes vacant
as disease takes over
your helpless body.
I wonder if you will make it.

Twila, I am so

sorry.

—Sarah Jordan

I can recognize at once in students' drafts the benefits of another craft lesson. This one involves the writing I do, and encourage students to try, apart from the draft itself. Although I've been writing professionally for thirty years, experience hasn't quelled the anxiety I feel when I start a new project. I'm still intimidated by a blank page. But if I can start elsewhere, on a piece of paper *over there*, off to the side, one that's in no way, shape, or form an actual page of draft, I'm able to free myself from the censor who lives in my head and doodle with language. I've learned how to use writing to generate writing—to take advantage of uncertainty by opening up to possibility.

By way of example, the winter I was on the Atkins diet, I was the happiest woman in America. I consider meat a reason for living. Inspired by Pablo Neruda's irregular odes, I decided to sing the praises of bacon. But I didn't begin by drafting. Instead, I jotted notes: my bacon rituals, bacon diction, and the curing ingredients listed on the package of bacon in my refrigerator (Figure 4.5). These doodles gave me specifics and momentum, until I was ready—eager—to begin the poem. I didn't use every idea I listed, and new thoughts and language surprised me as I drafted, but the ode was jump-started and sustained by free-form but focused notes.

ODE TO BACON

O, bacon,
you are the carnivore's
dream come true.
Your briny
mahogany crispiness
is the epitome
of meat.
Your pink-veined fat,
hermetically sealed
in plastic
and cured
with water, salt, sugar,
and scary chemicals
that end in *—ate* and *—ite,*

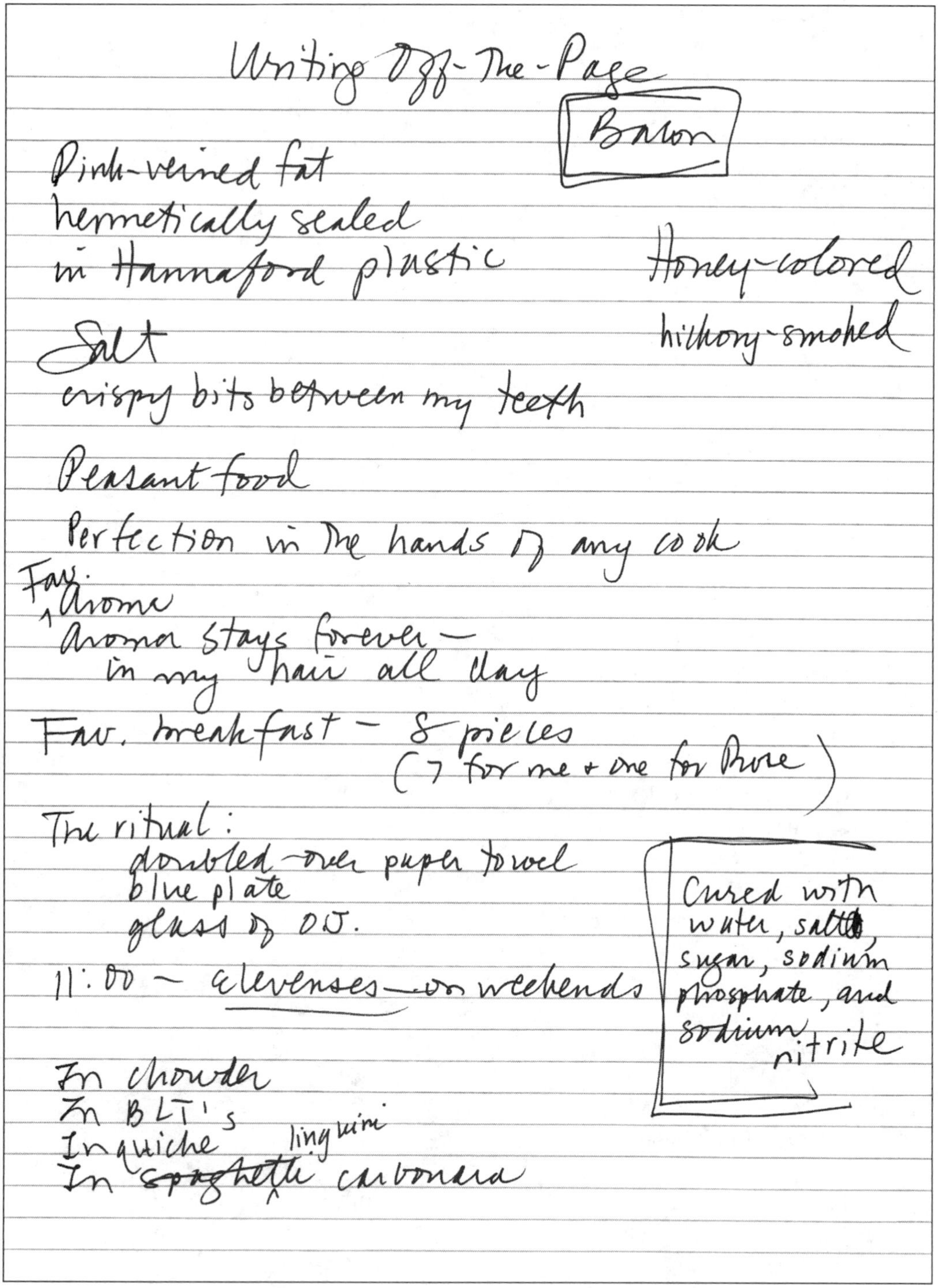

Writing Off-The-Page

Bacon

Pink-veined fat
hermetically sealed
in Hannaford plastic

Honey-colored
hickory-smoked

Salt
crispy bits between my teeth

Peasant food

Perfection in the hands of any cook

Fav: Aroma
Aroma stays forever —
in my hair all day

Fav. breakfast — 8 pieces
(7 for me + one for Rose)

The ritual:
doubled-over paper towel
blue plate
glass of OJ.

11:00 — elevenses — on weekends

In chowder
In BLT's
In quiche
In spaghetti carbonara   linguini

Cured with water, salt, sugar, sodium phosphate, and sodium nitrite

Figure 4.5 *Nancie's Writing off-the-Page About Bacon*

achieves perfection
in the fry pan of any cook,
from the peasant's BLT,
to a diner's
bacon and eggs,
to the gourmand's
linguini carbonara.
You are my favorite
weekend elevenses:
eight hickory-smoked
strips of you,
seven for me
and one for the dog.
I love your rituals,
bacon,
from scissoring open
the bright package
to severing your slices,
dialing the heat to high,
doubling a white paper towel,
retrieving the Fat Can
to gather your drippings,
and pouring a tall glass
of cold o.j.
I love
the spark and crackle
as you sing to me,
as you buckle and shrink
and your aroma
anoints the kitchen
and lingers
in my hair,
a smoky souvenir.
After the dog and I
have wolfed you down,
I lick your crumbs
and wish I had grilled
nine slices.
Fire was invented
for you, bacon.
So were fingers,
not to mention Bounty.

You are the crown
of civilization
and the reason
I haul my corpus
out of bed
on a weekend morning.

I write off-the-page every time: it is an integral part of my process. When I compose evaluation comments at the end of a trimester, I start each set by making notes off-the-page about the student's writing and reading. When I write a personal essay, I begin off-the-page by collecting sensory imagery and details. In drafting this book, I played off-the-page countless times—generated ideas, anecdotes, examples, arguments, diction choices, and quotes that I wove into the draft. Writing off-the-page is a relaxed but concentrated way to *pay attention*.

In a September minilesson, I show the class examples of my own and previous students' writing off-the-page and talk about how it made our writing—process and product—stronger. I give them a list to tape into their handbooks of all the ways students and I have benefited from what Donald Murray calls *writing before writing* (2003).

Writing off-the-Page

Writing off-the-page happens on a piece of paper apart from a draft. It's a place to let your mind play—gather words, images, and ideas; capture and store what you might otherwise lose or forget; get unstuck when you're stuck; and use writing to generate writing.

Write off-the-page to:

- relieve the pressure of a blank page
- help you get a piece started
- brainstorm words, ideas, and images
- play with different leads
- collect sensory details
- record words and phrases as they occur to you
- capture and store an idea that comes to you while you're drafting
- focus on a problem in a draft
- try out different ways of saying something
- rough out a new idea
- play with diction options
- figure out an order or organization for your information
- sketch a timeline
- explore possibilities for what might happen next
- brainstorm titles

- gain or regain momentum
- collect relevant quotes or statistics
- search for a theme or *so what?*
- experiment with different conclusions

I ask everyone to give this a try—to see if writing off-the-page makes first drafts or revisions easier and more productive. Afterward, at least half my students write off-the-page every time they draft anything. As the genres they write increase in complexity—as we move into reviews, short short stories, essays, and original research—almost everyone uses writing to plan writing.

In twenty years of teaching this lesson, I encountered three kids who never wrote off-the-page. They didn't need to—they were able to plan in their heads, bring internal selections and solutions directly to a first draft, and produce extraordinary texts. A *requirement* to write off-the-page would have wasted their time. It's also important to note that writing off-the-page isn't a web, graphic organizer, four boxes, six boxes, or one-size-fits-all. What matters is that kids understand they can play, think, plan, and pre-see their drafts, *before* and *as* they draft, on that other piece of paper.

Hope wrote off-the-page to help her plan the memoir that became "A Rip in Invincible," which appears in Chapter 10. During the process, she discovered her real topic. In Figure 4.6, we can observe Hope's thinking as she moves from a memoir that was centered on her bout with mononucleosis to a reconsideration of her illness in comparison with the permanent disabilities her mom and dad endure.

As Sophia was drafting a memoir about the first time she purchased something with her own money, she was stymied about its theme. She put the draft aside and doodled with language (Figure 4.7) to brainstorm and discover the *so what?* of her experience.

Anna also solved a writing problem in the midst of drafting, this time the short story that appears in Chapter 11. She stopped drafting and sketched a rough version of the exchange of dialogue that became the climax of her narrative (Figure 4.8).

Before Nate wrote a letter-essay about *I Am the Messenger* by Marcus Zusak, he brainstormed off-the-page (Figure 4.9) about features of the novel and his responses to it. The specifics he gathered here about characters, plot, theme, and author's style became evidence in his critique of the book

In the first week of January, when we return from winter break, I teach my students about the art of handwritten thank-you notes. I buy packs of inexpensive blank note cards, make overhead transparencies of notes of thanks I received from friends and family as good examples, and level with my kids:

> I understand why people can find it hard to write thank-you notes. It's not that they're ungrateful or lazy. It's that they don't know what to say after *thank you*, which means one note can take forever to write.

The secret? Write off-the-page first. Sketch what you like about a gift, what you'll do with it, what's special about it. Then bring these words and ideas to a note card.

I promise: writing off-the-page will make this essential responsibility of mature, considerate people both faster and easier for you. And the thoughtful people who give you gifts will appreciate—and remember—your thoughtfulness. Check out how Heidi wrote off-the-page to plan a specific note of thanks to her aunt and uncle [Figure 4.10].

Sometimes my students can't name exactly what it is they're doing as they fool around with ideas and images off-the-page. I celebrate it when I see this kind of generative play, because I recognize how productive it can be. In Figure 4.11, her label at the top shows that Sarah doesn't know yet if this is a draft of a poem or a plan for one. It doesn't matter. What's important is she understands how to think on paper. She made significant progress on a poem about a day with her mom in New York City, instead of staring into space and trying to figure out how to start it. Here's where her doodling with language led her.

SOUVENIR

We wander crowded streets
side by side,
our arms brushing as we weave
through masses of people.

The air is choked with the stench
of ominous smoke that drifts from cars
mixed with the sweet aromas
of candied nuts and hotdogs.

We duck in and out of stores
that line the sidewalk,
bags stuffed with new clothes
clutched in our hands.

Right now, we do as we please.
We have no plans
but to wander these crowded streets
together.

Right now, you and I.

—*Sarah Jordan*

I've also observed students use writing off-the-page to spare themselves the prolonged torture of drafting away at a dead-end topic. Adrienne had narrowed her memoir topic choices to two: Thanksgiving at her aunt's house in New Jersey, or her last time sailing at camp the previous summer. She wrote off-the-page about both experiences (Figure 4.12) and discovered that although the sunset sail evoked some lovely imagery, her memories of Thanksgiving offered the potential of a theme. She saved herself time and energy, and she went on to craft a memoir that captured for all time her wild but loving extended family.

Students tell me they find it helpful to play off-the-page with prose leads. They look for *the* way into a narrative, essay, or review, the one that makes them happiest, fuels them as writers, and suggests a direction for the piece. Figure 4.13 reproduces Brandon's experiments off-the-page with three narrative leads for a memoir he wrote about going hunting for the first time with his father: the two of them in *dialogue*, Brandon's *thoughts and feelings* during a moment from the experience, and Brandon and his dad in *action*. As a writer, he was pleased with and propelled by the third lead, and on he went to capture the story and meaning of that day.

Donald Murray calls writing before writing an act of "perception *and* conception" (2003). My students build successful texts on the foundation of perceptions they remember and conceptions they invent as they scribble on the scraps of paper that litter their writing folders. I show them my writing off-the-page and explain how it helps me. As soon as a student follows suit, I request permission to reproduce it, and the writer presents it to the group in a minilesson. Donald Murray said it best about the generative power of writing: we English teachers need to "understand that such a process takes place, that it is significant, and that it can be made clear to our students. Students who are not writing, or not writing well, may have a second chance if they are able to experience the writer's counsel to write before writing" (2003).

I'm often asked by teachers what to do about a student who won't write. My first response is, "Relieve their self-consciousness: show them how to write off-the-page and get their juices flowing." The second is a warning. Math teachers wouldn't tolerate for a minute a "blocked" mathematician. Writing is a school subject. Writing teachers should never indicate or accept that students might not write. This is a vestige of the old fallacy that writing is a creative art not a workmanlike craft.

Another essential craft lesson involves convincing kids of the benefits of drafting double-spaced. I photocopy a page of one of my handwritten drafts (Figure 4.14 shows an example) and ask kids to examine it and brainstorm in response to the question *What does double-spacing allow a writer to do?* Students meet in small groups to note, discuss, and name the range of my activities. Then the small groups report out, and I create a master list on an overhead transparency; an example appears on page 137.

Lead :- Reflection / Action = Mom w/ headache
- The Doctor's office ——— Flashback
- Weeks of staying home - my shoulders became bony ——— Flashback
- Coming into school late - how people made remarks — Flashback
- Some scene that had to do with Swimming —— Flashback
- Now — conclusion
——————— Flashforward

New Topic : My Dad and His Fake Leg

The leg lies at the foot of my father's dresser, with a plastic foot, the cloth padding around the rest until the top, a plastic shell that holds my father's stump. All of it painted tan but the hole in the knee hole in the knee betrays its tacky disguise and exposes what it truly is: shiny metal.

"So What?"
Connection Purpose of Memoir
theme, THEME
Now :
my parents   Mono has opened me up to see that all about
dad and his leg and her toe/surgeries or lost of one. It's shown me
that anything can be overcome / healed with time
and on sort of a heroes for doing all the stuff they
do. Because I don't think of them as amputities.

Figure 4.6 *Hope's Writing off-the-Page for a Memoir*

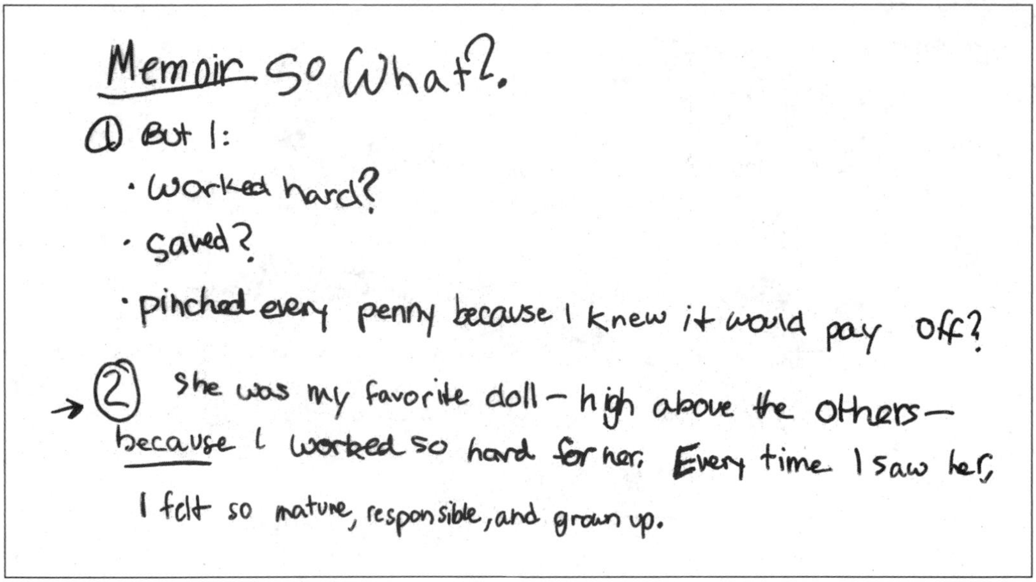

Memoir So What?.

① But I:
  · worked hard?
  · saved?
  · pinched every penny because I knew it would pay off?

→ ② She was my favorite doll — high above the others — because I worked so hard for her. Every time I saw her, I felt so mature, responsible, and grown up.

Figure 4.7 *Sophie's Writing off-the-Page for a Theme*

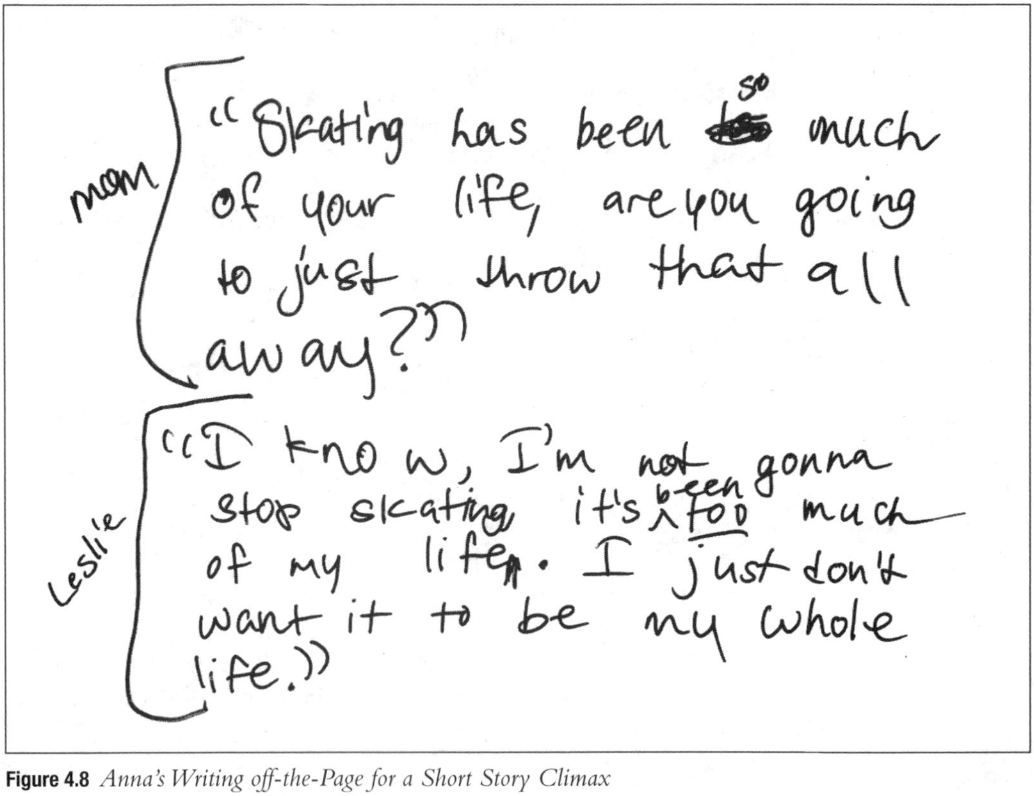

mom { "Skating has been so much of your life, are you going to just throw that all away?"

Leslie { "I know, I'm not gonna stop skating, it's been too much of my life. I just don't want it to be my whole life."

Figure 4.8 *Anna's Writing off-the-Page for a Short Story Climax*

Lead = incredible

word flow

1st mission really draws you in to the rest of them

Never knew what the new mission was going to be

• description of scenery really helped make the movie

Character development

• Tons of memorable lovable characters

• Poetic-ness of text

• mystery that follows all the way through book Keeps you on edge flow of text

{10 out of 10}

• so many twists

• amazing plot

• People description was really effective

Cover is kind of ties in with him (Ed) being "joker at the end"?

• So many lines in this book that I wished I had written

favorite Characters:
• Doorman
• Ed
• Milla

Ed = perfect main character: funny, loveable, clumbsy, ordinary (but not) and kind

Theme(s): anyone can make something of themselves, anyone can be a contribution to the world

Figure 4.9 *Nate's Writing off-the-Page to Plan a Letter-Essay*

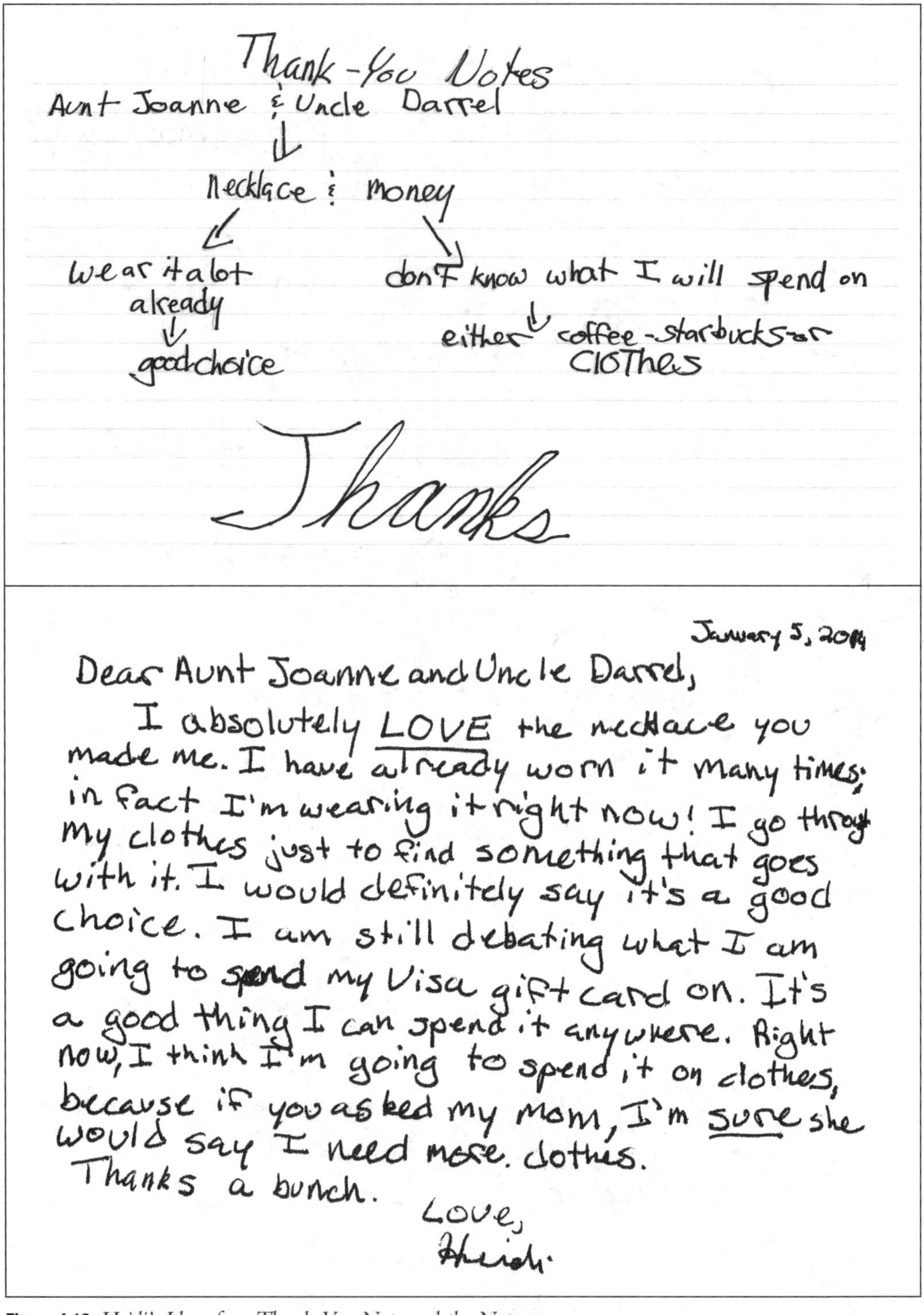

Thank-You Notes

Aunt Joanne & Uncle Darrel
↓
Necklace & money
↙ ↘
wear it a lot   don't know what I will spend on
already
↓   either↓ coffee - starbucks or
good choice   CloThes

Thanks

January 5, 2014

Dear Aunt Joanne and Uncle Darrel,
    I absolutely LOVE the necklace you made me. I have already worn it many times; in fact I'm wearing it right now! I go through my clothes just to find something that goes with it. I would definitely say it's a good choice. I am still debating what I am going to spend my Visa gift card on. It's a good thing I can spend it anywhere. Right now, I think I'm going to spend it on clothes, because if you asked my mom, I'm sure she would say I need more clothes.
    Thanks a bunch.
                    Love,
                    Heidi.

Figure 4.10 *Heidi's Ideas for a Thank-You Note and the Note*

10/16

Either Draft One or Planning for a Poem

we
~~we~~ wander ~~down~~ through the

crowded streets, ~~to go shopping~~

our bags clutched in our hands,

use somewhere else

we duck in and out of the stores

that line the sidewalk.

we stop by the stands,
out
~~bags~~ checking all of the items on the table,

as hopeful vendors force

things into our hands.

~~and~~ You shrug away

from their hopeful pleas.

~~we~~ we weave through the

crowded streets,

the ominous drifting
smoke from the pavement

- lots of people &
cars
- you always try
to pull me closer—
out of protectiveness
- ducking in and
out of shops
our hands filled
with shopping
bags
- We do whatever
we want—go into
any stores—try any-
thing on, etc.
- yummy smell of
those nut cart things
- checking out
all the little stands

WANDER
ramble
stroll
walk

maybe it
1st
stanza

Line

Possible
1st stanza

we wander through the crowded streets
that are choked with
the smelly of ominous smoke
drifting from the cars
~~and~~ the mixed with the
sweet aroma of candied
nuts and hot dog stands

Figure 4.11 *Sarah's Writing to Generate a Poem*

ThanksGiving?

- Going to Get ice cream at markt Julie's
- Uncle Peter taking me to play paddle ball @ his fancy club and how he yells at me when I play wrong
- Pool with cousins, + Dad helping me
- Shopping @ the Short hills Mall with Grandma
- Helping Aunt Bah cook + set up
- Getting the ThanxGiving outfits
- Theme: It's always crazy and someone is always mad at someone else but once the food is served and we're all together, everyone's happy.

Sailing in the Evening?

- Getting soaking wet
- Sarah being thrown over the bow, holding onto the mast, so tipping the boat
- We crashed into the American and Becky got mad, and we lied and said we didn't hit it
- There was one moment when we all stopped talking and just stared @ the amazing sunset
- theme?

Figure 4.12 *Adrienne's Writing off-the-Page to Weigh Topic Choices*

<u>Leads</u>   10/21

✱ We Slink through the forest and try not to give our Selfs away. I high step, avoiding Small twigs and young Sapplings that are Sprouting out of the ground. The Constant Crunch of leaves underfoot Makes it hard to stay quiet.

✱ I Start into the forest and head for the broken Stone wall, with excitement filling me: the first time that I will get to hunt. I keep Moving at a Steady pace, with the gun Craddeled in my arms. I can finnally find out if my years of target practice will pay off.

✱ "We're about to go into the woods. So we need to be Smart and quiet."
    He Swiftly strides through the trail, and I follow behind, Trudging ontop of the leaves, with a Crunch underneath every step.
    "Shhhh," he wispers with a grin on his face. "To walk Swiftly, you need to place your heel first, then follow through with the rest of your foot."
    I try the directions that he tells me. They help Create a little less noise.

Figure 4.13 *Brandon's Experiments off-the-Page with Memoir Leads*

WHY DO SERIOUS WRITERS DRAFT DOUBLE-SPACED?

It allows a writer to:

- add new language and ideas
- invent and insert whole lines of new text
- cross out words and phrases and substitute stronger, more accurate diction
- capture an idea before it gets lost
- plan what might come next
- switch or move parts around with arrows and asterisks
- accommodate surprises
- create breathing space: enough room on the page so the writer doesn't get lost in the draft
- approach the page as a canvas, one that can be considered, reconsidered, and made clearer, more convincing, and more satisfying
- in short, extra white space gives a writer room for the serious—and playful—*thinking* that leads to good writing

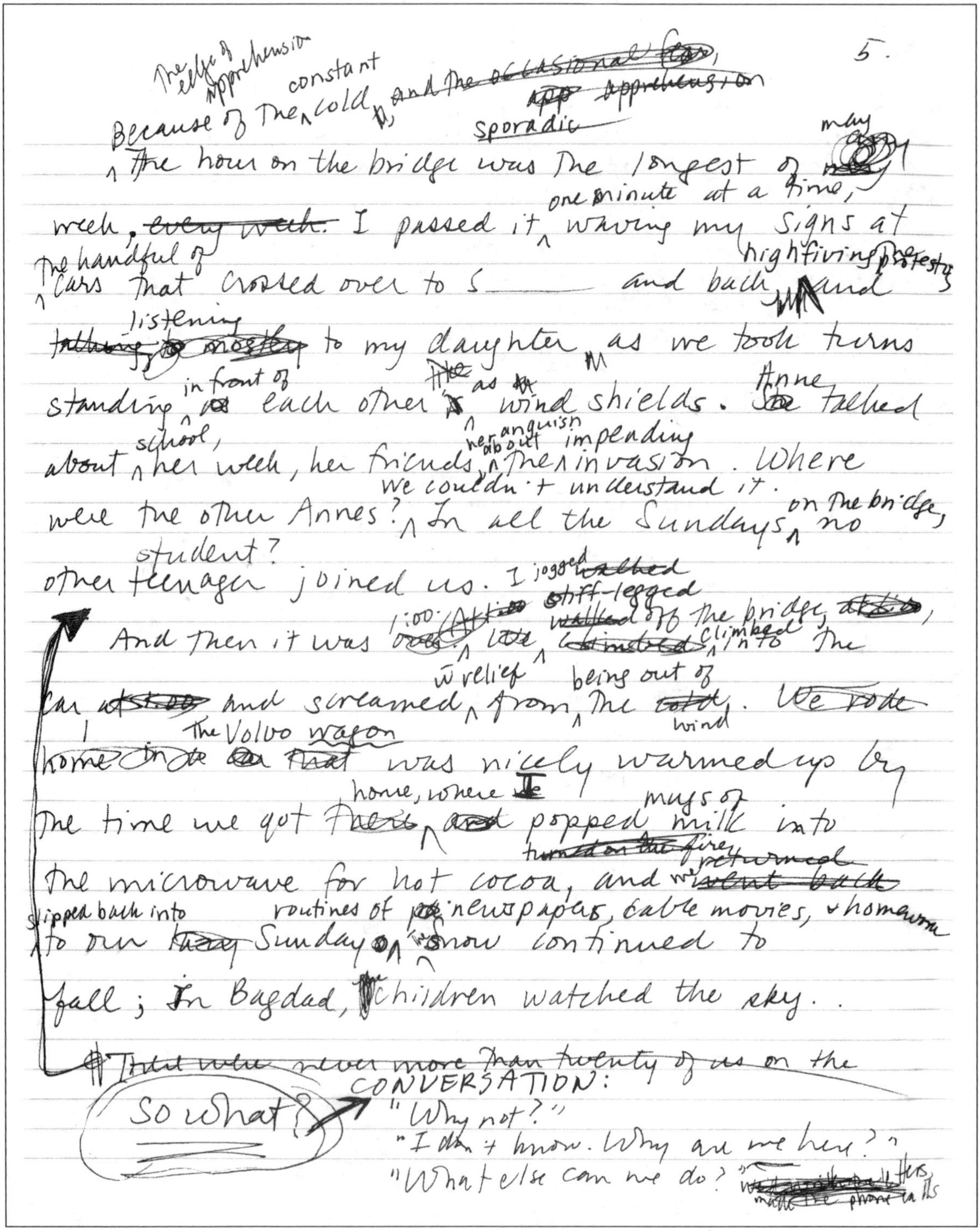

The edge of apprehension

Because of the constant cold, and the occasional ~~one~~ sporadic apprehension ~~app~~ ~~of the occasional~~

the hour on the bridge was the longest of my week. ~~every week.~~ I passed it one minute at a time, waving my signs at the handful of cars that crossed over to S____ and back, and ~~talking~~ ~~mostly~~ listening to my daughter as we took turns standing in front of each other as ~~the~~ windshields. ~~She~~ Anne talked about school, her week, her friends, her anguish about the impending invasion. Where were the other Annes? In all the Sundays on the bridge, no other teenager ~~student?~~ joined us. We couldn't understand it.

And then it was ~~over~~ ~~late~~ 1:00, and we jogged ~~walked~~ stiff-legged off the bridge, ~~and into~~ climbed into the car ~~and stood~~ and screamed in relief from being out of the ~~cold~~ wind. We ~~rode~~ home ~~in the car that~~ The Volvo wagon was nicely warmed up by the time we got ~~there~~ home, where ~~I~~ popped mugs of milk into the microwave for hot cocoa, and ~~turned on the fire~~ ~~warmed~~ ~~went back~~ slipped back into routines of ~~pa~~ newspaper, cable movies, + homework. ~~to our~~ Our Sunday ~~snow~~ continued to fall; In Bagdad, children watched the sky..

There were never more than twenty of us on the

CONVERSATION:
"Why not?"
"I don't know. Why are we here?"
"What else can we do?"

So what?

Figure 4.14 *A Page of Nancie's Double-Spaced Draft*

I type up the list, make photocopies, and distribute them the next day for kids to tape into their handbooks. Then we read, highlight, and discuss it around the circle.

A simple craft lesson, the first that many beginning writers apply to their texts, concerns titles. While a title is the briefest part of a piece of writing, a good one is memorable. It cues readers, whets our appetites, and opens the door into a text. Title generation is an occasion for any student to craft deliberately—to generate options and make a choice—but especially for inexperienced writers, whose titles are often labels. Alex, an inexperienced writer, titled his first poem with a label.

BOAT RIDE

I speed down the river,
watching for rocks
and other hazards.
The wind in my face
is cool and refreshing.
A seal pops his head up
between the foaming waves.
The motor's loud
and steady purr echoes
through my head.
I turn around
the corner of an island
and head back
toward the float,
ready for the final
challenge: docking.
                    —*Alex Graves*

In a conference, I gave Alex a nudge. "You know, I'd call 'Boat Ride' a working title. It's a kind of placeholder. It's what your poem is *about*, for sure, but for me, as a reader, it's not memorable or inviting, which is what you want as a writer, yes?"

"Yeah," he agreed.

"Donald Murray taught me to wait until *after* a piece of writing is done—until I've figured out what it's about—and then brainstorm titles: to push for quantity and let my mind play. Can you grab a piece of paper, read your poem, and let your mind play?"

Alex's title brainstorm (Figure 4.15) generated a strong, literary title, one that names a place, creates cadence, and uses alliteration. Alex and I presented a minilesson about his process for coming up with a title, and then the group and I collaborated on a theory of titles.

A GOOD TITLE . . .

- isn't a label
- invites a reader's interest
- is memorable
- matches and sets the mood for a piece of writing
- is specific
- is crafted
- might be found inside the piece of writing
- can be the first line of the piece
- can replace a working title the writer gave the piece
- fits the whole piece of writing
- fits or echoes the *so what?* or theme
- results from brainstorming: listing as many options a writer can come up with by cheating the censor in his or her brain and inviting captured ideas to inspire new ones
- usually comes last, after a writer has discovered what the piece is really about—its true focus or meaning

Figure 4.15 *Alex's Brainstormed List of Titles*

Alex, like other beginning writers I've taught, made his entry into the arena of craft via the simple act of generating and selecting the best words to appear at the top of the page.

Craft minilessons that focus on diction show students how to work toward language that's vivid, sensory, direct, and active. I teach them about weak verbs vs. sensory ones, passive voice vs. active, when and how to use a thesaurus, Ken Macrorie's "Really Bad Words" (1988), the power of simple color words, and clichés vs. fresh images.

I planned one diction minilesson after I noticed how adverbs were cluttering my students' short stories. When I had conferred with writers that day, I noticed sensory verbs weakened by unnecessary adverbs and way too many diminishers and intensifiers: adverbs writers had sprinkled in to prop up weak verbs. As a follower of Strunk and White and an advocate for plain language, I took action.

Why Smart Writers Think Twice About Adverbs

What's an adverb? It's a word that describes a verb—it tells *how* someone is doing or feeling something: for example, I love my dog *madly,* or I spoke to her *sharply.* Just so you know, an adverb can also describe an adjective (a *bright* or *really* red apple) or another adverb (he ran *seriously* fast). Most of the time, you can spot an adverb by the *-ly* at the end.

What's wrong with adverbs? They can draw away energy, overwhelm verbs, and weaken your writing. Inexperienced writers add them for needless effect (see [A] on the next page) or sprinkle them around in an attempt to prop up unsensory verbs (see [B]).

(A) *She whimpered softly.* (As opposed to what, loud whimpering?)

He wandered slowly down the hall. (Is it possible to wander quickly?)

I quickly ripped off the Band-aid. (Can you rip off something slowly?)

She smiled happily. (Arrgghh.)

(B) *She quietly walked into my room.* (How about a sensory verb like *tiptoed, crept, slipped,* or *padded?*)

He spoke loudly. (Did he yell? Shout? Scream? Bark?)

She looked at me meanly. (Did she glare? Glower? Scowl? Narrow her eyes?)

What's the solution? In the first set of examples, delete the unnecessary adverb. In the second set, delete the weak verb and its weak friend. Substitute a sensory verb, one a reader can see, hear, feel, taste, or smell. This is where a thesaurus is your friend. *Roget's* is packed with juicy, alternative verbs.

Here's an unsensory sentence: *I ate the cupcake hungrily.* An adverb, *hungrily,* is trying to prop up an unsensory verb, *ate.* To look up *ate* in a thesaurus, I have to start with its present-tense version, *eat.* Here, the thesaurus sends me to *food.* There I find two strong verbs: *devour* and *gulp.* But the thesaurus also says *see gluttony.* There I spy two more, *bolt down* and *gobble up. Any* of these verbs will create the image of an eager eater. Now I get to choose the verb that best fits my vision as a writer.

In a follow-up lesson, my students and I created lists of sensory synonyms for two weak verbs that were overwhelming their poems and narratives: people were *looking* and *walking* all over the place. Kids taped these thesauri into their handbooks and consulted them when they revised and polished stories and poetry. I included them here as Appendix H.

Lessons about craft help my students take on the perspective of insiders. They develop a repertoire of ways to generate writing, reflect on it, get themselves unstuck, reveal specifics, create imagery, discover their intentions and bring them to life, and move their writing into the realm of voiced, themed literature.

CONVENTIONS

The word *convention* comes from the Latin term for "agreement." I prefer it to *skills, mechanics, usage,* or *grammar* because it includes all of these and because it's a more accurate word to describe the rules of standard edited American English.

Conventions govern our everyday lives. We say "Hello" when we answer the phone, drive on the right side of the road, put the fork to the left of the plate, shake with our right hands, affix a stamp to the upper right-hand corner of an envelope, and say "I do" when we marry. It's healthy for English teachers to remember, and our students to learn, that *writers* invented the conventions in the texts we read—printing words left to right and top to bottom, creating spaces between them, putting periods at the ends of sentences and capital letters at the beginnings, quoting conversations, indenting for new paragraphs.

Writers developed these standards so others could read their writing with ease and as they intended. Conventionality matters because *readers count on it*. Think about what happens when you're reading a book and hit a typographical error, say, *the* appears as *hte*. Now imagine that the same book contains three comparable typos on every page. It's unlikely you or anyone would continue reading it. It's essential for students to understand that textual conventionality makes reading predictable and possible. Their writing won't be read, at least not for long, if they haven't held up their end of the bargain.

I approach conventions not as minutiae to be mastered but as means for helping students honor the agreement. Their writing needs to look and sound as they intend, invite readers and sustain their engagement, and ensure that what they've written will be taken seriously. Lessons about conventions that meet these criteria give kids accurate information, clear examples, and opportunities to put the rules to work.

I teach most of my conventions minilessons in the winter and spring, in response to patterns of error I find as an editor and gaps I notice in kids' knowledge—the omission of commas, apostrophes, dashes, double dashes, colons, and semicolons. One exception is the difference between a dash and a hyphen, which I address every fall. After I've inserted dashes in pieces of writing as I edit them, kids invariably type them as hyphens on final copies.

Conventions minilessons should help students take responsibility for perfecting their writing before it goes public. We need to be careful not to base them on such so-called skills as the five kinds of sentences, the six traits, labeling of parts of speech and the plethora of clauses and phrases, main ideas and supporting details, rules of paragraph development, topic outlines, or topic sentences. Our own experiences as readers and writers should teach us that this kind of information is irrelevant—even an impediment—when it comes to producing effective writing.

MINILESSONS ABOUT CONVENTIONS OF WRITING

- what conventions of writing are and how they make reading possible
- how to record the first three items on your individual proofreading list, edit a piece of writing, use standard editing symbols, consult your individual proofreading list when filling out an editing checksheet, and why to use a red pen: so the teacher can observe the errors you found and corrected
- how and why to proofread

- how to use a dictionary and a handheld spellchecker
- prose margins: how they work and what readers expect from them
- paragraphing while drafting and how to indicate new paragraphs when editing
- indenting run-over lines of poems
- keeping a consistent narrative point of view: *I*, *he/she*, or *you*
- keeping a consistent verb tense: past or present
- capitalization: basic conventions and common confusions
- treatment of titles: when to quote, underline, or merely capitalize
- origins of tone marks, the ancient cultures in which they originated, and how they changed over time
- comma usage and the most common omissions
- hyphens and how they function as spelling marks
- dashes and how they function as voice and meaning marks
- what's wrong with exclamation points and parentheses
- double dashes to set off information
- colons to signal a list or an explanation
- comma splices and run-on sentences as errors
- semicolons as a way to avoid comma splices, join independent clauses when you want to show a relationship between them, and avoid confusion when items in a list already contain commas
- apostrophes to show contraction
- apostrophes to show possession with a singular noun, show possession on words already ending in *s* and plural possessives, and form plurals of a letter, sign, number, or word discussed as a word
- quotation marks: how to put spoken words within quotation marks, punctuate before and after a quoted remark, use single quotation marks to indicate quotes within quotes, and paragraph for changes in speaker in written conversations
- writing numbers: when as numerals and when as words
- when to use *an* versus *a*
- when to write *Dad* versus *dad*, etc.
- verb confusions: *lie* and *lay*, *take* and *bring*, *affect* and *effect*, etc.
- friendly and business letter formats
- addressing an envelope; how to fold a business letter and insert it into an envelope; official U.S. Postal Service abbreviations; formats for the address and return address
- subject- and object-case pronouns and how to test for which case is correct when subjects or objects are compound
- abbreviations permissible in American texts
- too-long and too-short paragraphs
- a running list of usage errors I notice in students' writing titled "Get Over It, Already" (See Figure 4.16 for a photocopy of one of my "Get Over It" overheads.)

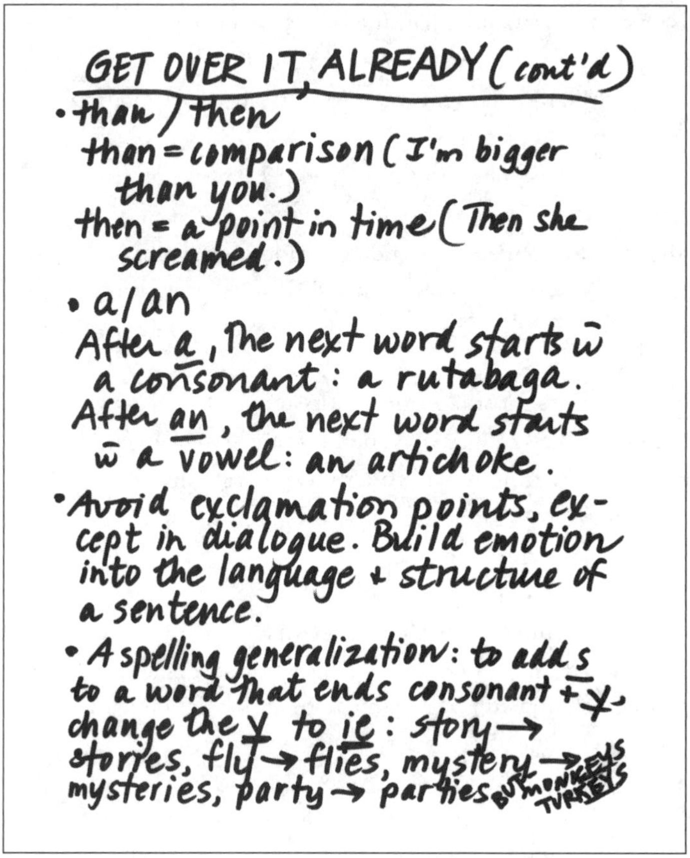

GET OVER IT, ALREADY (cont'd)

- than/then
  than = comparison (I'm bigger than you.)
  then = a point in time (Then she screamed.)
- a/an
  After a, the next word starts w̄ a consonant: a rutabaga.
  After an, the next word starts w̄ a vowel: an artichoke.
- Avoid exclamation points, except in dialogue. Build emotion into the language + structure of a sentence.
- A spelling generalization: to add s to a word that ends consonant + y, change the y to ie: story → stories, fly → flies, mystery → mysteries, party → parties BUT MONKEYS TURKEYS

Figure 4.16 *A Sample "Get Over It, Already" Overhead*

By the second week of school, some students will be ready to edit their poems. My first lesson about conventions addresses how to begin and maintain an individual proofreading list and complete an editing checksheet for each piece of writing. I ask everyone to start his or her proofreading list with the same three items:

1. Check obvious stuff.
2. Circle and look up every word I'm not 100 percent certain of.
3. Capitalize the first, last, and important words in a title.

By this point in their careers as writers, students have mastered some level of "obvious stuff." Do they put names on pieces of their writing, capital letters at the beginnings of sentences and on people's names, quotation marks around words spoken aloud, and periods at the end of sentences? Seventh and eighth graders shouldn't waste time listing every convention they've learned since first grade, so we sum up whatever their preexisting knowledge is as the "obvious stuff."

The second convention they record is the bottom-line procedure for finding and correcting spelling errors. Students need to learn to slow down, focus on every word in a piece of writing, and circle it if they're the *least* bit uncertain of its spelling. Then, after they've finished checking the whole text for potential misspellings, they should consult a dictionary, a handheld spellchecker, or the computer's spellchecker to look up the circled words. This will take a while, and that's fine with me. Identifying spelling errors and learning how to spell words are goals for every writer of any age.

The final common item on the proofreading list addresses how to capitalize titles. The "important" words in a title carry the meaning: nouns, pronouns, verbs, adverbs, and adjectives. The unimportant words show relationships—articles, conjunctions, and prepositions, like as *a, the, and so, but, of, in, with,* and *to.*

After these three entries, every student's proofreading list is individualized. Although I have tried to further standardize the list, I learned that any whole-class convention beyond these is a waste of time. For students who already have a mature grasp of edited English, a standardized list is an exercise in tedium. For my less knowledgeable writers, it's an exercise in mystification: without the supporting context of specific errors in pieces of their writing, the rules go right over their heads. I've also learned to intervene when students, of their own volition, add items to their proofreading lists, for example, *punctuation* or *margins.* Items such as these are broad, vague, and unhelpful.

Figure 4.17 shows Claire's proofreading list during eighth grade. It's personal to her, and it's specific: the discrete goals she needed to focus on and list on editing checksheets before she edits pieces of her writing. As I saw that Claire had mastered a convention or technique, I put a check mark next to it, to indicate that she no longer had to copy it on her editing checksheets.

Figure 4.18 reproduces the editing checksheet Claire attached to an essay she wrote in May, before she submitted it to me for editing. She omitted the conventions I had checkmarked on her proofreading list, and then recorded the relevant items. She borrowed a red pen from the materials center and did her best to edit for each of them. Then she paper-clipped the checksheet to the top of the edited essay and its drafts and put the packet in her class' stack tray.

When I edited kids' writing that night at home, I used a black pen to correct *every* error Claire missed: students need to be able to create perfect, reader-ready, final copies from my corrections. But I won't teach a student about every error—just one or two, so the writer can attend to and remember them. On Claire's editing checksheet I noted a convention I wanted to review with her, along with three misspellings I found. These became the basis for my editing conference with her in the next day's writing workshop. The symbols I use when I edit—and that I teach students each fall—appear as Appendix I.

_____Claire_____'s **Proofreading List**

1. Obvious stuff

2. Look at every word, circle those I'm not 100% sure of, and look them up.

✓ 3. Capitalize first, last, and all important words in a title.

4. Adjectives before nouns: no comma between the final adjective and the noun.

5. Beware of comma splices

6. Listen for — and fix — ineffective repetition.

7. Keep a consistent verb tense: all past or all present.

8. Beware of too-long paragraphs. Keep #'s friendly.

✓ 9. Avoid "you" unless "you" means the one person I wrote this for or to.

10. Shifts in time in narratives need to be signaled with transitional phrases.

11. Indent new paragraphs, i.e., no block style.

✓ 12. Review and refer to the rules for indicating titles.

13. Check for apostrophes on possessive nouns.

14.

Figure 4.17 *Claire's Individual Proofreading List*

EDITING CHECKSHEET

TO BE PAPER CLIPPED TO THE TOP OF YOUR WRITING SUBMITTED FOR TEACHER EDITING

NAME _Claire_

TITLE OF PIECE _Whose Body? or Depends who You're Fighting For_

DATE OF PIECE _5/1_

CONVENTION	EDITED (✓)	TEACHER'S COMMENTS
Look at every word, circle those I'm not 100% sure of, and look them up.	✓	Check for apostrophes on possessive nouns.
Obvious stuff and Capitalize first, last, and all important words in a title	✓	
Adjectives before a noun: no comma between the final adj. and the noun	✓	
Beware of comma splices	✓	
Listen for—and fix—ineffective repetition	✓	
Keep a constant verb tense: all past or all present	✓	
Beware of too-long paragraphs	✓	**WORDS TO ADD TO MY PERSONAL SPELLING LIST**
Shifts in time in narratives need to be signaled with transitional phrases	✓	who's = who is whose = belongs to a who
Indent new paragraphs	✓	liable reconcile

Figure 4.18 *Claire's Editing Checksheet*

An essential conventions minilesson, one that opens kids' eyes to the purposefulness of punctuation, tells the stories of five of the tone marks. When I conducted some research, I discovered that an ancient Greek named Aristophanes of Byzantium played a major role in the standardization of punctuation. The librarian at Alexandria, he is acknowledged as the inventor of some of the Greek diacritical marks. Figure 4.19 reproduces the summary I give kids to tape into their handbooks; I flesh it out in a minilecture.

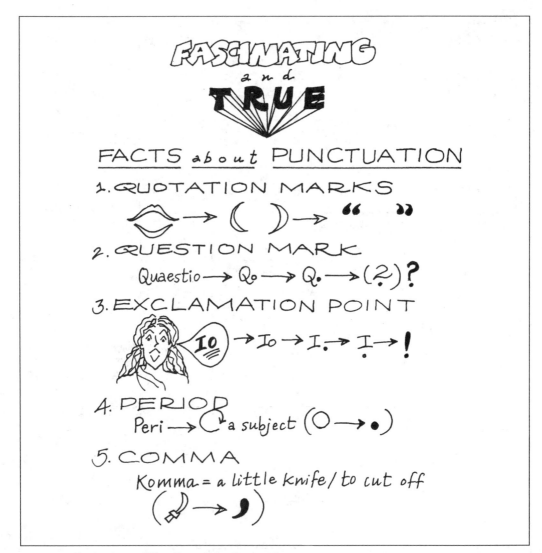

Figure 4.19 *Fascinating and True Facts About Punctuation*

Did you ever wonder about punctuation—about where all the dots and lines came from? I love English, so I love this stuff. I'm also a writer, so I was curious about the history of the marks I use to show readers how to read.

I discovered that quotation marks began in ancient Greece as drawings of two *lips* turned on their sides. When writers wanted to indicate that words they were writing were a direct quote—had been spoken by someone—they used these curved marks to represent the mouth of a speaker, one lip at the beginning of a quotation and the other at the end. Over time, the big lips evolved into the tiny sets of double lips we use today. Cool, right?

The question mark started out in ancient Roman texts as the Latin word *quaestio*, which means *question*. Writers inserted *quaestio* to show they were asking the reader a question. Over time, *quaestio* was abbreviated as *Qo*, and then just *Q*. The Roman letter for *Q* resembles our Arabic number *2*, and the question mark was born.

I love the history of the exclamation point. *Io* was a word in ancient Greece that expressed excitement—an early equivalent of *wow*. Writers inserted it into texts to show strong emotion. Over time, scholars changed the *o* to a dot, and, over more time, the dot came to rest under the *I*. The result was the exclamation point. *Io!*

The word *period* comes from the ancient Greek word *peri*, which means *round*. Writers inserted a circle at the end of a group of words to show they'd gone *all around* a subject—that they'd written a statement that was well-rounded and complete. Maybe they got tired of writing a circle each time, or maybe they wanted to save on parchment. In any event, the *O* became the dot we use today.

Finally, the word *comma* comes from the Greek word *komma*, which means "little knife" or "to cut off." Writers inserted the little curved blade of a knife whenever they wanted to create a pause or set off a group of words a bit—but not completely—from the body of a sentence.

I love it that these voice or *tone* marks were so concrete and practical right from the start. I think their evolution is fascinating. And I was inspired to issue a challenge.

If ancient writers and scholars could invent marks to show their readers how to read their texts, isn't it time for some new ones? Your homework tonight is to invent one or two punctuation marks for the twenty-first century. The mood, inflection, purpose, and appearance of the marks are up to you. The point is to create punctuation that indicates something brand new for a writer to show a reader about how to read a text. And, yes, they can be funny. We'll gather them on transparencies starting tomorrow.

If you skim any usage handbook, it's possible to imagine devoting an entire school year to the intricacies of American punctuation. Again, I narrow my focus to the errors and omissions I find with most frequency when I edit students' writing. When I teach my kids about the commas they most often omit, I start with the notes that follow.

SOME WAYS TO USE COMMAS

1. in a list (including before the *and*, aka the Harvard or Oxford comma)
   We ate, drank, and regurgitated.

2. between adjectives that can be flipped and can be joined by *and*
   Wallace is a sincere, thoughtful, witty mammal.

3. between two sentences joined by a FANBOY (*for, and, nor, but, or, yet*)
   Xander somersaulted down to the Barn, and Kate cartwheeled behind him.

4. with extra information that's *not* essential to the sentence making sense
   Diamonds, which are known to last forever, are the perfect teacher-appreciation gift.

5. after mild interjections
   Well, what if I don't feel like snorkeling?
   So, last weekend, like, I saw, like, this movie, like, about snorkelers.
   Okay, you may snorkel now.

6. in a direct address to someone, using his or her name
   Charlotte, put Madyson down this minute.

7. with dates
   Jordan, CTL's leapling, was born on February 29, 2003, in the afternoon.

8. with cities and states
   Helena flew to St. Louis, Missouri, to worship at the Bowling Hall of Fame.

9. before and after *e.g.* or *i.e.*
   Emily "enjoys" her siblings, i.e., Aidan, Katie, and Tristam.
   Amelia "enjoys" playing competitive games with her brothers, e.g., Ping-Pong, soccer, and Monopoly.

10. to introduce dialogue
    Glenn said, "Please, I beg you—show me your wiggly tooth."

11. in dialogue, between a quoted statement and its *he said* or tag phrase
    "Wiggle away," he said.

So kids can practice applying the rules and discuss their decisions, I create practice sheets: a paper copy for each student and another on an overhead transparency. Figure 4.20 shows a typical, silly practice. It's one of a series of fabrications I invented about the kindergarten class and Helene, their teacher. My kids had a laugh, consulted the guidelines in their handbooks to help themselves add commas, and then took turns at the overhead projector, inserting commas and explaining why.

In addition to giving students technical information about comma usage, I also advise them to go alone to one of the peer conference areas, read their drafts softly aloud,

COMMA REVIEW AND a few Periods, Too
OR
Helene's Group & the Easter Bunny

"Don't forget my darlings" Helene admonished her group of angel babies "You must be especially good because the Easter Bunny is coming soon"

"Helene don't be a fool" Kaden piped up

"Yeah Helene. Don't you know the Easter Bunny is a hoax perpetuated on naïve American youths by cynical adults as part of a crude plot to manipulate our behavior distract us with pleasant fantasies and warp our psyches?" Jasper queried.

"I ditto that J-Man" Sam proclaimed and he poked Helene in the eye to demonstrate his enthusiasm.

Nelly took the floor. "Well alls I know is I better git plenty o' chocolate on Sunday or I'm gonna be in a powerful bad mood on Monday so you better watch yourself then Helene baby."

"I'm not afraid of you Stafford" Helene huffed from inside the closet. Lexi grinned and held up the key. She inserted it in the lock jiggled it and turned it until the lock clicked as her teeny tiny bratty buddies cheered her on.

Then they built a fire and went looking for the Easter Bunny.

Figure 4.20 *Sample Comma Review*

and *listen*. Writers who read their texts in a normal inflection can hear many of the omitted commas.

To teach about semicolons and colons, I distribute guidelines that describe the functions of each mark, teach these in minilessons, and then assign hunting expeditions: as students are reading that night, they should skim their books, find places where the writer used a colon or semicolon, and copy the sentences onto 5 × 8–inch cards. The next day I collect the cards, cut and tape them to make one long document, photocopy it for each student, and lead a discussion: "Okay, given what we learned the other day about what colons (or semicolons) do, *why* did these writers use the mark? What are they indicating in each instance?"

Sometimes I broaden the focus and give everyone a photocopy of a piece of published writing to examine. I've used a column from the *Boston Globe*, a "Talk of the Town" essay from *The New Yorker*, a page of a foreword I wrote for a friend's book, and the highlights-of-the-week I submit to each Friday's CTL newsletter. The assignment is to *notice the punctuation*. Working with two pens of different colors, students use one color to highlight marks they understand, in terms of their function in the piece, and the other to highlight marks they don't get. In the next day's minilesson, kids meet in small groups to talk about what they understood and didn't, discuss their confusions, and tap my expertise as I circulate among them.

During a ten-year period when I polled my classes at the end of each trimester about minilessons—about whether anything I taught had changed them as writers—the most cited lesson came as a surprise. Students told me they valued above all others a lesson about pronoun case, about when to use *I* or *me*. Between you and me, it's a lesson that's dear to me and my English teacher friends.

Me *or* I?

You may already know that a noun is a word that names a person, place, thing, or idea. A *pronoun* is a word used in place of a noun. So instead of saying *Nancie* all the time, I can say *I* or *me*. When I address *the class*, I can say *you*. When you talk about *the class*, you can use the pronouns *we* or *us*.

The *case* of a pronoun tells how it relates to the other words in a sentence. There are two kinds of pronoun cases, and it's time for some notes. Please turn to the next clean page in the notes section of your writing–reading handbook and copy my notes from the transparency as I talk you through them.

Pronoun Case, or Me *or* I?

- Nominative-case pronouns are used as *actors*, as *subjects of sentences*: *I, he, she, we, they, you,* and *it.* They usually come at the beginning of a sentence.
- Objective-case pronouns *receive the action* in a sentence: *me, him, her, us, them, you,* and *it.* They usually come in the middle or at the end of a sentence.

The point of this lesson is to help you with the *me*-or-*I* conundrum. You seldom make errors in pronoun case when the subject or object is *single*. In other words, I never hear you say, "Me went to the movies" instead of "I went to the movies." And I've never heard anyone here announce, "My parents gave I a phone."

The difficulty comes when subjects or objects are compound—when there are two or more actors or recipients of the action. Let's return to the overhead transparency and note-taking:

- Errors in pronoun case usually occur when the subject or object is *compound*: more than one person.

  Examples: *Jake and me love mashed potatoes.* (wrong)
  Jake and I love mashed potatoes. (correct)
  Renée made mashed potatoes for Jake and I. (wrong)
  Renée made mashed potatoes for Jake and me. (correct)

The technical way to test for the right case is to determine if the pronoun is the subject of a verb or the recipient of the action. But there's a simpler test for correct pronoun case, one you can perform when you're confused about *I/me*, *she/her*, *he/him*, *we/us*, and *they/them*. Please copy it into your notes:

- To test for the correct case of a pronoun when there's a compound construction (e.g., *[name] and I/me*), drop the *[name] and* part, and ask yourself: is it *I* or *me*? In other words, test the pronoun *by itself* with the verb.

  Examples: *[Jake and]* _____ *love mashed potatoes.* (*I* or *me?*)
  Renée made mashed potatoes for [Jake and] _____ . (*I* or *me?*)

Take the next two minutes to create two examples of your own for practice. Give one sentence a compound *subject*: make one of the words a name and the other a pronoun—*I*, *he*, *she*, *we*, or *they*. Give the second sentence a compound *object*, with one of the words a name and the other a pronoun: *me*, *him*, *her*, *we*, or *them*. We'll read your examples around the circle. And, yes, these can be funny.

When my students leave CTL, they matriculate at local public high schools, independent day schools, and private boarding schools. No matter what kind of secondary school they attend, they're expected by their teachers to know how to produce standard, edited American English. In other words, high school English teachers don't provide much instruction about usage, but they do take points off for mistakes. I want my students to find success beyond CTL with teachers who attend to their ideas, not their errors. So I teach writers in the workshop how to edit and proofread their writing, hold them responsible over time for the rules and guidelines I introduce in editing conferences, and present lessons to the whole group about common errors of usage. This is my responsibility, not just as an English teacher but as someone who cares about my students, their writing, and their lives after my classroom.

SPELLING

Over the years I swear I tried every spelling approach ever developed—high-frequency words, grade-level words, content-area vocabulary, you name it. What I learned in the end is that there's little if any benefit to telling a whole class to study and memorize the same words. The students who are challenged as spellers can't learn fifteen new words a week, and a student with a strong visual memory will already know most of them.

Individual students need to focus on the individual words they don't know how to spell yet. Each week, each of my students works with just five of his or her spelling confusions—few enough that, studying them in-depth and with purpose, kids can learn and retain them. At CTL, every teacher is a spelling teacher. In grades 3–8, students and teachers of all subjects take a student's spelling words from his or her writing across the curriculum. Writers carry their spelling folders with them to every class. Before teachers return work, we circle any misspellings, write the correct spellings on Post-it notes, and attach these to the work. Students add the words to their individual master lists.

This means that the spelling words my students record include those I find when I edit their drafts, misspellings I correct as their history teacher, errors the math and science teachers spot, and words misspelled in their letter-essays about books, which I note on Post-its and stick to the covers of their marble notebooks. As my students draft, they're supposed to—and often do—record the words they're unsure of on Post-its, to add later to their master lists. I also teach them not to spellcheck on the computer until the final stages of a piece of writing, as part of the editing process, and then to record all the actual misspellings, as opposed to typos.

I ask the lucky spellers—the ones who inherited a visual memory gene—to work with atlases and place names, science and math terms, foreign words used in English texts, and lists of frequent misspellings that I download from the Internet. Identifying five unknown spellings is every student's responsibility every week.

Spelling study takes about ten minutes of class time. On Tuesday at the start of writing workshop, I walk the inside of the minilesson circle and scan each student's word-study sheet, to make sure that five words are recorded and spelled correctly. Figure 4.21 shows one of Sophia's word-study slips. That morning I paused at her beanbag because her fifth word, *altar*, represented half of a pair of homonyms: in a piece I edited, she'd written about an *altar* but spelled it *alter*. To learn the difference between the two, she needed to study both words and their definitions. So I asked her to add a sixth word—*alter*—and write brief definitions for each. After I okay or correct the words in the first column, students complete the study process (Figure 4.22) for homework, due Thursday.

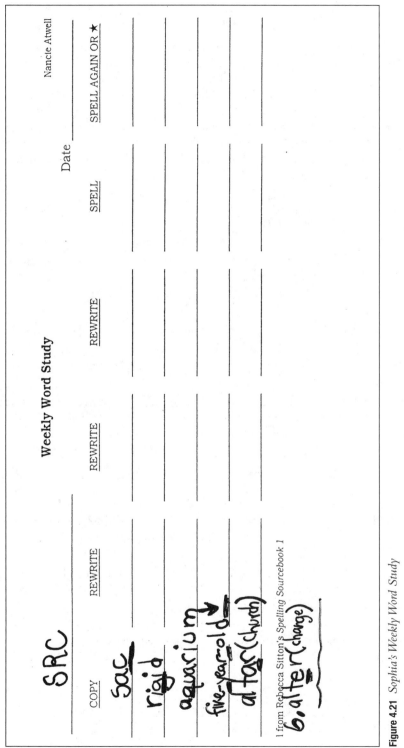

Weekly Word Study

Nancie Atwell

Date

SRC				
COPY	REWRITE	REWRITE	REWRITE	SPELL	SPELL AGAIN OR ★
sac					
rigid					
aquarium					
five-year-old					
altar (church)					
6. alter (change)					

1 from Rebecca Sitton's *Spelling Sourcebook 1*

Figure 4.21 *Sophia's Weekly Word Study*

Every week, prior to class on Tuesday, copy five words from your personal spelling list into the first column of a weekly word study slip. Copy exactly as the words appear on your list so you *don't learn misspellings*. Please *print*, rather than using cursive, so the individual letters are separate and distinct. Show the word study slip to me at the start of writing workshop on Tuesday morning, so we can be sure you don't study—and end up learning—any misspellings. Then, on Tuesday or Wednesday for homework, study your five words, using every step of the procedure described below, in preparation for a partner test on Thursday. It should take you at least twenty minutes to complete the following steps with your five words:

1. Identify the tricky part of the first word and underline it. Then read the first word: look at it and *say* it.

2. Spell the word to yourself: touch each letter with your pencil point and say the letter.

3. Close your eyes. See the word in your mind. Say each of its individual letters.

4. Put your muscle memory to work. Carefully and slowly *print* the word in the next three columns, and say each of the individual letters as you write it. When you come to the tricky part of the word, say those letters louder and write them darker.

5. Now, take a break of five or more minutes to give your long-term memory time to process the appearance of the word, its letters, and their order. Fold your spelling slip in half and read a book, listen to your iPod, watch TV, your choice.

6. Unfold your spelling slip, cover the correct spelling with your hand, and print the word in the "Spell" column.

7. Proofread: check the word you just wrote *letter for letter* against the original version in the *spell* column. Go back and forth, using the tip of your pencil.

8. If you spelled the word correctly, put a star in the final column and go on to the next word. If you misspelled it, repeat the process above, steps 1–6, this time printing the word in the "Spell Again" column.

9. Repeat the procedure with each remaining word. Again, a complete study of five words will take at least twenty minutes.

Adapted from *Spelling Resource 1* by Rebecca Sitton

Figure 4.22 *Procedure for Independent Word Study*

I adapted the word-study procedure from the work of Rebecca Sitton (1996); however, I do not use or recommend her word lists. In addition, I tried to make the process more involving for kids, so they can create a strong sense of what a word is supposed to look like, by tapping every kind of memory I can think of: short-term, long-term, visual, auditory, small motor, and muscle. It takes at least twenty minutes for students to study five words using the word-study procedure.

Teaching kids how to identify and master their own misspellings works better than anything I've tried to improve the correctness of daily schoolwork. Unless a student has an identified visual-processing disability, the goal is for drafts to be at least 98 percent correct by the time they graduate from eighth grade. By and large, they meet the goal.

On Thursday, at the start of the workshop, I ask to see the completed spelling study slips. I walk the inside of the minilesson circle again and check that the words in the last column are spelled correctly. Figure 4.23 shows Sophia's completed word study. If I discover that a word in the "Spell" column is misspelled, I tell the student, "I don't see how you could have checked this word letter-for-letter against the original. You're not using all the steps, and the study procedure won't help you unless you do. I don't want to see this again. Don't take a test on this word today. Study it again next week."

After I finish checking the study slips, pairs of students test each other on their five words on scrap paper. So a speller can learn from it, the procedure for giving and self-correcting a partner test is also particular and specific (Figure 4.24). I circulate while students are partner-testing and intervene as necessary. Testers have a tendency to rush when providing a correct spelling and not give spellers enough time to touch each letter with their pencil tips as they proofread themselves.

I don't collect or grade the word-study slips. Instead, I ask students around the circle, "How did you do?" If a student answers, "Four out of five," I respond with, "What word? Which part of it?" Then the rest of the class and I coach the student by describing our tricks or techniques for remembering the correct spelling. For example, when Ben omitted the second *s* in *embarrassed*, Nate said, "It helps me to think about what a strong feeling it is to be embarrassed—that after the prefix *em-*, it needs all the *r*'s and *s*'s it can get."

Each third week of September, I initiate the spelling program with a pep talk:

> Over the years, I tried to teach spelling so many different ways I've lost track. But since I found this approach, I've stuck to it like glue because it *works*. The way I'm going to teach spelling to you, and you're going to learn it, will change your spelling forever. That's because the basis of the program is *you*. Your spelling words will be *your own spelling words*: the ones you don't know how to spell yet, your old bad habits, your confusions, and your uncertainties.
>
> Spelling matters. Spelling *shows*. When educated adults read misspelled writing, they assume one of two things. Either the writer is *ignorant* and

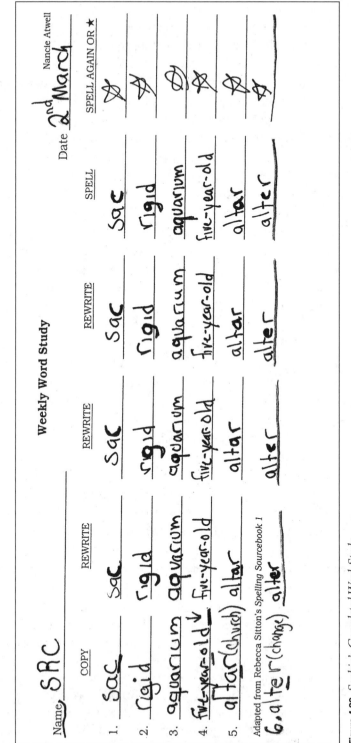

Figure 4.23 *Sophia's Completed Word Study*

PROCEDURE FOR PARTNER TESTS

Tester: Say the word, use it in a sentence, and say it again.

Speller: Print the word.

Do the whole list. Then:

Tester: Spell each word out loud *slowly*, so the speller can proofread.

Speller: Proofread by touching each letter of the word with your pencil point. On any word you've misspelled, circle *the part of the word* with the error.

Then, on your personal spelling list, use a star or checkmark to indicate the words that you spelled correctly on the test. Either circle a word you missed, or re-add it to the bottom of the list. Be sure to circle the *part* of the word you misspelled, so you can focus on the area of confusion when you study the word again next week.

Figure 4.24 *Procedure for Partner Tests*

doesn't know any better. Or the writer is *arrogant*: he or she doesn't care. I don't want anyone to judge you this way. I'll bet you don't either. So every week, you're going to focus like a laser on five words you don't know how to spell yet and, over time, master them.

Each student gets a spelling folder with pockets and brass fasteners, two blank master spelling lists, procedures for independent word study, procedures for partner tests, a half-dozen weekly word-study slips to start with, and the lists I downloaded of frequently misspelled words. I demonstrate the study procedure on an overhead transparency with one of my own spelling demons, asking the class to coach me through the process by reading the steps aloud to me. At the fifth step, when I pause to let my long-term memory digest the spelling of a word, I read aloud to the group for five minutes.

I end the spelling-study introduction by assigning students to come to class the next day with five spelling demons of their own, recorded in two places: on their master spelling list and on a word-study slip. By now I've already gathered words on Post-its to pass along to individuals—misspellings I found in the September writing and reading surveys or noted when I circulated during the first two weeks of independent writing time.

As the next day's minilesson, after I walk the circle and make sure that everyone has five words and that they're spelled correctly, I talk the class through the twenty-minute study procedure. At the point in the process when they take a break to encourage a correct spelling to filter into their long-term memories, I read aloud from a short story. Then each student attempts to spell the word he or she just studied. Afterward, we talk: "How did you do? What did you notice? What steps helped you most? How do you think you'll do on a test of these words in two days? On a test next month?"

I repeat this minilesson—everyone working through the twenty-minute procedure together but with his or her own words—in late November and again in mid-March, at the start of the second and third trimesters, to reinforce the steps and the reasons behind them. Once a month, I schedule a pop quiz on previously mastered words. Pairs of students trade spelling folders and put dots next to fifteen words that their partner has checked off as studied and learned. If a word is part of a pair or trio of homonyms, they dot each of them. Then the pairs number sheets of paper, 1 to 15, and take turns testing each other.

These tests I do collect and correct. I want to see which words kids are retaining, where they're still uncertain, who's spending twenty minutes a week on the study process, and who's madly filling out the study sheet in homeroom on Thursday morning.

When I return the tests the next day, I ask students to add any words they misspelled to the bottom of their master lists, to be studied again, and then assign students to research their test results and set goals. The goal for a student who scored 100 percent is to continue to take the study process seriously. Others' goals will depend on the nature of their mistakes. Over the years, my students and I developed a list of goals that applies to most spelling errors. With my help, individuals review it and copy down appropriate goals on index cards. They staple the cards to a pocket of their spelling folders as a reminder of what they should focus on during the coming month. Progress toward individual spelling goals becomes one basis for my evaluation of writers at the end of a trimester.

POTENTIAL SPELLING GOALS

Continue to be serious about the study process.

Underline/write darker *the correct letters of the tricky part(s)* of my misspellings during the study process.

Say *the correct letter(s)* of the tricky parts louder during the study process.

Develop mnemonics for the tricky parts, e.g., *broccoli* wants two *c*'s because it's so rich in vitamin C; *millennium* needs two *l*'s and two *n*'s because it's a major occasion; *success* deserves all its *c*'s and *s*'s; *possession* is greedy and wants lots of *s*'s.

Invent ways to say a habitual misspelling to myself so I remember its trick: *sub*-tle; se*par*ate*; re*-commend; si-*mile*; pro-*bab*-ly; memo-ir; de-*finite*-ly.

Recognize words inside words, e.g., *science* in *conscience* and—almost—*conscien*tious; *critic* inside *critic*ism.

Recognize where a prefix ends and a base word begins, e.g., the prefix *dis* + *appear* = *disappear*; *dis* + *satisfied* = *dissatisfied*; *un* + *necessary* = *unnecessary*; *re* + *commend* = *recommend*.

Recognize where a base word ends and a suffix begins, e.g., *totally* = *total* + *ly*; *definitely* = *definite* + *ly*; *absolutely* = *absolute* + *ly*; *awesome* = *awe* + *some*.

Break long, hard words into their syllables: say and write each one, one at a time, e.g., *cir-cum-fer-ence*.

Focus on tricky short vowels, e.g., exper*i*ment.

Focus on tricky double consonants, e.g., begi*nn*ing.

Remember that it's *usually* i before e, but that after a *c*, it's almost always *ei*.

Memorize the sound or rhythm of a sequence of letters, à la *n-e-c-e-s-s-a-r-y*.

Recognize the words that are my old, bad habits and concentrate on breaking them.

Write and say the correct spelling of a bad-habit word more than the four times required on the spelling-study slip.

Remember what foreign language a word is derived from and how that affects its vowels, e.g., arch*ae*ology from the Greek; man*eu*ver, mem*o*ir, and rest*au*rant from the French; lasa*gne* from the Italian.

Choose more realistic words to study.

Do a visual check of a word after I've written it during the partner test: take a moment to be sure.

Spend more time on the study process, do it exactly as prescribed, and commit to every step.

As effective as this approach has proven in helping my students learn correct spelling, I recognize that some of my students will have more difficulty than others. Students with visual-processing disabilities should own handheld spellcheckers and carry them with them everywhere, and everyone should learn deliberate approaches to *proofreading*: ways to identify potential misspellings in pieces of writing.

TECHNIQUES FOR PROOFREADING SPELLING

- Circle *each* and *every* word you're not absolutely, 100 percent certain of. Once you've proofed the whole piece, go back and look up the spellings of the circled words. In other words, maintain your focus as a proofreader until you've finished the actual proofreading. A dictionary or handheld spellchecker should come into play only after you've identified *every* potential misspelling.
- Scan each line of writing backward, from right to left, to focus on one word at a time and stop your eyes and mind from getting caught up in the meaning of the piece.

- Slow down on common homonyms (*your* and *you're*; *to*, *too*, and *two*; *its* and *it's*; *their*, *there*, and *they're*) and other homonym-type confusions (*college* and *collage*, *effect* and *affect*, *chose* and *choose*, *than* and *then*). Check the word in question against what you know, use a resource, or ask me.

- Slow down on demons, your own and the usual suspects. You know which words you've confused in the past or continue to struggle with. Give them particular attention, e.g., *necessary, recommend, separate, a lot, all right, definitely, truly, restaurant, eighth, twelfth.*

- Slow down on words with prefixes and suffixes:
  - words in which the doubling of letters becomes an issue, like *unnecessary, disappoint, disappear, granddaughter, occurred, writing, written, traveled, beginning,* and *finally*
  - words in which the dropping of letters becomes an issue, like *judgment, absolutely, ninth, lonely,* and *believable*

- Slow down on nouns with an *s* at the end. Ask yourself: is that word a possessive noun, requiring an apostrophe? *(I borrowed my brother's CD.)* Or is it a plural? *(I have two brothers.)*

- Use the resources in the classroom to help you check for correct spellings. These include a college dictionary, a handheld spellchecker, a good speller in the class, the master lists of frequently misspelled words in your spelling folder, the computer spellchecker, your personal spelling list, and, later on, your writing–reading handbook, especially the lessons "Homonyms," "The Truth About I before E," "A Rule That Mostly Works: Prefixes," "Suffix Rules That Mostly Work," and "Get Over It, Already."

In other spelling minilessons in writing workshop, the group and I focus on particular problems and solutions:

- personal survival spellings: words students need to know how to spell, like their mother's middle and maiden names and their own place and hospital of birth, allergies, ethnic background, and home address

- a brief history of the British Isles, the English language, and its multiple sources, which account for why only 46 percent of English words are spelled the way they sound

- a brief history of the Romance languages, with vulgar Latin as their source, which accounts for a strong correlation between sound and spelling in these languages; for example, in Spanish, the letter *e* is only ever pronounced one way, vs. the almost twenty ways *e* can be pronounced in English

- how to develop personal mnemonics for tricky spellings

- spelling demons, e.g., *necessary, tomorrow, absence, embarrass, beautiful, weird, occur, occurred, definitely, vacuum, character, psychology, genre*

- homonym pairs, trios, and close calls, for example, *desert* and *dessert, affect* and *effect, than* and *then, college* and *collage,* and *quiet* and *quite,* along with traditional homonym demons: *it's* and *its; your* and *you're; their, they're,* and *there; to, too,* and *two; past* and *passed;* and *weather* and *whether*
- mispronunciation confusions, for example, *diffrent, intrest, Febuary, goverment, probly, would of, seperate, discription, sophmore, alot, allright*
- foreign words, phrases, and abbreviations that appear in English texts, for example, *cliché, naïve, ad hoc, déjà vu, ad infinitum, versus, vice versa, via, etc., i.e., e.g.*
- contractions, for example, *let's, that's, doesn't, haven't, they'll, what's, who's, we're, isn't, won't, she's,* and, in dialogue, *could've, would've,* and *should've*
- the truth about *i* before *e* and the many exceptions to the generalization, aka *the weird words*
- The handful of generalizations that can be applied, most of the time, to American spellings:
  - adding a prefix doesn't affect the spelling of a base word
  - drop the *y* and substitute *i* when adding *-ed* to a word: *try* and *tried*
  - drop the *y* and substitute *ie* when making a word plural: *story* and *stories*
  - drop the silent *e* when adding a suffix that begins with a vowel: *experience* and *experiencing, confuse* and *confusing*
  - keep the silent *e* when adding a suffix that starts with a consonant: *definite* and *definitely, hope* and *hopeless*
  - double the final consonant of a one-syllable word when adding a suffix that starts with a vowel: *get* and *getting*
  - double the final consonant of a multisyllable word that ends with a single consonant *and* is accented on the final syllable before adding a suffix that begins with a vowel: *confer* and *conferring* vs. *gossip* and *gossiping*

My book *Lessons That Change Writers* (2002) is packed with usage and spelling mini-lessons, along with practice sheets and reviews. My most reliable sources for accurate information about conventions of usage and spelling are *Writers Inc: A Student Handbook for Writing and Learning* by Patrick Sebranek, Dave Kemper, and Verne Meyer (2001), *Teaching Grammar in Context* by Constance Weaver (1996), Kate Turabian's *The Student's Guide for Writing College Papers* (1976), *Eats, Shoots & Leaves* by Lynne Truss (2006), and *Grammar Girl's Quick and Dirty Tips for Better Writing* by Mignon Fogarty (2008).

I want students to be respected as writers beyond my classroom. I want them to be read. So I shoot straight about the expectations of readers and the limits of their tolerance for errors, and I work to provide the accurate information, practical applications, pertinent examples, sufficient time, and high expectations that kids need to produce writing that people will want to read.

Stuffed Maine Shrimp

1 lb. shelled, uncooked, frozen Maine shrimp, thawed
1 shallot, chopped fine
½ red bell pepper, chopped fine
1 c. sliced cremini mushrooms
Dash of crushed red pepper flakes
1 tsp. lemon zest
3 tbs. butter, plus more for the dish
1⅓ c. dry, seasoned stuffing
Chicken stock

Set the oven at 450°.

Sauté the shallot, red pepper, mushrooms, and crushed red pepper flakes in the butter until softened. Add the stuffing and just enough chicken stock to moisten but not soak it. Butter a shallow casserole or glass pie plate, and arrange the raw shrimp in the bottom. Sprinkle with lemon zest. Top with the stuffing mixture. Bake for ten minutes, or until the topping turns crisp and golden. Serves three.

CHAPTER 5

ESSENTIAL LESSONS FOR READERS

'Tis the good reader that makes the good book.

—RALPH WALDO EMERSON

In my eyes at least, I'm an old-guard kind of English teacher. I read literature, and I love it. And while it is true that I consider many of the books and poems written in the past fifty years to be literature, I maintain standards as a classroom librarian, and my goals for my student readers are robust. I expect they will seek immersion, gain stamina, experience a range of genres and authors, respond to their reading as someone else's *writing*, develop literary preferences and articulate and defend them, become discerning critics, use critical vocabulary to form and express opinions, make judgments based on textual evidence, and become better, smarter, more just, and compassionate people because of the poems and stories they take into their lives.

As a teacher of reading since the early 1970s, I've witnessed a lot of methods and movements. Along the way, I learned that it's easier to waste a student's time as a reader than in any other discipline, given the revolving door of programs, approaches, critical theories, magic bullets, shortcuts, and shiny technologies that promise proficiency for everyone. I continue to offer my kids the only entrée that has ever created lifelong, literary readers: frequent, voluminous experiences with books they choose combined with opportunities to talk and write about the choices authors make, language they use, effects they create, and themes they develop. I try not to squander precious class time on information that's inaccurate, advice that's impractical, and activities that don't extend or enrich a student's experience as a habitual reader and insightful critic.

What happens in reading minilessons matters a lot. We elevate reading workshop and give it literary bona fides when we teach students how to be literary—how to

165

identify their criteria for book selection and rejection, unpack a poem, observe and comment on the features of works of literature, figure out what they like and why, identify forms, notice figurative language and symbolism, differentiate between reading for pleasure and reading to learn, and plan for and manage their experiences as readers across a school year.

PROCEDURES

In the first two weeks of school, in addition to teaching students the routines of writing workshop, I introduce the procedures for reading workshop and the reasons behind them. The first-day scavenger hunt touches on topics I'll expand on in subsequent lessons—the kinds of books I've collected in the classroom library, where each subgenre is shelved, how to sign a book out and in, how to schedule a booktalk, where and how to record books finished and abandoned, and what I expect will happen in every reading workshop for every reader. The sooner I cover the basics and get the majority of readers settled and engaged, the better I can focus on any kids who are adrift or struggling.

MINILESSONS ABOUT PROCEDURES OF READING WORKSHOP

- expectations for reading workshop
- rules for reading workshop
- how the classroom library is organized
- how to determine the genre of a book
- how to sign out books on individual card packets and sign them back in with me
- nightly reading homework—why it's essential, when and where it will happen at each student's house, and how I'll keep tabs on it: checking each day that everyone is at least twenty pages ahead of yesterday
- why the room has to be silent during reading workshop
- how to keep track of titles read and abandoned on the form in reading folders
- how and why to rate books on a scale of 1–10, plus bella for an extraordinary title
- when to add a title to the books-we-love display: a title rated 9, 10, or bella
- how to schedule a booktalk and conduct one
- how and when to deliver a letter-essay; how to answer a peer's letter-essay; and how and when to return a peer's marble notebook after answering a letter-essay
- considerations in adding titles to CTL's Kids Recommend page on the school website
- how to self-assess experiences, criteria, strengths, challenges, and goals as a reader of books and poems at the end of a trimester
- how to sign out books for the summer and return them to school in September

To help students understand why reading workshop has to be quiet, I kick off a first-week workshop with a lesson about immersion:

> All summer long, I read novels in a room by myself, except for the dog asleep upside down on the chair next to mine. I'd become so engrossed that I jumped when Toby entered the room. It was easy to go deep, get lost, and fall in love with a good book because there were so few distractions.

> I want the same possibility for you every day—to journey into the reading zone, live with characters who intrigue you, and stay there. So I'm going to insist on silence during reading workshop. Even when you're bursting to turn to a friend and read aloud or tell about a good part, as cool as I think that is, I ask that you stifle the impulse and wait until it's time to segue out of the reading zone. In other words, please make an effort every day not to be a distraction to other readers.

> When I move among you and check in—to see what page you're on, make sure you're happy, and confer with you about your book—I'll be as quiet as I can. Please whisper back when you respond to me. Remember that whispering happens in the front of your mouth. Soft talking happens in the back, in your throat. Try to keep your voices up front.

> As I said, I've been reading in solitude for two and a half months. Today, if I get a chance to pick up a book and join you in the zone, I know it's bound to feel awkward—to read as a member of a crowd that's breathing, sneezing, coughing, sighing, laughing, turning pages, and shifting on their beanbags. At the end of independent reading time today and tomorrow, we'll talk about how we're adjusting as readers, en masse and immersion-wise.

In another procedural minilesson, I introduce the system for rating books and explain how it will be useful to individual readers and their peers.

> Every time you finish or abandon a book, I'll ask you to rate it, on a scale of 1 to 10. You'll notice there's a column on the record sheets in your reading folder to note your rating of each title. If 10 and bella are high—ratings for a fantastic story you absolutely loved—1 is, obviously, low. No one should ever finish a book that's a 1—or, for that matter, a 2, 3, 4, 5, or 6—without an agenda. Numbers this low indicate a book that doesn't deserve to be finished—*unless* it's a book that's so bad you decide to keep going because you want to write a pan of it, that is, a letter-essay or review that takes the author to task for choices that didn't work.

> Any title you decide you'd like to booktalk—to recommend to the group—should be at least a 9, 10, or bella. Otherwise, what's the point? A booktalk is an opportunity to rave about a favorite and let the rest of us in on it. Let your ratings be your guide before you decide to present one.

Your ratings will be useful at the end of a trimester, when you self-assess, select the best one of the books you read, and describe what the author did to make it so good. And your ratings will serve you as you look for patterns in your reading, notice which genres and authors you rated highest, and think about why.

Finally, your ratings of books will help readers beyond our school. At the end of each trimester, I'll ask if you have any new titles to add to the Kids Recommend pages of our website, c-t-l.org. These lists average thousands of visits every week from teachers, kids, and parents from around the country. You'll want to make sure that any book you rated a 10 or bella shows up here, so other students have access to your nominations of intriguing, meaningful, and well-written books.

PRACTICE

Students who choose and read books that are accessible and interesting to them comprehend as a matter of course. They use what they've learned about phonetics and patterns of syntax and semantics to predict text, chunk it, guess at or skip the few words they don't know, and make meaning. When students read stories that engage them, and when the difficulty of a book falls within their abilities as readers, reading *is* comprehension. This is the goal. Even as an old-guard teacher, I can't justify an instructional context that requires students in an English class to read books they don't like or can't understand.

But as a teacher of history, when I move into content-area reading, I do isolate comprehension, and I do consider how to help my students understand and retain facts, ideas, causes, and consequences; later in this chapter I'll touch on the study methods I teach in my history classes. But as *a teacher of English*, my focus is on helping students develop the habits of independent, intentional, critical readers of stories and poems.

MINILESSONS ABOUT PRACTICE
- why we have reading workshop
- reading in the zone
- why students read books that tell stories, vs. guidebooks, manuals, books of lists, or magazines
- ways to choose a book and develop criteria for book selection
- how and when to decide to abandon a book; the development of individual criteria for abandonment
- Daniel Pennac's "Reader's Bill of Rights" (1992)
- *plans* as a hallmark of good readers: awareness of what they want to read next and the authors and genres that intrigue them
- why and how to keep lists of "someday" books

- why rereading beloved books is something good readers can do
- personal reading rituals: when, how, and where individual students escape at home into the reading zone
- how the act of naming favorites—books, authors, genres, poems, and poets—creates a literary identity
- the different stances that readers take toward texts: the *aesthetic*, when we read stories and poems for the pleasure of a "lived-through experience," and the *efferent*, when we read to acquire information (Rosenblatt 1980, 1983)
- how good readers shift stance according to the kind of text they're reading
- why, when, and how good readers consider *pace*: when to skip, skim, slow down, reread, look ahead, or decide to read just the ending
- what students and the teacher do when we come across a word we don't know
- the psycholinguistic theory of reading and how the eyes and brain of a fluent reader attend to print (Smith 2004)
- bad reading habits: vocalizing, word-by-word reading, and underlining with a pencil or bookmark
- Shannon's game, cloze exercises, and tests of hidden assumptions to explore textual patterns, redundancy, and schemas
- tips on how to read aloud
- tips on how to read a book of poems
- why to memorize poetry
- how to approach a standardized reading test
- "summer slide" in reading and how to avoid it

An essential September lesson about practice addresses why I ask students to choose their own books and read them. I pose a question—what are all the reasons you can think of that we have reading workshop?—and record students' theories. This was a recent whole-group response.

WHY WE HAVE READING WORKSHOP
- to act like real, grown-up readers
- to learn how to choose books
- to find books we love
- to discover authors we love
- to figure out our favorite genres
- to try new books, authors, and genres
- to learn how and when to abandon books
- to learn new words and ideas
- to encounter different kinds of characters and people

- to learn from other authors how to write well
- to learn from one another about good books, authors, and genres
- to help us figure out the kinds of people we want to be
- to have experiences and feelings we couldn't have in the real world
- to escape
- to learn, period

As their teacher of reading, I added a crucial principle:

- To practice, practice, practice—to read often and a lot, accumulate experiences with texts and vicarious experiences, store these in long-term memory, and acquire the habits of lifelong readers.

And then I talked about reading in the zone:

> A few years ago, my students and I read and loved an article by Tom Newkirk about what he calls "the reading state" (2000). Newkirk was concerned about the kids who don't love reading because they never had the experience of getting lost in a good story, never felt the "heightened form of pleasure" that book readers find ourselves in all the time.
>
> When Jed, a seventh grader, joked that it was more like a zone than a state, the phrase stuck. That's why the place readers go when they leave our classroom behind and live inside a story is, officially, *the reading zone.*
>
> I want you to be able to enter the zone in every reading workshop—to get lost, be happy, and, over time, turn so many pages that you accumulate the volume of practice that transforms an okay reader into a great one.
>
> Reading is one of the wonders of the whole history of humankind for a ton of reasons, but here is one of my favorites: the way to get better at this glorious pastime is to do it. At the same time that you're lost in the reading zone and loving a great story, you're also increasing your fluency, awareness of how print works, knowledge of the world, vocabulary, and sophistication as a reader. We'll talk another day about how this works—how your brain accumulates knowledge, stores it as you read, and helps you make use of it the next time you read. In the meantime? Read a lot, and read happily.

In *Better Than Life* (1992, Stenhouse Publishers), his paean to the act of reading, Daniel Pennac declared a Reader's Bill of Rights:

1. The right not to read something
2. The right to skip pages
3. The right not to finish
4. The right to reread
5. The right to read anything

6. The right to escapism

7. The right to read anywhere

8. The right to browse

9. The right to read aloud

10. The right not to defend your tastes

In a minilesson, I ask students to review Pennac's list and talk about rights they agree with and don't and whether there's anything missing. While they agree with everything, some of my kids have added the phrase "or just read the ending" to Pennac's "the right not to finish," and, every time I teach this lesson, they append an eleventh: some version of "the right to access to good books."

Book abandonment is a minilesson topic because it's an act that doesn't occur to my students new to reading workshop. Either they've been taught never to give up on a book, or their expectations of book reading are so low they believe they're supposed to tolerate boredom, confusion, or bad writing.

I introduce abandonment as something that smart, critical readers do when a book fails to satisfy them. I tell my own stories of books that had a slow start but I hung in there and found myself captivated, as well as times when it was clear by twenty pages in that a writer's style was going to drive me crazy and that I *could not* read this book, along with occasions when I wasn't convinced by the premise of plot, didn't believe in or care about the main character, or had to work so hard to understand it that the book became a task instead of a pleasure. On our shelves at home, these are the titles with bookmarks still in them that indicate where I gave up on an author and moved on to a story I could enjoy.

I assign students a long-term project: develop your own criteria for book abandonment, including the maximum number of pages you'll give an author before you shelve a book and move on to another. Students list their criteria in their writing–reading handbooks, and we return a month or so later to discuss their initial ideas and revise them.

We've also had great minilesson conversations about why people reread books— why returning to a beloved title is one of the hallmarks of a habitual, literary reader. Here, we're not reading to discover what happens. Instead, we seek to live with characters again, savor an author's craft again, and think about his or her themes again. I love *To the Lighthouse, The French Lieutenant's Woman, Howard's End, The Age of Innocence, Pride and Prejudice, Lucky Jim, Atonement, Middlemarch, The Poisonwood Bible, The Great Gatsby, Behind the Scenes at the Museum, Hamlet, Regeneration, The Hours, The Handmaid's Tale,* and the short stories of Alice Munro. I'm confident I'll have a satisfying experience when I return to each story and cast of characters. I'll notice something new about how the book was written, and some part of me will hope that the stories with tragic endings will conclude happily this time around.

Frank Smith and Louise Rosenblatt are the reading theorists whose work has most influenced my practice as a reading teacher, including the development of reading workshop itself. Rosenblatt helped me understand how readers engage with and respond to different kinds of texts. From Smith, especially his book *Understanding Reading* (2004), I learned about psycholinguistic theory.

Psycholinguistic theorists posit that fluent readers don't read every word of a text. *We don't need to.* Instead, we predict our way through. We eliminate some of the alternatives based on the knowledge we acquired from previous reading experiences, and by tapping the built-in redundancies created by textual structure and meaning. Our eyes sample the visual information on a page, and our brains eliminate the irrelevant alternatives.

The implication for reading teachers is that our students need tons of experience reading interesting, accessible books to become fluent and skillful—thousands of hours spent with the richness and diversity of examples, contrasts, and *evidence* that only time with books can provide. Smith, a constructivist, asserts that children's brains are learning all the time, but that kids learn best and most when they perceive what they're being asked to do as meaningful and worthwhile. His book *Reading Without Nonsense* (1997) is a teacher-friendly presentation of his idea that only through reading—through continuous, pleasurable, easy, and meaningful encounters with books—will young children learn to read and older students come to read well.

In the fall, I teach students a simplified version of Smith's psycholinguistic theory. I illustrate how the eye and brain process print (see Figure 5.1), demonstrate why voluminous reading is *the* route to fluency, help kids set relevant goals as readers, and amuse and amaze them with trick questions built on hidden assumptions—on information that the brains of experienced readers have learned to supply. Everyone receives a photocopy of the booklet, and they highlight as I read it aloud.

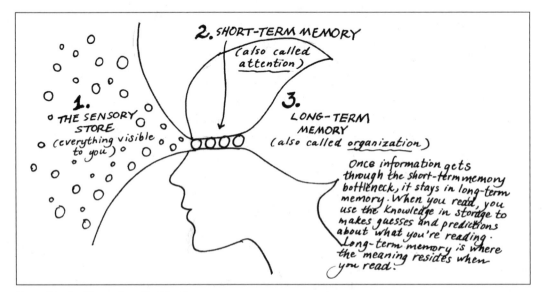

Figure 5.1 *An Illustration of a Fixation*

Reading: A Psycholinguistic Model

Every reader goes through the process depicted here. Your eye picks up "elements" from the scene before you, also known as your *sensory store*. You can only pay attention to four or so elements at a time; attention is also called *short-term memory*. About every five seconds or so, one of the elements you hold in your short-term memory will make it into your long-term memory, where it stays. For example, among the first bits of information you put into storage, when you were a baby, was your mother's face. Once you picked out her face from your sensory store, held it in your short-term memory, and then stored it in your long-term memory, you never had to learn her again.

A long time ago, as a reader, you stored elements like *and* or *the* in your long-term memory. Once you did, you never had to learn them again. Long-term memory is like a file cabinet. Yours is much fuller than that of a beginning reader, who's storing such information as the difference between *b* and *d*. Right now, you're storing words like *assonance* and *elegy*.

A good reader is someone who can get a lot of information through the bottleneck of short-term memory into long-term memory. What's important here is the *size* of the elements. An inexperienced reader is trying to get four *letters* or *words* through short-term memory into long-term memory. But a *fluent* reader is getting four packages of meaning—usually phrases, and sometimes even whole sentences—through the short-term memory bottleneck. Again, only about four elements can get through at a time, but each element can be as large as a phrase or a sentence.

So while a beginning reader is putting four words or parts of words into long-term memory, an experienced reader is putting four *chunks of meaning* into storage. The fluent reader also makes good use of all the information he or she has already stored in long-term memory—about how print works—to make *predictions* about the new information that's coming through the bottleneck. Frank Smith calls this "informed guessing"—making reasonable guesses from a relatively small set of possibilities (1997). In fact, research shows that fluent readers skip more than 30 percent of the words in a text (Just and Carpenter 1987) because they already "know" they're there.

The fluent reader relies on his or her memory of letter patterns and sound patterns. For example, good readers understand, whether they're conscious of it or not, that in recognizing words, consonants are more important than vowels, beginnings of words are more important than middles and ends, and ends are more important than middles. Nonproficient readers haven't built up enough experience yet to know to attend to the *parts of words* that contain the most information. Whether you realize it or not, this is what you're doing when you zip through a phrase like "on_ _ _p_n a ti_e."

The difference between long-term memory and short-term memory can be summed up in one word: *organization*. Short-term memory holds unrelated images, while long-term memory is a network, a structure of knowledge, a way to make sense. Constance Weaver says that long-term memory is a series of *schemas* (1994). Only when we have adequate schemas, and only when the appropriate schemas are activated, can we understand or recall what we read.

For example, read this passage from a book by Weaver (1994) *once*, and try to retell it in your own words.

Passage 1: Cost or Other Basis
(on the topic of capital gains and losses)

In general, the cost or other basis is the cost of the property plus purchase commissions, improvements, and minus depreciation, amortization, and depletion. If you inherited the property or got it as a gift, in a tax-free exchange, involuntary conversion, or "wash sale" of stock, you may not be able to use the actual cash cost as the basis. If you do not use cash cost, attach an explanation of your basis.

—Internal Revenue Service, 1989 booklet on
1040 Federal Income Tax Forms and Instructions

Because we don't already know something about capital gains and losses, we can't understand or paraphrase what we've read. There's not enough information in our long-term memory file cabinets to support understanding—we have *no cognitive schemas* for this topic.

Now try again with another passage from Weaver's book (1994). Can you retell this one?

The procedure is actually quite simple. First you arrange things into different groups. Of course one pile may be sufficient depending on how much there is to do. If you have to go somewhere else due to lack of facilities, that is the next step; otherwise you are pretty well set. It is important not to overdo things. That is, it is better to do too few things at once than too many. In the short run this may not seem important, but complications can easily arise. A mistake can be expensive as well. At first the whole procedure will seem complicated. Soon, however, it will just become another facet of life. It is difficult to foresee any end to the necessity for this task in the immediate future, but then one can never tell. After the procedure is completed, one arranges the materials into different groups again. Then they can be put into their appropriate places. Eventually they will be used once more, and the whole cycle will then have to be repeated. However, that is a part of life.

—John D. Bransford and Nancy S. McCarrell, 1974,
"A Sketch of a Cognitive Approach to Comprehension"

What would your retelling be like if you knew beforehand that this passage was about *washing clothes*? The point is, even when we do have a schema for a particular topic, if the schema isn't *activated*, it does us no good.

Now, let's shift gears and consider the *physical side* of reading.

If you could closely watch people while they're reading, you'd notice their eyes make a lot of brief, abrupt stops. That's because your eyes don't see when they're moving, only when they stop. Below I've illustrated these stops—they're called *fixations*—as they might occur for different kinds of readers. The dots above the line show where a reader's eye might pause. Remember—it's during a stop that reading occurs. Fixations typically last one-quarter of a second.

VERY SLOW READER

•   •   • • •   •   •   •   •

Some books are to be read only in parts, others to be read

Try to fix on each word: it's hard, and it takes forever.

READER OF FAIR SPEED

•   •   •   •   •

Some books are to be read only in parts, others to be read

Try this one. Still too slow?

FAST READER

•   •   •

Some books are to be read only in parts, others to be read

How's this?

One reason a fluent reader can read with fewer stops is because he or she is able to see more during each fixation. Look back at that illustration of a reader on the first page. It depicts a fixation. During a normal eye fixation of about a quarter of a second, we can identify four unrelated letters, *or* about ten or twelve letters organized into two or three unrelated words, *or* about twenty-five letters organized into a sequence of four related words.

This means that during a normal eye fixation, we might be able to identify an arbitrary list of letters like *hgibl*, or a sequence like *will make her cry*, or a phrase like *he lives in a nice house filled with nice toys*. Our perceptual span increases based on the *relatedness* of the units. We can identify more letters when they're organized into words, and more words when they're chunked into a meaningful phrase or sentence.

Context—the words and ideas *around* words—helps us identify words when we read. We have two kinds of context, or schemas, in long-term memory that aid us in figuring out words. *Syntactic context* describes the signals we get from word endings and the order in which words appear in English sentences. *Semantic context* describes relationships of meaning among words. In short, *syntax* means grammar, *semantics* means meaning, and both inform the guesses you make as a reader.

To see how grammar and meaning help us identify words, look at four strings of words from Weaver's book (1994). Which string is the easiest for you to process? Which is the hardest? Why?

1. Furry wildcats fight furious battles. *(Easiest: it has grammar and meaning)*
2. Furry jewelers create distressed stains. *(Has grammar only)*
3. Furry fight furious wildcats battles. *(Has meaning only)*
4. Furry create distressed jewelers stains. *(Hardest: a string of words that has neither grammar nor meaning)*

Some Goals for Readers in the Zone, Based on Psycholinguistic Theory

1. First, read a lot and often. Store tons of schemas in your long-term memory. As with any skill, you need a lot of experience to become an *expert*—Malcolm Gladwell says ten thousand hours of committed practice (2008).
2. Try to pick up *chunks of meaning* rather than individual words.
3. Try to concentrate on key words, the ones that carry meaning. Researchers call these *contentives*, and research shows that good readers fix more and longer on the contentives in a sentence.
4. Try to eliminate bad habits, like moving your lips or vocal cords while you're reading or *regressing:* continually going back to reread something you've already read. These behaviors slow you down, overload short-term memory, and force you to attend to single words instead of reading for chunks of meaning. Forge ahead: speed can *increase* your comprehension because it diminishes distractions. Count on the context that's built into English phrases and sentences to help you straighten things out.
5. Don't use a pencil or a card to "underline" each line you read. Syntactic and semantic context—chunking—is prevented when you limit your view of the page.

I ask students to continue the list independently in their writing–reading handbooks. The prompt is: *Given what I learned today, what are other new goals for my reading?* Afterward they read their responses around the circle, and I extend the list on the easel pad. Here's one class' response.

6. Read more genres: it creates more schemas in long-term memory.

7. On occasion, practice reading deliberately for a moment: where do your eyes stop? How much are you seeing at each stop?

8. Try to recognize words by their shapes.

9. Time yourself during independent reading: how many pages do you read in half an hour this month? Next month? In June?

10. When you don't have an adequate schema for a text, like with a history or science assignment or a difficult poem, you need to slow down.

11. When a book is easy—when your schema for this kind of writing is thick and packed—you can feel free to speed up.

In other minilessons, we play games that reinforce psycholinguistic theory. I type passages from different kinds of books—for example, a history text by Joy Hakim, a young-adult novel, and an op-ed piece from the *New York Times*—but delete every fifth word. Kids guess at the missing words in these cloze exercises, and afterward I ask them how and when they were able—or not—to use semantic context, syntactic context, and prior knowledge to help them make close or accurate guesses.

We also play Shannon's Game. Like its cousin Hangman, which is based on the predictability of letter order, Shannon's Game taps schemas about word order that are stored in long-term memory. To play it, I think of a sentence, then draw lines to represent each of its words. Starting with the first blank, kids call out their guesses, and I tick off the number of attempts it takes to identify a word. When they reach fifteen, I give them the word and move on to the next one. At the end of the sentence, we discuss the schemas that were activated, when they were activated, and how. Some sentences are easier to predict than others, but in general, after the first few words, kids and their long-term memories fill in the rest in the snap of a finger.

Shannon's Game

I'm	looking	forward	to	Columbus	Day	weekend.
~~////~~ ~~////~~ /	~~////~~ ///	/		//		

The	Popham	Colony	is	known	as	Jamestown's	lost	twin.
//	~~////~~			/	////			

I also collect trick questions that play on the assumptions that experienced readers have learned to make—that is, when long-term memory switches into gear, unbidden, and supplies information that isn't on the page or doesn't fit the situation. On the next page are thirteen of my favorite trick questions. The answers, as well as my interpretation of how each one fools a fluent reader, appear at the end of the chapter.

THIRTEEN QUESTIONS

1. *Before* Mount Everest was discovered, what was the highest mountain on Earth?

2. Answer this question within five seconds, and do not return to check your answer: How many animals of each species did Moses take aboard the ark with him? *(Note: the question is not how many pairs, but how many animals.)*

3. An archaeologist reported he had discovered two gold coins in the desert near Jerusalem dated 430 B.C. Many of his fellow scientists refused to take his claim seriously. Why?

4. If you have *only one* match and you entered a room to start a kerosene lamp, an oil heater, and a wood burning stove, which would you light first? Why?

5. Here's a question on *international law*: if an *international* airliner crashed exactly on the U.S.-Mexican border, where would officials be required by law to bury the survivors?

6. Some months have thirty days; some have thirty-one. How many have twenty-eight?

7. A farmer had seventeen sheep. All but nine died. How many are left?

8. You have a dime in an otherwise empty wine bottle. The bottle is corked. Your job is to get the dime out of the bottle without taking the cork out. You must do this without damaging the bottle in any way. How do you do it?

9. Explain the following true boast: "In my bedroom, the nearest lamp that I usually keep turned on is twelve feet from my bed. Alone in the room, without using wire, strings, or any other aids or contraptions, I can turn out the light on that lamp and get into bed before the room is dark."

10. If two U.S. coins total 35¢ and one is *not a quarter* (please keep this in mind) what are the two coins?

11. To writers knowledgeable about proper English grammar, which is correct: "The yolk of the egg *are* white" or "The yoke of the egg *is* white?"

12. Read this sentence aloud:

    FINISHED FILES ARE THE RE-
    SULT OF YEARS OF SCIENTIF-
    IC STUDY COMBINED WITH
    THE EXPERIENCE OF YEARS.

    Now, count the letter *F*s in the sentence. Count them only once—don't go back and count them again. How many *F*s are there?

13. Memorize the phrases below. As soon as you do this, turn the paper over and write them on the back of this page. Don't look at the phrases again once you've turned your paper over.

PARIS	ONCE
IN THE	IN A
THE SPRING	A LIFETIME

BIRD   SLOW
IN THE   MEN AT
THE HAND   AT WORK

Turning to the influence of Louise Rosenblatt, in *Literature as Exploration* (1938, 1983), her classic book about reader response, she describes two modes of reading, *efferent* and *aesthetic*. She posits that these are parallel frames of mind existing in a continuum. We bring them to bear whenever we engage with text in order to help us make meaning.

Efferent is from the Latin *effere*, which means "to carry away." When we approach a piece of writing in an efferent frame of mind, we're reading to acquire information, and we focus our attention on what we'll learn. I was reading efferently the other night when I reread my favorite of Rosenblatt's essays, "What Facts Does This Poem Teach You?" (1980). Other examples of my efferent reading include the first section of today's *New York Times*, the side-effect warnings that accompanied a new prescription, and a chapter from John Abbott's *The History of Maine* (1875), about the colonial settlement at Pemaquid, Maine, where I'll be taking my kids on a history field trip. In each instance, I was focused on facts and ideas to carry away and, perhaps, use or act on in some way.

The aesthetic stance runs parallel to the efferent. Here, a reader fuses affective and cognitive elements into what Rosenblatt describes as "a personally lived-through poem or story" (1978). Aesthetic reading occurs for its own sake, for the pleasures and rewards of living vicariously inside someone else's literary world. My students know and love this mode of interacting with text: it's what they call "reading in the zone." They're not searching for facts or information—or, for that matter, connections, predictions, visual imagery, or a-ha moments. They are *living through* a narrative and experiencing "the attractions of the journey itself" (1978).

The experience of reading aesthetically is a natural, wonderful outcome of reading workshop. Here, every day, students get lost in stories they choose, like, and understand. As Rosenblatt once cautioned teachers, "Doing justice to the aesthetic mode of language behavior does not require discovery of a new array of teaching techniques" (1980). It only takes books that tell great stories and teachers who understand immersion and know how to invite students into the zone.

Since I also teach history to the students in my writing–reading workshop, it's my responsibility to help them understand that comprehension is different from one genre to the next. When my students read aesthetically in reading workshop, my goal is for them to get lost in stories. When they read efferently in history class, I teach them how to focus on information—how *not* to get lost.

To teach strategies for efferent reading, I drew on work by Stephanie Harvey and Anne Goudvis (2002, 2003), combined it with old-fashioned study skills and a few new techniques (Harvey and Daniels 2009), and collaborated with CTL's science teacher to introduce and reinforce an approach that helps our students read history and science for understanding and retention.

In the content areas, kids do benefit from a strategic approach to reading. Because the texts CTL students are working with are the real thing—books, charts and graphs, timelines, editorials, summaries, magazine and newspaper articles, and book excerpts that the science teacher and I select as worthy and relevant—there are powerful reasons for students to practice strategic reading as an aid to learning facts and concepts.

HOW TO READ HISTORY AND SCIENCE FOR UNDERSTANDING AND RETENTION

1. *Skim* the assigned reading and any illustrations, headings, and sidebars. Create a mental road map of the material, turn on the lights in your brainpan, and activate your long-term memory.

2. Choose a writing utensil that's not a highlighter—in other words, one you can write with. Then, as you read a paragraph, underline what seems significant to you.

3. After you finish a paragraph, stop and react to it. Jot a symbol—or two—in the margin.

   Symbols*

   ✓ = I already knew this.
   ★ = This is important.
   ? = I have a question, or I'm confused.
   ! = This is surprising or fascinating to me.
   L = I learned something new.

4. In addition to using the symbols, write a note to yourself in the margin whenever you can, to push your thinking and create a verbal map you can retrace. *Think* about significant information by using writing to make tracks of your thinking.

5. Monitor yourself. Notice when you've become distracted—when you're saying the words without thinking about them or when your brain has gone off on a little adventure. Bring yourself back to the text, and reread what you missed.

6. Read history and science selections twice. Take a break to let your long-term memory do its thing, and then, the second time, move to a different room in your house. Research shows that changing the background improves retention. This time, read the tracks of your thinking, too.

7. Now comes the most important part. When you've finished a reading for the second time, put the text aside and engage in an oral retrieval practice. Test yourself by saying what you can remember about the paragraphs you gave stars and *L*s to. Ask: what events, names, vocabulary, phenomena, and big ideas can I recall? If you can't answer yourself, that's a cue to give the material and your tracks another skim or reread, especially your stars and *L*s. Then test yourself again.

---

*Adapted from Harvey and Daniels (2009).

I'm not a fan of integrated curricula. As the concept is most often realized, it means an English teacher takes on the work of content-area colleagues—for example, covers "the research paper." But a research report isn't a literary genre, and scientists report about science in particular ways as do historians about history. Teachers of science and history should show students the ropes of their disciplines and invite and respond to relevant writing assignments.

Content integration hurts the teaching of reading and writing. It robs time from lessons and practice in basic skills. No one asks math teachers to integrate history or science into their classes—the integrity of math instruction is a given. English teachers have to stand up for the integrity of our subjects. Students need us to introduce and nurture all that matters about writing and literature. It's a monumental task and obligation. We can't afford to surrender a single one of our precious 180 days to the work of other disciplines.

LITERATURE

The majority of my reading minilessons are about literature—genres, forms, features, authors and poets, literary terms, analysis, and criticism. Like the craft lessons I teach in writing workshop, they perform a double duty. They teach concepts that inform students' efforts as writers but also as people who read and respond to writing. While the Rule of *So What?* is essential in writing workshop as an invitation to craft purposeful writing, it provides a prism for students to identify purpose and theme in the published writing they read. When we discuss poetic forms or review a glossary of poetic terms in reading workshop, students are often inspired to experiment in writing workshop—to play with caesuras, the tritina form, hyperbole, or alliteration.

Familiarity with the vocabulary of craft invites students to assume the perspective of insiders—of literary writers and readers. This, I think, is the essential reading–writing connection: when teachers hand over a critical lexicon and provide opportunities for kids to draw on their reading experiences to write literature of their own, and when student writers perceive a work of literature as an accumulation of the choices made by its author.

MINILESSONS ABOUT LITERATURE
- the genres and subgenres represented by the titles in the classroom library
- how to read a poem as a critic
- how to unpack a poem
- how free-verse poetry works: sound patterns and effects, diction, tone, compression, figurative language, imagery, line and stanza breaks
- a glossary of poetic terms
- poetic forms: free verse, tritinas, sestinas, couplets, haikus, senryus, pantoums, villanelles, sonnets, abecedarias, irregular odes à la Pablo Neruda, "ways" poems à la Wallace Stevens, parallel structures, found poems, concrete poems, etc.

- kinds of figurative language: metaphor, simile, personification, hyperbole
- sound patterns in poems: alliteration, assonance, onomatopoeia
- rhythm in poetry: stress, pause, meter, repetition, cadence, tricolons
- poems grouped by theme or topic: personal identity, the diversity of topics poems can address, finding ideas in things à la William Carlos Williams, sports and games, pets, the five senses, growing up, language play, the natural world, childhood memories, gender, political and social issues, war and antiwar, prejudice, reading and writing, winter, Christmas and Hanukkah, Mother's Day, Father's Day, etc.
- the lives, styles, techniques, subjects, themes, and verse of poets Gwendolyn Brooks, Billy Collins, E. E. Cummings, Emily Dickinson, Robert Frost, Allen Ginsberg, Jim Harrison, Tony Hoagland, Langston Hughes, Ted Kooser, Pablo Neruda, Naomi Shihab Nye, Mary Oliver, Marge Piercy, Edwin Arlington Robinson, William Shakespeare, William Stafford, Wallace Stevens, Walt Whitman, and William Carlos Williams
- how to select a poem to present to others, prepare to present it, design a response task, and orchestrate a group discussion
- a lexicon of literary terms
- authors who write well for young adults
- booktalks about beloved titles
- qualities of effective letter-essays: how to write a critical response to a book
- how to indicate the titles of different kinds of literary works: quotes, italics, or mere caps and how to capitalize titles
- read-alouds and discussions of works from the genre being studied in writing workshop: poems, memoirs, parodies and homages, micro and flash fiction, reviews, essays, advocacy journalism, profiles
- forms of fiction: micro fiction, flash fiction, short stories, novellas, novels, sequels, prequels, trilogies, quartets, series
- elements of fiction: problem, conflict, main character, character development, protagonist, antagonist, plot, structure, pace, plausibility, point of view, tone, lead, conclusion, imagery, diction, transition, climax, resolution, theme
- methods of character development: reflection, dialogue, action, history, flashback, reaction, relationships and interactions with other characters, habits, patterns, quirks, tastes and preferences, talent, hobby, intimate setting, possession, pet, letters, e-mails, diary entries
- a brief history of young adult literature
- popular vs. literary fiction and the problem with best-seller lists
- publication jargon: pseudonym or nom de plume, first edition, printing, remainder, advance, royalty, editor, hardcover to paperback, jacket copy, blurb, gutter, typeface, typo, cover art

- what a copyright page reveals; how to use the Library of Congress Cataloging-in-Publication data when investigating a book selection
- developments and controversies in the world of book publication
- National Banned Books Week (every last week of September)
- National African American Read-In (every February)
- marginalia: in relation to the Billy Collins poem of that title, students inscribe creative marginalia in CTL books for students of the future to discover
- literary awards and annual winners: Newbery, Caldecott, Pulitzer Prize for Fiction, Alex Award Winners, etc.
- relevant articles about writing, reading, literature, criticism, the arts, and education from *The New York Times*, *The New Yorker*, *Rolling Stone*, *New York*, etc.
- transitional books and authors: titles and writers that show young teens what comes next for them as readers
- what makes a classic a classic
- individuals' selection and analyses of the best poems and books at the end of each trimester
- where and how to find good books beyond CTL

Because we read a poem or two at the start of every workshop, I'm eager for kids to pull up their socks intellectually, respond as discerning readers, and form an opinion about each poem. A second-week-of-school minilesson addresses my expectations for them as unpackers and critics of poetry. This is a substantial nudge, delivered in the form of a document for them to tape in their writing–reading handbooks, highlight as I read it aloud, and take home to annotate in response to these questions: *What do you understand? What don't you get? What do you agree or disagree with? What hadn't you considered before?* In the subsequent minilesson, they discuss their reactions, and I defend my method.

Reading Poetry as a Critic

I'll ask you to enter a poem with me at the start of class each day, and we'll read and talk about it *as critics*. I don't mean a critic in the sense of thumbs up or down or three stars out of four. But I also don't mean how you may have responded to poems in the past. Young kids tend to react to poetry in terms of personal associations, and that's just right for their age. Back in the day, you may have liked a poem about a dog because you had a dog, too.

When I say we'll read poetry as critics, I mean we're going to *talk about the experience of reading poems*—what you notice or like about how a poet built a poem, how it makes you feel, what it helps you understand, and what the poet did to give rise to your feelings and understandings. This kind of close reading is what critics do.

One reason we'll read poetry together is to improve your ability to experience poems on your own—to enter them independently, notice their features, understand or *unpack* them, and bring them into your life. Another reason is to learn the language of criticism—to experience what's meant by such terms as *allegory, alliteration, allusion, assonance, cadence, caesura, coded language, diction, enjambment, form, hyperbole, imagery, irony, line break and stanza break, metaphor, personification, rhyme scheme, sensory description, simile, symbol, theme, tone,* and *turn.*

Because one reader of a poem might respond differently than another, we'll discover which of our responses to a poem are supported by something the poet did and which are idiosyncratic, for example, *This poem about a dog is good 'cause I have a dog.* Our critical reactions are affected by our previous experiences. The more we read poetry, the smarter we'll understand it, respond to it, and understand our responses.

But no reader's response is ever as good as the poem itself, can ever "say" what the poem "says." No matter how well someone can explain all the words, images, and references in Robert Frost's "Nothing Gold Can Stay"—and I could talk about that poem all day—its meaning is complete only in the poem.

"*How* does a poem mean?" is as useful a question as "*What* does a poem mean?" The way meaning is coded in a good poem is as interesting and important as meaning itself. Because of the coded nature of poetry, some poems need multiple readings to discover how and what they mean. Writing and talking can help a critic unpack a poem. So can a dictionary. Great poems can be read a hundred times and yield new pleasure and surprises. I'm *still* learning things about "Nothing Gold Can Stay."

When a reader unpacks a poem, its words, lines, images, and metaphors need to be considered in context—in relation to the other words, lines, images, and metaphors. This means a critic can't build a theory about a poem based on one line if the theory doesn't fit the other lines, too.

Some of the words, lines, images, and metaphors in a poem are more important than others: they carry a greater weight. A productive approach to experiencing a poem is to look for significant words, lines, images, or metaphors. *Turns* and *conclusions* are especially productive junctures.

We'll also read poetry to inspire to craft verse that matters to our lives and will resonate for other people, too. The poems we read will help you, as a writer yourself, appreciate the difference between a word that's good enough and one that's perfect.

Finally, poems can refer or *allude* to other poems—to all of literature. No poem is completely original. If it were, we wouldn't be able to read or understand it. This isn't an argument for plagiarism; it is a reminder that critics can consider *a poem* in relation to *other poems and poets.*

Two September minilessons that come on the heels of this one involve glossaries. The first is a glossary of poetic terms (Figure 5.2). I make two copies for each student. They tuck the first in a pocket of their poetry folders, for easy reference all year as we're unpacking poems. They tape the other into their writing–reading handbooks and read and annotate it for homework—mark with a plus sign the terms they can already use with confidence and put a minus in front of any term that's new or they're uncertain about. The next day, we discuss their prior knowledge, discoveries, and the uncertainties that need clarification.

The second glossary is a running list of literary terms that come up in discussions, booktalks, and writing and reading minilessons. I ask students to flip to the backs of their writing–reading handbooks and number the last four pages as 94–97. This pagination takes into account the three unnumbered pages at the front of the spiral notebooks, which will become a table of contents later in the fall. I pass out fluorescent Post-it flags and ask kids to attach one to page 94, so they can locate it with ease throughout the year, and give it the heading *A Lexicon of Literary Terms*.

Figure 5.3 shows this glossary of literary terms from a student handbook at the end of the first trimester. Whenever I or a student use or encounter a new term, I write its definition on the easel pad, and students add it to their handbooks. On the bookcase next to my rocking chair I keep a college dictionary and copies of *The Teachers and Writers Handbook of Poetic Forms* by Ron Padgett (1987), *The Oxford Dictionary of Literary Terms* by Chris Baldick (2008), *Literary Terms: A Dictionary* by Karl Beckson and Arthur Ganz (1989), and *Benet's Reader's Encyclopedia* (1996) edited by Bruce Murphy, so I can be precise in the definitions I provide.

Minilessons I conduct about poetic techniques are straightforward: definitions accompanied by phrases, lines, or whole poems that illustrate a term and bring it to life. Because most of the poetry published in the United States today doesn't rhyme, I teach the craft techniques it relies upon instead—cadence, sound effects, figurative language, tangible nouns, sensory verbs, diction, imagery, tone, turns, and experiments with form. I want students to be able to identify and discuss these craft effects—first in poems, where they're most apparent, and then in the prose they read and respond to as critics. By way of example, this is the lesson about alliteration, assonance, and onomatopoeia that my students attach in their writing–reading handbooks in the fall.

Sound Effects

Repetition is an important tool in a poet's toolbox. It can give poetry a kind of tune. Patterns of sounds in free verse slow a reader down, focus his or her attention, create a tone or mood, and support a subject, image, or theme. Poets use repetition to create rhythm and harmony in their free verse and also to satisfy the demands of forms that depend on it, like tritinas, sestinas, pantoums, and villanelles.

alliteration—the repetition of initial sounds, usually consonants, in neighboring words

allusion—within a poem, a reference, usually brief, to a historic or literary work, event, person, or place beyond the world of the poem

anthology—a book of selected writings by different poets

assonance—the repetition of vowel sounds in neighboring words

blank verse—a poem written in iambic pentameter (duhDUH five times per line) that doesn't rhyme, e.g., *Hamlet* or Yeats' "The Second Coming," not to be confused with *free verse* (see below)

cadence—a rhythmic pattern based on the repetitions and emphases in speech

caesura (si·ZHOOR·uh)—a slight but definite pause *inside* a line of a poem, which is created by the rhythm of language or a punctuation mark, e.g., a period, dash, or colon in the middle of a line

close form—poetry that conforms to an established pattern, e.g., sonnet, limerick, villanelle, pantoum, tritina, sestina, rondel

collection—a book of selected writings by one poet

couplet—a pair of lines, usually written in the same form

diction—a poet's choice of words

elegy—a poem of mourning or somber meditation

end-stopped line—when sense *and* grammar pause at the end of a line: a line-break at a normal pause in speech, generally at a punctuation mark

enjambed line—when the sense and grammar of a line continue from one line to the next; also called *run-on lines*

epigraph—a quotation placed at the beginning of a poem to make the writing more resonant

figurative language—comparisons between unrelated things or ideas: metaphors, similes, personification, and allusions are all types of figurative language, which reveals the familiar in surprising ways

free verse—poetry that doesn't have a set rhythm, line length, or rhyme scheme; it relies, instead, on the natural rhythms of speech

hyperbole—when a poet exaggerates on purpose for effect

imagery—a sensory response that the language of a poem produces in the mind of a reader; not just visual but any sensory impression—sound, touch, odor—that is evoked by language

Figure 5.2 *Glossary of Poetic Terms*

(continues)

irony—when a poet says one thing but means something else

line—a group of words in a row; the unit of a poem

line break—the most important point in a line of poetry: the breath or pause at the end of a row of words

lyric poetry—short poems (fewer than sixty lines) about personal experiences and feelings (vs. *narrative poetry* or epic poems about communal events like *Beowulf* or the *Iliad*); most verse written and published today is lyric poetry

metaphor—from the Greek, meaning *transference*; a comparison in which the poet writes about one thing as if it is something else: A = B, with the qualities of B transferred to A

narrative poetry—a long poem (more than sixty lines) that tells a story at a leisurely pace: a short story in verse form

open form—see *free verse*

personification—from the Greek *prosopa*, meaning face or mask: a comparison that gives human qualities to an object, animal, idea, or phenomenon

prose poem—a piece of writing that has poetic features—rhythm, imagery, compression—but doesn't rhyme or break into lines

rhyme scheme—the pattern of rhyming in a poem; to describe the pattern, each line is assigned a letter, and lines that rhyme are given the same letter

sensory diction—language in a poem that evokes one of the five senses

simile—from the Latin *similes*, meaning similar: a kind of metaphor that uses *like* or *as* to compare two things: A is like B

speaker/persona—the identity of the voice that speaks the words of a poem; not necessarily the same person as the poet

stanza—a line or group of lines in a poem separated from other groups of lines by extra white space; a division in a poem that occurs at a natural pause or at a point where the poet wants to speed up or slow down the poem, shift its tone, change the setting, or introduce a new idea or character

symbol—a thing or an action that suggests, in addition to itself, another meaning

tone—the attitude of the speaker or poet toward the subject of the poem

turn—a point in a poem when its meaning moves in a new and significant direction or its theme emerges

Figure 5.2 *Continued*

A Lexicon of Literary Terms

Epistolary Novel: a novel written in the form of letters or emails

poet laureate: a title given to an outstanding U.S. poet for 1-2 years by the Library of Congress

Marginalia: comments handwritten in the margins of a book

Oeuvre: a French word for the total body of work produced by one writer

roman á clef: a French phrase ("novel with a key") that describes a novel in which real people, thinly disguised, appear under fictional names

(a) cliché: an expression that has been used so much it's lost its freshness, e.g., a rainbow of colors, busy as bees, a white blanket of snow (Note: use _clichéd_ as the adjective form, as in those lyrics are so clichéd.)

epigraph: a quotation that an author places at the beginning of a book, chapter, or poem that suggests something about its theme

oxymoron: a figure of speech that combines two contradictory words, e.g., _bittersweet_, _jumbo shrimp_, _living death_, _wise folly_

palindrome: a word or sentence that reads the same backwards and forwards, e.g., _Madam, I'm Adam_, _eye_, _deed_

Protagonist: the main character in a play or story; may be opposed by an _antagonist_

Figure 5.3 _A Lexicon of Literary Terms—Page One_

Alliteration is the term that describes the close repetition of *consonant sounds*, usually at the beginnings of words. Listen to the repetition of the hard *c* sound in these two lines from Tennyson's poem "The Eagle":

He clasps the crag with crooked hands;
Close to the sun in lonely lands

Because the subject of the poem—the eagle—is a brutal one, the hard *c*'s reinforce Tennyson's take on the harsh nature of a predatory bird.

Here's another classic example of alliteration. The poem "Eight O'Clock" by A. E. Housman tells the story of a public hanging that's set to take place at eight in the morning. Here, the *quarters* are the quarter hours being struck by the clock in the church steeple; *nighing* means nearing.

Eight O'Clock

He stood, and heard the steeple
    Sprinkle the quarters in the morning town.
One, two, three, four, to market place and people
    It tossed them down.
Strapped, noosed, nighing his hour,
    He stood and counted them and cursed his luck;
And then the clock collected in the tower
    Its strength, and struck.

Can you notice the heavy use of alliteration, both at the beginnings of words *and* inside them? How the repetition of hard sounds emphasizes the prisoner's terror at what's about to happen to him?

The repetition of *vowel* sounds inside words is called *assonance*. The phrase *holy smoke* is an example of assonance; so are *Coca-Cola*, *slow motion*, *queen bee*, and *Hula-Hoop*. Note that the vowels don't repeat in the last example, but the vowel *sounds* do.

We noticed in "The Eagle" how Tennyson creates a brutal tone by hitting hard consonant sounds. In this poem by Janet Lewis, about a young woman who's working a summer job as a chambermaid, listen to the softness of the vowels. They convey the wistfulness of a girl as she sweeps out a guest's room and dreams of her own grown-up, domestic life.

Girl Help

Mild and slow and young,
She moves about the room
And stirs the summer dust
With her wide broom.

In the warm, lofted air,
Soft lips together pressed,

Soft wispy hair,
She stops to rest.

And stops to breathe,
Amid the summer hum,
The great white lilac bloom,
Scented with days to come.

It's good to recognize that a little alliteration or assonance can go a long way. Try to avoid dumping it on like salt on French fries. You'll end up creating the infuriating repetition of television ads, like the invitation from a local used-car dealer to "Join Jolly John for a July joy ride!"

For me, using alliteration and assonance in poems is an act of discovery, not force. Their value is the subtle way they link sounds and words to create tone, emphasis, relationships, and theme. I tend to add them as I'm revising and polishing a poem.

Finally, some words carry their meanings *in their sound*. When a poet uses a word in which its pronunciation suggests what it means, or when sound and meaning match, that's an example of *onomatopoeia*. Examples of onomatopoeia include *bang*, *boom*, *buzz*, *caw*, *clink*, *cluck*, *crackle*, *gulp*, *honk*, *meow*, *moan*, *murmur*, *pop*, *sizzle*, *slurp*, *snap*, *snore*, *smash*, *splash*, *whisper*, *whistle*, *woof*, and *zoom*. The way we pronounce some words with short vowels also seems to me to suggest their meaning, for example, the short *i* in *little*, *skinny*, *slim*, and *thin*. I think the hard consonants in other words emphasize their heft: *gross*, *humongous*, *ponderous*, and *thick*.

The best-known example of onomatopoeia in English is the poem "The Bells" by Edgar Allan Poe. It is *way* over the top, but I have to confess I've loved it ever since it was set to music by Phil Ochs and its melodic effects became an actual song. Here's one of the verses, about the bells on a sleigh. Can you hear them?

Hear the sledges with the bells—
Silver bells!
What a world of merriment their melody foretells!
How they tinkle, tinkle, tinkle
In the icy air of night!
While the stars oversprinkle
All the heavens seem to twinkle
With a crystalline delight;
Keeping time, time, time,
In a sort of Runic rhyme.
To the tintinnabulation that so musically wells
From the bells, bell, bells, bells,
Bells, bells, bells, —
From the jingling and the tinkling of the bells.

Of the poets I love and teach to my students, the most influential is William Carlos Williams. His "Say it—no ideas but in things" (1951) is my mantra as a teacher of young poets, who often want to write about big, deep subjects—love, death, peace, war, prejudice, injustice. Williams helps them see that the best poems about big, deep topics address ordinary moments. The details and images of a writer's everyday experience evoke a reader's imagination and empathy, and the "things" create a larger meaning that can be felt and shared.

Although my students don't end up writing like Williams—no one will ever match his perspective or the precision of his diction—they take from him the essential lesson that a poet needs to begin with perceptions of the tangible—with observations of people, animals, objects, events, phenomena, life. I introduce Williams in the context of three of his poems:

William Carlos Williams (1883–1963)

If I had to name the most important poem of the twentieth century, I'd nominate "The Red Wheelbarrow" by William Carlos Williams. By *important* I mean the influence it has had on the poets who came after Williams. In just sixteen words he expresses a view of the world—a *vision*—that helps us understand that a good poem *and* a good life begin with the act of paying attention. Read along with me:

THE RED WHEELBARROW

so much depends
upon

the red wheel
barrow

glazed with rain
water

beside the white
chickens.

Williams is showing us how so much depends upon *noticing*, on using our senses to apprehend and appreciate the details of the world. Any quest for meaning begins with observation. *Look*, he says. *Stop*. Perceive your everyday life. Take in the fact of "a red wheelbarrow glazed with rain water beside the white chickens." So much—*the quality of your life*—depends on it. And then, what else can you notice?

As a poetry teacher, I live by two quotes from William Carlos Williams. The first is his admonition to all poets: "Say it—no ideas but in things." He's reminding us that particular moments and tangible objects are the way to reveal ideas, attitudes, and life itself. The second quote is "Perception is the first act of the imagination." In other words, get out there and perceive: *see*, *hear*, *taste*, *touch*, *smell*. That's where you'll find your vision as a poet.

Let's look together at two more short, famous poems by Williams. The first exemplifies his theory of poetry: in the way his cat scales the furniture in his kitchen, Williams perceives a living poem.

POEM

As the cat
climbed over
the top of

the jamcloset
first the right
forefoot

carefully
then the hind
stepped down

into the pit of
the empty flowerpot.

Before we read the third poem, you might be interested to know that in addition to being a poet, Williams was, for forty years, a family doctor who delivered more than two thousand babies. He often "saw" poems as he made his rounds at his hospital in New Jersey, and he jotted down his perceptions on the pages of his prescription pad. I think that's where "Between Walls" might have begun.

BETWEEN WALLS

the back wings
of the

hospital where
nothing

will grow lie
cinders

in which shine
the broken

pieces of a green
bottle

Notice how these poems rely on everyday diction, the language is cut to the bone, and each poem is a single sentence without punctuation, except for the period at the end of "The Red Wheelbarrow." Notice how Williams creates his own forms. Notice how he forgoes figurative language and writes direct descriptions, including strong, unadorned color words that create visual imagery: *red*, *white*, *green*. And notice how each poem is grounded in the concrete, in his observations of ordinary scenes and actions.

I'll not ask you to imitate Williams' style—it's unique to him. But I will ask that you appreciate his philosophy. A poet's vision begins in his or her actual *vision*—not in flowery performances, highfalutin' theories, or dreamy reveries but through paying attention to the details of the world and seeking meaning there.

So let's memorize "The Red Wheelbarrow" and, in our minds, insert the word *noticing* after Williams' *upon*, because for a poet, everything depends on *what we perceive*.

Other Williams poems we read and discuss include "To a Poor Old Woman," "Silence," "Complete Destruction," "Stormy," "The Maneuver," "Primrose," "Nantucket," and "This Is Just to Say." We finish with "A Sort of a Song," the poem in which he expounds on his battle cry of "No ideas but in thing" by showing how the words of a poem should capture sensations of the real world, not make pretty sounds.

I collect student poems about *things*, written under the influence of Williams, in my poetry binder. And I invite my classes to defy Williams: to rewrite badly on purpose. When kids collaborate in wrecking a poem, it's another way to demonstrate what they understand about good and bad poetry. With her permission, Natalie's classmates subverted her lovely Williams-inspired poem "My Father's Shirt" by recasting it as "My Dad Has Lots of Shirts." Small groups of students took responsibility for each of its four stanzas and proceeded to generalize, philosophize, revel in clutter, and spell out meaning.

MY FATHER'S SHIRT

I step into his closet and feast
on the familiar colors and patterns
of the shirts that swing on seven hangers.
I search for the one I love.

It's cotton and covered
with blue and white stripes.
I pluck it off the hanger
and put it to my face.
An aroma of cigar smoke,
metal, cut grass, and laundry detergent
wraps itself around me.

I remember times he wore it:
when he drove me to school, mowed the lawn,

when he lounged on the back porch
reading the Sunday paper and smoking a cigar.
He wore it to school conferences and plays.
He wore it to the funeral of a loved pet.
I remember cuddling up against him
on a winter night and feeling the worn
material on my cheek.

I slide it back on the hanger.
I button each button.
I cherish my memories
and my father.

         —*Natalie Brown*

My Dad Has Lots of Shirts

(aka Natalie's Evil Twin Poem)

Because I love my dad so, so much
I open his closet
and look at all his shirts
that hang there on a bunch of hangers.
His shirts
make me smile at his love for me.
Love is the greatest gift of all.
I take a pretty shirt off a hanger
and smell it.

There's a smell of smelly smoke
and the tangy, hard smell of the sheets of metal
that he works with every day at work
because he is a professional blacksmith
and the smell of the lawn,
which he cuts with a lawnmower.
The scent of the scented laundry detergent
used in a washing machine
flops off, and I smell it, too.
This shirt is a symbol
of my father.

He wears it all the time
to lots of stuff.
He's always there for me
when I need him.
He comes to all my things.

He would wear it everywhere,
to all kinds of places.
When I would hug him,
I would feel the specialness
of this really special shirt
and our special bond
as a father and his daughter.

I hang the shirt back on one of the hangers,
and I come out of the closet.
                    —*The Parodists of Grades 7–8*

Emily Dickinson is a difficult poet for my students to read and me to teach, but she is worth it. Many kids become besotted with her—the story of her life, the emotional uses she makes of poetry, and the brilliant, startling imagery of her poems. This is the summary of Dickinson's life and work that my students include in their writing–reading handbooks.

Emily Dickinson (1830–1886)

Emily Dickinson is one of the great American poets and a major influence on poets of the twentieth and twenty-first centuries. She was one of three children born to an affluent lawyer in Amherst, Massachusetts. She never married, and in her thirties she became a virtual hermit—a "ghost" in her father's big house. I've been intrigued by her since I was your age.

As a girl, Emily attended Amherst Academy, the local school, for seven years and took lots of science courses. At sixteen, she went away to college for a year—to Mount Holyoke Female Seminary, seven miles away, a school that trained lady missionaries to go off into the wilds and convert the "heathen" to Christianity. One-third of the students were already born-again Christians; one-third wanted to be; and one-third were "without hope," meaning they couldn't recognize Jesus Christ as their savior.

Emily fell into the last category. She never heard Christ's call—she felt herself "one of the lingering bad ones." She was too honest to fake being born again. She never joined a church, and, after age thirty, never attended the church of her father. Amherst was a Puritan community, and her absence was noticed and disapproved of.

The chief tension in Dickinson's poetry is her inability to accept religion *and* her need to believe in it. She called immortality "the flood subject," and she both yearned for its reassurance—of a heaven and everlasting life after death—and rejected it.

Most of Dickinson's poems were written between 1858 and 1865. Colonel Thomas Higginson, editor of the *Atlantic Monthly* magazine, was the first person she showed her poetry to. He was baffled by its strangeness compared with the verse of the time, and he discouraged her from trying to get it published. In her lifetime, she published only eleven poems. After her death, her relatives found almost eighteen hundred poems in her bureau drawers, sewn together into little packets.

Emily's poems are a diary of her insides, of her private feelings and observations. She had a powerful father whom she revered *and* rebelled against. There was no poetry in the Dickinson homestead, because her father wanted *his* life to be the focus of the household. Besides, the images of women in the poetry of her time were submissive to husband, father, and God.

Nature was viewed by most American poets in romantic terms—as an extension of the moods and emotions of the poet. Dickinson knew too much about nature to view it romantically—nature was apart from her. She was a knowledgeable botanist, geologist, and astronomer, and she based her nature poetry on a foundation of facts, not emotions.

Dickinson creates direct, surprising images. Her rhymes are irregular, her diction gemlike, and her metaphors surprising—startling, even. Her poetry is witty, morbid, passionate, and harrowing. She draws on the languages of carpentry, geology, blacksmithing, botany, biology, geology, and astronomy to craft metaphors about her feelings and to explore the tensions inside her between control and chaos. The ideas of science helped her express the complexity of her existence—of human existence. In the spring of 1862, her first poem was accepted for publication. Around this time she may have suffered a crisis: some kind of psychological or physical distress. Some of her poems are love poems, but to whom? God? A real lover? An imaginary lover? No one knows for sure.

Dickinson adopted the "white habit" at around age thirty, when she put on a white dress each day and remained within the Dickinson compound. She could have spent her life receiving and making calls, as other women of her class and station did. Instead, she became a recluse who saw a few close friends—worthwhile people who she felt could appreciate her work and ideas. She longed for real intimacy, but she couldn't achieve it. Most of the few friendships she did have failed because she asked too much of others. Dickinson was intense and hard to talk to; I think she must have been exhausting. In the end, she chose her own society.

My favorite quote of Emily Dickinson's is, "My business is circumference." I think she meant that her job as a poet was to journey the boundaries of human existence in her imagination and, with her words, to create unity—to lasso the chaos of life through poetry.

Then, as daily poems, we read, unpack, and appreciate "As imperceptibly as grief," "A narrow fellow in the grass," "There's a certain slant of light," "Because I could not stop for Death," "I'm nobody! Who are you?," "I never saw a moor," "The Soul selects her own Society," "After great pain, a formal feeling comes," "I died for Beauty," "I heard a fly buzz–when I died," and "Hope is the thing with Feathers."

My students also enjoy contemporary verse about Dickinson, including "Altitudes" by Richard Wilbur, "Emily Dickinson" by Linda Pastan, "Emily Dickinson's Defunct" by Marilyn Nelson, "Emily Dickinson's To-Do List" by Andrea Carlisle, "Emily Dickinson and Elvis Presley in Heaven" by Hans Ostrom, and "Narrow Fellowship" by Henry Braun, as well as a read-aloud of the picture book *Emily* by Michael Bedard, with illustrations of Amherst, Massachusetts, by the incomparable Barbara Cooney. Cooney based her illustrations on the actual architecture of Amherst, including the homes of Dickinson's brother and father and Emily's bedroom. I tempt students with the idea that they can visit the Dickinson homestead someday and see her room with its little writing table, her white dress, and her gardens still abloom.

I love to teach about Walt Whitman. He is the inventor of American free-verse poetry. His style and themes were astonishing for his time, they are so bold, and his insistence on poetry as a democratic language, for and *of the people*, changed it forever. As the self-professed "poet of the body and the soul," Whitman speaks from the heart of life's mystery in a language that regular people can understand—although the regular people of his time were shocked and offended at first. He's important to teach because of his generosity to the "poets to come," his diction and style, and the essential American themes he evokes. I teach eight lessons about Whitman, beginning with an enthusiastic account of his life, a description of his masterpiece, and a children's picture book rendition of one of his greatest hits.

Walt Whitman (1819–1892)

Walt Whitman was born on Long Island, New York, on a farm owned by his father. He left school when he was eleven and worked at various jobs, including printing, teaching, reporting, editing newspapers, and the building trades. Along the way he published a few poems, but there was no hint of what was to come.

In 1855, Whitman self-published eight hundred copies of an original, astonishing volume of poetry called *Leaves of Grass*, which consisted of twelve untitled poems. It wasn't well received, and only a few copies sold. Walt had offended the sensibilities of people of the Victorian era.

He cast aside verse traditions, rejected rhyming, used slang, championed the equality of all people, and celebrated the human body at a time so repressed that women *and* men wore layers of clothing that restricted their movement and bared only their faces. Out of modesty, they even covered up the legs of their pianos.

Today Whitman is regarded, along with Emily Dickinson, as the inventor of American poetry. Walt is the father of free verse. He rebelled against rhyme, regular metrical patterns, and language that was ornate and heavy. He substituted assonance, alliteration, cadence, inverse word order, and only the loosest of structures. I love his experiments.

For an example of Whitman's style, read the lines along with me on the overhead transparency:

> For we cannot tarry here;
> We must march, my darlings, we must bear the brunt of danger,
> We the youthful sinewy races, all the rest on us depend,
> Pioneers! O Pioneers!

Can you hear the assonance in *cannot* and *tarry*? In *march* and *darlings*? The alliteration in *bear the brunt* and *must march my*? Cadence means a repeating word or group of words, and here it appears as *Pioneers! O Pioneers!* Inverse word order is a deliberate violation of the usual subject-word-object order in English sentences. Instead of the conventional *All the rest depend on us*, Whitman writes *All the rest on us depend*. As you'll see, he also loved long lines and present-tense verbs, and he frequently put his own thoughts about the subjects of his poems inside parentheses.

Whitman's breaking of the old rules is one reason we remember him, but what he said is as important as how he said it. He celebrated everything and everyone as good and worthy. There's only one speaker in his poems—Walt himself—but he speaks for all of us, for every person on earth, urging each human being to discover his or her individual self. He loves all, feels compassion for all, and revels in the oneness of all creation. He is ecstatic about the whole of life, but especially about truth, poetry, freedom, and America. In the preface to the first edition of *Leaves of Grass*, Whitman wrote, "The United States themselves are essentially the greatest poem . . ." I think Whitman is his own greatest poem—he created himself as a man and a poet, and what a self, what a poet.

Whitman sent a copy of the first edition of *Leaves of Grass* to the famous writer and philosopher Ralph Waldo Emerson. Emerson's praise inspired a second edition, and from there Walt kept revising the book until by his death, almost forty years later, he had produced ten editions of *Leaves of Grass*. The last one, published in 1892, contained 383 poems. The major poem and his greatest is "Song of Myself." It's thirty-two pages long, consists of fifty-two sections of varying lengths, and is the purest, wildest, most generous version of Whitman's voice. In "Song of Myself" he wrote, "I send my barbaric yawp over the roofs of the world." His barbaric yawp is still sounding today.

Let's start reading Whitman with one of his most famous poems, "I Hear America Singing." It's one of his catalogue poems: these are long lists that put everything on the same level and, at the same time, make everything special. Here we meet people at work all over nineteenth-century America. Each is singing his or her own carol, and each is distinctive and important. I think this picture book version, with illustrations by Robert Sabuda, captures the tone and themes of the poem (1991).

In the following days, we read "Song of the Open Road" and compare it with "The Norseman," a poem by Whitman's contemporary, John Greenleaf Whittier, so kids will have a sense of the poetic tradition Whitman was rebelling against. I read aloud a lovely picture book version of "When I Heard the Learn'd Astronomer" (Long 2004) and distribute copies of the poem for kids to annotate Whtiman's use of assonance, alliteration, cadence, and inverse word order. Over several days we read excerpts from "Song of Myself" and discuss the imagery and themes, starting with his use of a blade of grass as a symbol—for all the miracles of the universe, growth, death, and the significance of every separate and distinct creation. Along the way, we note how verbose Whitman can be, how he rambles, rants, and repeats himself, and how stretches of dullness in "Song of Myself" are broken by sudden patches of sheer brilliance.

We also listen to a CD of an old wax-cylinder recording of Whitman reciting lines from his poem "America" and talk about his passion for the promise of the new nation. I teach about Walt's experiences as a wound dresser in Washington during the Civil War; *Drum Taps*, his collection of ballads about the war; and his love for Abraham Lincoln. Before we read his elegy for Lincoln, "Captain! My Captain," I explain that this is the only one of Whitman's poems that was popular in his lifetime. It's a poem he never liked. I agree: compared with his other work, it's trite and conventional. I try to persuade kids that "When Lilacs Last in the Dooryard Bloom'd" is a far superior elegy for Lincoln, and mostly they disagree with me—it's a lively debate. We conclude the study of Whitman with three poems: one I created for inclusion in *Naming the World*, "From the Preface to the First Edition of *Leaves of Grass*," which consists of Whitman's advice on how to make "a great poem" of one's life;"Poets to Come," which he directs to the young poets of every age; and Section 52 of "Song of Myself," the beautiful, moving conclusion, which brings me to tears every time.

After Whitman, we read and discuss poems by his literary descendant, Allen Ginsberg, about the lost promise of America—"A Supermarket in California," in which Walt makes an appearance, selections from "Howl," and Ginsberg's twentieth-century take on "America."

Teachers savvy about the Common Core State Standards may have noticed that my teaching of poems ranges beyond the four corners of the page. The CCSS adhere to a literary theory called the New Criticism, in which students are meant to analyze a work of literature as an autonomous whole and eliminate any consideration of context or personal response. This means a reader shouldn't relate a piece of writing to the time, place, or reason it was written, the author's life or other work, other authors' lives and work, a literary tradition, or the reader's own reactions to the work.

The theory of New Criticism, no longer so new, reached the peak of its popularity in the 1950s. By the time I was an English major in the 1970s, the professors I studied under had rejected most of its tenets. Although they did teach me how to analyze and annotate works of literature, they also asked me what I thought about them and introduced background information about authors and poets. When I read poems in college by Gwendolyn Brooks, Countee Cullen, Langston Hughes, and LeRoi Jones, it was in the contexts of the Great Black Migration, Jim Crow segregation, the Harlem Renaissance, the Civil Rights movement, and my own feelings and beliefs about racism in America. My readings were the richer for it.

Of course students should learn how to analyze literature and critique it using textual evidence. Because I teach my students critical vocabulary and perspectives, because I ask them, every day, to discuss a poem or two, they become adept at identifying literary features and their effects. But I also honor kids' reactions, the contexts in which particular writers created particular works, and the impact of the writing.

The result is that my students know poets. They have favorites. They take them into their lives, memorize poems, tape them inside their lockers and on their bedroom walls, and recite them in graduation speeches—I'm thinking of Helena, who channeled Whitman one June, and Curt who performed Shakespeare's St. Crispian's Day speech with passion and a sword. Poets and poetry are alive for them. It's personal, and it's political.

Literature isn't neutral. The study of literature isn't an objective science. Stories, poems, and plays are the heart of the humanities, and English teachers should never feel compelled to ignore the values that literature teaches, starting with compassion, passion, tolerance, courage, justice, a sense of wonder, and an appreciation for the power of an individual voice. Kids can read closely *and* widely *and* deeply.

Some of the literature we read and discuss in minilessons is nonfiction. If I could bestow one gift on every teacher in America, it would be a daily subscription to *The New York Times*. Reading the Paper of Record makes everyone smarter and more aware, including adolescents.

In my history classes, we read and talk about articles from the *Times* about current events. We also unpack the weekly roundups of political cartoons from the *Boston Globe* and *Maine Sunday Telegram*. We analyze Charles Blow's graphs from the op-ed pages of the *Times*, and we enjoy Calvin Trillin's political doggerel from *The Nation*.

As an English teacher, across a school year I find as many as three dozen articles from *The New Yorker, Time, Rolling Stone*, and, mainly, *The New York Times* that I reproduce to discuss with kids in reading minilessons. These have included articles about the new U.S. poet laureate and Newbery-Medalist, the rise of e-books, titles that appear on the current children's and adults' best-seller lists, the difference between trade and mass-market paperbacks, and smart reviews of books, films, and television programs.

We also read and debate works of advocacy journalism by *Times* columnists Nicholas Kristof, Thomas Friedman, Maureen Dowd, Charles Blow, and Gail Collins. And we have been intrigued by articles and opinion pieces about a range of topics relevant to kids: a study that indicates that tests are the most effective way for students to remember new material, the "summer slide" that occurs when kids don't read for three months, adult stereotypes of boy readers, President Obama's pronoun-case errors, the genre called *paranormal romance*, how adult readers decide whether to abandon books, the cult of adults who are crazy about young adult literature, a proposal that literary journals should only publish positive reviews of books, the Figment.com website as a place for students to publish online, and the art of writing in the margins of books. The last, in combination with Billy Collins' poem "Marginalia," led my kids and me to craft marginalia for books in the classroom library. We scrawled deep or ironical observations about works of literature, as well as silly non sequiturs, for future student readers to find and wonder at.

A handful of my students cajole their parents to buy the Sunday *New York Times* and attempt to read it on their own, but all of my students get to experience and engage with strong nonfiction prose by the best of the best. Along the way, I hope they'll be tantalized by opinions, theories, arguments, and evidence, including graphs and statistics. I want them to be able to read and understand journalism and essays; more importantly, I hope they'll grow up to be informed, thoughtful citizen-readers.

In the week or so before eighth graders take standardized reading assessments, mini-lessons become a context for teaching them about the conventions of standardized tests. Students who understand how they work and have experience with the format are more confident going into a test situation and more adept at demonstrating their competence as readers. It's only fair to prep them. But it's unfair—to them and to literature—to turn reading class into a year of test prep. Engaged, voluminous time with books is the key. A few days of background and training in how to approach a particular standardized assessment does more than enough to acclimate students to its demands and format:

> Something you should know about standardized tests in reading is that, when it comes right down to it, there are four kinds of questions. One group of questions asks for the best title, best topic sentence, main idea, or general idea—whatever terminology the test makers use, all of these test items get at one thing: what the passage is mostly about or is getting at.
>
> Next are the inference questions. Inferences are meanings that are implied by the passage, rather than spelled out in black and white. Often, an inference is just plain common sense: based on the evidence the test maker gives you in a reading selection, what can you understand and conclude?
>
> There are always detail questions. These ask for specific information you can look up in the passage. I think these are the easiest—unless the test maker decides to get tricky and word a question ambiguously, which is plainly unfair.
>
> Finally, when test makers ask you for the meaning of a word *in context*, they want to know if you can figure out what a word means *in the sentence or passage in which it appears*.
>
> I downloaded and photocopied test selections and sets of questions of the type you'll encounter next week. Let's start by looking at the questions that go with the first passage and analyzing them, in terms of what the test maker is asking of you as a test taker.

Together students and I analyze how the passages and questions are constructed. Then, in another minilesson, I teach a procedure for reading a passage and answering the questions.

PROCEDURE FOR STANDARDIZED READING TESTS

1. First, read the first couple of sentences in the selection, the last couple of sentences, *and the test questions*. This way you'll have an idea of what you'll be reading and what you should be looking for.

2. Next, read the selection, *with the goal of looking for the answers to the questions*.

3. When you answer a question, start by eliminating the alternatives that show the least merit: usually there are two that are easy to discount. Then reread the question and the remaining two answers. Always use a process of elimination.

4. Return to the reading selection whenever you need to, using a skimming/ scanning approach.

5. When a question asks for the meaning of a word, *read the whole sentence or group of sentences in which the word appears*. You're not being tested on whether you already know the definition of a word. The challenge here is whether you can figure out its meaning in the selection by using the words around it as clues.

Students work with several more sample passages, individually and in pairs; the whole group and I decide on the correct answers; and kids explain how they arrived at them or what confused them.

The final reading lesson of the school year addresses a well-documented phenomenon: summer slide. Students who don't read over the summer hiatus lose three months or more of reading ability. After all my students have accomplished as readers, September to June, the prospect of a loss of this degree haunted me.

A handful of my students' parents do take them to bookstores and libraries during the summer months. Others live in homes with few books or the money to buy them. There is no public transportation in rural Maine, and local public libraries offer limited hours and resources for adolescent readers. This meant little or no summer access to books for many students unless I did something about it.

Groundbreaking research (Allington and McGill-Franzen 2013) found that disadvantaged students from high-poverty schools who chose and took home books over the summer demonstrated significantly higher reading scores compared with those who didn't. Each of the 852 children in the study selected a dozen story books in June, which he or she got to keep. These modest collections of paperbacks resulted in an upsurge in students' summer reading *and* subsequent gains in their reading proficiency that were equivalent to having attended summer school.

I found the results to be heartening but also a cause for serious soul-searching. Although I'd always taught minilessons in June about how to find good books beyond

CTL, I had yet to acknowledge that many of my students wouldn't be able to follow through. It was a breakdown of handover in the reading workshop.

I took a deep breath and acknowledged that I needed to care more about the reading of my kids than the sanctity of my library. While it may sound risky to allow students to sign out books for the summer, it is necessary, and it works.

In June I ask the local supermarket for a donation of brown paper bags, two for each student. I double these, and kids and I booktalk like mad. The goal is for every student to select at least six books to read over the summer. On index cards students sign out the loans and write a note describing their plan for returning the books to me by September 1. I photocopy the index cards, and students staple the original to the brown paper bag as a reminder.

In three years, I lost two books—worth it, considering that my students participated in "the single summer activity that is most strongly and consistently related to summer learning" (Heyns 1978). The rest of the teachers at CTL joined me, and now all our students choose, borrow, read, and love stories in the summertime.

The reading lessons I teach are based on what I love of literature, understand about reading, and discover about my students as readers. Each September some of the new kids don't trust there's such a thing as a good book, their experiences of literature have been that limited, while others make their way to me from the classrooms of my book-loving colleagues or from homes where owning books and talking about them are as natural as breathing. Reading workshop reaches and embraces every one of them.

The workshop taps the strengths of young adolescents. Most can decode to some degree. They all love a good story. They're willing to experiment and are uninhibited about showing enthusiasm. They delight in quality, and when they see it, they acknowledge it. They are generous—more than willing to recommend stories they love to others. They stand on the threshold of analytical reading, ready to be invited to go beyond plot. In reading minilessons, teachers escort them inside books and poems, demonstrate the skills of critical readers, and teach the happiest lesson of all—how the minds of good readers interact with the words on the page to create a lifetime of good books.

ANSWERS TO THIRTEEN QUESTIONS

1. Mount Everest has always been Earth's highest peak. The italics tell an experienced reader to approach this as a question about chronology.

2. Moses didn't build the ark; Noah did. Prior experience tells readers to assume that test questions contain correct information, but also that we should direct our attention to instructions and italics.

3. The date "B.C." could not have been used to date a coin: how could someone have foreseen the future birth of Jesus Christ? Our eyes have learned to skim over a commonplace abbreviation like "B.C." without stopping to unpack it.

4. You'd light the match first. Long-term memory automatically fills in the "missing" information that the match is already lit.

5. Survivors can't be buried. Again, prior experience with text tells us to focus on the words in italics. The emphasis on *international airliner* shifts focus off the crucial word, *survivors*.

6. All of them. Here, schemas in a reader's long-term memory insert a word: *only*.

7. Nine. Experience with word problems in math classes has taught us we should expect to perform an arithmetical operation—in this case, subtraction.

8. Push the cork into the bottle, and shake the dime out. Experience tells us that corks are for pulling out of bottles, not for pushing in.

9. He does it in the daytime. Again, schemas in long-term memory supply the "missing" information that if darkness is mentioned, it must be nighttime.

10. A dime and a quarter. Schemas about the wording of math problems, plus the italics and special directions in parentheses, misdirect our attention: maybe one coin can't be a quarter, but the *other* one can.

11. Egg yolks are yellow. The structure and tone of the question cue a reader's long-term memory to focus on grammar instead of meaning.

12. There are six *F*s, not three. Reading the sentence aloud orients readers to the sound of the hard *F* in the first two words, *finished files*. When the word *scientific* is hyphenated at the hard *F* sound, it reinforces the pronunciation link. This makes it easy to miss the soft *F* of *of*.

13. Paris in *the the* spring. Bird in *the the* hand. Once in *a a* lifetime. Slow men *at at* work. An experienced reader perceives a chunk of meaning, as he or she should, and fixates on the contentives, the words that carry meaning.

CHAPTER 6

RESPONDING TO WRITERS AND WRITING

What a child can do in cooperation today he can do alone tomorrow.

—*L. S. VYGOTSKY*

In the September survey about students' attitudes and backgrounds as writers, among my questions is, "What kind of responses from others helps you improve your writing?" Every year their answers demonstrate how aspiring, intentional, and brave young writers can be:

- comments that push my writing
- when a teacher or friend tells me what's good *and* what I can do to improve it
- when someone tells me what isn't clear yet, if the language is weak in places, or if they can't see it yet
- when someone tells me what they don't understand or need more of
- constructive criticism—it doesn't hurt, and it does show you the ways you can improve as a writer and make your writing stronger
- specific responses that help me decide a direction
- criticism that's specific so I don't embarrass myself
- specific comments I can think about and maybe use
- specific suggestions to make my writing sound better
- advice that's specific about what I'm trying to do

These writers aren't looking for praise, bland neutrality, or adherence to rubrics or standards. They want guidance from a teacher—and classmates—who know that writers write to be read, understood, and appreciated.

My essential stance as a responder to writing is that of a veteran reader. I've been reading for more than fifty years, including tens of thousands of pieces written by students. This background informs my every response. Teachers anxious about talking with kids about drafts of writing might count the number of years they've been reading and draw confidence from their own experience with words on the page.

As readers, we've noticed features of poems, stories, and expository pieces that work, and that don't. In conferences I teach writers what I've gleaned as a reader about such literary features as leads and conclusions, titles, tone, reflection, logic, information, purpose, theme, imagery, clarity, diction, sensory verbs, verb tense, concrete specifics, organization, transitions, paragraphing, colons, dashes, you name it. Writing teachers don't need formulas or rubrics of response. We begin with our strengths as literary *readers*.

My conversations with writers are the highlight of my teaching day. This wasn't always the case. At the start I was so caught up in the orthodoxies of conference etiquette that my meetings with students were filled with tension. I could feel myself watching and listening over my own shoulder, I was so consumed with saying the right thing or not saying the wrong one. But when I began to focus on conferences as an opportunity for handover—for drawing on my history as a reader, remembering my own failures and successes as a writer, observing what a student had done, listening to the writer's intentions, and offering relevant advice—I realized the satisfaction of *teaching* in these conversations.

In September, when I read Daniel's first draft of his first poem of seventh grade, I recognized it wasn't working yet. Something—someone—had gone missing. The conference began when I pulled up my little folding chair next to his table and asked, "How's it going?"

Daniel: Okay. I think I'm done.

Nancie: May I read it?

Daniel: Sure.

D.1

Click, click, click:
the rhythmical clicking
as we press the "next song" button.
We find it odd how we can like an inanimate item
so much. But yet, we do.

Click, click, click:
we find a song.
We wait for a second, think, shrug,
put in our earbuds, sit back, and enjoy.

NANCIE: Is this about your iPod?

DANIEL: Yeah. I think I'm ready to edit it.

NANCIE: I'm curious—how did you decide to write about this?

DANIEL: Well, I was thinking about how much time I spend with it. I'm kind of obsessed. It's like I'm with it more than I am with my friends, and it's just a machine.

NANCIE: That's a cool observation. I like how the clicks are almost a voice—like a dialogue with a machine. And I like your tone—it's clear you're reluctant to be obsessed with a machine. The problem I'm having as a reader is I'm not *getting* your obsession. I think it's the *we* voice, Daniel. A writer can't tell his own thoughts and feelings in a *we* voice. You need an *I* to do that. Would you try a second draft, recast with an *I* voice, to see what happens?

DANIEL: Well, I sort of like it the way it is—it could be about anyone with an iPod.

NANCIE: That's the problem. A reader needs a *someone*. Just try it, and see what happens. Trust me—I think it'll make a difference.

DANIEL: Well, all right.

This is Daniel's final version of his iPod poem.

I Try Not to Think About It

Click, click, click—
I love the familiar rhythm.
I press the "next song" button again and again—
click, click, click.
I find it odd that I enjoy an inanimate item
this much.
Yet I do.
And this one was assembled
by other inanimate objects.

Click, click, click—
I find the song I'm looking for.
I pause for a second.
I ponder my pleasure
over a piece of plastic.
I accept my identity:
child of the twenty-first century.
I shrug, put in my earbuds,
sit back, relax,
and enjoy.

—*Daniel Mayer*

A first-person presence gave Daniel a way to include personal reflections. Personal reflections—his thoughts and feelings—led to a theme, the same one Daniel explained in our conference but now voiced in the poem with humor and clarity. His strong title, too, is a result of the shift to first person. I think the poem was transformed. And a seed was planted: Daniel is learning that readers want a first-person experience to be narrated by a first-person voice, so we can journey inside the writer's head and heart.

I was direct and directive with Daniel. I troubleshot a poem he said was done and, after he described his intentions, advised him how to try it again from another angle. I identified my problem as a reader and handed over a solution. His *we* was a red flag. It took me a while, as a responder to writers, to be able to articulate it and some of the other red flags I'll describe in this chapter. But once I recognized the power of *I* in personal writing, I didn't hesitate to hand it over.

My responses to writers are predictable. They know I'll talk with them *while* they're writing, not write comments on finished work. After-the-fact response comes too late. It assumes students will not only hold a teacher's advice in their heads until the next writing occasion and apply it to a new situation, but that they actually read a teacher's comments in the first place. Any teacher who has spent a Sunday writing marginal notes on class sets of papers has harbored the suspicion that she is shouting down a hole. Donald Murray's suspicion was so strong he conducted an experiment one Sunday afternoon and wrote purposely bad advice all over his students' papers: "Do this backward," "Add adverbs," "Be general and abstract." When Murray passed back the papers, not one student questioned his comments (1982). Writing workshop provides time in school for students to work on their writing, and it provides time in school for teachers to work with students on their writing.

Another constant of writing conferences is *where* I meet with students: I go to them. I move in order to control the length of the meetings, see many students each day, and keep on top of classroom behavior. One fall I experimented with a conference table, where I parked for the duration of the workshop and met with writers one at a time. There were problems. I couldn't get students to leave once they joined me at the table: they had Ms. Atwell at their disposal until they decided they were done with me. Worse, I saw only four or five writers each period, and I was distracted by the kids on line, not to mention the shenanigans in the corners of the classroom.

When I move, I can keep conferences short, work with many writers each day, and monitor classroom behavior. I travel in a random fashion, not from one table to the next, so my kids understand I could be anywhere in the room in a second. I carry the status-of-the-class survey on a clipboard, a pad of 4 × 6–inch Post-it notes so I can demonstrate examples and solutions, a pen, and my folding chair.

Students anticipate that I'll initiate a writing conversation with one of the open-ended questions that are a writing workshop teacher's stock in trade: "How's it going (or coming)?" "Where are you?" "How can I help you?" "What's happening?" "Where did this come from?" "Where are you going with this?" By November I often don't have to say a word. When I pull up my chair, writers start right in, telling me how it's going, asking for help, describing what they're trying to do, or waving me off politely because they're on a roll.

In a conference I listen to the writer, read the draft, ask questions about what I don't understand or want to know more about, identify problems the writer hasn't, suggest how the writer might solve them, and find out what he or she plans to do next. My goal is what Vygotsky terms "mediated" learning: "What a child can do in cooperation today he can do alone tomorrow" (1962). Today, I cooperate with Daniel by telling him that switching the narrative voice will serve his intentions, so that tomorrow he can raise his *I* flag on his own. This is my chief responsibility as a responder: to help kids meet their intentions by demonstrating ways that other writers have met theirs.

When I stopped next to Graydon's computer, perched, and looked over his shoulder at the screen, I saw the draft of a poem. "How's it going?" I wondered.

GRAYDON: I'm stuck. I'm trying to write a tritina about when we were in India. I want to give it to my mom as a gift.

NANCIE: What's the problem?

GRAYDON: I can't think of a line that ends in "Agra." And the last line—the envoy one—is too long.

NANCIE: May I read it?

GRAYDON: Yeah.

I recognized right away that in his attempt at a tritina, Graydon's meaning and purpose had been subsumed by the dictates of the form:

NEXT TO YOU

I'm sleeping, or trying to, behind you in the back of the van,
screaming through the streets of Agra,
marinated in the liquid heat.

After four weeks though, we get used to the heat.
You are gripping the handle above your head, tucked away in the left corner
 of the van.

In the muck of Agra,
the beautiful Taj Mahal lies, basking in the heat.
The heat stops me from going to sleep. And no, the windows only make it
 a humid van.

This moment of silence in our van bubble (besides the dries of Agra),
swimming in the heat, will always remind me of just sitting here, knowing
you're there.

NANCIE: Gray, why are you writing about this?

GRAYDON: It was such a special time, you know, with my mother. I want to let her know I remember it and what we were like together.

NANCIE: That's lovely. I'm wondering, how wedded are you to using the tritina form?

GRAYDON: What do you mean?

NANCIE: I think that trying to fit your story and theme into a form—working with the three words you chose—is making it hard for you to write what you want to say to your mom. I can't feel the specialness of this time. Let me leave you with a couple of ideas. In your next draft, you could stick with the tritina form but reconsider your three end words—I don't know if *van* holds a lot of promise. A good word might be *you*, meaning your mom, to ensure that she's in the poem. Or you could recast the experience as free verse, which is one of your strengths, and craft the best way to say directly what you want to say. What do you think?

GRAYDON: So I could write a second draft that's not a tritina?

NANCIE: Absolutely—it's up to you.

That's what he did. His next draft captured the experience in India and his pleasure in his mother's company.

COMFORT

"Hey, Mom?" I ask.
"Yes?" you respond.
"Oh, um, never mind."
The truth is, I just want to hear your voice
after long hours in a hot van.
My body is aching, stomach splitting.
But sleep mutes it.
I've been lying back here for hours,
holding your hand, rubbing your shoulder.
Your cool fingers feel smooth.
Your arm wraps around the back of the seat.
Mine rests on your suspended fingers.
We are headed towards the hotel,
and tomorrow, at six in the morning,
the legendary Taj Mahal.
"Mom?"
"Yes?"
"How long have we been driving?"
"Six hours."
"Okay."
"Okay."

"Love you, Mom."
"Love you, too."
On the streets of Agra,
I am at home.

—Graydon Nuki

Having listened to Graydon's intentions, recognized how form can get in the way, and considered what I knew about him as a writer, I figured he needed options for creating a poem worthy of his mother. The next time he couldn't make a poetic form work for him, he decided on his own to switch to free verse. On the other hand, he crafted an elegant Elizabethan sonnet as a Christmas present for his family.

In conferences about content and craft, I try to help writers see and name problems, attempt solutions, recognize successes, make plans, and develop a repertoire of strategies for drafting and revising toward literature. These are the guidelines that help make my meetings with student writers efficient, substantive, and productive.

WRITING CONFERENCE GUIDELINES

1. Keep an eye on the clock, and remember you're responsible to every writer in the room. Meet with as many as possible. At the end of class, put a check mark on the status-of-the-class record by the names of those you conferred with, and start with those you didn't in the subsequent workshop.

   In the beginning, as I was learning the ropes, my conferences ran long. Today I meet with at least a dozen writers in a thirty-minute independent writing session. A group of teachers visiting CTL bought a stopwatch so they could time my conferences. The shortest lasted thirty seconds, and the longest, three and a half minutes.

   Among the many good reasons to kick off a year of writing instruction with a genre study of poetry is that shorter pieces don't take long for students to write or me to read and respond to. Poems give me opportunities for many meetings with every student in September and early October. I confer with lots of them each day and get to know everyone as a writer sooner.

2. Bring the concepts and vocabulary of minilessons to writing conferences. I can keep mine relatively brief because I reference techniques of craft and genre that we discussed as a whole group and individuals recorded in their writing–reading handbooks. Our shared language becomes a reliable shorthand for troubleshooting writing problems: "Uh-oh, I think you've got pebbles instead of a pebble." "Without *T* and *F*, I don't have anyone to be with in your story." "Your paragraphs are making me hiccough." "Your essay lead is one of those ambiguous ones—I can't tell where you stand."

3. Be aware that some pieces of writing are too long to read in class. Once students move into extended prose pieces—some of my students' memoirs are as long as six typed, double-spaced pages—I can't read and respond to the whole text without stealing time from the other kids. I work with parts of prose pieces in class, and I take home a long draft in order to eyeball the whole thing. Kids put these in my rocking chair with a Post-it note attached that tells me what they want me to pay attention to: "Please eyeball this tonight. Can you follow the transitions when I flash back and forward?" "Can you tell what the *so what?* is?" "Does the information go in a logical order?" "Did I go off the track here?" "Are there enough thoughts and feelings?" "I need help with the ending, I think it just stops." "Are my arguments and evidence strong?"

   I skim the draft that night and make notes on another Post-it in response to the writer's query and about any other problems with content or organization. I don't write on the draft—my job at this juncture is to eyeball, not edit. The next day in class, I meet with the writer and discuss my reactions, cued by my notes.

4. Make conferences feel personal—intimate even. This means sitting shoulder-to-shoulder with writers, looking into their eyes, whispering, and asking students to whisper to you. Remember that voices louder than this will make it hard for the other writers in the room to concentrate and stay on task.

5. Try not to be discouraged, as least in front of the kids. One year I thought I'd laid the most fertile groundwork ever for student memoirs. I kicked off the genre study by asking them to analyze one of my memoirs. Then we read, critiqued, and identified the features of successful memoirs by professional authors and former students. I was filled with anticipation as my savvy, articulate kids began to craft memoirs of their own. Then I was filled with dismay as I circulated during independent writing time and skimmed the unfolding drafts.

   Problems I'd warned against were everywhere: dialogue bereft of visuals, people with names but no indication of their relationship to the memoirist, zero thoughts and feelings, and, after a grabbing lead, no context for it. I was reminded of the limits of so-called *mentor texts*. As young writers move into new prose genres, they can only focus on so much at a time. They're bound to create problems. But with the teacher's help in minilessons and conferences, along with their own realizations as they step back and reflect on what's on the page, they're bound to solve them. Students build their prose pieces layer by layer. A piece of writing that isn't working *isn't working yet*. It's not a failure. Neither is the writer. Neither is the teacher. Eventually, my students' memoirs were wonderful.

6. When it seems like it would be useful to demonstrate a solution to a problem on the draft, ask the writer's permission: "May I write on your draft, to show you what I mean?" I've never had a student say no. If you understand a writer's intentions and have a good idea about how he or she can meet them, by all means say, "Let me

show you a way to do this." Follow-up with, "Does this work with what you're trying to do?"

7. Notice strengths. *Name* what makes a piece of writing work, so the writer can do it the next time: "Your lead brings me right into the essay and your opinion." "This diction is so sensory, I can *see* it, especially your verbs." "Your conclusion resonates—I have goose bumps, and I'm left *thinking*." "The examples you chose are convincing and carry real power." "This is one witty description." "I love the way you build your arguments, from major to minor." "The theme of this poem is so strong I forgot about the form, but you nailed the form, too." "I can feel what you were feeling—I get why this matters so much to you—because of the thoughts and feelings you describe." "These simple color words are strong in creating imagery." "The shift in verb tense makes the whole thing more immediate." "Thank you for the paragraphs and the little rests between your ideas—it's much easier for me to take them in now." "It feels like you're channeling J. D. Salinger, your main character is so quirky and sincere." "This dialogue really shows who the people are and what their relationship is like."

8. Don't hesitate to be direct, as long as your response is specific. It's okay to say to a student, "I'm lost," "I'm confused," or even "I'm having a hard time caring about this." But you need to follow up with *why* and *what the writer can do* to address the problem.

9. Be patient with kids and yourself. Writing is a slow-growth process. When students write a lot across a school year, this translates into many opportunities to teach each of them, help them tap the power of craft and genre minilessons, and get better at responding to writing and writers.

RED FLAGS AND RESPONSES

By this time in my career, there is nothing new under the sun when it comes to the problems I encounter in drafts of student writing. Being able to identify sources of trouble and talk with kids in ways they can follow about how to revise helps me stay patient and helps them develop a repertoire of techniques they can use on their own. Over the years I've noticed a dozen or so red flags that wave in the drafts of seventh and eighth graders.

• *There isn't enough information.*

Readers want information: specifics that enlighten, exemplify, signify, convince, provoke, create images, and bring life to a piece of writing. With inexperienced writers, or when writers move to a new genre, teachers need to be prepared for problems with information—occasionally too much but, more often, not enough on the page to engage and satisfy a reader. In my conferences with students, a suggestion that they write off-the-page is the obvious solution because it focuses them on the quantity and quality of their specifics.

Helena was drafting a review of *Fahrenheit 451* by Ray Bradbury for CTL's book blog. Reviews were the first expository genre of the school year, following two months of personal writing—poetry and memoirs. She was having a hard time making the switch.

After a brief plot summary, Helena's draft became a rant about the teacher of a friend, a freshman at a local high school. The friend had spent eight weeks in English class reading *Fahrenheit 451* paragraph by paragraph and parsing each one. In a state of high dudgeon, Helena contrasted her friend's frustration with the novel and her own satisfied reading. The draft was voiced, for sure, but it was not a book review.

NANCIE: Wow, you're really hot about this.

HELENA: It just made me so mad. That teacher ruined the book for her, and it's such a great book.

NANCIE: You've got a worthwhile point. The problem is, this is the wrong genre to make it. Readers of the blog are looking for information about *Fahrenheit 451* and insights into Bradbury's writing, to help them decide whether they want to read it. How informed do you think they'll be by this draft?

HELENA: Yeah, but it's what I'm feeling.

NANCIE: Yes, and there's another genre that'll do that, that'll let you express strong opinions and feelings. It's called an *essay*. We'll study it soon. You could write an essay about questionable methods for teaching novels if you still feel hot about the topic. Add the idea to your territories section, so you don't forget it.

HELENA: So, what should I do now?

NANCIE: Have you written off-the-page about the book?

HELENA: Not really.

NANCIE: That's how you'll be able to generate the particulars that readers of reviews crave. Grab a sheet of paper and a copy of the novel, and gather specifics about Bradbury's writing and your experience of it. Then start a second draft. I know you loved this book. Give it its due. Okay?

HELENA: Okay.

Helena's review of *Fahrenheit 451* is packed with relevant details about Bradbury's plot, style, and themes, many of which she generated in her notes off-the-page. She does mention her friend's experience of the book, but in the context now of how the richness of the writing requires a reader to go slow, but not that slow.

A FIREMAN WHO STARTS FIRES

Ray Bradbury's *Fahrenheit 451* follows a protagonist named Montag. Montag is a fireman, but not the kind who puts them out. In the world of this dystopian novel, Montag *starts* fires: if someone owns a book and is found out, the fire brigade is called, and his or her house is burned down. Books are forbidden. But when Montag's curiosity is aroused and he reads a book or two on his own, his life goes spinning out of control.

In only 179 pages, Bradbury packs in just about every appropriate metaphor and simile. That's one of the things I love about the novel. One of my favorite metaphors describes Montag looking at his wife's eyes: "Two moonstones looked up at him, in the light of his small handheld fire; two moonstones buried in a creek of clear water over which the life of the world ran, not touching them." I never would have thought of eyes looking the way Bradbury describes them, but it makes glorious sense as a description of beauty that is empty.

Although the metaphors are awesome, sometimes I had to go back and reread them. This is a book you can't skim; you have to take it slow and unpack it as you go. My friend read *Fahrenheit 451* in her ninth grade English class. They spent two months going over each page and finding all the hidden jewels—or, as Billy Collins might have put it, they beat the novel with a hose. This shows how much there is to unpack on each page, as well as how some English teachers can torture a great story.

Fahrenheit 451 is dystopian science fiction and moves at a pretty good pace: not so fast that it got ahead of me, and not so slow that I was bored. I did read it a little slower than most novels though, so I could take in the maximum imagery and meaning.

Speaking of meaning, this book has multiple themes. The first is not to take what we have for granted. In the world of *Fahrenheit 451*, the government has taken away the right to think for yourself. I learned that thinking for myself and freedom of speech are rights I should be grateful for and fight to keep.

Another theme is that, for those in power, books can be dangerous. They make people think. This means that there will always be those who want to ban certain books. We have to stand up for our right to read.

I rated this book a ten because I loved Bradbury's plot, his concept, and how Montag grew and developed. I especially loved the way it is written. Although it was a bit confusing at times, it was worth it. *Fahrenheit 451* is a surprising, moving, and amazing book that I will read again. It's a novel that you shouldn't leave this life without reading and thinking about.

By the way, 451 degrees Fahrenheit is the temperature at which paper burns.

—*Helena Solorzano*

• *A first-person genre isn't written in a first-person voice.*

Beware of an insufficient *I* presence, a *we* voice, or lots of passive sentences in pieces about kids' ideas and experiences. These writers are hiding. It's a risk to lay claim to one's *I*, but without it, a writer can't reflect, develop a theme, or involve a reader.

Samantha, a seventh grader, deposited a draft of a memoir in my rocking chair for me to eyeball overnight. When I did, I was knocked out by the humorous descriptions and sensory diction. It began:

> "It's the cops! Bike for it!"
>
> We skid to a stop, my front tire sliding precariously close to the edge of the asphalt, turn hectically around, and pedal like our lives depend on it, gasping hysterical giggles. The ranger is occupied with some speeding camper, but we are absolutely sure that once he's done with that, he'll turn into Joe Friday with a fast car and a gun. Then he'll make it his top priority to chase after Morganne, Josie, Eloise, and me, the little delinquents, and throw us in the pen for the heinous crime of biking without helmets. My heart hurls itself against my ribcage, caught up in the pretend terror.
>
> We make it to safety, screeching around hairpin turns and screaming for no reason other than making noise. We bark and make faces at the unfortunate people in the campsite next to ours, then sail into our little clan of tents. I jump off my bike, throw the poor, battered thing aside onto a patch of gravel, and dive into our tent, with the other three sprinting alongside me.
>
> We stay hunkered down for about ten minutes, during which we laugh raucously, hear the ranger drive by three times, and yell at Josie for staying outside the tent. ("But I was wearing my helmet!" "Josie, he *saw* you with us! Now he'll *know* that this is our campsite. Get in here before we *disown* you!") Soon we decide it's safe, mainly because we don't have the patience to hide any longer.

This is, technically, a fine piece of writing, but there is only one line on the first page—and, as it turned out, the entire first draft of the memoir—that describes Sam's thoughts and feelings. She is missing from her own story, a not uncommon occurrence among self-conscious seventh-grade girls. The next day we talked.

NANCIE: Sam, you're so funny and observant. You capture the telling details of what your gang of girls is like when you're together. And I love your diction, especially the verbs. In your Post-it to me, you wondered if they were sensory. Yes, indeed. You write prose like a poet.

SAM: Thanks. It's my first memoir.

NANCIE: I thought it might be. I started to read it with such pleasure. And then you lost me, or I lost you. Where are you in the story, Sam?

SAM: What do you mean?

NANCIE: We talked about the rule of thoughts and feelings—how personal reflections give readers someone to be with, stay with, see through the eyes of, feel through the heart of. Yours aren't here yet. Although I can tell this camping trip was fun, I can't tell why you're writing about it. Why are you?

SAM: I don't know . . . well, maybe because camping at Sea Wall's a tradition.

NANCIE: One you love?

SAM: Yeah.

NANCIE: Can you give readers that side of your experience—weave in your love of these girls, their families, and this tradition?

SAM: Um, how would I do it?

NANCIE: What I'd do is read the draft and put an asterisk at every point where I think a reader might wonder what I'm thinking and feeling. Then go back and start crafting thoughts and feelings around the asterisks. You've got this perfect bit of reflection to use as a jumping-off point: "My heart hurls itself against my ribcage, caught up in the pretend terror." I love that line—it put me inside you. Can you give your readers more of these, so we can *get* the Sea Wall experience, and you can develop your *so what?*

SAM: I could try.

She did, and she succeeded. Here's the conclusion to the final draft of Sam's memoir. It is rich with reflections, personal meaning, and theme.

> In the quiet darkness, the rest of the Hyperactive Insomniac Gang and I giggle, shush each other, and snort into our sleeping bags in pathetic attempts to muffle the noise we're making even now. I have the strange feeling that I'm in a dream, and I act as though I am. I slip out of the tent with Morganne into the frigid, pneumonia-inducing night and look up at the sky. I gaze in awe at the steady little pinpricks of light that are the stars, and I marvel at how clear the air is here, how easily I can see the constellations. We crane our necks back so far that we fall with muffled thumps onto our butts in the damp grass. I'm dizzily ecstatic at being alive.
>
> After a while my feet are so numb I can't ignore them, and we crawl back into our sleeping bags as dawn creeps up on the evergreens and dyes their tips pink as a practical joke. It colors in the tents, returns them to their normal yellows and greens, and bleaches out the sky so that it's no longer navy blue.
>
> The second-to-last of us succumbs to sleep, snoring in synchrony with the multi-colored lumps surrounding her. Then it's time for my last thought, before I surrender to the hectic world of my subconscious and the crazy dreams that lie in wait for me there. And it's this: if there's any meaning to life, other than the pursuit of happiness, other than living out my time to the fullest, making lasting impressions on people I'll never meet again and being a lunatic with my friends, then I don't want to live it.
>
> *—Samantha Herter*

• *The writing is cluttered.*

William Zinsser is my guru when it comes to strong diction and straightforward language. He observes, "Clutter is the disease of American writing. We are a society strangling in unnecessary words" (2006). Kids should learn that deletion and compression are also acts of revision.

Lilly, inspired by Jim Harrison's poem "Child Fears," decided to experiment with caesuras and describe what she was afraid of when she was a little girl. This is the draft I read when I perched alongside her chair and looked over her shoulder.

CHILDHOOD FEARS

Hairy spiders. Movies with gore. Growling grizzly bears.
Clowns with their ridiculous yet terrifying painted faces.
The dead of night. The dark hiding in my closet. Huge crowds of people.
Drowning in my dreams. Being smothered by my sheets. Lord Voldemort.
Bristly black hogs. Ferocious roosters. The edges of cliffs threatening to
  crumble.
The fact that when I wake up, I might be the only one here.

NANCIE: You were inspired by Jim Harrison?

LILLY: Yeah. I really liked that poem yesterday.

NANCIE: Lil, one of the things we noticed about Harrison's poem is how cut-to-the-bone it is. Do you remember, when we unpacked "Child Fears," how precise his nouns were?

LILLY: Yeah.

NANCIE: You've got some specific nouns here, but they get lost in the modifiers. Some of the modifiers are obvious—they're descriptions that don't add to the poem. They're *redundant*. Do you know what that means?

LILLY: Is that, like, saying something more than once?

NANCIE: Yes. Take a look at the line "Clowns with their ridiculous yet terrifying painted faces." Isn't it a given, in clown world, that they all have "ridiculous yet terrifying painted faces"?

LILLY: Yeah . . . so it could just be "clowns"?

NANCIE: Yes. What about "Huge crowds of people"? Isn't a crowd, by definition, huge, and isn't it made up of people?

LILLY: So just "crowds"?

NANCIE: Absolutely. You've got a powerful poem hiding inside these extra words. Can you have a go at the rest of it?

LILLY: I think so.

In her final draft of the poem, Lilly cut the clutter and rearranged her ideas—I'd taught a minilesson about alliteration, and she wanted to try some. This was another occasion when I was grateful my kids have access to computers. It was easy for Lilly to experiment with the form of her poem.

FEARS OF A SIX-YEAR-OLD

Grizzly bears. Gory movies. Ghosts.
The dead of night. Drowning in my dreams.
Clowns. Crowds. Cliff edges.
The dark hiding in my closet. Smothered by my sheets.
Spiders. Roosters. Black hogs.
Locked out of the house. Lakes on fire. Lord Voldemort.

Then when I wake up, I might be the only one here.

—*Lilly Richardson*

Eloise is another writer who needed help with clutter. In the draft below, notice how she piled on the modifiers, included every single detail of an event and her every reaction to it, and left nothing for readers to unpack.

EXPRESS YOUR INNER DOG

I drape my head out the Subaru window
and howl in a wolf-like manner,
my tongue flapping in the breeze.
I challenge the world with huge, innocent, puppy eyes.
I bark at each unsuspecting couple,
yap at every disgusted mother,
and ruff at each curious child.

The beautiful canine sound
that escapes my young lips is music to my ears,
accompanied by Catherine's happy giggle fits,
her chest heaving uncontrollably in laughter,
which causes me to chuckle
as I attempt another howl.
I pause mid howl to gaze at the silver car ahead,
loaded with another pack of yapping girls,
Sophia, Samantha, and Josie.
I can faintly hear their ruffs and growls
and laugh loudly at the trail of startled tourists
they leave behind them in their wake.

You will never get the chance
to relive this moment,
so live it as fully as you can.
I yap once more, curling my lip
and twitching my nose.
The sound bursts from my lips,

my last beautiful bark.
A couple holding hands
startles and questions me with their wide eyes.
I absorb their quizzical faces,
then roll up the car window.
I spot the other retired dogs
sink into their leather-like seats
a couple of yards ahead.

When we reach the campground
it seems too quiet,
so very still, so free of our disruptive yaps.
But the memory is engraved
in our minds.

Nothing matters to me except this one moment,
all of us together creating a scene
of ourselves,
barking like madwomen
and yapping like dogs.
I can imagine what our witnesses,
going about their daily business,
must be thinking.
But who cares?

Why shouldn't you bark at a stranger
you will never cross paths with again?
Why shouldn't you experience
the look of pure shock,
raised eyebrows, dropped jaws
of the victims of your growls?

Why shouldn't you raise
your imagined, whiskered snout
to the clear blue summer sky and howl?

I skimmed the draft and then turned to Eloise.

NANCIE: I think there's a funny, true poem inside this one that's fighting to get out. Should we set it free?

ELOISE: What do you mean?

NANCIE: One of the great things about writing poetry is the trick of doing more with less— of paring the language down so a reader has to work a little. Readers of poems *like* a challenge. And they like language that creates strong images. You've got some images here that are dying to burst forth. Let me show you what I mean.

Eloise: Okay.

Nancie: About the first two lines: *drape* is a sensory verb, but I don't know if you can drape your head—drape means to fall like a cloth does. And I'm concerned about "howl in a wolf-like manner." Weren't you, in fact, hanging your head out a car window and howling like a dog?

Eloise (laughing): Yeah. We all were.

Nancie: You girls. So why not just revise it as—may I write on your draft?

Eloise: Sure.

Nancie: How about: *I hang my head out the Subaru window and howl like a dog?*

Eloise: That sounds better. It's funnier. I like the three *h*'s.

Nancie: And it's more like the way people talk, right?

Eloise: Yeah.

Nancie: That's one challenge of free-verse poetry—to write as if you're someone who loves language, imagery, and sound effects *and* who's just talking *but* to a smart friend. Let's see what you can do with this. Here's your assignment, Ms. Eloise: cut the language and the story *to the bone*. Do you accept this mission?

Eloise (laughing): Yes.

Each Friday, the CTL newsletter to parents concludes with a poem. Most of these are by students. The following week, Eloise's "Express Your Inner Dog"—compressed, voiced, and cadenced—was appreciated by the whole school community.

Express Your Inner Dog

I hang my head out the Subaru window
and howl like a dog.
My tongue flapping in the breeze,
I challenge Bar Harbor with huge puppy eyes.
I bark at each unsuspecting couple,
yap at every disgusted mother,
ruff at each curious child.

The canine sound
that escapes my lips becomes a tune
to the accompaniment of Catherine's giggle fits.
Her chest heaves with laughter
before I let loose another howl.
The silver car ahead
is loaded with another pack
of yapping girlfriends:
Sophia, Samantha, and Josie.
I hear their ruffs and growls
and laugh at the trail

of startled tourists
they leave in their wake.

Nothing matters except this moment.
We are creating a scene
of ourselves.
We bark like madwomen
and yap like mutts.
And why not?

Why shouldn't I bark at a stranger
I will never cross paths with again?
Why shouldn't I experience
the expression of pure shock—
raised eyebrows, dropped jaws—
on the faces of the victims of my yowls?

Why shouldn't I raise
my imagined snout
to the clear blue sky
and howl?

      —Eloise Kelly

• *The writer addresses a broad topic.*

Think *pebbles* instead of *a pebble*. This is another way writers hide or stay on the sur-face—by writing about general topics like summer, a sport, kittens, or ice cream. The writing is flat. Clichés abound. The voice is often second-person—*when you play hockey, it's so much fun.* A reader can't enter the writing or care about the topic because it lacks a particular experience and a particular perception of a particular *thing.* This red flag shows up across genres—in a memoir about a summer camp, an essay about how war is wrong, a poem about the four seasons.

 Amelia decided to write a poem for her father as a gift for his birthday. Her first two drafts were lists of things they did together: it was pebbles about Dad. Since I'd just taught the class the Rule of Write About *a* Pebble, my meeting with Amelia presented an opportunity to reinforce it.

NANCIE: How's it coming?

AMELIA: Okay, I guess. My dad's birthday is next week. I'm trying to thank him in a poem, you know, for being a great dad.

NANCIE: May I read what you have so far?

AMELIA: Sure.

Nancie: It's a list, isn't it? These are sweet memories, but it's a handful of pebbles, instead of *the* pebble, the one that'll illuminate your relationship. Amelia, don't be afraid to choose one experience and let it stand for others. Can you pick one of these to flesh out and attach your thoughts and feelings to, to *show* what you and your dad are like?

Amelia: I don't know which one . . . Well, maybe when we took a walk one night, just the two of us?

Nancie: Go for it.

Amelia's final version of the birthday poem for her father is lovely. It captures the joy of time spent with her dad, and it's a gem of a pebble.

> HARVESTED
>
> No one to hear us,
> we pack the cavernous night
> with our voices—
> the breeze that ruffles the reeds
> carries our conversation
> across the moon-paled marsh.
> Odd spurts of song and laughter echo
> up the paved hill where tree shadows
> connect with ours
> to create kaleidoscopic designs
> on the asphalt.
>
> On the journey home
> we slip into comfortable silence,
> wade through the pool of rusty lamp light,
> and emerge under a star-studded sky.
> We tilt our faces
> to greet the winking points,
> as you and I breathe deep to harvest
> this moment with each other
> and the patterns etched above.
>
> *—Amelia Neilson*

• *The conclusion doesn't resonate or even conclude.*

A writer should leave a reader thinking or feeling something *on purpose*. I think the conclusion is the most important part of any piece of writing. Inexperienced writers' conclusions can be confusing, go on too long, drop off a cliff, or send a reader in the wrong direction. Students need to learn not to settle for the first ending that occurs to them and to experiment off-the-page until they find the one that conveys the tone and makes the meaning they intend.

Brian was working on his second poem of seventh grade. He and his family visited Niagara Falls over the summer, and he loved the *Maid of the Mist*, the tourist boat that travels behind the Falls.

MAID OF THE MIST

The white water crashes down all around,
tumbling from the cliffs that surround me.
Spray thrown into my face stings,
and the only smell is water.
The barrage of droplets *almost*
makes me look away.

To the side of the boat, seagulls are everywhere.
One swoops down and plucks a fish
out of the blue water.
In the mist a rainbow
casts its colors on the shifting white wall.
The voice on the loudspeaker blares, "This is Niagara Falls."

NANCIE: Oh, Brian. I know what it's like to ride the *Maid of the Mist*. You've captured it—the sights, sensations, even the smell of the water.

BRIAN: It was really fun.

NANCIE: Unforgettable, yes?

BRIAN: Yeah.

NANCIE: I'm wondering something as a reader. In the end, what did *you* make of the experience? I can feel you building toward a conclusion in which you'll tell us, but the poem ends with the tour guide's voice, not yours.

BRIAN: What do you mean?

NANCIE: I mean, *how do you feel* standing there on the deck of that boat?

BRIAN: It was awesome.

NANCIE: Well, there you go: *And I'm in awe.* Does that work?

BRIAN: Yeah. Thanks.

NANCIE: You're welcome. Next time, approach the conclusion as a separate step in your writing process. Think about how you want to leave your reader, and play off-the-page with options.

Wallace's first conclusion to his memoir didn't conclude the story; it stopped it cold. When I read this version of "Four-Legged Sister," I recognized in it a writer who got tired.

FOUR-LEGGED SISTER

My hands clutch the red rubber ring as I wave it in front of Hannah, my grandparents' yellow Lab. Her strong jaws grip the toy. Patrick starts counting: "One Mississippi, two Mississippi." Hannah thrashes her neck and bounds across the room, while I slip and bounce behind her, knuckles white from grasping the ring. I'm four years old and so is Hannah, my canine counterpart.

Then I'm seven, and Hannah is, too. The starched collar of my yellow shirt digs into my neck, and an aroma of creamed onions and the fifteen-pound roast my grandmother has been cooking for the past six hours wafts in the air.

"Hey, Wallace, can you pull the roast out?" my grandmother calls from the other room. Thousands of potential outcomes run through my head—all the ways I could mess this up—as I slip on the charred oven mitt, blackened from decades of use. I reach into the oven and pull out the pan. I set it on the counter to cool, sigh in relief, and wander to the porch, where Hannah is waiting patiently to be let in. I open the screen door, and she brushes me as she slips inside, leaving a nap of white hair on my khakis. I step onto the porch, into crisp November air.

When I hear a stifled scream from inside, I slam back through the screen door and rush to the kitchen, where my grandmother is staring blankly, her hand over her mouth, at Hannah, who is gnawing on her hours of labor. I watch as the Lab is dragged down into the basement, where she collapses in a heap under a photograph of her and me on our sixth birthday.

Hannah and I are ten. I open the door to bitter wind and biting cold. She tugs at her leash as a plow truck passes by. The loop slips my grip, and she bounds off through neighbors' yards and up onto their porches. I call her name over and over again. I can barely see her, almost invisible against the snow, darting onto the dark ski trail. I run to the driveway to get help and glance behind me to see Hannah trotting to catch up with me. Relieved I won't have to tell my family she ran off, I scratch her neck and open the door to the ever-inviting house.

At thirteen, I'm strong enough to lift Hannah into the trunk of the Volvo. Her legs splay on the beige rug, her head rests on a leg, and she lets out a deep sigh. A squirrel darts through what used to be her line of vision, but she doesn't move. The Hannah I grew up with would have leapt up and barked that squirrel down into its hole under the woodpile. Now her foggy eyes lazily rotate in the direction of the car. With every breath, her chest shakes and her tumors bulge.

A year later my bare feet stick to the wooden steps, weighted down by a fourteen-year-old Lab. My arms encircle her shaking torso and rattling throat. My hand is pressed against a tumor on her stomach; my arms feel two more. Her fur sticks to my shirt and tickles my neck. I set her down in the mudroom, clip on her red leash, and open the door to the bitter wind and biting cold.

A plow truck charges by, and I slip, fall on black ice, and let go of her leash without thinking. I get up instantly. Oh, no—she'll already be yards away. Instead she meanders over to a soft, fresh snow bank and lies down. I pick up the leash and walk inside. I'm not sure if I'm relieved or heartbroken.

Hannah died at age fifteen.

NANCIE: Wallace, this is stunning—visual, specific, and *moving*. The transitions are clear, and the reflections are so heartfelt. You don't have to say *I loved her*. It's here in every line.

WALLACE: Thanks.

NANCIE: You really worked hard on this.

WALLACE: Yeah. It's the most I ever polished a piece of writing.

NANCIE: I was wondering if it wore you out.

WALLACE: Why?

NANCIE: Because it doesn't conclude really—it just stops.

WALLACE: Well, I didn't know what to do, because she died. There wasn't anything more to tell.

NANCIE: I understand, but you still need to leave a reader feeling or thinking something. You need to find a way to give Hannah the dignity and the conclusion she deserves. Maybe consider the red rubber ring—what happened to it? Or is there a way to pull a thread through all the different memories of her? Please take some time to play off-the-page until you find the approach that will bring closure *and* celebrate Hannah. Okay?

WALLACE: Okay.

This is the conclusion that Wallace crafted:

Now the red rubber ring resides in a pen at the local animal shelter, along with all the other donated toys scattered among different cages for different dogs. Christmas roasts are set carelessly on the edge of counters. Screen doors are left wide open and unwatched—no need for the attention of the past. The trunk of the Volvo is teeming with crates of pecans as a fund-raiser for some society. Under the piano lies an empty bed. They say they're getting a new dog to fill it. They just don't want to forget the last one. Neither do I.

• *The writer can't get started, or the lead he or she has drafted isn't inviting.*

Students' leads suffer in predictable ways. Inexperienced writers pile background information up front and keep a reader waiting around for the story, poem, or opinion to begin. Or they omit information that's crucial for a reader to be able to enter the piece of writing and make sense of the topic. Or they provide irrelevant information. Or they convey the wrong tone. Or they don't give a sense of direction—or the appropriate direction—for the rest of the piece. These leads are the products of writers who settle for the first beginning they draft, instead of writing off-the-page until they find *the one* that will fuel the piece, or trying out the types of leads I showed them in minilessons.

When Nate decided to write a review of the Lady Gaga album *The Fame Monster: Deluxe Edition*, he began by making notes about pop music before Gaga, the techno and dance genres, his favorite songs on the CD, and her skills as a songwriter and singer. But he had a hard time starting the first draft.

NANCIE: What's happening?

NATE: I'm stuck.

NANCIE: What's the problem?

NATE: I can't figure out what to put first. I have all this stuff in my writing off-the-page, but what should I start with?

NANCIE: Have you looked at the CD reviews we read together last week? Get your prose folder, and let's look at how the professional reviewers began.

NATE: This one's got a quote from a song. I like that idea.

NANCIE: Is there a particular song, or a line from one, that conveys what you like about the album?

NATE: I'm not sure.

NANCIE: Check out her lyrics on the Internet, and write down all the lines that have possibilities. Then you can choose the one you want to work and play with. Okay?

NATE: Okay.

Nate found three Gaga lyrics that worked. He narrowed down to the one that worked best to set the tone he was after. He had already generated lots of data; he needed to experiment until he found the way in that would smooth his path and give the review a direction:

> "I do not accept anything less than something just as real, as fabulous," Lady Gaga belts out in her song "Papa Gangsta" from her twenty-song album, *The Fame Monster: Deluxe Version*. She definitely follows through on that pledge. The deluxe version includes eight fresh and fabulous songs—the *Monster* part of the album—plus all the songs you love from her debut album, *The Fame*. It is classic, inspirational, *real* and *fabulous* Lady Gaga.

Charlotte was starting a piece of advocacy journalism, with the goal of convincing younger students at CTL to award a grant to a nonprofit organization whose work she believed in. But her lead was a list of facts and place-names:

> Friends of Merrymeeting Bay is an organization that protects the bay and preserves the eco-system there. The Kennebec and Androscoggin Rivers flow into a fresh-water estuary that is bordered by Richmond, Dresden, Bowdoinham, Woolwich, Bath, Brunswick, and Topsham. That is Merrymeeting Bay.

When I read Charlotte's lead, I recognized its weakness, especially as the beginning of a piece of persuasive writing.

NANCIE: Charlotte, in the minilesson I taught about essay leads, I showed you examples of different kinds—anecdote, quotation, news, announcement, scenario, description. I think that's all of them. Which kind of lead is this?

CHARLOTTE: Uh. Um . . . none of them?

NANCIE: I agree. This is a who-what-where lead. It's not inviting. The point about the other kinds is they have the potential to invite a reader by setting a tone, establishing a voice, and getting to the point. Please put this lead aside and play with some alternatives. Do you have the essay lead examples I gave you?

CHARLOTTE: Yeah, they're in my prose folder.

NANCIE: Sit back and reread them. Then draft different ways in until you find the best one— the one that'll fuel the rest of the draft for you *and* get a voice and direction going, plus one that'll hook a reader. Okay?

CHARLOTTE: Okay.

NANCIE: Off you go.

The kind of lead Charlotte developed for her advocacy journalism is a scenario. The first and second graders of CTL were hooked by it and the essay that followed, and they voted to award one of CTL's small grants to Friends of Merrymeeting Bay.

It Starts with One Eel

Imagine you are a great eel, easily forty years old and thick as an adult's wrist. You start your once-in-a-lifetime trek from a fresh-water estuary in Richmond, Maine, to the Sargasso Sea, far off the coast of Florida. But first you have to find your way there without getting ripped up or killed in one of the hundreds of dams and turbines on the rivers of Maine. Luckily, Friends of Merrymeeting Bay (FOMB) is working their hardest to protect you and the other eels and fish who swim in these rivers.

FOMB protects eels and fish by persuading the owners of private dams to put up a simple sheet of metal with holes in it that allows water to go through, but not eels and fish. The sheet leads them to an alternate route, so they don't get killed. Doing this brings the death rate down from 95% to 0%.

That's only one thing Friends of Merrymeeting Bay does. They also protect the bay as a whole and preserve the ecosystems there. The Kennebec and Androscoggin Rivers flow into a fresh-water estuary that is bordered by Richmond, Dresden, Bowdoinham, Woolwich, Bath, Brunswick, and Topsham. That's Merrymeeting Bay.

FOMB tests the water for unwanted chemicals, finds out where they come from, and discovers how to fix it. For example, last year FOMB water tests found a concentration of tar. They tracked it down and found the plant that produced it. They found it created puddles of toxic waste that were leaking into Merrymeeting Bay. Representatives from FOMB talked to the company, and they soon cleaned up their facilities, saved the lives of fish, and made the water cleaner.

Another creature that Friends of Merrymeeting Bay is trying to save is the sturgeon, a prehistoric fish that is practically a living dinosaur. They can grow up to twenty feet long and have been living for millions of years. Friends of Merrymeeting Bay are putting screens over the turbines and undamming the rivers, so the sturgeon can go on its migratory path with no problem.

Most of FOMB's work is done by volunteers. Each year they organize Bay Days, educational trips that schools make once or twice a year. FOMB teaches kids about the eels, sturgeons, and ecosystems in the bay. They offer activities from archaeology to fish printing. This is a unique experience for students because they learn a lot, have fun, and become aware of the beauty and significance of the bay.

Friends of Merrymeeting Bay would use a grant from CTL to fund more testing of water and to support Bay Day. Since most schools today don't have money to spare, FOMB would pay for the cost of buses to transport three or four school groups to Bay Day.

So as you, that imaginary eel, successfully make your way down to the Sargasso Sea, you can thank Friends of Merrymeeting Bay for clean water, blocked-off turbines, and the once-in-a-lifetime trip that will start a new generation.

—*Charlotte Collins*

• *A reader can't make the movie.*

An effective story in any genre inspires imagery in the mind of a reader. Readers love to hear, feel, taste, and touch in our imaginations, but the essential information we want is visual. We crave ocular specifics—fresh descriptions of people, places, things, colors, shapes, and actions that we can picture in our mind's eye.

Tristan, a seventh grader, loved Saturday evenings, aka pizza-and-movie night at his house, but his first draft was bereft of the sensory details that would bring his Saturday nights to life. I couldn't see a thing.

> The fresh pizza is pulled
> out of the oven,
> and an aroma fills the room.
> I love these nights where
> the family gets together,
>
> and we eat pizza,
> and watch movies together
> as a family.

It's these Saturdays that I
witness our family weave
a bond as tight as rope

NANCIE: What are you up to?

TRISTAN: I just finished the first draft of my pizza poem. Wanna read it?

NANCIE: Okay. . . . You sure do love your Saturday nights.

TRISTAN: Yeah.

NANCIE: I'm thinking this could become a poem you'll read years from now and it'll bring back the memories of Saturday nights like a home movie. Tris, remember the lesson I did about making a movie?

TRISTAN: Yeah, I think so.

NANCIE: Well, can you help me make a movie in my mind? Right now, I can't see this. Like, are you pulling the pizza out of the oven?

TRISTAN: It's my mom. She always makes two pizzas, a square one and a round one. Her oven mitts are all burned from other pizza nights. I'm standing there watching her and waiting for her to tell me when to start the movie.

NANCIE: Okay, now I'm picturing your family sitting around the kitchen table, eating pizza, and watching a movie on a TV in the kitchen, like I have at my house.

TRISTAN: No, no—we watch down in the basement. I'm standing by the basement door, ready to run down and put in the Netflix movie. We have this cool, old couch down there.

NANCIE: These are the kinds of details that will make the poem visual for your readers and memorable for you. Your conclusion is strong. I like the simile—how it conveys your love of this ritual and your family. Can you bring the rest of the poem to life by closing your eyes and making a movie of its details?

TRISTAN: I could try.

He could. He did.

SATURDAY NIGHTS

I watch as
the round pizza and the square one
are pulled from the oven by Mom
with her charred mitts.

I charge down the stairs
to the basement,
where our green couch
and old 42" TV wait.

I insert the latest Netflix movie,
and when everybody is settled, I press *play*.

We are transported together
into the film.

It's these nights that I love—
when my family comes together,
and we
weave a bond

that's as tight as rope.

—*Tristan Geboskie*

Telling a writer who hasn't provided sufficient information what I picture in my mind, based on what's on the page, is a response technique I learned from Mary Ellen Giacobbe. It shows students that readers need specifics if a writer wants clarity. Tristan learned the lesson. His next poem, "Pieces of Life," is rich with visual information.

PIECES OF LIFE

I used to lay Lego men body parts
across the field,
along with smashed vehicles
with round yellow heads sticking out the windows.
A general in an orange running suit
surveyed the field with binoculars
from the future.
And Harry Potter and Indiana Jones
both held rifles,
instead of whips and wands,
while I moved civilians to lock their homes
with oversized keys,
wooden axes and clubs in hand,
ready to defend.

Now, vehicles and soldiers wait forever
on my blue bedroom shelf,
and glossy heads rest upon scarred bodies:
spectators
to my ever-changing life.

—*Tristan Geboskie*

• *The information in the draft isn't organized or logical.*

I can remember telling students in early writing conferences, "The information in this essay is all over the place—please organize it." I might as well have been speaking Greek.

If they'd known *how* to gather like information with like and create an order for it, they would have done it.

Now I know to show kids how to go back into a mess of information and untangle it. I ask them either to gather colored markers and annotate a draft, or take scissors to it: cut the draft into its separate sentences and then manipulate the information to join like with like. Abe's essay "The Lawn" began with a successful scenario-type lead:

> Imagine a beautiful, hot, sunny Saturday afternoon, when you could be swimming in a lake or at the beach. Maybe you would rather be reading a book in the shade. But instead you're cutting the grass with an old riding mower that spills noxious fumes into the air. Its roaring assaults your ears and heats up the already-baking air. Sweat is pouring down your face and into your eyes. Why give up every Saturday to mow the lawn, when growing a small field is better for the environment, wildlife, and your own health and peace of mind?

After his promising lead, Abe piled up arguments and evidence for letting a lawn go to seed. But there was no logic, structure, or paragraphing, just a solid block of non sequiturs. When we conferred, I asked him to consider the direction he'd promised in his lead—that "growing a small field is better for the environment, wildlife, and your own health." Then I asked him to grab four markers of different colors.

"Abe," I instructed, "please underline in red everything in your draft that's about damage to the environment. Use the blue marker to underline all the benefits to wildlife of not mowing. Use the green marker to highlight the dangers to humans, and the orange one on sentences about why we have lawns—and mow them—to begin with. Then your job is to revise by putting the red sentences together, the blue ones together, and so on: to match like information with like. If there's information that doesn't fit any of these categories, you need to consider whether it belongs in your essay."

Abe color-coded his draft and then, on the computer, moved sentences around to form coherent points. The next time we conferred, I told him, "Look at your four chunks now. Logically, which would a reader need first?"

Abe said, "The one about why we mow lawns in the first place?"

I agreed. "Where will you go from there?"

"To the environment, then wildlife, then people. Does that make sense?" he wondered.

"Try it and see what you think," I advised. "And remember that each chunk should be its own paragraph—its own unit of thought."

It worked. "The Lawn," Abe's first essay ever, was a success: evidence-rich, convincing, and logical in its organization.

- ***The writer has told a story in the conditional mood.***

This might seem like a small issue, but *would* is a large flag. The action it creates is conditional and vague rather than direct and palpable. "I would do this, and then I would do that" is a narrative perspective that's difficult to experience vicariously or envision. By recasting the verbs as either present or past tense, a writer can make the action vivid *and* create a context for including his or her reflections.

Heidi was working on a memoir about the Sundays she spent at her great-aunt Gertrude's house. She started the draft in a *would* mood:

> At the age of seven, I loved Aunt Gertrude's little house with the big tree in the back yard. Carolyn and I would climb up and down it and run into the kitchen with red noses, numb fingers, and, often, a scraped knee or elbow. Aunt Gertrude would make hot chocolate. Then she'd talk to Mom and Dad, and we would sip our steaming cups. It would always be the best hot chocolate.

I skimmed Heidi's lead and told her, "There's a word here that's getting in the way of my experiencing your story. It's *would*. I think I know why you're using it—because you're summarizing lots of different visits to your aunt's. But it prevents your story from coming to life because it's general. Plus, *would* makes it impossible for you to describe your thoughts and feelings: it's awkward to saw how you *would* feel. Does this make sense?"

Heidi agreed. I followed up with, "So, now your choice is tense—past or present? Which do you think you want to use here?"

Heidi said, "I think past, because I want to flash forward to the present at the end," which she did. Heidi's final version of her memoir is rich with descriptions of images, actions, and reactions.

LITTLE OLD LADY

> I remember the beds in my room were pushed together and I was almost asleep, stretched across their middles, when my mom slipped in. I squinted through the light and saw the tears that welled in her eyes. She bent over me and whispered, "Aunt Gertrude died."
>
> I'm not sure if those were her exact words or what she said after. All I remember is watching her lips move and thinking—nothing. My brain had gone blank, but soon tears were stinging my eyes, too. Great-Aunt Gertrude was my first relative to die. I should have seen it coming.
>
> At the age of seven I loved Aunt Gertrude's little house with the big tree in the backyard. Carolyn and I climbed up and down it and ran into the kitchen with red noses, numb fingers, and, often, a scraped knee or elbow. Aunt Gertrude made us hot chocolate, and then talked to Mom and Dad as we sipped from our steaming cups. It was the best hot chocolate.

I remember she asked me questions: "How old are you now?" and "What's your favorite subject in school?" I felt important as I jibber-jabbered about what I wanted to be when I grew up and described the dramas of second-grade life. I told her about swim team and our animals. She listened and watched as I explained with the enthusiasm that little kids feel when they know they have a good audience.

Then she led Carolyn and me into her sewing room, with Mom and Dad trailing behind. She showed us a dancing Elmo doll that I thought was cool and wished I could have. He and I danced together. After, we sat and talked some more, and Aunt Gertrude asked me, "How old are you now?" and "What's your favorite subject in school?" I was puzzled, but I answered her all over again. I assumed it was just a mistake, because everyone makes mistakes—we learned that in kindergarten.

One Sunday, on the car ride home, I asked my parents why Aunt Gertrude asked the same questions over and over. I realize now how hard a question that was for them to answer. How do you tell a seven-year-old that her aunt has Alzheimer's disease? I remember that Carolyn, three years older than I, looked out the window and wouldn't meet my eye. My parents evaded the question by asking new ones—questions that took my mind off my troubled aunt.

And I remember her funeral. It was the sixteenth of December—my eleventh birthday. It's the only birthday when I cried, and I mean *cried*, not just a few selfish tears because I didn't get something I wanted. I sat in the front row. Hot tears wanted to run down my chilled cheeks, but I wouldn't let them, not yet. At the cemetery, after I threw a handful of soil on the grave, a lady I didn't know gave me a beautiful purple flower.

It wasn't until I was in the car, riding away from the cemetery, that I let the tears flow. I crushed the purple flower in my dirty hands, and I thought about her and me dancing and about the big tree and the sweet, sweet hot chocolate and the rugs she made and the funny smells in her house and the way she asked me questions and wanted to be a part of my life. I let the tears cascade and sobbed, my head pressed against the cold glass of the window. Everyone—Mom, Carolyn, Dad—had tears staining their cheeks, too.

In the will I was mentioned, along with Carolyn, Mom, Grandpa, and others. She left me many things, but the one that mattered was Elmo. I know that even through the darkness of her disease she *remembered* the way I danced around her old house. And she remembered the way I talked about school, my enthusiasm as I babbled on about what I wanted to be when I grew up. Aunt Gertrude left me the money that my parents are using to pay my tuition to a better school. I think she'd be happy to know that she helped me venture a step closer to my goals. But I think she'd be happiest to know how she taught me to dream big, accept loss, and remember.

—*Heidi Ziegra*

- **The writer is stuck for a topic.**

I'm using the adjective *stuck* rather than *blocked* because the latter implies a persistent condition, not a particular problem a particular writer is experiencing on a particular day. When a writer is flummoxed, the solution I suggest most often is to write off-the-page.

When I approached Natalie during a March writing workshop, she had been paging through the territories section of her handbook for a good fifteen minutes.

NANCIE: What's up?

NATALIE: I finished my review—I put it in the editing tray—and now I want to write a poem.

NANCIE: Do you know what about?

NATALIE: No. I've got so many pages of ideas here, it's kind of overwhelming. I'm having trouble choosing.

NANCIE: I'd be overwhelmed, too. It's a lot. Here's what I'd do if I were you. Grab a sheet of paper for writing off-the-page, skim the whole territories section with a pencil in your hand, and record every idea that seems attractive, that feels like a possibility for today. Try this, okay? In the end, you'll probably be selecting from six or eight high-quality ideas, instead of trying to navigate a gazillion topics.

Figure 6.1 shows Natalie's writing off-the-page. The star indicates the topic she chose: a memory from when she was five, when she wore her mom's sunglasses and viewed the world from a grown-up's perspective.

List of Possible Poetry Ideas 3-2

- a snapshot poem —scoring my first goal in soccer
⭐ • An early childhood memory— putting my mother's sunglasses on
- A pet poem— my hamster?
- Boating for the first time
- Hershey's factory
- The tornado
- Colorado zoo
- mom's roses—the fragrance, images, softness

Figure 6.1 *Natalie's Writing off-the-Page to Select a Topic*

Brian, a writer in Natalie's class, got stuck often. When I sat next to him one morning, he was staring at a blank computer screen with his fingers resting on the keyboard. As I'd been circulating the room, I'd noticed him out of the corner of my eye. He'd been frozen in this position for a while.

NANCIE: Brian, how can I help you today?

BRIAN: I'm trying to start a new micro fiction, but I can't come up with a good idea.

NANCIE: Have you tried writing off-the-page?

BRIAN: No—I forgot about that.

NANCIE: I'm happy to remind you again. At some point, though, writing off-the-page needs to become the jack in your writer's toolbox, the technique you remember to use to lift yourself up when you get stuck. Right now, pull up a chair at an empty table and start playing around with ideas. Think on paper—it's much more productive than thinking in air, because you can capture and *see* your thinking. Plus what's on the page will inspire new thoughts. Okay?

BRIAN: Okay.

That's what happened to Brian. His writing off-the-page (Figure 6.2) led him to a short short story that his class read and unpacked with appreciation and laughter.

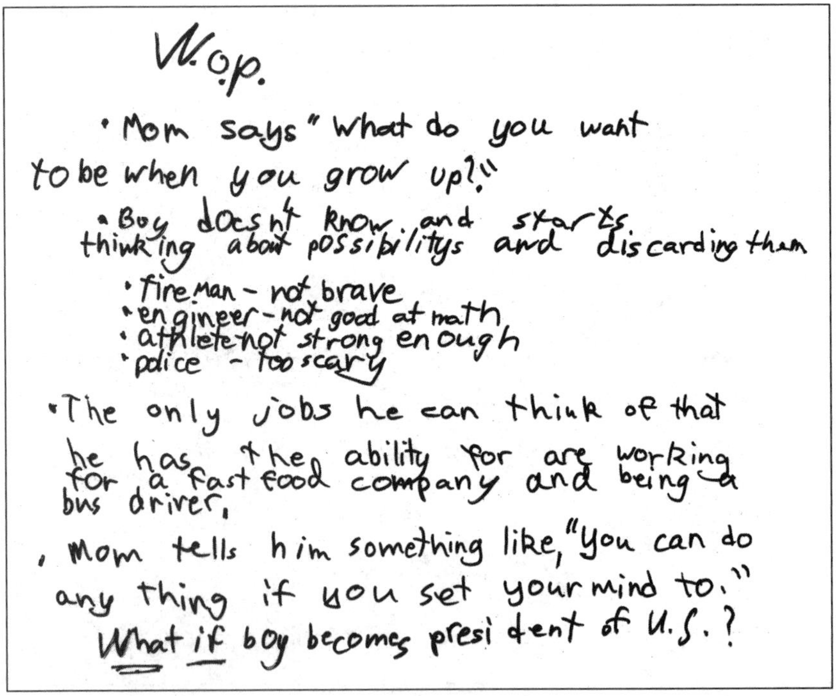

Figure 6.2 *Brian's Writing off-the-Page to Get Unstuck*

P.O.T.U.S.

"What do you want to be when you grow up, Barry?" Mom asked me, as we were sitting on the couch watching television.

I didn't know. I wasn't strong enough to be an athlete, not skilled enough to be a musician, not brave enough to be a fireman or a police officer. "The only thing that I can do is work at a fast food restaurant," I decided. "I'm not good enough to do anything else."

"Don't worry about that: you're only in third grade," she responded. "If you work and study, you can do anything you want to."

I realized that she was right. I was young and had many more years of school to get ready for my grown-up life.

Now, looking out over my rose garden and my wife's vegetable garden, I appreciate my mother's faith in me.

—*Brian McGrath*

When students get stuck after they've started drafting, I urge them to go off-the-page to generate possibilities for what might come next. When they're stuck for a lead, a conclusion, the right word, or a title, I nudge them to experiment off-the-page. I don't believe in writer's block. I put my faith in the power of writing to generate writing.

Finally, a stuck writer in a workshop who tells the teacher, "I'm sitting here staring into space because I don't have anything to write about" needs to be reminded that he or she has a handbook with a territories section that's filled with ideas for poems and, eventually, memoirs, reviews, essays, parodies, and short short fiction.

• *The draft is unintelligible.*

I'm referring here to a lack of sense, not problems with legibility, spelling, or usage. Sometimes writers have an idea of what they want to say but haven't represented it on the page and don't yet have a developed enough sense of audience to consider a draft from the perspective of an *other*.

These writers need to learn that readers expect sense—that we need to be able to understand a piece without a Q and A session with the writer. And they need ways to separate themselves from their drafts and read themselves over their own shoulders.

Gabrielle made room for me at her table and said, "I've written a poem about how it's starting to feel like spring."

"Let me see," I replied.

Just Spring

One eyelash bats me.
Brown wheels skim,
as I notice my reflection, jumping from each car.

Brown hair wipes green Subaru
and pinned against tan ears.
A red short-sleeve shirt flaps in the sunlight.

A smile
curls on my face, *Hey look—*
the ice has melted!

Inside I sighed. I'd read similar first drafts by Gabby—poems and prose I couldn't understand. I began my response by reminding her of a strategy I'd given her. "So, did you read this one aloud to yourself out in the stairwell?" I asked.

GABBY: Oops. No, not yet.

NANCIE: You've got to start there, Gabs: begin by catching the missing words and sense. You'll *hear* it if you slow down and read your writing aloud. For instance, "Brown hair wipes green Subaru and pinned against tan ear" doesn't make sense yet. What did you mean to say?

GABBY: I'm riding in the Subaru with my head hanging out the window, and my hair's whipping the car.

NANCIE: *You're* in the car? I couldn't tell. I'm also trying to figure out "One eyelash bats me."

GABBY: They're my eyelashes on my left eye, batting my face from the wind.

NANCIE: Okay. And about "brown wheels"—do you mean the black tires of the Subaru?

GABBY: Yeah.

NANCIE: And the red shirt is what you're wearing?

GABBY: Yeah.

NANCIE: And are you jumping between cars? Or is your reflection jumping at you from other cars? Help! You're making me work too hard here. It's my job, so I'll grit my teeth and do it, but other readers won't tolerate this much confusion. They'll just give up. Please start a second draft, and this time give 20 percent of your attention to a pretend reader. What does he or she need to see and understand? Okay?

GABBY: Okay.

NANCIE: When you've finished a second draft, go out in the stairwell, read it softly aloud to yourself, and listen for sense and completeness.

GABBY: Okay.

NANCIE: Tell me what you're going to do now.

GABBY: I'm gonna write a second draft and pretend someone else is there reading it.

NANCIE: Yup. Someone who needs to understand the things that confused me. Then what?

GABBY: Then take it out in the hall and read it out loud.

NANCIE: And listen to it.

GABBY: And listen.

NANCIE: Off you go.

It took Gabrielle two more drafts to make sense. She also used the third draft to play with caesuras, a technique I'd taught the class when we read poems by William Stafford. This was by no means the last time she and I talked about omissions or I reminded her about reading aloud and listening to herself. Gabby needed my reader's eye and ear, and my patience as a teacher, in ways different from her peers. But she was worth it. Her voice, exuberance, and the images of this moment shine through in the final version.

> JUST SPRING
>
> My brown hair whips the green Subaru
> as I hang my head
> outside. My red shirt flaps in the sunlight.
>
> My left eyelashes bat against my cheek,
> hard. Black tires at sixty miles per hour
> fly. I notice my reflection in the opposite cars.
>
> A smile
> curls on my face. *Hey, look—*
> *the ice is melting!*
> —*Gabrielle Nuki*

• *The diction is weak.*

Diction means a writer's choice of words. Diction can make the difference between an okay piece of writing and one that reads as literature. My diction and style gurus are Donald Murray (2003), Ken Macrorie (1988), Strunk and White (1979), and William Zinsser (2006). They preach that good writing is sensory, lean, and straightforward. As a writer, I try to follow their advice when I draft, but especially when I revise. As a teacher, I point out diction problems during writing conferences and help kids solve them.

My students' issues with diction include unnecessary or redundant adverbs and adjectives, participles instead of sentences with actors, awkward repetitions, overwrought descriptions, quoted dialogue without contractions, and shifts in verb tense or pronoun case. Kids and I refer to these infelicities in their writing as *clunkiness*.

In this clunky stanza from a draft of a poem about a lizard, the sentence structure could use a bit of smoothing, but adverbs are the issue.

> He crawls slowly forward
> and snaps his jaws shut firmly
> on a harmless cricket
> and quickly darts away.

After I skimmed the draft, I told the writer, "I love your sensory verbs—*crawls, snaps*, and *darts*. They have the potential to create strong visual images for readers. What's getting in my way, though, are adverbs. They weaken your description of what should be straightforward action. For example, doesn't the verb *crawl* already connote slowness? Can someone snap his jaws any way but *shut firmly*? And the verb *dart* means a quick motion, right? These intense verbs don't need to be intensified. See what happens if you delete the adverbs." Without them, the clunky stanza became concise and sensory.

> He crawls forward,
> snaps his jaws
> on a harmless cricket,
> and darts away.

In another example of unnecessary modifiers, a memoirist wrote, "I am so giddy and ecstatic when I see the title of the book for tonight." When we conferred, I asked, "Do you need both *giddy* and *ecstatic*—don't they mean close to the same thing? Either adjective is strong. And neither needs to be propped up with *so*. Polish this sentence and see what happens." In her final draft, she wrote, "I am giddy when I see what book she's going to read to me tonight."

Participles loom large as diction issues. They're nonfinite verbs that function as adjectives. When students try to use them as the subjects of sentences, actors disappear and action turns vague. Here's an example, a lead from a draft of a memoir.

> Wading in the river, doubting I am going to just drift under that old, wooden, rickety bridge looking as if it's going to topple over me any second.

When I conferred with the writer, I said, "I'm trying to enter your story, but there's a *kind* of word that's keeping me at arm's length. *Participle* is its technical name. You can identify it by the *-ing* at the end: *wading, doubting, looking*. The problem with participles is they kidnap the actors of sentences and deprive readers of someone to be with. How could you revise the first sentence of your lead so it starts with you engaged in an action—with an *I*?"

She responded, "I wade into the river?"

"Exactly," I said. "Now I'm with you. What are you feeling?"

"Well, I'm scared."

"Why?"

"Because I'm supposed to swim under this bridge that looks as if it's going to fall down it's so old."

"*That's* to-the-point diction," I said. "Tell your story as an actor with a voice. Revise this by cutting the participles, and then whistle me back when you're done." Ten minutes later, I circled around to her table and read:

> As I wade into the river, I'm scared. I'm worried that I won't be able to swim under that rickety wooden bridge and come out alive on the other side. It looks as if it could topple over any second with me underneath it. But I took my brother's dare, so here I am.

A diction problem that takes a while for beginning writers to identify is close repetition. For a host of reasons I urge students to spend at least as much time reading their drafts as they do writing them; one is to slow down, listen to their diction, and hear the clunkiness of words repeated in close proximity. This paragraph from a draft of a student essay exemplifies the problem.

> Every town in Maine, by law, has to educate its children, K–12. The children have to be put through school. Arrowsic doesn't have a school. Because of the huge expense of building a school, Arrowsic probably never will. So, by Maine law, Arrowsic has to pay for our tuition to CTL and other schools.

When the writer and I conferred, I said, "Some words in this paragraph are grating on my eyes and ears because they're repeated so close together. Listen as I read the paragraph aloud and see if you can hear them." She did—*children, school, Arrowsic, Maine, law.*

I followed up, "There are a couple of ways to fix this when you revise. One is to replace a repeated word with a synonym—a word close to it in meaning. Or you could substitute a pronoun, like *it, he, she,* or *they.* Another is to delete the repeated word or phrase if your piece doesn't need it to make sense. Let's tackle your second use of *children.* What word could you substitute?"

"Students?" she suggested.

"Hmm. I'm not sure that's a synonym, because these children aren't students yet. What about the pronoun *they?*"

"That would work."

"Okay. I think your first two mentions of *school* work, because here they mean different things. What about the third? Read along with me, and see if a solution doesn't emerge: 'They have to be put through school. Arrowsic doesn't have a school. Because of the expense of building . . .'"

"One," the writer supplied.

"Great. Now read these three sentences aloud again, and see what you can do about the next *Arrowsic*. Then tackle *Maine* and *law*." The final version of her lead read:

> Every town in Maine, by law, has to educate its children, K–12; they have to be put through school. Arrowsic doesn't have a school. Because of the huge expense of building one, it probably never will. This means the town has to pay for our tuition to CTL and other state-certified schools.

Overwriting is another diction issue for young writers. They pile on descriptions, mix metaphors, and sacrifice sense to ornate vocabulary and imagery. I try not to crush creativity or discourage experiments with language, but part of my job as a writing teacher is to help them recognize when their diction doesn't convey their meaning.

For example, a draft of a memoir about watching a hockey game included the line "All tired lips raised in unison to join in for one last roar of the crowd." This is a bad sentence: it's *throats* that tire from being raised, not lips; the lips "join in" in redundant "unison"; and the *roar of the crowd* is a cliché. My conference question was "Can you put your draft aside and tell me what was happening at this point?"

The writer said, "We'd been yelling for two hours, so our voices were tired. But we all yelled one more time when they scored the goal."

"That's a description I can understand, compared with the sentence in your draft. When you revise it, try to be as direct as when you told me about it." His sentence became, "We were exhausted from yelling for two hours, but we raised our voices for one last roar when they scored the winning goal."

In another example of overwriting, in a draft about the first time he played a baseball game using his father's childhood glove, the writer included the line "The bright sunlight reflected off of my dad's bright, shiny, red, Chevy GMC pickup." I pointed out the close repetition of *bright* and the redundancy of the phrase *off of*, and then addressed the essential problem with this sentence: it diverts a reader's attention from the glove to the truck. The writer gave it too much space, although I understood why. This was one cool truck.

I ended our conference by saying, "I'll leave it to you. You can tighten the description of your dad's pickup. Or you can delete it and focus your reader's imagination on your subject, which is the legacy of the baseball glove. Maybe you'll write an ode to the truck someday?" That's what he did.

Stilted dialogue is another diction issue. When students write dialogue without contractions, sometimes it's because they're not confident about how to spell them, but most of the time it's because they're not listening to their drafts. When I notice an exchange like the one below, my conference approach, once again, is to read it aloud. "*Listen*," I tell the writer. "What strikes you when you hear this conversation?"

"I am waiting for Miles," he said.

"I think he is coming," I reply back.

"You do not know Miles," he said back to me.

When I read their dialogue to them, students hear the overformal clunkiness. I tell them, "English speakers use shorthand when we talk. We say *I'm, he's, don't, aren't, what's,* and *they've,* instead of *I am, he is, do not, are not, what is,* and *they have.* From now on, check your dialogue. Does it *sound like* regular people in conversation, using contractions like regular people do?"

The exchange of dialogue above illustrates another issue: problematic tag lines. Students need to learn *I say back, I reply back,* and *I tell to him* are unconventional and clunky. In addition, I'll point out that a line of dialogue like *We said, "That's not the way to play four-square"* is unrealistic unless all the people in a story have decided to speak chorally.

Another phrase I respond to in students' drafts is *I think to myself.* There is no other way to think. And I help them with such awkward constructions as *"I must be super-human," I thought* by teaching them how to describe personal reflections without quotation marks: *I thought I must be superhuman* or *I felt superhuman.*

Shifts in verb tense are a major diction issue in my workshop. In the clunky stanza below, the writer begins to tell a story in past tense and finishes in present; in addition, the subject of the poem, a squirrel, transforms from a *she* to an *it.*

> The squirrel
> glanced up and noticed me,
> so I kept really still
> and hoped she would keep eating
> the sunflower seed
> that I drop on the ground.
> It cautiously
> strolls toward me.

In a conference, I said, "A writer of a story has to make a choice: will I tell it as if it's happening now, using present tense verbs, *or* after it happened, in past? You need to orient your readers in time. When you jump around, we can't follow the thread of your story. So which tense do you think you'll settle on?" After she selected past tense, I addressed the flip in pronouns, which often happens in narratives that feature animals; she decided to call the squirrel an *it* throughout. In a follow-up conference, I reminded her of a recent minilesson about *-ly* words, or adverbs: "Is there any difference between *still* and *really still?* Also, please think about *cautiously strolls.* A *stroll* is a casual kind of walk. Can someone walk casually *and* cautiously at the same time? Check out your handbook thesaurus for *walk* and find a verb that creates a visual image of how the squirrel approached you that day." In the end, she said it *inched* toward her.

One of Carl's poems was about his frustrations as a poet. He worked hard on his free verse. He also learned he could count on me for help if a draft crashed and burned. According to Carl, in writing conferences with my kids, I get to be the Triple-A guy who shows up to save the day.

RESCUED

Do other poets draft their poems
without turning their brains inside out?
No time wasted trying to make that line fit,
this word work?
Is there someone out there
who can snap his fingers
and BAAM
it appears out of green smoke?
While I'm left
coughing in the clouds
with page upon page of leads,
searching
every crevice of my mind
for an idea,
one small hint
that will give my poem the fumes
to carry it over the next hill?
Until, as usual,

it stalls

and rolls back to where I started,
leaving me to push it back up again,
straining my creative back,
which already feels broken
by the onslaught of words?

When I finally
make it over the hill
to glimpse the paradise
of a finished poem,
I don't watch where I'm writing,
and my poem veers off the narrow road
and crashes into a tree.
So I scramble out of the mangled mess

and wait for the one person
who can tow me
and my hissing poem
home.

—Carl Johanson

Do I make mistakes or misjudgments in conferences? Yes. Most often they occur when I haven't understood a writer's intention or I've made a wrong assumption about the content. When this happens, I apologize, rewind, and start again.

When I suggested to Avery that he spell out that he and his father had built a model airplane out of a cardboard box, Avery refocused me on his draft: "There was no model airplane. That was the point." His poem was about an empty cardboard box to which he and his dad had brought their large imaginations. Okay, Avery. Sorry.

Morganne drafted a memoir about riding with her father in his truck. From time to time the italicized lyrics to John Lennon's "Imagine" interrupted the flow of the narrative. I assumed the song was playing on the radio and suggested she say so. "No," she replied. "It's a motif I'm using to develop the theme of the piece. We're mourning John Lennon together on what would have been his seventieth birthday. The memoir's about how my dad and I are dreamers, too." Okay, Morganne. Sorry.

My students mostly take my advice. They learn they can—mostly—trust it and use it to improve their writing. But I tell the group, "If I cross the line, you need to tell me." Another benefit of students developing their own topics and purposes as writers is the ability to describe and defend what they're attempting to do.

When I don't have a solution to suggest for a troubled draft, I say so and press *pause:* "Let's put this problem in the back of our brainpans and come back to it tomorrow." I can't count the number of times I've been standing under the shower or driving my car when a solution has come to me, making me delighted and excited about the next workshop and my next conversation with the writer.

Conversations with students about works-in-progress are a radical departure from what I used to do as an English teacher. It took me a while to get a handle on how to consult with young writers, but conferences *work*. They work for a lifetime of teaching writing. And their quality improves with experience. When I read, write, and keep in touch with each writer's intentions, I pay kids the ultimate compliment of sitting side by side with them and handing over what I've learned about how to compose a poem, a story, an essay, a life.

CHAPTER 7

RESPONDING TO READERS AND READING

For all the reading research we have financed, we are certain only that good readers pick their own way to literacy in the company of friends who encourage and sustain them and that . . . the enthusiasm of a trusted adult can make all the difference.

—MARGARET MEEK

Right from the start, the metaphor that informs my vision of reading workshop has been the dining room table around which my family, friends, and I talk about what we're reading. My goal is for students and me to describe, defend, delight in, analyze, criticize, and compare works of literature as the insightful, enthusiastic readers who sit around my table do.

If reading workshop is a dining room table, its legs are our conversations: the chats that occur off-the-clock about books we're reading, my daily check-ins with readers, and the every-three-week letter-essays kids exchange with classmates and me. Forming literary relationships grounds the reading workshop, gives it rigor, ensures that it's not a study hall, and helps kids develop and refine critical vocabulary, literary criteria, and knowledge of books, authors, and genres.

I work hard to become Meek's "trusted adult" in the lives of my students. I read young adult and transitional titles, and I booktalk the good ones. I learn about the tastes of individual readers and search for books that will satisfy and challenge them. I read reviews and spend every penny I and the school can afford on building an adequate, intriguing classroom library. And I talk, talk, talk with kids about books—at lunch, before and after class and school, in my car on field trips, and every day in reading workshop. I assume the most influential teacher identity of all—a passionate adult reader—so hand-over in reading workshop can be compelling and authentic.

Reading Check-Ins

As much as I love to talk about literature, I watch the length of minilessons and book-talks so readers can read and so I can teach them one at a time: bump them out of the zone and ask them to reflect just enough that I can monitor their progress, understandings, and level of satisfaction.

Check-ins take place wherever students are sprawled with their books during independent reading time. I travel among them with a pen, a pack of Post-it notes, the reading status-of-the-class surveys attached to a clipboard, and the padded stool I drag along with me now that my knees are shot.

I tape-recorded my check-ins with one class during a Monday reading workshop, to illustrate what can happen in our conversations besides me recording titles and page numbers. Notice how I ask readers questions, answer their questions, initial titles back in, monitor the classroom library, introduce literary terms, provide background information, and give advice.

NANCIE: Hi, Sam. You're still reading *Extremely Loud*. Where are you?

SAMANTHA: Page 167.

NANCIE: How's the writing?

SAMANTHA: It's really excellent. Foer does the experimental-type things you talked about, but, like you said, they aren't distracting because they fit with the main character, with the way his mind works.

NANCIE: What do you make of Oskar?

SAMANTHA: Does he have, like, autism?

NANCIE: Probably a mild form of it. It's called Asperger's syndrome. I love this character—he's so innocent and brave in the midst of that tragedy. But you also have to consider his reliability as a narrator. And the *ending*—we'll talk.

SAMANTHA: Okay.

NANCIE: Hi, Avery. How's *11/22/63* moving along?

AVERY: I'm on page 362. I am loving it.

NANCIE: How is it compared to the other King's?

AVERY: I can still tell it's King, but it's much better written than, like, *Christine*. Jake is *such* a great main character. He feels more complicated and real.

NANCIE: I thought so, too—so did the reviewers. How are your arms holding up?

AVERY: Okay. It helps that King wrote it in sections. I'm taking it, like, one section at a time.

NANCIE: Good plan. Hi, Em. What do you have today?

EMILY: *Bunheads.*

NANCIE: The one I bought for you. How's the writing?

EMILY: It's great. It's the best book I've ever read about ballet.

NANCIE: Wow. What page are you on?

EMILY: A hundred and forty-one.

NANCIE: You read all that in one night?

EMILY: I couldn't put it down. I love the main character and the way the author tells the truth about professional ballet. Most of the girls are anorexic.

NANCIE: That's so sad. Flack's a former ballerina, right? So the details ring true?

EMILY: Yeah.

NANCIE: What happened to *Divergent?*

EMILY: It's at home—I decided to read this one first.

NANCIE: I appreciate that you wanted to take both books home to interview them, but *Divergent* should have come back today. Josie's looking for it. Okay?

EMILY: Okay.

NANCIE: Please bring it in tomorrow. Hi, Bri. How's it going?

BRIAN: It's good. I like it.

NANCIE: As much as the first two?

BRIAN: I still think *Game of Thrones* was the best, maybe because it was my first one. But the plots are still complicated and pretty harsh.

NANCIE: A different fantasy world than Eddings', right?

BRIAN: Yeah. It's more realistic. More about medieval Europe.

NANCIE: Do you think you'll go on to the next one, or take a break?

BRIAN: Do we have it?

NANCIE: Not yet. Do you know the title?

BRIAN: Yeah, it's here on the back: *A Feast of Crows.*

NANCIE: Okay. I'm making a note to order it.

BRIAN: Thanks.

NANCIE: You're welcome. Can I see your page number?

BRIAN: It's 222.

NANCIE: Abe, what do you have?

ABE: It's a book of my mother's that I found, *The Master and Margarita.*

NANCIE: You're kidding—you're reading Bulgakov? Toby and I just saw a play about him. It was one of the National Theatre plays from London that they show at Lincoln Theater. It was about how he was censored and tormented by Stalin. I've never read this. How is it?

ABE: It's weird. The devil is visiting Moscow, and a novel the "Master" is writing about Pontius Pilate gets mixed up with Bulgakov's novel.

NANCIE: You're understanding it? Enjoying it?

ABE: I am.

NANCIE: You're amazing. First Homer, then *The Prince*, now this.

ABE: I still haven't been able to persuade anyone to read *The Prince.*

NANCIE: I'm afraid you may be an outlier on that one. What page are you on?

ABE: Seventy-one.

NANCIE: Hi, Gabby. Did you finish *Life of Pi*?

GABRIELLE: Yes. Will you sign it back in for me?

NANCIE: Sure. What did you rate it?

GABRIELLE: I gave it a bella.

NANCIE: You and I talked about how it was an allegory. In the end, who do you think Richard Parker was?

GABRIELLE: I thought he was God?

NANCIE: I did, too. So what do you make now of the first hundred pages—of what Patel was doing?

GABRIELLE: Well, when Pi was going to all the churches and trying all the different religions, was Patel showing how spiritual he was?

NANCIE: I think so. Because he was on a quest for God, he found Him. He was, literally, saved. Will you write a letter-essay about this one?

GABRIELLE: I think so. I'm still thinking about it.

NANCIE: What are you reading now?

GABRIELLE: *The Year of Secret Assignments.*

NANCIE: Now, there's a contrast. But it's a great y.a. title—one of my favorites. What do you think so far?

GABRIELLE: I'm just starting it—page 5.

NANCIE: I hope you like it. Hey, Catherine. How's *Dreamland*?

CATHERINE: I'm not sure. Okay, I guess.

NANCIE: Was this on your someday list?

CATHERINE: Yeah, after Morganne booktalked it.

NANCIE: Is it different from the other Dessen's you've read?

CATHERINE: Yeah. I don't like the main character as much. I can't be with her like I could the other girls.

NANCIE: Are you going to stick with it?

CATHERINE: For a while longer. I usually give a book fifty pages before I abandon it, so that's what I'm going to do.

NANCIE: What page are you on now?

CATHERINE: Thirty-seven.

NANCIE: Good luck.

CATHERINE: Thanks.

NANCIE: Xander, what do you think of *No Country for Old Men*?

XANDER: It's really action-packed. The lead is great—McCarthy jumps right in with the excitement.

Nancie: How are you doing with his stylistic choices?

Xander: You mean like how he doesn't use quotation marks? It's really confusing, actually.

Nancie: Hang in there. You may be surprised at how quickly you adapt to his style. It matches the rawness of the characters and the plot—he's doing this on purpose.

Xander: Okay. Oh, I'm on page 29.

Nancie: Thanks. Josie, I see you've jumped on the *Vera Dietz* bandwagon.

Josie: Sam and Eloise are making me read it so I can take a side about Charlie.

Nancie: Well, that's one reason to read it. It's also a great story with great themes. I know Sam's drawn to that bad boy Charlie, but I loved Vera and her father. How far in are you?

Josie: I just started it—page 7.

Nancie: I'll check with you tomorrow and see how you're liking it.

Josie: Okay.

Nancie: Nathaniel, I thought you started *Crackback*. Now you've got *Marching Powder*. What happened?

Nathaniel: I left my book at home. But I did read it last night.

Nancie: I believe you. But I don't want you starting another book. It's going to mess with your pleasure in both books—your whole experience of each one. There are at least a half dozen sports collections in the short story bookcase. Read a short story today—check out Chris Crutcher's collection—and bring your book to school tomorrow.

Nathaniel: Okay. Sorry.

Nancie: Helena, what do you think of *Glass Castle*?

Helena: Her parents are *evil*. All I can think of is how glad I am to not have parents like hers. They never should have had children.

Nancie: I agree. And yet Glass is so forgiving. Do you remember what *tone* is?

Helena: Yeah, it's like the author's attitude, right?

Nancie: Right. Glass' tone is never bitter, which moved me and made me respect the book, despite the horrors. She *used* the memoir to figure things out and develop some insight—get some perspective on her parents. I really admire that.

Helena: I hadn't thought about that. You're right. It's not like those Dave Pelzer books I read last year.

Nancie: His so-called memoirs of experiences that his siblings have no memory of?

Helena: Really?

Nancie: Yup. What page are you on?

Helena: A hundred and sixty-three. I read for four hours last night.

Nancie: Wow. You're amazing.

Helena: Thanks.

Nancie: Hey, Kate. How's *Persepolis*?

Kate: It's good. So, what genre is this?

NANCIE: Good question. I'd call it a graphic memoir.

KATE: So all of this really happened to her?

NANCIE: Yes. Can you imagine being a smart, ambitious girl growing up in Iran?

KATE: Is Iran still like that?

NANCIE: For girls and dissidents—intellectuals like her parents—yes.

KATE: Yikes.

NANCIE: Double yikes. The way you care about politics—can you imagine?

KATE: Never.

NANCIE: What page are you on?

KATE: Sixty.

NANCIE: Noelle, did you finish *Why We Broke Up*?

NOELLE: Yeah. It was great.

NANCIE: Where is it?

NOELLE: In my locker.

NANCIE: Please go get it after I finish checking in. And don't forget to enter it on your reading record.

NOELLE: Okay.

NANCIE: So, you're starting *It's Kind of a Funny Story*?

NOELLE: Yeah. Catherine recommended it.

NANCIE: Did she tell you it's a roman à clef?

NOELLE: I don't remember what that means.

NANCIE: It's fiction with a real-life basis. Craig's experiences are a version of Vizzini's. He spent five days in a psychiatric ward, when he was a freshman in a selective high school in New York City, because the academic pressure was making him feel suicidal. Despite what I just told you, it's a funny book. Did you read *Be More Chill*?

NOELLE: No, not yet. But it's on my someday list.

NANCIE: I hope you like this Vizzini. Now, go get *Why We Broke Up*, and I'll sign it back in on your card.

NOELLE: Okay.

NANCIE: Lilly, did you start *Fault in Our Stars* over the weekend?

LILLY: Yeah, I'm on page 99.

NANCIE: What do you think so far?

LILLY: You were right. It's a bella already. I love it.

NANCIE: Is it too soon to compare it to the other Green's?

LILLY: Like you said, it's so different. There's no mysterious, missing girl, which was getting really old. Hazel's the narrator and the main character. Her voice is so real—it's sad and funny.

NANCIE: Hazel and Augustus are my two favorite John Green characters ever, and *Fault* is my favorite Green. It's a story of a true love.

Lilly: I hope I don't cry.

Nancie: I think you're going to cry. It's okay to cry. Hi, Weezie. How's *Octavian*?

Eloise: It's great. It's nothing like the other Anderson's, but it's great.

Nancie: What genre would you call it?

Eloise: Historical fiction?

Nancie: For sure. You're the first person in your class who's stuck with it. I know it's about a kid, but is this a kid's book?

Eloise: It's a good question. It's not easy—it took me a while to get into it.

Nancie: What page are you on?

Eloise: A hundred and forty-two.

Nancie: I loved it. I think it's Anderson's masterpiece. It probably doesn't reach his core audience, but I'm so glad and proud it's reaching you.

Eloise: Thanks.

Nancie: You're welcome. Morganne, thanks for grabbing *Alice Bliss* after my booktalk. It got great reviews, but, like I said, I haven't had a chance to read it yet. If you like it, will you booktalk it?

Morganne: I'm only on page 17, but so far I do like it—I like her, Alice.

Nancie: Great. Hi, Wallace. How's *Johnny Got His Gun*?

Wallace: The style is strange—not like any book I've read.

Nancie: It's called *stream of consciousness*. Trumbo's creating a stream of all the thoughts and memories running through Joe's head as he lies there, unable to move, see, hear, or speak. What genre would you call it?

Wallace: It's definitely antiwar. Which war is it?

Nancie: Let's check the copyright page for the publication date.

Wallace: It says 1939 and then 1970.

Nancie: Well, the United States didn't join World War II until 1941, so what war do you think?

Wallace: World War I?

Nancie: Yup. In fact, its publication just before World War II really hurt it. It was so shocking and tragic that people about to fight another war wouldn't read it—they couldn't bear to, I suppose.

Wallace: Is that why there's so many years between the two dates?

Nancie: Uh-huh. That and the blacklist of the 1950s. Trumbo was blacklisted. But that's another story. So why 1970, do you suppose? What was happening that might have made an antiwar book relevant again?

Wallace: The Vietnam War?

Nancie: You've got it. Hey, Claire. How's *Me, Earl, and the Dying Girl*?

Claire: It's hysterical, like you said. I'm on page 201.

Nancie: If you were going to rate it now, what would you give it?

Claire: At least a 10.

Nancie: Do you think you'll booktalk it?

Claire: Yeah, I'd really like to.

Nancie: Great. It needs a kid reviewer. Sometimes what I think is funny doesn't jibe with what kids think is funny.

In one workshop, a class and I covered a range of literary topics:

- what students notice or might notice about an author's style
- how a book compares with others by an author
- the status of a book that should have been returned to the classroom library
- what a student plans to do next as a reader
- whether a reader is understanding a difficult book
- what a student understood about a book he or she finished
- whether a student should abandon a book he or she isn't enjoying
- why a student decided to read a book
- why a student shouldn't read two books at one time
- the structure of a book
- the genre of a book
- background information about a book or author
- what a main character is like
- at what pace a student is reading a book
- how to use the information on a copyright page
- whether a title is booktalk-worthy
- what the teacher knows, thinks, or has noticed about a book

In this particular reading workshop, some of the other issues that I address with kids didn't happen to arise:

- How did you choose this book—what was your process? What were your criteria?
- What problem or conflict has the author given the main character?
- Are you convinced by the main character? What's the character development like?
- What's the narrative voice? What do you think of that choice?
- Why are you still reading a book you say is only a 5?
- Can you skim the parts that drag?
- Can you just read the ending—find out what happens—and move on to a book you will enjoy?

- If you're liking this book/author, here's another book/author to add to your someday list, while I'm thinking of it and you.
- Why aren't you twenty pages ahead of yesterday—what happened last night?
- I see you're close to finishing this book. What do you plan to read next?

Students learn in my September check-ins not to synopsize plot. Our conversations aren't an oral book report or a test. Nor do I request them to speculate about the theme of a book until a student has finished it. Readers only know for sure about the ideas that will emerge from a story and its characters after the whole literary work has settled inside them. *Theme* becomes a significant topic in the letter-essays they write to me and one another.

The overarching purposes of a check-in are to monitor my students' experiences with books and offer help that sustains and enlarges them as readers. So I observe them, find out what they're noticing and thinking, unburden them, teach them, and share my own enthusiasms as a trusted, adult reader.

LETTER-ESSAYS ABOUT LITERATURE

In the 1980s, when I was teaching at Boothbay Elementary School, I was intrigued by research conducted by Jana Staton (1980) that described dialogues that Leslee Reed, a sixth-grade teacher, exchanged with her students—letters about students' lives written back and forth in bound journals. My interest was piqued because I knew that my students had more to say about their reading than time allowed for in my workshop check-ins, and because I'd learned by then what a rich mode for thinking writing could be. I wondered where written-down conversations about books might lead my students as readers and critics.

I gave each of my seventy-five kids a notebook with a personalized letter inside that invited them to write to me about their reading. I hoped that written dialogues would help them reflect on books more deeply, specifically, and analytically. Thirty years later, I am still corresponding with students about their reading—and still experimenting with the method, in search of the most productive and manageable version.

I recognize that, inspired by the first two editions of *In the Middle*, other teachers initiated literary correspondence, too, and at a cost. The paper load that results from written exchanges with every student every week is exhausting. At some point, out of exhaustion, I cut my paper load in half by asking kids to alternate the audience for their letters: three exchanges back and forth with me, then three back and forth with one classmate of their choosing.

This adaptation made my teaching life more manageable. More importantly, it cre-ated regular occasions for peers to become members of Meeks' "company of friends who encourage and sustain" one another as readers. But it didn't resolve another issue with the weekly letters: sometimes my students didn't have much to say about a book. They might have just started it, or they may have become so engrossed in a story that it was frustrating and unproductive to detach from the zone and try to consider an author's choices so far.

The best letters were written after a student had finished a book. These responses were longer and more engaged, referred with more specificity to the text and the author's choices, delved more into theme, and, in general, functioned more as literary—albeit still informal—criticism.

I went back to the drawing board. Literary correspondence in my reading workshop today takes the form of *letter-essays* that students write to me or a classmate every three weeks about a title they have finished reading. Although still conversational in tone, letter-essays have proved more demanding, more forgiving, and more valuable to my students than weekly correspondence.

Students' letter-essays fill at least three pages of a marble notebook. By looking back, choosing *the one* book of the past three weeks that they wish to criticize, and considering it at length, students engage as critics. Because writing about their thinking makes anyone think better, my students are more insightful than ever about literature—about recognizing authors' techniques and purposes. And because their high school and college English teachers will ask them to write critical responses in which they develop arguments based on textual evidence, the letter-essays provide a stronger bridge into what comes next for middle schoolers as students of literature.

By way of example, here's a letter-essay to me by seventh grader Brian about Joseph Heller's *Catch-22*, followed by my response. Notice how Brian rates the novel, considers its structure, has a go at its themes, includes a passage that illustrates something he observed about the writing, gives his opinion as to genre, and responds to Yossarian, the main character.

3/11

Dear Nancie,

I'm writing about *Catch-22* by Joseph Heller. I rated it a 10 out of 10 because I liked how it was written and the plot.

It was sort of confusing how sometimes the timeline jumped around, like at one point in the book, Yossarian was lying in bed, then the next paragraph he's flying a bombing mission with just about no transition, but whenever that happened I just re-read the part.

I think the themes of *Catch-22* are about the power of bureaucrats like Colonel Cathcart, because of the fact that someone who only flew a few missions is making a whole squadron put their lives in danger 80 times, for his credit and the law Catch-22. Another big theme I thought was the uselessness, or lack, of communication. Several times people are either talking about different things, or have no idea what they're talking about, like when the chaplain is getting interrogated to figure out what, if any, crime he has committed. Here's an excerpt showing one of these times when everyone is talking but nobody is listening.

> "Well, Metcalf, suppose you try keeping that stupid mouth of yours shut and maybe that's the way you'll learn how. Now, where were we? Read me back the last line."
>
> "'Read me back the last line,'" read back the corporal who could take shorthand.
>
> "Not my last line, stupid!" the colonel shouted. "Somebody else's."
>
> "'Read me back the last line,'" read back the corporal.
>
> "That's my last line again!" shrieked the colonel, turning purple with anger.
>
> "Oh, no, sir," corrected the corporal. "That's my last line. I read it to you just a moment ago. Don't you remember, sir? It was only a moment ago."
>
> "Oh, my God! Read me back his last line, stupid. Say, what the hell's your name, anyway?"
>
> "Popinjay, sir."
>
> "Well, you're next, Popinjay. As soon as this trial ends, your trial begins. Get it?" (p. 79)

Heller is showing how insane the military can be.

I like how even though World War II is a grim subject, Heller makes *Catch-22* pretty funny in some spots. It is dark humor, so that would make it easier.

The genre is historical fiction I think, because it's set in World War II, and it is sort of realistic.

I think Yossarian is a great character because he's realistic and I can easily relate to him, the only "sane" person, surrounded by a lot of complete lunatics. I also liked how everything he did was so thought out.

Sincerely,
Brian

3/13

Dear Bri,

I'm not sure how to categorize *Catch-22:* as a war story? Black humor? The novel is based on Heller's own experience in WWII—he is, at some level, Yossarian. Heller was a bombardier. It's an *anti*-war story, for sure. I don't think anyone could read it and emerge with respect for the military.

Yossarian functions as an *antihero*: a protagonist who lacks the more traditional heroic virtues, who's some combination of inept, cowardly, or dishonest, but also a good guy. There's the realism you mentioned.

For my money, Yossarian is a perfect antihero. I adore him.
Thanks for a solid letter-essay.

Love,
Nancie

P.S. Heller says the original title was *Catch-14*. It doesn't have quite the same ring, does it?

In my response, I speculate about the genre of the book, introduce the concept of an antihero protagonist, share some literary gossip, and let Brian know he did a fair job of thinking critically about *Catch-22*.

When I asked students to move with me to this new genre, I planned three modes of handover. I wrote a letter-essay of my own that demonstrated what I had in mind; another letter to each reader that specified format and content; and a list of paragraph openers that invited students to think and respond as critics. My letter-essay was in reaction to the young-adult novel *Stupid Fast* by Geoff Herbach. Figure 7.1 shows the writing off-the-page I did prior to composing it: an essential first step when a critic wants to write with information.

9/15

Dear Gang of Readers,

I read *Stupid Fast* by Geoff Herbach on Saturday morning—got up early, hours before Toby and Rosie, and inhaled it. It's a 10 for sure: funny, heartbreaking, and *hopeful*. I loved it and Felton Reinstein, Herbach's main character.

Felton is fifteen and lives with his hippie mother, Jerri, and younger brother, Andrew, in a college town in rural Wisconsin. His father, who taught at the college, committed suicide ten years before; it was Felton who discovered the body. The setting feels real, especially the divisions at the high school between the townies, who Felton and his friend Gus call *honkies*, and the faculty brats—nerds and creative types like Felton, Gus, and Andrew—whom the locals persecute.

Things change when Felton experiences an extreme version of puberty. Suddenly he's way bigger and so athletic he vibrates. All he wants to do is run. Herbach shows the transformation so vividly I could practically feel the testosterone coursing through Felton.

In this excerpt, the high school football coach has just recruited Felton and taken his measurements. Felton's alarmed to learn that he's six-one and weighs 168 pounds.

How did I grow so much? Am I driving Jerri crazy by eating everything? Maybe Jerri really needs my paper route money? I probably ate ten thousand pounds of food in the last year. Oh my God. We're running out of money and that's why Jerri is so stressed out and has to go to a therapist and is crazy and calls

W.O.P.

Stupid Fast by Geoff Herbach (10)

CRF but also a mystery

About sports, family, family secrets and discoveries, puberty and growing up, friendship, h.s. insiders and outsiders, and first love

Squirrel Nuts + honkies

Felton = great male protagonist — funny (amazing T+F), sincere, endearing, well-meaning, lots of layers/complicated — a real boy → Supporting char. all rich + believable, too, except Jerri

Setting = college town in Wisconsin — townies/locals (honkies) vs. faculty brats/nerds/creative types

Inhaled it on a long Sat. a.m.

Funny dialogue — reveals people + relationships + absurdities of adolescence

Excerpt — p. 79? 111?

I understood why he needs to run — cd. feel the testosterone coursing through him

Why does F. have no mem. of what he looked like? And why does F. ... (Why does J. lie to boys about what Dad looked like?)

Thought of Sherman Alexie (Absolutely True...), Pete Hautman (Godless), and Gordon Korman (Schooled) — that kind of memorable, likable boy

BUT holes in plot strain credibility, esp. regarding F.'s father, who took own life when F. was 5 (F. found him hanging in garage). Nat'l tennis champ and academic? Suicidal and mean cheater? Plus what do they live on? How does Jerri support F. + Andrew?

Figure 7.1 *Nancie's Writing off-the-Page for a Letter-Essay*

me the f-bomber. I am eating Jerri and Andrew out of house and home! I ate that bagel! I ate an extra bagel! Oh, Jesus, I'm eating my family! Oh, my God!

Coach Johnson talked, and Cody talked, and I spun out in my brain, and Ken Johnson shook his head, and then Cody motioned for me to follow him, which, thankfully, I did.

As we climbed the stairs to the weights, Cody said, "See, I thought you were big, Reinstein."

"I don't feel big, man."

"You gotta start carrying yourself like you're that big. Really, Reinstein. Nobody will ever mess with you again."

"Nobody messes with me now."

"Are you kidding me? Everybody does. I used to, and I don't mess with anybody because I think messing with people is dumb."

"Really? You messed with me?" Duh. I knew that. People messed with me all the time, and I hated them for it. (pp. 79–80)

The excerpt shows how Herbach balances Felton's crazed but honest thoughts with dialogue that reveals characters and their relationships. Herbach is fair to all his characters, including jocks like Cody.

But it's Felton who readers live inside of, and it's a great place to be. He's a terrific male protagonist: sincere, manic, self-aware, observant, funny, awkward, and *complicated*. As I read *Stupid Fast*, I thought of boy main characters of other novels I love—Alexie's *Absolutely True Story of a Part-Time Indian*, Korman's *Schooled*, and Pete Hautman's *Godless*. Felton's personality and voice—the narrative is first-person—ring true and compelling in the same way.

Although technically contemporary realistic fiction, *Stupid Fast* is also a mystery. When Jerri bottoms out—withdraws to her bedroom and abandons her sons—Felton and Andrew try to carry on without her and solve the puzzle of Jerri and their father. This is where I lost some of my confidence in Herbach. The holes in this part of the plot strain credibility.

But I was willing to put aside my misgivings about plausibility because of Felton and the themes of the novel. *Stupid Fast* is about the pleasure and power of sports. It's also about family, sibling rivalry, secrets, truth, puberty, identity, friendship, insiders and outsiders, and first love. I haven't mentioned Aleah, Felton's first love, who happens to be African American, a fact that Herbach mentions in passing and no one makes a big deal of, which is another reason to appreciate this novel.

I think both boys and girls will like *Stupid Fast*. Herbach writes in the author's note that he grew up in Platteville, Wisconsin, where he was "both a dork and a jock." That's the perspective he writes from and, because of Felton's humanity, I think *Stupid Fast* will appeal to the dork or jock in everyone.

Love,
Nancie

In my letter-essay, I rated the novel, summarized the problem the main character is facing, compared the author to others, told about the narrative voice and genre, selected an excerpt that provided evidence for my opinion about the development of the main character, appreciated the dialogue, analyzed—and criticized—plot and character development, and described the themes that emerge from the narrative. I wrote in a casual, first-person voice in the form of a friendly letter, one draft only.

My second invitation to students to become critics was a letter I wrote to each of them, personalized on the computer, which I asked kids to glue to the inside of the front cover of their marble notebooks. It defines the letter-essay genre and spells out the requirements.

9/5

Dear _____ ,

Your critic's notebook is a place for you, me, and your friends to consider books, authors, and writing. You'll think about books in informal essays directed to me and classmates, and we'll write back to you about your ideas and observations. Your letter-essays and our responses will become a record of the reading, critiquing, learning, and teaching we accomplished together.

Each of your letter-essays should be at least three pages long and written in response to *one book*—in other words, not a series of paragraphs about a series of books, but a long look at one title that intrigued you. You should write a letter-essay to me or a friend in your own notebook every three weeks, due on Thursday mornings. We'll correspond in cycles: you'll write two letter-essays to me, then two to one friend of your choosing, then two to me again.

Before you write a letter-essay, look back over your reading record. Which title that you've finished would be enjoyable to revisit as a fan? What book you abandoned—or remained hopeful about to the bitter end—would be interesting to revisit in a slam? Once you've decided, return to the book, skim it to refresh your memory, write off-the-page about it, and select at least one passage that you think is significant, in terms of the theme, character development, or author's style: a chunk of text you think *shows something essential* about how the book is written. Hand copy or photocopy the passage you chose, include it in your letter-essay, and explain what it shows about the writing and your response to it.

What else might you do in a letter-essay? Describe what you noticed about how the author wrote. Tell about your experience as a reader of the book. Offer your opinions and pose your questions about the author, characters, plot structure, details, and voice. Definitely try the paragraph openers to fuel your thinking and writing. And *always* tell what you think the theme or *so what?* of a book is.

Once you've written your letter-essay, hand deliver your critic's notebook to your correspondent. If that's me, put it in my rocking chair on Thursday morning. When a friend gives you his or her notebook, you should answer in at least paragraph length by Monday morning. After you've written back, hand deliver your friend's notebook—don't put it in his or her locker or backpack. You may not lose or damage another's notebook.

Date your letter-essays in the upper right-hand corner, and use a conventional greeting (*Dear* _____ *,*) and closing (*Love, Your friend, Sincerely*). Always cite the name of the author and the book title in the first paragraph. Indicate the title by capitalizing and underlining it, e.g., <u>The Outsiders</u> by S. E. Hinton.

I'm already looking forward to reading and thinking about literature with you in this serious-but-friendly way. I can't wait for your first letter-essay and a year of chances to learn from you, learn with you, and help you learn more about the power and pleasures of books.

Love,
Nancie

As the final act of handover, I created potential paragraph openers for the letter-essays, and students glued these inside the back cover of their critic's notebooks.

WRITING ABOUT READING: Some Openers

I was surprised when / angry about / moved by / amused at / confused when

I liked/didn't like the way the author

I admired

I noticed how the author

I don't get why the author

I wondered why

If I were the author, I would have

Compared with this author's other books,

This author's writing reminded me of

I thought the title was

I thought the lead was

I thought the main character's problem

I thought the main character's thoughts and feelings

I thought the character development

I thought the author's choice of narrative voice

The visual details and other descriptions

The dialogue

I thought the setting

The structure of the plot

The climax of the plot

I thought the way the author resolved the main character's problem

I thought the ending was

The genre of this book is

I wish that the author

I agreed with / didn't agree with how the author

I was satisfied/dissatisfied with how the author

This is how I read this book

Next time I read a book like this, I'll

I rated this one _____ because

AND ALWAYS: I was struck / impressed / convinced / intrigued by this passage. It shows . . . about the writing. (INSERT A SIGNIFICANT EXCERPT FROM THE BOOK AND ITS PAGE NUMBER)

My students preferred letter-essays to the briefer, weekly correspondence I'd been assigning. When I surveyed the eighth graders, who had experienced both approaches, they said they liked writing in-depth about a whole book. It was also more satisfying to choose the one title they wanted to write about. They noticed and thought more about the author's writing and themes, responded more as critics than readers, and appreciated that these were still letters—that friends and I would read and respond to them.

Letter-essays are rich, interesting to read, and easier for me to reply to than weekly correspondence because there's more literary meat to them. When I write back, I affirm students' insights or challenge them, offer my opinions, make suggestions and recommendations, float theories, provide information, compliment their ideas or observations, and, when necessary, give pointers for the next letter-essay.

Cole entered our school as a seventh grader. He wrote his second letter-essay about his disappointment with *Mockingjay* by Suzanne Collins.

Oct. 13

Dear Nancie,

I finished *Mockingjay* by Suzanne Collins. I rated it a 7 out of 10 because it wasn't deserving enough to be the final volume to such a trilogy as the one that started with *The Hunger Games*.

I think the big reason that I wasn't too fond of this book is that the two books that came before it, mostly the first, were action-packed from start to finish. The big thing is that for the most part, in *Mockingjay*, for a good amount of the book, Katniss isn't really doing anything but talking, listening to others talk, and posing in front of a camera.

If not for the end of the book, I would rate *Mockingjay* even lower. The end of the book was both sad *and* action-packed. But one problem with the action-packed ending was in some parts it was so chaotic it took me a while to understand what was happening.

One thing that made the book really harsh is that over the course of 100ish pages, they killed all but four of the characters that I had grown to love over the first two books. I guess Collins couldn't end a series like this with everyone alive, but I just wish she'd left a few more other than the bare minimum.

Throughout this book I caught myself skipping a few lines here and there, looking for that first-book pizzazz, but up until the last pages, there was little.

Which brings me to my excerpt, which shows a little flare of what Katniss used to be, before she went out.

> I feel the bow purring in my hand. Reach back and grasp the arrow. Position it, aim at the rose, but watch his face. He coughs and a bloody dribble runs down his chin. His tongue flicks over his puffy lips. I search his eyes for the slightest sign of anything, fear, remorse, anger. But there's only the same look of amusement that ended our last conversation. It's as if he's speaking the words again. "Oh, my dear Miss Everdeen. I thought we had agreed not to lie to each other."
>
> He's right. We did.
>
> The point of my arrow shifts upward. I release the string. And President Coin collapses over the side of the balcony and plunges to the ground. Dead. (p. 262)

This passage reminded me so much of the old Katniss. It makes me want to brush off the first book and reread it. What first brought me to this series was that it was highly recommended dystopian science fiction, which was a genre I was being pulled to around that time.

I think the theme of this book is that no matter how bad some leaders are, others that rise to power may do so in dark ways, too.

That last chapter made me glad I didn't abandon this book. I hope other people who read it know that it's not as good as the others and for those who are in the dull parts: hang in there.

Your student,
Cole

10/15

Dear Cole,

I haven't read *Mockingjay*—I can't get my hands on one of the copies because they're both always in circulation—but I appreciate your response in the midst of the general moaning coming from your disappointed classmates.

I'm glad you put the novel in the company of the first two in Collins' trilogy, because this is how it needs to be approached and discussed, in relation to her body of work and how Katniss is developed and portrayed across the three volumes. In the lit. crit. biz, this is called *coherence:* a piece of writing—in this case, a trilogy—should be consistent, connected, and logical. Does *Mockingjay* lack coherence with the other volumes?

It's interesting to me that the reviewers—adults, obviously—have been more positive about *Mockingjay* than you guys, who have a different set of expectations in terms of Katniss and action. Did Collins become more theoretical/philosophical in the third book? The theme you've identified seems to say so—a smart observation, by the way.

Cole, at one point, in describing how *Mockingjay* is authored, you refer to a *they* and, at another, a *she*. Suzanne Collins is the one-and-only author, yes? It's essential for you to think about a novel as the creation of *a* mind and to criticize or appreciate the choices that *an* author made—just as you're *the one* making choices for your own writing in writing workshop.

Love,
Nancie

P.S. Thanks for the paragraphs—they really helped me.

I was honest: I hadn't read *Mockingjay* yet. But Cole's letter-essay gave me some things to say in response to a novice critic. I appreciated his consideration of coherence within the trilogy and taught him the term in context, speculated about the schism between reviewers' responses and those of his classmates, and gave him a nudge about how to attribute a work of literature: no more *they*. Kids new to writing–reading workshop often make this mistake. As literary outsiders, they assume books are produced by anonymous committees.

Holt, another seventh grader but a CTL veteran, wrote a semipan, too, about *After* by Francine Prose. It shows the specificity a more experienced critic is able to bring to a letter-essay. It also shows he can still require a nudge.

10/13

Dear Nancie,

I just read *After* by Francine Prose, and I was amazed. The way she wrote from a kid's perspective was fantastic. How she told characters' thoughts and feelings so well, after such a tragedy, is something I hope to be able to do as a writer someday.

The character development and the way Prose described how teens act around each other was convincing and smart, like how she described that one of the boys was black, but how they always tiptoed around it. That's a hard thing to write, but she pulled it off.

The way the characters reacted is exactly how I would have. She got it dead on, and in the process made me just wanna sock that grief counselor. It reminds me of that thing you have on the wall: "No tears in the writer, no tears in the reader." I love that sign. I'm sure Prose wanted to knock that guy's lights out just as much as I did, right?

Now, I really liked the book, but there were some times when I didn't think it was logical, like the e-mails brainwashing parents? Kids getting sent to boot camps? Dying there? That just doesn't click for me. Like below—how could Silas' mom fall for this? It isn't plausible at all.

> "Take it easy, man," we said. "Take care, dude." "See you soon."
>
> And then a weird thing happened. Silas's mom left the room, possibly so we'd have a few seconds together, or possibly just to position herself to say good-bye to us at the front door. As soon as she was gone, Silas got kind of wild-eyed. He grabbed the tape box that *Invasion of the Body Snatchers* had come in. He pointed to it, and he pointed in the general direction of his mom. He pointed to it again, and he pointed to his mom.
>
> I said, "Man, what are you saying here? Are you kidding?" But I didn't think he was.
>
> Before Silas could answer, his mom's voice drifted in from the hall.
> (p. 219)

And about the end. Now, I heard your booktalk and how you said the ending was bad, but I had kind of forgotten. Within the last three pages, it was like jumping off a cliff. It wasn't crazy, it was stupid. How in the world could the guy know they were at Pleasant Valley? Why would his girlfriend just hop in the car, let's go—no questions asked? Often, when a book doesn't have a clear-cut ending, I like to keep writing the story in my head. But here I couldn't—it's like Prose switched genres into straight sci-fi. How in the world could she write such an excellent book and end it like that? It made me think she got bored and needed to end it fast.

Overall, it was only the last seven pages that stunk in this excellent book, so I would rate it an 8 and still recommend it to every single person in the class.

Hang ten,
Holt

10/15

Dear Holt,

You appreciated everything I love about Francine Prose and everything I objected to in *After*. I'd like to have a one-to-one with her editor about what he or she was thinking in letting that conclusion go to print. It's not that teen readers can't deal with ambiguity or open-endedness. As you said, and it's a great point, an ambiguous ending can leave the reader writing in his head, and that's an intriguing situation to be in. But the lack of logic—*sense*, even—at the end of *After* undercuts the novel and takes attention away from the theme Prose had developed so powerfully.

So, now we come to theme, a topic missing from your letter-essay. It's Prose's theme that kept me hanging in there, because I think it's an important one: how far are we willing to let the government and its institutions go, in terms of surrendering our rights and liberties, in order to keep us "safe"? *After* fits into the discussion we had last month during Banned Books Week, about the intentions of some of the people who want to "protect" kids from books, aka ideas.

I assume you got so caught up in the passion of writing a pan that the need to consider the theme of *After* slipped your mind. Please don't forget it ever again when you write about a novel—theme makes a book *literature*, yes?

Love,
Nancie

A letter from Sophia about *I Am Number Four* by Pittacus Lore gave me a chance to clear up a confusion and share some literary gossip.

November 3rd
8:46 PM

Dear Nancie,

I recently read *I Am Number Four* by Pittacus Lore. I rated it a 9 out of 10. It is a fairly good book—lots of action, good theme—but the diction was not anything spectacular. I think that Lore writes in a very down-to-earth (haha) way, but it is not sensory so it was sometimes hard to get a good image.

I really liked John Smith/Daniel Jones as a character, he seemed realistic and sometimes that's hard to do with sci-fi/dystopian books that are all about plot. Lore uses dialogue effectively to give John a great personality.

Lore's style is more action, and less visuals. I really like this scene because it's one of the few where I can see what the characters are doing. I wish he'd done more of this.

> I see Sam, hunched over a small oak desk with headphones on. I push the door open and he looks over his shoulder. He isn't wearing his glasses, and without them his eyes look very small and beady, almost cartoonlike.
>
> "What's up?" I ask casually, as if I'm at his house every day.
>
> He looks shocked and scared and he frantically pulls the headphones off to reach into one of the drawers. I look at his desk and see that he's reading a copy of *They Walk Among Us*. When I look back up he is pointing a gun at me. (p. 181)

I would say that the themes in this book are about family and power. The family part has to do with John and Henri and their bond, and it also has to do with the Loric memories of his grandparents and Henri and what they mean to John. The war part is about the Mogadarians and what they did to Lorien, and what they are going to do to Earth if we don't watch out. It is about how that would affect everybody, not just the characters in *I Am Number Four*.

I definitely think that this book will have a sequel, maybe two. The series will be called Lorien Legacies. (Do I underline the name of a series, not just the books?)

I would actually compare this book to The Knife of Never Letting Go series by Patrick Ness. The basic plot outlines are similar, but the roles of Todd and John are reversed—human and nonhuman. In both books the main character is on a new planet because the old planet is being destroyed. They then have to run to save their lives and save someone they love, too. The plots may be the same but the writing styles are extremely different. I like Ness better.

I would recommend this book anytime you want a great, fast-paced, action/adventure-sci-fi-part-way-contemporary-realistic-fiction read. It was the perfect novel to read over a lazy weekend.

Sincerely,
Sophia

11/6
5:52 PM

Dear Sophia,

You are a generous rater. The best I could give Lore's *I Am Number Four* is a 7, especially in comparison with Patrick Ness' trilogy. *I Am Number Four* felt formulaic to me and, as you pointed out, not crafted diction-wise, while Ness reads as literature—as books that will stand the test of time—right from the first page. My point? I think there's more than one point, ratings-wise, between Lore and Ness.

About trilogies and series: their titles take capitals only—no underlines or italics.

While I've been writing this letter, my crack research team (Toby) has been on the trail of Pittacus Lore: that's a pseudonym if I ever heard one. It turns out he's James Frey, famous for being outed on "Oprah" as a liar. He wrote a "memoir" about surviving drug and alcohol addiction and jail that was later determined to be pure fiction.

Seems Frey knows there's major money to be made in the young adult market—everyone wants to be Stephenie Meyer and Suzanne Collins, right? So he started a y. a. novel factory to crank out books like *Twilight*. He's been accused of hiring college students—young writers getting their Masters of Fine Arts degrees—as cheap labor to churn out books that he doesn't give them author credit for. For that matter, the Lorien Legacies series was coauthored at first by Frey and another writer named Tobie Hughes, until Frey removed Hughes from the project.

So there's the skinny on Pittacus. I don't like the guy. Should that affect how I feel about the Lorien Legacies? Hmm.

Ponderingly,
Nancie

It's exciting to work with students over two years and observe their growth as critics. Here's a letter-essay by an eighth grader, Xander, about Hemingway's *The Old Man and the Sea*. This is specific, insightful, mature criticism. Xander's ready for the lit crit assignments that high school and college will bring—and more. He has a passion for literature and a voice to express it.

March 12

Dear Nancie,

I am writing to you about *The Old Man and the Sea* by Ernest Hemingway, a book I truly enjoyed. It was a definite 10.

Hemingway's writing style is simple and accessible, with short sentences and brief, straightforward descriptions of setting and characters. He writes with almost no figurative language, and I thought that his diction reveals a lot about who Hemingway was and the kind of life he lived. To me, his frank writing style revealed how down to earth he was and how unnecessary it was to him to embellish small details. He was famous for being macho, and I think his diction reflects that. He saw things as a "real man" would: simply, with no overdramatic symbols or contemplation. A sense of bravery, strength, and toughness is omnipresent in *The Old Man and the Sea*, a reflection, I believe, of Hemingway's own perspective on life.

The novel is written entirely in third person, with no *I* presence, but the way Santiago, the old man, talks to himself, he acts as an *I*. When he is alone on his boat steps back and considers his situation as an onlooker would, and through his conversations with himself he introduces his state of mind into the book. This style is very interesting, and used in few other books I've read. Today, if it were to be attempted, the main character might seem crazy, but in *The Old Man and the Sea*, it fits in with the plot and really works to create the lonely atmosphere I'm sure Hemingway wanted. He makes sure to stress that it really is only the old man and the sea.

Because of his isolation, the old man creates an interesting relationship with the fish, one similar to how early cultures respected and admired their prey.

With no one to talk to but the marlin, he becomes a friend and companion. Throughout their journey Santiago talks to him as one would a friend or even a lover, at times in awe of its beauty, and other times playful, teasing its strength and willpower. This excerpt shows the respect Santiago has for the fish and how Hemingway reveals his thoughts and feelings.

> Then he was sorry for the great fish that had nothing to eat and his determination to kill him never relaxed in his sorrow for him. How many people will he feed, he thought. But are they worthy to eat him? No, of course not. There is no one worthy of eating him from the manner of his behavior and his great dignity. (p. 77)

This predator-prey relationship is a key difference between hunting then and now. In many places hunting has shifted from necessary for survival to a sport. Hunting with high-powered guns is much less pure than it used to be. It has turned into mindless killing for bragging rights instead of survival.

Because of the connection the old man and the fish share, it seems that once he finally kills him, the marlin is still around, silent and strong, just as beautiful and great as always. The final desecration is when the sharks come, and the old man can do nothing to stave them off. The sacred body of the marlin is torn apart and destroyed, and this, not the defeat of the man, is what is truly sad about the book for me.

He loses his friend, his luck, and a large sum of money. The skeleton of the gigantic marlin was more saddening than many books written solely to bring tears to the reader.

The old man, as Hemingway describes him at the beginning of the book, is truly "saloa" or unlucky. He touches perfection and victory, and then it escapes from his grip and falls back into the sea.

The Old Man and the Sea is a book that remains important to our culture because of the timeless story it tells. The universal themes of man's struggle with nature, heartbreaking loss, and courage are ones that touch every life at some point, whether fisherman or businessman. I loved it.

Sincerely,
Xander

3/14

Dear Xander,

And I love you. This is a rich letter-essay. You *got* Hemingway and *The Old Man and the Sea*. And you did so with eloquence and specificity. Bravo.

I've ordered a copy of *The Sun Also Rises* for you. I think it's Hemingway's best book. It's a novel about what's known as "the lost generation": men who survived WWI (Hemingway was an ambulance driver) and their sense of rootlessness and disillusionment after the war. I think you'll find cool parallels between the mystery and beauty of bullfighting and Santiago's battle with the marlin. Please check it out when it arrives.

You might be interested to know that *The Old Man and the Sea* is a *novella:* a form that, lengthwise, falls between a short story and a novel.

Love,
Nancie

In September, everyone's first letter-essay is written to me. I want to make sure kids understand what I'm asking for and catch any omissions before they become bad habits: every year, about half the seventh graders forget the excerpt the first time around. After that, my students write two letter-essays to me, then two to a friend, then two to me, and so on. They choose their peer correspondents as I call the roll; I keep track of who is writing to whom on the reading status-of-the-class record. The names written in the bottom row on Figure 2.4 indicate the recipient of each student's next letter-essay. I'm the only reader who corresponds with more than one student.

The ways my students write to one another are different from the ways they write to me—different just as conversations between peers are. They doodle, exclaim all over the place, invent pen names and signatures, and postscript into tomorrow. There are more accounts of affect. They tell each other about crying, laughing out loud, screaming with surprise, or slamming a book down in anger. Peer correspondents make and follow up on more recommendations. They're more playful with one another and more direct. Bottom line, student correspondence about literature puts social relationships to work and deepens them.

Here, Lilly informs Morganne about her latest bella, *Where Things Come Back* by John Corey Whaley.

12/8

Dear Morganne,

First of all, wow! This is an amazing book. It is called *Where Things Come Back* by John Corey Whaley. He did an amazing job crafting this book! It is a complete and absolute bella because of the strong characters and Whaley's style.

I love smart, funny main characters, and in this case, there are two. The first is Cullen Witter. I think he is supposed to be about seventeen. He is living in Lily (!), Arkansas, with his parents and his fifteen-year-old brother Gabriel. His life is pretty good until one day, Gabriel disappears, and nobody knows why.

Despite this tragedy, everyone is shocked by the reappearance of a woodpecker that everyone had thought to be extinct. This brings me to our co-main character, Benton Sage. He is eighteen and working as a missionary for his church. I got the feeling almost right away that he had a hard home life. More than once he speaks about his father's beatings and anger.

Early on in the book, Benton gets fired from his job as a missionary and begins having dreams about the angel Gabriel and, of course, this also happens to be the name of Cullen's brother who has disappeared! Interesting, huh? These two characters alternate chapters.

The genre of the book is contemporary realistic fiction, with a little mystery. I really appreciated the fact that despite the sadness in this book, it is also incredibly funny! I admire the fact that Whaley combined humor, sadness, and, in a way, beauty.

I chose this excerpt because I think it shows Whaley's skill with thoughts and feelings, a character's voice, and cadence:

> I was getting tired of my parents hugging me every night. I was getting tired of Lucas Cader sleeping on my floor. I was tired of Aunt Julia's crying every single day, whether I saw it in person or heard it through the phone. Mostly, though, I was getting sick and damn tired of hearing and reading and seeing shit about that damn woodpecker. And sitting up one night in my bed as Lucas flipped through channels on my TV, I wrote this sentence down in my book, the same one I keep my titles in: If I had a gun, I would shoot the Lazarus woodpecker in the face. (p. 78)

That excerpt is from the perspective of Cullen, and the book he's talking about is one he uses so if he thinks of a good title for a future book, he can write it down.

I think the themes of this book are about love, friendship, and hope for a second chance, which is *important!* I hope that the rest of Whaley's books are similar in theme. This is his first novel and, hopefully, he will continue to write.

I definitely think that you should read it if you haven't already! It is one of the best books I've read all year, and I know a lot of people besides me have loved it (including Sam).

Love ya,
Lilly

P.S. Thanks for putting up with my rambling!
P.P.S. I think I know who your Secret Holiday Buddy is!!

Dec. 11

Dear Lilly,

Where Things Come Back sounds awesome! I think I kinda have to read it now after this letter and your booktalk!! Is the woodpecker important in the plot? I know that it's on the cover . . . I think . . . maybe. I'll find out.

Anyways, great letter! I'm in need of a bella. I hope no one has it, so I can read it Monday.

I just heated up apple cider and cinnamon and burned the pot. Mom's gonna be mad. (I put that random little fact in so this wouldn't sound like a robotic/nonpersonal letter.)

Anyways, I'll see you at school Monday. Happy weekend!

Love you,
Morganne

In this exchange between Xander and Nathaniel about Elie Wiesel's *Night*, the boys' tone matches the seriousness of the topic. Xander conveys the impact the memoir had on him, and Nathaniel's response is respectful, thoughtful, and empathetic.

4/30

Dear Nathaniel,

I am writing about *Night* by Elie Wiesel—the other famous documentation of the Holocaust besides *The Diary of a Young Girl* by Anne Frank. I loved it, and I rated it a 10.

One of the reasons this memoir is so powerful to me is because of the writing style. I'm not sure how much of this is the translation/translator and how much is Wiesel, but nevertheless I enjoyed the prose. It's bare—like Hemingway's—with no elaborate descriptions of the surroundings. Everything in the book is cut to the bone: the reason it is only about one hundred pages long.

Wiesel describes the world around him with beautiful clarity and just enough description so the reader can picture the horrifying scenes of the concentration camps. Wiesel's descriptions of Auschwitz and Buchenwald are more moving to me than anything I saw in any documentary or read in Hakim because they included his thoughts and feelings. He wrote T & F into the memoir in a method that complemented his prose style. He describes how he felt in short bursts—generally 1–2 sentences—that sum up the range of his emotions. These T & F descriptions help create a definite tone.

The tone is dark and mostly depressing—constant fear translated into words. He created this through his T & F but also dialogue and tag lines within the dialogue. Wiesel's punctuation and word choices also helped create a picture of how he felt. In his tag lines, he showed many different things, from his emotions to his physical state. This excerpt shows his writing style.

> He seemed to be telling the truth. Not far from us, flames, huge flames, were rising from a ditch. Something was being burned there. A truck drew close and unloaded its hold: small children. Babies! Yes, I did see this, with my own eyes . . . children thrown into the flames. (Is it any wonder that ever since then, sleep tends to elude me?)

So that was where we were going. A little farther on, there was another, larger pit for adults.

I pinched myself. Was I still alive? Was I awake? How was it possible that men, women, and children were being burned and that the world kept silent? No. All this could not be real. A nightmare perhaps . . . Soon I would wake up with a start, my heart pounding, and find that I was back in the room of my childhood, with my books . . .

My father's voice tore me from my daydreams. (p. 32)

This excerpt is a perfect example. In the first paragraph, it shows how simple and concise Wiesel's diction is, especially the short sentences I underlined. The T & F in the third paragraph are a little longer than usual, but in the same style: short statements or questions that are strong and to the point.

"Don't talk like that, Father." I was on the verge of breaking into sobs. "I don't want you to say such things. Keep the spoon and knife. You will need them as much as I. We'll see each other tonight, after work." (p. 25)

In this short excerpt, the dialogue reveals his emotions: he is terrified. The tag line "I was on the verge of breaking into sobs" helps solidify the feelings in the dialogue and reveals his fear of losing his father forever.

Wiesel was about the same age as us when he was thrust into the concentration camp system. This fact made the book even more horrifying for me, as I pictured myself in his place. Some of the unthinkably horrible things they were forced to do are impossibly cruel. They had to run over forty miles, malnourished, without a break, during the middle of the night. The fact that I could picture myself in his place—I couldn't from Hakim or even the Anne Frank documentary—helped solidify in my heart the horror that was the Holocaust.

The themes of *Night* are buried within the reason this book was written—to show how dreadful and cruel the Holocaust was. Below this, there are themes of hope, but overshadowed by the horrors of the Holocaust.

With such stunning documentation like *Night* and *The Diary of Anne Frank*, I find it impossible to believe how anyone can believe that the Holocaust didn't happen. These stories have such emotion in them it would be *impossible* to fake. *Night* forces us to look at humans and see how cruel we can be, but also strong. This powerful memoir of the Holocaust is a book I will remember forever.

Sincerely,
Xander

5/2

Dear Xander,

Your letter-essay was great. Wiesel's style of writing sounds different, interesting, and just right for this book. The topic is dreadful and harsh. I feel the same as you that I could definitely not imagine being in a Holocaust victim's shoes, especially at our age. He was just a kid.

Night is now on my "someday" list. I will definitely give it a try. I'm grateful you told me about it.

Your friend,
Nathaniel

My students created the protocol for responding to a friend's letter-essay. In a mini-lesson we discussed and debated what they wanted from their correspondents.

PROTOCOL FOR WRITING BACK TO A CRITIC FRIEND

- Write a letter—with a greeting and closing—that's about half a page in length.
- Respond to what the critic wrote about the book. Don't assess the letter-essay—that's Nancie's job. But if you have trouble reading the handwriting, by all means say so politely ("It was hard to read your letter-essay. Next time could you . . .?").
- What else? Give your own opinions of the book or the author, ask a question, tell about the book you're reading, recommend another book or author, and, if you'd like, throw in a bit of personal news.

It helps me to look at my literary correspondence with students not just as a vehicle for teaching them but also as a forum to learn from them. Here, Morganne critiques a title that's new to me, one she purchased at a book store with her birthday money. Figure 7.2 shows how she wrote off-the-page beforehand to generate ideas for a letter-essay about Jennifer Donnelly's novel *Revolution*.

Feb. 3

Dear Nancie,

The book I am writing about is *Revolution* by Jennifer Donnelly. I rated it a bella, for tone, diction choices, and theme, which were all strong and beautiful. *Revolution* is narrated by Andi, a 21st-century girl who goes to a private school in Brooklyn, but who is taken with her physician father to Paris to research a human heart and use DNA to identify it.

Honestly, Andi's pretty messed up. She is seriously depressed to the point of being suicidal. Sometimes it sounds like the only thing that keeps her alive is her music—she plays guitar. I know that sounds incredibly clichéd. But music—specifically a composer and guitarist of the 18th century, Amade Malherbeau—plays a huge part in the novel. Anyway, Andi and her guitar travel to Paris. I won't say why, exactly, but it's got to do with an end-of-the-year paper due at Andi's school.

w o+p

Book: _Revolution_ by Jennifer Donnelly

rated: Bella b/c strong descriptive diction & theme *french revolution*

theme: history repeats learn from mistakes world goes on love *music*

tone: sad dismal bleak hopeful then love

genre: ? historical fiction but she lives now (Andi)
& Alex 1790②-95 but she travels through the
Catacombs meets Amade guitarist she's studying...
but written real

excerpt: 2? 1 from Alex & 1 from Andi?
or compare 2 of Andi how she changes as
a narrator? pg. 8 or 317.

also the part w/ sparrow incorporated into diary...
she sees a sparrow & Alex's journal she's (Alex) called
la sparrow she sees stuff death thinks its from
anti depresents but...

Figure 7.2 *Morganne's off-the-Page Writing for a Letter-Essay*

Once in Paris, Andi finds the diary of a girl named Alex, written during the French Revolution, 1790–1795—maybe a bit earlier, but when Paris was a filthy blood bath.

I'm not sure what the genre is. Donnelly made me believe (up until Paris) that it was contemporary realistic fiction. Then she introduces long segments of diary, which seem like historical fiction, and then

WARNING! SPOILER! WARNING!

Andi travels back in time and *becomes* Alex, or Alex is dead and everyone thinks Andi is Alex . . .

My excerpt is a section right after Andi time travels and is starting to figure out what happened. The amazing part is that it's totally believable. Donnelly has created "excuses" for Andi to explain to herself what's going on: throughout the novel, whenever Andi sees a dead person, she says it's the Quells (antidepressants) she's taking, or that she shouldn't drink wine.

> The Green Man. That's what they called Alex, but Alex lived over two centuries ago. There was a bounty on her, too. I start to shiver. I feel dizzy again. And scared. It's too perfect, this movie set. This fake world. Something's wrong. (p. 197)

Another thing I like about this novel is Donnelly's sentence structure. As you can tell from the excerpt, sentences are short and clipped, making the novel read more like poetry than prose. Also, it keeps the action in motion and the t & f realistic.

Theme in *Revolution* is complicated. Donnelly has woven so many elements into the novel that there are, in fact, multiple themes, including love, revolution (not just the French one but also Andi's personal revolution), family, loss, and that the world goes on. These are just the biggest ideas, embedded over and over, along with music theory.

Revolution is a sad book. Diction and tone choices give it a lonely, sad feel, which gradually is transformed as Andi starts to feel happy. Through the process of reading Alex's diary, Andi can finally feel better about herself.

The way past and present interweave is magical, but the novel feels completely realistic, like it could happen. I loved it. There's so much more I want to say, but I can't, because you need to read it first. This and *Before I Fall* may be my favorite books ever. And *The Book Thief.*

See you Monday!

Love,
Morganne

Feb. 4

Dear Morganne,

I didn't even finish your letter-essay before I made a note to myself to order *Revolution* for the classroom library. Thank you for a specific and convincing review, not to mention smart book browsing, not to mention the spoiler alert. Any book that you put up there with Zusak's *Book Thief* is one I want to read and your classmates will, too.

I wonder if you've read Donnelly's *A Northern Light.* It's about a sixteen-year-old girl who takes a job at a summer inn, where one of the guests, a young woman, is murdered. It's set in the early 1900s and based on a true story. I like it a lot. It's in our library, in the historical fiction section.

Thanks for the great lead. When *Revolution* arrives, will you booktalk it?

Love,
Nancie

I don't edit the letter-essays. In my replies I do point out format issues—for example, when insufficient paragraphing doesn't give me breathing space. I jot down misspellings on Post-it notes, which I stick to the cover of the marble notebooks. After I return them, students copy the words onto their master spelling lists and work with them in a weekly word study.

In evaluating the letter-essays, I look for the baseline features. If each of them is present, a student gets a ✓+; if most are there a ✓; and if a letter-essay doesn't contain crucial features, like a discussion of theme or a glossed excerpt, it's a ✓– with an explanation in my response about why. When kids switch correspondents at the end of a cycle, I read and put the appropriate check mark on the two letter-essays that were written to a classmate, before I read the new one that's written to me.

Baseline features became clearer to my students, and their letter-essays were more sustained and specific, after another change I made a few years ago. My colleague Glenn Powers, who works with CTL's fifth and sixth graders, adapted my letter of invitation and paragraph openers for his reading workshop. These days most incoming seventh graders are experienced writers of what Glenn calls *lit letters*. This gave me an opportunity to up the ante and ask my students to approach letter-essays in a genre study.

Today I introduce letter-essays by asking kids to research a collection of good ones from previous years. In the second half of this book, where I describe the genre studies I conduct in writing workshop, I cite this approach a lot. It's the ideal jumping-off point. When students analyze models and tease out and name genre features, they understand them better and are more likely to include them when they produce writing in the genre. No teacher-made rubric is as powerful.

On Monday of the fourth week of school, I give each student a packet of photocopies of five strong letter-essays from the year before, including the writing off-the-page that preceded them, and I explain the assignment:

> As readers and critics, you and I chat about literature every day in reading workshop. Starting this week, every three weeks I'll ask you to go deeper than our check-in discussions and *write* about literature: select one book and explore what its author did. I call this genre a *letter-essay*. It's longer and richer than the lit letters you wrote in the younger grades, and it will provide you with a strong bridge into the literary criticism you'll write in high school and college.
>
> To help you understand the features of the letter-essay genre, here are five good ones. Tonight for homework, please read and study them. You'll be gathering data in response to two questions. Open your writing–reading handbooks to the next two clean pages in the class notes section, and write the questions as headings, one to a page:
>
> What Does a Critic Always Do in a Good Letter-Essay?
>
> What Else Might a Good Critic Comment On?

Tonight read the examples with a pen in your hand. Underline every feature you notice. Try to name them in the margins. Some features you'll observe in every letter-essay. Some topics you might find addressed only once. That's the reason for the two lists: *always* versus *what else*. Notice the format, too—what the letter-essays look like and how they're structured. Tomorrow, as the minilesson, we'll combine your individual notes and create master lists of elements to include every time, plus other features you might notice and comment on about how a book was written. Your own first letter-essays will be due Thursday.

Questions? Comments? Observations?

The next morning, before I send the kids off in small groups with their writing–reading handbook notes and either a pad of paper or a laptop, I tell them, "Today the group recorder will be the person whose birthday comes next. You have ten minutes to describe what you found in the letter-essays you read and help your recorder create two lists of letter-essay features." I circulate among the small groups, nudge them with my ideas, and keep them on track.

At the end of ten minutes, when students return to the minilesson circle, I fire up the overhead projector and the recorders take turns reporting out each group's observations as I write like mad to capture them. If every group misses something essential, I introduce it and add it.

I tell kids not to take notes; my own on the transparencies will be littered with arcane abbreviations. That night I flesh out and organize them; if I teach this lesson to more than one class, I combine their different sets of data as one. Then I type the two documents for distribution and discussion as the Wednesday minilesson, students glue the two lists inside the front and back covers of their marble notebooks, and they read and highlight them around the minilesson circle.

Figures 7.3 and 7.4 represent the most recent version of the letter-essay lists I compiled from students' research. I organized the required features of a letter-essay into two categories, format and contents. To exemplify what a theme is, the kids and I brainstormed every literary theme we could think of. When I created the second list of features a critic might consider, I used literary vocabulary and built in the definitions, because this is the terminology I want students to use.

This particular list of critical topics happened to be especially smart. The temptation is to reproduce it for next year's students. It doesn't work that way. The criteria were helpful in prompting strong letter-essays because students had identified them in context—had observed how other young critics had analyzed and appreciated literature. But I do save lists as good as these. Next time around, I'll put a copy on the corner of my overhead projector stand and add to the conversation any essential features my new kids didn't observe.

IN A GOOD LETTER-ESSAY, A CRITIC ALWAYS . . .

FORMAT-WISE:

- Writes off-the-page to gather ideas, impressions, opinions, and evidence. The *back* of the preceding page in your marble notebook is a good place to plan.

- Writes the date in the upper right-hand corner, a greeting that isn't indented (*Dear* _____,) on the left, and a conventional closing at the end (*Your friend, Love, Yours truly, Sincerely*), followed by a signature.

- Mentions the title of the book and its author in the first paragraph, capitalizes the title correctly, and underlines it.

- Indents the first line of the letter, i.e., the first sentence of the first paragraph.

- First time around, refers to the author by his or her first and last names and, after that, by last name only.

- Writes at least three pages.

- Creates paragraphs and tries to focus each one on an idea about the book; follows up, in the rest of the paragraph, with examples, reasons, or evidence.

CONTENT-WISE:

- Explores *theme*: ideas about life that emerge from the story. Based on *changes in the main character*, potential themes include coping with change or loss, discovering what matters, growing up, stereotyping, loneliness, peer pressure, pride, prejudice, choices, conscience, competition, courage, responsibility, betrayal, being true to oneself, perseverance, success and failures, facing reality, trauma, human nature, false values, religious beliefs, political beliefs, an apocalypse or war; the need for acceptance, love, family, community, identity, a voice, friendship, or survival; and the power of truth, lies, love, friendship, teammates, family, self-expression, art, nature, society, authority figures, institutions, government, gossip, jealousy, or shame.

- Has a *voice* that expresses and explains opinions, ideas, feelings, connections, likes, and dislikes.

- Explains *why* about his or her reactions: cites evidence from the book.

- Selects a passage that shows something important about the writing and isn't too long or too short; then either copies it by hand into the letter-essay or photocopies it and tapes it in, with the page number in parentheses at the end.

- Introduces the excerpt by telling why he or she selected this passage—what it shows about the author's choices or style of writing or a theme of the book.

- Identifies the genre of the book.

- Rates the book and explains reasons for the rating.

Figure 7.3 *In a Good Letter-Essay, a Critic Always . . .*

IN A GOOD LETTER-ESSAY, A CRITIC MIGHT COMMENT ON . . .

- a book you loved (a **rave**), disliked (a **pan**), or have **mixed** feelings about
- the **narrative voice** the author chose—first person? third limited? third omniscient? a rare second?—and how it worked out. If first person, what do you think of how the author took on a persona? And if the narrator turned out to be unreliable, comment on this, too.
- how the author **develops the** *so what?* or theme
- the **tone of the narrative:** the attitude of the author or persona
- the **descriptions** and **sensory details:** could you see it? feel it? hear it?
- the **plot** and how it's structured, makes sense, transitions among situations, coheres, or doesn't
- the **climax**—or high point—of the plot
- the **dialogue:** is the conversation realistic? how does it reveal character? did the author create a style or break rules?
- the **setting** and how the author describes and includes it—or doesn't
- the **plausibility of the main character** as an **invented person:** could you believe in him or her?
- how the author **developed the main character**, for example,
  - name—or lack of one
  - a change in him or her (note: this is often a source of *so what?* or theme)
  - problem or worry
  - desires
  - reflections, i.e., thoughts and feelings
  - personality traits
  - actions and reactions
  - relationships with others, including family and friends
  - dialogue with others
  - possessions, habits, hobbies, and interests
  - clothing, hairstyle, and ornamentation
- the resolution of his or her problem—where the character goes from here
- how and whether you **connected with the main character**
- the **supporting characters:** their roles and plausibility
- what you **would have done differently** as the author of this book
- your **first impressions** as a reader of the book *vs.* your **final impressions**
- how this book **compares** with another by **this author**
- how this book **compares** with another from the **same genre**
- how this book **compares** with one by **another author**
- how a **book resembles another genre**, e.g., a novel with diction that reads like a poem
- how **a character resembles a character from another book**
- the **one thing** that redeemed a book or left a negative impression of a good one
- the **conclusion:** satisfying? logical? confusing? a surprise? too fast? too slow? memorable? unsatisfying? ambiguous? thought-provoking?
- the **lead:** slow? gripping? inviting? confusing? misleading?
- the **format** of the book
- the author's **diction** and writing style
- the **cadence** or rhythm of the language
- the **illustrations**, if any
- the **title or cover design** of the book and its relationship—or lack of same—to the story

Figure 7.4 *In a Good Letter-Essay, a Critic Might Count On . . .*   *(continues)*

IN A GOOD LETTER-ESSAY, A CRITIC MIGHT COMMENT ON . . .

- the book's role as a **sequel** or part of a **trilogy, quartet,** or **series**
- **how you read the book,** for example, in one sitting or savoring it
- **how many times** you've **read the book** if it's a reread, and why
- what you **noticed, learned, or appreciated as a writer** yourself
- an **allusion or reference** to another piece of writing that you noticed
- your **reaction to another reader's response** to the book
- your **judgment of the harshness of the content**: is this one an adult or transitional title?
- your **overall response** to the book

Figure 7.4 *Continued*

I ask students to begin the first letter-essays of the school year in class—to devote the rest of Wednesday's writing workshop to selecting a book to critique, writing off-the-page about it, finding a revealing passage, and referring to the student examples and the lists their class created. I circulate, answer questions, and provide guidance. It's more likely their first attempts will resemble criticism if I'm around to help students get on track.

They finish up for homework and, in the morning, deliver the first letter-essays to my rocking chair. When I read them that weekend, I'll make a note to myself about the especially good ones. Three weeks hence, before the next round of letter-essays is due, I'll copy these as overhead transparencies, show them to the class, and lead a discussion about the features that make them successful examples of literary criticism.

When teachers help students focus on craft and literary response—on how a book is written and how its author's choices affected them—we encourage an active, critical stance. We teach them to go beyond plot, stop letting stories happen to them, and start making decisions about what is and isn't working in pieces of their reading. We show them how to pull up their chairs at the dining room table, engage with their whole hearts and minds, and become better, bigger, smarter people.

The most important thing I can do as a teacher, to ensure that students' lives turn out to be good ones, is to invite them, again and again, to discover the richest possible version of life. That's the one to be found in the words and ideas of authors and the pages of books, books, books.

CHAPTER 8

VALUING AND EVALUATING

The days that make us happy make us wise.

—JOHN MASEFIELD

Whether I'm teaching in a school that requires letter grades, number grades, or doesn't grade, if I'm teaching writing and reading in a workshop, I have to figure out how to put students' appraisals of their work at the heart of the evaluation process. Otherwise, assessment becomes a betrayal of the workshop—of the ways I've asked students to think and act as writers and readers over the previous months. Kids in a workshop are in a constant state of reflection and assessment as they consider where they've been, where they are, where they might go next, what they don't understand yet, and what they need to know, try, and do.

Self-assessment begins in writing conferences, when I ask, "How's it coming?" or "How can I help you?" and the student responds. It's manifest in the choices individuals make as they plan, draft, revise, and edit their writing. When they tell a friend what kind of assistance they're seeking in a peer writing conference, decide whether to type or handwrite a draft, review their territories lists for the most compelling topic, determine whether a piece of writing is finished, or take a particular focus when they edit a draft, students are assessing themselves as writers.

Evaluation of *other* writers drives my students' growth as readers of literature. It shows up in our daily check-ins in reading workshop and their letter-essays about books. When they rate a title 1–10, decide whether to booktalk it, do booktalk it, or consider such literary features as diction, plausibility, coherence, reflection, character development, structure, theme, and point of view, students are assessing authors.

At the end of each trimester, my K–8 colleagues and I stop teaching for a week and invite our students to pause, reflect on the work of the previous twelve weeks, and make plans for the trimester to come. Every class in every subject becomes an evaluation workshop as children examine collections of their work, complete self-assessment questionnaires, make photocopies of selected evidence, and assemble the contents of their portfolios. These are three-ring binders with plastic sleeves inside that display the self-assessment questionnaires, photographs that teachers have taken of students at work, captioned copies of kids' record-keeping forms, and captioned samples of writing, responses to reading, spelling, mathematics, history, science, and art.

Our goal in using portfolios is for students to analyze their processes, products, growth, and challenges. The self-assessment questionnaires give them a prism to examine their evidence, reflect on it, and set goals for their work. Teachers pose the questions that kids consider and list what the portfolios should include, sometimes with student input.

Only after students have finished self-assessing do teachers step in as evaluators. The goals that appear on a child's progress report are coauthored: a combination of the objectives the student named in the self-assessment and others the teacher believes the child needs to tackle. Teachers also create a document that summarizes the minilessons, discussions, activities, projects, and readings of the trimester. I ask each of my students to highlight this trimester summary to indicate what was most useful or meaningful, so their parents can enjoy the benefit of the child's governing gaze when reviewing it. Both documents become part of a student's permanent record.

At CTL, students lead the evaluation conference. A child opens his or her portfolio and talks parents and teacher through its contents. Then the teacher delivers and discusses his or her progress report and sets formal goals for the subsequent trimester. The conference closes with the teacher asking, "Do you have any questions or observations, for me or your child?" Afterward, parents take the portfolios home to peruse and show to grandparents. We ask that they be returned to school within two weeks. The DVD included with my book *Systems* (2014) shows two parent-teacher-student evaluation conferences, along with examples of K–8 self-assessment questionnaires and teacher reports.

Because the end of the school year is so frantic, we don't schedule evaluation conferences in June. Instead, students compile their third-trimester portfolios and they and their teachers coauthor a final report that provides a portrait of the child as a learner at the completion of the school year. It consists of summative self-assessments in writing, reading, and mathematics, accompanied by teachers' concluding observations of a child's strengths and the goals he or she needs to work toward the following September.

If I were teaching in a school where portfolios were impracticable, I'd still develop and assign self-assessment questionnaires—the process is that enlightening and productive for kids, teachers, and parents. Before sending it home, I'd attach a copy of the student's best writing and response to literature of the trimester, so parents could glean a basis for their child's reflections and goals.

CTL's assessment scheme provides a detailed picture of a student's abilities, activities, and progress. It reflects what happens day-to-day in our classes. It involves parents in a meaningful—often delightful—way. The information it conveys to mothers, fathers, and the next year's teacher is specific and *useful*. It is individualized and goal-oriented, and the goals are based on the observations of a professional teacher, in collaboration with an engaged learner. It holds students accountable. And it begins with their judgments about what they know, can do, have done, and need to do next. I can't imagine a more worthwhile use of my time or that of my students when it comes to evaluating their progress and nurturing their growth as writers and readers.

SELF-ASSESSMENT

At the end of each trimester, I spend a Sunday paging back through my lesson plans and taking notes on emphases and key concepts. Based on these, I create open-ended questions for students to reflect on about their work as writers and readers. I format my queries as two-page questionnaires, one each for writing and reading. My questions ask kids to collect data about productivity, articulate criteria for good writing and criticism, describe improvement and accomplishments, assess the progress they made toward the goals of the previous trimester, and set new ones. I don't ask for complete sentences; instead, I push for bulleted lists of data. I learned that kids can hide a lack of knowledge amidst paragraphs of long sentences. Lists cut to the chase.

Figure 8.1 shows a first-trimester writing self-assessment as completed by Avery, a seventh grader who entered CTL that fall and, after an initial couple of weeks of flailing around in an alien environment, adapted to and embraced the workshop. The first question is standard—I ask it every time. The number of pieces finished and genres produced represent the hard data of writing workshop. It matters to students, who gain perspective on what they've accomplished; to parents, who understand quantity as one measure of achievement; and to me, so I can see who met the expectations for writing workshop. If I had a say in establishing national standards for writing, I'd propose the number of finished pieces as a criterion, I'm so convinced of the correlation between quantity and quality.

The second question is standard, too. It motivates students to reflect on pieces of their writing as critics and articulate the features that make them effective. I'm nudging them to go beyond "My poem about my dad is good because he's a great dad" and use the vocabulary I introduced in minilessons and conferences to consider what *works*, literature-wise. When they can observe and name a technique, they own it—it becomes part of their repertoires as writers and critics. Avery is able to critique his two best pieces by identifying his use of *thoughts and feelings*, *cadence*, *effective repetition*, *transitions*, *sensory verbs*, *visuals*, and a *strong conclusion*. These were all subjects of first-trimester poetry discussions, minilessons, and conversations he and I had about his drafts. To ground Avery's observations, Figure 8.2 reproduces the writing he was analyzing: two of his first poems ever.

WRITING SELF-EVALUATION

NAME *Avery*   DATE *11/15*

1. How many pieces of writing did you finish this trimester? *7*
   What genres are represented among these pieces?

   Free-verse poem   *List poem*
   Collaborative parody

2. Which two pieces do you consider your most effective? Why? *List* what you did as the author in crafting each one.

   "Leftover Memories"

   - *I used a lot of thoughts & feelings.*
   - *I created a cadence.*
   - *I used effective repetition by repeating a specific phrase near the end of every stanza.*
   - *When I shifted through time, I did the transitions smoothly.*

   "My Backyard"

   - *I created cadence to show I was constantly observing*
   - *I used tons of specific describing words.*
   - *I used a lot of sensory verbs to try to create visuals.*
   - *I had a strong conclusion.*
   - *I gave examples: what's unique to my back yard, not just any old nature.*

3. How did you stretch as a writer this trimester? Think in terms of topics, approaches, productivity, your writing process, writing off the page, and attention to diction, purpose, form, technique, and theme.

   - *At first, I wasn't writing off the page, but I started getting more into the habit farther into the trimester.*
   - *I began to go into topics about my family and my younger childhood.*
   - *I imitated the style of e.e. cummings.*
   - *I experimented with a poem that had no I presence, but it didn't turn out well because I learned that I need to know what I'm writing about to be able to write it.*
   - *I wrote period.*

4. In your own words, why are strong conclusions crucial to effective writing?
   A strong conclusion is important because you don't want readers to be left hanging when they finish a piece of writing. You want to leave something in their brain for them to think about.

Figure 8.1 *Avery's First-Trimester Writing Self-Assessment*   *(continues)*

5. In your own words, why are sensory verbs crucial to effective writing?

Sensory verbs are important in a piece of writing because you want to create a visual for the reader. You want them to be able to <u>see</u> what you're doing, not just read about it.

6. What is the best memoir of those we read in class? What made it best? As a critic, please list its successful features.

"Triathlon" by Martin Shott is my favorite because he:
- *told specific but unusual feelings, e.g., knives in his chest when he was breathing*
- *cued time shifts smoothly, so I was with him the whole time*
- *used an action-dialogue lead that roped the reader right in*
- *told tons of thoughts and feelings and sensory verbs*
- *put his "So what?" right at the end so it really hit me*

7. What lessons about memoir do you need to take to heart as you draft your memoir?

- *To keep a balance among action, reflection, dialogue, and description*
- *To embed the context and ground the reader about the setting*
- *To remember the importance of the lead for the writer & reader*

8. Based on three entries in the territories section of your handbook—"New Poetry Inspirations," "After Our First Poetry Reading," and "Twenty Places I Found Poems Hiding"—along with "Some Things a Poet Does When Trying to Write a Good Poem," what are five smart, relevant goals you have for yourself as a poet?

- *Make sure each word is the right word.*
- *Cut out unnecessary cliches.*
- *Brainstorm titles that aren't cheesy and that aren't labels.*
- *Adopt a persona for a poem that actually has a "so what?"*
- *Write a poem about a household object that has sentimental value to me.*

9. What else do you intend to accomplish as a writer during the 2nd trimester in terms of:
 · your productivity (e.g., number of pages of draft per week, plus your weekend homework)? *Draft more over the weekend so I can have a better start the upcoming Monday: at least 2 full pages, plus 3-5 during the week.*
 · your spelling?
   - *Continue to be serious about the study process.*
 · your mastery of other conventions (e.g., commas, capitals, prose margins and paragraphing, apostrophes, etc.)?
   - *Correct punctuation, like commas and periods at the ends of lines of poems only when I need them.*
 · crafting your writing?

   - *Make sure there's an I presence in my poems, and make sure each line is concrete and sensory.*

Figure 8.1 *Continued*

LEFTOVER MEMORY

Scritch, scritch, scritch—
my black sharpie
etches a cockpit and wings
onto the flaps of a brown
cardboard box.

I climb inside,
grip the edges
with my three-year-old hands,
stretch my tiny legs.

Whoosh, whoosh, whoosh—
Dad lifts my
cardboard box—
now
a cardboard airplane—
and flies me around the blue Holland house.

Zoom, zoom, zoom—
I soar in and out of hallways,
through our kitchen,
past the brick fireplace that doesn't work anymore.
I extend my arms
and add another set of wings.

Laughing and smiling,
I glide past my mom.
She waves.
I glance back at my dad,
see the gleam in his eyes as he propels
me around the world
in a
cardboard airplane.

Nothing matters
but this moment.
I feel like I'm twenty thousand feet high.
Although in real life I'm only five feet high,
I'm in my
cardboard airplane.

Figure 8.2 *Avery's Best Writing of the First Trimester*   *(continues)*

Today, I'm too big
to fit into
a cardboard box.
Certain things fly away
as I grow up.
My
cardboard box
is gone with the wind.

But
not really.

—*Avery Genus*

MY BACKYARD

When I gaze upon
the forest
in what seems to be my backyard,

what do I see?

I see
the peacefulness of trees swaying in a breeze.
Green ferns sigh
as they wave plumy hands.

I see
light
filtered through
the spiny fingers of evergreens,
Shedding trickles of golden radiance
across the forest floor.

I see
roots spread themselves
and grasp for purchase in the rocky terrain.

And I lose
myself amidst
the calm sensation
that washes over me.

Figure 8.2 *Continued*

(continues)

But then I look closer.
The trees have broken branches.
The green ferns are brown.
Needles dropped from evergreens are dead.
Roots are withering from lack of rain.

I notice
that everything has a flaw.
Nothing
is absolute perfection.

If everything
were perfect,
perfection would be
nothing.

In my
backyard, everything
is just
fine.

—*Avery Genus*

Figure 8.2 *Continued*

I always pose some variation on the third question, "How did you stretch as a writer this trimester?" It's essential because it asks students to step back and reflect on the big picture of themselves as writers, to measure the distance between where they were and where they are and to celebrate their accomplishments.

The next five questions refer to lessons and activities of the particular trimester—our work with conclusions, sensory verbs, memoir as a genre, and poetic techniques and topics. Avery's answers provide a snapshot of what he noticed, valued, and learned about writing, September to November.

In other trimesters of writing workshop, depending on the focus of the genre studies and minilessons, I'll ask students to self-assess in response to such questions as:

- What did you learn about yourself as a writer this trimester?
- Describe all the changes you can think of in your writing, and yourself as a writer, over the past trimester.
- What's something new you tried as a writer that worked for you?
- What are the five most significant lessons you learned about writing free-verse poetry?

- How did you use the territories section of your handbook this trimester?
- Evaluate the process of writing a memoir (or review, short short story, essay, parody, profile, or advocacy journalism). What were the challenges? How did you solve them? What are the big lessons you'll take away about writing this genre? What are its significant features?
- What are you working on—or struggling with—as a poet (or memoirist, reviewer, writer of fiction, essayist, or reporter)?
- If you wrote off-the-page this trimester, *why*? What did it do for you as a writer?
- What are new conventions of usage you understand now and can use correctly as you draft?
- Please create sentences that demonstrate the usage of a colon and a semicolon.
- What were the most useful, meaningful writing minilessons of the trimester—which will stick with you, and why?
- What have I or people in your class done in writing workshop this trimester that helped you be a better writer?
- If you could rewrite the trimester, what would you do differently as a writer?
- And, always, in second- and third-trimester questionnaires, describe the progress you made toward each of your writing goals of the previous trimester.

A student's writing self-assessment concludes with goal setting in at least four areas: productivity, craft, spelling, and mastery of other conventions. In his self-assessment, Avery indicates that he wants to maintain his pace as a writer during the school week and increase it on the weekends. His spelling goal is the one I ask students to set if they've mostly aced the monthly spelling reviews and the end-of-trimester test. Avery selected his goals for conventions of writing from the proofreading list inside his writing-in-process folder. His craft goals are issues he and I had talked about in conferences.

As self-evaluators, my students tackle writing first, and then move on to reading. Avery's reading questionnaire appears as Figure 8.3. It, too, begins with the essential data: the number of books he finished and the range of genres they represent. I want students to pause and take pride in their accomplishments as readers; I've also learned that for parents, there is no number more important or impressive. Even if they aren't readers, parents recognize what book reading represents. The number of books a child finishes is the most significant statistic of all, it represents and predicts so much about his or her academic future. I ask students to identify the genres they read because it's useful for them and me to consider their preferences—which often shift across a year of reading workshop—as another kind of growth.

The "best book" question, another standard, nudges kids to focus on an author's craft rather than their reactions to a beloved story or character. It provides another snapshot of their critical abilities. Avery analyzes *Rocket Boys* in terms of the techniques Homer Hickam Jr. uses as a memoirist. He comments on Hickam's reflections, realistic

READING SELF-EVALUATION

NAME _Avery_   DATE _11/17_

1. How many books did you finish this trimester? _13_
   What genres are represented among these titles?

   Contemporary Realistic Fiction   _Dystopian Science Fiction_   _____

   Thriller   _Memoir_   _____

   Fantasy   _____   _____

2. What was the best book? _Rocket Boys by Homer H. Hickam_

   What made it the best? List what the author did in crafting this as a work of literature.

   - A _lot_ of thoughts and feelings
   - Describes his family environment and the relationship between himself and the members of his family realistically, but gracefully at the same time
   - Described the specific sounds, sights, and feelings he experienced, so I could too
   - Made amazing and realistic characters who actually seemed like they were alive to me, & they were alive: the book is a memoir.

3. What were the two best poems? Why? List what the poet did in crafting each.

   "This Is Just to Say" William Carlos Williams

   - Cut it to the bone
   - Created specifics, like saying the plums were in the "ice box"
   - Used line and stanza breaks to make up for no punctuation
   - Used the line and stanza breaks to create cadence
   - Created an ironic tone

   "America" Tony Hoagland

   - Had a form but let topics flow from stanza to stanza
   - Told specific details of "America" e.g., Radio Shacks, Burger King, and MTV
   - Used a tone of irony to create humor
   - Created a cadence & a form that helped the "so what?" build up to the end

4. How did you stretch as a reader this trimester? Think in terms of new authors and genres, new tastes and preferences, and new strengths as a reader and critic of prose and poetry. List them.

   - I've never turned a critical eye to poetry & prose, so that alone is a new step for me. I feel like I'm becoming better at noticing the details & techniques of crafted writing
   - I started reading memoirs. I've never done that before.

Figure 8.3 _Avery's First-Trimester Reading Evaluation_   _(continues)_

- I started becoming interested in contemporary realistic fiction, & I tried out a thriller, too.
- Now I can notice how a writer uses sensory verbs and describing words to make a poem visual for a reader.
- In writing letter essays, I'm getting better at thinking about what the theme is and the ideas the writer might be trying to get across.

5. From the glossary of poetic terms, what are two new terms that you can use as a critic of poetry in our daily discussions? List and define them.
- Cadence: the rhythm or pattern of the language in a poem
- Hyperbole: when you exaggerate something in your writing on purpose

6. What are two new literary terms that you can use with confidence? List and define them..
- Vicarious: when you read something and you feel like you're in the story and not just sitting there reading the words.
- Roman á clef: when real people are described in a story but have fictitious names in the story

7. What's a personal reading goal that you took away from the lesson about psycholinguistic reading theory?
- I'm going to try to have my eyes stop less when I read because it means I can put bigger chunks of information in my long-term memory.

8. What are your other reading goals for the second trimester, in terms of:
- your productivity and pace (number of books or number of pages/night)?
  - I'm going to try to get at least 40 pages per night, so I can finish more books at a faster pace.
- your choices of books?
  - Extremely Loud & Incredibly Close   • Paper Towns
  - No Country for Old Men   • The City of Thieves
- your experiments with authors and genres?
  - Two new genres I'd like to try: action/adventure & mystery
  - Two new authors I'd like to try: M.T. Anderson & Stephen King
- your letter-essays?
  - I've got the basics down, so I'd like to start getting ideas from the "A Critic Might Comment On" list.
- your participation in our daily poetry discussions?
  - 4 times per week
- your booktalks?
  - 3 times in the second trimester

Figure 8.3 *Continued*

descriptions, writing style, sensory imagery, and character development, all elements we discussed in our genre study of memoirs in writing workshop.

The questions about best poems of the trimester are also standard. Students' answers show them—and me—what they learned about literary features in particular and criticism in general. Students page through their poetry folders, make their choices from among the poems we read together, read and reread them, and take notes on what their preferred poets did. The emphasis is on techniques of craft, so students will be able to identify them again in other works and, perhaps, bring them to writing of their own.

Through reading and unpacking poems every day for twelve weeks, Avery began to establish a critical eye and ear. He recognizes compression (*cut to the bone*), concrete specifics and details, use of line and stanza breaks to offset punctuation and create cadence, irony, tone, stanza form, cadence and form as ways to build tension, and theme (the *so what?*). As a critic, Avery is on his way. As his teacher, I recognize that he has been paying attention.

"How did you stretch as a reader?" is another consistent focus in reading self-evaluations. The question asks readers to reflect on and describe their growth. My follow-up comment, which begins "Think in terms of . . . ," is a nudge to students to consider their strengths as people who choose books, attend to authors and genres, and respond to literature. In his self-analysis, Avery observes that he has begun to read poetry and prose as a critic who can identify "techniques of crafted writing." He is also trying and enjoying new genres. He notices that he's turning from fantasy, an old love, to contemporary realistic fiction. He appreciates how sensory verbs and descriptions create visuals, and he has begun to consider the themes of books in his letter-essays.

The fifth, sixth, and seventh questions are specific to the work of the trimester, when students annotated a glossary of poetic terms, created a running lexicon of the literary terms that emerged in class discussions, and engaged in the study of psycholinguistics that I described in Chapter 5.

In other trimesters, in connection with particular reading emphases, I ask students to self-assess in response to such questions as:

- What were the most important lessons you learned about reading a poem?
- What are five features of free-verse poetry you're confident you can recognize as a reader and unpacker of poems?
- What were your breakthroughs as a reader of prose and poetry this trimester?
- What are five important things you're able to notice and consider as a reader of narrative literature?
- Who are your favorite poets these days? Why?
- Who are your favorite authors? Why?

- What will you take away from our work as unpackers of the poetry of Emily Dickinson (or Whitman, Williams, Stevens, Hughes, etc.)?

- What's your own best definition of theme (or tone, character development, turn, etc.)?

- Who is a new favorite author you discovered this trimester? What appeals to you about his or her style, subject matter, and themes?

- What do you think happens in a good booktalk?

- What do you think, understand, or realize now about Shakespeare?

- What are all the ways you vary your approach when reading to learn vs. reading for pleasure?

- What have I or people in your class done in reading workshop this trimester that helped you be a better reader and critic?

- Evaluate the process of finding a poem that resonates for you, preparing to present it to your class, and presenting it. What were the challenges? What did you do to meet them? How satisfied were you with your presentation? What did you learn about poetry?

- What would you do differently as a reader if you could rewrite the trimester?

- And, always, in second- and third-trimester questionnaires, describe the progress you made toward each of your reading goals of the previous trimester.

Students set individual reading goals in six areas: productivity and pace, book selections, experiments with authors and genres, letter-essays, participation in poetry discussions, and number of booktalks. These goals reinforce my priorities for students as readers. They should read a lot, make plans, stretch, respond as critics, and recommend good books to other readers.

Avery's reading goals for his second trimester of seventh grade are ambitious. He wants to read double the required number of pages per night; read four of the books he listed on the "someday pages" of his writing–reading handbook; try an action/adventure novel, a mystery, M. T. Anderson, and Stephen King; add, to the basics requirements of letter-essays, some of the literary features a critic *might* comment on; speak four times a week in poetry discussions; and present three booktalks.

Avery is a reader with plans. He attended to booktalks, his peers' letter-essays, minilessons, and class discussions, and he's ready to put to use what he learned to imagine his future as a reader. The specificity of Avery's goals shows me that reading workshop is working for him.

In introducing the concept of self-assessment to my classes, I try to be deliberate and thoughtful, so students will take the work of this week seriously, *learn* from it, and inform their parents and me about their discoveries. On a Monday in November, before Avery and his peers began to self-evaluate, I talked with them about what they were about to do and why it mattered:

> This is one of the three most important weeks of the school year. It's time for you to pause, reflect, and assess yourselves as writers and readers—to look back at your efforts and accomplishments and look ahead to what you want to work on and accomplish next.
>
> Please view self-evaluation as a research project. Your subject is *yourself*—your growth and achievements since Labor Day. Each researcher will gather a collection of evidence to examine: your writing-in-process folder, finished writing folder, writing record, writing–reading handbook, reading record, poetry and prose folders, and letter-essays. You'll use this evidence to help you answer three big questions: *What did I accomplish this trimester? What did I learn? What do I want to accomplish and learn next?*
>
> *Engage.* Stretch. Go and be as deep as you can. Show how knowledgeable and observant you've become about literary writing. Think. Spend time. Sift through your evidence: read it and take notes about what you find. Notice and describe the specifics that will create a portrait of you as a writer and reader, right here and right now. Try to be *interesting*—to yourself, your parents, and me—in the information and insights you generate.

I distribute copies of the writing self-assessment and explain my rationale for each question. I ask for their questions. I remind them about how to handle titles of literary works—when to quote and when to underline. Then I distribute and ask them to use a second, blank copy of the questionnaire as a place to gather data off-the-page as they mine and examine their evidence.

As Avery researched himself as a writer, he took notes on the extra questionnaire. Then he drafted his responses in pencil on the other copy. I reviewed it, lightly circled his misspellings in pencil, indicated his punctuation errors, and returned it to him for correction. Last June I changed the procedure slightly and asked kids to photocopy the first drafts of their questionnaires. I edited the photocopies, and they made my corrections on their originals: this worked even better. When I first began asking students to self-assess, I required them to produce complete first drafts, which I edited, followed by pen-and-ink final copies, until I recognized that copying over is an exercise in tedium. In a self-evaluation, it's the information and ideas that matter—the *meat*.

After Avery finished his first-trimester writing and reading self-evaluations, he compiled his portfolio. He worked from a checklist that his class and I created in collaboration. These were the items we determined were representative of the work of the trimester.

PORTFOLIO CHECKLIST—FIRST TRIMESTER

Writing and Spelling

- your self-evaluation questionnaire

- the two effective pieces of writing (photocopies) you mentioned in your self-evaluation (no captions necessary)

- your writing record (photocopy), with a long caption about what it shows about you as a writer in terms of your productivity, pace, choice of topics, and growth

- three of the most useful writing entries from the class notes section of your writing–reading handbook (photocopies), captioned as to why each lesson is significant for you as a writer

- the best memoir reading of the trimester (photocopy), labeled *This is the memoir I analyzed in my self-evaluation*

- your proofreading list (photocopy), labeled as to what it is, with a caption about what you're focusing on, conventions-wise

- your first-trimester spelling test (already captioned with your goals as a speller)

- writing and spelling photos

Reading

- your self-evaluation questionnaire

- your reading record (photocopy) of the first trimester, with a long caption about what it shows about you as a reader in terms of your tastes, pace, patterns, risks, growth, work with genres and authors, and challenges you've taken on

- photocopies of five of the best poems of the trimester, including the two you mentioned in your self-evaluation, with captions on the remaining three as to why they resonated for you as a critic, reader, and writer

- your independent response to the new poem I just gave you, with a caption that describes your goals as an unpacker of poetry

- your best letter-essay of the trimester (photocopy), highlighted and with a caption that lists the features that make it an effective piece of criticism

- your note card list of beloved children's books, labeled as to what it represents

- reading photos, including those of you and a kindergartner reading your beloved childhood books

While the checklist is typical, it also reflects our first-trimester emphases on memoir, poetry, and a project my students took on as a favor to Helene Coffin, the kindergarten teacher. She was concerned that some of her better readers were already dismissing picture books in favor of beginning "chapter" books. My students reminisced about their own beloved picture books, raided Helene's library and borrowed favorites, learned pointers for reading aloud from Helene and me, and spent a morning with the kindergartners on their laps, reveling in the stories, characters, and illustrations and showing our littlest ones that even the biggest ones aren't too cool for picture books.

Many of the items on the portfolio checklist call for captions. Students write these on 4 × 6–inch lined Post-its and stick them to the documents. For example, this is the caption Avery attached to his best letter-essay of the trimester, which he wrote about *House of the Scorpion* by Nancy Farmer.

> In my best letter-essay I:
>
> - told how the book was plotted
>
> - described the realism of the characters
>
> - described how Farmer shows the change in Matt when he realizes what people think of him
>
> - compared *House of the Scorpion* to Farmer's other books
>
> - identified two themes—that just because something is legal, that doesn't mean it's right, and that we shouldn't let what defines us as human be controlled by a government

At the end of the third trimester, the process changes. My students and I coauthor a writing–reading assessment that becomes part of their permanent record. Figure 8.4 represents Avery's contribution to the document. It demonstrates his productivity and versatility as a writer (twenty-eight finished pieces in eleven genres) and a reader (seventy-five books and nineteen genres). These are numbers to celebrate.

At the end of eighth grade, Avery writes about himself and the literature he reads as an *insider*. He can name his intentions as a writer, the techniques that bring them to life, the approaches that work for him, his writing strengths, and his challenges. As a reader, he can express his preferences, identify authors' techniques that appeal to him, and describe his accomplishments, strengths as a responder to literature, and goals.

Avery's answers are thoughtful, specific, and *useful* to him. Self-assessing gives him a platform to show what he knows, lay claim to his knowledge in a formal way, and recognize what he needs to attend to next. The process of evaluating himself made Avery a stronger writer and reader—more self-aware, purposeful, and *ambitious* in all the best senses of the word.

Your Name __Avery__

Date __June__

Final Self-Evaluation in Writing and Reading and Final Teacher Comments

General

What were your favorite school subjects this year? history and math

What are you proudest of, in terms of your academic and social accomplishments at CTL this year?
I made friends quickly, I adjusted to the school well, I've done good work, and I got a lot of writing done.

Writing and Spelling

How many pieces of writing did you finish this year? 28

What genres are represented?
free-verse poetry — ode
haiku — review
abcedaria — essay
— profile
memoir
short-short
flash fiction
gift of writing

What are your favorite genres to write, in order of preference? short-short, ode, and memoir

Which two pieces of writing are most effective? Why? List what you did as the author.
"Two and a Half Deaths"   "Leftover Memory"

• I created multiple scenes and transitioned among them smoothly.
• I used specific details.
• I had metaphors and similes.
• I wrote a conclusion that had to be unpacked.
• I used strong verbs.
• I used dialogue effectively.
• I used a specific memory and brought it to life with sensory details.
• I created cadence.
• I shifted through time smoothly.
• I used effective repetition by repeating a phrase at the end of each stanza.
• I told lots of thoughts and feelings.
• I used simple color words to create visuals.

What were your major accomplishments this year as a writer? Your most significant changes? Please list them:
I tried an abcedaria, I wrote off the page more because I found it gives me better results in terms of the final draft of a piece of writing, I used

What rules and conventions of writing do you still need to master? Please list them: ____
• flexible paragraphing
• comma splices
• (single) spelling lists

Please list twenty words you learned how to spell this year. Choose representative words; choose words you've made part of your spelling repertoire forever.
necessary, dialogue, recommend, laid, subconscious, explanation, commiserative, awkward, epitome, memoir, fictitious, whether, embarrassed, presence, evidence, judgments, similes, positive, exercising

Reading

How many books did you finish this year? 35

What genres are represented?
contemporary realistic fiction — horror/thriller
dystopian fiction — political satire
fantasy — poetry/anthology
memoir — journalism
humor — science fiction
adventure/survival — classic
supernatural
historical fiction
modern Western
mystery-plot
graphic novel

What are your favorite genres to read, in order of preference? dystopian fiction, memoir, contemporary realistic fiction, horror/thriller, fantasy

Which two books were the best? Why? List what the authors did in crafting each.

Marching Powder by Rusty Young; Them McFallen   The Reapers Are the Angels by Alden Bell

• They gave specific details about people.
• The setting that brought the story to life.
• They created smooth time shifts that weren't confusing.
• They went off on seemingly unrelated topics that at the end revealed something about fiction.
• McFallen & his co-prisoners

• It created amazing visual details.
• It developed the main character brilliantly.
• He created a fast-moving plot.
• He made everything seem lifelike through specific details and strong diction.
• They built a strong anti-drug theme.

(continues)

Figure 8.4 Avery's June Evaluation in Writing and Reading

Who are your current favorite authors? Homer Hickam, Alden Bell, Patrick Ness, David Benioff, Neil Gaiman, Aaron Draper, Markus Zusak, Ned Vizzini

Who are your current favorite poets? Pablo Neruda, Gwendolyn Brooks, Robert Frost, Ted Kooser, and William Carlos Williams

Which poems of this year were the best? Please list them (title and poet). Include your favorites of all three trimesters.
"Carbon Physics, Part 1" by Nick Flynn, "Tree Heartbeat" by Siobhan Alderson, "Sims: The Game" by Elizabeth Spires, "America" by Tony Hoagland, "This Is Lost to Say" by William Carlos Williams, "Ode to the Onion" by Pablo Neruda, "Everything I Need to Know" by Karl Elder, "Opera" by Kevin Young, "The Fish" by Elizabeth Bishop, "Gwendolyn Brooks" by Haki Madhubuti, and "Let Evening Come" by Jane Kenyon

What were your major accomplishments this year as a reader of and responder to prose and poetry? Please list them:
- I read more books in one school year than ever before.
- I can unpack a poem and find the theme, rhyme scheme, and effects like alliteration and assonance.
- I novel beyond authors like James Patterson and Scott Westerfeld.
- I started reading memoirs and journalism.
- I did a lot of booktalks.
- I found two new favorite genres: dystopian fiction and contemporary realistic fiction.
- I moved beyond reading a ton of fantasy, although I still enjoy it once in awhile.

What are your strengths as a reader? What do you know how to do as someone who chooses books, reads them, reads and critiques poems, has literary opinions and tastes, recognizes good writing, and responds to literature as a critic? Please list your strengths:
- I can find the theme in a poem & in prose.
- I recognize that a good poem narrative balance of character development and plot.
- Now I don't just pick up any book and see if I like it—now I know what I tend to

sarcasm and irony in some of my poems; I used themes from my memories of my past; I craft work by hand now; I don't just accept a draft the way it is; I always try to make it better; I found that I really enjoy writing odes and memoirs; I like a lot of writing to my mom.
I kept a pace of about 7-11 pieces of writing per trimester; I found that I prefer typing to the third draft of a piece of writing but hand writing everything before that.

What are your strengths as a writer: the specific things you can do well at this juncture? Please list them:
- I can use thoughts & feelings to develop a theme.
- I can put sensory diction & realistic details in my writing.
- I can recognize comma splices.
- I can tell when it's appropriate to use numerals or whether I should write out the numbers.
- I can create cadence.
- I can use repetition and avoid ineffective repetition.
- I write off the page at the start of every new piece.

What are the areas in which you can improve as a writer? Please list them:
- I need to master the semicolon.
- I need to watch out for adverbs.
- I need to remember to write off the page with conclusions & experiment.
- I need to beware of clichés.
- I need to keep the dialogue and the speaker's information in the same paragraph.
- I need to remember the importance of keeping the balance in narratives among dialogue, action, reflection, and description.

Figure 8.4 Continued

(continues)

like, so I can focus on specific authors and books.
- I can find the tone in literature.
- I notice the turn in a poem.
- I can describe what makes an effective piece of writing in a certain genre, e.g., a review or essay.

What are the areas in which you can improve as a reader of and responder to prose and poetry? Please list them: _____
- I need to continue my current pace of booktalks, i.e., 3-5/trimester.
- I need to continue to speak daily and compose thoughtful, sustained letter-essays.
- I need to be discerning in adding titles to my Someday list: books that genuinely interest me.
- I need to move into more transitional titles.

Figure 8.4 *Continued*

TEACHER ASSESSMENT

No matter where I've taught English—urban middle school, rural elementary school, and, now, independent demonstration school—I have never graded individual pieces of writing. Growth in writing is slow. It's seldom straightforward, and it varies tremendously among young writers. It also happens on a wide array of fronts, as writers learn to generate, experiment, plan, select, question, draft, read themselves, anticipate, organize, craft, assess, review, revise, format, spell, punctuate, edit, and proofread. One piece of writing can never provide an accurate picture of a student's abilities; rather, it represents a step in a writer's growth—and not always a step forward, as new techniques, forms, or genres can overload any writer of any age.

Reliability—fairness to students and my understandings of the processes, genres, and conventions of writing—has to be one of my evaluation criteria. Validity is another. Assessment should reflect the expectations I communicate to my kids, day in and out, in the workshop. For evaluation to be valid, I can't turn around at the end of twelve weeks and impose "objective" standards for "good" writing on the collections in their finished writing folders. Avery's first poems weren't great. Clichés abounded, and there were few visuals, little to no *I* presence, and lots of woolly philosophizing; instead of concluding, his poems stopped. I didn't punish Avery's attempts in a grade book or view them as failures. Kids' writing and my own history as a writer have taught me that it's hard to write well while also experiencing writing-as-a-process for the first time, working in new genres, filling a toolbox with techniques of craft, and learning how to use it.

Teacher evaluation in writing—and reading—workshop has to step back and focus on the big picture of a student's experiments and growth and, within it, the revealing details. At the end of a trimester I read their self-assessments and gather and sift through the same evidence that students do: their finished-writing folders, marble notebooks of letter-essays, and the portfolio collections, which include their best pieces and letter-essays, writing and reading records, annotated best poems they read, proofreading lists, and selected handbook entries, all of it captioned. I add my status-of-the-class records to the pile. Based on these data, I write notes off-the-page about a student's writing and reading and then draw on these to write the progress report.

Figure 8.5 shows my progress report for Avery for the first trimester. In evaluating his writing, I began by describing the specific areas in which he improved, his motivation as a writer, and his control of conventions of usage and spelling. Then I listed the goals he needs to work toward in the second trimester. The first three were set by Avery; I took them directly from his writing self-assessment. To these I added my goals, which addressed problems I observed in his writing: premature titles that were labels, weak conclusions, clichés, ineffective repetition, and, in his emerging memoir, an overreliance on dialogue and action at the expense of reflection.

Next, I identified Avery's reading preferences, commented on his comprehension and vocabulary, and assessed the growth in his letter-essays and contributions to poetry discussions. To the goals he stated in his reading self-assessment, I added two book titles I thought he'd enjoy, nudged him to use the new vocabulary he'd been exposed to when he comments on the daily poems, and advised him to be more selective in adding books to his someday list—he was recording every booktalked title, which didn't help him make plans as a reader.

Parent-student-teacher evaluation conferences take place in the evenings and on four early-release afternoons. When they're over, I give each student a photocopy of his or her first-trimester progress report and two bright-colored tag cards, one headed "My Second-Trimester Goals for Writing" and the other "My Second-Trimester Goals for Reading." They copy the goals from their progress reports and then staple the cards inside their writing-in-process and reading folders. I tell them that a major part of their next self-assessment, and mine of them, will be determining the progress they made toward the goals. The colorful cards are intended as prominent, daily reminders of what each student is supposed to concentrate on over the subsequent twelve weeks.

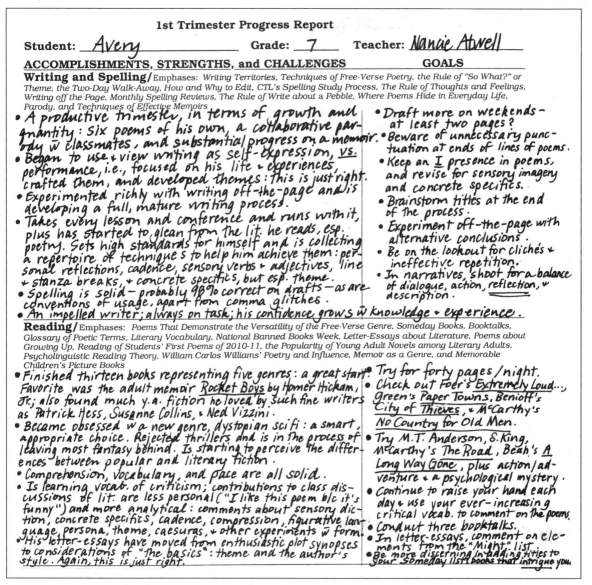

Figure 8.5 *Nancie's First-Trimester Progress Report for Avery*

The goals my students and I set for their writing and reading run the gamut, from conventions of usage and work habits to techniques, strategies, procedures, genres, authors, forms, and topics. The goals also represent the range of students I teach, from a quick-learning novice like Avery to those with identified learning disabilities, low ability or motivation, and attention deficit disorder. The lists that follow illustrate the nature and specificity of the objectives I've recorded in the second column of progress reports over the last few years.

POTENTIAL GOALS FOR WRITERS

- Push for a *so what?* or theme in everything you write.
- Brainstorm titles at the end.
- Experiment with cadence.
- Experiment with alliteration and assonance.
- Listen for and fix ineffective repetition.
- Write off-the-page to help develop your *so what?*s or themes.
- Establish an *I* presence in your poems to convey your thoughts, feelings, and perceptions.
- Experiment with a poem in the style of E. E. Cummings.
- Experiment with short poems and forms: *compress.*
- Take breaks from demanding prose pieces with poems.
- Cut your poetry to the bone.
- Include thoughts and feelings in poems and memoirs: use them as a basis for theme.
- Beware of writing about pebbles; focus on the tangible specifics of *a thing.*
- Take advantage of the two-day walk-away to give yourself perspective as a reviser.
- Write off-the-page *whenever* you're stuck or uncertain.
- Go to a peer conference area by yourself, read your draft softly aloud, and listen for a lack of sense or missing words.
- Refer to your territories list and become independent as a planner of your writing.
- View writing not as a performance (or exercise) but as an occasion for reflection: push yourself to name your thoughts, feelings, ideas, and experiences and discover what matters to you.
- Provide the sensory verbs, nouns, and adjectives that will help your readers see, hear, and feel.
- Write alternative leads off-the-page, and then work with the most promising—the one that fuels you as a writer.
- Write alternative conclusions off-the-page, and then work with the most promising—the one that will leave readers thinking and feeling as you want them to.
- In expository writing, focus on coherence: plan an order for your information off-the-page.
- In expository writing, anticipate a reader's questions and need for information.
- Finish your profile of *X* and try to get it published.
- Try a parody.
- Try a poem that uses a given form (e.g., tritina, sonnet, pantoum, or villanelle).

- In narratives, remember to revise for a balance among dialogue, reflections, descriptions, and action.
- Include more of your reflections in your prose—your thoughts and feelings about why events or ideas are significant.
- Focus on clarity: can a reader understand what you're saying without an oral explanation from you?
- Beware of adverbs (-*ly* words). Search for sensory verbs.
- Beware of *would* constructions. Use active verbs.
- Identify and replace weak verbs when you revise.
- When you revise and polish, slow down. Gut-check each word, phrase, and sentence.
- Consider deletion as an act of revision. What don't you need? What have you already said? What doesn't add to the theme or argument?
- Identify and replace clichés.
- Bring your eye and ear as a poet to your prose: make its diction sing, too.
- Spend less time conferring with peers. Bull through difficulty on your own. Have no more than one peer conference per week.
- Finish two more pieces of writing next trimester. Bull through difficulty, and don't abandon so much or so soon.
- Produce at least three to five pages of rough draft each week, no questions asked.
- Push for four to five pages of rough draft each week—you need to stretch for fluency.
- Be more scrupulous about record-keeping: record the titles of finished pieces and file them chronologically, with all drafts and notes, in your finished writing folder.
- Take time at the end of each workshop to organize your writing-in-process folder and file your drafts and notes. Make a special place in your locker to store your folder.
- Tape a note to yourself inside your locker: a list of what you need to bring each day to writing–reading workshop.
- Record new conventions on your proofreading list immediately after each editing conference with me.
- Slow down your handwriting.
- Make your handwriting larger.
- Work on legibility: close *o*, *a*, and *d*, and extend the tails of *g*, *f*, *p*, etc.
- Abandon cursive, except for your signature. From now on, print when you write by hand.
- When you've finished creating a final copy, proofread it s-l-o-w-l-y with a pen in your hand.
- Always draft double-spaced.

- Proofread for missing word endings (*s* and *ed*).
- Attend to conventions while you're drafting: punctuate, capitalize, and paragraph as well as you can right from the start.
- Spell as conventionally as you can as you draft.
- Draft your poems in lines and stanzas.
- Draft your prose in paragraphs.
- Watch out for too many paragraphs. Readers need to be able to relax into chunks of text instead of having the hiccoughs.
- Watch out for too few paragraphs. Readers need spaces to rest and breathe.
- When a correct spelling is available to you, consult it.
- As an editor, check every noun that ends in *s:* is it a plural, or is it a possessive noun that needs an apostrophe?
- Self-edit for spelling by circling, then looking up, every single word you're not absolutely sure of: conduct a slow, careful visual check.
- Proofread your drafts backward for misspellings.
- Be sure to record all your misspellings on your master list.
- When you study a misspelling, focus on the word *part* that confuses you: say it louder and write it darker.
- As a speller, break long polysyllabic words into their syllables when you write them.
- Acquire a handheld spellchecker and use it in every subject.
- As a speller, beware of your old, bad habits, e.g., *sentance, mabe, sence, tamorrow, recieve.*
- Develop mnemonics for your habitual misspellings.
- Pay particular attention to homonyms (especially *your/you're, their/they're/there,* and *its/it's*) when you edit.
- At the ends of words, change *y* to *ie* when you create plurals.
- *Listen* for periods: where does your voice drop and stop?
- *Listen* for commas: where does your voice pause?
- Experiement with new marks to give your writing greater voice: try ; : and —.
- Focus as an editor on the rules we studied governing commas, and apply them.
- Master hyphens vs. dashes.
- Keep a consistent verb tense in narratives: past or present.
- Shoot for active constructions: *I did this*, not *I would do this* or *This was done.*
- Make more use of direct quotes: bring speakers' words to life instead of para-phrasing them.
- Master how to indicate titles: when to quote, underline/italicize, or merely capitalize.
- Review your handbook entry on how to handle titles whenever you're uncertain.

- Indent for every new paragraph, including the first one.
- Capitalize only when you intend to.
- Identify and correct comma splices; then connect the independent clauses with a FANBOY (*for, and, nor, but, or, yet*), start a new sentence, or use a semicolon, colon, or dash.
- Put punctuation—! or ? or ,—after a quote and before its tagline: *never* use a period here.
- Keep the name of the speaker, the tagline, and the quote in the same paragraph.
- Use apostrophes on contractions to show missing letters: *don't, let's, that's, there's,* etc.
- Except in dialogue, eliminate the qualifiers and diminishers that clutter writing: *so, really, very, sort of, kind of, definitely.*
- Watch out for convoluted sentences: too many clauses hooked together with commas and conjunctions can lose a reader and the thread of sense.
- Practice keyboarding at home: sign out a laptop.
- Use your handbook as a resource when you're uncertain or stuck.
- Stop talking to others during writing workshop.

POTENTIAL GOALS FOR READERS

- Read with a finger on your mouth to prevent lipreading, which slows your reading rate and prevents you from chunking text.
- Read with a finger on your throat to prevent word-by-word inner vocalizing, which slows your reading rate and prevents you from chunking text.
- Try to see "chunks" instead of one word at a time. Read for meaning, not to say each word.
- Get out of the habit of using a bookmark to underline your reading: it checks peripheral vision, and it slows you down.
- Experiment with pushing your reading rate: skip, skim, and scan.
- When you get bogged down in an uninteresting passage in a novel, try skimming or skipping: what happens?
- Time yourself: how many pages do you read in half an hour? Can you increase the average number of pages over time?
- Read for at least half an hour every night, seven days a week.
- Ask your parents for a bedside lamp.
- Develop a consistent reading habit: *the* time and *the* place you'll get lost in a book at home.
- Make sure you read at least twenty pages a night.
- Shoot for forty pages a night.

- Read one book at a time, so your experiences with books are literary and coherent and you can criticize them in literary, coherent ways.
- Don't stick with a book you're not enjoying. Give the author [some number of] pages and, if you aren't happy with the writing, abandon the book.
- Try to finish three more books than last trimester.
- Begin to identify authors you love, and follow through by trying more of their books.
- Attend to booktalks, update your someday list, and use it.
- Don't settle for books that don't compel you.
- Try more books by _____.
- Try _____ as a genre, and see what you think.
- Try _____ as an author, and see what you think.
- Try the book _____ by _____.
- Refer to your someday list when you're book browsing: carry it with you to the bookshelves.
- Pay more attention to your peers' booktalks: they're experts about great stories.
- Be more discerning about recording someday titles during booktalks: only note the ones that intrigue you.
- Move beyond graphic novels as your most reliable source of pleasure reading: it's time.
- Keep complete reading records: you'll want to remember the authors whose books you rated as tens.
- Check in with me when you record the genres of books you finish, so you can be precise.
- Try some poetry on your own. Stick Post-it notes to, photocopy, and collect your favorite new poems.
- Try one of Shakespeare's plays on your own.
- Try a classic: *Jane Eyre*? *Pride and Prejudice*? *The Scarlet Letter*? *Lord of the Flies*? *All Quiet on the Western Front*? *Brave New World*?
- Put your hand up every day in our poetry discussions and get your mouth around the vocabulary of criticism.
- In our poetry discussions, focus less on a poem's form and more on the poet's diction, imagery, and figurative language.
- Begin to identify authors of adult fiction to whom you can look for satisfying reading experiences.
- Discern the differences between commercial and literary fiction, while continuing to enjoy both.
- Try some of the transitional and adult titles and authors I've been booktalking: you're ready.

- Give a booktalk to the group about _____.
- In your letter-essays, synopsize plot less and analyze writing more: tell what you think about how an author wrote a book.
- In your letter-essays, *always* describe theme.
- In your letter-essays, *always* introduce or follow up the excerpt with a sentence or two about what it shows about the writing.
- In your letter-essays, start at least three sentences with the author's name, to help you focus on the choices he or she made.
- Receive a ✓+ on every letter-essay.
- When you like a book or feel strongly about it, think about what the author did that gave rise to your feelings.
- When you're dissatisfied with a novel's conclusion (an ambiguous or unhappy ending), consider why the author made this choice. Is there a theme he or she might be pointing?
- Write letter-essays of at least three pages every time.
- Stay on-topic in your letter-essays and minimize the peer shenanigans.
- Remember to bring your book to school with you every day; put a Post-it reminder on your door at home.
- Return the books you borrow as soon as you finish them.
- Remember to sign out every book you borrow on your cards.
- Remember to sign in with me every book you return.

This evaluation scheme—student self-assessment and goal-setting combined with teacher analysis and goal-setting—fits my school, its philosophy, and our methods. Teachers do not assign grades at CTL. Here, a student's incentive is the work itself—engaging, working toward goals, and experiencing increasing power and pleasure as writers, readers, critics, mathematicians, historians, and scientists. I acknowledge this is a luxury. I know I'm lucky not to have to stick numbers or letters on my kids. But I also know that without the incentive of grades, my methods have to be strong enough to impel kids—to convince them that what I'm asking them to do has intrinsic worth and meaning. Without the reward or punishment of grades, CTL students work hard, achieve, and, often, excel.

When I taught at Boothbay Region Elementary School, I was required to assign letter grades four times a year to the students in my writing and reading workshops. The challenge was to make sure the grades reflected what I was asking them to do. The solution was to base grades on the progress students made toward their individual goals as writers and readers. I had too many students to write progress reports that detailed everyone's accomplishments, but I could, and did, focus on each student's goals.

If a student satisfied my expectations for writing and reading workshop and met all of his or her goals, the report card grade was an A. If there was solid or more than adequate progress, I assigned a B. Adequate or fair work earned a C. Students who did little received D's. The one student to whom I ever gave a failing grade had "lost" everything on purpose in June: there was no evidence for either of us to assess.

On the writing self-assessment I created at the end of Avery's second trimester as a seventh grader, among my questions was "Describe the progress you made toward your second-trimester writing goals." He answered:

- I did remember the importance of keeping the balance among dialogue, description, action, and reflection in narratives.
- I did keep an *I* presence and revise for sensory imagery and concrete specifics.
- I was aware of the negative potential of clichés and ineffective repetition.
- I did keep an eye on punctuation at the ends of lines of poems.
- I didn't experiment off-the-page with conclusions.
- I didn't brainstorm titles at the end of writing a piece.
- I didn't always draft two pages over the weekend.

I agreed with Avery's analysis—the evidence in his finished writing folder confirmed it. If he had been my student at Boothbay Elementary, his report card grade would have been B+.

Implementing this grading system at Boothbay meant that my mainstreamed special education students could work hard, accomplish their goals, and earn A's. It also meant that, on occasion, a so-called gifted writer or reader did not receive an A because the evidence to merit it was lacking.

At CTL, students of grades 1–8 start school in September with goals for writing, reading, and math already established by the previous year's teacher. When Avery matriculated to CTL as a seventh grader, the records from his sending school indicated no goals for him as a writer or a reader, but at the start of eighth grade, he went right to work on the objectives he and I had established the previous June (Figure 8.6).

If I were teaching in a system where students didn't end one school year with goals for the next, I'd be comfortable starting every writer with similar goals for the first trimester:

- Find meaningful topics for poems and a memoir.
- Produce three to five pages of rough draft per week.
- Finish three to five poems.
- Experiment with the techniques introduced in minilessons.
- Follow the rule of *so what?* or theme.
- Follow the rules and meet the expectations of writing workshop.

At Boothbay Elementary, when it came to reading workshop, I based first-quarter grades on the degree to which a student had conformed to workshop rules and expectations.

Teacher's Comments

Reading Strengths	Reading Challenges	Writing Strengths	Writing Challenges
• Avery is a passionate reader with strong comprehension, both literal and literary. Vocabulary, pace, and fluency are all mature. • He has learned to select books w̄ discretion: to recognize literary prose, be particular about his choices, and identify formulaic writing and characters. • His contributions to class discussions of poetry in the third trimester were impressive. He's becoming adept at analysis and identifying significant features of text, although theme can sometimes still elude him. • His letter-essays about books showed growth, as he learned how to attend to and describe authorial choices, styles, and techniques. • He discusses books with peers as an easy, natural extension of his friendships. • He uses the study process in history and science to good effect and understands, retains, and connects information and implications.	• Take the lead next fall in poetry discussions: show your new peers how to unpack a poem using critical vocabulary. • Continue to push your book choices into new authors + genres, as well as more adult-transitional titles and selected classics. • Continue the current pace and enthusiasm level of your book-talks.	• Avery is a teachable writer who desires significance and excellence. He's purposeful and ambitious, and he worked to acquire a repertoire of techniques and approaches, which he applied appropriately and smartly. He also experimented with forms, styles, genres, etc., and was able to learn from his successes and failures. • Poetry became a strength. He attends to diction at the single-word level and plays with cadence, figurative language, imagery and form. • Essays and reviews are new strengths, too. He knows how to gather information, order it, and give it a voice. • He developed a full, productive writing process; pays particular attention to revision and polishing. Generating writing off-the-page, both before and during drafting, serves him well. • Conventions of usage, including spelling, commas, capitalization, and paragraphing, are mature, with a few glitches.	• Continue to experiment and generate off-the-page. WOP makes a huge difference in the quality of your products. • Watch out for overusing adverbs and for excess verbiage in general; remember that deletion is also an act of revision. • Keep complete spelling records: make certain that every word you study appears on your master list. • Get the knack of the semicolon. • Edit for comma splices. • In your narratives, shoot for a balance of action, dialogue, description, and <u>reflection</u>.

Figure 8.6 *Nancie's June Progress Report for Avery*

I created a system that gave them points for each day they brought a book, read it in class, and had read at least twenty pages at home the night before. Then I averaged in my ratings of their letter-essays: each ✓+, ✓, and ✓− became an A, a B, C, or D. After the first quarter, I added to the mix the progress each student had made toward the individual goals we set at the end of the previous marking period.

Tom Romano observes about evaluation, "Our responses and grades should nurture" (1987). Evaluation of writing and reading in a workshop should focus on the writers and the readers and how a teacher promotes their growth by encouraging them and showing them ways to do better next time.

When we transform an English class into a workshop—when the language arts program is based on what writers, readers, and critics do and need—we send students unmistakable signals about the importance of initiative, commitment, and reflection. Making assessment an occasion for students to analyze their work, describe their progress, and set goals extends and enriches their development as writers and readers. It affords teachers a crucial perspective to learn about our students' learning. And it strengthens what happens in the workshop across all the days and weeks of a school year.

PART II

GENRE STUDIES

A WORD ABOUT GENRES

In writing workshop, I introduce and require kinds of texts found in the world of publishing: writing a reader can find in a newspaper, bookstore, or library. I avoid what I call "school genres," and I try not to water down too much the real-world genres that my students attempt.

In the category of school genres I'd include book reports vs. book reviews or critical essays; what-I-did-on-my-summer-vacation reports instead of memoirs; cutesy poetic formats vs. free verse; something called "fiction pieces" instead of short stories or flash fiction; five-paragraph essays rather than opinion pieces or letters to the editor; reports pasted together from Internet research vs. essays, feature articles, and arguments based on data a writer gathers firsthand; and a whole host of forms of writing no one ever borrowed from a library: compare-contrast essays, descriptive paragraphs, acrostic poetry, annotated bibliographies, and the steps in making a peanut butter and jelly sandwich.

When it comes to genre, the real thing is so compelling and worthwhile I don't want to waste one minute of students' time teaching them forms that delay the satisfactions of writing. Composing the real thing answers a crucial question: "What can writing *do?*" I collect examples of strong writing across the genres, and I sleep well at night thinking about the binders I've packed full of poems, narratives, exposition, and original research that I appreciate and think kids will, too. When they have opportunities to observe and identify the features of a kind of writing, it's more likely they'll produce effective, meaningful versions of their own.

I prepare and present courses of study: poetry in September, many days in October and November focused on memoirs, November and December devoted to reviews and gifts of writing; and an emphasis in winter and spring on micro fiction, essays, humor, and original research in the form of profiles and advocacy journalism. I ask students not to attempt a genre until I teach it. This means they develop repertoires as writers as they work with each genre across a school year and I present targeted minilessons.

Poetry is the exception. I teach it throughout the school year, September until June. Poetry offers so many possibilities, does so many things for students as writers and readers of literature, works in so many ways, speaks to so many facets of the human experience, and so affects my kids' feelings and ideas that it is impossible to ever teach it completely. Because of its generosity as a genre, the diversity of its content, its usefulness in young people's lives, and the compactness and versatility of the form, I think poetry is the essential genre to teach in grades K–12.

One day over lunch at CTL, I asked my K–6 colleagues to list for me the genres they teach in their writing workshops. Their answers, which appear as the following figure, demonstrate two kinds of expertise. Helene, Ted, Jill, and Glenn know their students— who they are developmentally, what they can do, and what engages and makes sense to them. And they know literature. They've matched the genres they teach to the children they teach with eyes toward authenticity and developmental appropriateness.

Genres overlap among our classes. Poetry and gifts of writing, which are usually poems, are written every year, as are memoirs. Teachers differentiate between simple memoirs in K–4 and reflective memoirs starting in grades 5 and 6: we're drawing a distinction between younger children's straightforward stories about events from their lives and our older students' push for significance and theme. Book reviews in grades 3–4 are briefer and less sophisticated in their attention to literary features than those written by seventh and eighth graders. And the business letters that advocate for change in grades 5–6 grow into full-blown advocacy journalism in 7–8.

The essential point about our work in genres is that these are kinds of writing that students find compelling and useful. A need for self-expression, coupled with meaningful modes in which to express themselves, drives our kids' excellence as writers. The faculty has not caved to standards that call for voiceless essays with "body paragraphs" of evidence under the misapprehension that this will transform children into masters of

GENRES TAUGHT IN CTL'S WRITING WORKSHOPS

K *(Helene Coffin)*
poetry
simple memoirs
alphabet books
counting books
lists
labels
cards
thank-you and get-well letters
gifts of writing

1–2 *(Ted DeMille)*
poetry
simple memoirs
lists
invitations
thank-you and other friendly letters
informational booklets
books to know and be known (about
    children's lives and families)
letters to authors
fairy tales
picture books
biographies
gifts of writing

3–4 *(Jill Cotta)*
poetry
simple memoirs
friendly letters
thank-you, get-well, and condolence letters
letters to authors
short stories

picture books
book reviews
personal essays and reports
peer profiles
gifts of writing
(*Note:* in reading workshop, regular letters about books)

5–6 *(Glenn Powers)*
poetry
memoirs (simple and reflective)
various short fiction genres
Letters about Literature (Library of Congress competition)
letters of change, i.e., complaint or persuasion
movie reviews, plus book reviews for the CTL blog
dramatic monologues
gifts of writing
(*Note:* in reading workshop, regular literary letters)

7–8 *(Nancie Atwell)*
poetry
reflective memoirs
micro and flash fiction
movie or television program reviews, plus book reviews
    for the CTL blog
essays
profiles
advocacy journalism
parodies
thank-you, get-well, and condolence letters
graduation speeches
gifts of writing
(*Note:* in reading workshop, regular letter-essays about
    literature)

Genres Taught in CTL's Writing Workshops

report writing who will wow future employers. We are preparing students for work—and academia—by inviting them to write *as children and adolescents write.*

Child writers learn best and most about logic, coherence, specificity, tone, evidence, diction, theme, usage, planning, drafting, and revision in the context of pieces of writing that matter to them. Engagement doesn't make writing simple. Instead, appropriate, authentic genres stretch kids in profound directions. They learn that concrete specificity is a hallmark of effective writing in every genre, that purpose is essential to any writer, and that clarity matters, always. Tempted by variety, by a wealth of opportunities for crafting their ideas, feelings, and experiences, they push themselves to become effective writers of any genre.

Colleen was a student in my writing workshop years ago. She was an enthusiastic poet, memoirist, and reviewer—a writer with a big voice and a deep investment in self-expression. She wrote to me as a second-year law student about how the writing she composed as a child has prepared her to write as a budding attorney.

> Much of my undergraduate degree involved writing, but nothing screams reading, analysis, and writing quite like law school. Although my writing has certainly evolved since my early years in middle school, your guidance and the passion for learning that you fostered early on have had the most profound effect on me as an adult.
>
> In the spring we were required to write an appellate brief for one of our classes, and the process included peer editing. I was astonished to see the drastic differences between my writing and that of my classmates. Certainly mine warranted heavy corrections by the professor, but the fundamental difference I noticed was that I was taught from a very young age, by you and the other teachers at CTL, to love writing and to practice regularly and passionately. I never considered that others did not have this same experience. It was not until I realized this that I began to appreciate the unique, and successful, methods practiced at CTL; it wasn't only about teaching us how to write professionally and effectively, but also to bestow the deeper appreciation and satisfaction that one derives from writing well.
>
> I approach writing today much the same way you instructed me, with an eye for creativity and analysis, and relentless dedication. I thank you from the bottom of my heart for providing me with this gift.

In her twenties, Colleen looked back and recognized that a school environment in which she was invited "to love writing and to practice regularly and passionately" taught her *how to write, period*. Her CTL teachers weren't preparing her for a career at the bar by backmapping the language arts curriculum. We were teaching a little girl how to think and express herself on paper.

Colleen's ambitions at the end of eighth grade were to star on Broadway and marry someone famous. Like other CTL students who grew up to become lawyers, authors, advertising copywriters, editors, academics, environmentalists, engineers, and business owners—adults who work at careers in which they write every day—she benefited from a child-centered curriculum that gave her the experience, advice, and tools to communicate her ideas to others with, as she put it, "an eye for creativity and analysis, and relentless dedication."

Writing workshop teaches children how to work as writers. Choosing their own topics and exploring their ideas in authentic, kid-friendly ways motivates and gives them a sense of purpose. Teachers who understand children, genres, and writing process create lessons that meet students' needs and produce writers.

CHAPTER 9

POETRY

Poets are not born in a country.
Poets are born in childhood.

—ILYA KAMINSKY

For years, I launched writing workshop with memoirs. I figured it was the genre most accessible to students because narrative was a familiar mode and memoirs described kids' real experiences. I suspect that teachers who followed my advice may have observed the same results I did.

Most of the memoirs were okay but not great. Instead of viewing personal stories as an opportunity to reflect on formative experiences and shape them as literature, students with limited writing experience had to use the genre as a vehicle for learning big, essential lessons about process and craft. The memoirs involved a tremendous amount of work, on my part and theirs, as kids experimented with the processes of writers in the context of multiple drafts of extended pieces of prose. I fretted because few students scratched the potential of personal narratives to illuminate their lives and reveal what was significant. They were more than ready to move on to the next genre study, free-verse poetry, and the pleasures to be found in its versatility, compactness of form, and tight focus on diction and meaning.

One summer, as I sketched my plans for September, it occurred to me that if students began with free verse, they might be able to learn and apply the initial, important lessons about process and craft *and* produce more satisfying, more significant, and just plain more writing sooner. Since I started each workshop with a poem, my kids were familiar with the genre from the first day of school. I decided to see what happened if we put poetry first, as the foundation of a year of writing workshop. Poetry changed everything.

My students showed me that no genre can match it in teaching about the craft of writing. Every lesson that matters, every essential feature of literature, can be highlighted easily and accessibly in free-verse poems: the need for a writer to find subjects he or she cares about, the importance of first-person voice and reflection, the value of tangible nouns and sensory verbs and adjectives, how to revise and polish and edit, what titles do, why readers want inviting leads and resonant conclusions, how punctuation gives voice to writing, and why and how writers develop and support a theme.

What's more, because of the compactness of poetry, every student finished two or three pieces of writing by the end of September. Kids applied the lessons they learned from the writing of one poem to the writing of the next. There was immediate improvement—a strong incentive to like writing and want to continue. And many of the poems were wonderful—themed, specific, and full of energy and imagery. Through reading a poem a day and writing poems of their own, my students learned how writers of every genre observe, select, shape ideas, identify feelings, and discover what matters and what is true—and it was still only September. The memoirs, reviews, short fiction, essays, and original research that followed were better than ever before—voiced, deeper, more eloquent, and more meaningful to writers and their readers.

A free-verse genre study is a foundation for a year of motivated writing. It gives focus and resonance to students' ideas and experiences. It makes them see, listen, think, feel, and remember. It changes their perspectives. Wallace Stevens writes that the poet's role "is to help people live their lives" (1951). Their poetry, more than any other genre, helps my adolescent students live their lives.

In Chapter 8, about evaluation, I introduced Avery as an incoming seventh grader discovering how poetry works and what it might mean in his life. By the end of eighth grade, poetry had informed his experience as a writer and transformed his experience of the world. His sense of purpose; control of diction, cadence, imagery, figurative language, and theme; and appreciation of what writing could do all began with poetry. Most important of all, his poems taught Avery how to pay attention.

Why I Write

I want to write a graceful poem
because I saw
the red yellow orange leaves
twitch on their skeletal limbs
and blend into a natural mosaic
(and i knew what i had found).

I want to write a concise poem
because
if I tried to explain
the way the smile
split his face,
too much

would not be enough
(so
i'll settle for less).

I want to write a sensory poem
so I can capture how the flaming sun
melted
into the horizon above
Singing Meadows
and saturated the sky
with her warm hues
(leaving fading streaks of color
as she disappeared).

This is why I write:
because life
would be death
if I forgot my memories
(because i need to remember
these snapshots
before they fall off the page of my mind).

—*Avery Genus*

FREE VERSE: BUILD A TOOLBOX

It's easy for inexperienced writers to misperceive the power and potential of poetry. Their rhyming poems often struggle to have something to say, and while their free verse is usually about something, it's weakened by a lack of knowledge of the conventions of the genre.

I realize this sounds like a contradiction—that a free genre should follow rules—but practicing free-verse poets understand some things, implicitly or explicitly, about how the genre works. Their knowledge raises free verse above the worst sins of the genre: cliché, clutter, cuteness, formlessness, voicelessness, intentional obscurity, and prose structures masquerading as poems—skinny paragraphs with arbitrary line breaks. Knowledgeable poets use the conventions of the genre to create voice, pattern, imagery, comparisons, sound effects, and resonance.

To learn about the conventions, I read tons of free verse and began to write some of my own. Both processes took me inside the genre. Multiple readings of good poems helped me understand how they cue readers, use white space, denote, and connote. My own poems showed me how hard it is to write a good one. I learned that a poet both has to create and resolve difficulty, and I wrestled with the minute choices and decisions of the genre. I've never written fewer than four drafts of any poem.

In figuring out how to introduce free verse in September, two ideas informed my plans: good poems take time and revision, and the techniques of good poets can be observed, learned, and put into practice, even by novices. I decided to approach both ideas in a series of minilessons about what a poem can do besides rhyme—about the tools of the free-verse poet. I illustrate each lesson with verse by pros and my former students. I've included lots of rich examples of the latter here, for teachers to choose among as models for your students.

In the first minilesson, we define the genre and explore the power of the first person.

LESSON 1: A DEFINITION OF FREE VERSE

I think you can already guess, based on my embarrassing enthusiasm for the poems we've read so far, how much I love poetry. More than any other genre, it helps me live my life. It connects me with others at the most essential level—one heart and mind touching another heart and mind—but it distances me, too. It invites me to see the familiar with fresh eyes. Poetry is the language of my feelings. It expresses my needs, hopes and dreams, ideas about life, perceptions, heartaches, and sources of happiness better than any other genre.

So I begin with a warning. Good poetry, the useful kind, is hard to write. Let's face it—it's easy to string together pretty words and parcel them into lines. What I'm talking about is the hard work of a good poet—observing, creating images others can perceive, finding a truth, choosing and arranging, cutting and playing, considering language at the single-word level, and writing from the heart.

There's a myth out there about writing a poem, that it's an exquisite experience in which beautiful language is delivered to a poet on the wings of a dove. Don't you believe it. Good poets work at it. They know what good poetry is because they read it, and they revise toward their sense of what a good poem does, is, and can do.

Emily Dickinson wrote: "If I feel physically as if the top of my head were taken off, I know that is poetry" (Bianchi 1924). She knew the *labor* of it.

So, how do you work as a poet? I know nine techniques for you to keep in mind as you draft, revise, and polish your free-verse poems. Please turn to the next clean page in the notes section of your writing–reading handbook and record this heading: My Free-Verse Poetry Toolbox. Please dog-ear the corners of the next four pages. I may teach other minilessons among and between these, and I want you to keep the free-verse lessons together. The turned-down corners are a reminder to save these pages.

Let's start with a formal definition, based on what I've learned as a reader and critic of free-verse poems. Copy it from the easel stand into your handbook, as the frame of your toolbox.

A Definition:

Free verse is poetry that doesn't have a regular rhythm, line length, or rhyme scheme. It relies on the natural rhythms of speech. Today it's the form of poetry that most American poets prefer. Free-verse poetry invents and follows its own forms, patterns, and rules.

So, if free-verse poets create and follow their own forms, how can there be rules? In fact, they're more like *conventions*—approaches that poets and their readers agree make poems strong. The first technique to add to your toolbox is "Tap the Power of *I*." Tape your copy of these notes right below the definition of free verse.

Tap the Power of **I**

First-person experiences need a first person. Make sure your *I* is acting, reacting, seeing, hearing, and feeling in your poems. Give readers someone to be with. Use *I* to create entry points to describe your thoughts and feelings, which will lead to your *so what?* or theme. Wave your *I* flag.

Never underestimate the power of *I* to ground a poem—to capture you in relation to the world of the poem and provide the single most important detail a reader craves: a human intelligence, a presence, a specific someone to be with. This year we'll read *I* poems by Billy Collins, Emily Dickinson, Mary Oliver, Robert Frost, Naomi Shihab Nye, Langston Hughes, William Carlos Williams, William Stafford, Pablo Neruda, Nikki Giovanni, Elizabeth Bishop—so many *lyric* poets. This means they wave their *I* flag. These are poets who have powerful first-person voices.

I know it's tempting to hide or be modest. But you are the only one who can tell your observations, ideas, feelings, and stories. Embrace them. Raise your voice as a poet. Give your readers someone to be with. Your poems will be stronger for it; your readers will love you for it.

Check out two versions of a poem by Heidi about her beloved Converse sneakers to see what I mean. In the first draft, there isn't an *I* in sight.

CONVERSE

God—
there's nothing like a new pair of
high-top Converse,
except an old worn pair.
But the feeling when you
slip
your

      foot

          in

and you tighten the laces
up your ankle.
It gives your ankle support
and, really,
no other shoe does.
They come in so many
colors and shades of colors
and different shades of those.
If you don't like high-tops,
you can get low cuts.
But the truth is no
other shoe feels the same.
The truth—
the best shoe in the world.

Now compare the first draft with Heidi's final version.

ODE TO MY CONVERSE

The truth?
There's nothing like a new pair
of Converse high-tops—
except an old, worn-in pair, that is.
The feeling when I
slip
my
       foot
            in
and tighten the laces
is better than
anything—
the support it gives my ankle,
the style,
the color,
the comfort,
oh, the comfort.

And the choices?
The colors, the colors,
a world full of shades.
Should I buy
red,
black,

purple?
Purple *definitely*:
a beautiful color
and my favorite.

The bottom line?
No other shoe feels the same.
No other fits my foot
so right.
The truth?
Best shoe in the world,
I adore you,
and I swear
I'll wear you
forever.

—*Heidi Ziegra*

What's different about the second version? What does shifting to a first-person voice allow Heidi to think, feel, and say? What does it do for you as a reader?

Next, check out Hope's first draft of her first poem of seventh grade. It's about how people don't notice the beauty around them because they're focused on where they're going. It's an interesting theme, but this draft doesn't bring it to life. Hope has written about a *they* and a *you*, instead of an *I* (Figure 9.1).

Figure 9.1 *Hope's First Draft*

(continues)

> Never do they stop and stare up into the cosmos,
> into the deep black of endless beyond.
> So far we might as well be blind.
> Pause, stop, look up.
>   To something that is closer then you think and
> farther away then you could ever imagine.
>
>   Notes: More visuals
>   More cut to the bone

Figure 9.1 *Continued*

Now notice what happened when Hope recast the poem in a first-person voice. We can see it, experience it, *get* it because we're with Hope, following her actions and thoughts.

PAUSE

I hustle along busy sidewalks.
I speed across stretching blacktop.
I dash through the familiar rooms of my house.
In constant motion, I feel the pulse
of the play button:
forward, forward, forward.

I stare ahead to the next goal.
Seldom do I look up.

Last night I pressed *pause.*
I stared up into the glittering cosmos
at something that was closer than I thought

and farther away than I'll ever imagine.

—*Hope Logan*

LESSON 2: BREAK LINES AND STANZAS

Beginning poets can be stymied about how to handle line breaks. Rhymed poems are obvious: lines end with words that rhyme. But in free verse, the length and content of a line are the poet's decision. So, how do you choose which words belong together? How do your mind, eyes, ears, and lungs help you decide?

First, it's important to know that poetry is written to be spoken. Free-verse poetry breaks its lines to emphasize pauses. The ends of lines signal the briefest of rests, breaths, or silences.

Next, it's important to recognize that most poets end their lines on meaning words: nouns, verbs, adjectives, and adverbs. Slicing a line at a weak word like *the*, *of*, or *and* tells your reader to pause at an insignificant moment in the poem, rather than a point of meaning. The poet Mary Oliver isn't tentative about this. She says, "The most important point in the line is the *end* of the line" (1994).

Check out Eloise's poem "Grandpa Mon's Blueberry Fingers" and pay attention to the strong words at the end of each line.

GRANDPA MON'S BLUEBERRY FINGERS

He hunched in fields of blue,
only his straw hat visible.
He filled bowls with berries:
one bowl equaled one pie.
Mom begged him to stop.
She warned him he would shrivel
under the August sun.
We laughed and plunked
blueberries into our mouths.

I spied on him from behind bushes
and snuck berries from the bowl.
He caught me,
and together we plucked the fruit.
His fingers turned sticky blue,
and when he wiggled them in my face,
I laughed.

I felt safe and warm
nestled in the blue bushes
with my head in his lap
as we plucked blueberries in unison:
one for the bowl,
two for us.

    —Eloise Kelly

Imagine if Eloise had broken the first line after *of*, or the third line at *with*, or the last line of the first stanza after *into*. Can you see and hear how her poem would have been weakened—how important the ends of her lines are in creating *meaning pauses*?

Free-verse poets are aware of how their poems look. Line and stanza breaks *are* a poem's form. Poetry is the only genre in which the form matters as much as the content.

Try to draft your free-verse poems in lines. You can always revise by shortening, lengthening, and moving them around, but it's important to enter into an act of poetry by visualizing the draft as poetry, not prose, right from the start.

Of course, it's okay to go back into a draft and divide it into lines, and then revise and polish based on the line breaks you created. That's what Brian did as a new free-verse poet. His first draft of "Lindt Truffle" went down on the page as a paragraph.

LINDT TRUFFLE

The green wrapper makes a crinkling noise as I spin it off and throw it in the garbage to reveal an orb of milk chocolate. I bite half way through and an explosion of chocolate fills my mouth, followed up with a big burst of strong mint. I savor it as it melts away and I look down at the white half sphere with its light brown shell remaining in my hand. I plop it in my mouth and the amazing taste fills my mouth again until, like all the good things in life, it ends with nothing left but a memory.

In a conference I showed Brian how to insert double slash marks at the points where he might break lines. I asked him to listen for groups of words that seemed to belong together, notice the junctures at which he breathed or paused when he read his poem aloud, and look for meaning words. This is how he marked it up.

LINDT TRUFFLE

The green wrapper makes a crinkling noise//as I spin it off and throw it in the garbage//to reveal an orb of milk chocolate.//I bite half way through//and an explosion of chocolate fills my mouth,//followed up with a big burst of strong mint.//I savor it as it melts away//and I look down at the white half sphere//with its light brown shell//remaining in my hand. I plop it in my mouth//and the amazing taste fills my mouth again//until, like all the good things in life,//it ends with nothing left//but a memory.

When Brian retyped the poem as a second draft, he began a new line each time he hit one of his slash marks. From there, he revised by cutting and polishing. Here's the final version.

LINDT TRUFFLE

The green wrapper crinkles
as I spin it off and throw it out
to reveal an orb of milk chocolate.
I bite halfway through,
and an explosion of chocolate fills my mouth
followed by a burst of mint.

I savor it as it melts
on my tongue.
I gaze at the white half-sphere
in the light brown shell
that remains between finger and thumb.
I plop it in my mouth,
and the amazing taste
fills me again
until, like all good things,
it ends with nothing
but a memory—
and a hint of mint.

—*Brian McGrath*

Take a look at Carolyn's poem about a swim meet. In the first three stanzas, she leaves words out and makes the lines short, so the form of her poem imitates her subject: as a swimmer, she's gasping for breath. In the last stanza, the form changes because the race is over. Carolyn relaxes as she returns to life on land and full sentences.

RHYTHM

Arms tired,
legs useless.
Want to stop—
Can't stop.
Hit the side.
Turn.
Legs slam wall.

Lungs scorch,
gulp air.
Keep the rhythm:
pull, kick,
pull, kick.

Halfway there.
Body screams.
Push forward.
Almost done.
Pull, kick.
Pull, kick.
Punch wall.
Stop timer.
Grasp wall.
Breathe.

I haul myself
out of the pool
and pant,
gulping the sticky
sweet air.
I shove my feet
into flip-flops,
and my jelly legs
plod me back to the bench
amidst high fives and *good jobs.*
I gasp my thanks, plop onto a seat,
and grab my water bottle.
I lean my head back.
Close my eyes.
Drift away.

—Carolyn MacDonald

A poem by Emma shows another way to play with line breaks. Her topic is the skill-crane game in the lobby of her local bowling alley. Notice how her poem is one sentence. Its form imitates the "twenty-second thrill" of the game.

THE CRANE AT YANKEE LANES

Two cool rusty quarters
are all it takes
to unleash the twenty-second thrill
that comes from sliding
the worn black gear
from right and left,
checking the angles,
finding the perfect spot,
and releasing
the claw
that never quite
grips a prize for the others
but always obeys me
by delivering
shiny plastic
victory.

—Emma Moorhead

A word about punctuation: sometimes a beginning poet will put a comma at the end of every line, maybe as a way to enforce a breath or rest. But since the white space at the end of a line already signals a reader to pause, the comma is redundant—it's not necessary. For now, punctuate your free-verse poems as if they're prose sentences: use commas, dashes, and periods as if the lines of the poem come one after another in a paragraph. Later, we'll talk about some of the ways poets play with—and without—punctuation and capitals.

About capitals. New poets who aren't sure how to capitalize lines sometimes play it safe by capitalizing the first word of every line. As a result, the power of a poem gets undercut. All those capital letters can look pompous, as if the poet were saying, "Every line I'm writing is so profound it must be capitalized." Today, most free-verse poets capitalize poems as they would prose: first words of sentences and proper nouns.

Let's talk stanza breaks, too. The word *stanza* means "stopping place" or "room" in Italian. Ron Padgett, a poet, says it's helpful to think of stanzas as rooms in the house that's your poem. He says, "The stanza break almost always indicates a pause, however slight, just as you have to slow down to go through a door" (1987).

Look at Ben's poem "Pumpkin Encounter." He creates three-line stanzas to separate the different actions in his story, almost like paragraph breaks in prose. In the first stanza, he and his pumpkin consider each other. In the next, he draws the design for the face. Then, he picks up a knife and hollows it out. Next, he carves the eyes and mouth. Finally, he and the pumpkin consider each other once again, and Ben closes with a one-line expression of satisfaction.

PUMPKIN ENCOUNTER

It glares at me,
an orange-headed monster
begging for a face.

I bite my tongue
as the Sharpie outlines
a ghoulish grin and two devilish eyes.

The cool grip of a knife
creases my palm,
and I start the operation: guts first.

With a shaky hand
I carve those eyes,
that mouth.

I step back to admire my creation.
It leers back a silent *thanks*.
I nod in response.

Our work is done.
　　　　　　　　　　—*Ben Dewey*

Tristan played with stanza breaks in a similar way, with each break signifying a shift in the action, in a poem he wrote about a heron sighting. Notice how he makes the title the first line of his poem.

Suddenly in the Middle of the Road

it stands like a statue.
Beady eyes stare through me —
I'm invisible.

Its body is covered in beautiful blue.
The wingtips are black and white.
Its head swings left, then right,

until the silence is broken
by the loud throbbing
of an SUV coming over the hill.

As awkward as can be, the heron flies
like a buoy in choppy water
and slips into graceful escape.

—Tristan Geboskie

And here's something cool Nate did with stanza breaks. In "Time," he's remembering a former best friendship. The long first stanza describes a memory—the day the two boys found an abandoned dock. In the second stanza, he switches to italics and transitions to the present. In unpacking this sensory poem, we readers understand that the friendship is over, a victim of the passage of time.

Time

They scurry through an endless maze
of bitter blueberry bushes
in and out, back and forth,
in sync as only best friends can be,
down crusty granite slopes,
racing to see who will reach the bottom first
until
they find it.
Cradled between two pines,
it creeks and retches,
swaying back and forth with the tide.
The boys look at each other
and grin, the words coming to both minds at once:
secret hideout.

They dash down soggy, moss-covered planks
and perch, not knowing what to do next
as the swirling leaves around them prove
swim season has passed.
But best friends don't care.
They stand at the edge, giggle,
and plunge into the deep, uncertain waters.

Seasons pass
and I return, alone,
drift back down the hard slopes,
back onto the dock.
I slouch on the rail,
watch baby waves lick the crusty planks,
think about jumping in, don't.
The old dock rolls in and out,
bent by an ever changing tide.
              —*Nate Friant*

In free-verse poetry, stanza breaks are up to the poet. Ron Padgett advises that you may want all the rooms in your house to be the same size, or you may want to vary the sizes of the rooms, depending on what they're for. He concludes: "The main thing is to make rooms that are big enough to be useful, shapely enough to be attractive, and not so empty as to be disappointing" (1987).

Line breaks and stanza breaks are techniques I'll help you with when we confer about your poems and when I edit them. Right now, experiment deliberately. Resist settling for the first form that goes down on the page. One of the benefits of computers is that it's easy to experiment with line and stanza breaks. Bump words down to another line, separate a phrase from the rest of its sentence, build white space around important words, and consider how your poem looks and reads strongest.

Let's summarize all of this. Tape this set of notes into your writing–reading handbook beneath "Tap the Power of *I*," and then we'll read and highlight it.

Breaking Lines and Stanzas

Poetry is written to be spoken. Break the lines of a poem to emphasize its breaths, pauses, and silences. Break on *meaning* words—nouns, verbs, adjectives—and avoid ending lines with words like *the*, *and*, or *with*. Breaking on little words like articles, conjunctions, and prepositions tells readers to pause at and emphasize points of insignificance.

Draft your poems in lines—jump in and guess. Then, when you revise, insert slashes (//) between words to create new line breaks. Use horizontal lines (═══) between lines to indicate a new stanza break. Experiment with the size, shape, and length of your lines and stanzas. See what you can achieve, in terms of meaning, emphasis, patterns, and attractiveness, through how you arrange words and the white spaces that surround them. The computer is your friend when it comes to this kind of play.

In general, punctuate and capitalize poems as if they're prose sentences—but don't be afraid to experiment with or without caps and punctuation. More on this to come.

LESSON 3: CUT TO THE BONE

To make maple syrup, a farmer collects the sap that runs inside a maple tree and boils it down. It takes twenty gallons of sap to make just one bottle of syrup. The result is the essence of maple. The process is called *distillation*.

The poet Gwendolyn Brooks believed that "poetry is life distilled" (1975). Poets boil down life to produce its essence. They *concentrate* it in as few words as possible. Another poet, Robert Wallace, put it another way: "Poetry is especially an act of *compression*" (1996). The verb *compress* means to force something into a small space. Poets suggest a lot in a small space by making sure every word is loaded and necessary. This is the significant difference between poetry and prose. Poets distill language. They compress it. They cut it to the bone.

The first and last things I do when I revise a poem are cut. When I write the first draft, I know I'll use more words than I need because I'm focused on generating all the details of an experience and my feelings about it. Then I let the draft sit for a two-day walk-away, return, and tighten it: find the one word that can do the work of three, cut the language a smart reader doesn't need, and examine every *a* and *the* and adverb to see if it's essential. I continue to revise and polish—to substitute better words, add strong ones, and distill, compress, *cut to the bone*.

Let me show you what I mean. Here's the uncut first draft of a poem I wrote about my daughter the year she graduated from high school. It might as well be prose, it's so undistilled and uncompressed.

JUNE (FIRST DRAFT)
I've noticed how in early summer
the light casts a special kind of shadow.
It seems to me to foretell the weather that's coming—
days that are somber, cold, damp.
Wrapped in veils of grayness,
they'll cancel
the brilliant greens of June.

My daughter knows this—
winter is coming, for the world and for her, too.
She sees and feels
the cycle of growth that starts
with warm, green Junes

and ends with December dusk.
She understands that like the petals
that drop from peony blossoms in June,
her own days
of girlhood
are coming to an end.
Fall will arrive,
and she will have to grow up,
lose her innocence,
and become a woman.

     —Nancie Atwell

Everything is explained here. There's nothing to intrigue or attract a reader, nothing to *unpack*. Compare it to my final version.

June (Draft 5)

Early summer casts its own shadows.
It foretells other weather:
somber days wrapped in veils of gray
will depose the green brilliance.

Well she knows it.
Her wise eyes and cool fingers
surmise the cycle
that starts with green light

and ends in dusk.
The peony will concede its petals.
The days of girlhood will shorten.
There will be a fall.

     —Nancie Atwell

Can you see and feel the differences? I weighed every word and tried to decide if it deserved the space it was taking up in my poem. I cut the clutter—unnecessary words, redundancies, distractions, and flourishes. And then I cut some more. In Gorän's poem "Tip Down," look at how purposefully he cut to the bone in this story about the sand forts he built with a friend when they were little boys.

Tip Down

Our little
hands slide
yellow shovels
through the dirt.

We are making
a sand fort,
Will and I,
under the shade
of the trampoline,

digging our hole
deep and wide,
piling up the walls,
filling our shovels.

On a summer afternoon
I take a walk
to our old sand pile,
dig into my past,

and remember
yellow,
Will,
and the days

I could make worlds.

—*Göran Johanson*

Göran distilled a childhood memory and captured its essence. In her poem "History of US," Josie distills and captures the essence of the American paradox: slavery in the land of the free.

History of US

There are more of us,
but we are nothing.

We have no voices,
our heads are empty.

Up we get and down we lie,
to we wander and fro we stagger.

Hands slip from hands.
The sun crosses the sky.

Eyes bulge, and moans echo.

Leaves turn, flakes fall.
Price rises, value lowers.

The world tilts beneath our feet.

Rats scurry, roaches scatter,
mosquitos breed, time lasts

like a fever.

Stripes run,
stars fade.

—Josephine Cotton

Josie's poem could have taken the form of paragraphs of prose describing the brutality of slavery and its forever-blemish on our history, but prose would and could not capture the sheer horror of slavery as does this handful of powerful words and images.

Here's a final example, with a lighter tone. Wallace was fishing with his brother and a friend. When their bait ran out, he had a brainstorm. He baited his hook with a Starburst candy and waited to see what would happen. This is the poem he ended up with, after he cut and cut some more.

THE DAY WE RAN OUT OF BAIT

the glutinous
chewy
chunk of candy
slides on the hook

then drifts
just below the surface
of the teal water
too light to sink

minnows swarm
create gentle ripples
try to eat it
can't

a fat black silhouette
glides toward the bait
and with an easy movement
of the jaw

he is hooked
and so am i

—Wallace Jackson

Let's put some words around the gist of this lesson. Please copy my notes from the overhead as the next entry in the free-verse toolbox in your handbook:

Cut to the Bone

Only when a poet can't find another word to cut is a poem finished. Weigh every word as you revise and polish. Does it do anything for your poem? Will a smart reader need it?

LESSON 4: CONCLUDE WITH PURPOSE

There are two places where readers find the deepest meanings in poems. The first is a *turn*: a point in a poem where the poet moves in a new, surprising direction. But the most important is a poem's conclusion.

Conclusions—last lines—are the parts of my poems I revise the most. I want to leave a reader thinking, maybe even trying to finish my thought. I want words that will resonate, will vibrate in a reader's mind. And I want to discover my own deepest meaning—to surprise myself so I can surprise my reader.

Read Sarah's poem "Flight" and notice her sensory diction. We can enter, see, and feel this poem because of her word choices, her *diction*. Then pay special attention to how she decided to end it.

FLIGHT

I sprang from the blue screen
of our trampoline
and wiggled grass-stained toes
as I soared.
My hair swirled around my face
as I leapt higher, higher.

I raised pudgy arms in the air,
pushed off,
and reached once more for the sky.

I could fly.

Today
I escape the tedious tasks of homework,
leave the sheets of graph paper
scattered across my desk,
and slip into the basement.
Cool air envelops me

as I trudge towards the fridge
to grab a soda.

Among the mounds of forgotten junk,
I spy a blue screen
coated with dust,
its circular metal frame
slippery with grime.

With my two size-eight feet planted
on cold concrete,

I mourn my wings.
                              —*Sarah Jordan*

Sarah's last line tells us everything about how she perceives the distance between the carefree little girl who jumped so high she flew, and the adolescent who's weighed down with homework and other responsibilities. The one-line conclusion echoes the title and sustains the image and metaphor of flight.

In his poem "Litter," Xander describes an encounter with a homeless man. The single-line stanza that concludes it mimics two others in his poem and helps give it a form. More importantly, it suggests the change in Xander's perception of the man's humanity.

LITTER

The man sits on the curb, arm extended.
He shakes a Dunkin' Donuts cup,
and a few coins clink inside
like a sad excuse for a paycheck.
His shopping cart lies off to the side,
a tarp thrown over it,
protection from the sun.
He wipes the sweat from his face
with a calloused hand,
then again on his torn T shirt.

He smiles at me, front tooth gone,
teeth stained, full of hope.

I walk away

until a scratchy voice cuts through the air,
soft and soothing.
It's okay, little ones. You'll get food soon.

I turn

as the man kneels on the pavement,
index finger poked through the bars of a metal cage
perched in his shopping cart.
Inside, snow-white kittens crowd toward his hand,
jumping and pawing one another
to lick his sweaty finger.
Play fighting erupts,
and a hissing, meowing snowball of kittens
rolls around on a padded floor.

The man grasps his coffee cup and stands,
arching his back and stretching his arms.
He yawns and takes his seat on the curb.
He scans the area, and our eyes meet.

He smiles at me, front tooth gone,
teeth stained, full of hope.

I smile back.

—Xander Bartone

Notice how Heidi's conclusion resonates in a poem about how her cat caught and killed a blue jay. She uses cadence—the repetition of the phrase *I remember*—to help move the story she tells in the poem. In her conclusion, she acknowledges something hard about the nature of nature.

BLUE JAY, BLACK CAT

I remember how you looked
in that sugar-dusted Christmas tree,
your blue wings shining between
white and green.

I remember how you flew
beneath the stone sky,
your delicate body
a contrast with steel gray.

I remember how I woke that morning
and blood spattered the snow,
how my black cat stalked away
with a glint in his eye
and your feathers on his chin.

I remember how that night
the cat curled on my lap

in a ball of seeming sinlessness,
how my fingers stroked his silk head
and he touched his cold nose to my palm.

Though I love him,
he is built to kill.
Your absence
in trees and beneath sky
is the brutal proof.
                    —*Heidi Ziegra*

Heidi played with two sound effects here, alliteration in the repetition of consonant sounds in *cat curled* and *seeming sinlessness*, and assonance when she repeated the *oo* vowel sound in *brutal proof*. File those terms in the back of your brainpan—I'll define and exemplify them formally in another lesson.

Here's another resonant conclusion. At the end of "Bottle," Alex invites us to continue writing his poem in our heads—to imagine what could have happened next.

BOTTLE

I slide across the slushy lawn
and scoop up the wet baseball.
Try-outs are tomorrow,
and I need to be ready.
But I'm not ready
for the sharp crack of ice
or the splash that follows
or the barks like a voice
calling for help.

I know it's my dog.
I'd seen him playing
with a plastic bottle
across the road
near the pond.
I throw my glove
toward the porch
and barrel
to the water's edge.
I see his yellow head
poking above
sheets of ice,
the plastic bottle
skittering beyond him.

And I freeze,
until my voice starts
yelling his name,
reeling him toward me.
He makes it, gasping,
to the muddy shore.
He shakes himself,
and cold water sprays
across my jacket.
I don't mind.
I rub his sopping coat
as we gaze at the bottle.
Together we watch it
fill with water

and sink
like a stone.

—*Alex Graves*

Next, notice how Göran's conclusion to "Night Walk" solves a riddle.

NIGHT WALK

Our boots
trample
the snow,

patches of yellow grass
scattered across
the barren field,

the sky dark
save for a few
stars.

My eyes
adjust to the blankness.
I pull up on my zipper

and listen to the crunch
that echoes
father and son.

—*Göran Johanson*

In cutting this poem to the bone, Göran omitted on purpose the identity of the companion who's signified by the *our* in the first line. By revealing that it's his father, the last line satisfies and resonates.

Finally, in his conclusion to this poem, Wallace uses an echo structure: the last line echoes the first one. He repeats it, but with a meaningful twist.

MY MOTHER TEACHES AT THE JAIL

I slouch in the leather seat.
Your fifteen minutes were up five minutes ago,
and I don't like hanging around here.
I close my book and notice a group of three emerge:
a man, a woman, a toddler.
The toddler is in the man's arms, the woman at his side.
Then I notice
the boy who follows feet behind.
He can't be more than ten.
He looks ashamed to be here.
What was the man in for? I imagine the worst.
From my vantage in our SUV,
he looks like a meth addict,
a thief, maybe a drunk driver.
Now the toddler is in the mom's arms,
and the boy in his father's.
I see tears soaking the generic football jersey—
the tears of his son.
I slouch even lower in the leather seat.

—Wallace Jackson

Wallace slouches "even lower" as he realizes, after the stereotypes he assigned to the released inmate, that he is a father who loves his son, with a son who loves him back.

None of these poets arrived at their conclusions in first drafts. They *sweated* these—played and experimented off-the-page until they found the words that gave their poems weight and meaning. This is an essential craft lesson for *every* genre, not just poetry. Please turn to your toolbox and tape "Conclude with Purpose" into your handbook under your notes about cutting to the bone. Then we'll read and highlight it.

Conclude with Purpose

The conclusion is the most important part of a poem. It needs to be strong—to resonate after a reader has finished the poem. The conclusion should leave a reader with a feeling, idea, image, question, understanding.

Give your conclusions the time and play they need—and your readers deserve. Use the two-day walk-away to get distance on a poem: allow ideas for an ending to percolate in your brainpan while you work on another piece of writing.

Then come back and experiment. Try different endings off-the-page until you find the one that best conveys your meaning, completes your poem, makes a reader pause.

LESSON 5: USE REPETITION

We know that free-verse poets don't pack rhyme in their toolboxes. But that doesn't mean they don't have poetic techniques at their disposal. Some of these are sound effects, and one of my favorites—also one of the easiest for beginning poets to experiment with—is repetition. Read "My Book" by Ethan, listen for the repetition of the title inside the poem, feel the pleasing rhythm or *cadence* it creates, and understand through the repeated emphasis how much this boy loves a good story.

MY BOOK

My book
my personal heaven
where I can be anything
My book
my best friend
who gets me in trouble
making homework disappear
until it's the night before
My book
my anti-car-sick pill:
mix with reclined seat
and wait for effect
My book
eclipses every responsibility
Who cares? it hisses
You can do it later
Good idea, I agree
as I sink to my doom
until the self-preservational part
of my brain prevails
Are you crazy?

You know you'll get butchered
Put that book down
In silent consent I obey
My book
whispers
my name

　　　　　　—*Ethan Rittershaus*

Alex played with repetition in "The Rope Swing," a poem he wrote as a Father's Day gift for his dad.

THE ROPE SWING

It hangs there:

a rope and a wooden chair
that you attached at the end
on a warm day one summer.

It hangs there.

I remember
when you pushed us so high
we could touch
the top of the giant oak.

Now it just hangs there:
a lonely rope swing
tied to an oak tree branch.
But when I grow up,

I will remember
flying
through the trees
because of your sturdy swing

that hangs there still.

　　　　　　—*Alex Graves*

By repeating variations on the line "it hangs there," Alex emphasizes the sturdiness of both the rope swing and his father's love. Alex knows that each will last, even when he's no longer a child.

In "knights of my bedroom," John writes about his three model airplanes. He repeats a line and also varies it, so by the end of the poem, a reader understands John's theme: the feeling of comfort and security he derives from these ever-present symbols of his boyhood.

KNIGHTS OF MY BEDROOM

i don't remember when i got them,
but there they are, three planes.
one dives straight for heaven.
another sets sights on the enemy.
there they are, three planes
that stalk the skies unpiloted,
forever haunted, because
there they are, three planes.
the third has double lift: my favorite.
there they are, three planes,
each crudely detailed
in a beautiful way.
they can't communicate,
yet somehow they sync.
there they are, my three planes.
there they are, my fleet.
there they are, three planes,
dusty, united, protectors of my airspace.

there they are.
there they have always been.

—*John Solorzano*

Repetition can also be used for humorous effect. In "Child Fears," Sophia borrows an idea from the poet Jim Harrison and crafts a list of things that scared her when she was a child. Apparently, death was a major concern for little Sophia back in the day.

CHILD FEARS

Dying. Losing my doll.
House fires. Scorpions.
Werewolves. The dark. Big kids.
Earwigs. Voldemort. Ken.™
Hands in the dark. *Dying.* Wasps. *Dying.*
No electricity. Throwing up. Turning green.
Asparagus. Peekachu. Bed time.
Big fish. *Dying.* Motorcycles.
Rubber bands snapping on my wrist.
Rotten avocados.
My death.

—*Sophia Carbonneau*

In creating cadence—in giving poems rhythm through repetition—consider something that rhetoricians call a *tricolon*. I call it "the power of three." A rhythm, emphasis, or pattern is apparent and effective when a writer uses it three times. Consider the impact of Jefferson's phrase "life, liberty, and the pursuit of happiness" without all three nouns, or Macbeth's "Tomorrow and tomorrow and tomorrow" speech with just two *tomorrows*, or the Protestant Lord's Prayer without its concluding tricolon: *the kingdom and the power and the glory*. Check out the power of the tricolon at the conclusion of Natalie's poem about sleeping outside in the summertime.

Ebony

Blackness curls around me
as I slip into the night sky
with stars as my light.

Constellations appear above,
and I merge into their embrace—
nature as my source,
blackness as soothing medicine.

I reach for a star

and fall

deep into the cosmos,
deep into its silence,
deep into my dream.

—*Natalie Brown*

By repeating "deep into . . ." three times in the last stanza, Natalie creates a kind of lullaby. We can feel her falling asleep under the stars.

Sophia wrote about the first snow of the season. Starting with an allusion to William Carlos Williams, she describes one snowflake and three things it does. By stretching the moment, her tricolon gives it significance.

So Much Depends Upon

a single
frozen flake that has
fallen on
melted on
selected
my quivering pinky

during the first
faltering snowfall
of November.

                                   —*Sophia Stafford*

In an autobiographical poem, Sophia tells three little stories or *anecdotes*. The poem builds from one to the next. Any two of the stories wouldn't suffice. In exploring her adolescent identities, Sophia needs the power of three.

ALTER EGO

I trudged by her
in the grocery store,
that girl in shorts
and a t-shirt,
her brown hair tied
into a ponytail with loose ends
flying.
Her right hand grasped
a soy energy smoothie
boasting protein and calcium.

I shouldered by the troop of girls
waving colorful banners
advertising "Girl Scout Cookies!"
One stood out—
average height, but a yellow
cord hung off one shoulder
and dangled from her khaki vest: patrol leader.
A busy mother
whispered
in her pink ear.

I whizzed by another girl
on her bike,
mud splattered
on the frame.
A green
sweater flew out
behind her as she pulled ahead
and went shooting
down the hill.

I know that girl.
She lives in me:

one of many
alter egos
ready to
burst forth
and sing.

—*Sophia Carbonneau*

Finally, here's one of Cody's first poems ever. He wrote it after this minilesson. Using repetition helped him create a form, a sound, and an elegy.

CHLOE

She was the dog who pranced
everywhere she went—
from our house, to the neighbor's,
and across the street to the pond.
She didn't need a leash on walks.
She was the dog who didn't run away.

Now, burdened by arthritis,
she hobbles wherever she goes—
not to a neighbor
or the pond these days.

She was the dog who retrieved
tennis balls thrown over the roof
and chewed through screen windows
when we left her behind.

She is the dog I lived with since my beginning,
the dog I wrote stories about in third grade,
the dog who rubs her head against a leg
and everyone knows she wants a pat.

Now she is the dog
who doesn't glance up
when I call her name,
the silent dog in the corner
asleep.

But when I stare into her
warm brown eyes,
she is the only dog
I will ever need.

—*Cody Graves*

Try to imagine a version of "Chloe" without the repetition of "She was/is the dog" or the power of three examples in the first, fourth, and fifth stanzas. I'm sure it would be a sincere and heartfelt piece of writing—Cody adored that dog. But would it have been a poem?

These poets used repetition on purpose and to good effect. But beware of the other, accidental kind. Repetition can sound awkward when writers don't read themselves with their ears. Let me show you what I mean. With Noelle's permission, I wrecked a poem she wrote comparing her hands to her mom's. Read it softly aloud, listen for the ineffective repetition I created, and underline it when you hear it.

Our Two Hands

I never noticed:
our two hands
are carbon copies.

When I held your two hands
I examined
your knuckles first:

your huge knuckles
from cracking your fingers
for years.

Then
I examined
our two palms:

I examined
the lines in our two palms
that lead to nowhere.

And last
I examined
the bluish veins

under our skin,
blue and purple veins
in perfect alignment.

Thanks to you, from me,
for passing down
your two hands to me.

Because of our two hands
I will always have
a part of you in me.

Where did you hear ineffective repetition? It sounds bad, right? Those inadvertent, purposeless repeats of words like *our, two, hands, examined, blue,* and *me*? Here's the real thing: "Part of Us" by Noelle Timberlake, with no ineffective repetition and cut to the bone. Listen again, as I read it aloud.

PART OF US

I never noticed:
our hands
are carbon copies.

When I held yours
I noticed
our knuckles first:

huge
from cracking fingers
for years.

Then
I examined
our palms:

traced
the lines
that lead to nowhere.

Last
I looked
at the veins

under our skin:
blue and purple
in perfect alignment.

Thank you
for passing down
your hands.

I will always
have a part of you
in me.

—*Noelle Timberlake*

It's time to capture this lesson in your toolbox. Please tape it beneath "Conclude with Purpose," and we'll review it together.

Use Repetition

Use *repetition* to stress an important word, phrase, idea, or theme; move a poem; build its momentum; set a tone; capture a feeling; and create *cadence*—a pleasing, rhythmic flow of sound.

Remember the power of a *tricolon*—three words, phrases, or examples that create music and please the eye, ear, and mind.

Beware of *ineffective repetition:* a word repeated in too-close proximity, to no purpose or effect, which sounds awkward when you read your writing aloud. When you revise, *listen* to your writing. Read it with your ears. When you hear an instance of ineffective repetition, substitute a pronoun or another word (a thesaurus can help) or see if you can cut one of the repetitions altogether.

LESSON 6: SEARCH FOR SENSORY DICTION

My favorite poems give me visual images—through the poet's choice of words, they create a picture in my mind's eye. This is called a *sensory image*. Poets can also use sensory diction to evoke images in our ears, fingertips, olfactory nerves—that's our sense of smell—and taste buds. Check out Max's sensory poem, and see if it doesn't make you thirsty.

FIZZED

I pop the tab
and foam rushes
to greet my lips
as I gulp
the sweet, carbonated bite
of root beer.

—*Maxim Jordan*

Diction means a writer's choice of words. What diction makes Max's poem sensory—which of his word choices can you see, feel, taste, hear? Note that these are all strong *nouns, verbs,* and *adjectives,* with not an adverb or *-ly* word in sight. Hold that thought—it's important.

Three questions you can ask of yourselves as poets attempting to be sensory are *Can a reader see it? Can a reader hear it? Can a reader feel it?* In other words, have you crafted diction that will bring your writing to life? In particular, have you selected nouns, verbs, and adjectives that will evoke sensations and images in a reader? Read Emma's poem "Just" with me, and we'll put it to the sensory test.

JUST

The boat hums as we putter past
waterfront mansions
abandoned seven months of the year.
A sweet breeze tickles my neck
when we approach the marsh.
Tomorrow we will ache
where the sun slyly slaps our backs.
Today, all around us, leaves
brown at their edges.

I remember a time when I sat in your lap
and you read to me and I imagined
you carrying me through a green forest
and it was just us.

I let my fingers slip down the side of the boat
and bounce through the shy water,
shatter the murky glaze,
and send slices of the river swimming through air.

We drift into a tangle of reeds.
I pull the motor up: spindly grass snakes through it.
We are stuck.
You could free us,
and I could flip the motor back on,
and we could rip through blue, back to our cabin,
where you could take a nap and I could try to watch T.V.

Instead I climb back to my bench,
and we sit in silence,
and it is just us.

—Emma Moorhead

Now read Eloise's sensory poem "Enough," as we join her and her friend Sam while they walk along railroad tracks at sunset.

ENOUGH

I wobble on the left rail
of the rusty track,
arms spread like wings for balance.
Sam teeters on the right rail,
aviators on, as she attempts
to stay upright.

The sun warms my back,
and the breeze plays with my hair.

The track runs around a bend
into the trees and a yellow field.
Sam and I step in sync.
Everything looks right out of a movie—
the light is perfect.
She hands me her sunglasses,
and I slide them on.
The world is

sharper.
Tracks and trees turn sepia.
Colors become richer and redder,
like a faded photograph.

This is the time of day:
late afternoon,
when the sun is disappearing
behind the treeline and seems so close
I could reach out my hand,
brush my fingertips against it,
and let its warmth run through me.

This is the time of life:
thirteen years old
and happy to walk the tracks.
And for now
that is enough.

—*Eloise Kelly*

Please go back into these two poems on your own and underline every word, phrase, and line you can see and feel. Then we'll talk about what you found.

So, what are we learning? In "Enough," we can feel and see specific verbs, like *wobble, teeter, warm, plays, slide,* and *brush.* In "Just," such specific verbs as *hums, putter, tickles, ache, slaps, slip, bounce, shatter, drift, snakes,* and *flip* create images. So do color words in both: *yellow, sepia, redder, green,* and *blue.* So do specific adjectives and nouns: *rusty track, right rail, aviators, faded photograph,* and *tree line* in Eloise's poem, and *waterfront mansion, marsh, shy water, murky glaze, slices of the river, tangle of reeds,* and *spindly grass* in Emma's.

Emma and Eloise sweated every word. They considered diction at the single-word level. They did much of this work as revisers and polishers—went back into their poems again and again until every word was the right one. Both used a real thesaurus, not the one on the computer, to help them make their poems sensory, especially in their choices of verbs.

Let's capture all of this as an addition to your free-verse toolbox. Please tape these notes in after "Use Repetition."

Search for Sensory Diction

Sensory diction involves and appeals to a reader's senses. These word choices bring life to writing by evoking vivid impressions a reader can see, hear, feel, taste, or smell. Some tips for creating sensory images in your poems:

- Verbs, nouns, and adjectives offer the most potential.
- Beware of adverbs (-*ly* words). Instead, shoot for strong verbs.
- Also beware of present-tense participles (-*ing* words). Instead, shoot for active constructions: *I love to run* instead of *running is fun.*
- A thesaurus is your friend when it comes to finding sensory verbs and adjectives and tangible nouns.
- Simple color words create powerful visuals.
- Ask yourself, as you read a draft of your poem, *Could a reader see this? Hear this? Feel this?*
- Revise and polish your poems at the single-word level: is each word choice the best one?

LESSON 7: COMPARE

The next toolbox technique is a tough one for me to put to work. My mind doesn't work this way. But if you can create figurative language—if you can say two things at once—it's guaranteed to transform your writing.

Let's start this lesson with the entry in your handbook. Turn to the next full, clean page in your toolbox section, and tape in "Compare." Then grab a highlighter, and we'll review it together.

Compare

Literal language is true to fact. It uses words according to their actual meanings.

Example: My dog is a carnivore.

Figurative language makes comparisons between unrelated things or ideas, in order to show something about the subject.

Example: My dog becomes a tap dancer when I put bacon on the griddle.

Three Kinds of Figurative Language

Metaphor (Greek): means, literally, "transference." The writer transfers qualities of one thing to another thing. A metaphor has two parts: A = B. Something *is* something else. The B part, the *something else*, shows how the poet feels about or perceives the A part.

Example:

THUMB

The odd, friendless boy raised by four aunts.

—Philip Dacey (1977)

Simile (from the Latin *similes*: "similar") is a figure of speech that uses *like* or *as* to compare two things: A is like B.

Example: Thunder threatens
like a sound that rolls around and around
in a mean dog's throat.

—Martha Sherwood (1982)

Personification (from the Greek *prósopa*, meaning "face" or "mask") is a comparison that gives human or physical qualities to an object, animal, or idea.

Example:

The yellow fog that rubs its back upon the window-panes

—T. S. Eliot (1920)

The right comparison can take a reader's breath away. The feeling of surprise and delight when I'm reading along and think *yes, of course,* makes me happy to be alive and human. A poem by Catherine makes me feel that way, as she compares her geometry homework to the candy corn she snacked on while doing it. Think about what kind of figurative language this is—and notice how her conclusion draws on the power of three.

MIDNIGHT MATH

White: the square root of 10:30 pm.
The product
of word wall and reading.
The base times height
divided by two.

Orange: the perimeter
of the Halloween addiction.
The distance between point A
and point B.

The mental equation
of finding the area
of a 30-60-90 triangle.

Yellow: the hypotenuse
of delicious,
varieties of chemicals
molded into seasonal
relief.
The snack intermission,
the corn of the hour,
the boost for midnight math.

—*Catherine Roy*

The title of the next poem gives away the kind of figurative language the poet is using. Enjoy the extended simile of Josie's "Your Life Is Like a Hobo" as I read it aloud.

YOUR LIFE IS LIKE A HOBO

You see him, pockets ragged.
A few favorites bulge: a half-deck of cards,
the broken remains of a pink pacifier,
an empty chocolate box filled with memories
of blissful delight. But the aroma
lingers.

His coat, once red, drags
tattered on concrete.
The knees of his pants hang
rusty with dirt,
like dried blood
from a war wound.

His eyes have lost
the sparkle of youth.
They sag near cheekbones bruised
from bricks, his only bed
at night.

He carries so much.
It slows him with each step.
But

he isn't homeless. He doesn't think so.
The world is his home.

Stray cats scrounge in his gutters,
mice scuttle in and out of his trash bin,
people parade down his sidewalk.
He sits in the dust—
eyes glazed—

and still smiles.

If you're ever out alone
in the dark
and you can't find a place you belong,
remember—
your life
is like a hobo. You belong
everywhere
you go.

—*Josephine Cotton*

In Eloise's poem about her father at work making a table, and in a poem by Daniel about reading late at night, notice how a few strong metaphors and similes give the poems their central images. Eloise's dad's back is "bent like a fish hook," while Daniel is hit by "the tsunami of the story."

CARPENTER

Proof of labor:
crooked back bent
like a fish hook
over a rough table top.

Sandpaper clutched
in both hands,
he scrubs away a rind
that turns to dust and hangs
in the air, prisoner of sunlight.
And then: a sticky coat of varnish
painted in smooth strokes
by a man who cares
about his art.

—*Eloise Kelly*

ALTERNATE UNIVERSE

Words
float from the page to my eyes,
which take them in like vacuums.

Suddenly I'm hit:
the tsunami of the story.
I am the boy waiting in a courthouse,
the warrior riding on a dragon's back,
the detective revealing the name of the murderer.
When fatigue tugs me from the flood of words,
I turn off the light and surrender
to my own
imagination.

—*Daniel Mayer*

Here's another of my favorites by a student. What kind of figurative language is Alex using in "Kayak"?

KAYAK

I climb onto the small
yellow back of a dragon.
Its wings stroke through
thick air as we take off.
We glide
over the lake.
When a gust of wind flips us,
I fall into warm water.
Underneath
I release from the dragon's embrace
and swim upside down.
I break through the surface,
breathe,
grab hold of its wings,
and climb back on.

—*Alex Graves*

Personification may help you find your way into figurative language. I think it's the easiest way to move from the literal to the figurative. Hope personified a rainstorm as an angry woman.

RAIN WAS HERE

She tiptoes
to where the sun hangs
and swallows him whole.
Earth holds its breath
as she starts her assault,
sneaky at first.

Then pitter patter
gives way to clacks
followed by pounds.
She releases her wrath—
great glassy bullets bore down.
With screams
she tears at Earth
'til everything is saturated
with her watery self,
'til the sun
finally
shoulders through.
Her clouds defeated,
she storms away,
still second best.

—*Hope Logan*

Please turn to the territories section of your handbook. At the top of the next clean page, write this heading: *Potential Things, Ideas, and Phenomena to Personify.*

Tonight for homework, become a seeker of things to personify. Look for objects that might be intriguing to bring to life. Think about concepts you could invest with human qualities, like hunger or equality. Consider natural phenomena, like wind, fog, snow, or a heat wave. See pets, other animals, and birds through new eyes, as rational beings with human thoughts, feelings, and motivations. Under the heading in your handbook, make a list of at least ten personification possibilities. And if one of your ideas grabs you and won't let go—that's a personification, by the way—start drafting.

Here's the list Nathaniel made (Figure 9.2). The cartoons were his idea. Of all the possibilities he generated, I thought a desk lamp had the least potential. I was wrong.

DESK LAMP

It squats,
heads hanging,
patient.
It watches through my skylight
as the sun fades into the trees,
then suddenly becomes alert,
preparing for the assault
of darkness.

When night creeps through,
it raises its metal-sheathed heads.

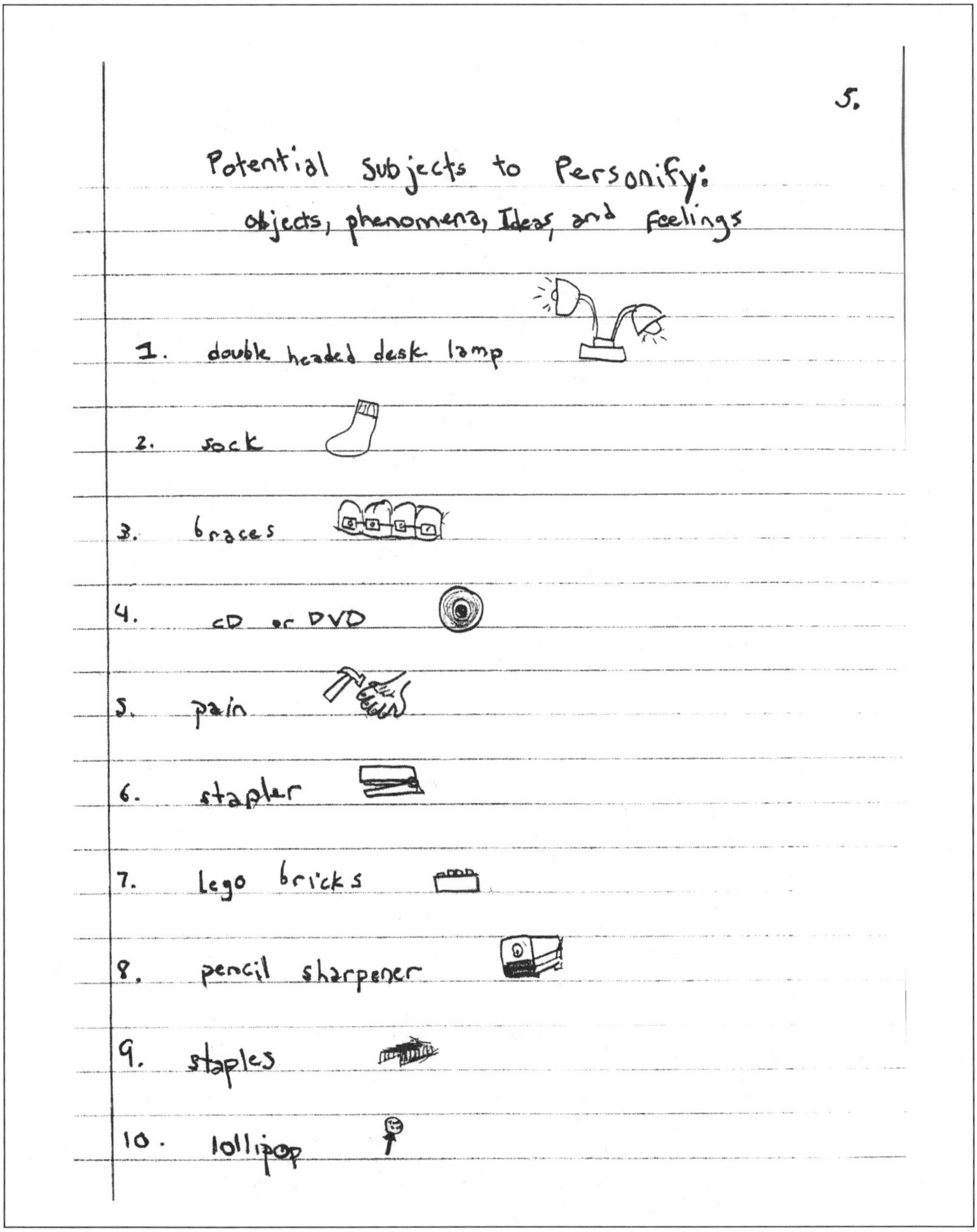

5.

Potential subjects to Personify:
objects, phenomena, Ideas, and Feelings

1. double headed desk lamp
2. sock
3. braces
4. CD or DVD
5. pain
6. stapler
7. lego bricks
8. pencil sharpener
9. staples
10. lollipop

Figure 9.2 *Nathaniel's Ideas for Personification*

Its linked necks swivel,
so its gaping mouths
face the oncoming foe.

Click.

Now it spits white fire from its circular jaws,
and the brightness of its flames
burns up the darkness.
The blackness
retreats to the windows
and slithers between the cracks.
The two-headed
defender of daytime
twists its necks,
shines silver beams
into all corners,
searches to destroy
the remaining
night.

Satisfied,
it stills,
training its attention
on shadows
still lurking
—under beds
and in closets—
and waits for the night
to attack
again.

—Nathaniel Williams

LESSON 8: EXPERIMENT WITH FORM

Let's begin this lesson by taping in and reading its toolbox entry. Then I'll illustrate it with poems by poets who took advantage of the generosity of free verse.

Experiment with Form

Depending on the subject and tone of a poem, free-verse poets play with how their words go down on the page. You can use form to follow, support, or emphasize your meaning.

Experiment. Consider stanzas of a set number of lines, some punctuation, no punctuation, no capitals, selected capitals, extra white space, repeated lines, a poem that's one sentence, a prose poem, a concrete poem, a poem in chapters or numbered sections, caesuras, and lists.

You may have noticed that some of the poems we've read have stanzas of a set length. Emily decided that a poem about her mom baking bread would take the form of triplets, or stanzas of three lines. In addition, Em created cadence by repeating a line in every stanza.

LOPSIDED LOVE

I watch you knead,
flour all over, fingers embedded in the ball of dough,
brows furrowed: you're concentrating on the recipe.

A lopsided sphere, off-white in color,
flour all over, fingers embedded in the ball of dough.
A pinch of flour leaps onto the counter.

The orb turns into a sweet-tasting cylinder—
flour all over, fingers embedded in the ball of dough.
A piece sticks to your finger, and you shake it off.

It drops into the loaf pan with a thunk—
flour all over, fingers embedded in the ball of dough.
You pat it into the shape of the pan.

Flour all over, fingers embedded in the ball of dough,
you knead
your love.

—*Emily Sanborn*

In a poem about her bedroom, Catherine settled on a form of five-line stanzas. Notice how she uses a repeating structure at the start of each stanza to give the poem cadence and shift back and forward in time.

MY ROOM

Then? Pepto-Bismol pink,
a setting for imaginary friends
and worn stuffed animals
waiting for me to dress them,
talk for them, create their story.

Now? A gentle blue.
Only I know about

the stuffed animals
that hide in the dusty closet,
waiting forever.

Then? White shelves
revealed Barbie's missing high-heel
and my nursery rhyme books,
their bindings stretched and pages stained
from years of love.

Now? The yearning to be a kid again—
to belong to layers
of costume jewelry, sticky earrings,
plastic high-heels,
and twisting feather boas.

Still, I have this room
if I ever need
an imaginary friend, a nursery book rhyme,
or a pause in ever-changing me.

                —*Catherine Roy*

Hope, a competitive swimmer, decided to abandon capital letters and punctuation—except for an exclamation point and a period—to capture the act of plunging into a lake and swimming for the pleasure of it, in contrast with the tension she feels whenever she swims in chlorine.

THE GOAL

I pound the dock in a sprint
bang bang bang
deep navy glints
lake descends to me
bang ba-
muscles tense then strain
I abandon solids
I am moses
I erupt calm waters
unafraid
I glide
through infinite liquid
this is not
gymnasts in my stomach
no roar of "GO!"

no harsh cold chlorine
no ache in my . . . everything
no endless movement
no burning chest
this is slow powerful strokes
this is warm silence only broken
by bubbles that escape my lips
swirling towards
a beautiful blurry sun
this is serenity
the only goal.

—*Hope Logan*

In "parabola" Emily uses line breaks as punctuation. Notice how she groups words on each line so the pauses at the ends do the work of commas and periods.

PARABOLA

i tiptoe across the beach
my toes gently grazing the sand
i spy the abandoned lifeguard chair
and sprint to its bulky frame
i glance at dad and climb hand over hand
onto the platform from the sand pile
scrambling like a monkey
i pause as i watch the others
assisted by dad
climb behind me
i wait for them
then glance sideways
stand
breathe
and feel majestic
i look from side to side
bend my knees
and spring into the air
i spread my arms
and begin the negative part of this parabola
drifting downward

my toes brush the sand
and i drop to my knees
somersault down the incline

cover myself with sand
and giggle insanely
i won't get the beach out of my hair for two weeks

but who says I wanted to
                        —*Emily Sanborn*

Sophia was a fan of E. E. Cummings. She adored his experiments with graphic elements and learned from him how to use paper as a canvas. She wrote this poem as an anniversary present for her parents, represented here as joy and sorrow.

when little Bell   rings
        to joy
to sorrow
up from the dawn
        she grows on

Becoming
        more than less
        but less than more
learning
to   love
        when morelike
hate
sometimes explodes
till now
she   calms
into the day
while
sorrowslips
into   aged night

and joy and sorrow
Love on
adoring
their Little belle

loving into the dark
until
        Gone
they love
no More
        But

little bells ring
still   in the day

giving
all she can
until the story continuesForever—

SorrowandJoy
and
Belle.

—S. R. Carbonneau
(After E. E. Cummings)

Inspired by Cummings, Avery wrote about a walk he took in the woods near his house one fall day. The white spaces around and between his words suggest footsteps on a wilderness ramble.

AND I THINK TO MYSELF

my galoshes sink
   into
      the
         bog
     bubbles float
        to the surface
   form a ring
             around my boots
      and burst
crisp wind
   nips my nose
    and ears
    i am silent
    nature
           is not
      rooks squawk   overhead
        blurs of blue flit
   through pines
        singing as they glide
   frogs kick through the wetland
           spitting whirlpools in their wake
red white planets
   bob like buoys
   rotate
      in liquid space
   i pluck
      tart orbs out of water
      my fingers tingle

the world around me is a painting

                                        monet

                                                      green pricks

                                        slurs of red

                              orange slashes

                                        rare

                purple dabs

as i trod home

                each step seeps

                            deeper

                                      into moss

and autumn

                —Avery Genus

In a poem about playing in the backyard with her brother when they were little, Morganne experimented with capital letters. By turning common nouns into proper ones, she suggests what was—and maybe still is—important to her and Parker, aka the Dragon.

MOUNTAINS

There were only two Mountains that mattered.
Of those, only one was Relevant.
Every morning, Spoon or Hammer or red Shovel in hand
I marched
straight in my angular way
to the four, two—one, my Mountain, and scaled its side
a returning Hero
to the Land of Dirt and Grasses.

The Hole started innocently enough
if War can ever be innocent.
In any case, the simple truth: I had a shortage
of ammunition
and Dried Clots of Mud
were my weapons of choice.

Here I was:
seven, maybe nine—expected
to Defend the Honor of Nature and Peace.
Fight fire with fire,
said the Dragon
and it was easy for Him, because he knew
how to Harvest Fire
and use it to Win.

As per expected, my Interest
dwindled
in throwing mud-bombs
at offending Trees and Rocks and Monsters.
None of it seemed to faze Society,
anyways. Coulda cared less about Two Warriors
for Truth and Light and All things Beautiful and Calm.
I suppose that's when
I was Expected to discontinue the continuation
of the Growing Hole.

But
the Dragon and I
met again, to formulate a Plan
to Strike back
against War and Hate
and greed and McDonalds and everything else
Wrong with the World.

Our Mission was clear: get in, get out.
Inform the Enemy
they aren't the Enemy
but their Acts are. Less Hate,
more Resolutions. Talk
to them, explain how much Happier
the Whole World could be
with everyone Digging Holes to Nowhere
only because they can
and want to
and laughing
and Counting Clovers
and Rain coming
to Wash Everyone Clean.

        —Morganne Elkins

Morganne set herself another challenge with form: to write a poem that's a single grammatical sentence. Her subject was her grandfather at Christmas time.

DON

his sack was filled
with toys
and his beard was white
and his suit was red

and over his shoulder
were slung
a pair of l.l. bean boots
and in his hand
a card to mom
and his glasses weren't
small and round
but big and square
but still
he was santa
until he wasn't
and i turned seven
and understood
my santa
was my grandpa
and he could fly.

                    —*Morganne Elkins*

Xander experimented with a form called a prose poem, which is a short piece that looks like prose but has poetic features. Notice Xander's diction, cadence, and imagery in this extended personification about the wind.

WHAT THE WIND KNOWS

She knows what we look like from her perch high above—tiny and meaningless—and she knows we can't do her harm. The wind recognizes us as black spots against a gray ground, and she smiles at our everyday humanity. She knows every hair on our heads, every ache in our bones, everything about us—even laughter as well. Across the world she has waltzed into every home and school and gently shaken our hands. She understands our intimacies, but she also feels our dread. Our fears come to her easily, and she loves them—uses them to whisper into our ears and spin us around, wide eyed and insecure. The wind knows how to taunt us, how to tickle our backs and blow hair in our faces on a tranquil day. She knows she can play with us—tap on our shoulders and then dance away, just out of reach. As many times as we grasp for her, she knows we'll never catch her. She will always slip away: through our hair, the faint branches, the holes in the sky.

                    —*Xander Bartone*

Here's another experiment with form. This is called a *concrete* poem, which means that its shape echoes its topic. Nate, famous for chewing pencils, wrote a pencil-shaped poem about his bad habit.

SNACK

I
gnaw
at the
yellow
flesh,
dissolve
the
school-
bus
paint,
tear
off the
dull
pink
eraser
with my
teeth
if you
chew
pencils
enough
they
become
a habit
your
bread
your life
an
addiction
and
soon
enough
all you
want
to do is

chew   chew

chew   CHEW

chew   chew   **CHEW**

CHEW   chew   chew   chew

chew   chew

—Nate Friant

Martin played with form by creating numbered sections, almost like chapters, in a poem about skiing.

SKIING: SEVEN MOMENTS

I.
I struggle into endless
layers of stuffy sweatshirts
and cotton socks.

II.
6:30 AM.
Drive-through at Dunkin Donuts.
Coffee.

III.
Billions of people
cram into one lodge.
The lift line is a mile long.

IV.
The glorified
super quad takes
hours.

V.
I reach
the top and follow the herd
to the trails.

VI.
I glide
down powder slopes
and zig-zag around boarders.
I have longed for this.
I have longed for this.

VII.
I am free.

—*Martin Shott*

Finally, a cool poetic structure to experiment with is the caesura. A *caesura* is a break or pause within a line of poetry, instead of at the end. It's how Teddy broke a poem about a moment in the tall grass behind his house.

If

I could lie here among
the crickets, listening to their
raw harmony, and not have
a thought in my head,
I would. I'd be willing
to let rain cascade
down my face and pamper
my lips. I'd invite a staring contest
with the hazy sky, ask the wind
to sweep across the bridge
of my nose and leave behind
a chill to linger on my cheeks.
I'd lie down in the knee-high grass
and let serenity overcome me: start
in my stomach as an ember,
then spread through my body.
And that moment when everything
is, I am.

—*Teddy Matel*

Two poets who influence students as creators of caesuras are Jim Harrison and William Stafford. Harrison's "Child Fears" and Stafford's "What's in My Journal," both of which take the form of lists with caesuras, inspire kid poets. Here's Graydon's take on his childhood fears.

Six-Year-Old Fears

The bed monster, the shower monster,
the attic monster, the basement monster,
the closet monster, the water monster,
hospitals, my piano teacher, preschool,
big kids, applesauce in my lunchbox,
timeouts, Ronald MacDonald, leftovers,
mice, deformed fingers,
mold, my own blood, fevers,
going crazy, rat poison,
thorn bushes, staying back,
soccer balls, my dog in a psycho state,
the Bermuda Triangle, showers, running away,

that Bambi isn't just a movie.

—*Graydon Nuki*

Max and Abbie borrowed this caesura-list form to write about what they believe in. In the process, they created vivid self-portraits of themselves aged thirteen.

MY BELIEFS

Flying cars. Duck ponds. Giant cliffs—steep and thick. The speck of a sailboat on the horizon. A white mug of coffee on a dark countertop. Long night flights. The glow of a city in the distance. Second-hand books littered with margina-lia. A room—everything dark, except for the blue glare of a television set. A bowl of almost-melted vanilla ice cream. The twinkling red light of a satellite passing the stars. Frost's cold blanket over grass—sweet no more, its color fad-ing. A marsh's dry, brittle grass against a grey November sky—thin passages of salty water winding toward the horizon. Restaurant speakers leaking jazz. The clinking of champagne flutes. A dead tree swaying in the breeze. A view from a mountain—the gold-specked evening sky—the same one that meets the sea

and never ends.

—*Maxim Jordan*

I BELIEVE

In worn tillers, rusted keels, dented hulls,
and sailing without a watch. In older brothers,
twin sisters, green cottages, riding in the back
of a rusty red pick-up, and eating
chocolate on chairlifts. In Harry Potter,
Holden Caulfield, Hester Prynne, and every
Disney princess. In good pizza, inspirational
graffiti, and red nail polish. In the plains of Colorado,
Vermont's foliage, and an island in Maine. In
streams, creeks, rivers, bays, ponds, lakes.
In oceans. In the dusty-sweet scent of rosin.
In cousins, cast parties, Halloween costumes,
and the box filled with journals
gathering dust under my bed.

—*Abbie Hinchman*

Finally, Avery used caesuras and a list structure to enumerate his pet peeves—an-other kind of self-portrait.

WHAT IRKS AVERY

Cold pizza, authors with pennames, wet towels, the sound
of teeth grinding, slimy stuff, people who chew with their
mouths open, unripe honeydew, slimy chicken,

dried toothpaste, outgrowing my jeans, slime, more slime,
dog-eared pages, when people say what goes around comes around,
squishy things, sea cucumbers, mystery gumbo, wax lips, wet
mittens, being late, and something, anything, everything slimy.

—*Avery Genus*

The ninth and final free-verse technique I ask students to include in their toolkits are the sound effects assonance, alliteration, and onomatopoeia, a lesson I described in Chapter 5. This two- or three-week introduction to free verse gives students tons of craft options to try as they draft and revise poems. It also exposes them to the topics and motivations of other students—kids who like poetry, find it useful to their lives, and put their toolboxes to work to craft poems that mean something to them.

IDEAS THAT MATTER

Of all the genres, poetry is the one made for feelings. It exists to help us notice and name what matters inside. Their poems make kids members of the coolest community ever, one that expresses love, sees through stereotypes, cares about the natural world, finds humor in the absurd, protests injustice, and celebrates the everyday. Many of the topics my students address as poetry come straight from their hearts.

In *Awakening the Heart* (1999), her brilliant book about exploring poetry in grades K–8, the poet Georgia Heard suggests that teachers ask kids to *draw* the place where feelings reside: to create maps of their hearts and explore the territory of their feelings. Of all the invitations I extend to students to develop meaningful topics for poems, Georgia's heart maps are the most productive in terms of quantity and quality of ideas.

To begin the process of heart mapping, students need to see one. Figure 9.3 is a map of the contents of my heart. At the center I placed its most beloved elements: my husband, daughter, dog, and mother. Around the edges I added my collections and comforts. I filled in the rest of my heart with the particular experiences, places, memories, moments, food, rituals, events, books, animals, and people that matter to me.

It's important to show kids a heart map that's rich with specifics so they can see how explicit and evocative a good one is. If my topics are general categories—*candy* instead of Halloween candy corn, Mary Jane's, and almond M&Ms—kids will record categories too, and the poems that result will be generic—bromides about broad topics like pets, friends, sports, and reading.

I introduce heart mapping in the third week of school, amidst the free-verse toolbox lessons. I make an overhead transparency of my heart map and talk about it—tell the stories behind some of the entries. Then I assign students to map their own hearts:

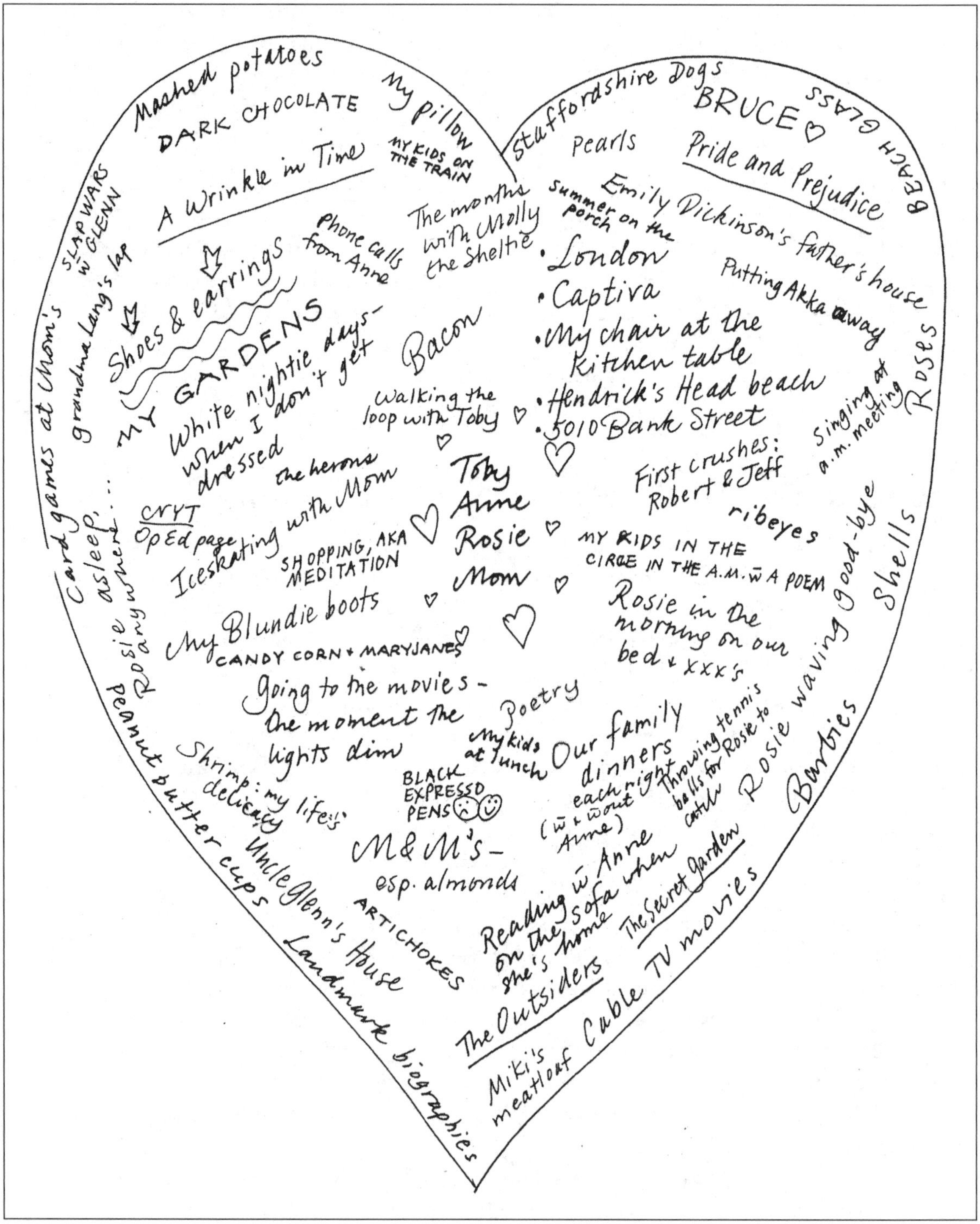

Figure 9.3 *Nancie's Heart Map*

THE LESSON

Do you see what happened because I mapped my heart? There are so many poems here waiting to be written—poems with the potential to *matter*. There's little in my heart that's general, clichéd, or cute. Instead, I've filled it with particular things, people, places, and experiences I care about. The act of drawing my heart and filling it in helped me remember and name them.

Please turn to the next clean page in the territories section of your handbook. Draw a big old heart—fill the page with it, so tonight you'll have plenty of room to mine its contents. Then tape the little nudge that I photocopied on slips of paper onto the right-hand bottom corner of the page:

> ### Questions to Help Mine Your Heart
>
> What has stayed in your heart? What moments, family members, pets, adventures, animals, objects, places, books, fears, scars, friends, teachers, things to eat, journeys, secrets, dreams, crushes, relationships, comforts, toys, tragedies, traditions? What's at the center? The edges? *What has stayed in your heart?*

Spend serious time with this assignment at home tonight—at least half an hour. You may want to take breaks and come back to it. Give your long-term memory time to do its work. Fill your heart with as much personal meaning as you can find.

The next day, at the start of the workshop, students gather in groups of three or four with their heart maps and pencils and take turns teaching one another about what has stayed in their hearts. I remind them that the purpose of sharing ideas is to listen for inspirations and record them, and I circulate, listen to the topics, laugh and cheer, and keep the groups on task.

Afterward, I convene the minilesson circle and conduct a fast Q and A: "What topics that stayed in your heart are yelling your name, you're so intrigued by them?"

Over the course of a school year, about a third of my kids' poems arise from ideas they captured on heart maps. I also encourage them to record new topics here as poetry inspirations occur to them. And I encourage the teachers in a K–8 school to conduct this exercise annually, which we do at CTL. Every year the contents of children's hearts vary, as they grow up and their vision of what matters changes and grows, too.

In addition, I help students generate ideas for poems that matter by asking them to set aside two pages in the territories sections of their handbooks to record techniques and topics inspired by the poems we read together each day. Students label these pages "Inspirations and Ideas from Other Poets." Each lesson that accompanies a poem in *Naming the World* ends with an invocation to students to act or think in response to the poem; many of these take the form of advice to poets.

For example, "You Can't Write a Poem About McDonald's" by Ronald Wallace is a sensory-in-the-extreme, funny, themed poem about the power of a poet's vision. After we've read and unpacked it, I offer this benediction: "Something you might try as a poet is a sensory, free-verse description of an unconventional topic. If a poet can write a great poem about McDonald's, what are other unlikely, amusing subjects to perceive as poets?" After the class and I generate some absurd ideas, I write a shorthand version of the benediction on the easel stand, and kids copy it onto the "Inspirations and Ideas from Other Poets" pages in their handbooks, for example, *A "nonpoetic" subject for a sensory poem, à la "You Can't Write a Poem About McDonald's" by Ronald Wallace.*

Class poetry anthologies and readings provide a similar benefit. Unless it's as part of a minilesson—when a writer demonstrates to classmates how he or she solved a writing problem—my students share only finished pieces of their writing, and only when everyone has a copy to read along with.

Oral reading is an art. As a teacher, I rehearse before I interpret anything aloud. If it's a poem, I annotate my copy in terms of the pauses, emphases, and grammatical structures I decide to create with my voice. Few of the students I teach can deliver a reading that's smooth and inflected. I don't think it's fair to kids, or pieces of their writing, to ask them to wing it. Nor do I think it's reasonable to expect the group to pay attention to a peer's reading without the visual support of the text. It's especially difficult to respond to an ears-only experience of poetry, since the audience can't register and appreciate the form, an essential component of any poem.

As soon as every student in a class has written a couple of poems—usually by the last week of September—I schedule a poetry reading. I collect final copies of the poems, cut and tape them onto sheets of 8½ × 11–inch paper, photocopy and collate them, and create a fast, inelegant anthology. Students in a class brainstorm and vote on a title and vie to create the cover design.

On the day of a poetry reading, we don't have writing workshop; instead, we celebrate the fruits of the workshop. I provide decaf coffee, decaf chai, cocoa, biscotti, and, to each poet, a copy of the class anthology. I ask them to take a few minutes to find their poems and rehearse them, while classmates collect their refreshments. I demonstrate how people respond at a poetry reading: at the end of each poem, snap your fingers. Then we relax around the circle, sip hot drinks, snack on "sophisticated baked goods," as one poet put it, and listen and follow along as students read aloud their poems in the order they appear in the anthology.

Across a school year, each of my classes enjoys three readings of anthologies of their poetry. Kids hear and read poems about intriguing topics, and they're exposed to new poetic techniques. So this knowledge doesn't get lost, at the end of each reading I give two index cards to every student, ask them to page back through the class anthology, and record on one card "Possible Topics for Poems" and on the other "Possible Approaches, Forms, and Techniques." I collect the cards and type up master lists (see Figure 9.4 as an

POSSIBLE APPROACHES, FORMS, AND TECHNIQUES

- Concrete poem (i.e., shaped to resemble the topic)
- Elegy
- Ode
- Use a repeating line to start each stanza
- No capitalization
- Short descriptive poem
- Short poem, in general
- Personification
- Center the poem on the page
- One short, packed line after another: a rapid-fire structure
- Experiment with italics
- One-sentence or one-line stanzas
- Dialogue
- Stanzas with a determined number of lines
- Staircase of lines or other kinds of play with the white space
- *Smell* as the chief sense, vs. vision
- Title that's part of the first line

POSSIBLE TOPICS

- What's-in-my-journal
- Singing/music
- Special place
- Family outing
- Moment-of-accomplishment
- Food experience
- My bedroom
- Being with Mom/Dad
- Fair ride
- Family tradition
- Pet peeve
- Poetic character study of someone
- Memorable board game
- Pet —dog, cat, etc.
- Key life moment: a memoir
- Sports moment or snapshot
- Early childhood memory
- Poem about *a thing that signifies*, e.g., Converse, blue highlighter
- Crazy invention or discovery
- Special time/place with friends
- Hiking
- Direct address to a thing or person
- Summer moment
- Conquering a fear
- Beloved hobby

Figure 9.4 *New Poetry Possibilities After Our First Reading*

example) for kids to tape onto the next clean page in the territories section of their handbooks. In the following day's writing workshop, they read and review the ideas around the minilesson circle. I encourage students to refer to the lists of peers' topics and techniques when they contemplate their own next poems.

From time to time during a school year, I ask kids to gather poetry ideas in relation to a particular theme, technique, or style. These include approaches to potential gifts of writing for the winter holidays, Mother's Day, and Father's Day; potential subjects for a "ways" poem in the style of Wallace Stevens or a "madeleine" à la Proust; and ideas for a potential tritina, pantoum, villanelle, or sonnet. My repetition of *potential* is intentional. None of these forms is a requirement. But the act of focusing, generating ideas, and capturing them in the territories sections of their handbooks makes the forms available, should students decide to turn their hand to them. The territories section exists so writers will never run out of options, but also so they can be selective and feel impelled about projects they choose to pursue.

Some of my students' most significant poems are written as gifts for parents and other family members. At a time in their lives when it isn't as easy as it used to be to express love or gratitude, adolescents can take a time-out, achieve perspective, and write poems that address and acknowledge the people who matter most. Those on the receiving end, especially parents trying to survive dry spells in their children's affections, appreciate the power and longevity of the poems. Gifts of writing *last*; they are a welcome substitute for boxes of candy, bottles of aftershave, and kitchen gadgets, which don't. I speak from experience as the grateful recipient of poems written for me by my daughter. Gifts of poetry provide an important occasion for kids to uncover and convey the *so what?*s in the relationships and rituals of their emotional lives.

In December I assemble a collection of gifts of writing by former students, one that represents a range of approaches. I photocopy a packet for each student, and as I read it aloud, volunteers identify the poetic techniques. Kids copy the list they create into the territories section of their handbooks, under the heading "Potential Approaches to Holiday Gifts of Writing." The list on the left, below, is typical. To the right I noted the titles of the poems my students were analyzing. These appear at the end of this chapter, as models for other teachers to share with their classes.

POTENTIAL APPROACHES TO HOLIDAY GIFTS OF WRITING

Cummings-style madeleine	"basketball Daddy" Max Jordan
Senryu(s)	"Holiday Senryus for Dad" Adrienne Jaeger
Funny résumé	"Résumé" Cole Wentworth
"Ways" poem à la Wallace Stevens	"Nine Ways of Looking at Mom" Carolyn MacDonald
Specific acknowledgment	"Thank You" Abbie Hinchman

Metaphor	"Mine" Noelle Timberlake
Tritina	"We Two" Xander Bartone
Symbolic experience	"In Your Shoes" Maura Anderson
Resonant memory	"A Gift from My Father" Sarah Jordan
Familiar moment	"Mom" Abe Steinberger
Couplets (with repetition)	"Delta, Alpha, Delta, Delta, Yankee" Helena Solorzano
Found poem	"Janet as Found on Google" Cole Wentworth
Six-word memoirs	"Five Six-Word Memoirs About Us" Sophia Stafford
Holiday memory of a brother	"Two Hours" Morganne Elkins
Significant memory of a sister	"Again" Sarah Jordan
Cummings-style poem for a brother	"love is longer" Tess Hinchman
Concrete poem for a brother	"Christmas Cracker" Cole Wentworth

I conclude the gifts-of-writing lesson by asking students to create a second list in their handbooks, below the first, headed "Potential Recipients of Gifts of Writing." I say, "Please spend the next three minutes thinking about the people for whom you might create a gift of writing. Look into your heart, and name the folks who need and would love your words. Then think about how you might touch their hearts forever with a piece of writing. Which forms interest you? Which styles? And what moments, feelings, and traditions stand out, signify, or symbolize?"

The subgenre of madeleines began in my classroom with a poem I wrote. I was walking with my dog in the woods behind our house one April afternoon, when some combination of the quality of the light and the rawness in the air transported me to the field behind the house where I grew up and the fantasy lives I made-believe there for me and another dog fifty years before. The sensation became a poem.

PIONEER DREAMS

In a green clearing
I clear my mind.
The air and the light
just right
reverse time.

I'm the girl
who escaped into green fields
with Lizzie the dog,
crashed through reeds,

whittled at sticks with a Girl Scout knife,
collected cockleburs,
and leapt the creek.
Heart brimful in love
with green,
solitude,
and adventures I pretended
with Rin Tin Tin,
Colin and Mary,
Annie Oakley,
and Francis Marion the Swamp Fox.
I was my own first romance.

Today in a green clearing,
the air and the light
just right,
I reclaim the green in me,
the daydream world,
and the lost girl.

I'd intended to use the drafts of "Pioneer Dreams" to illustrate a lesson about re-vision and polishing, but my kids were more taken with the subject of the poem than my objective. We had a rich discussion along the lines of "Whenever I eat one of those round butterscotch candies, I'm back at my great-grandmother's house," or "When I see the first dandelions, I remember how I used to have these dandelion battles in my backyard with pretend swords."

I told the kids the story of Proust's *madeleine*: the sugar cookie Marcel nibbles at the beginning of *Remembrance of Things Past* that summons up the first of many "privileged moments" of memory and allows him to live in the past and present and glimpse the essence of both. Some of the kids began to write their own madeleines, and I began to notice and collect published poems that seemed, to me at least, Proustian.

There's a selection of madeleines in *Naming the World*. I think "On Turning Ten" by Billy Collins is the best, but all of them inspire students to nostalgia and the creation of poems that flash back to their early childhoods. John flashed back to his make-believe friends, Joe and Joey, and the adventures they once shared and then flashed forward to his sense of loss, all these years later.

UNDER THE PORCH
This is where they lived?
Three feet of air space,
a floor of dirt and rocks,
bugs and cobwebs in every corner.

Sure didn't choose the best home,
but they never seemed to mind.
Never mentioned it when we played war,
hide-and-seek, truth-or-dare.

Must have been those vacations:
Hawaii, China, Disneyland, cruises (that thing rich people did),
New York, York, Mexico, Canada,
the moon.

They were anything I wanted to be
and, at some point, everything.

We haven't been in touch lately,
Joe, Joey, and I.
We kind of drifted apart.
"Hey! Hey, John! C'mon.

Let's get this done, huh?" Dad teases.
"Oh, yeah, let's fix this dumb porch,"
I say, in my deep, changing voice.
"Hand me that hammer."

I don't run into Joe and Joey,
but I need to believe
they're still having loads of fun
wherever they are.

—*John Solorzano*

Amelia remembered the days when her imagination transformed Lego people into the cast of characters of her beloved Harry Potter books.

NAMELESS

The cool kids at Hogwarts
wear hats—red and blue.
They swerve open-topped cars
amidst the mismatched buildings
and sneak out at night
to host parties at the caf
(Hagrid's hut: the only structure
that withstood the great
Instruction Rebellion).

At Hogwarts, Draco Malfoy
is God in student eyes—
after all, he has a *penthouse*

on the fourth level of the Tower.
The lower levels include
reception/gift shop,
Snape's shadowy lair,
the Treasury and Jail Department.
When mischief is managed,
they sleep in their plastic beds
and wait for a new day.

Now the Legos lie still,
smiles on their faces and hats on tight,
unaware that I don't return
to invent their dawn.
Hagrid's hut is silent,
the cars overturned
and the Tower toppled.
If they were to wake up now,
I have a horrible hunch
they wouldn't recall
their own names.

—Amelia Neilson

In a madeleine about her mother teaching her to read, Helena's use of sensory details flashes readers back in time with her.

TIME AND I

The breeze sways us,
and my eyes droop.
Warm rays try to persuade me
to give in to sleep.
I fight the urge
and continue to read to Mom.
My voice is slurred; I stutter,
and my reading is choppy,
unlike the smooth flow in my head.
But she listens all the same,
helping me along
as I struggle to pronounce
even the simple words.

The air smells of salt and pine.
The grass looks as if God
laid down a plush green carpet,

the sky as if He painted it blue
to welcome His son
into the kingdom of clouds.

Do you want me to read?

Mom asks, rousing me from dreamland.
I hand her the book as an answer,
and she picks up where I left off,
reeling me into another world,
one where it is snowing
and a child is dying,
a world not nearly as perfect
as this one.
I let my eyes drift closed
and lose myself in the song
of my mother's voice.

Time and I fall asleep in the summer sun.
                              —Helena Solorzano

A present-day encounter with a snake was Wallace's sugar cookie. It hurtled him back to the perilous days of little boyhood.

SNAKE BITES

I watch, Xander and Patrick by my side,
as a slim pink tongue escapes from the stone wall.
Next a quick black head explores the heat of an August sun.
The slender body ripples and squirms
while seamlessly floating over dirt and grass.
My hand shoots down to what I think is the head
but ends up being the tail.
A snake can bite its tail.
It latches onto my callused thumb.

And I'm four again,
but instead of Xander and Patrick,
there's Haize, my best friend before the move.
We run wailing to the stream
and soak our hands in the muddy water to cleanse the poison.
I wipe a mixture of mud and blood on my corduroys.
I'm close to tears, but I have experience, and I hold it in.
Steve Irwin never cries.

He taught us everything—
from what frogs are poisonous to which are docile,
that bullfrogs are the equivalent of a poison dart frog,
that some snakes are for catching and some must be left alone.
But we got cocky and tried to catch the deadliest of all,
the garden snake.

These days, when I see what I once thought
was the coolest thing in the world,
I do notice, and sometimes I will toy with it,
but mostly
I'm too old for the thrill
of frog catching,
of crocodile hunting,
of the deadliest menace of them all.

—Wallace Jackson

Some Forms

As the school year progresses, I introduce students to poetic possibilities beyond the effects of free verse. I show them formats that depend on stanza length and number, cadence, brevity, hyperbole, a knowledge of the alphabet, or, in the case of sonnets, rhyme and syllable counts

Tritinas, pantoums, and villanelles are repeating forms that create lovely rhythms and powerful emphases and are doable by middle school poets. A tritina consists of three stanzas, plus an envoy. The three lines of each stanza end in one of three words, repeated in the order below. The final one-line stanza, the envoy, contains all three words.

Tritina Form

Stanza I.	1
	2
	3
Stanza II.	3
	1
	2
Stanza III.	2
	3
	1

Envoy: 1, 2, 3

Brandon wrote a tritina about hunting with his father. His three words are *together*, *deer*, and *you*.

HUNTING

We rest in brittle leaves together
as I scan burnt fields for a deer,
grateful for the presence of a hunter like you.

I sneak glances at you
in the little time we have together
before dark, before we can't spy the deer,

. . . and nothing emerges—the deer
remain hidden. But a memory is born, of you
and me, alone together.

There will always be deer, but never enough time together with you.
—Brandon Blake

Tess wrote a tritina for and about her twin sister, Abbie.

PAIR: A TRITINA FOR ABS

We sit crossed-legged on one bed, although there are two.
I can barely hear over the blare of music.
The best part of my day? I spend it here with you.

When we walk, I share secrets I'd only tell you
as we count down the months until summer: just two
to go. I almost hear it in a swallow's music.

Later we dance to the TV's cheesy music.
I grab your hands and spin you.
Our parents are asleep: it's just we two.

Let the others see us as two halves—music sounds sweeter with you.
—Tess Hinchman

I encourage students who want to write a tritina to brainstorm diction in connection with a topic they've chosen and consult a dictionary and thesaurus to help them select three words that have a lot to offer. For example, *light* can function as four parts of speech. *Promise, talk,* and *wonder* can be both nouns and verbs. *Long* is an adjective and a verb, and *you, me,* and *it* are versatile pronouns.

A pantoum consists of four-line stanzas, with whole lines repeated in a set pattern. The second and fourth lines of each stanza reappear as the first and third of the next. Its length—the number of stanzas—is up to the pantoumist.

Pantoum Form

Stanza I: Line 1

Line 2

Line 3

Line 4

Stanza II.   Line 5: Same as Line 2

Line 6

Line 7: Same as Line 4

Line 8

Stanza III.   Line 9: Same as Line 6

Line 10

Line 11: Same as Line 8

Line 12

Emma wrote a sensory pantoum about Maine's Kennebec River in winter.

KENNEBEC PANTOUM

Steam rolls off the river.
Snow slides down its banks
and stifles
the brown grass.

Snow slides down its banks.
Old leaves dance on
the brown grass,
leaving the maples lonely.

Old leaves dance on
frosted rooftops,
leaving the maples lonely
with the weight of winter.

Frosted rooftops
sag and leak
with the weight of winter
along my stony Kennebec.

—*Emma Moorhead*

A villanelle is a more complicated form—almost like working a jigsaw puzzle. It consists of six stanzas. The first five have three lines, and the final stanza is four lines. The first and last lines of the first stanza take turns repeating as the final line in the next four stanza; then they rejoin as the last two lines of the poem. The rhyme scheme is ABA, except for the last stanza:

Villanelle Form

A1
b
A2

a
b
A1

a
b
A2

a
b
A1

a
b
A2

a
b
A1
A2

"Do Not Go Gentle into That Good Night," written by Dylan Thomas for his father, is the best-known villanelle. I also like "The Waking" by Theodore Roethke and "Deer Island Villanelle" by seventh grader Parker Elkins.

DEER ISLAND VILLANELLE

The waves lap against the shore.
The home my ancestors built for each other:
the ancient cabin with the pink door.

The abandoned rowboat rots with the oar—
the one once captured by a great-grandmother.
The waves lap against the shore.

The sunlight beams onto the hardwood floor
of a hut: the summer home of my mother:
the ancient cabin with the pink door.

The kayaks land ashore
on Heart Island and none other.
The waves lap against the shore.

The pinecones fall to the forest floor—
a currency of sister and brother,
the ancient cabin with the pink door.

My family will come here no more.
Soon it will pass to another.
The waves lap against the shore,
the ancient cabin with the pink door.

—Parker Elkins

Once I've introduced a poetic form that rhymes, I present a minilesson about how to use a rhyming dictionary. This is another occasion when I want writers to work from quantity and be selective, rather than putting down the first rhyme that comes to mind. Students tape these instructions into their writing–reading handbooks.

How to Use a Rhyming Dictionary

1. Take off the first consonant(s) of the word you're trying to find a rhyme for. Then search for its rhyming sound by its *beginning vowel: A, E, I, O, U,* or sometimes *Y.*
2. Locate the appropriate section in the rhyming dictionary by vowel: *A, E, I, O,* or *U.*
3. Within that section, use alphabetical order to locate your rhyming sound.

Example:
    The word I want to find a rhyme for is *well.* I take off the *w* and get *ell.* I turn to the *e* section of the rhyming dictionary and, using alphabetical order and the key sounds at the tops of the pages, search for a list of words with the *ell* sound. I find it on the page with *egal-ell* at the top.

The rhyming dictionary gives me more than sixty rhyme options for *ell*. As I skim them, I jot down any word that shows potential for my poem. Then I close the rhyming dictionary and play with my list of possibilities until I find the one that makes the best sound and the best meaning.

Josie decided to use a rhyme scheme in a poem about the life she imagined for a woman whose job is distributing free samples at a supermarket. With help from a rhyming dictionary, she made the best sounds and the best meanings.

ONE OF THOSE LADIES

She stands, plastic gloves wrinkling
over pale fingernails, polished.
Lines crease her face—an inkling
of secrets hidden, hope demolished
in her broad smile—
crooked teeth splashed with white.
Her laugh echoes on tile,
brushes the buzzing fluorescent light—
a thunderous cry.

She holds out a plastic cup
of Stonyfield Lowfat Frozen Yogurt ("Please buy. . . ."):
an offering to customers who look up
and take but never think.
She stuffs fish rolls in her purse
for the cat at home. Pink
lipstick smeared on napkins, a disperse
of crumbs scattered.

Days to months to years
of service, waiting, though shattered,
for someone who hears
her crying from the inside
to come, remove her white apron,
be her lover, her guide.

For now she throws used spoons, one by one,
into a plastic bag,
waves at small faces in bright coats
who stare as they are dragged
away by mothers who dote
on them as they endlessly shop.

And she wonders—
will the cycle ever stop?
　　　　　　　—*Josephine Cotton*

An Elizabethan sonnet is another rhyming form—fourteen lines with the scheme *ababcdcdefefgg*, or three quatrains and a couplet. The first eight lines, or octave, establish a situation or scene; the next six, the sestet, reach a conclusion about it. The rhythm is iambic pentameter: five stressed beats in each line, alternating with unstressed syllables, for a total of ten or eleven syllables per line.

I don't hold seventh and eighth graders to the full requirements. After all, these are the sonnets Shakespeare composed. We read and unpack some of his, and I encourage those who want to give it a try to focus on the rhyme scheme. In her first sonnet ever, that's what Josie did. She wrote it as a gift for a big sister who was about to move halfway around the world.

Sonnet to Anina

On the dock below the boiling sun,
we watched the waves lap the boats
that tilted as the water spun
from motors gurgling in their throats.
The buoys bobbled on the surface,
growing algae on the ropes
that kept them tied to one place,
like me at home, not lifting my hopes
while you go drifting away.
When you've left, my tears will flow,
though nothing will end this perfect day.
I'd always hoped you'd never go
but stay with me, at home, forever.
For now, we sit alone together.

—*Josephine Cotton*

Göran achieved the basics in his "River Sonnet," along with ten-syllable lines throughout, an octave, and a sestet. The poem almost killed him, but it's a stunner.

River Sonnet

Our paddles dip into murky water.
The bow cuts through small whitecaps. On nothing
but the slap of the boat, we teeter-totter.
A bird sings, and down the river it rings.
Looking behind I glimpse his orange jacket.
Two strokes switch, two strokes switch, propelling us.
Our paddles sing a duet. The sunset
casts pinks and purples across the sky, thus
calling us homeward and lighting our way.

Connections formed, time falls away, modern
life a footnote. We've escaped from the fray,
two brothers rounding the bend. No downturn—
we are this moment, together, two boys
paddling our duet of synchronized joy.

—*Göran Johanson*

Pablo Neruda, regarded as the greatest Latin American poet of them all, is a hero to my kids. He developed a loose form called an irregular ode by retrofitting the intricate, choral odes of the ancient Greeks. Neruda abandoned weighty topics, threw out the rules about stanzas and meters, and went over-the-top singing the praises of common things—an apple, an onion, socks, salt. His *Odes to Common Things* (1994) is one of the most popular books of poetry in my classroom library. Avery ventured into Neruda territory by emoting at length about his favorite fruit.

ODE TO THE POMEGRANATE

O, Pomegranate,
you are
the epitome
of delight,
the essence
of pleasure,
the eye
of the hurricane
of natural cuisine.

You, pomegranate,
are the quintessence
of perfection.
I can feel
the juicy treasure
seep out of your sphere
before
I break open
your smooth
rosy shell
with a satisfying
crunch
and feel
red drops of dew
squirt
from your ruby core.

My eyes
feast
on your interlocking,
radiant
crimson gems.
When I plop a spark
of you
on my tongue,
your flavor bursts
across it
like a red tsunami
of joy.
I chew
on a single seed,
and a tidal wave
of refreshment
rolls through
my mouth
and down my throat
to settle, finally,
in the pit
of my grateful stomach.

Pomegranate,
how does such a luscious,
succulent
taste spurt forth
from the tiny,
precious packets of life
that inhabit
your scarlet husk?

Alas,
my worst fear
is that someday
you will
vanish
and leave the human race
without its ambrosial companion.

Never leave,
pomegranate.
I
need you,

the world
needs you,
O, darling friend,
O, inanimate lover.

> —*Avery Genus*

After we've read some of Neruda's odes, I ask students to create a list in the territories section of their handbooks headed "Potential Subjects for an Ode" and identify at least six things in their everyday lives that they adore and might want to exalt someday. Then, for those who decide to follow through, I offer these guidelines:

TIPS FOR NERUDA-ESQUE ODES

- Choose an ordinary subject from your everyday life that you love, appreciate, *get*.
- Begin by writing off-the-page. Note everything you feel, think, like, notice, taste, smell, hear, or wonder about your subject.
- Exaggerate its admirable qualities until it becomes central to human existence: hyberbole rules.
- Tap all five senses.
- Use metaphors and similes.
- Directly address the subject of the ode.
- Tell your feelings about the subject *and* give exalted descriptions of its qualities: a balance.
- Keep the lines short.
- Push for sensory diction, plus language that's packed with meaning and cut to the bone.

Another poetic form, the abecedaria, is just what it sounds like: a poem with twenty-six lines that begin, in consecutive order, with the letters of the alphabet. When I teach it, I give kids an example of a good one and send them off in small groups with the direction, "Tease out the form of this poem." With a good one—where the content outshines the form—it can take a while. Abecedarias are a hit with my students. These are two of my favorites.

RULES TO PLAY BY

Always keep your back to the basket.
Balance the court, fill the open spaces,
Coach reiterates.
Diagonal cuts work best,
even against a zone defense.
Forgetting can be embarrassing—
go up lefty for a lefty lay-up,

head up when you're dribbling,
ignore the cowbells in the stands,
jump-shots need form to fly, and
keep your feet on the ground for a foul shot.
"Live in the moment," Dad tells me.
Many times *he's* the distraction, his camera flashing.
Now that I'm older I should remember to
overplay a bad ball-handler and
press full-court on a slow or small team.
Questions later, we've got to talk about sideline, Coach says.
Remember to use a drop-step on post moves.
Shooting is always the first option.
Turnovers decrease morale and give
us an advantage; we need to use
V-cuts against slow players.
Whispering, Coach describes our out-of-bounds play:
X's are us, O's are them.
You have to read the defense—then
zoom to the basket.

Nice hoop, Hotshot.

—Sophia Carbonneau

JOHN'S THIRTEENTH

A day is all I get.
Best to make it meaningful,
'cause I'll only turn teen once.
Dad's planning a gigantic bonfire.
Emmett—a friend—says, "Birthdays suck.
For every one, you're one year closer to death!"
God! How depressing, a thought like that, and
hearing it from such a joyful person, too.
In just a week
"John" will be an exalted name, like
King John. For a day I'll be the center of the universe.
Long ago, in what seems like a galaxy far away, I dreamed,
more than anything, to be this age.
Now that it's coming true, I'm freaked.
Or maybe I'm just being melodramatic.
Possibly, on October 25, I'll simply . . . turn thirteen.
Quietly. I've been getting
ready all my life for this moment, yet I feel unprepared.

Soon it's so long to kid and hello to adolescent.
Try to slow down the process?
Until a time machine is invented, good luck.
Voting, driving, drinking (not at the same time) are inching closer.
What would Dad say if I got an ear pierced?
X-ing out previous choices, I search catalogues for presents.
Young never again!
(Zits are the downside.)

—*John Solorzano*

When I teach about haiku and its cousin, senryu, the first step is to disabuse kids of the notion of a five-seven-five syllable structure. The traditional Japanese haiku doesn't count syllables—it counts *sounds*. Seventeen Japanese sounds take about as long to say out loud as twelve to fifteen English syllables. The poet Robert Hass, who translates the Japanese masters Bashō, Buson, and Issa into English, rarely writes them as five-seven-five syllables.

It's more accurate to think of haikus and senryus as *meditative nuggets*: brief descriptions or observations of nature (haiku) or people (senryu). Their essence lies less in the number of syllables and more in their tone, diction, and brevity. They are a marvelous form for teaching about concision.

My students and I read many haikus and senryus, by the Japanese masters but also by Jim Harrison and Ted Kooser from their book *Braided Creek: A Conversation in Poetry* (2003), which collects the correspondence they conducted in the form of brief poems after Kooser was diagnosed with cancer. From our readings and discussions, my students and I teased out these criteria.

GUIDELINES FOR WRITING HAIKUS (NATURE) AND SENRYUS (PEOPLE)

- Examine the literal world of the senses: what you can see, hear, taste, touch, and smell. ("To learn about a tree, go to a tree." —Bashō)
- Use concrete details to ground the poem in a specific moment.
- Avoid metaphors and similes.
- Write in the present tense. ("Haiku is simply what is happening in this place at this moment." —Bashō)
- Make every word count: few adjectives and no adverbs or conjunctions, if you can avoid them.
- Use strong diction, especially tangible nouns and sensory verbs.
- Take a direct tone.
- Make the reader feel something.
- Don't rhyme.

- Keep to a form of three short lines.
- Think *meditative nuggets*: tone and sensory specifics are the essence of a good haiku or senryu.

Sam was brooding about ninth grade, when she'd be away at boarding school and parted from her mom; her ruminations took the form of a senryu.

NEXT YEAR

you won't be able to kidnap me
from the bus stop and take me to café crème.
if i cry, that will be one reason.

—*Samantha Herter*

Awakened on a stormy night, Lilly remembered it with a senryu.

Rain hammers at the window.
Midnight lurks at the door.
Wind scatters my dreams.

—*Lilly Richardson*

In March, Cole protested springing forward with a senryu.

DAYLIGHT SAVINGS

Sheets pulled back.
Eyes open angry.
One hour early.

—*Cole Wentworth*

One of Gabrielle's responses to the death of an elderly family member was a snapshot she took at the cemetery.

CEMETERY STROLLERS

Among graves,
silver spirals of hair lean
over their canes.

—*Gabrielle Nuki*

And here's Sam again, who never wore a coat or real shoes to school if she could help it.

DEFYING WINTER

Goose bumps on bare arms.
Snow clumps on sidewalks but
flip-flops prevail.

—*Sam Herter*

To inspire my twenty-first century students to write haikus—or any poetry about nature—first I have to get them to go outside. Even in a beautiful place like the coast of Maine, it's a struggle.

When I moved here in the 1970s, the students I encountered at Boothbay Harbor Grammar School didn't need nudges to act as naturalists. They navigated the local woods on loops of trails, built forts and camps, and enjoyed sleepovers in tents. Kids could identify birds and birdcalls, animal tracks, marine critters, and edible leaves and berries. Boys owned knives, guns, fishing gear, land traps, and lobster traps, and they ate or sold what they caught.

Everyone—boys and girls—knew how to split a piece of field grass and make a whistle, tell fortunes with a buttercup, choose a good bouncer and send it skipping across the surface of a pond, and direct you, if you wanted to see one, to an osprey's nest or a beaver dam. They brought to school snake skins and bird nests, and they raised the hair on the back of my neck with tales of the fisher, the vicious mystery mammal of Maine that eats housecats and porcupines. Everyone's family owned a CB radio. When a call came over the scanner for a county sheriff because a driver had collided with a deer, locals raced to the scene to try to claim the road kill.

It's not that they were untouched by popular culture. They were mad for *Star Wars*, Kiss, *General Hospital*, Leif Garrett, and *Tiger Beat*, the same way my current generation of kids is obsessed with Justin Bieber, dubstep, Katy Perry, One Direction, and *The Voice*. But they also lived in and amidst Maine's flora and fauna. These days, when my students and I update one another about our weekends, some will announce that they didn't go outside once between Friday afternoon and the ride to school on Monday morning.

If we want this generation to care about the natural world, teachers of writing need to kick our students outdoors and tell them to pay attention. William Carlos Williams wrote, "Perception is the first act of the imagination" (1963). I would add that imagination—*empathy*—is the first act of caring about something. My kids' best poems about any subject begin with concrete experiences and direct observations. They need to perceive first, because this is where they'll find their visions and voices: *in the particular*. Then, as they craft verse about the particular, they adopt an attitude and convey a tone. They figure out what it means; they *give it* meaning.

Haikus are the ideal place to begin to find meaning in nature. Every few months I give each student a clipboard, blank paper, a pencil, and a set of instructions, and then we head outdoors:

HOW TO GO OUTSIDE
- Stay on CTL's property.
- Stay apart from other kids.
- Look hard—at eye level, down, and up.
- Be quiet: *listen*.

- Touch.
- Smell.
- Fill the page with sensory details.
- Remember: "To learn about a tree, go to a tree." —Matsuo Bashō

After fifteen minutes, students return to writing workshop with their pages of sensory information, and I invite them to try at least one haiku based on their data. Everyone always obliges, I think because the imagery they collect is so juicy. What they notice and how they craft their observations teaches them about the local environment, its rhythms, and their relationship to it. These are a handful of haikus that resulted from an early March ramble on CTL's grounds.

Tips of green
try to burst through winter's shell—
not yet.

—*Patrick Jackson*

THE EVERGREEN

A brush stroke
among brown skeletons
waiting for leaves.

—*Graydon Nuki*

HATS OFF

Acorns shed
their fractal berets in preparation
for warm weather.

—*Avery Genus*

POE ON THE PLAYGROUND

a mystery
is brewing in the murder
of crows.

—*Xander Bartone*

A white pebble hides
in the brown field: souvenir of a child's
adventure.

—*Teagan Guenther*

Colonies of buds open
their red beaks, show off
their green tongues.

—Avery Genus

The annual River of Words poetry competition, founded by Pamela Michaels and former U.S. poet laureate Robert Hass, is a major incentive for my students to perceive and write about the natural world. Like any teacher anywhere, I have to teach the kids I've got. River of Words motivates twenty-first-century students to have perceptions beyond the four walls of their wired bedrooms, pay attention to local watersheds and landscapes, and bring their imaginations to the world out there.

I inform kids in September that the River of Words deadline is December first. Throughout the fall, we read and unpack nature poems by former CTL students, previous winners of the contest, and professionals. I assign weekend homework: "Go outside. Spend time. Look close. Listen. Smell. Touch. Take notes of your perceptions. Search for moments of connection. We'll talk about them on Monday."

That Monday morning they arrive with stories about adventures in the woods, along streams and rivers, by the seashore, on their front lawns, in puddles. It doesn't matter. It's the *act of perception* that matters, even if they think they haven't perceived a thing. That's what Maura started to say, in a poem she wrote about writing a nature poem. The Mary of the title is Oliver, famous at CTL for "The Summer Day," our official school poem, to which Maura alludes.

This Is for You, Mary

It's snowing.
I am outside,
and it is snowing.
I'm sure the fire inside is nice right now,
but nope,
I'm out here Catching the Moment.
I'm freezing my fingers off
with a pen and a pad of paper,
hoping to maybe get down some choice words.
I won't say that when the wind blows through the trees
it sounds like whispering
because, well, it doesn't.
It's hard to capture a moment of nature
when maybe your mind is on something else.
I don't know how Mary Oliver does it.
There have to be other things on her mind than
dogs and fields.

But, according to nature and Mary,
here it is:
The ground is cold.
The trees are swaying.
The wind's blowing.
The clouds are dark.
The sky is snowy.
And I'm not Mary Oliver.
I'll put down the facts and throw in some metaphors and similes,
but not one of the ideas in my head is Mary material.
I won't watch a grasshopper eat sugar out of my hand.
But I will laugh and have perfect summer days.
I will watch my dog prance through the grass,
having fun like there's no tomorrow.
I will lie on that splendid green carpet
and watch the sun melt its fiery colors
over the distant pine trees.
And Mary?
I do know exactly
what a prayer is.

—*Maura Anderson*

Despite herself, Maura paid attention, made connections, and took a stand.

One weekend, as a poet fulfilling his teacher's assignment to observe the natural world, Avery got lucky. He was astonished.

Lucky

I watched the doe stop, perch
on the edge
of man and nature, swivel her head

and glance behind her.
Then my eyes caught sight of the calf
a few yards away, knock-kneed

and unsteady.
Tranquil, the doe clipped across the road
and paused once more

to look back at her calf and then at our car.
I was astonished.
The waning sun shed pools of illumination

through the pines,
bathed her in radiance, and set her sleek fur
ablaze.

For what seemed an eternity, she pondered
my existence and dissected my soul
with luminous eyes,

unfazed by our rumbling presence.
Then slim legs
whisked her slender body away

towards the forest. I saw the calf scramble,
hooves clattering about the tarmac,
after its mother.

As the calf reached the brink of the woodland,
it cast a final, doubtful gaze
in my direction,

then vanished into the brush.
One day I watched a doe stop, perch
on the edge

of man and nature,
and teach me about splendor.

—*Avery Genus*

After a weekend spent saying good-bye to her family's summer cottage, Tess channeled her sadness and the beauty of the setting into a poem about her relationship with a place.

LEAVING EDEN

The wind stings my skin,
makes my eyes water,
blurs my view of the glassy sea.
Trees are tinged with red.
The aromas of autumn tickle the back of my throat
and remind me that this is my last ride on the island.
I wish I could lean into the wind forever.
I pedal harder and push the thought away.
Afternoon sun slants through the trees,
bathing everything in golden glow.
Streets I've biked every day

are peaceful without tourists,
and ocean smells mingle with wood smoke.
I wish winter would never come.
I dread leaving the simplicity of the island,
returning to school and structured life.
Maybe autumn is the island's sunset:
its brilliance before the sun disappears.
I just wish it didn't have to.

—Tess Hinchman

Josie found an abecedaria on a Saturday in spring.

APRIL WIND

Already the grass wears
braids of green, but a few leaves
continue to cling in
desperation to their branches: if the rumors
ever prevail, they'll be the
first to know. The bark on every tree is smudged by
gray and laced in lichen. Crows can't
hide in snow or burrow
into scarlet leaves
jostled by the vicious wind. Thorns,
kicked and tangled, hang
limp and dangle spider webs.
Moss crawls like caterpillars and
nestles among rocks, frozen
over the dehydrated stream,
puckered by crinkled leaves.
Questions linger after the
rigid ice melts, when it bubbles to the
surface and sings again. Will
the lilies still blossom
underneath the bridge? Will the birdhouse still sit
vacant, or will voices echo from above?
Weeping willows wilt, waiting for the
xanthous flowers of the forsythia to bloom: a
yellow umbrella for sparrows who float on the
zephyr of wind that reaches all corners,

whispering of spring.

—Josephine Cotton

Josie also found inspiration for a piece of alliterative twitterature.

TWITTERATURE

the drop drips,
delicately diving,
descending diligently
through dismal daylight,
determined to
ricochet off
a desolate puddle
gone dry.

—*Josephine Cotton*

Wallace was one of my rare outdoorsmen of recent years. He skied, sailed, and went fishing with his father. Our study of nature poetry invited him to consider his adventures in the out-of-doors as material for poems, to which he brought voice, specificity, and feeling.

SEVEN TWISTER

We sit in the canoe—
he's in the back, I'm in the front.
A tapered leader twists in the evening breeze.
He hands me the green fly box,
and I open it in awe:
thirty years of collection and selection.

But I don't want the green box.
I reach for the steel case—
the selection of flies like no other
That box was handmade in England, you know.
Your grandpa tied all the flies in there.
I pop it open.

Fingers touch
the strong black bristles
of a leech pattern grasshopper.
Eyes scan
the streaming yellow feather of a Mickey Finn.

Finally,
I find it,
the perfect fly:
small brown plumes on both sides
with a soft white tuft on top.

I remove it from the foam ridge.
That's a great fly, Dad comments.
I slip the line through the eye
and tie it on.

Such a little knot
never made
such a strong connection.
            —*Wallace Jackson*

And Abe discovered a perfect sonnet on a spring day in the fields beyond his house. The philosophy and diction of his concluding couplet make me think of Robert Frost and William Shakespeare, and make me grateful for Abraham Steinberger—that I enjoyed the privilege of teaching writing to this "one small man."

SONNET

By my stone wall with its wild brush I walk,
my ears alive with lovely sound. The birds
they sing—so clear—a joyful song. They talk
of worms and seeds and nests, their cries like words,
describing the bodily things they need.
They don't take flight when I walk by, for I
am one small man, not nests or worms or seed.
I'm not a threat: I'm only worth a sigh.
My thoughts go out to them, these birds. Their lives
I feel so close and vital, though I'm not
so foolish to believe a bird that strives
to survive would share my leisurely thought.
The birds will forget me now forever,
but I wrote these words, so I'll remember.
            —*Abraham Steinberger*

Through the observed and felt experiences they shape as poems, my students are changed—as sons and daughters, young men and women, observers and critics, thinkers and writers, stewards and citizens, and humans alive on the planet.

Poetry is *useful* to them. Poems won't keep them safe, ensure a successful life, heal their pain, or make them rich. But poetry teaches them what craft means. It sharpens their perceptions and opens their hearts. It consoles them, inspires them, and gives voice and meaning to the experiences of their lives.

That seems enough to ask of it.

GIFTS OF WRITING

BASKETBALL DADDY

i

i gazed up at Dad
as he descended
the stairs in sweat pants
and lingered
on the last step
smiling at me
my pudgy hands
reached
up to him
when he exclaimed
Hey big guy!
and i hugged him
and declared
with two year old joy
basketball Daddy!

and we drove
to the gym
and he plucked
me off the ground
and set me atop
his shoulders
and handed me the ball
and i trembled from
this new vantage
of six feet two inches

clasping the ball i
stretched
toward the orange rim
(oh how i strained)
and let it
drop

down

through the net
and it bounced

from me
to the ground

lower
and

lower
until it rolled
away

ii

Now I stand
only inches shorter than he is
on the same floor where I'd shivered
atop his shoulders
with a ball
between
my palms,
and I raise it
and
I
shoot.

—Maxim Jordan

Holiday Senryus for Dad

We tiptoe downstairs,
rattle our gifts, and solve the mysteries
beneath bright paper.

On the last night of Hanukkah
eight dancing heads glow by a dark window.
Two hands dare to brush through them.

The date:
December 24th, and we are still hunting
for the perfect tree.

Under a sky spattered with stars
we glide on black ice, numb fingers
buried in our pockets.

—Anna Jaeger

Résumé

Belly dancer, dice roller,
cruise taker, baker queen,
cookbook writer, recipe inventor,
the bane of crossword puzzles everywhere,
ruler of Birch Point Road,
giver and receiver of immeasurable love,
my grandmother,
my own Grammy.

—Cole Wentworth

Nine Ways of Looking at Mom

I.   Among my family lazing around
on a Saturday morning,
the only one working is my mom.

II.   I don't know which to prefer:
the story
or the sound of Mom's voice reading it.

III.   Dad, David, and I are three.
Mom, Dad, David, and I are a family.

IV.   I know cryptoquips
and what my hair looks like in French braids.
But I know, too,
that Mom is involved in what I know.

V.   Mom sings my violin pieces offbeat.
It is a big part of everyday life.

VI.   At the sight and smell
of Mom cooking dinner,
even a picky eater would cry out in hunger.

VII.   I was of two minds—
like trying to decide whether Mom should read me
Anne of Green Gables or *Ramona the Pest*.

VIII.   Mom and I were baking all afternoon.
We were mixing the dough,
and we were going to put it on trays.

IX.   A split cookie, ready to share, waited on the counter.

X.   The earth is spinning.
        I must be loving my mother.

—*Carolyn MacDonald*

THANK YOU

for singing along to my god-awful music,
for keeping in touch with old girlfriends,
for putting another blanket on me at five a.m.
on a snow day, for teaching me to make
scrambled eggs, for never acting your age,
for painting your toenails red, for being stubborn
and tough and brave, for talking to at least four of your five
children everyday, for pulling gourmet meals out of an empty
cupboard, for never judging, for watching Brad Pitt movies
on mute, for injuring your foot a hundred ways,
for the time we took a right turn instead of a left
on our way to my violin lesson and drove and drove
and drove until we saw the sea, for hot chocolate,
foreign swear words, advice, laughter, friendship, love,

and for the hugs.

—*Abbie Hinchman*

MINE

My flashlight in the darkness.

My teacher of patience and generosity.

My blanket in the freezing night.

My mender of broken hearts.

My constant in a world of confusion.

My defender of happiness and truth.

My friend in the lonely forest.

My landmark of life and love.

My mother.

My mother.

My mother.

—*Noelle Timberlake*

WE TWO

The Volkswagen grumbles beneath its cargo of two.
Your hands on the steering wheel of the car you love,
you guide us home through the soupy dark.

You stand there, enveloped in crisp dark-
ness, hand raised in a wave I pretend is just between us two.
Your face shines with love.

You dash around the kitchen, your love
evident in cookies baked from dawn to dark,
until you're done and the only ones awake are we two.

The dark is never loveless when it's shared by two.
                    —*Xander Bartone*

IN YOUR SHOES

I sprint
despite my limp
as crisp air blows
through sweat-drenched hair.
You pass me,
look back,
and frown:
a frown
that says you know
I should have known
better.
I look at my shoes.
They might as well be
bedroom slippers.
Examining
the flimsy, archless material
makes my feet hurt
even more.
You gaze down
at my mistake,
then
at your perfect running shoes.
You crouch,
untie them,
and trade with me.

In your shoes,
I follow your footsteps
and run off
into my future.

—Maura Anderson

A Gift from My Father

Together we stand in the woods,
the faded orange Husqevarna clutched
in the grimy gloves that envelop my hands.
My heart races as the engine growls.

Sensing my fear,
you smile and nod
and ease my nerves.

I position the whirring blade on the tree,
and dust flies everywhere
The slice in the wood deepens,
then breaks off.
I glance over to see you grinning.

Want to try it again?
Yup.

Later, as I lie in bed,
faint scents of sawdust and gasoline
cling to my hands—

an aroma that belongs
to your fingers
now lingers on mine.

—Sarah Jordan

Mom

You sit
in the same red chair
at the same computer.
I read
on the same green couch.
Every night
our breaths
a discordant chorus
of in and out.

The sharp tap of your keys
is the perfect contrast
to the rasp
of my pages turning
until
slowly
our breaths merge
and we are
one.

—*Abe Steinberger*

DELTA, ALPHA, DELTA, DELTA, YANKEE

One word. Two syllables.
My whole world.

Daddy would make sure Private Ryan
got home safely.

Daddy makes perfect carne asada papas,
not to mention tacos.

Daddy never lets problem get out of hand
and never is unfair.

Daddy knows whether to use Neosporin or Bactine.
Not that he is ever sick.

Daddy always remembers when it's trash day.
Don't forget to take out the trash!

Daddy will play Little Big Planet *and* MW2 with me.
Don't even get us started on Black Ops.

To make it clear,
Daddy loves me and I love Daddy.

—*Helena Solorzano*

JANET AS FOUND ON GOOGLE

Janet is hungry.
Janet is ageless.
Janet is coming to a city near you.
Janet is always fab.
Janet is the founder of a vocal group called MAMA SAYS!
Janet is going on Letterman.

Janet is a force all her own.
Janet is waiting for you.
Janet is a little more latte than bittersweet.
Janet is right on.
Janet is like a hug from baby Jesus.
Janet is only swimming ten meters per second.
Janet, is that you?

Janet is a great mom.
Janet is Cole's mom.
Cole loves Janet.

—Cole Wentworth

FIVE SIX-WORD MEMOIRS ABOUT US

You get the last word. Again.

Okay, I'll put on something "appropriate."

Wherever swimming takes me, you follow.

Mom, I'm thirteen now; I hang out.

So pathetic: *The Voice* = our life.

—Sophia Stafford

TWO HOURS

A single, blinking red light
warns us it is only four a.m.
Mom said at least six, you whisper,
but I slide out of my sleeping bag,
and you slide out of yours,
and together we creep down the stairs
like burglars in a silent movie
and stumble towards the tree that glows
in red, purple, and green
with a sea of wrapping paper clinging
to its trunk, and you squeal,
and so do I, as we grab our stockings,
race up the stairs, and clamber into your room,
where we spread the contents in neat piles,
suck on sweet chocolate, and play cards until,
at last, it is six, and, at last,

we can wake our parents
and discover the tree.
But for now, it is just us,
and for now, that is all we need.

—Morganne Elkins

AGAIN

The black envelops us
as we slip through darkness—
the only sound
the heavy breathing of our parents,
who succumbed to the night
hours ago.

My sister turns to me.
The moon that peeks through a window
casts its eerie glow on her face.

Tomorrow, when I wake up,
she'll be gone
again.

She pulls me toward her,
wraps me in a hug,
rests her head on my shoulder.

We stand in the darkness
together.

I love you, Sar,
she whispers.
Then she slinks into her room.

Saying goodbye
was supposed to get easier,
but the knot in my stomach
that loosened with time
ties itself back up again,
and, same as the day we left her at college,
my heart is hollow.

I stand in the darkness
alone.

—Sarah Jordan

love is longer than the snow
shorter than a stone

quieter than music through the bedroom wall

it is farther than the sun
less sane than the sky

bigger than all the words I'll ever say

love is plainer than a song
and more alive than spring

it is waiting all year to see you again

—Tess Hinchman

CHRISTMAS CRACKER

This is our love
We fight
We hate
We make up
We play
We fight
We hate

This is the cycle
That I wish to break

This is the cycle that tears us apart
And pulls us back together

This is the cycle of our friendship
This is the cycle of our love

This is the cycle I wish to break
But until then

We fight
We hate
We make up
We play
We fight
We hate
This is our love

—Cole Wentworth

CHAPTER 10

MEMOIRS

Most of the basic material a writer works with is acquired before the age of fifteen.
—WILLA CATHER

I believe Willa Cather. The themes of my life had pretty much unspooled by the time I hit fifteen, and I've been acting on them, or choosing not to, ever since. Memoirs are how writers consider our pasts. We figure out who we were, who we've become, and why. We gain perspective on experiences and learn from them. We question or confirm decisions. We recognize and explore moments along the way to becoming ourselves. We distill the essence of an event through what we decide to include and exclude. We consider ourselves in relation to the others in our lives—memoirs celebrate people and places no one else has heard of. And memoirs invite writers to tell our own truths, give them shape, and understand what they mean.

Göran knows this. His memoir about working with his dad to haul a tractor out of a muddy field tells the truth about growing up on a farm: hard, sometimes dangerous work, a connection to the land, and a heritage. The title says it all.

STUCK

The 826 tractor rumbles down the road. The yellow line skips by as I sit on the hub and watch Dad shift into high range as we gain speed. The fields slip out of sight—the B1 North, the Big Wedge, their crops turning brown, corn stalks crumpled, rotten tomatoes clinging to their stakes, the harvest over. Zipping my jacket to my chin, I fight the wind that whips at our bodies. I glance over at Dad, whose eyes point straight ahead down the never-ending road. I look at his rough hands gripping the wheel, worn from a lifetime of farm work, and I remember some of the stories he told me, about when he was young. I think how hard he had it compared to me.

Dad pulls the tractor onto the farm road, and I see a glint of green and red where he was seeding cover crops. Now the other tractor, the 766, comes into view. Its tires sit a foot deep in mud, and the John Deere planter hitched onto it looks too big for the sunken machine.

We pull up alongside the 766. Dad pushes in the clutch and taps the brake. The tractor comes to a full stop. He flips the emergency brake and pulls the kill-switch. I know what I'm supposed to do—I hop off and start to unravel the chain that's circled around the three-point hitch. It feels heavy in my hands, but its rusted links don't seem strong enough to pull two tons of steel. I know it will work: he's done this before. But a flicker of doubt still lingers at the edge of my mind.

"Göran, get up there and lower the hitch to about the axle," Dad instructs. "That way it has a less likely chance of flipping over."

Flipping over. Man, I hadn't thought of that possibility.

"Okayyyyy," I reply.

I watch the hitch drift down. I stop the lever, and when it comes to a rest, Dad slips the chain through the U hitch and hooks it back to itself; then he circles the chain through the front of the 766. With the two tractors chained together, he hops on the 766 and yells one last instruction.

"See that pedal next to the seat? That's the differential lock, and that will make the tires spin together. So when you first feel a tug, I want you to push down on that. It will give the tractor more grip."

"Got it." I go through the motions: push in the clutch, lift up the E brake, and tap the throttle till I hear the familiar click. Then I push the black button, and the 826 roars to life. I hear Dad's tractor do the same. I push on the throttle until I get it up to about 15,000 RPM and look for the thumbs-up. Okay, here we go.

I put the 826 in gear and let off on the clutch. The tractor creeps forward. As I watch the slack disappear, my foot slides over to the small pedal. The thought of flipping over comes back to me—I've got to hit that pedal. I feel a slight tug, slam my foot down, look over my shoulder, and watch as the 766 creeps out of the mess of mud and broken corn stalks.

We pull both tractors and the planter up to dry ground. I clamber down the steps, hop onto the field, unhook the chain, and start to ravel it up around the hitch.

"Good job, son," my father says.

"No problem, Dad." I look over at the sun sinking below the tree tops, casting pinks and purples across the sky, and hop back on the 826. "I'll see you at the house," I yell over the rumble.

And I remember a poem we read in my English class—Wendell Berry's "The Current." Its last lines describe how a current flows through the earth from one generation of farmers to the next. For a moment I feel the power of that current and the pull of this land and my heritage. Then I put the tractor in gear and follow my father home.

—*Göran Johanson*

Michael used a memoir to capture for all time his take on a famous fifth-grade field trip. Written as a vignette for the eighth-grade yearbook, "One Child, Every Night" shows the influence of a quote I'd posted in the classroom from Gore Vidal's *Palimpsest* (1996): "A memoir is how one remembers one's own life, while an autobiography is history, requiring research, dates, facts double-checked." Michael knows he can be playful as a memoirist—that it's okay to embroider and elide in writing his version of an event. Here he's working in the tradition of Dave Barry and David Sedaris, two of his favorite memoirists and humorists.

ONE CHILD, EVERY NIGHT

The smoke drifted toward the ceiling of the car. It was blue, and it smelled of burning plastic. I rummaged for more trash to brand with a cigarette lighter; there was one in each door of Katie's old car, even in the back seat. It was my only form of entertainment during the four-hour drive to Hammond Castle.

"Where is all this smoke coming from?" Katie yelled back from the driver's seat. Alison sat next to her in the passenger's seat, with Sierra and me in the back.

"I have no idea," I lied, facing the window.

Alison glanced back. "Michael's burning stuff again," she said nonchalantly. I dropped the lighter and bonfire materials.

"Stop that, Michael. We're all gonna suffocate!" Katie frantically tried to turn in the seat to look behind her while keeping an eye on the road.

"Okay," I lied, again.

"Ooh, forty-six!" Sierra exclaimed. Forty-six brown UPS trucks had passed us so far today. If she saw one more freaking truck, I'd light myself on fire.

When we finally arrived at Hammond Castle, I flopped out of the back seat and onto the pavement: both legs had passed out in the car. The Castle loomed against the dark blue waves behind it, worn gray stone spiraling up into great towers. I took out my disposable camera.

Our class filed through the grand archway, into the dark interior of the stone building. It became cooler, and the lights dimmed for a moment. We entered a huge room with a tall ceiling that rose up and up. A guide joined us and started explaining about the life of John Hammond, inventor and practical joker.

We unloaded our stuff. We were, apparently, sleeping on the cold floors of the Great Hall. But before we retired, our guide returned. "Before you go to sleep, would anyone care for a ghost story, perhaps?"

Julia volunteered to tell us a chilling story about a clown and a dog. When she finished, the crowd silenced, in shock. Then Carl spoke up.

"I've got one," he said. He walked to the front of the room, flashlight in hand. I'll never forget his haunted words or the ghastly plot of doom and despair. He took a seat and launched his dreadful tale.

"It was a dark and stormy night," he began. "All was still, and the fifth and sixth grade class slept silently." We glanced around. Something about this story seemed familiar. "But the creature stirred under the prison's grate." He pointed with a white finger at an iron grate over a gaping gap in the stone floor. I hadn't noticed it before. The dark pooled inside it. Even the pitch black seemed to cast shadows. Carl continued.

"Every night, the creature left its lair. It found the children and took one back down with it. It took one child, every night, and another on the next night. It did this every night, taking someone every single night. It always took someone; none could escape. Every night it took someone with it, just one person every night. It took one of them. Every. Single. Night. It would—"

"Every single night?" someone called out.

"Yes, it would always take one, every single—"

"It took just one of them?"

"Yes, it—"

"So you're saying that it took one of them every single night?"

Everyone broke into laughter.

"Are you sure it—took one—every night?" someone said between uncontrollable bursts of laughter.

Carl's story was remembered for years. Even as we attempted to laugh him off stage, he continued to spin his wheels and try to invent an ending for his tale about the scary monster who, according to legend and Carl, took *one child, every single night.*

—*Michael Carter*

Morganne used an elegiac memoir to capture some basic material of her young life—memories of her beloved great-grandmother—and explore the power of love, grief, and memory.

The Key

I remember lying in my bed, the one painted with ladybugs, listening to her coughing. The dry, wracking sound exploded through the thin wall that separated our rooms. Splinters of opera slithered from under her door, taunting me, and the air felt heavy with sherry and painkillers. I slipped out of my bed. My nightgown trailed the hardwood floor as, a glass of water clutched in my hand, I paused at her door and knocked.

"Petshop?" she rasped. "Is that you?" Stars lit up her room. She lay like the broken doll a little girl loves too much, propped by pillows and swaths of blankets. Her hair fanned by her ears, haloing her in cotton and snow. I nodded, handed her the water glass, and crawled into the mahogany bed next to her. She stroked my hair and smiled.

"Thanks, love," she murmured. I nodded again and smiled back. For a while, we watched the opera in silence.

Maybe it was the singing characters on the rabbit-eared television that comforted me, or how I fit, perfectly, under her arm, her voice melodic over theirs as she reminisced about journeys to Japan and France and Germany— *Over there's a piece of the Berlin Wall. Go on and fetch it for us, Petshop, please, and I'll tell you how I managed to smuggle it out.* Finally, I fell asleep, always just before she did.

I realize now how lucky I was to know her. When you live with a grown-up for almost two-thirds of your life, she becomes an extended parent, one who critiques your art and reads you Robert Burns. It never occurred to me that the other five-year-olds at my nursery school didn't go home to their eighty-seven-year-old great-grandmothers. She was as permanent a fixture in our home as the lovebirds singing in the sunroom.

I remember standing barefoot in the garden. It was November, and the fallen leaves were crusted with frost. I had on my lilac wings and the shimmering dress I'd worn for Halloween. As the first car pulled into our driveway, Parker, my brother, darted down the long walkway to inform the adults already waiting inside. I stood still, hidden behind a birch. Only when the mile-long driveway was choked with sedans did I enter, trailing behind the mink throws and silk scarves.

The parties she threw were never quiet or simple. This one, in honor of the Scottish poet Robert Burns, was annual—like clockwork or Christmas. There were always bagpipes, several men dressed in kilts, and haggis. Throughout the night guests spouted lines in Scottish accents, all leading up to her own rendition of "To a Mouse."

I remember weaving through legs sheathed in cocktail dresses and khakis, and champagne flutes dangling from fingers. There were so many people— the women with their sensible heels or stilettos, the men in black dress shoes. Feet overlapped feet until I felt there was no room for me to stand and the crush of bodies was stifling. I pushed my way through the throngs of people clogging the porches and dining room and escaped to an abandoned hallway.

The bagpipes started up again. Sitting with my back against the wall, cross-legged in the dark, I didn't find the lull of voices imposing. The hall was empty except for a sagging cardboard box, tucked in the corner behind the door. I fingered the satin hem of my dress, unready to return to the mass of poets, neighbors, and foreign diplomats. I searched for an excuse to delay my return.

I'd paraded through this hall so many times that I'd never stopped to explore it. Outside, I knew every chipmunk hole and fallen tree. A mundane hallway had never before held my attention. Maybe it was because I lacked anything better to do, but the mildewed cardboard box suddenly shone with possibilities.

I imagined lifting the cardboard flaps and uncovering a beautiful porcelain doll. Her locks of real black hair would be faded from years of love. She'd be wearing a cornflower-blue petticoat the exact shade of her eyes. I would lift her, gently, and run to Grandma––she would have been hers, originally, of course—and ask her name. If she couldn't remember, I would call her Ella for Eleanor or Polly for Grandma.

Eager now, I crawled to the corner. Running my fingers along the edge of the yellowed tape holding everything together, I sent a quick prayer in the general vicinity of God and Fate that I would find Ella or Polly or something equally amazing. When I lifted the box's wings, yellowed paper like old lace fluttered out. A key was nestled on a blue ribbon––the color my doll's eyes would have been. I slipped it into my pocket and stood. Brushing invisible cobwebs off my skirt, I floated back to the voices calling my name.

I hate it when grown-ups tell you that you never know how good a thing is until it's gone. I hate it because they're right. I was eight when Grandma went to the Lincoln Home, a big, yellow assisted living alternative. The past year she'd been in and out of hospitals, and with my parents' new business it was difficult to take care of her the way she needed. For the first time in my life she wasn't at home, sitting at her desk writing. Instead we visited her at the Home almost every day after school. She told me about the gardens— Grandma was a famous gardener—and we walked along the shore. In its own way, this was almost better. Now I treasured my time with her. She died there, in the big, yellow hospital disguised as a community.

I have tried to visit her grave.

We didn't have school—it was April break. We ate breakfast with Nana and Don at a bakery in town. I got a croissant, and Nana tried to convince Mom to let me go on a cruise with her.

"Benny," she'd scolded, "the tickets are half off. We gotta get this girl out of America." She broke off a piece of cinnamon roll and dunked it in her tea.

Mom rolled her eyes at me. "Yeah," she agreed, "that's because it's hurricane season." Nana frowned and bent over her iPod, where she reviewed the websites of cruise lines. Parker flipped through *Time* magazine, and Grandpa Don showed me how to eat a sugar cube. We said goodbye, promising to come by later and pick them up for a gallery opening in Rockland.

In the car I switched on the radio. Mom turned it down, and I opened my mouth to protest. "Morganne," she began, before I could, "I think we should visit your grandma. She loved spring. The promise of it. I think––" Her words sounded mechanical, like she'd rehearsed them in front of a mirror. She was still talking when I nodded, mute. I didn't try to turn up the radio again, just stared out the window as green trees budding with new life blurred my eyes.

We pulled up the narrow dirt road cutting through grave sites and eased to a stop next to our family plot. I couldn't get out of the car. I sat, staring straight ahead at a tomb marked with a marble lamb. *Beloved Baby Son* read the marker. The lamb was moldy and forgotten, ivy crawling up its skin. Beloved baby son. Beloved baby son.

My whole body started to shake. Parker stared at me. Mom asked if I wanted to get out. *What do you think?* I screamed at her inside my head. *What do you think?* Instead, I whipped my head back and forth. Tears flung themselves from my eyes. I stared down at the grease-blotted paper wrapped around my half croissant.

Maybe holding tight is the only way to let go. My fist clenched around a key, knuckles white. I held on so long that the gradual numbness of my joints loosening didn't shock me. I didn't fight it until my palms bled, rusted metal indenting flesh—until it didn't feel like betrayal.

That day in the car was two years ago. I haven't tried to visit her since. I don't know when I will, or what may happen if I do. But I can feel my fist opening. I wouldn't call it moving on so much as accepting. I've lost the cornflower-blue ribbon. Now I thread the key where it beats next to my heart on a silver chain. When people ask, I shrug or tell them in a sappy voice, like I'm joking, that it's the key to my heart. I know I can't hold on forever. I know nostalgia won't bring her back. But when I wear the key, she's with me, locked in years of memories.

— *Morganne Elkins*

A teacher friend and I were discussing memoir as a school genre. She told me she's required to teach her fifth graders a four-step formula for writing a personal narrative: develop the main character (the first-person narrator), describe the setting, introduce the narrator's problem, and explain how it was solved. If only real life were that tidy.

For my students, there is no resolution to some of their memoirs. At the end of "The Key," Morganne still can't bring herself to visit her great-grandmother's grave—she hasn't "solved" her "problem." But the memoir was useful to her. It helped her create a record of essential memories, give shape to them, express inchoate feelings, and even grow up a little. Plus it's a beautiful piece of writing. The Scholastic Art and Writing competition awarded Morganne a Gold Key and an American Voices Medal on the strength of it.

To help students understand what *can* happen in authentic works of memoir, I marinate them in strong examples of the genre. In early October, I begin to read aloud short memoirs I love during the ten minutes between the end of writing workshop and the beginning of independent reading time; kids will also read good ones for homework. As writers, students are still working on poems. But as critics, they begin to turn their attention to memoirs.

Many of the memoirs we read together, like those I included in this chapter, are written by students. I also rely on the "Lives" feature that appears on the last page of each Sunday's *New York Times Magazine*: about once a month a memoir published here will be appropriate for and useful to middle schoolers. And I love Cynthia Rylant's *But I'll Be Back Again* (1993), which collects memories of her childhood and adolescence. Each chapter is a read-aloud, and each concludes with an explicit statement of its theme, of what Rylant learned, gained, or understood from a time in her life and the people who were a part of it.

I find other memoirs on the op-ed pages of the *Boston Globe* and *New York Times*. I read aloud chapters from books by David Sedaris, Anna Quindlen, and Dave Barry, as well as excerpts from such book-length memoirs as *The Glass Castle* by Jeannette Walls, *Rocket Boys* by Homer Hickam Jr., *Breaking Night* by Liz Murray, and *Black Boy* by Richard Wright. I share college application essays written by former students, which confirm my theory that successful ones are nothing other than CTL memoirs written to a word count. And I ask students to read and discuss memoirs I write about my childhood, adolescence, and experiences as a mother, teacher, and activist.

Students keep the memoir examples I give them in the final folder of writing workshop, the one dedicated to prose. I assign them to set aside fifteen pages toward the back of their writing–reading handbooks—pages 78–93—for the notes they'll take on the prose selections we'll read and critique together during the rest of the school year. I launch this section of the handbook by asking them to tape onto the back of page 77 a list of questions that will inform their critiques of memoirs:

GENRE STUDY OF MEMOIRS: Responding to Readings

- How does the title invite you as a reader *and* fit the story?
- What kind of lead did the memoirist choose: action, dialogue, reflection, or description? What does the lead do for you as a reader?
- What verb tense did the memoirist choose: past *or* present? How is the tense choice effective here?
- How is the memoir structured, e.g., vignettes, flashbacks, flash-forwards? How does the memoirist move events through time and space? How does he or she indicate transitions in time?
- What does the memoirist do to help you make a movie behind your eyelids? What sensory details help you to be *there*, in the scene, and see, hear, and feel it?
- Do any *things*, à la William Carlos Williams, help reveal the memoirist and this time and place in his or her life?
- What kinds of diction choices—especially verbs—bring the story to life?
- Is there dialogue? Does it sound real? What does it reveal about people, their feelings, and their relationships?
- Is there a climax, or high point, to the action? How can you tell what it is?
- How and where does the memoirist describe thoughts and feelings and invite you into his or her head and heart?
- What's the theme or *so what?* How does it grow from the memoirist's thoughts and feelings?

- How does the conclusion affect you as a reader—what feeling or insight does it leave you with, and how did the memoirist achieve it?
- What else do you notice, like, and want to remember as you prepare to write a memoir of your own?

I used to ask kids to talk off the top of their heads in class discussions about what they noticed in prose readings. But as always happens, once I nudged them to write about their observations, the written-down insights that emerged were more specific and more useful to them when it came time to make similar decisions about drafts of their own.

One October, the first memoir reading was "The History of a Girl Obsessed" by CTL graduate Marley Witham. I gave the kids copies, reviewed the "Genre Study of Memoirs" questions with them, introduced the term *vignette*, since Marley's memoir is a series of brief, related stories, and read it aloud as they followed along.

The History of a Girl Obsessed

Shiny, bright, new: my boots. Even now I can close my eyes and envision them, their purple soles, teal bodies, and, in the center, Pocahontas, hair flowing, in glowing Disney colors. They were my favorite shoes—I begged to wear them everywhere—and the start of my first obsession.

I never saw the movie. I'm not quite sure how this infatuation began. Probably a love for Indians sparked it; in my four-year-old mind, Indian royalty must have been the best thing anyone could aspire to. For years I made my parents read every Pocahontas book available. I was Pocahontas for Halloween. A photograph shows me grinning next to Erin—who was a slime monster—adorned with tan felt and leggings, a feather in my hair, and at the bottom of the picture, I can just make out the beginnings of teal boots. I remember my excitement that night as I dressed as my idol. I refused to wear a coat over the costume. I wanted the world to see Indian royalty running in my veins.

I faded out of my Pocahontas stage only to enter the lair of another Disney character, Peter Pan. The idea of a flying boy who could never grow up was incredible to a five-year-old. I had always dreamed of flying, and I sat on the edge of the bed as I watched the animated movie for the first time. Captain Hook was the perfect villain to face the heroic Peter. In the end, when Hook was devoured, I jumped off the bed and cheered. This was the first time a movie had this effect on me. I chanted, "I won't grow up." When I was finally taken to see the stage play, I was astounded. I clapped the loudest I could when Tinkerbell's light started to fade, yelling, "I believe! I believe in fairies." I went to bed happy after every performance I saw, knowing I had helped saved Tinkerbell.

Another Halloween costume was sewn. I still have the green cap in my basement, though the moths have taken their toll on the body. Back then I thought I knew the play and movie inside-out. Now I realize I only knew the first layer of the story—not the darker themes that lie beneath.

But then it was time to dip briefly into the world of the fairy-tale princess. Cinderella? No, too whiny. Sleeping Beauty? Too scary. Snow White was the perfect mixture of grace, kindness, and capability. Her love of animals is what I fell in love with. Then I saw the dwarves, and I was captivated by their world, too. Every time my parents went to the video store, I begged them to rent *Snow White*, so I could giggle, smile, and scream along. I know my parents were afraid I'd be influenced by the Disney images. I was. I galloped through our woods singing. I asked my mirror questions. I hoped for an evil stepmother so I could escape to the dwarves I was sure I would meet.

When I tired of Snow White, I fell in love with wolves. They were so mysterious, so elusive. They were the fairy and witch version of dogs. I built a wolf piñata for my birthday; I remember shaping its long snout. It was in this stage I got Palio, my stuffed coyote, who I pretended was a wolf. He was my keeper of tears and screams, my guardian as I slept. My mother took me along with her to a conference where there was going to be a wolf. I was so excited at the thought of viewing a real, live wolf. My stomach flipped as I blocked out the speeches about facts I already knew. I stared at the crate, willing it to break open, willing the wolf to come leaping out. I would hop on its back, and we would run away and live in the woods together—happily ever after, of course.

The next love of my life was a place: India. Even the name sparked a wild joy and sense of awe. I stared at my dad's photographs, soaking up the images. Soon every single book I read was about India. I even bought travel guides. In my mind I embarked on a journey to India. I glided through the streets, looking at all the people. I skipped through the jungles, at peace with the tigers and elephants. I trudged through the mountains, inhaling the fragrant air. I wanted to run away there, to get lost in a world that was foreign and tantalizing.

But I also loved France. That love started with the musical version of *Les Misérables*. I don't remember what song I heard first or where I heard it. I do remember walking everywhere with headphones covering my ears, letting the story, the voices of characters I loved, flow over me. I memorized every song until I could run around my house, dancing and singing along, until I became part of the musical. Not only did I know all the characters, their goals and their songs, I could also name what made them human, what part of them was inside me. I remember days when my house became Paris in the 1800's.

Today I can argue that *Lord of the Rings* is one of the best-crafted works of literature ever written. I fell in love with Tolkien. I wanted more than anything to live in the extravagant world he created. These books became my infatuation in the months prior to September 11, 2001. It was in these great adventure novels that I found hope for peace. I disappeared into Middle Earth for hours and hours, again and again. Some days I was a heroic Rohan soldieress. Or I was a hobbit, overwhelmed by the world outside my safe corner. I could even become a wizard, wise and mysterious. I fell in love with every character—except those I hated with a passion. I picked out my Middle Earth family. To me, these books weren't fantasy. They were history: this world existed.

In second grade I'd liked Harry Potter books; now I realize how awful they are—how unoriginal J.K. Rowling is with her plots, so different from the fantasy world of my beloved Tolkien. Even so, I took away from Rowling a love of her characters. I discovered a Harry Potter Fanfiction website, where people, even I, could write whatever we wanted about the characters and settings Rowling had created. I could make the characters fall in love with whomever I wanted. I could even kill off Harry. It was a perfect way to love the characters while hating the plots, and I became a part of a whole Internet community of Harry Potter fanfiction.

Starting with Pocahontas, some part of each of these obsessions has stayed with me. I was looking for ways to identify myself, to find something in the world to help me know who I was, to name something or someone I could be for a while, and to escape from the real world. I am still obsessed with my fantasies.

When I was little, they helped me become an avid reader. Today they help me imagine a world for myself when the one I live in becomes too much. They help me think and feel in ways I never would have otherwise. They help create me. They let me become someone else and, finally, myself.

—*Marley Witham*

After I finished reading aloud Marley's memoir, I gave the class five minutes to take notes about it. By way of example, Figure 10.1 shows the observations Sarah recorded in her writing–reading handbook. Then, as Sarah and her classmates talked about the features they observed, I captured their comments on the easel pad, so students who hadn't picked up on something could add it to the notes in their handbooks.

After students had read another couple of memoirs and we'd unpacked them, I formally launched the course of study. Again, most students were still writing poems, and that was fine—for now. I told them, "Everyone needs to finish your current poetry project by next week, as we officially transition into our next genre study. I'd like the memoir lessons to be fresh in your minds when you make the transition."

In order for students to create memoirs of significance, they need topics of significance. Eighth graders write a memoir in the course of the genre study, as well as vignettes for their yearbook. Seventh graders produce just one memoir. This means *a lot* hinges on the particular slice of their lives students decide to focus on. The first memoir minilesson invites kids to go deep and be deep.

Responses to Memoir Readings

1. "The History of a Girl Obsessed" by Marley Witham

- title is funny, strong diction, hints but doesn't give topic away

- description lead — I could see the boots

- past tense — good choice b/c so many vignettes

- easy to follow transitions between vignettes

- good visuals

- lots of things — boots, P.P. costume, stuffed coyote, India books, Tolkien

- sensory verbs — begged, sparked, devoured, etc.

- no dialogue — good choice b/c so many little stories

- no climax — good choice b/c so many little stories

- about ½ is T & F?

- Conclusion — shows how all the phases make her who she is & helped her. A strong "so what?" at end but little ones in some of the vignettes too.

→ • remember how much I like her T & F

Figure 10.1 *Sarah's Responses to a Memoir Reading*

THE LESSON

I have this teacher fantasy. It's twenty years from now, and your parents are sick and tired of the boxes of your stuff that are clogging their attic. They beg you to come home and deal with it.

So you do. You're slapping aside cobwebs and rummaging through boxes, until you chance on the one that holds your papers from middle school. And there it is: the memoir you wrote twenty years before. You sit back on your heels, read it, and think three things:

How cool was I, to be this thoughtful and perceptive as a thirteen-year-old? What a good writer I was at such a young age. And, *reading this memoir, I can draw a line between the kid I was then and the person I am today.*

I hope our genre study of memoirs will make my dream come true—that the stories you write about your lives will matter and resonate now and in years to come. You'll start by selecting an experience that matters, one that's interesting to shape as literature, one that will help you figure out who you are, who you were, and who you might become.

A big hurdle in writing a successful memoir is choosing the topic and angle. If a memoirist's heart isn't in his or her subject, if there's no *itch* to discover how and what an experience signifies in a writer's life, it's likely the memoir will fall flat.

I'm remembering student memoirs that never had a chance, written about topics like "Our Trip to Disney World," "The Day I Got My Braces," and "My New Racing Bike." These ideas don't have a lot of potential for a *so what?* or theme. The stories that resulted were a version of "And then we did this, and then I said that, and it was all so much fun/ really terrible." It's hard to call them *memoirs*, there was so little meaning.

Today I invite you to begin the process of investing in a memoir by identifying multiple events from your lives that have significance and potential: *meaty* memories. Please turn to the next clean page in the territories section of your handbook. At the top, write the heading *Memoir-Worthy Experiences*. Then, on the *back* of the previous page, tape this document, "Questions for Memoirists." When you lay your handbook open and flat, the questions should appear on the left and your heading "Memoir-Worthy Experiences" on the right.

QUESTIONS FOR MEMOIRISTS

- What are my earliest memories? How far back can I remember?
- What *things* have signified for me—have had an important presence in my life?
- What relationship, over time, has helped shape who I am, what I'm like, what I care about?
- What's something I've seen that I can't forget?
- What's an incident that shows what my family and I are like?
- What's an incident that shows what my friends and I are like?
- What's an incident that shows what my pet and I are like?
- What's something that happened to me at school that I'll always remember?
- What's something that happened to me at home that I'll always remember?
- What's an experience that changed how I think about something or someone?
- What's a time or place that I was perfectly happy?
- What's a time or place that I laughed a lot?
- What's a time when I felt as if my heart were breaking?

- What's a time with Mom that shows what our relationship is like? A time with Dad?
- What's a time with a grandparent that shows our relationship?
- What's a time with a brother or sister that shows our relationship?
- What's a time with a cousin or another relative that shows our relationship?
- Can I remember when I learned something, or tried something for the first time?
- What memories emerge when I make a timeline of my life so far and note the most important things that happened to me each year?
- What experience over time, captured in vignettes, might show a lot about who I was and who I am? Think: birthdays, Halloween costumes, favorite TV shows, sports, beloved books or songs, performing, family meals, shoes, bedroom redecorations, or visits to one camp, pond, lake, or beach over time.

Let's start the process of mining your memories together. What are your earliest memories? Close your eyes—how far back can you go? Write those down. . . .

Consider the second question: Is there a *thing* that's significant for you, that's had a lasting presence in your life? Maybe a special stuffie, toy, book, gift, or souvenir? Write it down. . . .

Consider the third question: What have been the central *relationships* in your life so far, the ones that influenced who you are and what you like and care about? Is it a brother or sister? A parent? A friend? A grandparent? Write them down. . . .

Tonight for homework, sit in a quiet place for at least a half an hour with your handbook and a pen or pencil. Consider the rest of the questions, and try to answer each one. Take your time. Search for memories that jog your identity in intriguing ways. Don't feel compelled to go into detail. Use just as many words as you need to capture the gist of a memory. Come in tomorrow with a list of meaty ones.

The novelist Willa Cather said, "Most of the basic material a writer works with is acquired before the age of fifteen." For sure, the themes of my life emerged in my childhood and adolescence. Yours are developing right now. Don't waste this opportunity to name and follow the threads of the themes of your life. Come to class tomorrow with a thoughtful list of the big ideas of *you*.

At the start of the next class, students gather in groups of three or four with pencils and their handbooks. They take turns describing the memories they captured, discuss one another's topics in terms of their potential, and jot down new inspirations. I circulate, listen, and ask questions. After ten or fifteen minutes, I convene the minilesson circle and ask kids to tell about one surprising or valuable nugget that surfaced when they mined their pasts. And I ask them to consider potential patterns: "Are there relationships among any of the memories on your list? Might some be combined as vignettes, like Marley did, to illustrate a common theme?"

Everyone's homework that night is to select a memoir topic: "a subject that has serious potential, calls your name, and will be interesting to write about now and read about later. The best way to determine a topic's possibilities is to write off-the-page about it—gather impressions, sensory images, and details and begin to discover what a subject might demonstrate or reveal, as Adrienne did (in Figure 4.13) when she weighed two memoir topics and discovered one had a theme and the other didn't. This is a critical occasion for writing off-the-page." Students need a nudge to explore the potential of different topics, and a strategy to help them avoid the trap of sticking to a poor choice to the bitter end.

In the next three minilessons, students establish formal criteria for an effective memoir. In the first, small groups research the observations they've accumulated in the back of their writing–reading handbooks. The group member whose last name starts closest to the end of the alphabet takes the role of recorder, and each trio or quartet has ten minutes to collaborate on a list of techniques they've noticed that contribute to a successful memoir. I collect these, to use as one basis for a whole-class master list of elements of an effective memoir. A teacher could stop here and collate a great set of criteria. I take it a step further.

In the next minilesson, I present a memoir I've written badly on purpose, one that suffers from the myriad problems I've encountered in student memoirs, from a lack of first-person presence and reflections, to a pace that's too fast, a deficit of sensory details, an off-putting lead, a conclusion that doesn't bring closure, too much or too little dialogue, no setting or context, no identification of the people in the story, titles that are labels, and zero theme. I've read so many of these I can practically write one in my sleep. One of my few *nevers* as a teacher is never to use a piece of student writing as a negative example. So I create negative examples of my own.

How I Spent Lots of Sundays One Winter

A Bad Memoir by Nancie M. Atwell

One winter, every Sunday, Toby, Anne, and I would drive to the Southport Bridge. We would take peace signs with us and stay on the Southport Bridge for an hour. It was very cold and really windy on the Southport Bridge! No matter what clothes we wore, we would still be really cold.

Once the police came to guard us because of the thing that happened to those two guys in Newcastle. Some drivers made obscene gestures at us; some would honk their horns at us. George waved at everyone, no matter what they did.

At 1:00, we were always glad to go home and drink hot chocolate!!!

The End

I must say, my students enjoy identifying the problems in a bad piece of my writing. When I ask them to name what's wrong, they take out their hatchets and have at it. It's interesting to me each October how many of their criticisms draw on knowledge and vocabulary they acquired as poets in September.

WHAT'S WRONG WITH NANCIE'S BAD MEMOIR?

- It has no thoughts and feelings.
- It ends "the end."
- It includes bad words: *really, very, would*.
- There's ineffective repetition: *Southport Bridge* 3×.
- There's no *so what?* or theme.
- There's no lead, just *who, what, when, where*.
- The conclusion doesn't resonate or even conclude.
- A reader can't see it, hear it, feel it—no sensory imagery.
- The title is a label.
- There's a *we* voice instead of an *I* voice, so there's no person for a reader to be, think, and feel with.
- Who *are* all these people?
- Why are these people on the bridge anyway?
- Nobody talks—we can't understand their feelings or relationships
- Exclamation marks!!!

Henry, who entered CTL as a seventh grader, finished four poems and his first memoir during the first trimester. In his November self-evaluation conference, he told me, "The lesson you did about the bad memoir was one of the most useful to me. Everything you did in that one, I would have done, from no *so what?* to exclamation points to ending with *the end*. You saved me a lot of time and mistakes." A bad-on-purpose model saves time for kids *and* for me, as a responder to the first drafts that would otherwise be versions of "How I Spent Lots of Sundays One Winter."

In the follow-up minilesson, I give students a written-to-the-best-of-my-ability version of the same story. I show them photocopies of my drafts, writing off-the-page, experiments with leads and conclusions, attempts to develop theme, and title brainstorm. A memoir is one of a handful of pieces I compose during the school year as a model for kids. If its influence is evident, I'll save the drafts and use the memoir again another year. My students don't need to perceive me as prolific. They do need to see what it looks like when an adult thinks on paper and tries to craft a piece of her life as literature.

SUNDAYS ON THE BRIDGE WITH GEORGE

I glanced up from the Sunday *Times* at the clock on the kitchen wall: 11:45. In the next room my husband began to pace; I knew he knew what time it was, too. Behind him, beyond the picture window, snow fell so thick

I couldn't see our pond. I pretended to read the paper as I waited to see what Toby would do.

"I'm going," he announced. "George hasn't e-mailed, so it must be on."

"I'll get dressed and tell Anne," I sighed. "Wait for us." Half of me was relieved that someone—George, the organizer of the weekly vigils—had the strength of character to decide that snow wouldn't stop us. The other half was reluctant in the extreme. Even on a sunny afternoon, the wind off Townsend Gut cut like knives. This promised to be the longest, coldest hour yet.

The cold—bitter, frigid, unrelenting—was the first surprise about standing on the Southport Bridge, holding onto a tagboard sign for dear life as blasts of wind fought me for it. In theory the Bridges for Peace campaign against the invasion of Iraq was a brilliant tactic. The rivers, bays, and bridges of Maine are potent symbols of the connectedness of living things and a powerful setting for demonstrating against war.

In practice the Bridges for Peace movement depended on the hardiness of a band of anti-warriors who could remain upright on a Maine bridge for an hour every wintry Sunday and live to tell the tale. I learned not to leave the house at noon without gloves inside mittens, a scarf tied around my hat, and two coats over two sweaters.

The second surprise was the public response to the protests. I was knocked out by the number of Southport oldtimers who honked their horns, smiled, and waved at us as they drove across the bridge we lined with our bodies and signs. Each friendly gesture felt like someone had turned up the thermostat a notch. After every honker, we smiled and high-fived one another. "All right! Peace!"

But some of the responses scared me and worried me for my daughter. I made a point of wearing my Southport hat, so islanders could recognize that the folks on the bridge weren't outside agitators from, say, Damariscotta. This didn't prevent a lot of dirty looks, and it never stopped one of my neighbors from making a famous obscene gesture as he cruised by. One Sunday he slowed his truck way down, I hoped to read my latest tome of a sign, but instead locked eyes with me, mouthed the name of a body part, and shook his fist.

The previous Sunday, on another Maine bridge, an angry selectman had driven his car into the protestors, sending two of them to the hospital. Although nothing that ugly happened on Southport, I was relieved when one of my old Boothbay students, now a sheriff, took to parking his cruiser near the end of the bridge.

The signs we waved in front of passing cars ran the gamut: ban-the-bomb symbols, American flags, and all manner of written messages. My signs were ridiculous, and I didn't care. On each one I presented, in large, careful block letters, my best argument to speeding vehicles about the injustice of this war ("50% OF IRAQIS ARE CHILDREN 15 AND YOUNGER") and the need for a change in U.S. policy ("WIN WITHOUT WAR: SAY YES TO INSPECTIONS AND CONTAINMENT"). While I tried to engage Southport in a political debate at thirty mph, Toby carried the same, wind-battered sign week in and week out: "No War."

Because of the constant cold, exposure to wind, and hum of apprehension, the hour on the bridge was the longest of my week. I passed it one minute at a time, anticipating the rumble of the snow tires of the next vehicle, waving my sign at it when it passed, and listening to my daughter as we took turns standing in front of each other as wind shields. Anne talked to me about her classes and teachers, her friends, and her anguish about the impending invasion. Where were the other Annes? In all our Sundays on the bridge, no other teenager joined our group.

"Why not?" I asked her. "Don't they know what's going on in the world, talk about Iraq, understand that the U.N.—"

"I don't know, Mom," she cut me off. "I'm not the spokesperson for the youth of America. You could just as well ask why we're even here. What is this accomplishing?"

I responded the only way I knew how, with another question. "What else can we do?" Any action, even putting my body on a bridge for an hour, felt better than seething in helpless rage over what my country was about to do.

And then it was 1:00. I said good-bye to George, jogged stiff-legged off the bridge, climbed into the car, and screamed with relief at being out of the wind. The Volvo warmed up by the time we reached the house, where I popped mugs of milk into the microwave for hot cocoa, and we slipped back into our Sunday routine of newspapers, cable movies, and homework. The snow continued to fall. In Baghdad, children watched the sky and waited.

—Nancie Atwell

This time, students met in small groups to name what worked in my better memoir. I collected their lists of observations, and I combined them with the features they'd noted about the other memoirs we'd read. The result was a master list of criteria identified and articulated by kids.

Students' criteria are more effective than any rubric or formula. Because they build their own standards as memoirists, they understand them from the inside and, over time, draft and craft literature in response to them. Figure 10.2 shows a typical list of memoir criteria created by my students.

I know the temptation—I've felt it myself—to save a list as good as this one and distribute it to next year's classes. It doesn't work that way. The examples of student-generated criteria in this book are meant to show what's possible—what student critics can notice, lay claim to, and, as appropriate, incorporate in their writing. I ask teachers not to distribute my kids' criteria to your kids. They'll only perceive it as another rubric. Please *do* use the pieces of effective student writing in this book and *Lessons That Change Writers*

AN EFFECTIVE MEMOIR . . .

- has a title that suggests the theme of the story *and* draws a reader in
- has a lead that's inviting—that brings a reader right into the story
- fills in or embeds the who-what-where-when-why information a reader needs after the lead
- is packed with sensory details—a reader can see, hear, feel it
- is packed with thoughts and feelings that bring the memoirist to life, give a reader someone to be with, and help develop a *so what?* or theme
- contains lots of specifics a reader can relate to
- includes specifics that *show*
- conveys details of setting: place *and* time
- uses dialogue to reveal people, their feelings, and the *so what?* or theme
- keeps a balance among dialogue, thoughts and feelings, actions, and descriptions
- has a strong conclusion—one that wraps up the memoir and its *so what?*
- can be a series of vignettes
- can flashback and flashforward in time
- can build to a climax
- can use *things* as symbols to which the memoirist attaches meaning
- can use or allude to songs or poems as symbols or themes
- can use one personal experience to explore a larger phenomenon, e.g., bullying
- can inform readers
- can roll a series of similar events into one narrative
- can be directed to a specific audience, e.g., the memoirist's mother
- can be humorous
- can be circular in structure, with a conclusion that echoes the lead
- can have a conclusion that draws together and wraps up different plot elements
- can include invented details, or combine different events, as long as the memoirist maintains the spirit of the experience

---

Figure 10.2 *An Effective Memoir . . .*

as one basis for your students to tease out and articulate their own criteria for excellence. And, if you'd like, do keep a copy of my kids' list at hand when your students are generating theirs, so you can throw into the pot anything they miss that's essential.

After my students tape the master list of memoir criteria into their handbooks and we read and highlight it around the circle, the next memoir minilesson is devoted to narrative leads. Its beginning gives shape to a story *and* the experience of writing it. For a *writer* of prose, the lead is the most important part.

A good lead sets the tone, determines direction, establishes the voice and verb tense, and grounds and impels the writer. When students produce a lead that works, the rest of the writing comes more easily. Left to their own devices, kids begin memoirs with background information—a roll call of who-what-when-where-why before they launch into the good parts. Readers of memoirs want good parts right from the start, as an invitation to enter the story.

In a minilesson I introduce four kinds of narrative leads (Figure 10.3), students to experiment with the entry points, and encourage them to choose the one that fuels them as a writer and gives direction to the rest of the story.

THE LESSON

Please tape a copy of "Narrative Leads" onto the next clean page in the notes section of your handbook, and let's talk about the ways you might invite readers to enter your memoir.

Scott, a seventh grader, had a great story to tell. A bunch of teenagers drove a car into Rangeley Lake, near his family's camp. When he and his dad hauled it out the next day, he was terrified they'd find a body. Under the heading "Typical" you'll find Scott's first lead for his memoir. Read along with me.

Scott has almost written a newspaper lead. He gives us the who-what-where-when-why information, but there's no voice, no sense of direction for the rest of the memoir, and no sense of *him*, Scott, so we can see, feel, and participate in his experience.

Together, Scott and I crafted four new entries to his story. First we drafted a lead that jumped into the *action*, with Scott *doing something*. Read along with me.

Then we started again, with *dialogue*, with people in the scene speaking. This is a different kind of action.

Next, Scott took me inside his head, and I wrote down his *reflections*, starting with him in midthought.

Finally, Scott told me what it looked, sounded, and felt like at his camp that morning, and I drafted a lead that captured *sensory details* of the scene.

Each of these beginnings does what a narrative lead should: it starts the story *in* the story. More importantly, having these alternatives helped Scott choose a starting point he liked and felt inspired to pursue, instead of suffering the sinking feeling a writer gets when he tries to pursue an uninspiring lead to the bitter end, while the writing collapses.

Writers create strong leads deliberately. When starting your memoir, craft several. Experiment with different ways in. *Choose* the lead that makes you happiest as a writer. It will make your readers happy, too.

Figure 4.11 shows how Brandon used this minilesson to experiment until he found the memoir lead he liked. Once they've crafted their leads, students will need help with what comes next: how to shift into the subsequent events of the story while also revealing the details of setting and relationships a reader needs. Embedding the context is the next lesson students tape into the notes section of their handbooks.

TYPICAL

It was a day at the end of June. My mom, dad, brother, and I were at our camp on Rangeley Lake. We arrived the night before at 10:00, so it was dark when we got there and unpacked. We went straight to bed. The next morning, when I was eating breakfast, my dad started yelling for me from the dock. He said there was a car in the lake. I ran down there.

- *Action:* The Main Character Doing Something

    I gulped my milk, pushed away from the table, and bolted out of the kitchen, slamming the screen door behind me. I ran to our dock as fast as my legs could carry me. My feet pounded on the old wood, hurrying me toward my dad's voice. "Scott!" he yelled again.

    "Coming, Dad!" I gasped. I couldn't see him yet—just the sails of the boats that had already put out into the lake for the day.

- *Dialogue:* The Main Character or Others Speaking

    "Scott! Get down here, on the double!" Dad yelled. His voice sounded far away.
    "Dad?" I hollered. "Where are you?" I squinted through the screen door but couldn't see him.
    "I'm down on the dock. MOVE IT. I need your help!"

- *Reaction:* The Main Character Thinking

    I couldn't imagine why my father was hollering for me at 7:00 in the morning. I thought fast about what I might have done to get him so riled. Had he found out about the way I talked to my mother the night before, when we got to camp and she asked me to help unpack the car? Did he discover the fishing reel I broke last week? Before I could consider a third possibility, Dad's voice shattered my thoughts.
    "Scott! Move it! I need your help!"

- *Description:* Relevant Sensory Details That Set the Scene and Tone

    A breeze pushed at the pines outside the window that cast patterns on the wall beside my bunk. The only sound was birdcall—it was June, too early for out-of-state jetskiers. The sun and my relief that the school year was over filled our camp with calmness. The sun kept rising as I slipped down the ladder, passed my brother asleep with his mouth open, and headed for the kitchen.

When beginning a story, craft several leads. Experiment. Choose the way in that makes you happiest. A lead you love will fuel you as a writer and give direction to your writing.

Figure 10.3 *Narrative Leads*

EMBED THE CONTEXT

Your grabbing lead invited readers straight into your head, your heart, your story. Now, how do you weave in the crucial information about *where* you are, *what* you're doing, *when* and *why* you're here, and *who* the other people are, so your reader can get the setting and other facts of the story straight and settle in without confusion?

This is called *embedding the context.* You need to look for points early in the story to drop in or embed the who-what-where-when-why, so your readers can get their bearings but without feeling like you just hammered them with a news bulletin.

This is a tricky balancing act, but you do need to both move your story and introduce enough context to make a reader feel comfortable.

Then we read and unpack a memoir like Nate's "Going Rogue at CTL." This time I ask students to pay particular attention to how Nate segues from his dialogue lead to the contextual information that grounds the opening conversation.

GOING ROGUE AT CTL

"Nate, buddy? Are you awake?"

"Mehhh," I mumbled, still groggy after only a few hours of sleep.

"Well, I don't think you want to know how it went last night," my mom said gently.

"NO!" I wailed and slammed my face into my pillow. *This can't be happening, this can't be happening. But I knew it was. I knew it.*

Last night was the big night: the night when the two political parties went head to head, Democrat vs. Republican. Until 11:30 I had stared at my computer screen, watching in disgust as state by state—*including* my own, Maine—turned from a neutral white to a disappointing blue, with specks of red scattered mostly at the bottom and middle of the map. Gotta love that South and Midwest.

As a politically-opinionated fourteen-year-old, I felt like I deserved a big win. I mean, I had watched pretty much all the political debates and interviews of the 2008 campaign, from the early presidential candidates all the way to the presidential and vice-presidential debates, mere weeks before the election. I even purchased a big sign and stuck it in our front lawn for the whole town to see, although my liberal mother didn't like it one bit.

At school we engaged in countless discussions and debates, mostly involving the question: *Who would be a better president, Barack Obama or John McCain?* As one of only three conservative-minded students in my class, it wasn't exactly a picnic trying to get my perspective across when all I heard was: *Hey, I could be a better vice-president than Sarah Palin, man. She's, like, the dumbest person ever.* Or *How could you even think of voting for John McCain once you've heard his views on abortion!* Or even the simple *Republicans suck, dude. They suck.* That's what I had to confront every Tuesday, Wednesday, and Thursday from 10:40 until 11:30.

But, of course, it didn't end in history class. The conversations extended into lunch, which turned into the Sarah Palin slam sessions my classmates held so dear to their hearts. I thought it was weird, unhelpful, but—at the same time—funny that my two fellow Republicans never joined me to stand up for their political beliefs. They just ate their sandwiches in silence.

One morning, a week before the election, I walked into school wearing a shirt I ordered from www.JohnMcCain.com. It read, in bold letters, **McCain–Palin 2008.** I guess I bought it to show everyone that no matter how much they trash-talked Republicans, they weren't going to change my mind. As soon as I walked through the doors of CTL, Jake, one of the kids in my class, approached me.

"Hey, Nate. Nice shirt ya got there, bud," he sneered.

"Oh, thank you, Jake. That is very kind of you," I shot back.

"Nate, why don't you just give it up? Obama is going to kill McCain next week."

"Oh, yes. I forgot that you are the political expert of the country, Jacob. Next time I will try to remember that." It wasn't one of my best comebacks.

Now, the morning after the election, I lay in my bed, eyes wide open, staring at the ceiling with too many thoughts reeling through my mind.

Why did this have to happen?

What was I going to say to Jake, to the whole class?

What did this mean for the country? And what would become of my sign?

I dragged myself out of bed and over to my closet. As usual, I pulled out a pair of jeans and found some socks. Then I clunked over to my dresser to choose a shirt. I opened the drawer and looked down. My eyes grew wide as I stared at what was sitting on the top of the pile. A sinister grin spread from one ear to the other. I grabbed it, pulled it on, and hustled down the stairs, now fully awake.

When I reached the mudroom and started putting on my shoes, Mom looked at me with a questioning expression. "Isn't it a little late to be wearing that shirt?" she asked.

And at that moment I was reminded of a Henry James quote that my English teacher introduced me to: "Try to be one of the people on whom nothing is lost." I realized that, yeah, we Republicans may have not *won* this particular election, but it wasn't forever. There would always be another election, another Republican to root for. We would be back.

"Nah," I replied to my mother. "We didn't lose, Mum. We just haven't won yet." She shook her head. I breezed out the door and into the car, eager to get to school and challenge the jeers, whoops, and hollers that I would argue against in the four years to come.

—*Nate Friant*

Even with all the minilessons and prep work, the first drafts of kids' memoirs will be thin. I learned to advise them to *build a scaffold*: "In your first draft, capture the events of the experience and create your chronology. Then, as you revise, you can begin to layer in your reflections and the sensory descriptions that give a memoir life, texture, and a *so what?* or theme."

This is the perfect time to introduce or review The Rule of Thoughts and Feelings (Chapter 4). I remind students that their reflections will be the most likely source of theme in their memoirs. I teach them how to read their drafts, place an asterisk or the abbreviation *T&F* wherever a reader might wonder or need to know what they're thinking and feeling, and layer in reflections at each point.

Figure 10.4 shows a page of the second draft of Amelia's memoir, after she had annotated it for thoughts and feelings. The final version, titled "Time for Treats," appears below. It captures a half an hour in a typical, fraught relationship between a preadolescent girl and her mother. But because of the reflections Amelia wove into the memoir, it became an opportunity to assess the relationship and acknowledge her love for her mom.

Time for Treats

I climbed into my mother's silver Volvo and abandoned my bag on the floor. Mom twisted in her seat to study me. Driving to after-school art was one of the few times we spent together these days, ever since she opened her restaurant. She seemed glad for the chance, but, as a sullen twelve-year-old, it wasn't that big a deal to me.

"Ready to go?" she asked. I nodded, and we headed for the exit of the school parking lot. I sank into the warm leather and relished the fact that I didn't have to deal with the carpool this Thursday afternoon. I wasn't in the mood to wage war over seating arrangements.

"How was school?"

"Fine," I said, following up with the usual sigh. Always, she tossed me this question. I didn't know if she expected some other answer.

"Did you do anything fun?" She smiled at me—a smile that grew wider at my resonant *no*.

We fell silent and watched bony trees slip past the windows. As the car turned onto the bridge, the trees surrendered to steely water. The sun peaked from a crack in the roof of gray clouds and forced me to squint as we drove straight at it.

"You mind if we stop at Treats?" Mom questioned. An answer wasn't required. It was Thursday: Treats, a local shop and café, was our designated stop before she dropped me at art class. She pulled in close to the crosswalk, and we hoisted ourselves out onto the road. I wished the weather would make up its mind already. The day seemed stuck between rain and sun.

My Awesome Memoir **Which I Will Title Later**

I climbed into Mom's silver Volvo and abandoned my bag on the floor. Mom twisted in her seat to look at me. **[T + F**

"Ready to go?" she asked. I nodded, and we headed for the exit of the school parking lot. I sank into the warm leather and relished the fact that I didn't have to deal with the carpool that Thursday afternoon. I wasn't in the mood to wage a war over seating arrangements.

T + F, T + F, WHEREFORE ART THOU, T + F?
Tired from school, a little irritable *getting a bit more annoyed*

"How was school?"

"Fine," I replied to Mom with the routine sigh of a twelve-year-old. Always, she tossed me this question.

"Did you do anything fun?" She smiled at me—a smile that grew wider at my resonant "No." ~~My repetative answers negative amused her, italicise but I didn't show any sign of mirth~~ *Another way to say this?*

We were silent for a bit, watching the bony trees slip past us. As the car turned onto the bridge, the trees became steely water. The sun peaked from a crack in the roof of gray clouds and forced me to squint while we drove straight at it.

"You mind if we stop at Treats?" questioned Mom, but my answer wasn't necessary. After all, it was Thursday: Treats was our stop before she dropped me at art class. She pulled in close to the crosswalk and we lifted ourselves out into the dreary world. **[T + F?**

T + F: NOTHING really - boredom perhaps...

The March wind flipped my hair and I bundled deeper inside my coat. Mom made *I was bored by the monochrome world before me.* to grab at my hand as we passed in front of waiting cars, but I tugged away.

MAJOR T + F

Figure 10.4 *Amelia's Annotations: Thoughts and Feelings*

The March wind flipped my hair, and I bundled deeper inside my coat, bored with the monochrome landscape. Mom made a grab at my hand as we crossed in front of waiting cars. I tugged away, appalled. I wasn't five; I didn't require assistance to cross a road. I hopped over the residue of grainy snow that coated creases in the street and heaved open the glass door to our weekly haunt.

Treats.

The dry warmth hit my face—a welcome change from bitter breeze. Loaves of bread reached out to me and begged to be torn, glass jars filled with fancy dips rose to the ceiling, and muffins nestled by the register. I headed for the drinks cooler in the back, where the contrast of the colored labels with the world outside cheered me up as I pretended to ponder the choices. Root beer? Orange soda? Of course, in the end, I clutched a sparkling lemonade; the familiar bumpy surface of the bottle was cold against my fingers.

Satisfied, I hurried back to my mom. She'd bagged a sour dough loaf, and five leaf-shaped chocolates lay next to it on the marble counter. She was just ordering: "Half coffee, half steamed skim milk." There was an undeniable rhythm to her mantra that amused me. The lady by the register strolled away to the steamer.

"What time is it?" I said, as my nervous feet began to tap.

"Early," Mom answered with a peek at her watch. I scoffed, skeptical because my mother was never early. Now she asked, "Do you want anything else? Soup?"

"No!" I protested. I let my shoulders sag and showed her wide *let's go* eyes. I hated to think I might be late for art again. But I knew what came next.

"Are you sure? It's tomato bisque." Mom had acquired her *I'll do it anyway* tone, and I went queasy at the thought of bursting into art class to find they'd already started.

"We don't have time," I argued.

"We have plenty of time," Mom insisted. She spoke to the woman behind the counter. "Can we have a small cup of tomato soup and two spoons?" I groaned. We always had "plenty of time." But then again we were always late. The soup was already ladled into a cup. I had no choice but to slump on a low, wooden stool beside my mom and dip a plastic spoon into the creamy soup while eyeing her wrist.

The soup scalded my mouth, and I jumped in surprise. My tongue felt as if it had blistered into a foreign object. I swigged my lemonade in a desperate attempt to soothe it, but my taste buds remained raw.

"Are you okay?" Mom asked. I detected a hint of a giggle in her voice.

"Haaaa!" was all I managed in response. I thought I'd never close my mouth again.

"Is it really that bad?"

I moaned, but Mom was apparently unconvinced by my display of suffering and had to prove it herself. She blew on a spoonful and then slurped some of the orange substance.

"Ooo!" Her face contorted as she exhaled many breaths in rapid succession. I cracked up at the sight, and soon she joined me. We laughed about our shared injuries, our joint foolishness, our long history of adventures and misadventures. At that moment, it didn't matter that Mom was forever late. I understood what was important was that we had this small window of time each week to spend together.

That knowledge was enough to stop my nagging, to stop the window from closing again. I was reluctant to return to real life, where Mom and I clashed and disagreed. I wanted to stay here in Treats.

But Mom glanced at the time and exclaimed, "Oh, gosh. We should get going." I grabbed the paper bag with the bread, while she trashed the wasted soup. We were definitely going to be late.

As we hustled through the narrow room, Mom turned to me. "Sorry, Melie," she said with an apologetic smile. I was quiet as I opened the heavy door, uncertain as to how I should reply. Should I tell her that it was okay? That I loved her? Mom instinctively gripped my hand as we crossed the road, and my words caught in my throat. For now it was enough to leave my hand wrapped in hers.

—*Amelia Neilson*

A memoir by seventh grader Maura, "Smooshed Coins," provides an opportunity for me to teach another layer-it-in minilesson, this one about sensory description. In first drafts, students often speed through the significant plot points, where the pace should be slowed down. When they revise, I want them to identify the junctures where readers should be able to enter a moment, stay in it, and understand what's important about it. Kids and I call this lesson *make the movie*.

THE LESSON

As poets, we talked a lot this fall about the importance of sensory details—of crafting images a reader can see, hear, feel, even smell and taste. Today the focus is on sight and sound—on how descriptions of visual and auditory details can slow down a moment in a story and bring it to life.

As readers, you make comments to me about stories you're enjoying along the lines of, "I was so in the zone, I felt like I was there." "I was in the story, seeing and hearing what the main character was seeing and hearing." Or even, "I forgot I was reading, it seemed so real." These are moments we love, when the prose is so thick with revealing details that the text disappears and we revel in a character's experience.

This level of richness isn't accidental. The author has slowed down the important moments in the story by describing them fully—by remembering or inventing the sights and sounds that make it feel real for readers.

Every day, after the status-of-the-class conference, I enjoin you to *work hard and make literature*. One way to make a literary memoir is to craft descriptions of sights and sounds. The best way to do that? Close your eyes, make a private movie behind your eyelids of a significant moment, and then open your eyes and craft language that captures what you saw and heard in your mind's eye.

Let me show you what I mean. Maura wrote this sensory memoir, "Smooshed Coins," when she was in seventh grade. It's about an adventure she had with her father when she was a little girl. As you read along with me, highlight every word, phrase, and sentence you can *see* or *hear*.

Smooshed Coins

"I'm frozen," I mumbled through the fabric of my scarf. Dad dropped the hand he'd held tight and zipped my red coat all the way to my chin. Our feet made tapping sounds as our boots hit the gravelly road. The sky grew darker.

"I wonder what would happen if we put a penny on top of a quarter," Dad said. He was as excited as I was. "You would think smooshing coins underneath train wheels would be a little *boy's* dream," he murmured, in reference to the brothers who had preferred to stay home and finish their video games.

But I liked being here, just Dad and I. We kids were never able to do things with him in the summer, when he was busy at the nursery, but now we had him for the whole winter, and I was not about to share all my Daddy moments with overexcited brothers.

"Eoin and Nolan can come next time," I whispered.

"Yeah, who needs them anyway?" Dad grabbed me in a headlock and ruffled my hair. Leaves crunched beneath our feet, and fire-scented air wafted though the fall sky.

We reached the tracks. When I bent down to touch them, the familiar feeling of cool rustiness came back to me. I smiled up at Dad as he bent down to my size and handed me two shiny coins. Remembering what he had said on the way here, I placed the penny on top of the quarter and began to tape them to the railroad track.

"You know . . . even if you tape them on, they're gonna fly off," Dad said matter-of-factly. But I set to work, concentrating on my project. Dad had his mind on other things: searching for metal or screws or pieces of train, which he always did. I taped the last coin on and stood up, proud of my accomplishment. The wind picked up. Trees swayed their bare branches. Pulling my mittens back on, I called out to Dad, who was somewhere along the tracks.

"Dad! Dad, it's time to go!" I scanned the area. As I expected, he had wandered off into the woods, getting more and more caught up in his thoughts and his quest.

"I'm coming! Hold on. Just a few more minutes." He jogged up to me and held out his hands, showing me the junk treasures he'd found. I smiled up at him as he sorted out what he wanted to take home this time before tossing a clanging collection of metal back into the forest.

"Let's get going." Dad brought his hand back to mine and squeezed it, and I remembered again why winter was my favorite season: because of the times when just Daddy and I collected sea glass on a cold beach or stopped at the side of the road to watch eagles feed and fly.

As we trudged home, I imagined us tomorrow, collecting the flattened coins. I walked faster, my steps in sync with his, and I thought about how today Dad was like a child again—going back through time and becoming the little boy he used to be. I felt like I was the grown-up. I frowned at the tar beneath my feet.

Suddenly I could see myself getting older. All this time, in our adventures together, had he been telling me to slow down, to stop growing up so fast? Now I wanted to be a little kid, too. I stared up at the autumn dusk and squeezed his hand. Dad squeezed back and said, "Take these moments and capture them, Maura." And that's exactly what I did.

—*Maura Anderson*

Were you able to enter Maura's memoir? Could you see and hear it in your mind's eye? Where—at what points?

Maura used a technique called *make the movie* when she drafted her memoir, but especially as she revised it. She slowed down the story, tried to see and hear it in her mind, and layered in the relevant sensory information. Please tape this lesson onto the next clean page of the notes section of your handbook. Use it to help you layer in the sensory information that will bring your memoir to life for others.

Make the Movie

This is a technique for slowing down the important parts of a story and creating sensory images—pictures readers can see and sounds they can hear.

1. Close your eyes. *Concentrate.*
2. Imagine the scene as if you're making a private movie in your mind. See and hear the setting, yourself, and the people in your story, in action and in real time.
3. Open your eyes and try to capture your mental movie on the page: the details of sight and sound, one frame at a time.

When *drafting*: close your eyes and make the movie, and then write down the sensory specifics you envisioned.

When *revising*: close your eyes and see and hear more and richer actions, reactions, gestures, expressions, dialogue, tones of voice, colors, and other visual details.

When *polishing*: close your eyes, envision the scene, and check it against the diction of your text, especially the verbs. Does the language you used to evoke people and action measure up to the images you saw and the sounds you heard in the movie in your mind?

This is hard work. The level of concentration it requires will make your brain hurt—I know it does mine. But the payoff is guaranteed, in terms of crafting narratives that involve readers by appealing to their senses.

Try it. I promise that no one in writing workshop will look at you funny if you're poised over a draft with your eyes squeezed shut.

In two other minilessons I teach kids about dialogue. Sometimes a student doesn't include any in a story in which people obviously spoke and what they said was revealing, in terms of mood, intentions, and relationships. Other times, almost the entire first draft is dialogue, which means the reader hasn't been afforded essential visual cues—reading one of these is like listening to an old-time radio play but without the sound effects. The first dialogue minilesson is a review of how to punctuate, capitalize, and paragraph a conversation, which I included in *Lessons That Change Writers*. The second taps a piece of successful student writing to demonstrate effective use of dialogue.

"Authority," a memoir Max wrote in seventh grade, provides kids with a good introduction to direct quotes and how they can reveal what people are like, create a mood, bring an event to life, and, when accompanied by thoughts, feelings, and sensory descriptions, move the plot.

AUTHORITY

A rusty Chevrolet pickup swerved into the parking slot next to ours, its red lights blinking like angry eyes as it skidded to a stop. My brother, cousin, and I gaped at the truck through the open windows of Mom's car—open just in case it got even hotter than we already were, which shows what a summer day at Pemaquid Beach can do to a person. Sweaty and sandy, the three of us waited for my mother to emerge from C.C. Reilly's and Son grocery store with ice cream.

Beside us, two teenaged boys had just started to get out of the pickup when a sheriff marched up to the truck and glared inside. He swung open the driver's side door, and I leaned towards my open window to listen in. I could tell this was going to be something to watch.

"Whatcha hidin'?" the cop demanded in a loud, flat monotone through gum he chewed with his mouth open. I was surprised by his rudeness. I had always looked at police in a positive way, especially when I was little, when I pleaded in every game of cops and robbers to be the police—the heroes. But this cop didn't seem like a hero. Will, my cousin, turned to glance at me in the back seat, and then gestured with his eyes towards the commotion outside.

"I saw ya fidgetin'. I don't know what you guys were doin', but I wanna know what's goin' on," the sheriff barked.

"I was trying to get my seat belt on," the boy in the driver's seat muttered.

The cop snorted like a bull. "Yeah. Pretty good excuse, but not gonna fly, son."

The driver cast his eyes downward.

"Outta the vehicle," the sheriff grunted, rolling his eyes. I couldn't believe this was happening.

Will glanced back at me again. He said, "You guys, he's getting him out of the car without a probable cause. You can't do that."

"You live in Virginia," I stated. "The laws in your state are different."

"That doesn't matter—it's the same here. The cop doesn't have a reason for getting this guy out of the car." I began to believe Will, because he was fourteen and I was only eleven. I nodded. So did my little brother, Noah, before our attention returned to what was happening outside.

Now the cop shouted, "Ya know what really *pisses* me off is when I have to *hunt* for the answers." And he began to inspect the truck, flipping seats over, yanking open the glove compartment, and even picking up a bottle of water. He opened the cap, sniffed inside, grunted, and slammed it down again.

I looked over at Noah. His eyes were wide and afraid.

The sheriff stalked around to the back of the pickup like a rhinoceros on a rampage. He reached over the side of the flat bed and, from the center, pulled over a big white bucket.

"What's in here? Crabs?" he asked in a gruff, sarcastic voice. The two boys nodded. He opened the lid, peeked inside, and grunted again. Then he stalked over to his squad car and rummaged inside it as the two boys, solemn faced, dialed numbers on their cell phones. When the sheriff returned, he handed the driver a ticket. I couldn't hear what he said, because right then my mom peeked through an open window and cheerfully greeted us.

"Hello, boys!"

Grateful for her interruption, I muttered, "Hey, Mom." Here was an adult who I knew I could count on, who would never use her authority this way. The sheriff drove away as the two teenagers retrieved the bucket of crabs and began to walk towards the grocery store to deliver them.

"Sorry, guys, they didn't have Dove Bars," my mother said, handing each of us a Ben and Jerry's.

"It's okay, Mom. Thanks."

"What was that all about? What was going on here?" she asked.

"This cop just searched their whole truck without a probable cause," Will replied, as the three of us ripped open the plastic wrappers.

"He was so mean about it, too," I said, as I licked my Ben and Jerry's, as I tried to forget about what I'd just seen, as I enjoyed the cool, sweet ice cream, as I grieved for all the pretend games of cops and robbers and my childish certainty that when I chose to be a cop, I was the good guy.

—*Max Jordan*

After we read "Authority," I asked students to consider these questions:

- Did Max somehow remember every single word that was spoken that afternoon? How *do* you think he arrived at this dialogue?
- What does the dialogue reveal about the sheriff?
- Although dialogue—especially the conversation Max, Will, and Noah overhear—is crucial to this memoir, what fraction of the story do you estimate is talk?
- How much of the story is sensory description, actions, and thoughts and feelings?

Although there isn't a formula for balancing dialogue, reflection, action, and description in a narrative, something is out of whack when a memoir doesn't work yet. Sometimes there's too much dialogue or reflection. Other times there's not enough reflection, too little action, or insufficient sensory description. The minilesson "Keep the Balance" addresses this concern. Students tape it into their handbooks, we review it, and then we read and discuss a well-balanced memoir, like Nathaniel's "Outline of a Broken Heart."

KEEP THE BALANCE AMONG REFLECTION, DIALOGUE, ACTION, AND DESCRIPTION

1. Are there enough of your reflections (thoughts and feelings) for a reader to enter and stay inside your head and heart throughout the story?
2. Is there so much dialogue—at the expense of action, sensory information, and thoughts and feelings—that a reader feels as if he or she is listening to your memoir from behind a closed door?
3. Are there so many thoughts and feelings that action and setting fade away, leaving the reader rudderless?
4. Is there enough sensory information so a reader can make the movie—can see, hear, and vicariously experience your story?

Nathaniel does such an effective job of keeping the balance that I've asked kids to color-code his memoir—to use four markers or colored pencils to highlight thoughts and feelings, dialogue, descriptions of action, and sensory details. The result is a colorful mess—some sentences contain two or more of the features. It makes an essential point about the variety of information a writer has to include to bring a memoir to life for a reader.

OUTLINE OF A BROKEN HEART

I threw myself on the couch and began to soak its cushions with my tears. Mom sat next to me, trying to comfort me, while her own grief leaked from her eyes.

"No!" I shouted at the pillow my face was buried in. "He's not . . . no way . . ."

"He's gone," Mom said, patting my heaving back.

Gone. I tried to remember the last time I saw him, curled on his bed under the piano. His brown eyes tried to tell me what was about to happen, but I remained oblivious. I wanted to see him again, bury my face in his black fur, never let him go.

I remembered the crayon pictures of my family that I'd drawn in preschool. In every one of them, next to four smiling people, sat Buster, the loyal dog. I felt as if someone had taken scissors and cut a hole in the portrait—a hole in my ten-year-old heart. And suddenly another preschool memory, forgotten until that moment, came back to me.

That day I had played with the plastic dinosaurs on the crumb-scattered rug, clutching my favorite one—a green T-rex with big teeth—and bashing it into the others. I looked up from my play as my best friend, Isaac, entered the room. His eyes were red, and he was hiccupping.

Isaac pulled off his boots and put on dry shoes as his mom kissed him good-bye. He padded his way over and plopped down next to me. We played in awkward silence as I wondered what could have made him so upset. Maybe he missed his mom? As a four-year-old, this was the most likely explanation my mind could conjure.

"Don't worry. School will be over real fast," I said, trying to comfort him. I couldn't stand him being so sad. Having my best friend sitting next to me, crying, felt terrible.

"Uh-huh," Isaac mumbled, and he looked down at the floor. I picked at a strap of my green overalls, confused.

"Wanna draw?" I asked him. "I could make a picture, and you could color it in." I grinned. This would cheer him up: it was our favorite thing to do. He liked to color, and I liked to draw. I stared at him, my broad smile starting to hurt my face. He didn't respond.

So I skipped to the art center, picked up a yellow crayon, and began to draw Isaac's dog, Brooke. The head came first—big, with long ears, brown eyes, and a black nose. Then I added the four legs, the body, and tail. I picked up the portrait and gave it a final glance. All it needed was to be colored in yellow.

With a triumphant smile on my face, I trotted back to Isaac. He was still half-heartedly playing with the dinosaurs. He positioned them on the table, knocked them off, and repeated the process. I handed him the picture and waited for his reaction. To my surprise, he burst into tears and ran into the cubby area, his light-up shoes blinking to the rhythm of his steps.

I sat on the dinosaur crate and puzzled over his reaction. What had I done wrong? Maybe my drawing was really bad? I stood, dragged myself over to where Isaac was sitting, and perched next to him on the shoe cubbies.

"I'm sorry . . ." I mumbled, not sure what I was apologizing for.

"It's not your fault," Isaac said. "Brooke died yesterday, and I'm still sad."

"I'm sorry . . ." I mumbled again. Of all the things I could have drawn for him—aliens, superheroes, boats—it had to be his dog. We sat in silence until we were called to snack. I ate my M&M cookie in two bites.

Over the next days, the drawing sat in Isaac's cubby, colorless and empty. But with each new morning of preschool, Isaac seemed happier. He joined me at the sand table, we played with blocks, and together we raced our favorite Matchbox cars. Pretty soon, he was back to the Isaac I knew.

Weeks passed, then months. One sunny March morning, as I was drawing a picture of my dog Buster, Isaac arrived at pre-school. He tugged off his boots and fuzzy red mittens and took the picture I'd drawn for him that fall from the top shelf of his cubby. I'd forgotten about the picture and watched him, perplexed. He pulled out a little blue chair next to me, set down the portrait of his dog, and smiled. He was ready to color it in.

"Can I have the yellow?" he asked.

Yesterday, aged thirteen, I paged through a trunk full of my artwork from years past. When I spotted a forgotten picture among the marker drawings of aliens and cats, I retrieved the crinkled paper and unleashed a landslide of memories.

I climbed the stairs to my room, clutching the picture. I sat at my desk and cleared away the clutter that engulfed it: homework, iPod, chewed-up pencils, Snickers wrappers. I pulled open a file cabinet drawer and rummaged through the mess. Finally, I found what I was looking for: a wrapperless nub of black crayon. I smiled as I gazed down at the unfinished preschool drawing—an outline of a black dog. Buster.

I knew I was ready. Three years had passed since his death, and my eyes had stopped tearing when I saw the white cross in our field. I was ready to accept that he had a good life with a loving family, and that he was gone, forever.

I positioned the crayon in my left hand, aligned the soon-to-be finished drawing in my right, and began to color it in.

—*Nathaniel Williams*

Nathaniel accomplished something else in "Outline of a Broken Heart." He created and signaled five shifts in time. I point this out in my introduction to the subsequent minilesson.

THE LESSON

Some of the memoirs we've been reading—and you've been drafting—aren't straightforward chronological accounts. For example, in "Outline of a Broken Heart," Nathaniel shifted time all over the place. He flashed back and forward. He told about Buster's death when he was ten, events from preschool when he was four, and himself in the present as a thirteen-year-old.

These time shifts are called *transitions*. Good writers signal them with words and phrases that cue readers a shift in time is about to happen. Transitional words and phrases usually appear *at the beginning of a paragraph*.

Please tape "Some Ways to Cue Transitions in Narratives" (Figure 10.5) onto the next page in the notes section of your handbook, and we'll review it together.

Tonight for homework, read the memoirs "A Rip in Invincible" and "Grandpa Eldon" and pay close attention to Hope's and Patrick's transitions. Notice and underline the shifts in time. Tomorrow we'll talk about how they cued us—plus everything else you notice they did as the authors of these meaty memoirs.

A RIP IN INVINCIBLE

The prosthetic leg lies at the foot of Dad's dresser, a tan plastic foot, tan padding around the calf and thigh, and the tan plastic shell that holds his stump. The shiny metal underneath shows at a rip in the knee and exposes its true nature: a fake.

For a long time, when I thought of my parents, I never considered how Mom had lost her toe to cancer, or the boating accident in New Zealand that led to the loss of Dad's leg. And the word *amputee* never occurred to me. *Dad* brought to mind his smiling stubble and the musty scent when I hug him. *Mom?* I conjured up her enthusiastic laugh and fine blond hair. Their real-life dramas happened so long ago they seemed like a musty photo album stacked on a shelf.

But all that changed. It was early December when I shuffled into the green-walled doctor's office. When I heaved myself onto the examination table, wax paper crackled beneath me. My body felt as if someone had stretched it out and then snapped it back like a rubber band. The doctor felt under my ribs and at the base of my neck. Then, in a concerned voice, she perched with her clipboard and began asking questions.

I had been exhausted for weeks, leaning against car windows to doze, snapping at classmates in school. My parents and the doctor juggled their

SOME WAYS TO CUE TRANSITIONS IN NARRATIVES

TO MOVE FORWARD IN TIME OR RETURN TO THE PRESENT:

- Now . . .
- The next morning/afternoon/day/week . . .
- Later that morning/afternoon/day/week . . .
- A month/week later . . .
- The following summer . . .
- The next time I . . .
- Suddenly . . .
- All of a sudden . . .
- After that . . .
- Still . . .
- When . . .
- Today . . .
- These days . . .
- Then . . .
- Then, in _____, . . .
- It was only a few minutes/hours/days later when . . .
- At three o'clock that afternoon . . .
- The next _____ I remember was . . .
- But all that changed when . . .
- A purposeful shift in verb tense, e.g., from past to present, or the use of italics to signify the past or present

TO MOVE BACKWARD TO AN EARLIER TIME:

- I remember . . .
- I used to . . .
- Once . . .
- Then . . .
- Before . . .
- Back when . . .
- Back then . . .
- For a long time . . .
- Yesterday . . .
- The day/night before . . .
- Earlier . . .
- An hour before . . .
- Last week/month/year . . .
- The previous week/month/year/summer . . .
- A purposeful shift in verb tense, e.g., from present to past, or the use of italics to signify the past or present

PARALLEL FRAMES OF TIME:

- At the same time . . .
- Meanwhile . . .
- While this was going on/happening/occurring . . .

Figure 10.5 *Some Ways to Cue Transitions in Narratives*

theories about what might be wrong, but nothing was certain until the blood test. Then I heard the word I would fear for the first time: mono. It became a life sentence to an isolation chamber that held me back from everything I loved by keeping me in bed, on the couch, in front of the TV.

Three weeks later, I trudged in late for school. I slipped off my orange coat and shoved my backpack in my locker. Then I climbed the stairs and to my classroom.

"Oh, here comes Hope, late as usual."

"Why are you late? You know, I had basketball practice last night, and I didn't get home until eight, and then I had to do my homework, but I still got here on time."

"Have a good sleep-in?"

Just words, I told myself, but they still stung. Every time someone called me lazy or told me I had it easy, a hollow nausea knotted in my stomach. I wanted to scream at them that I was *sick* and I *couldn't help it*, that coming in late after extra sleep was what I needed to do to get better. I felt no one understood that I'd rather be going to class, to swim team, to voice lessons, than lying in bed and watching the Disney Channel.

I remembered a two-hour swim practice, pre-diagnosis, when I had to leave early. My limbs felt like wooden logs as I plowed through the water, and when I climbed out after an hour, my head ached I was so drained of energy. In silent defeat I waved goodbye to my coaches and pulled open the heavy metal door. Sitting in the Y lobby, cell phone to my ear, I snapped at my mother for being late to pick me up.

A month later, after I had been diagnosed, I lay in bed at night, exhausted but unable to sleep. My swim season was shot, I had endless math work to make up, and I felt as if I had lost touch with my entire world. All I could do to get better was the one task that felt impossible: falling asleep. The clock ticked on.

The worst wasn't the sinking feeling in my stomach every time someone doubted my virus or the longing for activity and competition. The worst was the waiting, the being told that in order to fight this illness, I had to do the exact opposite: be passive, rest, and wait. This oxymoron perturbed me no end, all through the school year and into the summer, when the illness was banished for good and I was free to taste salt water and feel the wind on my face from the prow of a sailboat.

Before my bout with mono, I was embarrassed to have to hold Mom's hand when it was slippery outside so she wouldn't fall. I was frustrated when she and I were in a hurry and had to wait because Dad couldn't run. But these days I get it. I understand that my parents' problems will never be fixed with time. Thanks to mono, I went through a tiny piece of what they experience every day. It made me realize how humble and diligent they are.

Now, while I still think of Mom's joyful laugh, I also appreciate her resilience. I picture Dad's smiling stubble, but I also think about his strong will. I know the rip in the knee of his false leg represents something more than the fact that it's not real. It shows that the prosthetic is worn; it displays the truth that every day, Dad rises and puts it on and gets going. I know that in my life I will be humbled again. I hope I've learned to pick myself up and persevere, just as my parents do.

—*Hope Logan*

GRANDPA ELDON

I am seven. I grip the mainsheet and help hoist *Ebb*'s mainsail. I think about how you were probably doing the same thing sixty years before. I unclip the brass hook from the mooring that's bobbing in the green Cape Cod water and push it away from the wooden Beetle, excited that I finally get to go sailing with you, just we two, on this boat that has been in our family for generations. I hop in next to you.

"Hey, why don't you give it a try?" you ask. I take it from you warily when you hand me the dark, varnished tiller, nervous because this boat is much bigger and more beloved than the Sunfish that Wallace and I sail, and this is the first time I've been trusted to steer. I handle the tiller, and with your help, we sail through the maze of boats in the inner harbor and wave to Mom as she watches from the porch. I wonder if someday I will teach my grandchildren to sail in *Ebb* in front of the Cape house.

I am five. I pick up a cork handle that you crafted in your workshop, and I look around at all the things you made or modified here. I think about how I would never want your beautiful old tools to be replaced by new ones. "Hey, let's go out back and see if we can cast it," you say, eager with excitement. You follow me out the back door, rod in hand. "Give it your best," you say in a soft voice. So I use all my strength to cast it a mere six feet.

"This isn't like the rod I'm used to," I use as an excuse.

"Oh, that was good. But I'll show you a little trick," you say. I hand over the rod and, with no effort, you flick the lure what looks to me like a mile, then hand the rod back to me.

"See, the trick is that when you cast, you have let go of the line right before you see it flick straight, and you step into your cast." Now it's my turn. I try to replicate what I saw you do, and I watch with awe as the hookless lure sails through the air. "See? I knew you could do it. I can't wait 'til we can do this on the water," you say with a smile. Neither can I.

I am ten. You open the cabinet drawer in the kitchen and pull out a round, worn leather case. "Open it," you say. I take it from your hands and feel leather that has been smoothed by time. I undo the brass latch and pull out a black compass trimmed in gold. You say it was your father's. You start talking about how to use it to find your bearing, but all I'm able to do is admire it. I instantly want the compass but know that's selfish. I understand how much it means to you. So I just admire its sleek blackness as you teach me how it works. After I learn about finding a bearing and backtracking, we put the compass back in its home until next time. There is no next time.

I am fourteen. It's been three years since the funeral at Maine Maritime Museum, where we know you would have wanted it to be. Still, whenever I hoist the mainsheet on *Ebb*, jump off the big pier, or catch a bluefish in Buzzards Bay, I think of you. Now the compass sits on my bureau, hardly ever opened because when I do, it brings back memories of us. Nini says you would have wanted me to have it. The rod that we practiced with gathers dust in our garage. I would trade it all for just one more cast with you, or one more minute of sailing. Your memory lives on whenever I step onto a sailboat or walk into the Cape house. The skills that you taught me will stay with me for the rest of my life. Grandpa Eldon, you live inside me.

—*Patrick Jackson*

Minilessons about narrative techniques give students a prism for reading their memoir drafts and a lexicon for requesting help. When I circulate during independent writing time, when they deposit drafts on my rocking chair for me to eyeball that night, they have agendas as memoirists, which they voice in the shorthand of minilessons: *Can you make the movie of this part? Do I have enough T and F? Does my lead invite you in? Can you understand the context? I wonder if I'm keeping the balance—is there too much dialogue? Can you follow my transitions? Is my so what? clear? Does the conclusion resonate for you?*

A resonant conclusion is key. If the lead of a memoir is the most important part for the writer, the conclusion matters most to a reader. I've seen okay memoirs that were transformed by strong conclusions; I've seen compelling memoirs collapse when a conclusion stops cold, meanders, or fails to make sense of the memory.

Because so many of my students are gymnasts, I came to appreciate a gymnastics analogy when I teach about narrative conclusions. Whether their routines are on the beam, horse, rings, or floor, gymnasts know that at the end they have to *stick it*—nail the landing by maintaining their balance and holding a position with power and grace. No matter how good the rest of the routine, if they fail to stick it, the result will be a significant drop in their score. The final image an athlete presents is crucial.

So is the final image or insight presented by a storyteller. A good ending satisfies. It leaves a reader thinking, wondering, seeing, or feeling. Another verb that captures what a memoir conclusion should do is *resonate*: the ending should continue to sound, ring, even sing in the reader's mind.

The way to help kids get there is to teach them to experiment off-the-page with conclusions—to play with possibilities and then select the one that best fits the story, its tone, and its meaning. Most often, the conclusion that satisfies these criteria is reflective. What a memoirist thinks and feels at the end is the surest source of theme.

Helena's memoir "A Series of Unfortunate Events" succeeds on many levels, but it's the conclusion that sticks it. The information she withholds from this series of vignettes about her father changes everything. The humorous tone shifts, and a reader is left gasping. The Scholastic Arts and Writing competition honored Helena with its best-in-grade award, along with a check for $250.

A Series of Unfortunate Events

I am five. I awake with an uneasy feeling in my stomach. My room is dark, and I strain to make out the fingers of trees outside the window. I rub sleep from my eyes and feel my way across the hall to my parents' room, where my dad snores like a giant. "Daddy?" I squeak. I twist my hands, the uneasiness growing.

"Yeah, sweetheart?" he groans. I let out a tiny breath. My eyes are adjusting, and I locate the lump of my sleeping mother.

"I think I'm gonna throw up," I say, a frown spreading across my face.

"Run to the bathroom." All the sleep is gone from his voice. "I'll be right there."

I scramble out the door, trip through the living room, and grab the railing to the spiral staircase: Daddy says always hold the railing. At the top of the stairs I flick on the kitchen light without pausing. I skitter to the bathroom and throw open the door, but I am too late. I empty my stomach while *looking* right at the toilet. I burst into tears as Dad flies up the stairs.

"I-I-I'm s-sorry," I choke out. I am afraid he will yell at me to clean up my mess and leave me here alone with only the skeleton trees for company.

Instead, he gathers me in a hug and wipes my face, saying, "It's okay, sweetie. It's okay." And it is.

I am seven. I feel the tug of the fishing line, and I'm surprised at how strong it is.

"Dad, Dad!" I shout, keeping my eyes trained on the agitated green water as he hurries to my side of the red *Trinket*.

"You got something!" I hear the smile in his voice and feel his warm hand on my sunburnt shoulder. "Now remember: give it a bit of slack. You don't want to pull too hard," he guides.

But I do pull too hard: I am too excited. With a quiet twang, all my hopes are lost to the sea. The string snaps, and my throat tightens. I worry he will sigh and give me a disappointed look. I hide my face beneath my sun-bleached hair.

Instead, he reassures me, reties my line, and casts it for me, farther than I can fathom. At the end of the day, I'm convinced we've caught a thousand fish.

I am nine. Tears stream down my face, hot and irritating. I have a brush stuck in my hair. It's July, and I haven't run a comb through it since June. I tiptoe to my mom and dad's room, wringing my hands.

"Um, Dad?" I ask tentatively. He sits in bed on top of the checkered quilt with a martial arts book propped in his lap. The lamp on his bedside table casts a yellowish light.

"Yeah, sweetie?" he looks up with a smile, but when he sees my tears, his face falls, and he asks, "What's wrong, Rosa?" I don't say anything. I bite the inside of my cheek and turn to show him the rat's nest that is my hair. I hear a small intake of breath.

I think he might yell, grab a pair of scissors, and chop it off. Instead, he sits me on a stool and gently works the brush out of my hair. He talks to me now and then. "Always work from bottom to top," he reminds me. I close my eyes, almost drifting off, never feeling a pull or yank, and by the end of ten minutes, my hair is silky and shining. I love when he brushes my hair. He never passes up the chance to hold me close and salvage the damage of my neglect.

I am fourteen. A hot breeze blows in my face. It smells like cow patties and goats. I wrinkle my nose and continue to stack wood. I glance at Dad. He is running a length of twine from one cedar tree to another parallel to it. I smile when I hear him humming "Poker Face" by Lady Gaga.

"All right, Lena, clip that level to the string," he instructs me. I produce from my pocket a small green level with hooks on top, and I reach over the woodpile, up to the twine. But the next thing I know, the small green level isn't in my hands. It's bouncing down the cracks between logs, stopping halfway down the pile just out of my reach. I risk a glance at Dad. I imagine him with slumped shoulders, tired and disappointed, a dismissive wave of the hand.

Instead, he breaks into a laugh. "Whoops," he chuckles. I breathe a sigh of relief and let a smile split my face. By the time we finish, I drop the green level twice more and even farther down. We have to unstack half the woodpile, and I have to lower myself, head to hips, into the hole.

We are trying to build a structure to cover the wood for the winter—the winter that he will be gone, the winter he will be stationed in Afghanistan, near Kabul, in the mountains.

When he leaves, I am sad, obviously, but also angry. I don't understand it. Why would he abandon me? Strand me here? But then I realize he left for the same reason he didn't yell when I emptied my stomach *in front* of the toilet, snapped my fishing line, neglected to brush my hair, or dropped that stupid green level.

Because he is my dad, and he loves his daughter and the country she lives in.

He will spend a year without me to keep me and our family safe. He will clean up my sick, retie my line, fix my hair, re-stack half a cord of wood, and deploy to a foreign country, all of it out of love.

That's why I'm not mad at my father for missing my eighth-grade grad-uation or my first day of high school, for leaving me for "no longer than four hundred days."

Because I am his daughter, and I love him.

One hundred and twelve days down. Two hundred eighty-eight to go.

—*Helena Solorzano*

The list below, of kinds of memoir conclusions, is one I compiled after reading many memoirs by students and professionals. Kids tape it to their handbooks and highlight it, and then they play off-the-page with the approaches they think have the most potential for sticking it.

A DOZEN APPROACHES TO MEMOIR CONCLUSIONS

- a summary of elements of the memoir: what they add up to meaning-wise
- a strong image of you in action
- a strong image of you thinking or feeling
- a strong exchange of dialogue
- the gift or the curse of this experience
- a reflection: what do you feel *as you look back*?
- an understanding: what do you realize or know *now*?
- an assessment: in the end, what did you take away from the experience? What did you learn?
- a prediction of or hope for the future
- the reason you wrote the memoir
- the revelation of a crucial piece of withheld information
- an echo, one that returns to images, ideas, or language from the title or lead

  Play off-the-page with conclusions, as you did with leads, until you find the one that reso-nates, satisfies, and sticks it.

The final memoir minilesson summarizes everything we observed and discussed. When students think their memoirs are done, I require that they take a two-day walk-away. They file the last draft in a pocket of their writing-in-process folders and work on a poem for a couple of days. At this juncture they need distance, followed by fresh eyes.

When they return from the walk-away, students try to read their memoirs from the perspective of an *other*. They hold the text in one hand, a pen in the other, and focus as critics. It's important that they don't read the memoir draft on a computer screen, where everything looks good, and that their governing gaze is literary. "Reading Your Memoir as a Critic" (Figure 10.6) is a checklist for students to assess what they've written and, as necessary, revise once more to balance narrative elements, cue transitions, develop or refine a theme, or rethink the conclusion.

READING YOUR MEMOIR AS A CRITIC

Print a double-spaced copy. Pen in hand, away from the computer, take this attitude: *If I were reading this memoir in a book . . .*

- would the lead bring a reader right into my story?

- is the context embedded early on: an explanation of *who, what, when, where, why,* to ground a reader in a time, a place, and who the other people are?

- are there enough thoughts and feelings throughout the story to take readers into my head and heart *and* keep them there *and* develop my *so what?* or theme?

- is there unnecessary reflection: thoughts and feelings that don't add anything new to the story or its *so what?*

- is there enough sensory description that a reader can make a movie at key points in the story?

- does the dialogue sound natural? Is all of it necessary, in terms of revealing something about me, the other people, and our relationships?

- is there too much conversation unaccompanied by sensory descriptions or thoughts and feelings?

- are there any gaps in information that might confuse a reader who isn't me?

- is every transition between one time and place and another signaled, so a reader can follow me from event to event without becoming confused?

- will a reader find the specifics—*the things*—that readers relate to and love?

- are the verbs sensory and strong?

- does the conclusion resonate? Does it stick it? Will it leave a reader satisfied *and* thinking?

- is there a *so what?* or theme yet: a point, a purpose, an understanding, an acceptance of something, a change in me?

- how are the conventions of usage? Is the verb tense consistent, past *or* present? Is punctuation and paragraphing of dialogue correct? Are there any comma splices? Spelling errors? Enough paragraphs for a reader to breathe? Paragraphs so short they make a reader hiccup?

Figure 10.6 *Reading Your Memoir as a Critic*

The memoir study ends with a class reading. I cut, paste, and photocopy a magazine of their stories, and kids and I spend a workshop reading them silently to ourselves. As we sip chai and decaf, we write and pass notes to authors about what we noticed and liked. It is a lovely time as, every year, I feel certain that my twenty-years-from-now dream will come true.

Memoirs aren't problems with solutions. Neither are they autobiographies. They are literature, fashioned deliberately. The best of them all, *Walden*, may read as a lyrical chronicle that unwinds with ease, but Thoreau crafted seven drafts over eight years. The possibilities of the genre lie in the portion of their lives memoirists decide to explore, how they craft it, and what they learn from it.

The teaching of memoirs calls for lessons and examples that help kids attend to diction, sensory imagery, reflections, rich specifics, telling details, theme, and *selection*. It is an important genre to teach in middle school, as young adolescents measure themselves against the adult world and begin to imagine their place in it. It is an essential genre to teach in high school, as young adults take control of their lives by crafting them as literature, and as they practice writing the most important genre of their K–12 school career, the personal essay.

The final examples of student memoirs, written by CTL alums Martin and Anne when they were high school seniors, were submitted with their college applications. Both draw on lessons they learned as middle school memoirists. In four years of high school English classes, neither student had been asked to write a memoir. But their college essays are voiced and sensory, with inviting leads, revealing specifics, resonant conclusions, and themes of growth and hope. It's a pleasure and privilege to hand over advice to seventh and eighth graders about how to craft memoirs, but especially so when I believe these lessons might stick it.

University of New Harbor

As one of the lucky few who have experience with the two o'clock luggage rush to Monhegan Island, I hauled abundant suitcases and coolers down the wobbly ramp to the Hardy Boat, the island ferry that I've worked on for the last two summers. We're based out of the fishing village of New Harbor, which lies far down Maine's Pemaquid peninsula. With salty lobstermen on one side of me and well-heeled tourists on the other, I am tasked with handling luggage, selling snacks, hosing down seasickness, and anything else Captain Al requires.

"How are we doing on cargo space?" he called from the pier.

"It's no fun if it all fits the first time," I returned.

"These people from away bring their whole houses with 'em," contributed Jesse, a sun-burnished, ocean-fragrant lobsterman who enjoyed color commentating from the dock about my storage challenges, while he sorted lobsters into shipping crates.

"It's a different world," I remarked, struggling with someone's painting easel.

"This is all I need," he replied, gesturing at the sunny harbor with a squirming lobster. "I learned everything I needed to know at UNH: University of New Harbor."

His last comment struck me as I jogged up the pier, searching for the next task. I hate standing still. After another twenty minutes of pre-departure chaos, I stopped to catch my breath. An elegant woman with a grandmotherly smile struck up a conversation with me while she waited to board.

"You boys work very hard," she said, observing one of my mates and an island carpenter negotiating a table saw through the narrow cabin door. "I hope they pay you well."

"It's a great summer job for a high school senior."

"Are you going to college next year?" she inquired. I nodded. "Where are you applying?"

I rattled off the list I had prepared for inquisitive adults and, thinking of Jesse, added, "and UNH."

"Well, best of luck. Going to college is the most important thing you'll ever do."

I smiled as she turned to make her way down the ramp, stopping only when her heel caught between the planking. As I was about to intervene, I watched Jesse gently extend a hand to assist her.

I was suddenly aware of standing at the nexus of two worlds. How tiny my slice of knowledge was compared to Jesse's and his life on the water, how limited compared to the well-educated vacationers whose luggage I hauled. As I hopped back onto the boat to cast off the lines, I resolved to absorb as much of the world as I could get my hands on, to learn from anyone who had anything to teach me. Captain Al pointed the boat toward Monhegan, a dim mound on the horizon, and I began my journey out to sea. There, perched at the bow, cool spray across my face, I felt ready to meet the wide ocean.

—*Martin Shott*

CONSTELLATIONS

"Do the constellations have different names in German?" I asked Anna, as we stared up at the sky. The air was cool, typical for Maine in early June, when the night hasn't yet noticed that the days were growing warmer. I shivered, whether from the breeze off the river or a sense of overwhelming change, I couldn't tell.

My junior year had ended that afternoon in a whirlwind of finals, yearbook inscriptions, and locker doors slamming shut. A year I had dreaded fiercely and fought against, hard, was over. As I sat on the edge of Damariscotta Mills with Anna, the German exchange student I'd befriended in the fall, listening to other friends splashing in the cold, dark water below, I considered the stars. They looked the same as they had thousands of years before, when they inspired myths that ignited the darkness. I was suddenly grateful that my own life wasn't similarly stationary, that what I'd once yearned for most—for things to stay the same—had not been granted me.

The previous August, at the start of junior year, my three closest friends left Maine for year-long European exchanges. They forged new paths, while I walked alone the halls we had filled with our laughter. I didn't know who to turn to, or even who to be. It was the greatest loss—of self, of control, of connectedness—I had ever experienced.

Now, the last day of school presented a surprising contrast. Earlier I'd watched the sun set over a lake as I sat before a bonfire, marshmallow roasting on a stick in the traditional summer salute, surrounded by new close friends: athletes I met on the cross country and track teams; friends I made during our school trip to Barcelona; a girl from elementary school with whom I reconnected; and students with whom I'd begun a conversation during class and allowed it to develop afterward, something I might never have risked if my clique had stayed in Maine. When dusk fell and individuals began to peel off from the group, I understood that farewell doesn't have to mean sorrow. And then a handful of us ended up here at the Mills, beneath the clear night sky, Anna and I among them.

This year of change had witnessed so many changes in me. I discovered what it meant to feel alone, and I learned how to rise from the ashes of a three-fold heartbreak and move on. I cemented an old friendship, so strong now it may last forever. I learned not to be tied down to one group—how to look past the labels and social classifications of high school and find my place in every constellation. I learned to dip churros in hot chocolate in Barcelona's cafes, to laugh so hard my stomach hurt during bus rides to track meets, to lie under the stars of early summer and feel completely at home.

"Most of the constellations have the same names everywhere—the ones that come from Latin," Anna told me. I looked up at stars that never change, with names that are universal, already anticipating the next shift in perspective and the transformations to come.

—*Anne Atwell-McLeod*

CHAPTER 11

SHORT FICTION

The house of fiction has . . . not one window, but a million.

—HENRY JAMES

In Chapter 1, I told the story of Nancy Martin and Toby McLeod, how they rhapsodized about Anthony Powell at our dining room table one night, while I and the rest of our guests headed to the beach to watch the sun set. The next morning I enjoyed my own face time with Nancy. I was the director then of a writing project at Boothbay Region Elementary School, where colleagues and I were adapting the methods of Donald Graves and Donald Murray to our K–8 classrooms. Nancy wanted to know all about it.

We walked and talked our way down the road to the beach and then stretched out side by side on one of the flat slabs of rock revealed at low tide. I launched into a description of Boothbay's writing workshops—how children had time to write every day, conferences with the teacher about their drafts, encouragement to experience writing as a process, and their choice of topics. About the last I clarified, "We ask that they write about what they know and care about. Of course, that means no fiction."

"No fiction?" Nancy asked. "Whyever not?"

"Well, we want them to learn how to revise—how to craft writing until it's focused and full of specifics. The truth of an experience is like a yardstick they can measure their drafts against. The kids are dying to write fiction, but their stories are these wild daydreams. Everything in fiction makes sense to the kid who's writing it. Our goal is to teach them how to revise their writing so it makes sense to others."

I can quote Nancy directly one more time. "That's *rubbish*," she pronounced. And then she spoke about the stories children create not as whimsical inventions but fables in which they remake their own lives and mingle in stories they've read or had read to them.

Nancy argued that since fiction is about what's possible, rather than what's actual, it gives children access to the *hypothetical:* they can begin to see how to improvise on their own experiences. She said story writing is essential, especially for primary students, because it's the genre that synthesizes their experiences, their preoccupations, and their emotions.

I was silent—lost for words. Only after Nancy sprang up to trawl the shoreline for sea glass did a response occur to me. It was a weak one, but it was the truth. I didn't know how to teach fiction—how to invite, respond to, and help children craft make-believe. My Boothbay colleagues and I wanted our students' writing to be good, and we hadn't a clue about how to elicit good fiction. So we steered children toward memoirs and poems, while as readers they lived hungrily and happily in fiction. We taught them *not* to make believe on paper, even as their minds and hearts yearned to.

Today, teachers of primary-grade students can learn how to nurture fiction from the book *Making Believe on Paper: Fiction Writing with Young Children* (2008) by Ted DeMille, CTL's teacher of grades 1 and 2. He shows how he taps the work of author-illustrators of children's picture books, as well as drawings and stories of his own, to demonstrate techniques of fiction and illustration to students who thrive as storytellers. Children bring their voices, needs, feelings, and perspectives—Nancy Martin's hypotheticals—to the fiction they craft in Ted's workshop.

In the 1980s and 1990s, as a teacher of seventh and eighth graders, I had no lessons to hand over to help adolescents craft fiction. From the start, the genres I taught were autobiographical and expository, and my minilessons focused on information—introducing it, structuring it, clarifying it, and presenting it. This wasn't surprising. Donald Murray, whose insights continue to influence and inform what I do as a writer and teach my kids to do, was a journalist. Information—conveyed with precision, logic, and grace—was his holy grail. When I taught about memoirs, essays, reviews, and lyric poetry, I handed over Murray's principles, and the lessons stuck. When it came to fiction, all I had in my teaching repertoire were the old chestnuts passed along by my high school English teachers: the three kinds of conflicts in literature and the structure of a short story.

But my students begged to write fiction. So I surrendered and let them have at it, and then I worked with them to try to fix the results. Since many of the kids defined fiction as a daydream on paper, their plots went wherever they took them— stories about talking goats, flying boys, and flight attendants who live in Hawaii but are really CIA spies. When someone actually reached the end of a story without giving up in frustration, more often than not it concluded with the classic escape clause *Then she woke up and realized it was all a dream.* While my students could make literature as poets, memoirists, and essayists, there was little that was literary about their fiction.

I was determined to design a genre study of fiction that would circumvent tangled, implausible plots, so I turned to young adult literature for models—not novels, because there would never be enough time in a school year for a kid to craft one, but short fiction.

I collected stories by writers who specialized in young adult fare, mostly in anthologies edited by Don Gallo, and began to build a study of contemporary realistic short fiction. My students and I read and discussed the stories, teased out their features, and created criteria for effective contemporary realism. We observed that the main characters were mostly teenagers confronting choices or problems, and we identified the techniques that the authors used to develop their protagonists—action, dialogue, reflection, reaction, setting, personal interests, and beloved objects.

To prevent the outlandish plots of yore, I focused on character development and created two documents for students' handbooks, "Considerations in Creating a Character" (Figure 11.1) and a "Main Character Questionnaire" (Figure 11.2). I mandated that kids use these scaffolds, and I pushed them to build characters close to their own ages and experiences—to write what they know and to preplan their stories. Before they could start a first draft, they had to review with me the *information* they'd generated. There's that word again.

The short fiction that emerged from this approach *was* character-driven, plausible, and themed. But much of it was also unmemorable and formulaic. By defining fiction one way, as information-based contemporary realism about teen characters, I created a kind of literary Levittown in my classroom. Although a few students were able to

---

CONSIDERATIONS IN CREATING A CHARACTER

The writer has to:

- create a meaningful, interesting problem for the character, one that holds possibilities for theme development
- choose a first name that doesn't take over the story and also fits the character's family background
- choose an age the writer can imagine
- choose a family background the writer can imagine, one that fits with the main character's problem
- choose a setting the writer can envision
- choose supporting characters for reasons that relate to the main character
- develop quirks—details of personality that reveal the main character
- use objects to signify and reveal the main character's character
- create a history: a life for the main character before the story starts
- make the main character change or realize something *vs.* requiring others to change as the solution to the character's dilemma
- resolve the main character's problem realistically, in a way consistent with his or her life and personality

Figure 11.1 *Considerations in Creating a Character*

MAIN CHARACTER QUESTIONNAIRE

1. What's your name?

2. How old are you? (Remember the age limits we set.)

3. What's the problem you're facing (and is it realistic)?

4. What's your family background (and is it familiar)?

5. Where do you live? (This should be familiar, too.)

6. What do you like to do?

7. What's different about you?

8. What do you care about?

9. What do you fear?

10. What are your dreams?

11. Who are the important people in your life?

12. What are the important things in your life?

13. How will you change through confronting your problem? Possibilities:

14. What will you understand about yourself and your world at the end of the story? Possibilities:

Figure 11.2 *Main Character Questionnaire*

produce fresh, compelling fiction within the parameters of the genre study, the majority of the stories were heavy-handed and predictable. Three plot premises prevailed:

- The main character has to choose between the cool group and an old friend.
- The main character is in, or is invited to join, the cool group and has to do something "bad."
- The main character is pressured by family or friends not to try something "different."

Anna's short story "New Steps" conforms to the third scenario. It's about Leslie, a figure skater with a stage mother and a twin who excels at the sport. Leslie has to choose between skating and a new interest, art. I include it here as an example—a good one—of a student attempt at contemporary realism.

New Steps

I lie in bed with my eyes squeezed shut and my comforter pulled way up to keep in the warmth. The light is still dim, and dark shadows cling to my bedroom walls. I hear the rustle of covers from across the hall, followed by the familiar thump of bare feet on a creaky wooden floor.

"Get *off* me," I mumble in a sleepy groan. As usual, Maddy, my twin, has run across the hall from her bedroom and leaped onto my bed. I don't understand how a human can be so alert at five in the morning. She has always been an early riser and, unfortunately, my wake-up call.

"Get up, Leslie! Get up and get out of bed, or you're gonna make us late!" Maddy whines. She pulls off my blankets before I'm awake enough to fight her.

"Okay, I'm up," I groan in response. The smell of bacon wafts up the hallway and seeps into our room. I stumble down the stairs, following the greasy aroma into the kitchen.

"Hey, honey! I made bacon and scrambled eggs, so eat up! You're gonna need the protein for a big day of practice," Mom says, placing a plate and a glass of orange juice in front of me.

Mom is always up early and always makes us a big breakfast. "Are you excited? Your program is really coming together. I'm so proud of both of you. You've been working so hard, and I'm sure you'll both place high," Mom says with a proud smile and a gleam in her eyes. She has never missed a single one of our skating competitions, and she shows up for almost every practice, too.

"Thanks, Mom," I say. I gulp down the rest of my orange juice.

"Well, I'll go warm up the car, and you finish getting ready," she says as she grabs the coat that's slung over a dining room chair.

"Okay," I reply. I run upstairs to my room—light has started to seep in the windows. I pull on sweatpants and the Winter Olympics fleece I got last Christmas. I slip on my Uggs, grab my bag, and run down the stairs and out to the driveway. When I get to the car, Maddy is already there and has claimed the front seat. I turn on my iPod, and the sound of my music puts me right to sleep. I never stay awake on the way to early morning practice.

An hour later, I rub my eyes as we pull into the rink parking lot. When I pull open the heavy metal door, Maddy runs in before me—she's dressed and ready and starts lacing up. I head into the changing room. When I come out, she's stepping onto the ice.

"Have you already stretched?" I ask.

"Yeah, I stretched at home while *you* were still getting dressed!" she calls back, then starts skating around the rink to warm-up. I sit down on the first bleacher row and begin my stretches. I watch Maddy skate; she always beams as she takes her first glides onto the ice. Right from the beginning, skating looked easy and natural for her. When we were little, she had a grin on her face as she flew through learning the basics, and she was always eager to learn more. For me, skating has been—still is—hard work. I finish lacing up my skates, step onto the ice, and glide out over the smooth glass.

Mom comes through the door. "Okay, see you then," she says, flips down her cell phone, and puts it in her purse. "Coach Shuler will be here in an hour," she yells. "She says to practice basics 'til she gets here." Coach Shuler has been with us for years now. She is the best in New England and coached three Olympic contenders. Still, I have never felt comfortable around her, but Maddy adores her, and she adores Maddy in equal measure.

I start to warm up with waltz jumps. When I look over, Maddy is already practicing her double-toe loops. I think back to a conversation from last night. We were in Maddy's room, lounging on her bed like lots of Saturday nights, with popcorn and coffee ice cream, watching movies on her computer.

Maddy was talking about skating. "I love the feeling when I'm gonna jump—worried at first, but once I'm in the air, my mind clears, and it's just pure excitement until my skates touch the ice again." As she spoke, I thought about my own emotions when I jump, and I wished I felt the same. I am always worried. There's so much pressure to get it right. I have to work through the steps in my head, and I hold my breath. I *do* love the feeling when I land: a feeling of accomplishment but, more than anything, relief when I can finally breathe again.

After a long day of salchows and toe loops and Coach Shuler noting my every mistake, I trudge back to Mom's car beneath a darkening sky. My mind is still running through steps: three-turn inside edge outside edge, half revolution scoop backwards, land. I try to shake the jumps out of my mind. On the way home Mom orders takeout, and that night I go to bed early—exhausted from the day but starting to feel okay about how my program is coming.

The next morning at school, I head down the hall to my first class: study hall. I take out my unfinished history notes and start to work. The sound of static comes from the intercom as the morning announcements begin. I continue to write, ignoring the usual reports about basketball games and swim meets and the upcoming canned food drive. But one announcement catches my attention. I stop and listen.

". . . there are two openings in a drawing class for eighth graders who have a first period study hall or who are taking an elective and would like to transfer. The sign-up list is in the main hallway on the bulletin board. Sign up today, and talk to your guidance counselor at your next meeting . . ."

I look over at Maddy, wondering if she has heard the announcement, but she's reading her book. I go back to my notes and try to start writing again, but my mind has drifted off: art class? It might be fun. I do lots of sketches on my binders . . . No, these kids will be way more experienced than I am. I'd be behind. My brain can't make up its mind: part of me wants to try it, but another part is telling me not to. The bell rings, and I try to forget the art class and go on with the rest of my school day.

That afternoon, when I step onto the bus and sit down, I'm still surprised at myself. I don't know why, but as I passed the bulletin board on the way outside, I saw the list—the sign-up sheet. The bold letters caught my eye: **First Period Art Class.** I went over, put my name on it, and strolled out to the bus. Every single class I have is with Maddy, and I haven't said a thing to her about it yet. She went home today with her friend Beth.

When I get home, I go up to my room and start on my homework. Mondays are the only days we don't have a practice after school. I finish quickly, go on my computer, and listen to my music, glancing every few minutes at the clock and wondering when Dad will be home and we'll sit down to dinner. I try to imagine what Mom will say when I tell about the class. I hear the door open and the jingle of keys being tossed on the kitchen counter.

"Maddy, Leslie, Dad's home! Come down for dinner!" Mom hollers up to us. I hear my sister skip down the stairs.

"Just a minute!" I call back. I turn off my computer and head down.

Salad is on the table as Mom pulls the chicken out of the oven. Maddy is already helping herself. "How was work?" Mom asks Dad.

"Things are pretty hectic at the firm. We've got a lot of big cases right now," he responds in a typical reply. He spends more time at his law office than he does at home. "How were your days, girls?" Dad asks, as he piles a big serving of salad onto his plate.

"Okay, sorta boring, nothing special," Maddy says, then stuffs a forkful of chicken in her mouth. The table is quiet except for the clanking of cutlery.

"I signed up for an art class, and it starts tomorrow," I blurt out. The clanking stops.

"Well, I guess that's okay," Mom says. "Just as long as it doesn't interfere with your skating."

"Yeah, that'll be fun," says Dad. "No reason one of my little skaters can't be an *artiste*, too," he jokes. Neither of them seems to think it's a big deal. I let out a sigh of relief.

"An art class? I am definitely not taking it with you. Why would you wanna replace a study hall?" Maddy asks.

"I, uh, thought it would be fun. I think I could like art. It's worth a try," I say. My voice is hesitant.

"You are so good at doodling. You should go for it," Maddy decides.

"Well, like I said," Mom says, "just as long as it doesn't affect your practice schedule." We finish dinner without another word.

Later, in my room, I think about how Maddy has always been better than I am at skating, school, making friends, but especially skating. I begin to hope this art class will give me something that I'm good at. Something that's mine. I climb in underneath my comforter and read until I drift off.

On the bus to school the next morning, I tap my fingers on my math book in anticipation and wonder about the first class. Will I know any of the kids? Will the teacher be nice? Am I any good at drawing? When the bus stops, I hop off and head to the art wing. I have never been in this part of the school before. I follow the corridor to room B27. Two girls overtake me in the hall.

"Hey, you look kinda lost. Are you looking for a class?" a girl with red hair asks. I open my mouth to respond, but before I can, the other girl interrupts.

"That's the new art class girl: Leslie," she says to her friend, nudging her with her elbow.

"I don't know how she knows this," the red-haired girl says to me as she gives her friend a sarcastic evil glare, "but we're in the class too. I'm Kayla, and this is Isabelle."

"Hi, I'm Leslie, but I guess you guys already know that," I say with a shy smile.

"I saw the name on the list, and I looked you up in last year's yearbook," Isabelle says. The second bell rings. "Come on, follow us. We'll show you where to go," she says, and I run behind them down the hall.

Kayla opens the door, and Isabelle and I follow her in. I look around the classroom. It's different than any in the school: its dull gray walls are awash in art. The tables are splattered with spots of bright paint. The door creaks, and a young woman pushes it open while trying to balance a stack of folders and a cup of coffee. She plops the stack down on the teacher desk, and I take the empty seat next to Isabelle. The class is small. I recognize two kids from the hallways, but I don't know their names.

"Okay, everyone, if you haven't already, take out your gum erasers and soft pencils and continue on your perspective projects. Keep in mind the lesson yesterday on the use of negative space," the teacher says to the class, then drains her coffee cup, tosses it into the trash, and looks over at me.

"Oh, I'm sorry. You must be one of our new artists. Uhhhh . . ."

"Leslie," I fill in.

"Right, okay, I'm Miss Ryan, and I'll go over yesterday's lesson with you, and then you can get a start on a drawing. We're working with two-point perspective," she says, while sifting through her pile of folders.

"Don't worry. You're not far behind, and Miss Ryan's really cool," Kayla whispers to me from across the table.

The class goes by quickly. I love the idea of combining geometry and drawing, and the building I create looks three-dimensional—I really like it. I walk out of class with Isabelle and Kayla. "What lunch period do you have?" Kayla asks me.

"Um, I've got period A this week," I respond.

"Hey, us too!" Isabelle says. "Okay, so we'll meet at the cafeteria door."

"Um, okay, I'll meet you there," I say and head the other way down the hall to my next class, which is math. Most girls aren't so willing to let someone they don't know sit with them. I can already tell these two are gonna be different. I slip into the math classroom and take my seat next to Maddy.

"So how was it?" she asks.

"Great!" I respond, a smile still on my face. "I met these two girls, and I'm sitting with them at lunch today," I say.

"Okay. I was gonna sit with Natalie and Beth anyways," she says. Mr. Weiss walks in before I can respond.

The class lasts an eternity, but once it's over, I walk down the hall to the cafeteria and see Kayla and Isabelle waiting there. They spot me and wave. We take a table at the back. A few other kids from the art class come join us. I've only known them since this morning, but already I feel comfortable around them—like I can be myself.

"Hey, Leslie. Kayla and I are going downtown after school to the coffee shop. Wanna come?" Isabelle asks.

"Sorry, I can't. I've got skating practice," I respond, disappointed. I wish I could hang out with them. "There's a big competition coming up, so I can't miss it. Another time though, definitely," I add.

"Yeah, okay," Isabelle says with a half smile.

The next days at school I continue to have to decline Kayla and Isabelle's invitations. Each time it gets harder. I want to spend time with them and be friends, but there is no time. Skating has to come first. I don't want them to think I think I'm too cool to hang out with them, but it starts to feel exactly like that's what's happening.

One morning, when I take my usual seat next to Isabelle in art class, Miss Ryan makes an announcement: "As most of you know, the annual county-wide student art show is a week from Saturday. I encourage you to submit a portfolio. I have a flyer for each of you with all the information you'll need." She passes one to each of us. I look at the date at the top: Saturday, February 10th, 4–6 p.m. That Saturday? It can't be that Saturday. Why does it have to be that Saturday? It's the date of the next skating competition.

"Hey, Leslie," Isabelle whispers. "There's a party afterwards at my house, after the art show. Everyone in the class is invited."

"Yeah, it's always really fun," Kayla adds, "except for those weird art games." She laughs.

"Pin the palette on Picasso," someone yells from across the room. The whole class bursts into laughter.

"It's a tradition, okay? And my mom made them up when I was like eight; it was not me," Isabelle argues.

"Settle down everyone," Miss Ryan says. She walks over to our table. "Leslie, I know you have fewer pieces than everyone else, but you're doing really great work. I think you have real potential. I'm encouraging you to take a collection of your watercolors and sketches to the show on Saturday," she says.

"Yeah, um, definitely," I lie, not knowing what else to say. I know I can't. I could never miss a competition, no matter how much I want to do something else—like go to the art show and hang out afterwards with my new friends. My mother would disown me. Skating comes first. It always has, and it seems like it always will.

I spend the next week worrying. I don't say a word to my mom. How can I tell her I don't want to compete? She would never in a million years let me miss a competition. But what will I say to Miss Ryan? That I'm not serious enough about art to do the show? I love the art class—not just the new social life I'm enjoying, although that's great. I love the feeling I have when I'm painting or sketching. I understand now how Maddy feels about skating: how your mind clears and you lose yourself when you're doing something you love. Questions flood my mind for the rest of the week, distracting me from everything.

It's Wednesday: three days until the skate competition *and* the art show. I have made up my mind. I come home from school and wait for my mom, whose note says she's at the grocery store. I sit on the couch and try to plan what I'm going to say. My knees shake as I watch the clock. When the sun starts to set, its light glares through half-open blinds.

Finally Mom returns, balancing two packed grocery bags. As she plops them down onto the island, I hurry to her before I lose my nerve.

"Hey, honey, how was your day? Leslie, is something wrong? You look . . ." she starts.

I cut her off. "Mom, there's something I need to talk to you about." My voice is shaky.

"What is it?" she responds, concerned.

"I can't compete on Saturday," I blurt.

"What are you talking about? Of course you can. You're ready, and you'll do great. Wait, are you sick? Did you injure yourself?" she asks, confused.

"I'm gonna be in an art show instead," I say, staring at the checkered linoleum.

"No. No, Leslie, you can't do that. This is the biggest competition of the year! You've been practicing for months for this! You can't miss it, especially not for an art show." Her voice is getting louder. She says the words *art show* like it's the dumbest thing she's ever heard—like it's a joke. "You want to give up what you've been working for your whole life—all your dreams?"

"Mom, I'm good at art. I love it. It's who I think I am—an artist. You've always been pushing for both of us to be skaters. I always thought there was no other option for me, except skating, but I found one. Art is important to me. It's my voice. And I'm sick of you telling me that who I am—me, Leslie, not one-half of the skating twin sisters—doesn't matter." I've never spoken like this to my mom. I've never been the one for confrontations. I've always been a keep-quiet-and-go-with-the-flow kind of person. I look at her, anxious about what her reaction will be.

"Well, you seem to have your mind made up," she says. I can hear her anger and disappointment. "Skating has been your whole life. Now you're going to throw all that away?" she tries again.

I take a deep breath. "Have you ever noticed that it's always been Maddy who loves skating? Who lives for it and who's good at it—much better than I am? I know skating is a part of my life. I'm not gonna stop; I just don't want it to be my whole life anymore," I say, calmer now. "Art has made me happier than skating ever did. I've thought a lot about this, and my mind is made up." I don't want to yell at my mom and make her angry with me. I just want her to *understand*.

"So, I guess I'll call and unregister you for Saturday," Mom says. Her voice is quieter now, but it still has an angry tone: her disappointed-in-you-tone. I know she hasn't heard what I mean, but maybe she'll learn to accept it. She'll have to accept it.

"Thanks," I say and trudge upstairs to my room. It is the last conversation I have with my mother for two whole days. In the meantime, at school, I assemble my portfolio, and I'm happy. The pressures and stresses of the last few weeks have lifted.

On Saturday morning, I run down the stairs to wish Maddy good luck as she's about to leave with Mom. We hug and then draw back, and our twin eyes tell each other what we don't need words to say: *I'm happy for you.* After Maddy heads to the car, Mom puts her hands on my shoulders. She looks deep into my eyes. I have no idea what she's going to say.

"Leslie, I'm sorry. I know you're not the kind of person to confront someone and sound off, so I realize how important this art show and your art must be to you. You know I always wanted you and Maddy to be skaters. It was my dream and Maddy's but not yours. But I guess I'm gonna have to want an artist now, too," she finishes. I know how hard this must be for her.

"It's okay. You were doing what you thought was best," I respond. "And so was I. But now I know better." Mom starts to head out the door to the car. "Kayla's mom is gonna pick me up at eleven-thirty," I holler after her.

"Okay. Have fun," she yells back. I wait at the window and wave as they pull out of the driveway. Maddy waves back with both hands. Then I plop down on the couch and turn on the TV, happier than I've been in a long time.

The past weeks I was jumping, although not on ice. I was worried about how to begin, and I was holding my breath. But this time, I made up my own steps, steps that led me to my own person, to *Leslie*, who's no longer just one of the skating twins. Now I've landed, with the feeling of accomplishment I always wanted and, finally, I can breathe.

—*Anna Jaeger*

Anna's story is a success within the constraints of the genre study. She does invent a person and a context, create a supporting cast, craft dialogue and reflection that reveal a conflict, build the plot to a climax, and resolve Leslie's problem. But there is nothing for a reader to unpack here. The longer Anna worked on it, the more predictable the story became.

It took her eight weeks to finish "New Steps" as she planned, researched skating moves and jumps, drafted, got bogged down, planned some more, strayed off track, conferred with me and classmates, revised, and edited. I watched her enthusiasm for fiction flag—everyone's did—as months of writing workshop were eaten up by contemporary realism. It was fiction. But it was the wrong kind. Instead of nurturing imagination and invention, I'd created a version of fiction that was as information-based as every other genre I taught.

Then Leigh Peake, an editor at Heinemann, gave my kids and me a copy of *Micro Fiction: An Anthology of Really Short Stories* edited by Jerome Stern (1996). In his introduction, Stern defines micro fiction as a story of three hundred words or fewer. He also points out that it's not a new genre: jokes, Aesop's fables, and the parables of the Old and New Testaments are all short short stories.

Leigh said, "I thought your kids might want to try their hands at this." I skimmed the book and said, "Thanks, but I don't think so." My first objection, as a literary purist, was that micro fiction wasn't a real genre. In addition, I didn't think seventh and eighth graders could write it—could compress, omit, imply, and surprise. Micro fiction is as much poetry as it is prose.

Well, exactly. And if my students are anything, they are poets. I mulled this over. First I had to overcome my prejudices as an old-guard English teacher about what constitutes a genre. Jokes, fables, and parables are, in fact, ancient micro fiction. Some of Chekhov's stories are only a page long, while Kafka wrote stories of a single paragraph. I'd become a fan of the short short stories of Lydia Davis, which push the boundaries of prose, and Dave Eggers, whose micro fiction Toby and I read online in the *Guardian* newspaper.

So I sat down with the Sterns anthology, really read it this time, and dog-eared stories I thought kids would like and could unpack: "Eclipsed" by Robert Shuster, "Carpathia" by Jesse Lee Kercheval, "Flu" by Stuart Dybek, and "We Eat Our Peas for the Souls in Purgatory" by Annette McPeters. I made copies of Eggers' "How the Water Feels to the Fishes" and "Thoughtful That Way," which he published in his collection *How the Water Feels to the Fishes* (2007). And then I introduced the new genre to my students by asking them to read micro fiction, note in the back pages of their handbooks the features they observed, discuss them in small groups, and then come back together to help me create a master list of attributes of effective short short stories.

Figure 11.3 reproduces the criteria my students developed the third year I taught micro fiction as a genre study. An insightful, thorough description of how and why short

---

FEATURES OF EFFECTIVE MICRO FICTION

- The lead jumps right into the action, as a poem does.
- Instead of a traditional short story structure (lead, introduction of main character and setting, rising action, climax, falling action, resolution), there's just rising action and a climax.
- It explores one scene or situation; it can be summarized in a sentence.
- It has a particular setting.
- Imagery brings the scene to life.
- Every word is essential: so compressed, it's as much a poem as a narrative.
- There's little dialogue *or* much: it depends on the writer's intentions for the story.
- There are lots of thoughts and feelings *or* few: again, it depends on the writer's intentions.
- The diction—choice of words—is sensory and precise, as in a poem.
- The reader has to slow down, as with a poem.
- It maintains a balance between implying and specifying: there's *just enough* information.
- The story turns: there's some kind of surprise or reversal.
- The end line is crucial: a twist, a realization, a change.
- The conclusion has to be unpacked: it implies rather than states.
- It implies a *so what?* or theme.
- It demands a strong title with a layered meaning.
- The paragraphs are friendly.
- The length limit is 300 words, and every one counts.

Figure 11.3 *Features of Effective Micro Fiction*

short stories work, the list is informed by their readings of successful micro fiction by professionals, as well as CTL alums.

I'm reluctant to make blanket statements about kids—what they all love to write or read—because they're no more uniform in their tastes than any group of adult writers or readers. But they do enjoy writing short short stories. I think this is *the* genre to hand over to middle school writers of fiction.

It starts with the variety of tales they get to spin. So far the fictional subgenres they've produced include action-adventure, contemporary realism with a twist, dystopian fiction, espionage, fantasy, historical fiction, homage, horror, humor, magic realism, metafiction, murder mystery, parody, psychological mystery, romance, science fiction, stream of consciousness, supernatural, and thriller.

Micro fiction invites genre play—and plain old play. It invites kids to ask "What if?" and to imagine answers that take myriad forms. As Henry James observed, "The house of fiction has . . . not one window, but a million" (1934). Micro fiction moved my kids out of the studio apartments I'd leased to them and into mansions of their own.

Wallace, an eighth grader, asked, "*What if* a guy's every move was dictated by a Magic 8 Ball?" The result is a microtragicomedy.

MAGIC 8 BALL

Dave limps down the street—socks got *my sources say no*—and opens the door to the diner. He sits at the counter, pulls out the 8 Ball, and puts his finger on the first item on the menu: "The Lumberjack Feast: three eggs, four sausage links, three pancakes/waffles, and two pieces of Texas toast." Dave shakes the black ball; the response is immediate and definite. *It is decidedly so* pops up on the triangle that floats in the mysterious blue liquid.

He sees Sheila sitting in the booth she does every night after her shift at the bowling alley. He has never said a word to her. He knows her name because of her nametag. *Don't count on it* says the ball when Dave asks the familiar question: does she recognize him? He asks again. *Very doubtful.*

"Oh, hey, I know you. I rented you shoes the other night," Sheila calls from across the diner. Dave trembles as he murmurs a hello. She walks over and sits next to him. "What do you have there?" she asks.

"Oh, it's just a toy," Dave responds. "Excuse me for a minute. I need some air." He walks outside. "Magic 8 Ball, is she the one? I like her. I think we might have something special." He shakes the ball.

The triangle lingers in nothingness, until—*My reply is no.*

He asks one final question. *Yes—definitely* is the response. His heart drops. His stomach sinks. He limps home.

—*Wallace Jackson*

Dave is an adult—way older than his thirteen-year-old creator. There isn't a diner or bowling alley anywhere near Wallace's house. The "Lumberjack Feast" is pure invention, and I'm not sure if Wallace even owns a Magic 8 Ball. In the past, when I told kids, "Write what you know," my definition of knowledge wasn't nearly generous enough. Wallace is alive in the world. He watches movies and television, and he reads. He's learned the conventions of lots of different kinds of stories and lived vicariously alongside lots of different kinds of characters. Given the opportunity, he has ideas about what he wants to experience vicariously—who it would be intriguing to become beyond his self, and how he might project his imagination into someone else's world.

Payton, Wallace's classmate, projected herself into an Amazonian rain forest in an action-adventure story.

OUT OF THE FRYING PAN

The water was warm but refreshing. Sarah's legs still stung, but at least the ants were gone. The world swirled around her as she floated face up in the river. Her stomach lurched as flashes of memory came back to her. *The army ants that came when she was sleeping. Her screams. How she opened her mouth and they crawled in. Branches whipping her arms and face . . . millions of insects devouring her . . . then . . . silence . . . water . . . life. And now . . .* the rainforest came into focus. Its moist canopy shone. She watched a pack of spider monkeys swing from vines. Then she glimpsed the clearing.

It was hardly a village. A dozen or so people milled about outside grass huts. But they wore clothes. They carried babies in slings. They probably had food. Sarah sobbed with relief. She waded to the muddy bank and stood slowly, tremulously, as if she couldn't believe what she was seeing was real, and limped into the village.

Faces peered out of huts to watch her pass. Sarah smiled as she stumbled to the center of the clearing, towards the charred remains of a fire. Jubilation flooded her, and she forgot the chunks of flesh the ants had taken and the gashes on her face from the thorny branches. It was then that she felt the first blow, to her neck, followed by a second to her left leg, and a third to her right side. Sarah slumped to the ground, the smile still etched on her startled face.

A bonfire was started. The villagers wouldn't starve after all.

—*Payton Sullivan*

A reader can feel the pleasure Payton takes in imagining army ants, spider monkeys, a lost tribe, and a ghastly, ironic conclusion. As a writer, she was in heaven. Compared with the twenty-page stories my student used to write, "Out of the Frying Pan" is like a bonsai tree. A sculpted, heightened slice of life, it resists formula because it's hard to write formulaic micro fiction. The conventions of a genre need an extended chunk of space to become predictable. In a collapsed space, Payton could be fresh as a writer—could forego a backstory, bypass character development, plunge right into the "good parts," make an impression, and discover freedom within the limits of scale.

When students do venture into contemporary teen realism in their micro fiction, they write toward a twist—a turn, surprise, reversal, or realization. Kate's conclusion is classic micro fiction. When I use it as model, it's a story students read twice.

GUARDIAN

I bubble the tape, attach it to the back of the White Knights poster, and stick it to my bedroom wall. It's the only poster I have, and it's the only poster I want. I lie down on my bed and beam at it. I focus to the far left, on the bass player. He has wavy brown hair and warm hazel eyes. He's wearing jeans and a leather jacket. He looks so trustworthy, so kind and caring.

"Honey, what are you doing?" My mother interrupts my daydream.

I don't respond.

Her eyes sweep my room. When she spots the poster, her eyes get big, and her mouth gets tight.

"I told you I didn't want you to buy that," she snaps.

I stay silent.

"That better be down by the time I come back up here," she orders. Then she stomps back downstairs.

But I don't move. I want to stare at it for as long as I can— to try to memorize its colors, shapes, and shades. I want to hug the bass player. I want to talk with him. I want to meet my knight in shining armor.

I want to meet my dad.

—*Kate Friant*

Avery captures the moment when a life changes forever. The conclusion to his realistic micro fiction sends readers back to his title to unpack its meaning.

TWO AND A HALF DEATHS

The black sedan practically flew off the interstate and onto the exit ramp at sixty-five miles per hour.

"Slow down! You're going too fast!" the woman yelled as she gripped the door handle, her white knuckles the same color as her painted fingernails.

"Honey, we're fine," the man admonished her. He was calm as he turned the wheel and pressed the brake. Suddenly the car fishtailed. He wrenched the wheel to the left in an effort to keep it on the road. But it spun out of control and slammed into the ledge that loomed alongside the ramp.

In an instant, the frame was ruptured beyond hope. The two passengers were sprayed with shards of inch-thick glass and tossed about like dice. And then they were still, disfigured, unrecognizable, in a car that was crumpled like tinfoil.

In the next town a boy stepped up to his front door. Rummaged in his pocket for the key. Twisted it in the lock and shoved the door open with his shoulder. Kicked off his shoes and trudged into the kitchen. Slung his backpack on the floor. Helped himself to a snack. Noticed the red voicemail light blinking on the phone. Pushed the button. Listened. Felt his childhood end.

—*Avery Genus*

Noah pushed into historical fiction. After his class studied the Holocaust in history, he read *Night* by Elie Wiesel and Anne Frank's *Diary of a Young Girl*. Under their influence, he projected himself into a micro fiction about a boy who is losing the love of his mother forever.

BUT IT WAS NEVER ALL RIGHT AGAIN

"It'll be all right." Her words echo in my head. Her cold fingers tremble in my palm. I can sense the fear in her voice. As we make our way out of the stinking boxcar, wind whips at our backs and jagged stones grate our bare feet. Though Allied bombs drop eight hundred miles away, no one is here to save us.

We march silently, grouped by the hundreds. An elderly man next to me, limbs like sticks, wheezes. He slows to catch his breath. An officer with a rifle strikes him in the back.

Pain—*"Help."* The word dangles at the end of his sputtering lips. Wide brown eyes, which his mother once called beautiful, fade. Shuffling feet clamber over him, and he's lost in the dust.

Here the group splits, dividing families into two lines.

"Go left," a man says, directing Mother. I follow, but he shoves me to the right. I stumble into place.

"I'll meet up with you when it's over." A voice, faint like a whisper, barely reaches my ears. *"It'll be all right."* I shuffle in shock, losing sight of her as the lines grow apart. Then her group disappears behind a chain link fence, and my mother's silhouette vanishes in smoke. Doubts of seeing her again consume me. Emptiness fills me. But I hobble on. And on.

Today I stare at a faded photo. It's Mother before the war, wearing a hopeful smile and optimistic eyes. Whispers echo in my head, the words she spoke to me last—It'll be all right. It'll be all right. It'll be all right.

—*Noah Jordan*

Gabrielle ventured into science fiction. She imagined a woman whose obsessive-compulsive disorder drives her to push others away, until it's too late to connect.

ALONE

She reaches for her spray bottle of Clorox and wipes down the bedside table. As she clenches the bottle her eyes tear up. She's thinking of the germs that might have attached themselves to her since last night. She reaches into a white bin, finds her plastic shoes, and slides them on. She rinses her hands in alcohol, snaps on medium-size plastic glove, hooks her finger around the curtain, and pushes it aside: a sunny day, as if it matters.

She strides into the kitchen, wipes down the handle of the teakettle, and pours in water from her filter machine. She perches on the shiny plastic cover of her white couch and then bounces up at the sound of the kettle's whistle.

She wipes down the handle of the cabinet, grabs a plastic-wrapped mug, wipes down the teakettle again, unwraps the mug and checks it for spots, and pours her tea. It's only when she settles down to gaze out the window that she realizes something is missing.

There are no cars. No birds. No people. Mrs. Kelly isn't packing up her nasty kids to drop them off at daycare. Mr. Brook isn't taking his defecating dog for its morning walk. Mrs. Russell isn't standing on her porch smoking a stinking, disgusting cigarette. She checks the time: 8:35. She takes a deep breath and screeches, "Hello? Hello?" Nothing and no one answers. It is then that she wishes for someone else—for humanity, with all its germs, filth, and color.

—*Gabrielle Nuki*

Parker was reading thrillers. Micro fiction let him channel his inner Jason Bourne and write about guns, knives, "curses," and an antihero protagonist. There's violence here because the thriller genre requires it; there's a reversal and theme because micro fiction requires them.

REVELATIONS OF AN ASSASSIN

The SCAR-H assault rifle slams into his wounded shoulder with his every stride across the desert sand. He rips a clip out of the gun and jams in another, noting the scant supply remaining in his vest pocket. He grimaces, thinking of his safehouse: food, clothing, ammo, weapons. *But he would make do. He would always make do.*

A sound behind him. He whirls, draws the rifle to his shoulder, and sinks into a crouch. Only the wind. He curses himself for being unprepared. Even a second of relaxation could mean his end. *Ahead: a voice. Take cover.* He glances around a boulder.

Two soldiers. He can take two. He exults silently, then grimaces. More tracks in the sand than two men would make. He strides toward the first soldier. *Act like you belong. They'll think you do.* He shoves the knife between one soldier's ribs, then slashes it across the second's throat. *He would make his own way. He would always make his own way.*

He pockets their pistols, leaving the heavier squad automatics behind. *An angry shout: drop your weapons.* A barrel is pressed against his back. He raises his hands, then whips around, grabs the gun, twists it, and sprays the sand with lead. He dives behind a rock and unslings his rifle. *Alone he would survive. Alone he would always survive.*

They come for him then. He shoves the rifle barrel over the boulder and fires blindly, rewarded by screams of agony as his shots hit their marks. Projectiles fire past him. His analytical mind identifies the weapon as a Barret .50 caliber heavy rifle. It also recognizes a new truth. *He will die. Alone, he will die. Here. Now.*

—*Parker Elkins*

Hope decided to try a romance. It's a lot for an eighth-grade girl to develop a fully blown story about teen love. Micro fiction allowed her to fantasize a little and, as a writer, elide, imply, and invite her readers to experience a friendship that turns into love.

LOVE IS THICKER THAN FORGET

His UCLA t-shirt brings a heavy silence to my doorstep. He hands me a small box; I tear off the newspaper wrapping to reveal a pen.

"Keith, I didn't get you . . ."

"It's not really a present, Mac. God." He grins, but it doesn't touch his pine-colored eyes. He pulls me in for a final hug, and as I breathe his scent of grass and soap, I remember us—

The first time I rode a bike. I was tottering down our driveway when a voice shouted. "Just do it." Red heat flooded my face. I pushed off, to *show him*, but tipped and crashed in an instant. I expected a cackle and a taunt, but to my surprise I looked up into furrowed pine eyes and an outstretched hand. "Don't fall next time."

The week I got flu. We lounged on my carpet with Monopoly and tissues after his baseball practices. When he left, I refused Mom's orders to clean up. I left the board intact, willing him to return.

The night after Izzy and Shannon saw my granny panties and broadcast it to the world. He told endless jokes as we lay side by side watching clouds. I laughed so hard I forgot about everything except his pine eyes that were laughing, too.

Now my eyes burn and threaten to burst. As we let go, I don't trust my voice. I guess he doesn't either, because he takes my hand and writes something with my new pen, before his parents' minivan can whisk him away. I glance at my palm: *write me* is scribbled in pine ink, my favorite color. Proof he'll be back. It's then I wonder—does he know why I love this color so?

—*Hope Logan*

Xander fell under the spell of Dave Eggers, whose short short stories are experimental and impressionistic: formatted in block style, peopled with nameless *he's* and *she's*, spare, and haunting.

Tsunami Dreams

He dug and he dug, and the hole grew while the dirty light faded. He pushed deeper and tossed the shovelfuls onto the mottled green lawn. He tunneled until he could not feel himself anymore—his arms and legs fell away and his mind eroded. He plowed past fire and water, blue days and green grass. Through layers of crust and mantle he dug until darkness enveloped him like a wet towel. Soon, the walls around him fell away, and the world was bright and familiar. The wind whispered in the palm trees, and across a clearing, a yellow house basked in the sunlight, his old house—the home he had lived in with his wife and child before the deluge. A deep roar crept into his ears, and he took the familiar step back, déjà vu swelling inside him like a broken wave.

—*Xander Bartone*

As a new author of micro fiction, Elizabeth didn't dither. She imagined something horrible—the doll from hell—and as a fan of horror stories, she went for it.

Rosily's Doll

Rosily was in love with her new doll. She loved how its hands looked so human, with faint veins on the wrists, creases where its fingers bent. She loved its outstretched hand, with five fingers posed as if it were waving.

When Rosily was almost asleep, she heard a yelp from downstairs. She rushed down to find her dog on the kitchen floor, dead. She noticed something next to its corpse. A finger. A doll's finger.

A shriek came from upstairs. There she found her brother, dead in his bed, with a finger on his pillow. Two more screams sounded. She knew what had happened, and she knew there was no escape. The doll sat on the floor between her recently deceased parents, staring blankly at its owner. Rosily stared at the doll's hand, missing all its fingers but one.

Rosily grabbed the doll and threw it down the stairs, ran to her room, and slammed and locked the door. She heard footsteps coming up the stairs. "Rosily, I'm coming. I'm almost to the top, Rosily. I'm at your door, Rosily." The door creaked open. "Hello, Rosily."

Months later, when she was clearing the house that had been her late sister's, Rosily's aunt found the doll. She noticed the missing fingers, so she donated it to a local charity. The cashier put the damaged doll in the not-for-sale bin—but not for long. She was pleased to discover the next morning that the doll had made a miraculous recovery. Five new fingers. It was almost like she was waving.

—Elizabeth DiGiulian

Finally, a work of micro meta fiction by Nicholas both tells a short short story and comments on the genre: as he explains how to write one, he writes one.

FIRST DRAFT

It begins with an idea: setting or event, not character. *How about . . . being sick?* Genre comes next: humor, mystery, thriller? And so on. *Contemporary realism fits, but with a twist.* Now, start drafting. You're limited to three hundred words, so know exactly what you're writing about. *A sick boy. With a dog.* Also: know your tone.

The lead sets the stage. *The boy was sick. The dog came to him, and its rough, warm tongue licked his hand.* Take a firm direction with the middle. *The boy smiled and slept. The dog made him happy, and he forgot about his fever.*

Next is a reveal that keeps the story interesting. Remember that the plot comes from your imagination. It's not constrained by a theme someone else chose. It's *yours.* If it's not fun anymore, you've done something wrong. *The boy's fever broke. And then he remembered: his dog had died five years ago.* Your ending must be strong, resonant, leave a reader thinking about the boy (or the dog).

So why would this happen? *He thought for a second before the answer came to him: he had needed to remember a time when he was happy. The dog always made him happy. Tonight it had helped him survive.*

—Nicholas Miaoulis

After I read Stern's book, I discovered anthologies (Figure 11.4) of other kinds of short short stories—flash fiction (a limit of 750 words), sudden fiction (1,750 words), and a bunch of ultra-short forms like Twitterature (140 characters), drabbles (100 words), and dribbles (50 words). My students aren't that taken with the most diminutive of the short forms: their drabbles and dribbles are mostly parodies. But some welcome the longer versions, which allow more elasticity.

Once my kids understand the principles of short short narratives—of starting inside the story, creating layers of meaning, keeping it spare and mysterious, focusing on the imagery of a scene, and ending with a powerful line that turns the story—I'm less concerned about whether they write to specific word counts. As they go longer, they bring with them the micro techniques they've learned, plus two other essentials: imagination and invention. My best advice is, "Beware of going too long, into too much detail, or you'll end up tangled in the weeds of conventional main characters, predictable plots, and too much information."

A SELECTED BIBLIOGRAPHY OF SHORT SHORT STORY ANTHOLOGIES AND COLLECTIONS

Beckel, Abigail and Kathleen Rooney, eds. 2006. *Brevity and Echo: An Anthology of Short Short Stories*. Boston: Rose Metal.

Eggers, Dave. 2007. *How the Water Feels to the Fishes*. San Francisco: McSweeney's Books.

Kafka, Franz. 1987. *Franz Kafka: The Complete Stories*. Nahum Glatzer, Ed., New York: Schocken. (The "Shorter Stories" Section)

Orner, Peter. 2013. *Last Car Over the Sagamore Bridge*. New York: Little, Brown and Company.

_____. 2001. *Esther Stories*. Boston: Houghton.

Perkins-Hazuka, Christine, Tom Hazuka, and Mark Budman. 2011. *Sudden Flash Youth*. New York: Persea Books.

Shapard, Robert and James Thomas. 1986. *Sudden Fiction*. Layton, VT: Gibbs Smith.

_____. 2006. *Flash Fiction Forward*. New York: W. W. Norton.

Stern, Jerome. 1996. *Micro Fiction*. New York: W. W. Norton.

Thomas, James, Denise Thomas, and Tom Hazuka. 1992. *Flash Fiction*. New York: W. W. Norton

Ziegler, Alan, ed. 2014. *Short*. New York: Persea Books.

Figure 11.4 *A Selected Bibliography of Short Short Story Anthologies and Collections*

In a flash fiction story, Helena entered the world of dystopian fiction to imagine and invent a brave girl whose existence is against the law. The surprise ending moves the story into a new fictional genre.

I Am Number Eight

I wipe sweat from my eyes with a dirty sleeve. Flanked by Seven and Four, my little sisters, the job is easier. It's illegal for girls to work in factories like this one, but we have to take the risk. Mom's sick, and there's no money.

I glance at the security feeds. What I see chills my blood. "Girls!" I hiss. "Owls!"

Like snakes, all sixteen illegals dart for cover; the legals feign obliviousness. Peering from inside a box, clutching my sisters' hands tight, I watch a gang of boys saunter in, hands in pockets, eyes scanning the room. From afar they look like the Lost Boys from that old fairy story. Up close they are immaculate: not a hair out of place.

Finding nothing, they depart. I breathe a sigh of relief. To be found by an Owl is to never return. Stories of torture plague my mind. Squeezing my sisters' hands, I realize how lucky it was I looked up.

Weird, I think. *This was an unusual time for a scouting party. They never come after noon.* A frantic Seven interrupts my thoughts. She points to the factory clock as it screams, "Go home, ya damn illegal rats!" Our shift is over. It's obvious that the Owls are still close enough to have heard it.

Before I can think, I pull my sisters to their feet, and we sprint from the building. Aware that the Owls are probably on our tail, I look to Four, then Seven. Each nods; I understand what it means. With a glance that says everything, I let go.

Moments later I'm trapped, my back against a wall, the Owls closing in. *Why did all five follow me?* I guess I'm glad. It means Four and Seven are safe. My eyes dart around the alley like a caged animal contemplating escape. Seeing this, the Head Owl grins.

He leans in, sets his hands on my shoulders, and looks down at me. I think of Seven and Four, and courage overtakes me. "I've seen you before, Owl," I whisper, as I study my feet. "Shows just how good you are at your job." His body stiffens, and I blanch, thinking *I can't believe I dared say that.*

He grasps my chin roughly, tilting it so I'm forced to look at him. His eyes are hard as they search mine. But then he smiles. His body relaxes. I contain a gasp as his face transforms into something of unbelievable beauty.

"You're brave," he murmurs, his forehead centimeters from mine. "I like that."

From behind him, I hear, "Ha, too bad we're gonna kill the rat, eh, boss?"

Without breaking eye contact, he snaps, "Yeah . . . too bad." He releases my chin, but I can't look away.

Unholstering his gun with one hand, he uses the other to tuck a stray lock of hair behind my ear, sending a shiver down my spine. Cocking back the hammer, the Owl takes my hand in his, his grip strong and, somehow, comforting. "Too bad," he repeats. Then he pivots and shoots down every Owl behind him.

Turning back to me he says, "I wish you wouldn't call me *Owl*. My name is Judas." His fingers find mine.

—*Helena Solorzano*

Sam loved to write fiction under the influence of beloved authors. In her flash fiction "Found Objects," she channels three of her favorites, J. D. Salinger, C. S. Lewis, and Stephen King, while envisioning a new world that is hers alone.

FOUND OBJECTS

Brown canvas thumps against her thigh. The strap is too long. The bag contains Band-aids, three pigeon feathers, a hairpin, and a battered copy of *The Chronicles of Narnia*. She has turned away from 513 Elizabeth Street, afraid Mommy and Dad have hired Marcy, the horrid babysitter, in one of their fits of guilt about leaving her alone so much.

She walks past the grey jaws of the abominable Wormwood Elementary School, passes Craig on the street, and throws a Band-aid into his Styrofoam cup. "Thank you, Miss Durkin," he says, ever polite, but the familiar knot of shyness represses her reply. She drifts past the park where she plays with the pigeons and runs and turns cartwheels. When she finally reaches the zoo, she slips through the back entrance that Jerry showed her.

Her feet scuff through the forest of leaves and past the steel bars holding back impassive creatures. The snake in her stomach prevents her from shouting when loud, dirty people poke the animals with sticks. She strides to her destination, reaches it, leans against the bars, and grips them like a prisoner yearning for freedom.

"Aslan." The name she has given him flutters into his jail on a whisper. Her eyes mourn the lion. They take in the gum matted in his mane, the ribs showing through his knotted fur. "We're going today."

His liberty is blocked only by a rusty padlock. She gropes for the hairpin in her bag, traps it with small fingers, and twists it in the keyhole. The gate gapes open.

Aslan lifts his blocky tan head. He starts towards the open door, slow at first, and then he bounds towards life. There are screams, but she doesn't hear them. She waits on the other side.

"Aslan," she trills in her eight-and-three-quarters voice. "We're gonna be free."

—*Samantha Herter*

Payton's sudden fiction, "Switched," takes advantage of the slightly longer form to use dialogue to establish tone and theme. Her story is as intense and troubling as a dream.

SWITCHED

"And," said Amy, as she blew a strand of hair out of her eyes, "Delia Smith has the prettiest dress. She loves chocolate, but she's trying not to eat too much—says it'll ruin her figure. She hates being stuck in a painting. She wants to get out."

"Amy, if you don't stop inventing tales, I'm going to call your mother," Teacher reprimanded. The hall was dim and silent except for the muffled voices of children from behind doors. Amy leaned against a locker and gazed up at Teacher, her eyes wide with bewilderment.

"You're a very bad influence on the other children. What if they start making up stories, too? You're a big girl—five years old. You shouldn't be telling lies anymore."

"But I'm not making up stories," Amy insisted, her bottom lip quivering. "Anywhere I go, the pictures come alive. Dr. Boo—he's one of the paintings in my room—says it's me who makes the paintings alive. He says I must be *magical*. Me! Magical! He told me whenever I say my words, photos and paintings will jump out of their frames. All I need to do is say them. But I won't. He gets very angry. He says the people in the pictures should be let out."

"Amy—"

"But I'm scared to let all the pictures out. I keep thinking of the dinosaur painting above my bed. He's all right in the painting, but I don't want him to come alive!"

"Amy, I can't think what's wrong with you," Teacher said. "I'm definitely going to speak with your parents. Now, we need to get back to class. Come on." Teacher grabbed Amy's arm and dragged her into the classroom, where two dozen children were occupied with Lego towers and baby dolls.

"No! Noooo!" screamed Amy. "You're hurting my arm. Let go! Let go, or I'll let them out. I swear I will. You won't like it if they come out."

The kindergartners looked up from their Legos and dolls. They stared as Teacher slapped her hand over Amy's mouth and knelt at the child's eye level. "Amy," she growled. "Stop it. Stop or I'll . . . I'll . . ."

Amy's eyes were wild, but she stopped crying. Teacher removed her hand. Amy quivered on the spot for a moment. Then she began to spin.

Her eyes traveled over the classroom walls. She stared at the posters of U.S. presidents, the print of Christopher Columbus, the black and white photograph of Martin Luther King, Jr. Her eyes pierced the children's paintings of Halloween mummies, ghosts, and vampires. Only after she had studied all the images did she begin to yell.

Teacher leapt at Amy. Her hand gripped Amy's arm like a vise. Amy was screeching words but in no language Teacher recognized. Then Teacher was yanked backwards, still clutching Amy's arm. She heard the children cry out in terror, smelled smoke, and saw a flash of brightest light.

Later that afternoon, when Mr. Charles wheeled his cart into classroom K3, he groaned at the mess that was left behind. Books, dolls, Legos, and art materials were strewn across the carpet. After cleaning up the toys, he swept crayon stubs, crumpled paper, and ash from the floor. *Ash*, he thought. *That's strange.* He emptied the trash and wiped down the tables. He was about to shut the door behind him when he heard a rustle from the other end of the room and glimpsed a dart of movement out of the corner of his eye. Mr. Charles turned back to the classroom.

Everything was perfectly still and in order. The toys were in their bins and the blackboard dark and blank. Evening light from the windows fell over the maps and building blocks. Mr. Charles' eyes traveled up the walls of the room. *Weird*, he thought.

The paintings had changed. The sheets of construction paper that had once depicted Halloween monsters now portrayed incredibly realistic children. Mr. Charles frowned. Some of the frames held nothing but blank canvas. He could have sworn the picture in the corner had been of Christopher Columbus, yet now its frame was empty. He heard a thump behind him. He wheeled around again, but everything was still. An eerie silence filled the room. Mr. Charles fled, slamming the door behind him.

He hadn't noticed the painting that hung directly above the teacher's desk. If he had, he would have seen a woman and a little girl. The woman's mouth was stretched in horror as she gripped the girl's arm. The little girl was laughing.

—*Payton Sullivan*

In his first piece of sudden fiction, Avery drops hints for an attentive reader to pick up and put together about the secret of Bobby, his main character. Avery tells *just enough*.

DNA

Bobby was ten years old when he first saw the man. He was sprinting out of school in the normal 2:45 rush and glimpsed a figure by a lamp post. The man was tall, gaunt, and wore a scruffy beard. His red sweatshirt was dirty, and his jeans rode up above his knobby ankles, making his torn sneakers blindingly obvious. Bobby didn't think much of it. Maybe the man was waiting to pick up his child from school?

He saw the man for the second time on the way back from Little League practice. His mother was working at the diner, so he had to walk home. Bobby was shuffling off the diamond, laughing with a friend, when he caught sight of the man again, leaning on the chain-link fence. His arms were crossed, and one ankle overlapped the other. He wore a heavy sweater this time, despite the sweltering June heat. Their eyes met, and Bobby thought he saw a smile start to inch across the man's face before he wiped the corner of his eye with a dirty finger. Bobby quickened his pace. When he glanced back over his shoulder, the man was watching him.

The third and final encounter came on a Saturday, the one day his mom had off from the diner. Bobby was outside, rolling around on a beat up skateboard he'd picked up at a yard sale. His mom was cleaning the house, and he was trying to stay out of the way. By the time he noticed he had company, the man was directly across the road from the end of their driveway. The man's hand flinched in what Bobby supposed was a greeting. He waved back, but a sense of unease swelled in his throat. He picked up his board and tried to stroll casually toward his front porch. When he got inside, he closed the door and pushed the dead-bolt into place. Circling around to the dim living room, Bobby knelt on the sagging couch, peeled back a fraying curtain, and peered out. The man was staring at their front door. Then, suddenly, he turned and loped away. A sense of déjà vu slithered in a corner of Bobby's mind, but he brushed it away.

That winter, back at school, Bobby leaned against a brick wall, crossed his arms, and lapped one ankle over the other. He was hanging out with Jamie at recess. Bobby didn't have gloves, so he curled his fists in his sleeves, a final defense against the freezing air.

"Man, it's brutal out here," he complained.

"I know," Jamie agreed. "But it's gonna be perfect for ice fishing soon. You ever been out to the lake?"

"No, I've never gone ice fishing," Bobby admitted.

"Oh. I go all the time with my dad."

Bobby fell silent and studied his scuffed shoes. Luckily, the bell split the frigid air, summoning them back to class. Jamie ran ahead, but Bobby, cold as he was, moved slowly, savoring his last seconds of freedom.

"Thompson! Pick up the pace!" the recess monitor screeched. Bobby ran the last few yards.

That afternoon, when Bobby got home, he fetched himself a pack of peanut butter crackers and plopped down in front of the TV. His thumb twitched, and the screen awoke. Mindlessly, he surfed the twelve channels they could afford. He was ready to turn it off when a story caught his attention.

"A tragic car accident has left one dead and two injured," a reporter shrouded in a winter coat droned. "The driver and passenger of the vehicle are being transported to Maine Medical as we speak. The cause of the accident is uncertain, but speed and dangerous conditions appear to be factors. The victim, a pedestrian named Robert Thompson, appears to have been homeless. The only ID found was an expired driver's license."

A picture flashed on the screen, and an overwhelming feeling of anguish flooded Bobby's senses. He turned off the television and stared at the blank screen. He had a lot of questions. The problem was, he didn't know where to start.

—Avery Genus

There is a coda to this chapter. A few years ago, Howard Gardner and one of his doctoral students at Harvard, Katie Davis, launched an investigation of the impact of digital technologies on U.S. adolescents—how "today's youth navigate identity, intimacy, and imagination." To do so, they sought samples of student fiction written over the previous two decades.

By that time, CTL's archives included twenty years' worth of *Acorns*, our school literary magazine. I invited a team from Harvard to borrow and peruse back issues of *Acorns* and analyze the short stories my students had written. For the sake of consistency, they focused on the years of contemporary realism and omitted the more recent micro fiction. They also looked elsewhere, at fiction written by high school students and examples of student artwork from the same period.

The way the Harvard researchers coded the writing samples is unique and intriguing. To assess short fiction for evidence of imagination, they characterized the plots as *everyday* stories about events that could occur on any day at any time of the year; *everyday with a twist* stories, which have mostly realistic plots but with at least one moment of action that couldn't happen every day; and *not everyday stories*, which feature impossible events or elements of fantasy. It doesn't take much imagination to predict how the researchers coded CTL's contemporary realism.

In their book *The App Generation* (2013), Howard Gardner and Katie Davis classify almost 90 percent of my students' stories as *everyday*. In fact, they use the adjective *mundane* to describe the plots. The paucity of invention and genre play was obvious, and it was my doing. I wrote to Howard about how my method had constrained kids' imaginations and possibly skewed his and Katie's conclusions. He kindly replied, "You properly remind us that every finding reflects the particular sample from which one draws," and he assured me that they drew most of their conclusions from the comparisons of high school writing. Still, to be busted in public by Howard Gardner for years of teaching the wrong genre is a humbling experience.

Not everyday is the perfect guideline for teaching fiction at the middle school level. My students invent people, places, and scenarios. They draw on their voluminou experiences as readers of all kinds of stories, as well as the vicarious knowledge they acquire along the way. They tap skills as poets to compress events, select diction, create imagery, suggest themes, and craft killer titles and end lines. They surprise and delight themselves, one another, and me as they envision many worlds through the abundant windows of their imaginations. It took me thirty years, but at last I became a teacher of the hypothetical, the unpredictable, the *not* everyday.

CHAPTER 12

TAKING CARE OF BUSINESS

Problems make good subjects.

—DONALD MURRAY

Problems are my bread and butter as a writer. In books and articles I identify problems of teaching, describe solutions, interpret results, and reach conclusions. I explain. I argue. I try to persuade. The big-tent name for writing that addresses problems is *exposition*. Most of my day-to-day writing is expository prose. It's my niche, and I'm not alone.

So far, one CTL alum has become a full-time writer of fiction. Among the others, an overwhelming number craft exposition every day. On the job they write reviews, press releases, advertising copy, blogs, lectures, submissions to academic journals, legal briefs, closing arguments, petitions, grant proposals, research reports, position papers, websites, ship's logs, lesson plans, curricula, progress reports, data analyses, business plans, recipes and menus, and articles and books about the environment. Their skills as writers are prized. I remember reading that the higher someone's salary, the more writing he or she does on the job. I believe it. Employers, clients, customers, and readers in general value writers who use precise language, present clear information, engage our interest, and help us untangle the problems of everyday living.

As an English teacher, I struggled with how to introduce exposition in genuine ways. It's easy and obvious to ask kids to write poems, narratives, and criticism—literary genres belong in an English class. It's harder to push out of the classroom into the world of problems and pull it back into the writing workshop in ways that feel purposeful and authentic—that bypass the bogus genres of reports and five-paragraph essays. And since my kids already know so much as writers about process, diction, specifics, tone, theme, leads and conclusions, titles, even paragraphing, I have to figure out how to build on this knowledge, so their expository prose will be as clear, coherent, enjoyable, and voiced as their poems, memoirs, short fiction, and letter-essays.

Letter-essays are a strong bridge into exposition in my workshop; from them, I launch a genre study of reviews. I tackle essays in the context of problems my students identify in their lives and the world. And I teach firsthand research and reportage in the form of advocacy journalism and profiles. Each of these is an authentic expository genre, each is similar enough to a genre I write that I can hand over lessons about it to my kids, and each can find a real audience.

Something happens with every piece of exposition my students produce. It goes public on CTL's book blog, Amazon.com, or other websites. Or it's published in *Teen Ink* magazine, a local newspaper, the school's newsletter or literary journal, a class magazine, or as part of a contest. It reaches an intended audience, and it gives readers something to think about.

I don't teach expository prose to prepare students for the essays on standardized tests. The version of exposition called for by these prompts is so odd and specific it's a genre unto itself and should be taught and practiced in the week or two before the test, using the test maker's sample prompts and under test-taking conditions. It's not necessary to devote a school year to test prep. But teachers do need to familiarize students with the format and demands of the writing task—to help them tease out and name the features of the writing samples provided by the test maker, create a protocol for writing one that includes writing off-the-page, produce a couple under timed conditions, and analyze their results against the list of genre features they created.

I teach exposition so students will learn how to make writing *work* for them in the world—advocate for causes they believe in, seek answers to questions that baffle them, shed light, weigh in, and clear the way. To paraphrase Murray, problems make great subjects, especially for young writers. Expository genres teach them how to articulate ideas, gather evidence, send both out into the world, and try to have an influence there.

REVIEWS

Although a well-written review does a lot of things, it has to do one big thing—answer the question *Is this book, film, television show, play, concert, CD, restaurant, exhibit, or dance performance worth someone's money and time?* A good review convinces readers through the power of the writing.

Good reviewers have deep knowledge of their subject areas. They voice opinions based on standards they've developed over time, and they cite evidence specific to the conventions of a genre. For these reasons, I narrowed the genres my students review to narrative forms they're familiar with: books, movies, and TV programs. By winter, when I launch a genre study of reviews, they've written four or five letter-essays about books and learned the basics of literary criticism. They can comment on plot structure and credibility, observe character development, and notice a writer's style, plus they've learned how to unpack theme. One winter, when the kids who wished to wrote reviews of CDs, I found that the learning curve was too steep for them to acquire sufficient background knowledge and vocabulary to be able to answer the one big question. Since then, we've stuck with narrative forms.

In the two weeks leading up to the genre study, I collect reviews of books, movies, and television shows so I can marinate the kids in current, relevant examples. In the beginning, I clipped reviews from an eclectic mix of publications, from *People* to *Rolling Stone;* then I realized that some of these were more postcards or fan letters than serious critiques. Today I sample just three sources.

For my money, the daily *New York Times*, the Sunday *New York Times Book Review*, and *The New Yorker* contain the best-written, most informative, most reliable reviews. Critics who write for these publications are strong writers and experts in their fields. Rather than introduce the review genre with less than stellar examples, it's worth it for teachers to purchase or download the *New York Times* and *New Yorker* for a couple of weeks and select reviews that are kid-friendly—not too long or scholarly and written in response to books, movies, and TV shows that middle schoolers will be interested in. I also seek a balance of raves, pans, and mixed reviews, so students get a sense of the range of positions a reviewer can take.

I photocopy and collate a packet that contains three each of the three kinds of reviews. Then I launch the study.

THE LESSON

There are lots of ways someone can write for a living besides becoming a poet, memoirist, or novelist. *Reviewing* is another occupation for a writer. Good reviews are some of my favorite reading material.

When a book is published, I'm eager to learn what the reviewers who work at the *New York Times* think about it. I won't go to a movie until I've read the critical takes on it in the *Times* and *The New Yorker*. And I count on reviewers to clue me in to the television shows I should check out.

Reviewers have a demanding audience. We expect to learn from them—about a particular book, film, or show, but also something about its genre, context, and creation. We expect expertise. And we expect advice about how we should spend our precious time and dollars. The best reviewers have opinions, support them with anecdotes and examples, try to convince us, and, along the way, inform and entertain us, too.

I've put together a collection for each of you of well-written reviews I think you'll enjoy. They include three each of critics' takes on books, movies, and TV shows. Please turn to the next three pages in the back section of your handbook, where you respond to prose readings. Then write these three headings, one to a page: Features of Book Reviews; Features of Movie Reviews; Features of TV Reviews.

For weekend homework, spend at least an hour reading, highlighting, and taking notes on the reviews. You'll be looking for and marking the *kinds of things reviewers write about and how they write them.* Afterward, under the three headings, create lists of the features you noticed and highlighted.

Questions? Comments? Observations? Happy reading—I think you'll enjoy this writing. It's smart, interesting, often funny, and helpful to readers, moviegoers, and TV viewers.

As Monday's minilesson, I ask kids to divide themselves into three groups, one dedicated to each genre, and collaborate to create a list of its features. Afterward, when the minilesson circle convenes, each group reports out to me as I take fast notes on overhead transparencies. After a group finishes, I open up its list to the rest of the class: "The kids who analyzed book reviews did a great job. Check out your own list of features. Did they miss anything crucial about reviews of books?"

This is a long minilesson but worth it. It puts kids inside a genre that's new to them, generates specific criteria they can use as guidelines when they draft reviews of their own, and allows them to learn from and with one another. Figures 12.1, 12.2, and 12.3 represent three features lists, which I typed up and gave to kids to add to their writing–reading handbooks the following day.

FEATURES OF AN EFFECTIVE BOOK REVIEW

- Starts with an inviting title
- Tells the author's name and the title of the book
- Takes a tone—a clear point of view about the book and its author, while avoiding *I* and *my*
- Is written in the present tense
- Provides an overview of the plot that sets up the problem but leaves a reader wanting more
- Tells about the main character and his or her problem or situation
- Compares the book to others by this author, others with similar themes by other authors, or movies with a similar plot, in order to make a point about the book or put it in context
- Describes or hints at what the book is *really* about, theme-wise
- Comments on: character development, structure or chapter set-up, descriptions, narrator or narrative voice, dialogue, humor, plot, plausibility, pacing, form, tone, lead, conclusion, genre
- Uses quotes or excerpts to capture the author's style or the book's situations, themes, and characters
- Starts with a deliberate lead that draws a reader in with a question, strong statement, comparison, overview, etc.
- Ends with a deliberate conclusion that has an attitude and wraps things up
- Describes elegantly, using sensory adjectives and verbs
- Tells if the book is a prequel, sequel, or part of a series or trilogy
- Tells what the book is missing or has too much of
- Hints at the ending but doesn't reveal it
- Suggests that a reader of the review either reads or avoids the book—spends or saves his or her time and money

Figure 12.1 *Features of an Effective Book Review*

FEATURES OF AN EFFECTIVE MOVIE REVIEW

- Starts with a strong title that draws a reader in
- Has a voiced lead—starts with an attitude—that includes the title of the film and name of its director
- Is written in the present tense and avoids first-person and second-person voice: no *I*, *my*, or *you*
- Synopsizes the plot
- States the genre of the movie
- Gives its running time
- Gives its official rating and explains the reason(s) behind it
- Touches on the film's theme(s)
- Tells who would like the film
- Quotes lines from the film
- Introduces the major characters and, in parentheses, the actors who play them
- Describes the personality, motive, and/or problem of the main character(s)
- Discusses the strengths and weaknesses of individual actors or their acting styles
- Compares the actors' performances to previous roles
- Talks about the director:
  - his idea or vision
  - how she conveyed the theme
  - how long he worked on the movie
  - her past work/other movies
- If it's an older film, may mention its cost, profit, box office success, and original release date or cites any awards or nominations it received
- Compares the film to movies, books, TV shows, etc., that have a similar plot or theme
- Speaks in a strong voice—jokes and sarcasm
- Gives evidence for the reviewer's opinions
- Tells where and when the movie is set
- Evaluates the film's plausibility, pace, special effects, costumes, mood, cinematography
- Describes what the reviewer felt like when watching the movie
- Mentions the screenwriters and critiques the script
- Tells what the script is based on or if it's an original screenplay
- Alerts the film-goers to any holes in the plot or other problems with the screenplay, like clichéd characters or predictable plot turns
- Describes the reviewer's hopes for the film
- Has a deliberate conclusion that conveys an attitude, wraps up the review, and implies or states a recommendation about whether the reader should spend time and money on this movie

Figure 12.2 *Features of an Effective Movie Review*

FEATURES OF AN EFFECTIVE REVIEW OF A TELEVISION SHOW

- Starts with a strong title that draws a reader in

- Has a voiced lead: begins with an attitude

- Maintains a definite opinion, voice, and tone, but without *I*, *my*, or *you*

- Is written in the present tense

- Tells the genre of the show—sitcom, reality, horror, melodrama, drama, anthology, mini-series, sketch humor, documentary, fake news, etc.

- Mentions the date the show premieres and its airtime

- Tells what network it's on

- Names the producer and/or creator

- Connects the show to other projects by its creator

- Describes the main character(s) and his/her/their problem or situation

- Names the characters and, in parentheses, the actors who portray them

- Might review roles previously played by the actors

- Rates the show in terms of its suitability for audiences of different ages

- Tells what it's based on if it's not an original series

- Tells where it's filmed

- Assesses the actors' performances and appearances

- Touches on the theme(s) of the show

- Tells who would like the show

- Compares it to other shows, past and present

- Alludes to books, movies, or lyrics

- Describes the quality of the screenplay or script: dialogue, plot premise, predictability, clichés, believability, character relationships

- Quotes revealing dialogue or critiques the quality of the dialogue

- Describes the reviewer's expectations for the program's future

- Tells what season this is for the program

- Lists any awards or nominations it received

- Assesses the show's production values

- Has a deliberate conclusion that conveys an attitude, wraps up the review, and indicates whether the show is worth a viewer's time and attention

Figure 12.3 *Features of an Effective Review of a Television Show*

In the next minilesson, I introduce the requirement that each student writes two reviews. Everyone produces one book review to add to the school's book blog "You Gotta Read This" as a service to other kids and their teachers who depend on the tastes and insights of CTL readers. The focus of their other review is up to them. In terms of deciding what to review, the best way, as always, is to select from among options rather than grinding away at the first prospect a writer comes up with.

THE LESSON

Please turn to the next clean page in the territories section of your handbook. You're going to record three headings on this page. Please leave six lines between a heading and the one that follows it. The headings are: Five Books I Might Like to Review; Five Movies I Might Like to Review; Five TV Shows I Might Like to Review.

Tonight for homework, take home your reading folder, which has your reading record for the year stapled inside. Consider the titles you finished or abandoned, and jot down at least five under the first heading that you might enjoy critiquing in a rave, a pan, or a mixed review. It's fine if the list includes books you wrote about in letter-essays, and more than fine if you want to bring the tone and ideas of your letter-essays to the book reviews you craft.

Under the next heading, record the titles of five movies that intrigue you, for good reasons or bad. Whether you choose current releases or movies you can rent, they should be films you're able to view *more than once*, so you have opportunities to note your observations and ideas. That means if it's currently in theaters, you'll need to see it twice. If it's a film that's available on DVD or Netflix, you'll need to watch the DVD or tune into Netflix twice. In short, as you make your list of five possibilities, take into consideration the fact that a single viewing will not be enough for a detailed review.

Finally, under the last heading, brainstorm the titles of five series that are on TV right now. They don't have to be current productions, as long as they're on major networks or basic cable on at least a weekly basis. So, for example, the old *Andy Griffith Show* is a possibility, since it's shown weekly or even nightly. But *The Voice* is on hiatus right now, which means you won't be able to gather the kind of firsthand observations that informative reviews depend upon. Finally, if your family doesn't watch television, you can just skip this category.

Tomorrow you'll have a chance to meet in groups of three, think out loud about the possibilities you generated, bounce ideas off one another, and prepare to narrow down and choose the book and movie, book and TV show, or book and book you'll take on as a reviewer.

The following day I introduce a process for writing a review, one I developed with students over years of teaching the genre and based on what I do when I write book reviews and forewords. It relies heavily on writing off-the-page—to gather specifics, find a lead that gives direction to the draft, plan and order the information, and wrap up the review.

A PROCESS FOR WRITING A REVIEW

- Review the master list of features we created for your genre.
- Skim the book or watch the film or TV show again and write off-the-page about it. Use the list of genre features we created to prompt specific opinions and observations.
- Research online what you don't know: also, consult the case of a DVD or the copyright page of a book.
- When you're filled up with information and opinions, begin the draft by experimenting with different leads until you find *the one* that takes an attitude, invites a reader, gives direction to the rest of the review, and makes you want to keep writing.
- Organize your writing off-the-page—with numbers, arrows, boxes, etc.—to help you pre-see a structure for the rest of your draft.
- Use the full name of the author/director/creator the first time you mention him or her; thereafter it's by last name only.
- Describe the book, film, or television program in the *present tense*.
- As you pull information from your writing off-the-page, give each kind of information its own paragraph, and keep your paragraphs friendly.
- Avoid *I, my, me,* and *you*. Instead, for the subjects of your sentences, consider:
  - the title of the book/movie/TV show
  - *This book . . .; This novel . . . ; This movie . . .*
  - the name of the author, director, or creator
  - the names of characters or actors
  - third-person pronouns: *he, she, his, her*
  - the theme, purpose, or aim of the book/movie/TV show
  - craft elements: the characters, author's style, focus, plot, story line, premise, beginning, end, genre, setting, conflict, production values, camera work, special effects, acting, etc.
  - implicit opinions: *It's not surprising that . . . ; The best part is . . . ; _____ makes this book _____; The only . . . ; The reason . . . ; The problem . . .*
  - *we, us, (a) reader(s), (a) viewer(s), teens, fans of _____*
- Just as you experimented off-the-page with leads, play with conclusions until you find an ending that wraps up the review and leaves a reader convinced and satisfied.
- If you get stuck, reread the reviews in your prose folder for inspiration.

- Don't lose sight of the goals of a review: stay true to the feelings you experienced while you read or watched and take seriously your responsibility to potential readers and viewers about how they should spend their money and time.
- When you feel done, take a two-day walk-away to gain perspective. Then reread a review from the appropriate genre, along with the master list of features, to get back into the review zone. Next, read your own review as a critic, with a pen in your hand: Are you in the ballpark? What do you need to do to make your review clear, coherent, convincing, and ready for the mind of a discerning reader?

This is a good time to talk with students about leads and reiterate the lesson I taught about beginnings back when they wrote their memoirs. With any kind of writing about information, whether it's personal narrative, a review or essay, or reportage, *the lead comes first*. Donald Murray once wrote, "I *never* proceed without an opening that I think will produce a good piece of writing. That's the only never in my personal toolbox" (1999). It has become the only never in my toolbox, too.

I hope other teachers won't weary of my harping on the importance of experimenting with leads and writing off-the-page. But I know firsthand the effect both have on my writing—how they make it possible—and I've seen the same effect on kids' expository prose. Generative writing-before-writing starts them off with a quantity of ideas and establishes the tone, direction, and structure of a draft. This groundwork makes a difficult genre doable. So does a deliberate lead. Figure 12.4 is a list of types of beginnings that one of my classes and I teased out from a collection of professional reviews. I'm sure there are others, but this document, intended for inclusion in students' handbooks, suggests a range and relieves some of the pressure of the blank page.

A topic I bring up in another minilesson is how to write a personal opinion without using first-person singular pronouns. Unless it's a celebrity reviewer, as is sometimes the case with the lead review in the *New York Times Book Review*, the convention is to forego *I*. A second-person *you* is also rare. Instead, reviewers state opinions by structuring their sentences so the subjects are aspects of the work, not the writer's perceptions of it. The list of ways to start sentences in "A Process for Writing a Review" is another that kids and I created by researching professional reviews. This is good preparation for the academic writing of high school and college as well as prose they might someday produce on the job. In another minilesson, I reteach the conventions for capitalizing and indicating titles.

As students are drafting and revising their reviews, I continue to reproduce and distribute newly published ones, to keep them in a review state of mind. When individuals think they're finished, they take a two-day walk-away and start their second review or a new poem. Before they return, I ask that they reread a model from the appropriate genre and the list of genre features and only then revisit their own reviews, pens in hand.

At the end of the study, I publish an issue of *CTLRBMT*, or the *Center for Teaching and Learning Review of Books, Movies, and TV Shows*, and we enjoy a class reading. In addition,

---

POSSIBLE LEADS FOR A REVIEW OF A BOOK/MOVIE/TV SHOW

- A quote from the _____ that shows something
- A question about the _____ (and an answer?)
- A strong positive statement (with brief evidence)
- A strong negative statement (with brief evidence)
- A brief plot synopsis of the _____, conveyed with a tone or attitude
- A metaphor or simile that conveys an attitude about the _____
- A list of features of the _____ that makes a point about it
- A bit of history behind the _____
- The approach taken by the author/director/creator, or his or her vision for the _____
- Advice to the reader/viewer
- A comparison of the _____ to other _____
- A comment about how the _____ does (or doesn't) fit within a particular genre
- A comparison with the original version of the _____
- Who the target audience for the _____ might be
- A highlight or an intriguing part of the _____
- A comment about how the _____ exemplifies (or doesn't) a cliché
- A sarcastic comment about the _____
- The likelihood of the _____ receiving an award or nomination

NECESSARY TO INCLUDE IN THE LEAD:

- The name of the author/director/creator
- The title of the book/film/television program

Always begin by playing with alternative beginnings. The lead you like best will fuel you as a writer and give direction to the rest of your review.

Figure 12.4 *Possible Leads for a Review of a Book/Movie/TV Show*

students post reviews of books on the school blog and comment back and forth on one another's critiques. Some kids, with parental permission, post on Amazon.com.

The movie and television reviews I've included here as examples won't be timely for long; I hope the reviews of books will stay relevant for a while. All of them represent convincing pans and raves, starting with Emma's paean to the TV show *The Office* and Tess' pan of the last season of *Scrubs*.

DOING WHAT IT SHOULDN'T

The Office shouldn't be so captivating. A dead-end day job at Dunder Mifflin, a paper supplier in Scranton, Pennsylvania, is a mundane subject. Yet *The Office* enthralls with its blunt humor, its outrageous characters, and their puzzling relationships.

The Office is streamlined to pack maximum humor into its twenty-odd minutes by taking the form of a mockumentary. This interview style cuts out the clumsiness of a narrator and replaces it with opportunities for the characters' opinions. It also leaves room for the audience to observe and judge, as the characters don't always tell the truth. The mockumentary format embeds the context seamlessly through realistic dialogue.

The characters are what really pull the pieces of *The Office* together. They make the unbelievable situations possible. The interweaving relationships among the characters provide for funny problems and constant tension. The actors in *The Office* have fantastic comedic timing and deliver their lines with perfect emotion. Each character has his or her own dramatic personality that brings each little situation to a boiling point; this is what keeps the plot alive.

The Office relies on situation comedy. Everything funny about the show comes from the actions and reactions of the characters. The writers have a clear sense of each individual, as the dialogue is consistent to each personality. But they keep things interesting by throwing a wrench or two into the plot every once in a while. On occasion they mess with *The Office* a little too much for this viewer's liking. But just when it seems the writers are about to jump the shark, they restore normality.

Jenna Fischer and John Krasinski star as Pam and Jim, the most adorable couple on NBC, and they provide the romance and sane perspective that *The Office* needs. Their quirky sense of humor and on-going jokes are a winning part of each episode. Steve Carrell plays the perfect, ignorant, funny boss who wants to fit in too badly. His incompetence, along with an office full of employees who recognize it, makes for a hilarious show.

There is a British TV show also entitled *The Office*, which the American version is based on. The UK version features incredibly talented Ricky Gervais as the boss, but it has a different take on the relationships among the characters. Ricky Gervais is the creator and producer of the U.S. version, too, but has a smaller role here.

The Office is shown on Thursdays at 9 pm as part of NBC's comedy night. It's one of the rare shows that keeps viewers on their toes. We never know what will happen next, and that keeps us coming back for more. *The Office* breaks the mold of situation comedy and does what it shouldn't: it captivates.

—*Emma Moorhead*

SCRUBS REINCARNATED

ABC has revived *Scrubs* for yet another season in an obvious attempt to squeeze the last bit of profit out of the former hit show. The beloved Sacred Heart Hospital was torn down, and a teaching hospital has been built where JD, Turk, Dr. Cox, and others teach a new group of med students. Obviously, the expression "too much of a good thing" means nothing to ABC.

While it would be near-impossible to compete with the original *Scrubs* cast, this show seems to be so out of ideas that the "new" characters are exactly like the old ones. Lucy is the new JD: a naïve, small-town girl who wants to help people but is completely lacking in the nerdy humor that made us love JD. Meanwhile, JD is so far from reality, this viewer can't be the only one wondering what he's on. Drew is a second-time med student with a dark sense of humor that screams Dr. Cox. Thankfully, Coxie is still ranting and torturing interns: not new, but hysterical as always. Drew, a funny, likeable character, is too much like Dr. Cox to be appreciated. Finally, the only original character is Cole, a spoiled rich boy who thinks he's God's gift to women. New? Yes. Annoying and clichéd? Definitely.

As for romance, Dr. Turk falls a little flat without his better half, Carla. She is the new show's greatest character loss, apart from The Janitor. Thankfully, a new dynamic duo is there to take their place, Denise and Drew. Dr. Denise is a returning character from season eight with a tough girl attitude and a sick sense of humor. Their adorable love/hate relationship is based on their shared hatred of "touchy-feely crap." But we watch them fall in love anyway. It's by far the best and funniest new aspect of the show, even if it's too similar to Cox and Jordan's relationship.

The pressures of med school, relationships, and patients they just can't help are some of the challenges the new doctors face. The actors do a reasonable job portraying the characters, but the new show misses the personality of the old one. From minor characters like Nurse Roberts to familiar hangouts like the cafeteria, the details of Sacred Heart gave life to the old version. Removed from their context, JD, Turk, and Dr. Cox lose half their personalities.

The wit of *Scrubs* and its quirky charm were beloved, but all good things must come to an end, and this premise has been sucked dry.

—*Tess Hinchman*

These three book reviews also represent raves and a pan. Max loved *I Am the Messenger* by Marcus Zusak. Sophia was appalled by Lauren Myracle's *Peace, Love, and Baby Ducks* when she began to read it but decided to stick with it so she could criticize it. Abbie's review of *Before I Fall* by Lauren Oliver provides an interesting contrast to Sophia's, as she analyzes how Oliver avoided the clichés of y.a. fiction that ruined Myracle's novel for Sophia.

THE THINGS THAT HAPPEN TO CAB DRIVERS THESE DAYS

Nothing ever happens to Ed Kennedy, a young cab driver. He does the same thing every day. When he's not working, he's at his friend Marcus' house with his other buds, where they play cards, something Ed isn't good at. He hasn't got one talent—echoing his mother's dialogue (**** you, Ed, you good for nothing . . .")—in this dark but hopeful novel, *I Am the Messenger* by Markus Zusak.

Things change when Ed arrives home late one night to find two strange men in his house eating meat pie. They force him to become someone called the "messenger" but answer few of his questions about his new role.

Then a playing card arrives in the mail; written on it are three addresses, and next to each address a specific time of day. Ed realizes what he must do. He arrives at each address at the specified time, witnesses both horrible and beautiful things, and always manages to help. Ed goes around town healing those who are depressed, patching up the wounded, making those whose problems he witnesses feel better, and, essentially, becoming a hero.

Zusak expresses Ed's thoughts and feelings with determination and hopefulness. He fills his main character with humor that brings a comforting, warm blanket to all the darkness, seriousness, and strangeness of the rest of the book. Apart from Ed's thoughts and feelings, the dialogue is also extremely realistic, filled with Zusak's magical humor that makes his characters so believable. This novel's darkness and its power to move the reader echo another Zusak, *The Book Thief*, which is about Nazi Germany. But the humor in *I Am the Messenger* puts this book in a category of its own.

The chapters are set up to echo the mystery of who is sending Ed the playing cards, and the book is divided into four parts. Each chapter represents a playing card, from ace to king, and the parts are titled with the names of the suits of cards: diamonds, clubs, spades, hearts.

This book is a ten out of ten, including the conclusion. It ties all the strings together, and Zusak uses humor here as well, creating a truly perfect ending. Readers, be sure to turn the page when you finish the book and check out the author's photograph. Then go back and reread the last few pages.

This is a novel for both boys and girls, though for ages twelve and up only because of the language and content. *I Am the Messenger* is serious, and could be depressing, but its humor, themes, and the way it ends on a note of hope for all of us make it a must-read.

—*Maxim Jordan*

UGLY DUCKLING

Lauren Myracle, did you want readers to skim your clichéd new novel *Peace, Love, and Baby Ducks*? Did you purposely make the characters flat? Why did you waste your time writing a novel that every seventh-grade girl has already read a million times?

This book is yet another story of a teenage girl living a complicated existence with petty girls and hot boys in a rich-kid school. Gawky sixteen-year-old Carly goes to a private Catholic school, Holy Redeemer, with her fifteen-year-old sister, Anna. Carly is surrounded by perfect Barbie-doll types who don't give her weird wardrobe and stay-true-to-herself personality a second glance. Anna has always been Carly's number one supporter, but things start to change when Anna grows a curvy silhouette and a moody personality. Boys at school take notice of this hot new Anna. As a result, Carly becomes jealous of her drop-dead gorgeous sister. But she has more important things to worry about, like the mysterious new hottie, Cole.

Myracle doesn't include one original idea in this y.a. novel, which makes the characters' emotions feel both unconvincing and predictable. Readers will feel lost because there is no protagonist convincing enough to agree with and no antagonist conniving enough to hate. This is fine for readers who like to be left wanting more. But those of us who want to develop *with* the characters and become a more intelligent reader will pick up a novel by A.S. King instead.

Throughout the plot, the relationship between Carly and Anna is bumpy. One minute they're BSFL (best sisters for life) and the next they don't want to look at each other. This constant tension is confusing for the reader and not necessary to the plot. In addition to the sister conflicts, Myracle includes random problems to try to keep readers engaged, but it just creates a distraction from the cheesiness of the ending.

Rodger is the only enjoyable character in the novel. He has been Carly's best friend ever since he enrolled at Holy Redeemer. His simple gestures and meaningful dialogue make it clear that he likes Carly. Unfortunately Rodger appears only occasionally in the story. This is a drag, because he's Myracle's best-crafted character and, honestly, the only reason any reader should continue reading the novel.

The theme of *Peace, Love, and Baby Ducks* is a cliché: be true to yourself and march to the beat of your own drum. But the book ends so abruptly that rereading the ending is a necessity if a readers wants to take away anything at all.

Overall, Lauren Myracle leaves readers disappointed. Her writing style is clumsy, the plot is old, and her theme overused and tired. Readers, don't waste time or money on *Peace, Love, and Baby Ducks*.

—*Sophia Stafford*

GROUNDHOG DAY FOR TEENAGE GIRLS

It's not a new concept: mean girl gets into a terrible accident, relives the same day over and over again, realizes her wicked ways, and finds redemption. I've seen multiple ads for movies and books with basically the same plot. But *Before I Fall*, Lauren Oliver's debut novel, somehow manages not to come across as worn-out and predictable, but beautiful and moving. Oliver accomplished this daunting task through poetry-like prose, a realistic narrative, and never letting her characters seem black or white, even the mean ones.

The book takes place on the Valentine's Day of Samantha Kingston's senior year of high school. Sam has everything she could want: the admiration and fear of her peers; a tight clique led by her best friend, the fearless but vicious Lindsay; and a gorgeous—but incredibly thoughtless—boyfriend, Rob, who she plans to lose her virginity to that night. Her plans are ruined when she and her friends get into a horrific car crash on the way home from a party. Now Sam has seven chances to relive that day—her last—and somehow change its conclusion. While doing so, she's forced to reexamine everything about her life and herself.

The biggest difference that sets this book apart from other mean-girl novels is that Oliver doesn't try to fit Sam's friends into the stereotypical mean girl box. Instead, she lets Sam realize, over time, how awfully she and her friends treated other students at their school, yet still recognize what she loves about them, like how Ally is a wonderful cook or Lindsay is fiercely loyal. This doesn't forgive the characters, but it helps the reader understand how they grew to this level of bullying and why Sam can still care about them.

Over the seven days, Sam encounters some of the other villains of their high school, like Anna, the bad girl who is sleeping with another girl's boyfriend. Sam sees a completely new side of Anna—someone who is surprisingly funny and cool but also vulnerable under her tough exterior, thanks to years of harassment from Sam and her friends. She realizes Anna is someone she could have been friends with.

Sam's good side is shown through the eyes of her little sister, Izzy. Izzy is a sharp contrast to Sam: open, honest, and endearingly weird. But she worships Sam, and Sam loves her more than she'd like to admit. The reader's heart drops alongside Sam's when she realizes that she might not be able to see Izzy grow up. It makes you root for Sam, if only for Izzy's sake.

Like most young adult fiction catered to girls, this book features a love interest. Kent was a childhood friend of Sam's and her first kiss. He's funny, quirky, and seems to have never given up on her. In the beginning, she thinks he's annoying, but as the book progresses, Sam begins to see that there's more to him than the silly cartoons he draws for the school newspaper. Kent is a likable enough character but not vital to the story, like Lindsay or Juliet Sykes, the girl who Sam and her friends torture for so long. He's simple and sweet: just another reminder of what could have been.

Oliver makes the book moving through her characters, but she makes the book beautiful through her prose. Nowadays, with *Twilight* knock-offs crowding the shelves of bookstores, it's refreshing to discover a new author who can, believe it or not, actually write. Like John Green, she maintains the tricky balance of realistic dialogue and strong themes. Sam's thoughts and feelings are fluid and chockfull of metaphors and symbols. The prologue and epilogue are even better. Oliver masterfully uses italics as she describes Sam's last thoughts. At first it comes across as eerie and unsettling, but it soon morphs into something beautiful and hopeful. *Before I Fall* has one of the most satisfying endings ever.

Again, readers won't find any new themes here. But Oliver manages to put her own twist on the age-old idea that no one is all bad or all good by revealing the flaws and strengths of all her characters and, in the process, making them seem undeniably human. *Before I Fall* is a book about life, loss, death, friendship, family, cruelty, love, redemption, but, most importantly, growing up.

—*Abbie Hinchman*

Finally, as examples of movie reviews, Cole and Lilly wrote raves, as do most of my students who write about films. Here I appreciated the contrast in genres, typical of girl and boy students, as Lilly takes on a teen romantic comedy and Cole delights in the undead.

A CHIVALROUS LIE

"What happened to chivalry?" asks seventeen-year-old Olive Penderghast. Maybe she'll find it in the sunshine state of Florida, where the high school student relies on the rumor mill to boost her social status. Although some viewers might not be thrilled with the plot of *Easy A*, a film written by Bert Royal and directed by Will Gluck, it teaches a valuable lesson about crashing, burning, and surviving.

Three cheers for casting director Lisa Miller Katz. Emma Stone—a newly emerging young actress—was chosen to play the role of the witty Olive Penderghast. Although this is one of Stone's first films, she portrays the character in a way that makes her hilarious to watch and completely lovable. Nominated for a Golden Globe for this role, she is clearly going to be something big. Also starring are actress and singer Alyson Michelka, playing Olive's best friend Rhiannon, and Amanda Bynes as Maryanne Bryant, known by the other characters as "a psycho religious Nazi prone to shoving her beliefs down other people's throats."

In the movie, Olive cites examples from the novel *The Scarlet Letter* by Nathaniel Hawthorne to show how closely her story relates to that of Hester Prynne. Both are focused on female characters who face mockery and judgment because of one decision. It is up to the viewer to decide whether Olive's is right or wrong.

After she is asked to lie for a friend (Dan Byrd), she must face the fact that honesty *is* the best policy. Her small lie grows, the growing lie turns into a rumor, and the rumor is spread throughout the school. Now known for a bad reputation that started as an exaggerated story, Olive must find a way to make things right, set the school straight, and regain her lost friends. This is not a movie with a great message about how to take on high school, but Olive handles the situation she creates with maturity and, yes, chivalry.

The movie's focus on essentials is enjoyable. Viewers can relate to the characters and their problems, rather than trying to follow a complicated plot. As we move through the story, we see more and more how the bullying and assumptions of others affect Olive. At first, she seems not to care about what everyone is saying about her, but as the movie progresses, we watch as she becomes more and more upset. Each character's reaction to Olive's unfairly ruined reputation carries a different meaning. Olive is there to show what we can lose from lying and how much we can gain from telling the truth.

This is a good movie, honest and true, with great acting and a solid plot. Although there is little to unpack, teen audiences will love *Easy A*. It shows the power of peers, love, friendship, and honesty. Olive's problem is brilliantly resolved as she learns to be more responsible for her words and actions. From *Easy A*'s humor, to the strong plot and its sly references to Hawthorne, this is a teen movie to appreciate.

—*Lilly Richardson*

IS IT OKAY TO EAT BURGERS?

That's the question a viewer will ask after seeing *Zombieland*, where mad cow disease turns into mad person disease and then into mad zombies. Directed by Ruben Fleischer, written by Paul Wernick and Rhett Reese, and released in 2009, *Zombieland* is funny, gory, action-packed, and downright unpredictable. Some scenes may make viewers cringe, but others will cause them to laugh their heads off.

In *Zombieland*, characters go by the names of their hometowns. The main character, Columbus, is played by Jesse Eisenberg. While Eisenberg does a good job playing a reclusive, easily shaken geek, Woody Harrelson steals the film. Harrelson plays Tallahassee, a redneck. With his hedge clippers, chainsaws, and other implements of zombie killing, he brings the gore—and much of the humor—to this movie. After Tallahassee decimates a crowd of zombies singlehandedly, he doesn't feel like a mere man anymore. This makes the film a less believable example of the zombie-horror-comedy genre, unlike *Shaun of the Dead*, a superior horror-comedy movie.

Columbus has survived the zombie apocalypse this long—two months—because he follows a code of rules. The way the writers embed the rules is one of the funniest things about the film. Whenever they introduce one, they show an unfortunate person breaking it. The first rule that comes up, "Cardio," is illustrated by an overweight guy being chased and eaten by a zombie in slow motion on a football field.

Shortly after Columbus meets Tallahassee and hitches a ride with him, the two stop to raid a grocery store, where they find Wichita (Emma Stone), a bright twenty-one-year-old girl who Columbus falls in love with, and her sister, Little Rock, who, despite being twelve, knows how to use it to her advantage. She is played by Abigail Breslin and is a funny character, from shooting zombies to trying to explain to Tallahassee that Miley Cyrus is only Hanna Montana when she puts on the wig and talks funny. She is an average twelve-year-old girl who loves pop and the Disney Channel but is trapped in a parallel universe.

Wichita is the kind of character who, at first, viewers love to hate. Tallahassee and Columbus decide to trust her, and she robs them of their food, truck, and weapons. But she grows on them and us. Halfway into the movie, she decides to trust them back.

Zombieland is not a kid's movie. It is rated R for blood, gore, strong language, and intense violence. This reviewer gave it 4.5 stars out of 5 for a great plot, lovable characters, and, by the end, a surprisingly positive experience. Here's hoping for a sequel.

—*Cole Wentworth*

Essays

In order to write essays, seventh and eighth graders have to read some. In the weeks prior to the genre study I start looking for examples of good essays, *good* meaning opinion pieces that are crafted, comprehensible, and about topics of interest to kids. Proven sources include the op-ed pages of the daily *New York Times* and *Boston Globe*, the Talk of the Town "Comment" in each week's *New Yorker*, opinion pieces in the Sunday *Times* sports and weekly review sections, and editorials and letters to the editor in local and regional newspapers.

I've clipped or downloaded essays about an intriguing range of topics—Barbie, Darwin, obesity in America, sugar consumption, drug use by athletes, whether U.S. sixteen-year-olds should have the vote, global warming, income inequality, child vaccinations and autism and the lack of a connection, black women's hair and Army regulations, foreign child laborers who produce cheap goods for the U.S. market, lengthening the school day and year, the validity of movie ratings, captive animal performances, the legalization of marijuana, the right (and wrong) way to make a Maine lobster roll, later school starting times for secondary students, prescription medication addiction in Maine, and the implications of his or her birth order for a child's adulthood.

Once I've collected a dozen essay candidates, I photocopy a packet for each student. At this juncture, as writers, students are still working on short fiction. Over the course of a week or so, I expect that everyone will segue into the new genre. I launch it with a definition.

THE LESSON

For the next few weeks, we're going to look at the genre that's made for writers to address their questions, concerns, ideas, opinions, and problems. This genre is the essay. How many of you would describe yourself as readers of essays?

I'm not surprised, and that's okay. Unless you read a daily paper, a habit you're still growing into, a reader doesn't have a lot of traffic with the essay genre. So I've collected a dozen—most by professional writers and a handful by students—that were enjoyable for me to read and that address topics I think you'll find interesting, too. As with every genre we've studied, I'll ask you to learn about essays by reading some and teasing out their features.

In the meantime, it will be helpful if you have a working definition of the genre. Please record it on the next clean page in the class-notes section of your handbook.

An Essay Definition

A short, literary composition that brings a problem, issue, situation, or opinion to the attention of readers; provides background; takes a stand, and backs it up with evidence. In general, essays *persuade*, *interpret*, or *analyze*.

Right under the definition, please write this heading: Features of Effective Essays.

For homework that's due the day after tomorrow—so you have two nights to read and think—please choose ten of the twelve essays to read, annotate, and take notes on under the heading. What do you notice about their titles, leads, conclusions, diction, tone, kinds of information, length, content, and style?

I'll quickly preview the subject of each essay in the packet, to give you an overview of the subjects the essayists bite off. Follow along as I flip through. . . .

As you can see, there's a range of topics and opinions. From among these, select the ten you're most interested in. Read them and mark them up. Then make as complete a list as you can of what you notice about form and content, and we'll debrief in two days.

The day their essay criteria are due, I ask students to form groups of four. Each small group collaborates on a list of what they discovered about essays; Figure 12.5 shows an example of the features teased out by one foursome.

After ten or fifteen minutes, I ask the class to join me in the minilesson circle, where recorders take turns reporting to me as I convert their small groups' lists to one on overhead transparencies. That night I organize, edit, and type the essay criteria and make a class set of photocopies. At the start of class the next day, students tape the list into their handbooks and, highlighters in hand, take turns reading "Features of an Effective Essay" around the circle. The list on the next page represents a typical final product.

Figure 12.5 *A Small Group's List of Essay Features*

FEATURES OF AN EFFECTIVE ESSAY

- addresses a subject the essayist cares about—an "itch" to "scratch"
- has a strong *I* presence and a conversational tone
- starts with an inviting title that suggests the problem and fits the whole essay
- the lead is focused and clear, grabs the reader's attention, introduces the problem, *and* takes a position on it
- the author communicates a definite opinion
- asks (and answers) a reader's questions
- flows and is crafted like literature: strong diction, even metaphors and similes
- sticks to the subject—no sidetracks
- cuts to the bone: no rambling
- takes advantage of *cadence* or repetition
- cites evidence that backs up the writer's opinion: survey or poll results, research findings, relevant quotes, experts' opinions, statistics, anecdotes, names, dates, places, personal examples and experiences, allusions, etc.
- weaves or embeds evidence into the essay vs. listing a bunch of facts

- provides the history or context of the problem
- points out pros *and* cons: includes the position of others and debates them
- balances opinions, information, and others' positions
- proposes a solution—or multiple solutions—to the problem
- is considerate of readers and tries to keep them engaged
- is coherent: the movement from one point to the next is logical, so the argument builds
- moves at a good pace
- uses transitional words and phrases to connect paragraphs and support the flow
- the conclusion wraps it up and alludes to the lead
- has a *so what?* a reader can paraphrase
- consists of friendly paragraphs and a balance of kinds of sentences, some long and elegant and some short and punched
- typically is between eight and eleven paragraphs in length

The essayist E. B. White wrote, "When a mosquito bites me—I scratch. When I write something, I guess I'm trying to get rid of the itchiness inside me" (1977). The question that invites me and my students to generate meaningful essay topics is, "What itch needs scratching?" This is the next minilesson. Before I teach it, I draft a list of problems I might address in an essay of my own (Figure 12.6), using a reproducible from *Lessons That Change Writers*. If I want kids to take on subjects that matter to them, a demonstration of subjects that matter to me is a meaningful invitation.

THE LESSON

Donald Murray is one of my favorite writing teachers. I quote him often because his advice is practical and true. Today's Murray quote is his assertion "Problems make good subjects."

As you gathered from the essays we read and discussed, this is the genre for writing about what you know, wonder about, think, observe, and can find out. You'll begin the process of writing your essay by generating topics that inspire you—mental itches you're interested in scratching. Here are the ideas that are tickling my cranium these days.

Please turn to the next clean page of the territories section of your handbook, tape the invitation "What Itch Needs Scratching?" at the top of the page, so there's room below for writing, and read along with me.

Tonight for homework please consider the questions. In the space below, list at least eight itches that intrigue you—topics that make you happy, sad, curious, furious, confused. Go for quantity and idiosyncrasy—a list of essay topics that no one but you could have generated.

WHAT ITCH NEEDS SCRATCHING?

("Problems make good subjects." —Donald Murray)

What problem needs solving?

What situation needs correcting?

What issue needs explaining?

What phenomenon needs exploring?

What choice I've made/stand I've taken/personal preference needs to be understood by others?

What area of my expertise needs sharing?

What subject that's close and familiar to me needs to be viewed and considered from a distance?

What point of view needs my powers of persuasion?

- Low reading scores in Maine and a proposal to the governor: make Maine the Reading State, with a statewide initiative to establish classroom libraries + reading workshops?
- Exercise is bad for people: my pet theory, as a slug.
- What's wrong with the Common Core State Standards for writing and reading?
- Learning how to cook in my sixties
- Dark chocolate: is it a health food? If so, how so?
- What first-time tourists should see + do in London
- How should a school handle religious + ethnic holidays? Celebrate none or embrace them all?
- The problem of even talking about eating issues with teen girls — after discussion of Lent, CTL girls decided to fast at lunchtime; 25% of US girls experience an eating disorder at some point. How to address/not provoke?
- The English springer spaniel is an ideal dog breed for a family pet.

Figure 12.6 *Nancie's Potential Essay Topics—"What Itch Needs Scratching?"*

The next overhead (Figure 12.7) shows the list of itches brainstormed by Jacob, a seventh grader. These are problems, questions, and issues he discovered mattered to him.

Tonight, as you make your list of itches that need scratching, spend at least half an hour poking into the corners of your ideas and experiences. Take breaks along the way so your long-term memory can do its work.

WHAT ITCH NEEDS SCRATCHING?

("Problems make good subjects." —Donald Murray)

What problem needs solving?

What situation needs correcting?

What issue needs explaining?

What phenomenon needs exploring?

What choice I've made/stand I've taken/personal preference needs to be understood by others?

What area of my expertise needs sharing?

What subject that's close and familiar to me needs to be viewed and considered from a distance?

What point of view needs my powers of persuasion?

- Football safety w/ concussions
- Russell Wilson playing for the Texas Rangers
- Should college athletes get paid or not?
- Why people should help out locally
- People should buy cage free eggs
- Swimming is an amazing sport
- Art should be encouraged at all high schools
- Kids & smoking
- Being a middle child

Figure 12.7 *Jacob's Potential Essay Topics*

In the next day's minilesson, students gather in groups of three or four and discuss their ideas in response to three questions:

- On a scale of 1–10, how do I rate the itchiness inside me about each topic on my list?
- How would I go about researching the itchiest topics—what sources might provide the specifics an essay needs?
- After hearing my friends' ideas, do any new essay topics occur to me?

That night for homework, based on degrees of itchiness and possible sources of evidence, kids make their final topic selections. They write their choice at the top of the next clean page in the notes section of their handbooks in the form of a *thesis statement or question*. Examples by previous student essayists include:

Global warming is a fact.

Does Coke taste better than Pepsi?

We need deer hunting in Maine.

Why are so many Americans obese?

The FDA and USDA should ban the use of artificial growth hormones and antibiotics in animals raised for food.

It's time for Maine to permit same-sex marriage.

Everyone should sing at CTL morning meetings.

While movies for children are original and captivating, movies for teens aren't.

Maine's apprenticeship program for young lobstermen is a worthwhile opportunity.

Creationism is a religious belief not a scientific theory.

Quentin Tarantino is a great filmmaker.

Do green M&Ms taste different from—*and* better than—the other colors?

Field trips and other direct experiences are the best way to learn about history.

Does the amount of sleep a student gets really affect school performance?

We need to stop a private company from developing Maine's Moosehead Lake Region.

Is green tea a health food?

An essayist's next step is to define the issue or problem. Students start by writing a list underneath their thesis in answer to the question *What do I need to find out about my topic to write a strong essay about it?* Afterward, I ask them to draw a line across the page, exchange handbooks with six to eight other students, and ask peers to add their questions: What do *they* wonder about this topic? This activity helps students focus as researchers on specific, relevant information, instead of launching into a rant, cobbling together clichés, or saying the same thing over and over again.

At this point, I give the class an outline of steps in writing an essay. Before we review it together, I let them know, "I'm handing over to you some of the things I do as a writer of expository prose. This is what works for me."

HOW DO I SCRATCH THE ITCH?

- **Define the problem.**
  - What do I need to know?
  - What do readers need to know?

- **Collect information for readers *and* for me. *Work from quantity.***
  - Note my own ideas, experiences, prior knowledge, arguments, questions, judgments, and interpretations.
  - Brainstorm reasons, benefits, disadvantages, solutions, and roadblocks.
  - Design and administer a survey; summarize and interpret the results.
  - Collect relevant quotes.
  - Collect relevant statistics: numbers that reveal the situation.
  - Collect relevant examples or stories.
  - Interview appropriate subjects.
- **Play with leads.**
  - Find the best way in: a lead that will give voice and direction to my message, information, and conclusion.
- **Focus the data.**
  - Create a plan that displays my information *and* gives it an order.
- **Draft the information.**
  - Use my plan as a foundation to draft my data, paragraph by paragraph, as a well-supported argument.
- **Experiment with conclusions.**
  - Play off-the-page until I find an ending that connects with the lead, clinches my argument, and leaves a reader thinking.
- **Revise. Clarify and tighten the information. Close the holes. Cut the rambling. Make it sing. Ask:**
  - Does the rest of the essay deliver on the promise of the lead?
  - Does the language flow?
  - Is the itch well and truly scratched in a convincing, complete, logical, coherent, enjoyable way?
- **Brainstorm a title.**
- **Take a two-day walk-away.**
  - When you return, read one of the essays in your prose folder—one you thought was especially good—to get back into the essay zone. Review the master list of features of an effective essay. Then, pen in hand, read your essay. What do you need to do to make it convincing, complete, logical, coherent, enjoyable, and ready for the eyes of a discerning reader?
- **Polish, edit, and publish.**

A lesson about kinds of information students might collect comes next. They tape "Write with Information" (Figure 12.8), adapted from Murray's *Write to Learn* (1999), in their handbooks, and after we've reviewed it together, I teach them how to use it.

Donald Murray says, "The writing act begins with the collection of the raw material of writing, information that will be arranged into meaning by the act of writing." Essayists write with information—specific, accurate data. And, Murray continues, "Readers read to satisfy their hunger for information—specific, accurate information they can use."

There are many forms of information and ways to collect it:

Process: your observations of the actions of someone affected by the issue

Questions: what readers will wonder

Answers: responses to the questions readers will ask

Facts: accurate details from magazine and newspaper articles, books, and the Internet

Statistics: numbers that reveal and illustrate the situation

Surveys and polls: statistics gathered first-hand, summarized, and interpreted

Quotations: statements by authorities and person-on-the street types

Examples: times and places the problem or situation occurs

Anecdotes: little stories that reveal the problem

Theories: your thoughts or the thoughts of others that explain the problem

Principles: the accepted way something is done or perceived (which may be wrong and which you may attack)

Interviews: voices of other people concerned about the problem

Solutions: steps readers or someone else can take to solve the problem

Roadblocks: what's stopping the problem from being solved

Arguments: reasons for your point of view, plus your responses to the roadblocks

Personal experiences: events from your life that illustrate the problem

Ideas: thoughts you want to consider in this essay

History: a problem's past or its traditions

Implications: the future of the problem

Background: the who-what-when-where-why of the problem

Murray advises writers: "Collect the material to fill out such a list, and you'll stop feeling empty. In fact, you'll feel so full that you'll be eager to write to relieve yourself of the information."

*Adapted from *Write to Learn* by Donald M. Murray (1999), Fort Worth, TX: Holt, Rinehart, and Winston

Figure 12.8 *Write with Information*

THE LESSON

Information comes in many forms. Your task as essayists is to gather more than you can use—lots of the specific, accurate data that readers crave. Take a good three or four days for this phase of the process, but begin your quest by narrowing its focus.

Write your thesis statement or question at the top of "Write with Information" and read through this list again on your own. This time, start to make some decisions. Given your essay topic, which forms of information are appropriate for you to gather? Make a tick mark next to each kind of information you think is relevant to your thesis.

For example, if your thesis is that global warming is a fact, will a survey of classmates provide you with scientific information? If it's about why your favorite kind of music should be taken seriously, will statistics provide useful evidence?

Tomorrow and the next day I'll meet with each of you, ask you to tell me about the sources of information you're considering, and help you hone your approaches as data collectors.

Then I let students have at it as researchers. They design surveys and administer them to classmates, students beyond the classroom, or, via the newsletter, CTL parents. I show them how to select Internet search terms—how to identify key words, come up with synonyms, search for pictures under "Images" and current developments under "News," and add new key words to narrow their research: *effects, facts, impact, implications, polls, quotations, solutions, statistics, studies,* and *testimonials.*

When students feel as if they're filled up with information, finding a direction for it is the next step. Generating a lead is the ideal way to focus an essay. I introduce seven kinds and provide examples of each. I also illustrate kinds of leads to avoid—ones that confuse, bore, or insult the intelligence of a reader.

Experiment with Essay Leads

Anecdote: Begin with a brief story that reveals something essential about your topic—that captures its essence.

SLEEP: DOES IT MATTER?

My dad is always telling me not to stay up late. He claims that not getting enough sleep will affect how I do in school. Every night he says, "Get to bed—you've got school tomorrow," and I always respond with an exasperated "I know." But then I got curious. What if the amount of sleep a student gets really does affect school performance? What if not getting eight or nine hours could mean I won't do as well on my test tomorrow? Curiosity got the better of me, so I decided to find out for myself. I decided to research teens and sleep.

Quotation: Start with a relevant quote or epigraph you can elaborate on by agreeing, disagreeing, or explaining its significance. It might come from something you've read in your research or a survey response.

WE HAVE THE ABILITY

"We, the human species, are confronting a planetary emergency—a threat to the survival of our civilization . . . But there is hopeful news as well: we have the ability to solve this crisis." So says Al

Gore, a leading activist in the cause of fighting global warming. Gore is right: unquestionable facts support the idea that global warming is here. Numerous graphs show a linear pattern in the increase of Earth's temperature and the amount of CO_2 in our atmosphere; each graph has a spike at the end, representing the 21st century. Global warming is real, and it's time to take action.

Scenario: Ask the reader to imagine him- or herself in a hypothetical situation, and then explain how it connects to the real-life issue you're addressing in your essay.

Living History

Imagine yourself in a history class. At the front of the room, your teacher assigns a chapter from the textbook after finishing his lecture on the Revolutionary War battles of April 19, 1775. You, meanwhile, have been carving your name into your desk. The kid in front of you is passing notes across the aisle, and the girl behind you is asleep. Not one student learned anything of substance from the lesson. Not one cares about the battles of Lexington and Concord.

Now, imagine yourself among the crowds of Americans who gather to stand twenty deep around the small triangle that is Lexington Green each April. Watch Major Pitcairn lead his troops onto the grass while William Diamond beats out his drum call to the militia. The annual Patriot's Day festivities begin, and you are a part of American history.

Announcement: Begin with a statement—a fact, series of facts, or strong opinion that takes a stance on an issue. The rest of your essay will back up the bold claim you make here.

What Is the Prize?

An elementary school principal dyes his hair green when students read 10,000 pages. Another school hosts a pizza party for students to celebrate a similar "achievement." Give me a break. Readers don't need prizes. Reading itself is the prize.

Background: Begin by providing a brief history of the problem. What will a reader need to know in order to enter your essay argument?

It's Not Over Yet

As a loyal viewer of *The Office* ever since it premiered on NBC, turning on the TV each Thursday night is a routine for me. But since July 16, the Writer's Guild of America has been refusing to work until the Alliance of Motion Picture and Television Producers compensates them fairly—which means that millions of fans will have to suffer the half-finished plot lines of sixty-three of our favorite shows until they can reach an agreement. As a viewer who believes that the writers should stand up to the networks until they get paid more fairly, I believe new episodes of *The Office* are worth the wait.

Description: Describe a real scene that illustrates your topic. Give your readers a word picture of a particular setting, so they can visualize it before you begin to make points and present evidence.

LEARNING MAGIC

It's early on a Sunday afternoon. I step into the small, cluttered shop on Main Street in Brunswick. Men and boys sit around solitary table in folding chairs, shuffling and chatting. Others wander with tattered trade binders, soda cans, and slices of pizza. I hear more male voices rising up the stairs. A line of players waits in front of the desk, patting their pockets to scrounge up five bucks for the Vintage tournament. This is the weekly Type I Magic: The Gathering tournament at J & R Cards.

News: Start with current developments about your topic or statistics that reveal the seriousness of the problem.

HERE TO STAY

Oil prices hit a record high this month of $53.90 a barrel, and experts predict there's no relief in the future. Oil prices have increased over 25% in the last eighteen months, and experts say they will grow even higher. Right now a gallon of gasoline costs an average of $3.50. The question on everyone's mind is why.

Some Leads to Avoid

- A dictionary definition ("*Webster's* defines *conformity* as . . ."). This is a cliché.
- A question to the reader ("How did that hamburger you had for dinner last night get to your supermarket?"). It presumes a reader cares about the answer, plus the tone is condescending.
- A bromide ("We've all heard the expression, 'Better safe than sorry.' But is that true of today's airline security procedures?"). Your reader is already snoring.
- A lead that isn't focused ("Adoption programs in this country have some flaws. They aren't completely bad, but they need to be dealt with. There are a couple of things I'm concerned about even though, overall, adoption is a good thing."). The reader is confused—and bored—before the writer has entered the heart of the essay.

Once kids have drafted a lead they like, I ask them to hone and polish it before they move on—to nail its language and information—because a crafted lead suggests the structure of the rest of the essay and sows the seeds for its conclusion. When I confer with them about their leads, we use this checklist, which I also adapted from Murray (1999).

CHECK YOUR ESSAY LEAD

- *Is it inviting?* Is it lively? Will it engage a reader's interest?
- *Is it clear?* Will a reader grasp the issue or problem?
- *Is it true?* Are your statements factual, accurate, and generally the case, so the rest of your essay will be convincing?
- *Is it focused?* Does it point a direction where the rest of your essay is headed?
- *Is there an attitude?* Does it sound like you, speaking with conviction?
- *Is it developed enough?* Is there enough information to establish what the problem is and where the essay is going?
- *Is the language clear and strong?* Are the words you've chosen and sentences you've structured straightforward and accessible? Are the verbs strong?

While students are perfecting their leads, I teach a lesson about the next step, focusing the information. I introduce four approaches to organizing the data they've gathered.

THE LESSON

Here's another essential quote from Donald Murray. He said, "There's no (one) way to outline. But you should find some way of presenting what you may write . . . Most of the time my drafts collapse unless I have outlines in my head or on paper" (1999).

Organizing your information—planning the rest of your essay—is the hardest part of the process. But it's necessary—a step that will keep your draft from collapsing on you. Hang in there. I'll show you four ways (Figure 12.9) to look at your notes and create some order.

As students begin drafting their essays, they'll be helped by a lesson about transitional words and phrases. In narratives, one event follows another, so unless they're shifting the time frame, writers can depend on chronology to hook their paragraphs together. In expository prose, readers need to be taken by the hand and led from the end of one paragraph to the beginning of the next and reoriented in the essay.

The kids and I skimmed a couple of weeks' worth of editorial and op-ed pages from the *New York Times* in search of words and phrases that writers used to graft a new paragraph to the one that precedes it. Figure 12.10 represents the fruits of our research—not every extant transitional word or phrase but a healthy sample to give to novice essayists as they learn how to cue readers. Also at this point, because many of them will cite statistics, kids need a lesson about the conventions for writing numbers—when as numerals and when as words.

FOUR WAYS TO ORGANIZE INFORMATION AND PLAN AN ESSAY

1. Donald Graves' method of three columns:
- Create three vertical columns on a big sheet of white construction paper. Head them Beginning, Middle, and End. Move ideas and items from your notes into the appropriate columns, based on where they seem to belong in the essay.
- Be aware that you may not use everything in your notes and that new ideas can be included as they occur to you.
- When you're done, number the items within each of the three lists in the order that makes sense to present them.

2. Colored paper frames:
- Gather large sheets of different-colored construction paper.
- Use scissors to separate your notes into kinds of data that might be grouped together, or beginning-middle-end.
- Place the strips of notes on the different-colored sheets of construction paper depending on what they're about or where they'll go in your essay. Move them around and look for new patterns.
- When you're satisfied with the order, tape them down.

3. Colored marker highlights:
- Gather colored markers. Underline your notes in different colors according to categories of information or beginning-middle-end.
- Use scissors to cut apart your notes. Then put together the information according to color. Move the strips of each color around to create an order, and then tape them down.

4. Nancie Atwell's method of writing off-the-page:
- Spread out your notes on a big surface, so you can eyeball them (I use my kitchen table or the floor).
- Scan them. As you do, write captions or labels on them: What are the *big ideas*? *Categories*? *Examples or points* that seem best to *start and end* the essay? Best *quotes* or *statistics*? Most revealing *anecdotes*?
- On a sheet of paper—or several—create your own form of outline: a plan that roughs in a sequence for your array of labeled information.

Figure 12.9 *Four Ways to Organize Information and Plan an Essay*

As soon as one or more of my students are on the verge of wrapping up first drafts, I conduct a lesson about endings. They tape "Experiment with Essay Conclusions" into their handbooks.

Experiment with Essay Conclusions

"The end must connect with the opening. What has been promised must have been delivered. Read the opening over to see what closing it implies."

—*Donald Murray*

SOME TRANSITIONAL WORDS AND PHRASES FOR EXPOSITORY WRITING

According to

Actually

After

After all

Again

Although

And

And once

Another

As soon as

As a (girl, future voter, etc.)

At a time when

At the same time

At this point/time

Because

But

Certainly

Chief among the (reasons, arguments, etc.)

Despite

During

Even so

Finally

First (Second, Third, etc.)

For example

For many (of us, millennials, teens, etc.)

For (months/years/hours etc.)

Fortunately

Here's the thing

However

If

In addition

In any case

Inevitably

In fact

In other words

In short

In the meantime

It's (obvious, clear, no surprise, surprising that, etc.)

Just consider

Last (week, month, year, time)

Let's say that

Many (people/voters/ parents, etc.)

Maybe

Meanwhile

Most important

Next

Now

No wonder that

Of course

On the one hand/the other hand

One of the (impacts, prob- lems, implications, etc.)

Or consider

Perhaps

Questions:
How . . . ?
What . . . ?
When . . . ?
Where . . . ?
Who . . . ?
Why . . . ?

Recently

Remember (that, when, why, who, what)

Since

So

Somehow

Sometimes

Soon

Still

That said

The answer/issue/problem/ reason

Then

This is how/what/where/who/ why

Today

Thus

Unfortunately

Until

Whatever

When

Which brings us

While

Yet

Figure 12.10 *Some Transitional Words and Phrases for Expository Writing*

SOME CONCLUSIONS TO TRY

- **an admonition or instruction:** what a reader can do about the issue
- **a prediction:** an insight into how the future might be different, better, or worse
- **a strong, punched statement**
- **an anecdote:** a brief story that reiterates the essence of the issue
- **a pointed question**
- **an echo:** language or ideas that circle back to the lead

A Conclusion to Avoid

"Only rarely in effective writing is the closing a formal summary in which the writer repeats . . . what has already been said."

—*Donald Murray*

And then I distribute copies of "Examples of Essay Conclusions" (Figure 12.11), which students store in a pocket of their writing-in-process folders after this lesson.

THE LESSON

No matter the genre, conclusions need to be strong. They should resonate—leave a reader thinking, feeling, or both. I've noticed six kinds of conclusions in the good essays I've read, plus a seventh kind that's tired, clichéd, and doesn't resonate one bit.

The first conclusion you might try is an *admonition* or *instruction* to the reader to take action. That's how Marley ended an essay about how her beloved rap and hip-hop don't, in fact, promote teen violence.

A prediction is another kind of strong conclusion. Emily *predicts* a future in which America's meat supply will be safer. Next, Hayley makes a brief, emphatic *statement* about the unhealthy body images that professional models represent. Zoe ends her essay, about the need to protect the alewives ladder near her home, with an *anecdote*—a brief story about a visit to this magical place. Cameron leaves his reader, especially the athletes among them, with a *question*. And Nate's conclusion returns to his beginning, which you have in the collection of essay leads I gave you. He *echoes* his opening anecdote about a debate with his dad about teens and sleep.

A conclusion to avoid is the one Murray refers to in his second quote—when essayists restate what they've already said. A reader shouldn't have to revisit, in a compressed form, all the points you've already made. I wrote one of these boring bad boys to show you what I mean.

To compose your conclusion, read your lead, and then start playing. Don't be satisfied with the first way your words go down on the page. Experiment with different ways out, just as you played with different ways in. Then choose the one that will leave a reader thinking the hardest and feeling the strongest about your essay topic.

An admonition or instruction:

"Whenever possible, we should buy local. If we buy meat raised locally, not only are we supporting independent businesses but also a healthier future for our communities. If enough people stop relying on factory farming for their meat, we can make a difference in our future as a healthy country."

A prediction:

"The problem of violence in today's society will not stop until Americans accept and take responsibility for our actions—including the way we allow easy access to firearms—instead of blaming violence on entertainers and musicians."

A strong, punched statement:

"Young girls need healthy role models to look up to, so they can grow up to be strong, dependable, kind, intelligent and—finally—themselves."

An anecdote:

"Today I walk out on the rocks by the alewives ladder at Damariscotta Mills. The geese are still squawking, and the alewives have just left. As I slip into the water, I hope this small piece of happiness remains protected forever."

A pointed question:

"So, when your teammate or friend reveals that he is taking steroids, will you reach out? Will you help save your friend's true athletic talent or let him get pulled into the lifestyle so many athletes have chosen? And when you're confronted with this problem yourself, will you have the strength—no steroids required—to say no?"

An echo:

Lead: "My dad is always telling me not to stay up late. He claims that not getting enough sleep will affect how I do in school. Every night he says, "Get to bed—you've got school tomorrow," and I always respond with an "I know." But then I got curious. What if the amount of sleep a student gets really does affect school performance?"

Conclusion: "No matter what your situation regarding sleep, remember teens need a good amount to function well. We need to be informed about the effects of lack of sleep. So the next time my dad reminds me not to stay up too late, I think I might even, for once, agree with him."

Figure 12.11 *Examples of Essay Conclusions*

The four student essays I chose for inclusion here represent different modes of data gathering and kinds of information. Nate wondered if the amount of sleep teens get makes a difference academically, so he designed an experiment. He borrowed a book about IQ tests from the classroom library, dragooned six student volunteers, assigned them to sleep six hours one night and eight the next, and administered comparable IQ tests each morning. He combined his experimental findings with Internet research as the bases for a convincing essay.

SLEEP: DOES IT MATTER?

My dad is always telling me not to stay up late. He claims that not getting enough sleep will affect how I do in school. Every night he says, "Get to bed—you've got school tomorrow," and I always respond with an exasperated "I *know*." But then I got curious. What if the amount of sleep a student gets really does affect school performance? What if not getting eight or nine hours could mean I won't do as well on my test tomorrow? Curiosity got the better of me, so I decided to find out for myself. I decided to research sleep and teens.

I administered two verbal I.Q. tests to six kids in my class. The tests came from the book *How Intelligent Are You?* by Victor Serebriankoff. Each test was of the same length and difficulty. For the first test, I asked the kids to get only six hours of sleep the previous night. Then, at school the next day, I gave them verbal test A. The next night they had to sleep for eight hours. Then they took verbal test B.

The test results surprised me. For the six-hours-of-sleep night, correct answers fell in the range of 4–10 out of 28. After the eight-hour-sleep night, the results ranged from 8–18. The results show that the number of correct responses almost doubled with more sleep. This is quite a big increase, and it does show that with more sleep, this group of kids did do better on the test.

Studies over the years have shown that the amount of sleep kids get has been dropping. The average is about six hours, which is depriving them of much-needed sleep, even though, as teens, we actually need more. Other studies of high school students have shown that kids who got twenty-five minutes less sleep each night and went to sleep forty minutes later than peers were getting C's, D's, and F's as grades, while kids who got more sleep and went to bed earlier were getting A's and B's.

Other problems, like sleeping disorders, can also come into play. These are more serious issues that require medication and even counselors. But for those of us who do have control over when we can go to sleep, we need to make the right decision.

All of this leads to my point. I've become convinced that teens need to get more sleep and make good decisions about it. If we don't it could seriously affect both school and the rest of our lives. Kids need to start going to bed earlier and managing our time better. Parents need to help, by having their children do things to help them unwind, telling them to stay away from caffeine during the evening, not letting them take naps, and restricting the viewing of stimulating TV shows or video games on school nights. They can even set a bedtime, even though most kids won't like it. Kids who have sleep problems or disorders may need to see a doctor. Sleep is important.

So no matter what your situation regarding sleep, remember teens need a good amount to function well. We need to be informed about the effects of lack of sleep. The next time my dad reminds me not to stay up too late, I think I might even, for once, agree with him.

—*Nate Miller*

Carolyn, a lover of gum, wanted to chew at school. On the Internet she found studies that described the benefits of gum chewing, but she also researched the roadblock—the objections of her teachers. Figure 12.12 shows the survey Carolyn administered to us and her summary notes of our responses. In her essay she presents our concerns and her counterarguments, and she proposes a solution.

NEW FLAVOR: GUM IN SCHOOL

Okay, I'll admit it. I *love* to chew gum. I am a gum addict. Sometimes, when I need something in my mouth to chomp on but I'm not hungry, I'll grab my mom's pocketbook and slip out a package of Trident Watermelon Twist. It tastes *so* good. And it's supposed to help people concentrate. If it does, and if it tastes so great, why isn't it allowed in school?

Of the teachers I surveyed at CTL, the answer that appeared most frequently is that kids don't dispose of gum properly. It ends up under chairs and tables, on the floor, in people's hair, and on their clothes. And it's tedious, if not impossible, to clean up.

I understand these complaints, and I have seen gum on sidewalks and other places it shouldn't be. I know it's disgusting to see and step on. But if students agree to not stick our "ABC" gum everywhere and dispose of it properly—in its wrapper, in the trash—this shouldn't be a problem.

Another teacher issue was that gum makes noise, because of bubbles being popped, so it's distracting and disruptive. Also noted was that gum looks bad when people are talking. These problems could be solved by setting rules for gum chewing, such as no chewing loudly and obnoxiously, or, as one student I surveyed put it, "like a cow."

Despite its few negative aspects, gum *is* good for you and your teeth. In fact, dentists now say that chewing sugarless gum is beneficial. Gum strengthens teeth, reduces plaque acids, and stimulates saliva, which is the most important defense we have against tooth decay. It also helps fight cavities, and, if chewed after eating, washes away food particles.

Other benefits of gum are school-related. Gum is proven to improve focus and concentration and help people think. Studies show that kids who chew gum during tests get higher scores than those who don't. The armed forces supplies soldiers with gum because it helps improve their concentration and reduce stress.

Studies also show that gum stimulates the human brain five times faster than the normal rate and helps us absorb more information. It opens blood

Survey for CTL Teachers

1. What are your reasons for not allowing gum chewing in your class?

Chewed gum ends up under doors, tables, on floors, Most can't chew w/out making noise/bubbles, kids focus on gum, not lesson, looks bad when talking, Against rules, distracting + disruptive, gum in hair, gum on clothes

2. As a teacher, have you had any negative experiences with gum chewing in class?

___ Yes ~~IIII~~ 83%

___ No I 17%

If you answered yes, please explain: gum under chairs and tables, even when not allowed, cleaning up gum difficult + tedious, gum on clothes, some kids not having gum, arguments, throwing gum

3. Do you chew gum? (Please be honest.)

___ Yes ~~IIII~~ 83%

___ No I 17%

If you answered yes, when and where? At home, on pc, in car, when they sing, after eating garlic or tuna

4. Is there any way someone could persuade you to allow gum chewing in your class? Are there conditions that would make this tolerable for you?

___ Yes II 33%

___ No IIII 67%

If you answered yes, please explain: If students made sure gum ended up wrapped up carefully in waste basket after they were through, Some studies show it helps students concentrate, If specialists recommended it

Figure 12.12 *Results of Carolyn's Survey of CTL Teachers*

vessels to the brain so we can remember and think at a higher rate. It also improves short-term memory.

I think that if students and teachers collaborate to establish rules, there is no reason why gum can't be allowed in school. We could have a week with gum permitted and see how well students abide by the rules. If people break them, gum chewing would be banned again.

In my opinion, there are more pros to gum chewing than cons, and if teachers listen to the facts and give it a chance, then they, too, will come to the conclusion that gum chewing will make their students smarter and happier.

—*Carolyn MacDonald*

Charlotte's essay topic was more personal. She felt she had reaped the benefits of an unusual upbringing for a girl, one that encouraged her to be independent and physically strong. Her data consist of anecdotes about her formative experiences and her parents' responses to interview questions she designed and posed.

Girls Can Be Strong; Parents Can Help

My parents told me a story of the birthday party when I turned two. As I was opening my presents, I ripped the paper off one and discovered a small bag. Inside it there were rocks. I squealed, ran to our pond, and promptly threw them in, one by one. Apparently, my parents had suggested to a party-goer that I'd love a bag of rocks. At the time I thought it was the best present ever. I loved throwing things, loved the big splash, and loved seeing how far I could throw. At age two, I wasn't conforming to the stereotypes of a little girl. I was my own person.

Recently I asked my parents why they raised my sister and me as tomboys and not girly girls. Both said that wasn't exactly what they had set out to do. "Instead," my dad replied, "it was important for our girls to have great personal power." This makes total sense. He pushes me every day to do my best and reach my highest potential.

My mom agreed: "(A parent of a girl) should impress upon your daughter that girls can achieve whatever they want to in life—gender should not be any kind of limiting factor."

And it hasn't been for me. I was eight when I began to play ice hockey. I started on a girls' team, but I wasn't pushed hard enough. We would glide through drills, and it wasn't fun. I barely got any exercise, and I didn't learn anything. When I told my dad, he quickly signed me up for a boys' team. I loved it. I was pushed hard, and because of that, I am now a devoted hockey player. I enjoy the game, I gain strength from playing, and I'm not afraid to skate hard and show that girls can be as strong as boys.

Ever since I moved to Maine, as a baby, I have lived on a farm. I also grow strong doing farm work: I haul water, deliver food to my chickens and turkeys, and fling hay bales to our sheep. My parents think that being strong physically helps build self-confidence. Also, life on a farm taught me how lambs are born. What's a bloody mess for some is a miracle to me. I was taught that it is okay to get my hands dirty and learn new things. I think the stereotype for strength is a big guy with big muscles, which is unfair to boys *and* girls. I don't want the definition of strength to be a big guy; I want it to be a strong-willed, able-bodied human being.

Cycling back to when I was little, at my third birthday party I tore the wrapping off a box, flipped it over, and found a Barbie. I set it down, and it quickly got buried by other presents. Later, when I wasn't looking, my parents threw the Barbie out. My mom hates it when girls feel they have to compare themselves to the false images of dolls or models in magazines. She says directly, to other parents of a girl, "She should be taught to look critically at all the images in magazines and advertising that perpetuate girls' insecurity about the way they look. They are not realistic!" This is typical of my mom—she expresses that opinion a lot around the house. I think it's important to stress this idea to girls, to help us understand the importance of not comparing our bodies and faces to those in teen magazines.

When I asked my parents about advice for other parents with daughters, they responded in similar fashion: "Don't give in to societal pressure," my dad urged. My mom spoke about body images in magazines, as well as sports that are centered on body image, like gymnastics, ballet, and figure skating. Personally, I think it is important for girls to be raised as equals to boys and to their highest potential. As my dad put it in his advice to other parents, "Enjoy your kids, and encourage them to be *strong, intelligent individuals.*"

That's what matters most.

Plus a bag of rocks wouldn't hurt.

—*Charlotte Collins*

Jordan's essay takes on Holocaust deniers. He begins with an epigraph, an excerpt from a poem entitled "I Cannot Forget" by Alexander Kimel, a Holocaust survivor. Then he combines statistics he gleaned at the U.S. Holocaust Memorial Museum, information from his reading and Internet research, survey responses from classmates and their parents, a personal encounter with a Holocaust survivor, and his own questions and challenges to deniers.

NEVER FORGET

Do I want to remember this world upside down?
Where the departed are blessed with an instant death.
While the living condemned to a short wretched life,
And a long tortuous journey into unnamed place,
Converting Living Souls, into ashes and gas.
No. I Have to Remember and Never Let You Forget.

—ALEXANDER KIMEL

As a practicing Jew in the 21st century, I am furious when a so-called "expert" tries to claim that the Holocaust didn't happen. It *did* happen. It's documented history. And as harrowing as it is "to remember this world upside down," we have to question the motives of anybody who says otherwise.

According to the U.S. Holocaust Memorial Museum, in 1933, prior to the Holocaust, 9.5 million Jews lived in Europe. That was 60% of the world's Jewish population. After World War II, in 1950, only 3.5 million were left alive. Of all the Jews in Europe, 66% were murdered; the rest fled to Israel, America, and other countries.

One of the reasons that some people deny the Holocaust is their belief that no specific document ordered it. But there was: Adolf Hitler's autobiography *Mein Kampf.* In 1919 he wrote, "Rational anti-Semitism must lead to systematic legal opposition. Its final objective must be the removal of Jews altogether." Also, at the Wannsee Conference on January 20, 1942, a meeting of the officials responsible for the systematic murder, the "Final Solution to the Jewish Problem," was enunciated by SS Lieutenant General Heinrich Müller, SS General Reinhard Heydrich, and SS Lieutenant Colonel Adolf Eichmann.

The movement of Holocaust deniers in the U.S., Canada, and Western Europe insists that the Allied Powers tortured Nazi perpetrators into "confessing" that they had murdered the victims of the Holocaust—Jews, Gypsies, homosexuals, blacks, Slavs, Freemasons, Jehovah's Witnesses, and also mentally and physically handicapped individuals. Deniers believe that the survivors of the Holocaust who testified about Nazi crimes were lying out of self-interest. They focus most of their attention on Auschwitz, the largest extermination camp in Europe, and believe that if they can disprove the fact that there were gas chambers in the large concentration camps in Poland, the whole history of the Holocaust will be discredited.

Out of curiosity about where my peers and their families stand on this issue, I administered a survey to seventh and eighth graders and their parents. My question was, do you think the Holocaust happened? Everyone answered yes; some appended questions that caught my attention, e.g., Do *you* think World War II happened? Or, why is your question about my opinion and not, *Did* the Holocaust happen? I thought those particular answers implied they thought I was suggesting that the Holocaust never occurred. Far from it.

In any event, it was unanimous: every respondent stated that the Holocaust happened. Of the four who knew survivors, two had family members and two had friends or acquaintances who were survivors. One person had missing family members. There were two who knew someone who was there at the time.

In the rest of their responses, my peers and their parents explained that they had read history books, listened to eyewitness accounts, and knew that there was concrete, physical evidence of the mass murder by the Nazis. Where would the brands on the arms of camp survivors have come from? Why would they burn themselves? How else could escapees explain why they are walking skeletons? What happened to the millions gone missing if the Nazis never killed any Jews, Gypsies, homosexuals, or handicapped citizens? What could have happened to them all?

I would like Holocaust deniers to think about these questions. They might also go to Germany, Poland, or Hungary and visit the remains of the concentration camps. I want them to visit the Simon Wiesenthal Center in Los Angeles, where I met a Holocaust survivor who talked to me about her experience in the concentration camps. I want them to go to the Holocaust Museum in New York City, to read *Night* by Elie Wiesel and *The Diary of a Young Girl* by Anne Frank, to enter the minds of Holocaust survivors as they tell their stories, stories that reveal the truth and remind us to learn from a time when Jews and others were not considered human beings, when the world was, truly and tragically, turned upside down.

—*Jordan Friedland*

As one culmination of the genre study, I help students who want to raise their voices beyond the school community find homes for their essays on Internet sites and as guest editorials and letters to the editor in Maine newspapers. Everyone submits his or her essay to *Acorns*, and pertinent ones also become attachments to the school newsletter. Finally, I compile a class magazine of essays and schedule a reading. Fortified with chai, hot chocolate, and decaf, kids silently read one another's essays and pass notes to each author. Figure 12.13 shows some of the notes student essayists received during a recent reading.

Because they write essays, others in their lives come to know my students for their opinions, passions, and perspectives. This is a heady kind of recognition for seventh and eighth graders. Sometimes it's also a challenge, as readers can question the kids' positions. Let's face it—it's scary for writers of any age to put ourselves out there. But when we teach students how to write with information and suggest solutions, we help them become *agents*—people brave enough and skilled enough to send ideas and evidence out into the world and make a difference there.

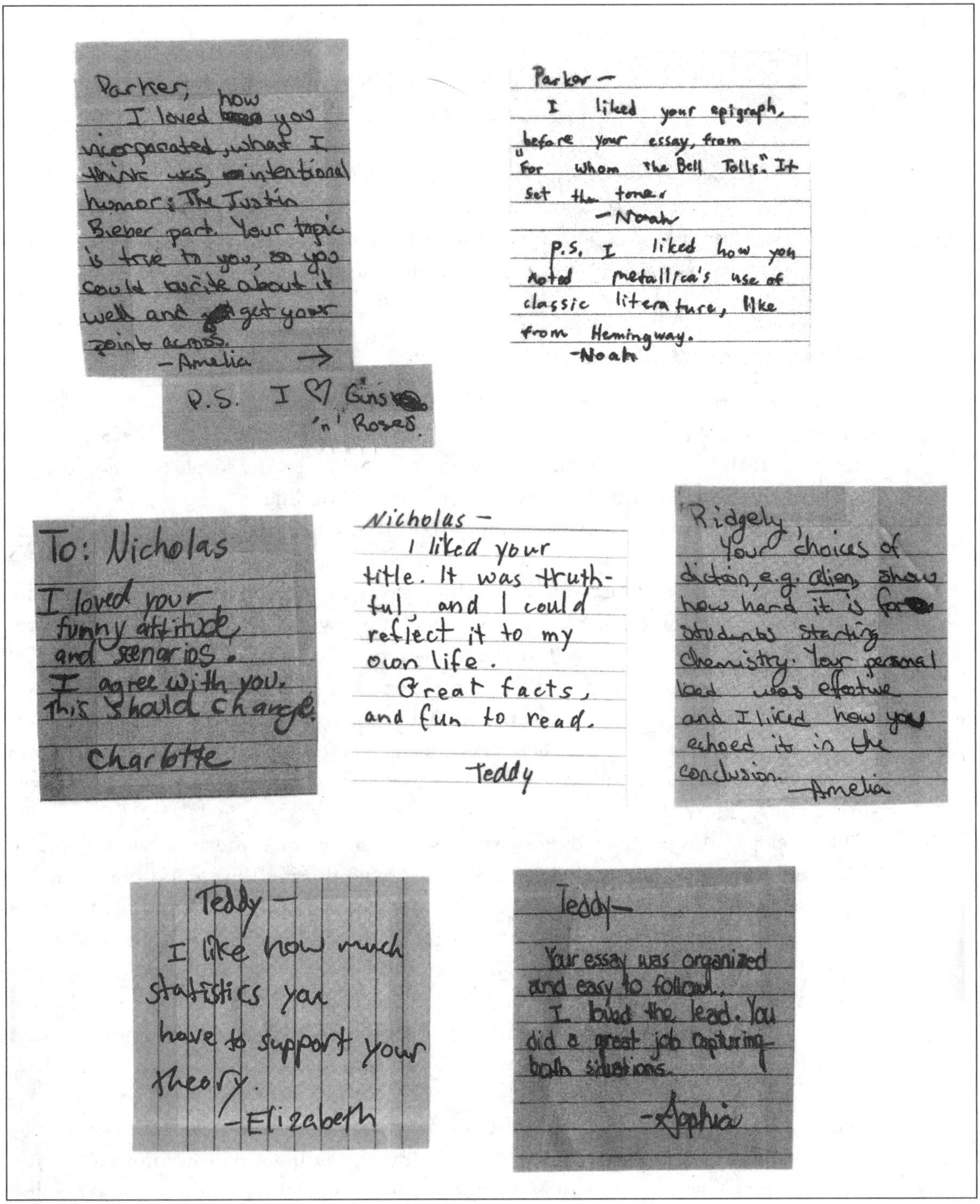

Parker;
I loved how you incorporated, what I think was, intentional humor: The Justin Bieber part. Your topic is true to you, so you could write about it well and get your point across.
—Amelia →

P.S. I ♡ Guns 'n' Roses.

Parker —
I liked your epigraph, before your essay, from "For whom the Bell Tolls." It set the tone.
—Noah
P.S. I liked how you noted metallica's use of classic literature, like from Hemingway.
—Noah

To: Nicholas
I loved your funny attitude, and scenarios. I agree with you. This should change.
Charlotte

Nicholas —
I liked your title. It was truthful, and I could reflect it to my own life.
Great facts, and fun to read.
Teddy

Ridgely,
Your choices of diction, e.g. alien, show how hard it is for students starting chemistry. Your personal lead was effective and I liked how you echoed it in the conclusion.
—Amelia

Teddy —
I like how much statistics you have to support your theory.
—Elizabeth

Teddy —
Your essay was organized and easy to follow.
I loved the lead. You did a great job capturing both situations.
—Sophia

Figure 12.13 *Students' Notes to Peer Essayists*

Advocacy Journalism

This has become an important genre in my workshop. Advocacy journalism gives kids firsthand experience in conducting and reporting original research, creates a platform for them to learn about local causes, and, for some, launches their involvement in community service. Maine is the least philanthropic state in the nation, according to national surveys and polls. I'd like to help reverse that trend. Our study begins in early May with a discussion of nonprofit organizations and *persuasive exposition*, which is what advocacy journalism is: a persuasive essay with something real at stake.

THE LESSON

CTL is a nonprofit organization or NPO. That means no one owns it or owns shares in it. If the school ever ended the year with our budget *in the black*—with more money coming in than we spent, which has never ever happened—the surplus would go right back into tuition assistance and improvements to the building or program.

We're one of almost a hundred nonprofit organizations in our part of Maine. Each one has a mission. CTL's is to be a demonstration school—to teach regular kids, develop new and powerful methods for teaching them, and share our practices with other teachers. What are some other local nonprofits? What would you say their missions are?

For the next few weeks we'll be learning about the work of local NPOs. Each of you will select one to research. You'll go there as a reporter, conduct an interview, observe what they do, and turn your notes into a persuasive essay about why this NPO is worthy of people's support. This genre is called *advocacy journalism.* You'll investigate an organization you believe in and *advocate* for it: write in support of it. At stake are three small grants—more about that in a minute.

I developed this genre study for two reasons. I hope you'll discover causes you care about and grow up to become the kind of citizen who donates time, goods, or money to help people, animals, and the environment. There are a handful of nonprofits I support because I care so much about their work—Planned Parenthood, Doctors Without Borders, Seas of Peace (which was started by CTL alum David Nutt), the Boothbay Region Food Pantry, Maine Public Broadcasting, and CTL. I can't write checks as big as I'd like, but every little bit helps. What I get, in return, is a feeling of satisfaction from lending a hand to people who need it and work I believe in. I want you to know that feeling in your lives.

The second reason you'll write advocacy journalism is to learn how to conduct firsthand research. Although you may start your investigation with an organization's website, to get your feet under you, the rest of the process will depend on information you gather on-site. You'll observe and take notes; you'll conduct interviews and take notes; and you'll put the skills you learned as essayists to work as you compose this special kind of persuasive essay.

Here's what's at stake. I applied for and received a grant of $750. This is money we'll give away, in the form of three grants to local nonprofits. When the pieces of advocacy journalism are complete, you'll divide into three groups, depending on the focus of your NPO, and present your essay to kids in grades 1–2, or grades 3–4, or grades 5–6. They'll rate them, and their ratings will determine which pieces of advocacy journalism are the most effective. Three NPOs will receive grants of $250 from CTL thanks to the advocacy journalists in this class. In addition, I hope every piece will find a home in a newspaper that's local to its subject, to inform people of its mission and methods and garner community support.

At this point, what are your questions and observations?

Each fall I apply for a small grant of up to $1,000—funds that CTL will distribute to nonprofits based on kids' research—and the money always materializes. Some foundations have an interest in nurturing philanthropical habits among young people. If I taught in a public or charter school, I'd post this project on DonorsChoose.org.

That night for homework, students meet with a parent to create as long a list as they can of local nonprofit organizations. I collect these, create a master list, and distribute it so students can begin to consider which NPOs call their names and fit with their families' interests. I also distribute a packet of examples of advocacy journalism.

Some of the essays were written by students in previous years—I've included three here for other teachers to use in their workshops. Others are columns I collect from the op-ed page of the *New York Times*, fund-raising appeals I receive in the mail, and articles from *The Boothbay Register* and *The Lincoln County News* about the needs of the local food pantry and animal shelter. Students read them, tease out their features, meet in small groups to talk about them, and collaborate on a master list:

FEATURES OF EFFECTIVE ADVOCACY JOURNALISM
- title that invites, fits, and isn't a label
- strong lead
- first paragraph that embeds the name of the organization, its location, and its purpose, in the voice of the reporter
- *I* voice
- description of the nature and severity of the problem the organization addresses
- evidence
  - programs they offer
  - typical day at the organization
  - accomplishments
  - geographical area they serve

- anecdotes: little stories about the organization in action
  - types and numbers of clients they help
  - statistics
  - impact of the organization on the community
- history
  - year founded and by whom
  - background on the founder(s)
  - goals/missions statement
  - funding sources
- quotes from people who work there
- quotes that echo a point the reporter has made
- info about who works or volunteers there
- description of the atmosphere at the organization
- explanation of how and where the organization raises awareness of its target issue and program
- suggestions of what the organization would use the grant for
- prose that moves logically and gracefully from point to point
- compression: no rambling
- short, friendly paragraphs
- strong, deliberate, persuasive conclusion that ties in with the lead
- focused message or argument
- about six hundred words in length

Each student creates a list of his or her top three choices of an NPO. It's important that they have more than one option, because more than one student may select the same nonprofit, or an organization might not be amenable to a visit from a cub reporter. And then I introduce a process for writing the genre:

A PROCESS FOR WRITING ADVOCACY JOURNALISM, AKA THE PERSUASIVE ESSAY

- **Define the problem.**
  What do I need to know? What do readers need to know, understand, *believe?*

- **Collect information for the reader *and* for me.**
  Work from quantity. See "Write with Information" in my handbook, plus write down *everything* when I conduct the site visit and interview.

- **Play with leads.**
  Experiment off-the-page until I find the best way in—the lead that gives voice and focus to my message, information, and conclusion; a lead that's clear, true, inviting, and to the point.

- **Develop a plan that focuses my information and brings order to it.**
  Cut up my notes as to beginning-middle-end, use colored markers or a system of numbers, or spread out my notes, label the different kinds of information I find, and, in notes off-the-page, create an order for it.

- **Draft the information.**
  Use my plan as a foundation to draft paragraphs of information as a logical, well-supported argument.

- **Revise. Clarify and tighten the information, close the holes, cut the rambling, and make it sing.**
  Does the rest of the essay deliver on the promise of the lead? Does it make sense throughout? Are the paragraphs friendly? Does each paragraph build on the one that came before it? Are there transitional words to help a reader move from one paragraph to the next? Is the language precise and interesting? Does it flow? Is there enough information—enough specifics—to convince a reader of the worth of this organization?

- **Experiment with conclusions.**
  Play off-the-page until I find the ending that connects with the lead, clinches my argument, and leaves a reader thinking about my NPO.

- **Brainstorm a title.**
  Play with alternatives until I find the combination of words that conveys my message and invites a reader.

- **Take a two-day walk-away.**
  When I return, read one of the pieces of advocacy journalism in my prose folder and the master list of genre features. Then, pen in hand, read my draft. What do I need to do to make it interesting, coherent, complete, and *convincing* to CTL's younger students?

Once everyone has determined which nonprofit organization to research, students use either the telephone in the classroom or my cell phone to contact their NPO and schedule a site visit. They're nervous wrecks about this, so I provide an outline of a script.

Telephone Script for Arranging an NPO Visit

Hello. My name is _____ _____. May I please speak to the director or manager? (*If he or she isn't there, ask:* When will he or she be available?)

Hello. My name is _____ _____. I'm a(n) _____th grade student at the Center for Teaching and Learning, a K–8 school in Edgecomb. Our school has a small philanthropy grant. Your nonprofit is one of the organizations the children at my school are considering donating to. We're making three awards of $250 each.

I'd like to research your organization as a possible grant recipient. Could I schedule a day and time when I might observe the work of your group, interview you, and collect any print materials you could make available?

The best days for me are _____

_____.

What's best for you? _____

_____.

That's great. Thank you. Where and when, exactly, should we meet? _____

_____

_____

_____.

That's _____

_____

_____ (confirmation).

(*If you need directions:* How do I get to your office?) _____

_____

_____

_____

_____

_____

I'll see you then. Thanks for your time. I'm looking forward to meeting you and learning about the work of your organization. If you need to get in touch with me before the interview, I can be reached at school at _____ or home at _____. Good-bye.

Kids conduct the site visits after school, on a Saturday, or during school hours with parental approval and assistance. I give them a window of a week and a half to get these set up and done. Meanwhile, I teach how to conduct an interview. These are the tips that have proved most helpful to my students.

INTERVIEW AND QUOTING TIPS

- Don't use a tape recorder: it's not writing, not getting the *meaning*, plus it takes about ten hours to transcribe one hour of taped conversation.

- Listen for the good quotes and capture exact words. Remember that writing comes alive when quotes—people's voices—are woven into it.

- When your interviewee speaks too fast, say, "Please, could you hold it a minute?" Write until you catch up; then look back up to show him or her you're ready.

- Develop abbreviations (@, w/, b/c, +, wd., shd., =, #); omit small words (*the, a, of, in*); write the first letter (or two) of a word and leave a space for the rest of it.

- Go with your list of principal questions. Listen well, and ask follow-up questions.

- Remember that the best follow-up questions start with *Why?*
- Try to chunk information as you record it—leave air around the different subtopics by skipping lines between them or drawing boxes around them.
- Take either a laptop and a cord, signed out with Krista, *or* a lined notebook and 3–4 sharp pencils or pens that flow well.
- Prepare the notebook (or laptop) by writing a question at the top of every other page. Don't write on the backs of pages, since it's likely you'll need to cut and tape the information later.
- Do your homework about the organization before you go: find out what you can about their purpose and history.
- Go through your notes right after the interview. Fill in the missing letters and words, and pick out the key quotes.

Students will need practice formulating questions, following up, and taking notes. I ask them to pair up, write a question I suggest or one we come up with together at the top of a piece of paper, and try the interview strategies on each other, while I circulate, sit in with the pairs, and offer guidance, especially about exact quotes, abbreviating, and follow-up questions. Practice questions that work involve topics like *family* (What are your family members' names and their relationship to you? How do you feel about each of them? Why?), *high school* (Where do you plan, or where would you like, to go to high school? Why?), and a *favorite book or movie* (Why this one?). We debrief afterward about what was difficult or surprising, and the next day students try it again, in new duos with a new question.

In another minilesson, the class and I generate a list of basic questions to ask about a nonprofit organization:

- How old is your organization?
- Who started it?
- Why?
- What's its purpose?
- Who do you serve?
- What exactly do you do to help?
- How many people/animals/visitors/women/children/citizens do you serve each year?
- What are some of your accomplishments?
- What might you use the grant for?
- Do volunteers help you with your work? How?
- Can you tell me an anecdote or two about your work?

- How do you feel about this work? Why?
- Is there anything else I should know about your organization that I can tell the children at my school?

Once students return from their site visits, the writing process is the same as for the essays they composed earlier in the year. They consult the relevant entries in their handbooks to review kinds of expository leads, ways to focus and organize their information, transitional words and phrases, and types of essay conclusions. A new minilesson is a discussion of explanatory phrases or tag lines to use when quoting an interviewee. *Said* is fine—it's the verb journalists use most often. Other possibilities my students brainstormed include *explained, commented, noted, clarified, suggested, stated, pointed out, confirmed,* and *acknowledged.*

One final task is to divide the persuasive essays into three groups, depending on the nature of the NPO's work. For example, my students decided that Head Start, a home for the elderly, and a boys' camp with a leadership program were appropriate subjects to present to the first- and second-grade class, while a battered women's shelter, a program for grieving children, and a group home for mentally challenged adults were deemed NPOs better suited for an audience of fifth and sixth graders.

Before their presentations, students generate a list of criteria for the younger children to base their ratings on. Because my kids worry that grades 1–6 kids might be swayed by personal relationships with presenters or a family history of involvement with an NPO, a version of the information below appears at the top of the ballot.

Criteria for Voting on a CTL Nonprofit Grant

Persuasiveness: after listening to and reading along with the presentations, *this* one was the most convincing to you because of the quality of the writing:

- an inviting lead that goes right to the point
- evidence and arguments that make you believe that this organization's work is the most important
- organized information that flows naturally from point to point
- a strong conclusion that connects with the lead and leaves you thinking

NOTE: *Do not* consider a favorite seventh or eighth grader, your brother or sister, or an organization your family is involved with. Your job is to judge the persuasive quality of the *writing*.

John's essay about a camp experience for veterans of Iraq and Afghanistan won a grant to support its continuation. It helped that John went beyond objective reporting and was himself involved in the program: he could bring to his advocacy journalism the little stories that are often the most convincing evidence of all.

"A Small Thing We Can Do to Help"

Quote by Maria Millard, Director of Camp Kieve's Veterans' Program

Three friends—soldiers—who had been deployed to Iraq were eating in a mess hall when it was hit by a suicide bomber. These three and other survivors were immediately evacuated by helicopter to European hospitals, to be treated for their physical injuries as well as PTSD, or Post Traumatic Stress Disorder. Once the men could walk, they were sent to US hospitals and, eventually, home. They lost touch with one another. Months later, the three happened to all sign up for a program at Camp Kieve in Nobleboro that serves veterans of Iraq and Afghanistan. At Kieve, they were miraculously, and joyously, reunited. This is exactly what Dick Kennedy and Maria Millard want: for soldiers to have a place where their experiences and memories will be shared with men and women who know firsthand what they went through after 9/11/01.

Dick Kennedy is the son of Don Kennedy, who started the boys' camp at Kieve in 1926. In 2001, Dick began a 9/11 camp session for children affected by the World Trade Center attacks. Then, in 2009, he had an idea for a similar camp for veterans of the armed forces. He knew there wasn't a place for soldiers to gather and talk. The army only provides a power-point presentation when a soldier's tour is over, basically saying "act normal." When they get home, soldiers are shoved into regular life, many of them emotionally damaged by their memories of what they saw and did.

My father, a sergeant first class, and my mother were two of about forty volunteers for the first two one-week sessions of the veterans' camp at Kieve. I got to accompany them and see the operation in action. At first light, some of the soldiers attended chapel, where a local pastor volunteered her services. At nine, everybody walked or drove to breakfast. The rest of the day included choices of snowshoeing, ice fishing, indoor rock climbing, pottery, spoon carving, and, for a lucky few, massages. Snacks were provided all day. At eight, everyone filtered into the building at the bottom of the hill for dinner and then an after-dinner activity.

Maria Millard related, "In the first two sessions of the program, we helped about forty people spend quality time with their families and make new friends who they could talk to and connect with." She said she wants to serve ten times as many veterans this year.

Maria said, "If we were to receive a grant from CTL, it would go into replication: to help fund another week of the Maine program this year. Kieve is also teaching veterans' camps in North Carolina, Texas, and Minnesota about what we did and learned from the program, so similar opportunities can be made available to veterans in other parts of the country."

At the end of his week at Kieve, a soldier presented a slide show of pictures he had taken while he was on tour in Iraq. The show was rewarded with frequent calls of "Hey, I remember that!" "Boy, do I have a story for that one!" "Hey, when did you take that?" and "That brings back memories." I watched as the soldiers' eyes lit up at certain images. They turned to new friends to tell them about a flashback, or old friends, like those in that mess hall in Iraq ten years ago, who had survived a nightmare.

The veterans' program at Kieve is the only place I know where this kind of healing happens. It's something I strongly support, and something you can, too.

—*John Solorzano*

Parker became a volunteer for the nonprofit organization he investigated and wrote about. Although he did not win a grant for the organization Rebuilding Together, he rolled up his sleeves and joined their efforts to repair and winterize the homes of elderly citizens. In his essay, below, he notes, "There is no age limit—the youngest volunteer is only twelve." That would be Parker.

"They Made My House Smile"

Imagine a house in this community, rotting away and falling down. It's a health hazard, but an old woman lives there, alone. She knows what needs to be done, but she can't do it herself, and she can't afford to pay someone to do it for her. Then along comes a group of volunteers. They tear off old siding and replace it, paint walls, and remove trash, all at their own expense. They are the Lincoln County branch of Rebuilding Together, a group of volunteers who fix local houses every spring. Later in the year, they will return and prepare the house for the season of snow, or, as they put it, "Winter-proof it."

Rebuilding Together is a national organization. It started over thirty years ago when a group of kind Texas neighbors worked together one April to repair houses in their area. Their selfless actions inspired the nation, and in 1988, Rebuilding Together was incorporated. Since then, they have worked nationally to repair houses and provide safe living conditions for homeowners.

Rebuilding Together began to make a local impact eleven years ago, when Boothbay selectman Joyce Armendaris, who had participated in the national effort, told local lawyer Chip Griffin about the organization and suggested they start a branch to cover Lincoln County. He was intrigued by the idea, so they gave it a shot.

However, they changed the main workday to May, because of the difficulty of working in Maine's April weather. As a rough estimate, Armendaris told me, "We help fifteen to twenty-five elderly, low-income residents each year, replacing siding, building ramps for disabled citizens, repairing roofs, and sometimes just applying a coat of paint or primer."

Every volunteer in the Rebuilding Together group lends his or her own skills: a carpenter handles woodworking, an electrician deals with the wiring, a plumber reroutes the pipes. All kinds of people help, even those without professional training. There is no age limit—the youngest volunteer is only twelve. The groups are organized by captains, based on their areas of expertise.

The official mission of Rebuilding Together in Lincoln County is to "Keep them warm, safe, and dry." However, their repairs extend further, sometimes to the psychological health of the homeowner, as when volunteers closed in a deck to keep animals from getting under a house. As one older homeowner put it, "They made my house smile."

Rebuilding Together would use a grant from CTL to fund their next large project, winter-proofing local houses in the fall. The money, combined with other donations, would go into a fund reserved for the purchase of raw materials such as wood, caulk, and insulation.

The house that had been rotting away stands proud now, braving the heavy rain and winds. The old woman lives there still, safe, warm, and dry. She is secure in her home, all because of the volunteer labor and generous hearts of Lincoln County Rebuilding Together.

—*Parker Elkins*

Seventh grader Sophia became aware of and then passionate about the work of Feed Our Scholars, an NPO that sends children from impoverished families home from school on Friday afternoons with backpacks full of food for weekend meals.

A SMALL SOLUTION TO A BIG PROBLEM

Gretchen Burleigh-Johnson was a Wiscasset teacher who had seen too many of her students suffer from hunger. She watched kids become lost in class and fall behind their peers because all they could think about was where their next meal might come from. Gretchen stated, "Child hunger is like a rolling snowball: the problem keeps getting bigger and bigger." Contacting folks at the regional nonprofit Feed Our Scholars was her response to this crucial issue. Gretchen presented the idea for the program to other retired Wiscasset teachers, as well as the Good Shepherd Food Bank. Today, this fundraising group aims to provide forty kids from the Wiscasset Primary and Middle Schools with a backpack full of healthy food every Friday afternoon.

Over the last few years, similar backpack programs have helped families all over New England. Thanks to Gretchen, Feed Our Scholars kicked off in Wiscasset this year. Their goal is to raise ten thousand dollars by August. This will be just enough to provide forty children with proper nutrients and a better chance to be successful students in the 2013–14 school year.

There are around seven hundred students in the Wiscasset school system, and half of them are on the free or reduced lunch program. This means that 54% of the children enrolled in the primary school, 64% of middle school-ers, and 47% of high school students come from families that are struggling financially. School cafeterias provide a Monday through Friday breakfast and lunch to these students. On weekends, many go hungry. Feed Our Scholars believes this isn't right.

Gretchen explained, "The children who receive this food aid are identified, confidentially, by Wiscasset school employees who are aware of each child's situation. The backpacks are quietly given to the chosen recipients to take home, ensuring that they, their siblings, and their parents have something to eat over the weekend." One Wiscasset teacher noted, "Children are eager to get their food on Fridays. They are proud to be taking food home to their families."

Feed Our Scholars relies on donations to continue providing meals for needy students and their families. If this organization receives CTL's grant, all of it will go directly to the purchase of food. A donation of $250 will be just enough to ensure that one child and his or her family have enough to eat for a school year of weekends.

When Gretchen Burleigh-Johnson brought this program to Wiscasset, she knew it was a small step towards solving a big problem. Hunger is everywhere. Your vote could make a huge impact on the lives of kids around you: in your neighborhood, on your sports team, even a friend. By supporting Feed Our Scholars, you give a hungry child the chance to be a learner.

—*Sophia Stafford*

Sophia's essay did not win over CTL's little kids. The kid it did win over is Sophia. She is on fire about food insecurity in America. As an eighth grader she devoted a dawn-to-dusk Saturday to baking cookies—hundreds of cookies—and on Sunday set up a bake sale at her church that raised over $700 for Feed Our Scholars, almost enough for a year of weekend food backpacks for three local families.

As writing teachers, we are at a critical juncture. We can refocus our instruction so it aligns with the bureaucratic language and goals of the standards movement. Or we can approach writing as one of the humanities and invite students to engage in worthwhile work that exceeds the standards—to learn what writing is good for and, in the process, contribute to making the world a better place.

Profiles

Because I teach my students for two years, I alternate the approach to conducting and reporting firsthand research. One May they write advocacy journalism; the next they craft profiles of local women who are engaged in interesting work.

While I recognize that rural Maine isn't the only place in the United States where the political and cultural agenda is mostly set by men, I want my students to observe, acknowledge, and call attention to the work of local women and the contributions they make to the life of our community. As a writing teacher, I also want them to learn how to bring people and their experiences to life on the page, and to find *so what?*s or themes for the brief biographies they create. So I collect, from magazines and newspapers, ten profiles of people I think my students will be interested in—athletes, actors, young adult authors, and ordinary people doing extraordinary things. Then I introduce the genre study:

THE LESSON

The genre we'll work with next is the profile. A profile is an informal biographical sketch—not a detailed summary of someone's whole life, but a close look at a person in action, often on a job. Like the reviews and essays you've written, it's an expository genre but more story-like than the others. The writer researches what makes a person different and important by observing and interviewing her and others in her environment, and then telling her story. By the way, those feminine gender references are intentional—I'll come back to this in a minute.

I love to read profiles—in *The New York Times, Entertainment Weekly, The New Yorker, Vanity Fair, Rolling Stone, Sports Illustrated,* even *People.* People *do* want to read about people; our curiosity about others is a natural condition of our humanity.

I'll ask you to research and write profiles as a way to learn how to conduct and report firsthand research—to become curious about someone or something; experience interviewing, observing, and note-taking; focus the data you gather; give it a pleasing shape; and, in this case, publish it so others can learn about someone who's doing cool work.

The subjects of your profiles will be local women. It's not that I'm prejudiced against men; it's that even in the twenty-first century, we still don't hear enough about women's contributions to society. So you'll be performing a public service by informing the readership of local papers about interesting women in our community. In addition to publishing the profiles in-house in *Acorns,* I'll help you contact local newspaper editors and submit your profiles as feature articles.

This weekend for homework, please choose and read six profiles from this packet of ten—sketches of interesting people from *Sports Illustrated, Rolling Stone, The New York Times,* and *The New Yorker* and by CTL alums—with a pencil in your hand. Underline kinds of information, titles, leads and conclusions, specific details, anecdotes, and technical vocabulary. Notice the structure, use of quotes, voice, verb tense, and *so what?* Then go back and look at what you underlined and create a list in your writing–reading handbook of the Genre Features of a Profile, just as you did earlier this year for memoirs, reviews, and essays.

Comments? Questions? Observations?

The next day students meet in small groups, discuss their features lists, collaborate on a group list, and then tell me what they noticed, while I take notes. This master list, created from one class' contributions, is typical.

FEATURES OF AN EFFECTIVE PROFILE

- a grabbing title that fits the whole piece
- a packed lead that points the direction and sets the tone for the rest of the profile
- the writer's voice and judgments about the subject, but without an *I*.
- inclusion of the subject's full name early on; thereafter, references to her by last name only
- key facts: who, what, where, when, why information
- revealing quotes from the subject about her life, her work, and what it means to her
- revealing quotes from the people around her about her work and life
- indirect quotes: summaries of things she or others said
- background information, e.g., where she lives, her work history, her personal history
- specifics that illustrate, demonstrate, and reveal her work
- the vocabulary of her work
- a physical description: her appearance
- a description of her work routine and the details of the job
- a description of the environment
- her process as a worker
- little stories that reveal the name of her work and what she's like
- her path to this line of work
- her heroes, mentors, or sources of inspiration
- visuals that show her in action
- sensory verbs and adjectives
- explanatory phrases (*she saids*) and descriptions of her in action that break up long quotes
- friendly paragraphs
- present-tense verbs except when describing her background
- a *so what?* or *focus*: a big idea about her and her work
- a conclusion that connects with the beginning and resonates

For homework that night, students talk with their parents about potential subjects for their profiles. I ask them to come up with names of three to five women from their immediate community who they might like to observe at work and interview, with the provision that they can't be their teachers, mothers, or other female relatives. Kids need distance from their subjects, so they'll be able to be curious and notice fresh, revealing specifics.

The next day, as the minilesson, I teach a process for writing a profile. Then I meet with individuals, review their choices with them, and help each settle on a subject who's suitable in terms of the location and nature of her work, and one no one else has claimed.

A PROCESS FOR WRITING A PROFILE

- **Collect information for the reader *and* for me.**

   During the site visit and interview, act as a sponge. Write down everything I can—observations and quotes—so later I'll be able to work from quantity and be selective. Observe the woman at work *before* I interview her—it will help me come up with new questions to ask her. Immediately after the site visit and interview, go over my notes, clarify and clean them up, and add anything I missed. (If there's time, type them up.)

- **Create a focus.**

   Read through my notes. What surprised me most? What's the most important thing I learned? Then, in one sentence, determine the *focus* of my profile—its big idea or dominant impression.

- **Play with leads.**

   Experiment off-the-page until I find the best way in—a lead that conveys the focus I've chosen for my information, plus one that's clear, packed, and intriguing. Then revise and polish it.

- **Experiment with conclusions.**

   Play off-the-page until I find an ending that connects with the lead and the focus I've chosen.

- **Develop a plan.**

   Select an approach to help me bring order to my notes, for example, cut them up as to beginning-middle-end, use colored markers or a number system, or spread out my notes, label the different kinds of information I find, and, off-the-page, create an order for what will happen between my lead and my conclusion.

- **Draft the information.**

   Use my plan as a foundation to draft paragraphs of information that unspool in a logical order, anticipate a reader's questions, and connect the lead and conclusion.

- **Revise. Clarify and tighten the information, close the holes, cut the rambling, and make it sing.**

   Does the rest of the profile deliver on the promise of the lead? Does it make sense throughout? Have I anticipated and answered a reader's questions? Does each paragraph build on the one that came before it? Are the paragraphs friendly? Are there transitional words to help a reader move from one paragraph to the next? Is the language precise and interesting? Is there enough information—enough specifics—to convince a reader that this woman and her work are an interesting, worthwhile subject for a profile?

- **Brainstorm a title.**

  Play with alternatives until I find the combination of words that conveys my focus and invites a reader.

- **Take a two-day walk-away.**

  When I return, reread the best profile in my prose folder *and* the profile checklist. Then, pen in hand, read my draft. What do I need to do to clarify the focus and make the profile more coherent, specific, and engaging?

- **Polish, edit, and publish.**

Students have a week to schedule their site visits. As I did with the advocacy journalism projects, I let them use my cell phone and the classroom telephone to make appointments, and I provide a script.

> ### Telephone Script for Arranging a Profile
>
> Hi, my name is _____. I'm in a writing class at the Center for Teaching and Learning. I think your work as a _____ is important and interesting, and I'd like to write a profile about you and what you do. If you agree, I'll attempt to get it published in _____ _____. Would you be willing to let me write about you and your work?
>
> If no: Thank you very much for your time. Good-bye.
>
> If yes: That's great. Thank you. I'd like to schedule a day when I can do two things: first, observe you at work, and then meet with you for about an hour to talk one-to-one. Is this okay? _____.
>
> The best days for me are _____. What's best for you? _____.
>
> That's great. I'd like to spend at least a few hours with you, so where and when shall we plan on meeting? That's _____ _____ (confirm the time, place, and date).
>
> I'll see you then. If you need to reach me in the meantime, my home phone is _____. You can also leave a message for me at school at _____.
>
> Thank you very much. Good-bye.

Students prepare for the site visits as they do for the advocacy journalism project: we review the list of tips for conducting an interview, and pairs of students practice the techniques. Then I suggest baseline questions for the interview and essential observations for them to capture.

OBSERVATIONS TO NOTE ON-SITE

- sensory details about the subject in action: her pace, movements, manner, and process as a worker, plus what she says while on the job
- sensory details about the subject's appearance that will bring her to life: her manner of speaking, gestures, clothing, physical size, hands, hair, eyes, habits
- sensory details of the physical environment
- details about other people in the environment
- details about how the subject interacts with others in her environment
- details about her and her work that surprise you
- **Remember: if you don't write it down, you don't have it to use later**

BASIC QUESTIONS FOR A PROFILE INTERVIEW

- How would you describe yourself and what you do?
- Why did you choose this work?
- How long have you been doing this?
- What got you interested in this work?
- What do you get from your job? How does it make you feel?
- What's the best part of the job?
- What's difficult? Easy? Satisfying? Frustrating?
- Can you tell me a story about _____ that shows what you mean?
- What gives you your feelings of greatest accomplishment?
- Where did you grow up?
- What was your preparation for this job?
- Did you have a mentor or mentors?
- **Note: Try to get both *what* she says and *how* she says it. Try to pose new questions based on your observations of her at work.**

Once students return from their site visits, they use the process I defined and the handbook lessons they learned as essayists to plan and draft their profiles. But first I introduce kinds of profile leads to play with, along with types of conclusions. In both lessons I push, hard, the idea of finding a focus for the profile. It's this quality that separates okay profiles from great ones—when a writer has brought his or her intelligence to bear on an accumulation of data and selected an essential issue, impression, or theme.

SOME IDEAS FOR PROFILE LEADS

- the hopes, dreams, or desires of this woman
- who, what, when, where, why information
- a description of her work environment
- a description of the woman in action as she engages in her work
- a packed-with-action lead to indicate a multitasking woman
- a revealing anecdote about her
- an overview—a bold statement about her and her work
- the woman speaking: a direct quote
- **BUT ALWAYS** an indication of the *focus*: an essential issue or theme of this woman's story

SOME IDEAS FOR PROFILE CONCLUSIONS

- a revealing anecdote
- a quote: the woman speaking or someone speaking about her
- a description of the scene
- a description of the woman in action
- a direct statement from you, the writer, about this woman: a final observation or conclusion
- **AND ALWAYS** circle back to the lead and echo the focus you selected

Once students have planned, drafted, and revised and feel as if their profiles are close to done, they take the traditional two-day walk-away. When they return to their profiles a couple of days older and smarter, they measure the draft against one of the good profiles in their prose folders. Then they use a checklist like the one that follows, based on the list of genre features, as a guide in reading their profiles as critics.

PROFILE CHECKLIST

- Is the title inviting? Does it fit the whole profile?
- Is the lead packed with information? Does it invite a reader to care? Does it establish a focus for the rest of the profile?
- Does the end connect with the beginning and the focus?
- Is the woman alive on the page? Can we see her, her physical appearance and on the job?
- Can we see her work environment?
- Do we hear her voice throughout the profile, directly quoted?
- Do we see her as she's speaking?
- Do we know why she does what she does?

- Do we understand how she feels about it—what it means to her?
- Do we know how she got here?
- Have you followed the conventions of no *I*, present-tense verbs except when describing background, last name only once you've introduced her whole name, friendly paragraphs, and correct punctuation and paragraphing of quotes?

In his profile of the proprietor of a new ice-cream shop in his hometown, Xander's notes led him to focus on her work ethic and the pride she takes—justifiably—in the fruits of her many labors.

MARY SREDEN: BATH'S DAIRY QUEEN

It's noon at Dot's ice cream shop in Bath, and Mary Sreden, owner and founder, is hard at work. Wrapped in a large white apron, her brown hair pulled back in a ponytail, she whips off a batch of chocolate chip cookies, then starts on the batter for whoopie pies. "Today is a slow day," she says. "When we're busy, we're always on the go, so I try to get everything done before that happens." She is busy, to say the least. Sreden is at Dot's seven days a week, sometimes for just a few hours but on busy days spending as many as twelve hours here. Since Dot's opened, she has done almost everything. "I manage the staff, the scheduling, the payroll, the bookkeeping, the ordering of supplies, and the baking," she counts off. She's an ambitious and committed entrepreneur.

Sreden grew up with a strong work ethic. In northern Minnesota, where she was born, her mother Dorothy-Jean—or Dot, for whom the shop is named—raised seven children. Sreden was the youngest. When she was in sixth grade, her mother went to work to pay for her sister's college tuition. "She did everything," Sreden confirms.

As a result of this great maternal role model, Sreden began her working life as a high school student, serving ice cream at the local parlor. As a kid she also painted houses, moved lawns, and served as a camp counselor. She sailed around the world as the chief medical officer on a boat and is still a registered nurse to this day.

But Sreden always wanted her own business. When she moved to Bath, there were no ice cream shops. She researched small businesses, read a lot about how they run, and created a business plan. She also went over all her mom's old recipes for baked goods. When Dot's first opened, she was scared it wouldn't do well. "I was always worried," she admits. Today she says her feeling of greatest accomplishment comes from getting the business up and running.

Sreden lives with her husband Hal and is mother to Sophie, a freshman in high school, Noa, a seventh grader, and Abby and Zoe, twins in fourth grade. Recently Zoe's class saw a video in which a nine-year-old girl from

Washington State died in a car crash while trying to raise funds to provide clean water in undeveloped countries. They decided this was an important cause and joined a community project called Charity Water. Their goal is to raise $5,000 to provide a well for an African school.

Sreden has been a frontrunner in the fundraising effort, teaming up with Shains of Maine, an ice cream maker, to create a new ice cream flavor, H2O. It stands for "Help To Others," as well as representing the chemical formula for water. A portion of every sale at Dot's goes to the fundraising effort.

On Dot's maize-colored walls, signs reading "1 out of 8 people does not have clean drinking water" and "Buy a $10 H2O shirt and get a quart of H2O ice cream free" hang next to the list of flavors of ice cream. The walls also feature many photographs: snapshots of Bath seniors, the Sreden family, other locals, and happy customers.

The small bell above the brown door rings, and a new customer—a self described "ice cream cone aficionado"—enters. She orders a medium java crunch and then asks about the newspaper article about Charity Water that hangs above the cash register. Sreden explains the project and expresses how proud she is of her daughter's class. She tells what she appreciates most about the effort: "It's expanded their little world from Bath, Maine, to a more global view."

The woman pays, and Sreden smiles, clearly delighted with Zoe's class's efforts and how the news is spreading. As the woman licks her ice cream, she pauses only to give a compliment. "This is great." she enthuses, and with that, Sreden's smile only grows, her pride evident.

As a stream of customers begins to stroll into Dot's, Sreden meets them all with a warm welcome and an ice cream scoop in hand. The customers range from regulars to first timers, but they all have compliments. A grey haired woman, ice cream sundae in hand, exclaims, "This is a nice place! I like coming here." A vacationing mother with four kids calls Dot's "an attractive little spot."

Sreden serves their ice cream with gusto, clearly happy with her life and job. "Hard work pays off," she says. "When you want something in life, you have to go out and work for it." The slow day has become a faster one. Sreden has worked hard on Dot's, and that work has paid off. It shows in every child and adult who walks through the brown door and leaves with a smile—and ice cream—on his or her face.

—*Xander Bartone*

In her profile of the owner of Morning Dew Farm, Eloise focuses on the diversity of tasks a successful farmer has to take on—the many hats her subject wears. Eloise brings life to the farm with sensory images, pertinent quotes, details that reveal, and the kind of specifics that readers love.

Fertile Ground for a Rich Life

Brady Hatch of Morning Dew Farm in Newcastle wears a lot of hats: she is a salesperson, accountant, plumber, and, most importantly farmer. Because farming involves a wide range of responsibilities, she is never bored. "I am motivated to get out of bed in the morning because I always know what to do next," Hatch says. "And of course, I love the good food," she adds. Hatch, who was born in Maine, once traveled abroad, thinking she would find herself on foreign shores. Then she came home and found her true calling—farming.

This reporter is greeted by Maxwell, an ecstatic yellow dog who bounds towards the car and licks the reporter's face. Hatch walks down the driveway in a red flannel shirt and khakis, her blonde hair tucked into a cap. Her husband, Brenden, her mother, and two apprentices, Whitney and Sam, join us for a delicious meal grown on the farm. It features fresh salad mix, peppers and corn, and a stir fry of pork made from last year's pigs. Everybody is seated on benches and gobbles up the food, while Brenden entertains with his impersonations of the men on *Pawn Stars*. "I love sitting down with my family and friends to share the food we've grown. We eat together about four times a week," Hatch comments.

Her biggest struggle as a Maine farmer is weather, but she finds the Damariscotta region to be an amazing place, a community that is very rewarding. "Maine has many programs to help aspiring farmers, like Coastal Enterprises Incorporated and Maine Organic Farmers, so what I thought would have been challenges weren't," Hatch states. She has offered a community share program since 2004. "It's been great," she enthuses. "I've met some really great people, and it just keeps growing every year. We now have 101 families involved."

The process of becoming profitable wasn't as hard as she anticipated because people in the area are happy to be part of a local food movement. Some of Hatch's friends and neighbors let her use bits of their land to plant additional crops. They don't ask for money, but she always gives them generous amounts of produce as a thank-you. She sells and delivers her food to the Damariscotta Farmer's Market, which she is helping to run this year, along with Miles Hospital, local banks, River Grill, Public House, Treats, and Rising Tide. She makes runs about twice a week and delivers right to their freezers. For Rising Tide, she also provides vegetable seedlings.

Hatch never has a set schedule but, rather, does what needs to be done. A typical day on Morning Dew Farm starts off with a good breakfast as she goes over the plans for the day. Then come the morning chores: dealing with the greenhouses and watering plants. On harvest days she coordinates the crew and harvests in the morning when it's still cool, and then does fieldwork and weeding as the day goes on. They stop for lunch and dinner breaks and work till dark. Her favorite thing to do on the farm is to weed because, she says, "I find it meditative."

Hatch's two apprentices, who live in a tent on her property, are trying to learn enough about organic farming to go off on their own. Morning Dew has been bringing apprentices onto their farm for four years. Hatch says, "We have been lucky, because each apprentice brings something new to the farm that wasn't here before—a skill, recipe, attitude, something that stays after they leave."

Greenhouses and hoop houses are scattered around the property. Lettuce mix, cilantro, tomatoes, ginger, herbs, turnips, peppers, and the seedlings for Rising Tide all grow in the houses. Hatch rotates the plants through, depending on which need more warmth. When it's time to move plants out to the field, the process is gradual, to gently expose them to cool weather. For the outside crops, Hatch pulls clear plastic sheets over the rows when they need more warmth. She rotates the crops each season so the bugs don't know where plants will be. "This method has worked quite well. I'm glad we have found a pesticide-free way of avoiding bugs," she states.

Twelve pigs are fenced in the woods with an automatic feeder given to Hatch by her father, so the pigs are never hungry. She and her husband move the pigs further into the woods when they get bored with their surroundings and need new dirt. The lucky pigs receive food scraps and water every day and are much loved by Hatch, who scratches their backs and talks to them. "I love the noises they make," she admits as she tosses wilted broccoli rabe at them. In the fall she will take them to West Gardner Beef to be slaughtered and then sell them by the half-a-pig. Fifteen chickens roam the farm, but they provide eggs for the family only.

Brady Hatch is a strong woman who loves her work and is excited about getting more people involved in the organic and local food movements. If you live in the Midcoast Region, you may already be eating food from her Morning Dew Farm and appreciating the bounty created by this wearer of many hats.

—*Eloise Kelly*

As the profiles are completed, students use the classroom phone or borrow my cell again, this time to contact editors of newspapers, depending on which town a subject lives in, and try to place their profiles. Again, I provide a script to ease their trauma.

1. Hello, my name is _____. I'm trying to reach _____(the editor)_____.

2. Hello, I'm a student at the Center for Teaching and Learning in Edgecomb. My writing class has been researching local women doing interesting work, and I've written a profile of one of them: _____(name)_____, who _____(does what and lives where)_____. I'd like to submit this profile as a feature article for a future issue of _____(this newspaper)_____. Can I send it to you for your consideration? If yes: What's the appropriate e-mail address? _____ If no: Thank you for your time anyway.

All my students find homes for their profiles in community newspapers, and for the remainder of the school year they page through local weeklies in search of their bylines. I never see kids as excited about finished writing as they are the published profiles. And I hear again and again from the profiled women about community members who approach them to say, "I never knew this about you." Feature articles written by students help great women become visible in their communities.

When Donald Murray asserts, "Problems make good subjects," I can almost hear the satisfaction he finds in the word *problems*. For a writer, a good problem is an adventure—a chance to feel curious, hang suspended in time between one idea and the glimmer of the next, use writing to solve the new problems that writing creates, and understand what inspiration feels like.

Problems make for good teaching, too. Writing workshop is a place where students and a teacher can say "This is a problem I care about" and realize "I can write about it." Or think "I don't know" and understand "I can find out." The tension between caring and acting, between not knowing and knowing, becomes a continuous adventure and a source of inspiration for a lifetime of raising and solving problems.

CHAPTER 13

HUMOR AND HOMAGE

Outside of a dog, a book is a man's best friend.
Inside of a dog, it's too dark to read.

—GROUCHO MARX

I picked up a crumpled Post-it from the floor of my classroom, smoothed it out, and discovered a note from Josie to Morganne.

> My father's dead, my mother's wed,
> my uncle's sleeping in his bed.
> My girl's a spy and so am I,
> but I'm completely off my head.
>
> Oh, Hamlet, Hamlet, Hamlet . . .
> what are you gonna do?
> Oh, Hamlet, Hamlet, Hamlet,
> gonna die or see this through?

I laughed, of course. I also indulged in a moment of pride—in Josie for passing such a witty note, in Morganne for Josie's confidence that she would get it, and in the underground curriculum that thrives among kids who are literary insiders.

There is always an underground curriculum. It begins in kindergarten with dinosaurs and Star Wars, proceeds to jokes about poop and underwear, and in middle school takes the form of sarcasm and poking fun. The highest compliment someone can pay one of my students is "You're so funny."

Mostly they don't confuse poking fun with bullying. Seventh and eighth graders recognize meanness when they hear it, and they avoid the blatant cruelty that can rear its head in the intermediate grades. Instead, they develop a sense of irony: they begin to notice ways that the adult world doesn't do what it says. In writing workshop, they raise their pens about it.

Sophia raised hers after a lesson I taught about poetry contests and how to recognize a scam. Legitimate competitions often ask for a check up front, in the form of a reader's fee. But beware any that requests money from a "winning" poet to purchase a copy of the anthology in which all the "winning" poems are published. Once, before I knew better, I sent in a large check, only to receive in return what looked like a phonebook. My student's lovely poem was squished on a page among dozens of unlovely ones.

Sophia, who thought this was a hoot, wrote a poem that was just horrible enough to be credible. She submitted it to a scam contest and, lo and behold, "won." We resisted buying the phonebook in which it appears.

> LOVE!
>
> Love is a snake is proud of his brand new scale.
> Love is a father who is telling a tale.
> Love is a dragon flying with glee.
> Love is a leprechaun who is very small, tiny, and wee.
> Love is a surfer riding a really sick wave.
> Love is a hermit who lives in a deep, dark cave.
> Love is a giant who's not mean at all!
> Love is an elf who has grown another half an inch tall.
>
>   *—Sophia Carbonneau*

Anyone who wants to see this phenomenon carried to the nth degree should read the correspondence in *More Letters from a Nut* between Ted L. Nancy and the International Library of Poets as he submits one seriously bad poem after another—"My Hate for Poetry Contests," "Why I Really Hate Poetry Contests," "Why I'm Going to Jump Off a 30 Story Building Because of Your Poetry Contests"—but, no matter how demented the writing, can't break his "winning" streak.

My students also raise their pens as satirists. While we were studying the art of William Carlos Williams, Catherine combined imagery from some of his best-known poems to craft a parody of "This Is Just to Say."

> This is just to say:
> I'm sorry
> for watching with amusement
> as the cat
> wiped its rainwater paws
> on your plum-colored car

and scratched off
the paint
in annoying chips
that formed a pile
on the cold gravel.
This is just to say that.

—*Catherine Roy*

And my students raise their pens to experiment with the styles of other writers and pay them homage. Avery played with inverse word order, a technique we observed when we unpacked poems by Walt Whitman, as well as E. E. Cummings' abandonment of capitals and punctuation, to create a poem that only he could have written. It's about a snapshot his eyes took, an approach he learned from William Carlos Williams. The title alludes to Whitman; the theme is one Avery observed in the work of all three poets.

SHREDS OF GRASS

on the concrete divider
bleak with shreds of grass
stood the man

battered cardboard
chest-high raised
and plea scratched
in black marker

and connection briefer was
than the gasp of a dying candle
but in that fraction
tangible the grief
in the oceans of his eyes

and as along we rolled
i stared and was ashamed
to be one of them
that passed

—*Avery Genus*

As a teacher of middle school English, I learned to embrace language play, parody, and homage and bring this part of the underground curriculum into the workshop. It's important for kids to know that writers have been messing around with the work of other writers since—at least—the ancient Greeks. And it's essential for teachers to recognize that parody and homage stretch students not just as writers, but as readers and critics, too. To lampoon someone else's writing requires close reading, attention to detail and tone, and understanding of theme. It may well be the ultimate form of literary analysis.

Unlike the other genres we study, the models of humor writing I present to students have to be relevant to their experience and up-to-date. They should be able to get the joke with minimal teacher explication. So I comb the sections of local bookstores devoted to humor and entertainment in search of writing that's clever, will make my kids laugh, and is clean enough for the classroom. I subscribe to *The New Yorker*, where "Shouts and Murmurs" is often a source of humorous inspiration; throughout the year I clip columns I think will work and file them in my binder of prose genres. *The New Yorker* is where I first encountered Simon Rich and David Sedaris. I also check out the online version of *The Onion* for their outrageous take on current events and trends. But I especially save funny work by students to share with future classes. Parodies by other kids are the surest-fire sources of inspiration.

To kick off a genre study of parody, I provide a definition for kids to record in their handbooks: "A parody is an imitation of a poem, story, song, or some other piece of writing in which the style is the same but the content and theme are ridiculously different." I read aloud a few of my favorites from the examples I've collected—Kenneth Koch's parodies of William Carlos Williams, included in *Knock at a Star* by X. J. Kennedy; Joan Murray's "Brush and Floss: To a Young Child," a ridiculous imitation of Gerard Manley Hopkins, sprung rhythm and all; Loren Goodman's "Traveling Through the Dark (2008)," which repeats William Stafford's poem word for word until a nihilistic twist of the end line; and "To a Stranger Born in Some Distant Country Hundreds of Years from Now" by Billy Collins, in which he skewers the dog poems of—and the pomposity of a remark made by—Mary Oliver.

Then I turn the kids loose in small groups to brainstorm and record answers to two questions: "What are kinds of writing and pieces of writing you know well enough to mess around with? Who are writers whose work you know well enough to poke fun at it?" Afterward, I turn on the overhead projector and create a master list of their ideas.

Figure 13.1 shows the list one of my classes generated with input from me along the way. It draws on diverse sources: our daily poems and the poets we study, the weekly newsletter and other school publications, teachers' styles of speaking and writing, songs we sing at our whole-school morning meetings, current events, our history textbook, children's literature, the classroom walls, and writing by the students themselves. The common features are familiarity and brevity. Kids *know* these texts, and each is manageable to take on as a project in writing workshop.

For me, the most effective student parodies are of poems. I'm impressed when a writer is able to step inside the architecture of the source poem, tease out its form and features, and recast it as a new work that demonstrates a mastery of the original *and* has something to say.

"Thirteen Ways of Looking at a Black-bird" Wallace Stevens

"Nothing Gold Can Stay" Robert Frost

CTL Newsletter:
Kudos
We're Grateful
Dates to Remember
A teacher's Highlights of the Week

Ancient Japanese haikus

A Shakespearean sonnet, speech, or scene

"The Red Wheelbarrow" or "This Is Just to Say" William Carlos Williams

"Hope Is the Thing with Feathers" Emily Dickinson

Another Emily Dickinson poem

"59th Street Bridge Song" Paul Simon

Joy Hakim's books about U.S. history

CTL Bill of Rights

CTL dance rules

"We Real Cool" Gwendolyn Brooks

Nancie's instructions for a spelling study

Nancie's "Get Over It, Already" minilessons

"What Not to Bring to School" from the CTL Parent Handbook

Guidelines for Behavior in Gr. 7–8

"The House Was Quiet and the World Was Calm" Wallace Stevens

"Digging for China" Richard Wilbur

CTL job list

CTL sledding rules

Rules for one of Pam's arcane games in P.E.

A book review from the CTL blog

A manufacturer's or drug company's warning

Poems from our last poetry reading

Nancie's minilesson about adverbs

"Inspirational" quotes for a classroom's walls

Hamlet's "To Be" soliloquy

"As freedom is a breakfastfood" E. E. Cummings

"anyone lived in a pretty how town" E. E. Cummings

A River of Words/celebration of nature poem

When not to send your ill child to school from the CTL Parent Handbook

One of Walt Whitman's catalogue poems

CTL's dress code from the Parent Handbook

A Pablo Neruda ode/anti-ode

"This Pretty Planet" Tom Chapin

"The Summer Day" Mary Oliver

Ted DeMille's "School on the Hill" song about CTL

One of Oliver's m-a-n-y poems about dogs

"Stopping by Woods on a Snowy Evening" Robert Frost

"who are you little i" E. E. Cummings

Ted's "Seven Nights to Read" song

"There's a Hole in the Bucket" song

Humanities Room presidents timeline, with new "accomplishments" for each president à la John Hodgman

"Down by the Bay" Raffi

A president's State of the Union address

A fairy tale

A well-known children's book

A well-known novel or story as retold by Dr. Seuss

CTL lunchtime questions

A poem by a peer

Potential scripts:
Morning meeting
Nancie's writing workshop
Katie on a tear in math class

A 7–8 lunchtime conversation, a.k.a., welcome to Non-Sequiturville

A business letter à la Ted L. Nancy

A wrecked version of a piece of your own or someone else's writing

Figure 13.1 *Writing and Writers We Might Parody*

With the help of *Roget's Thesaurus*, Noelle took on Hamlet's most famous soliloquy and transformed it as a critique of the human propensity to talk too much.

Words, Words, Words

To speak, or not to speak, that is the question.
Whether 'tis vulgar in the mouth to make
Phrases and clauses of outrageous verbosity
Or to take arms against the sea of letters
And by opposing end them.
To verbalize: to form;
No more;
And by a lull to say we end
The distress of the million man-made words
That flesh is heir to,
'Tis a translation
Wordlessly to be wished.
To verbalize, to form;
To form, perchance to babble:
Ay, there's the rub;
For in that state of gab what expressions may erupt
When we have shuffled off this wordy coil
Must give us pause:
There's the respect
That makes misfortune of great diction;
For who would bear the acronyms and profanities of time,
The teenager's slang, the businessman's insult,
The pangs of despised speech, the law's phrase,
The ignorance of office and the disdain
That hearing words of the unintelligent takes
When he himself his blather makes
Without a censor?
Who would fardels bear,
To discuss and consult under a weary word,
But that the dread of something after quietude,
The undiscovered thoughts from whose brain
No sane man returns,
Puzzles the mind,
And makes us rather bear the palaver
Than risk the repose that we know not of?
Thus connotation does make cowards of us all;
And thus the native hue of conversation
Is sickled o'er with the pale cast of thought,

And action of great brainwork
With this regard their ideas turn awry,
And lose the name of knowledge.

The rest is silence.

—*Noelle Timberlake*

Nathaniel's father works at the Naval Shipyard in Bath, Maine, which is a scene of continuous layoffs and rehires; it became the subject of his parody of "Nothing Gold Can Stay" by Robert Frost.

NOTHING SILVER CAN STAY

Shipyard's first metal is silver,
Its hardest hue to deliver.
Its early scraps are dear;
But only so a year.
Then rust subsides to rust.
So the shipyard sinks to dust.
So unemployment's up today.
Nothing silver can stay.

—*Nathaniel Sinibaldi*

After a plague of poems by classmates in the style of E. E. Cummings, Samantha had had enough. She called them on it in a poem.

c
(h
ol
y)
rap

does
    (no)one
       w
   r
   i
   te
a straight
      forward
   poem
     {any} more
?

—*s herter*
after e. e. cummings

Xander took aim at Emily Dickinson and "as imperceptibly as Grief" in a poem about a long wait on a plane parked on the tarmac of an airport. His playfulness with Dickinson's slant rhymes, dashes, capitals, and line breaks demonstrates his critical attention to her style.

> 'Twas so slow, it was a Relief
> When the Airplane left the runway.
> Alas, it took so long to leave
> It seemed like Treachery.
>
> Then Quietness was killed,
> As engines began to growl.
> The passengers, their anxious selves
> Released breath held all Afternoon—
> The plane gathered speed—
> At last began to Soar.
> Inside, grateful, relieved faces
> On the guests, smiles shone.
> And so, with metal Wings
> And tiny spinning Wheels—
> The Airplane made its loud escape
> From the gate at Idaho Falls.
>
> —*Xander Bartone*
> *(after Emily Dickinson)*

Charlotte and Emma took on the form and style of "Thirteen Ways of Looking at a Blackbird" by Wallace Stevens to poke gentle fun at their parents. It seems that in an attempt to cure herself of swearing, Charlotte's mother promised to give a dime to any of her children who caught her cursing. Charlotte and her siblings reaped the benefits.

THIRTEEN WAYS OF LOOKING AT A SWEAR

I
Among six members
of our family,
the only one swearing
is my mother.

II
I was of three minds,
like the thirty cents
presented to me by Mum
after three swears.

III

A swear whirled around the house.
It was a small part of the nutt–house chaos.

IV

My mum and a swear
are worth ten cents.
My mum and 293 swears
are almost thirty bucks in my pocket.

V

Mum's face was rimmed
with happiness.
A swear crossed it, to and fro.
I giggled
but said nothing.

VI

I don't know which to prefer,
the beauty of a full–throttle swear,
or the money I gain afterward.

VII

O wise Jasper,
why should you clean up?
Can't we split the profits?

VIII

I know many swears,
but only some will make money.
I know, too, that
"No, that one doesn't count!"
is involved in what I know.

IX

When the swear flew out of sight,
it marked the edge
of one of many obscenities.

X

At the sound of the swears
when Mum spills her earrings again,
even Dad would cry out sharply.

XI

The swear galloped
on a bright white stallion

to pluck the princess from her prison.
"That's ten cents!" she cried.

XII
My mother's mouth is moving.
This must be the start of a great career.

XIII
She was swearing all afternoon.
I was reeling in cash
and I was going to reel in cash.
Mum sat in her chair at the table,
laughter pouring
from her heart-shaped face.

—Charlotte Nutt
(with apologies to Wallace Stevens)

Emma's father, an inveterate punster, reader, and coffee drinker, is the children's librarian in Lewiston, Maine. Stevens is the prism through which she views him in a poem she composed as a birthday present. In the process, she notices and appreciates both the original poem and her father in ways she wouldn't have otherwise. As she noted, "I loved imitating Stevens while adding my own twists. I poked fun at my father without being mean, and I used little details that show his personality. Above all, this poem is specific to him and couldn't be about anyone else."

THIRTEEN WAYS OF LOOKING AT MY FATHER

1.
Among five cars pulling into Dunkin Donuts
the only one not going to the drive-thru
was steered by my father.

2.
I was of three minds:
like my father
with three clean shirts.

3.
The coffee dripped from the machine.
It was a small part of my father's day.

4.
A chair and a book
are one.
A chair and a book and my father
are one.

5.
I do not know which to prefer,
the beauty of Pokemon
or the thrill of Harry Potter.
The silence of my father
or just after.

6.
Books filled the long shelves
with barbaric tales.
The shadow of my father
lumbered to and fro.
The mood
traced in the sunlight
an indecipherable pun.

7.
O' small children of Lewiston,
why do you imagine computers?
Do you not see how my father
waits at the desk
to answer your questions?

8.
I know late-night oatmeal
and weapons of mass destruction;
but I know, too,
that my father is involved
in what I know.

9.
When my father meandered out of sight,
he marked the edge
of one of many long walks.

10.
At the sight of my father
making something non-microwavable,
even my mother
would cry out sharply.

11.
He rode over Wisconsin
on a plane, in coach.
Once, a fear pierced him,
in that he mistook

the blackness of the screen
as broken.

12.
The earth is revolving.
My father must be reading.

13.
It was gorgeous all morning.
It was sunny
and it was going to be sunny.
My father sat on the white couch
watching the football game
and drinking a beer.

—*Emma Moorhead*
(with gratitude to Wallace Stevens)

Nathaniel cracked up his class with a parody he wrote as an attachment to a letter in the style of Ted L. Nancy, the pseudonym used by someone who writes absurd business letters to corporations and institutions and then publishes the responses he receives in his Letters from a Nut series. In his letter from a nut, Nathaniel achieves the subtle balance of obsession, verbosity, and sincerity that makes for a successful example of the genre—and, along the way, mastered business-letter format. But it's the attachment, his perfectly silly parody of the song "The Confrontation" from the musical *Les Misérables*, that clinched the deal and earned him the only prize sought by writers of nutty letters: a letter in response. A consumer affairs supervisor at L'Oréal wrote to thank him and let him know she had forwarded his idea to their marketing department. Nathaniel's still waiting for L'Oréal to take him up on his offer.

L'Oréal USA, Inc.
575 5th Avenue
New York, NY 10017-2422

Dear L'Oréal Shampoo Company:

I have been a diligent user of your fine hair products for years. As a result of my excessive consumption—some might call it an obsession—I watch and tape each new commercial that your brilliant advertising team comes up with. Sometimes, to maximize the experience, I sniff a bottle of your finest watermelon eye-friendly shampoo. I find this makes for the most satisfying viewing.

My other passion in life is listening to Broadway show tunes. Several days ago, as I was in the shower scrubbing my head clean, I had an idea—why not put the two together in a commercial? I think it would be a great marketing strategy: you could not only attract consumers concerned about hair hygiene, but also draw Broadway fans into your ever-growing pool of satisfied customers.

In honor of your company, I sniffed some L'Oréal watermelon shampoo for inspiration and wrote the script for a commercial. The final draft is included with this letter.

Please note that I am one of your company's greatest fans. Because I love your products so much, you will not be required to pay me. I would not accept payment. The only thing I ask in return is a bottle of shampoo *straight from the factory*.

The enclosed is set to the tune of "The Confrontation" from *Les Misérables*. I hope you will consider using it. It would make my day.

Thank you.

Sincerely,
Dominic Weatherbee
(Nathaniel Williams)

THE CONFRONTATION—À LA L'ORÉAL

Adapted from *Les Misérables*.
Javert: Ja-VAIR (rhymes with *hair*)
Valgean: VAL-jon (rhymes with *gone*)

A bottle of shampoo sits between the two men.

Javert:
Valgean, you cow,
I see the shampoo now.
M'sier le Mayor,
it's time to wash my hair!

Valgean:
Before you say another word, Javert,
it is I who will wash my hair.
Listen to me:
I need that shampoo!
The smell of my hair is irritating me.
When I approach, everybody flees!
In Mercy's name,
I even killed a tree!
It won't be returned, you silly bird!
It won't be returned—

Javert:
You are making me mad!
I hunted it across the years.
It's time to wash behind my ears.
Shampoo
is not for you!

Valgean (in counterpoint):
Believe of me what you will.
I smell so bad I could kill.
The L'Oréal is to be mine!
Your hair's smell is probably fine.
When I go into a church,
people's stomachs start to lurch.
They hate dandruff, I can tell—
I was told to go to Hell!
Do you believe in me, Javert?
If you don't, then here's a dare:
lean over and sniff my hair!
You'll find out the smell's not fair!
I am begging you, Javert!
I want it to smell peachy-pear!
I don't like it when people stare!
Don't make me hit you with this chair.

Javert (in counterpoint):
My hair's scent must really change.
It smells so bad I'm quite deranged.
No! It's not very fun!
My hair smells worse than yours!
It is worse than the breath of a boar!
Listen to me—
or I'll pull out my gun!
The shampoo is meant for me.
Now, Valgean, please let me be.
Do you think I'd tell a lie?
I'd like to smell like apple pie.
People's nostrils start to fry!
When I'm upwind, they start to cry!
Insults and names begin to fly—
they say I belong in a sty!
You know nothing of my plight.
If you want to, I will fight.
I need that shampoo more than you!

Valgean:
This I swear to you tonight . . .
Javert:
C'mon, it's on, let's start a fight.
Valgean:
The L'Oréal is to be mine!

Javert:
It's time my frizz starts to decline!
Valgean:
My hair is worse than Frankenstein's!
Both:
I swear to you,
I'll wash my hair!

Through peer writing conferences and class poetry readings, students in a workshop come to know friends' writing, too. Göran's poem "Pull" was complimented by classmates for its sensory diction and imagery, while his buddy Cody recognized an opportunity for a different kind of compliment. With Göran's permission, his poem about an adventure with his brother was transformed by Cody into a tale of attempted fratricide.

PULL

Carl flicks his wrist.
A fluorescent disk
spins across the white field.
Gun shouldered,
I pull the trigger,
but the orange disk floats down.
Miss.
I blame Carl for the bad throw
and ask him to do it again.
He sticks the red
into the hot water from the evaporator
and slips another skeet
into the U.
"Ready?" I call.
Carl repeats the motion,
and another disk twirls out.
My shotgun ready,
my finger twitches.
Shards of orange fall
like rain onto the white snow.
And it's just Carl and me and the aroma

of gunpowder.

—*Göran Johanson*

PULL (OR WHAT REALLY HAPPENS WHEN GÖRAN TAKES POSSESSION OF A GUN)

Carl flicks his wrist.
A fluorescent disk
spins across the white field.
Gun shouldered,
I pull the trigger,
but the orange disk floats down.
Miss.
I turn to blame Carl for the bad throw,
but then I notice the hole in his knee
and the blood that is streaming out of it
and the fact that he's writhing in pain.
I blame him for getting in the way.
I insist that he throw me another.
"Ready?" I call.
My finger has a nervous twitch,
and, just like that, Carl's other knee is gone.
"Let's just call it a day," he begs.
"Oh, come on, don't be such a baby!"
But the drama queen drags himself home
as I fire off one last warning shot over his head.
And, well, I guess now it's just me and the aroma

of gunpowder.

—*Cody Graves*

I want students to explore what writing can do for them. This includes bonding with friends and channeling an adolescent sense of humor. A small group of students bonded over a script they wrote in the workshop and performed in drama class. This time they nailed my voice and affect and the rituals of writing workshop.

EXTREME WRITING WORKSHOP

(Everyone is talking loudly—Nancie walks in; immediately everyone is silent and terrified.)

NANCIE: Hi, kids!

(A few students mutter, "Hi, Nancie.")

NANCIE: AHHHEEMMM. Let's try that again. Hi, kids.

(All loud:) Hi, Nancie!

NANCIE: Today's poem is by a former CTL-er, our old friend Rush Limbaugh, who graduated in June and is now a freshman at the Maine State Juvenile Facility.

(Reads with deep feeling: "Dragon: Flying overhead, smoke coming out of your nostrils, guarding your kids. A soldier appears out of the mist. You shoot a fireball. He burns to a crisp. Your kids are safe.")

NANCIE: Now I want you to go back into this remarkable poem *(pause)* and, if you can, unpack its deepest meaning *(pause)*. And *(pause)* mark all the lines you love and *(pause)* want to talk about.

(All students write for two seconds)

NANCIE: Take a few seconds to finish up . . . Now, what gems did you mine from this moving masterpiece?

(Tristan raises his hand.)

NANCIE: Tristan?

TRISTAN: I loved the line, "Guarding your kids." I just think it's very descriptive and so, so true.

(Nancie overlaps Tristan's comment with "Yeah . . . yeah . . .")

(Emma raises her hand.)

NANCIE: Emma?

EMMA: I thought the line "smoke coming out of your nostrils" was really sensory and visual, like, I could *see* it. With my *eyes*.

(Nancie overlaps Emma's comment with "Yeah . . . yeah . . .")

MAX: It's pretty obvious that the smoke in this poem is love, and the theme is we must all join hands and fight to stop dragon abuse.

ALL: Yes! I agree! Brilliant! (etc.)

NANCIE: *(weeping)* Beautiful, so beautiful. Now rate this poem, tuck it away in your poetry folders, and take out your spelling homework. I need some ocular proof. Or else.

(Nancie walks the circle, checking each each student's five spelling words.)

NANCIE: Perfect . . . perfection . . . more perfection . . . the height of perfection . . . the definition of perfect . . . the epitome of perfection . . . the zenith of perfection . . .

(Ben has forgotten his homework.)

NANCIE: Where are your five words, Dewey?

BEN: Uh, I—uh . . . um . . . I accidentally put my spelling folder on the roof of our car, and when we drove off, the folder, kinda, blew off.

NANCIE: Didn't Solorzano try that one last week? That's a *pass*, Dewey *(evil cackle)*. It's time for the status-of-the-class check-in. Ben, what are you going to do today as a writer?

BEN: I'm gonna stare out the window at the old oak tree and wait for inspiration.

NANCIE: Nate?

NATE: I'll either be moping or checking out my Facebook page.

NANCIE: Hope?

HOPE: I'll be consulting the thesaurus to find a more sensory word for *poop*.

NANCIE: Nice. Emma?

EMMA: I'm hoping to get my writing folder open.

NANCIE: John?

JOHN: Dance a little jig. Wanna see it?

NANCIE: In your dreams. Heidi?

HEIDI: Nothing.

NANCIE: Natalie?

NATALIE: I'm starting draft twenty-one of my poem about tree frogs.

NANCIE: Sophia?

SOPHIA: I'm gonna go downstairs, like I have to use the bathroom, but I'll actually be pigging out on my snack.

NANCIE: Great. Tristan?

TRISTAN: Do my science homework.

NANCIE: Abbie?

ABBIE: Surf the Web.

NANCIE: Tess?

TESS: I'll be reading the quotes on the wall for the next forty-five minutes.

NANCIE: Patrick?

PATRICK: I found a new game to play on the Internet.

NANCIE: Max?

MAX: I'll probably add a comma to the fifth line of my ode to flamingoes. Then I'll log on the Internet and hack into the U.S. government's secret files, as I continue my quest for world domination.

NANCIE: Okay. Graydon?

GRAYDON: Find the best position for sleeping in a chair.

NANCIE: Cole?

COLE: Light a fire.

NANCIE: Sounds *great*. Off you go. Work hard, and make . . . um, uh, um, er . . .

EVERYONE: *Literature!*

With the exception of parody, I don't allow students to collaborate in writing workshop. With the rest of the genres, it's important for me to know whose ideas, information, diction, and conventions I'm reading and responding to, so I can teach the writer. But in crafting parody, two heads can be better than one as kids set each other off. A lot of heads worked together to compile a running list of first names for the new millennium after I groaned about the trendiness of the children's names in the incoming kindergarten class. A student posted two sheets of construction paper on the bulletin board, and everyone went to town (Figure 13.2).

Parodies of school policies and documents are perennial favorites among my kids. Since they already notice and comment on teachers' tics, we might as well give them

FIRST NAMES FOR THE NEW MILLENNIUM

BOYS:

Rockefeller	Cement	Jeep
Oak	Triscuit	Moxie
Jeeves	Transom	Zen
Callow	Shilling	Samson
Throckmorton	Tundra	Spew
Bentley	Chevy	Hoover
Puma	Jebediahzeph	Slab
Grass	Jive	Quincy
Maple	Dewdrop	Denim
Curry	Winchester	Millennium
Slate	Ford	Stony
Orlando	Asphalt	Nabob
Average	Ruger	Raw
Dirt	Tigger	Pilgrim
Macro	Stainless Steel	Veto
Dodge	Nano	Almond
Gauge	Flint	Random

GIRLS:

Vanderbilt	Peach Blossom	Saffron
Brighton	Saran	Savory
Feather	Basil	Glee
Winston	Nonchalance	Camembert
Portmanteau	Weed	Hortensia
Miillee	Una	Tinsel
Pond	Lilac	Bluebell
Opiate	Tapestry	Minion
Magma	Wyoming	Lattice
Adieu	Bagel	Inca
Lemon	Lady Gaga	Calliope
Cotton	Rahrahohlala…	Ecstasy
Mauve	Flame	Plume
Heliotrope	Free	Naiveté
Balm	Chaos	Utopia
Oolong	Snow	Eurasia
Activia	Hawthorne	Levi 501

Figure 13.2 *First Names for the New Millennium*

opportunities to mock with impunity as well as skill and style. A small group of eighth graders took the guidelines I'd written for behavior in grades 7–8 and recast each one, the little devils.

GUIDELINES FOR GRADES 7–8

Brush off your shoes WELL before you enter the building; otherwise it's back to inside shoes, strictly enforced.

Never brush off your shoes before entering the building. Watch Nancie's head explode.

Remove hats, headcoverings, hoods, and sunglasses in the building.

Remove all clothes in the building.

Dress for school

Please don't dress for school. At all.

Don't chew gum or eat candy at school or during field trips, unless the candy is packed as part of your snack or lunch or given to the whole group by a teacher.

Chew gum everywhere all the time with your mouth wide open.

Raise your hand when you wish to speak in whole group meetings.

Scream out your comments with veins in your neck.

Wait to talk when a teacher or another student is speaking: it's common courtesy.

Scream whenever a teacher or another student is screaming.

Contribute as much as you can in class: raise your voice, listen, become engaged and smarter, teach others, and help make the time go faster. There are so many ways to consider issues and approach problems, it's important that you explain your ideas, too.

Don't even try in school. It's not like an education is going to help you in later life. Besides, there are so many other things to do, like napping.

Keep all personal belongings inside your locker. There should be *nothing on top and nothing on the floor.* Your backpack must fit inside your locker. We're sorry but you can't apply stickers or tape to your locker, outside or in, attach anything to the newsletter clip, or cover or obscure your name. It's fine to bring in clips and magnets from home or to create shelves if this helps your organization.

Keep all your stuff on the floor so others will trip over it.

Come to each class prepared with the materials you'll need.

Don't bother coming to school prepared—it's so last year.

Remember what your school job is. Do it.

Remember what your school job is. Nothing.

Include others—and yourself—in the lunchtime group.

Sit alone during lunch. Exclude everyone. If people try to join you, throw ramen at them.

Use a placemat or paper towel at lunchtime.

Use a kindergartner as a placemat.

Clean up your own messes.

Then make him or her clean up your mess.

Return supplies and materials to whenever you found them.

Leave supplies wherever you feel like. The cluttered look is in.

If you become part of a boy-girl couple, observe the CTL couples policy.

If your friends are part of a boy-girl couple, leave them alone in peace so they can "do things."

Don't bring to school items that might cause injury to yourself or others.

Bring knives, grenades, fireworks, flamethrowers, and other dangerous and illegal weapons to school. Preserve and defend your Second Amendment rights.

Don't download anything onto CTL computers or surf the net inappropriately.

Download viruses onto CTL computers and surf all the nasty sites you can find.

Bear in mind the rules governing the inside-recess privilege: don't blow it.

Burn the rules for inside recess. In fact, as often as possible, start a fire.

Do your homework.

Don't even think about doing homework or you'll pay the consequences: peers will remove your fingernails.

Live the CTL Bill of Rights.

You can say, "You can't play." So say it, with gusto.

Be good to one another. Before you speak, think: is it true? is it kind? is it necessary?

Fight with each other like there's no tomorrow.

Joy Hakim's series The Story of US is my choice of text as a teacher of American history. Her information is accurate, her perspective both generous and critical, and her writing style, for better or worse, unmistakable. Abe had a wonderful time taking on Hakim's voice to "explain" the Magna Carta, including Hakim-esque sidebars (Figure 13.3).

Moving beyond parody, some of the kids' play with language celebrates the pure joy of creating combinations of sounds and images. Göran spent a writing workshop with a rhyming dictionary; by the end of class, he'd composed an infectious ode.

ODE TO ODES

ode to a Red Box
ode to the Red Sox
ode to Fort Knox

ode to jocks
ode to knock knock
ode to gridlock

ode to punk rock
ode to a padlock
ode to "what's up, doc"

irish odes to shamrocks
california odes to aftershocks
locker room odes to smelly socks

odes around the clock
odes around the block
odes until there's culture shock

odes to the tomahawk
odes to writer's block
odes to cuckoo clocks

ode to a chatterbox
ode to chickenpox
ode to Mr. Lunch Box

ode to all livestock
and baby back ribs
—*Göran Johanson*

Sophia's poem for two voices is the same story told twice. On the left, she delivers a play-by-play of the action in a game of field hockey as if she's wearing her mouthguard; on the right she translates herself.

THE MAGNA CARTA ACCORDING TO JOY HAKIM AND ABE STEINBERGER

On the eighteenth of October, 1216, at roughly (ruff-**leee**) 1:39 in the afternoon, when the sun was still hot in the sky, a peasant by the name of John was shot through the leg with an arrow and trampled to death by a horse!

John was a happy man, and everyone liked him. Today we will follow his story through this part of the Medieval Ages; we will see just how common his story is and how horrible his life was! What was it like to be a peasant (**pez**-ant)? I don't know and neither do you! To learn this, we will have to travel back in time in our space capsule, so hold on! We will travel to December 24, 1166, England. This was when John was born. He was the youngest son of four, William, Henry, and Geoffrey (jeff-o-**reee**). But John quickly turned into an only child as his brothers soon died of disease. This was very, very sad.

John grew up like most peasants, in a hole. Also, like most peasants, he lived under the feudal (**feww**-doll) system. This was very, very good for the very, very rich, while being very, very bad for the very, very poor. Do you think this was a good thing? I do. Not.

Being a filthy, poor, and completely worthless peasant was not all bad. There were some bonuses, like having nothing on your mind but surviving (sur-**vi**-v-ing). Peasants didn't have to worry about rival farmers because all of them were just as poor and no one ever got richer. I don't know if this is really a blessing. Do you think it is a blessing?

Then, in 1215, a bunch of really rich people called barons (**bear**-ons) got together and said they wanted to get even richer. To do this, they decided they would have to take more money from the very poor, and to do this they had to have more power than the King. So all the barons made the King sign something called the Magna Carta, which said they had the power to oppress people just like he did. This was a great step forward in the freedom of the common people. There is no question about it.

The Magna Carta makes 63 points. I will review a few of them. 1. The Church (chur-**Ch**) has the right to beat up whomever it wants, whenever it wants, however it wants. 8. A widow doesn't have to marry again, as long as she promises her baron not to do so without him giving the okay. 23. The barons will stop forcing random people to dig moats. 40. The barons will stop killing people for no reason at all. 54. No one will have to trust the word of a woman (**Whoa-**man) ever again.

Things were different back then. Knowing all you do now, who would you have been if you lived during medieval times? Don't say a baron, because if I ever saw someone who came from peasant stock, it's you.

Hunger: to be hungry

The Medieval Ages or Dark Ages were from the 5th century to 15th century A.C. This was roughly 10,500 to 3,500 dog years ago.

The Feudal System is a system of government where nothing ever gets done, nothing is ever worth doing, and nothing ever works. This system of government was especially popular in the Middle Ages because it allowed rich people to do whatever they wanted! Some people thought this was a good thing. Do you think so? It does not matter anyway, because you cannot change a thing.

Figure 13.3 *The Magna Carta According to Joy Hakim and Abe Steinberger*

A Gem wiv Owa Moutgas In

The official signals
for us to slip in our mouthguards.
The whistle blows.

Abbe, owa golie,
sands in da gole,
and wiv aw dat paddin,
she loos like one ob dose
Twansfomas my wittul cothin
pwayth wif.

Owa lef fowad, Noma,
hath da baw
and ith wunnin up da feewd—
dwibbin bak an foth.
I well, see doethnt
unnerthand, an Evuh
Fwom Boobay
cwathes inoo haw
fwom behine
and wacs da baw back
up da feewd.

I wun backwas,
atipayin evy moov.
Fo evy step I tayk
I nee to bay
too thepth fatter
dan dem.
Evy mooove I mayke
cood win da gem
or loothe i'.

Ash da baw ish shlapped
toarths me,
I dot fowad
to whok it
to baiwe'.
Ah no see cawn hi' i'
hawd enou to mak i' pat
mid feewd.

A Game with Our Mouthguards Out

The official signals
for us to slip in our mouthguards.
The whistle blows.

Abbie, our goalie,
stands in the goal,
and with all that padding,
she looks like one of those
Transformers my little cousin
plays with.

Our left forward, Norma,
has the ball
and is running up the field—
dribbling back and forth.
I yell, but she doesn't
understand, and Eva
from Boothbay
crashes into her
from behind
and whacks the ball back
up the field.

I run backwards,
anticipating every move.
For every step I take
I need to be
two steps faster
than them.
Every move I make
could win the game
or lose it.

As the ball is slapped
towards me,
I dart forward
to whack it
to Bailey.
I know she can hit it
hard enough to make it past
midfield.

Afer it cwotheth	After it crosses
da wine, Tai Wee	the line, Thai Lee
dwibbeth inoo	dribbles into
da corcwe,	the circle,
and see swapth it	and she slaps it
inoo dee appodin gole.	into the opposing goal.
Oh, yes. We	Oh, yes. We
score!	*score!*

—*Sophia Carbonneau*

A new comic genre that captivates some kids is the six-word memoir. My daughter turned me on to the SMITH magazine website sixwordmemoirs.com. I bought their book *I Can't Keep My Own Secrets: Six-Word Memoirs by Teens Famous and Obscure* (2009) and in a minilesson read aloud a sampling of funny and ironic stories, ones with content appropriate for seventh and eighth graders. Sophia and Amelia were the first writers to take up the challenge.

SIX WORDS CAN MAKE A DIFFERENCE

I've accidentally washed three iPod shuffles.
I'm the oldest and the least responsible.
I get lost everywhere I go.
74% on test—life goes on.

—*Sophia Stafford*

SIX WORDS ABOUT ME

i love cats, but i'm allergic
no sleepovers: so much for that
One Direction is the only direction

—*Amelia Genus*

I can never know the impact or reach of a minilesson. After I conducted one about the irregularity of English spelling to demonstrate why kids need to do a visual check when they self-edit, Charlotte's response was to start a new poem, this one about English spelling.

TRIUMPH OF ORTHOGRAPHY

Shee strugles
tryeing to graspe
the Werd.

Its ulmost
their. Her fayce
swets, end she squirmes

inn discomfert. A longe
siegh eskapes, end shee
tryes agen. Butt, agen,

lyke unncooked foode,
itt dosnt taist rite,
dosnt loock rite.

So she scribles owt
thi misteak
end rerites. The Werd

is ulmost their. Shee
ads anuther ingrediant,
anuther lettr.

Finaly: shee loocks
bak att hir werk,
sattisfied.

—*Charlotte Nutt*

After I conducted a minilesson about personification, Wallace wrote his first love poem.

TRAGEDY

We swayed rhythmically,
you humming a mindless tune.
We wandered our lawn for hours.
You loved the smell of freshly cut crabgrass.
I loved how you felt in my hands.

This winter you fell ill:
an unidentified sickness
that not even I could ignore.
You were never the same:
a constant rattle and hack.
You wanted to sleep all day.
One bright afternoon
I carried your corpse to a vile and rusty graveyard.

O weed-wacker, how I loved you.

—*Wallace Jackson*

And after a discussion of the poem "The Lanyard" by Billy Collins that centered on his ironic use of symbolism, Göran was inspired to find irony in a symbol of his own.

THE SAUSAGE

the other day I was ricocheting
from the frying pan to the refrigerator
to the cookbooks when I found myself
at the *S* section in Farmer John's Recipes
and my eyes fell upon the word *sausage*

no cookie devoured by some writer
could bring one so suddenly back
two days ago I was sitting at our table
thinking of what to eat when
imagine that: I thought of you
so I started to cook a sausage

you gave me backpack rides through the fields
and I cooked you a sausage
you gave me platefuls of food
and I gave you a sausage

you said here is a warm bed and house
and I replied here is your sausage
you gave me dish after dish of Swedish pancakes
and here is a sausage that I nuked in the microwave
and I know now that I can never repay you
but two days ago I was as sure as a thirteen-year-old boy
could be that these little scrumptious sausages (let's face it—I
cooked one for myself, too) would be enough to make us even

> —*Göran Johanson*
> *(with apologies to Billy Collins)*

Göran was more than influenced by the Collins poem; much of his phrasing and structure is borrowed directly from "The Lanyard." He and his classmates learned from me how one poet acknowledges another, as Göran did with *with apologies* and Sophia did below with *after Wallace Stevens*. She loved his "The Night Was Quiet and the World Was Calm" and appropriated its form and language for a poem about a battle that raged between her and her mother about whose music would play on the family radio.

MY RADIO WAS QUIET AND MY MOTHER WAS CALM
After Wallace Stevens

My radio was quiet and my mother was calm.
My pop became her jazz. African drums

Were like the conscious being of the music.
My radio was quiet and my mother was calm.

I sang in my head because there was no song,
Except that her sound system blazed,

Wanted to be heard, wanted much to be
The maestro to whom his orchestra is true, to whom

The summer night is like a perfection of waltz.
My radio was quiet because it had to be.

The radio is part of my meaning, part of my mind,
The access to all the perfect stations.

And my mother was calm. The truth in a calm mother,
In which there is no other music, herself

Is calm, herself is jazz and soul, herself
Is the speaker playing late and singing there.

   —Sophia Carbonneau

Wallace composed his poem "Seal" as a Mother's Day gift of writing. In it he empathizes with his mom's hectic life as a single parent of three by borrowing language and a theme from "Stopping by Woods on a Snowy Evening" by Robert Frost.

SEAL

You gaze out the sliding glass door
at the eddies that sink then swell.
Every few moments
a glistening gray head
rises from the brown water
and floats down the back river,
no schedule to keep or bills to pay.
You watch her,
unaware of the pasta boiling over
or the older son
calling on the phone, asking for a ride.
You stand, though, finally.
The water is lovely, dark and deep.
But you've got promises to keep
and miles to drive before you sleep,
and miles to drive before you sleep.

   —Wallace Jackson
   (after Robert Frost)

When we read and unpacked poetry about World War I, Amelia was struck by the irony in Wilfred Owen's masterpiece "Dulce et Decorum Est"—the distance between the "old lie" that it's sweet and honorable to die for one's country and the grotesque conditions of the war. Amelia, a dancer, borrowed Owen's diction, tone, and structure to explore the distance between sugar plum fairy stereotypes and the pain and pressure of "this daunting art."

A DANCER'S HOMAGE TO WILFRED OWEN'S "DULCE ET DECORUM EST"

Straight-backed, like steel rods of a tower,
Faint-headed, panting like hounds, we cursed through combination,
Till, on tip-toes, we curved our arms
And towards the center, our cheeks were turned.
Girls adorned in blue. Many had lost their spirit
But lugged on, limp-limbed. All went slack; all weary;
Drunk with fatigue; oblivious to the pain
Of tired, beat-up toes that point behind.

Thirty-two jumps! Quick, girls!—An ecstasy of fumbling,
Turning the bottle cap just in time;
But someone was still fixing her skirt
And stumbling, only to trip and fall . . .
Dim, through blurry eyes and soft yellow light,
As in that pale glow, I saw her slumping.
In all my memory, before my helpless sight,
She pitches forward first, screeching, sinking, drowning.

If in some smothering memory you too could stand
By the wall she clung to
And watch her eyes flood with tears,
Her drowning eyes, like an ocean to a droplet;
If you could hear, at every step, the whine
Come forced, through pursed lips,
Obscene as broken limbs, bitter as the screech
Of hawks, incurable sores on innocent tongues—
My friend, you would not tell with such high zest
To boys dismissive of this daunting art,
The old lie: Saltatio est
tantummodo puellis.

Ballet is only for girls.
            —*Amelia Genus*

One morning in March, the worst thing that could happen happened. An eighth-grade boy from another school jumped to his death off the Bath Bridge. It weighed heavily on my kids. Although they didn't know him, they felt they did. He was their age. He lived up or down the road from them. What could have possessed him to give up on his life, to forgo its small and precious pleasures forever? Tess was the first to try to make sense of it in a poem.

March 15

They never mattered much before:
the cashier who smiles as she bags Mom's groceries,
the ocean pock-marked by rain,
Abbie's sympathetic eye roll,
the tangy aroma of sharp pencils,
a cool brush of balm sinking into dry lips,
the ghost bag that floats above a dirty alleyway,
a kiss grazing my cheek as I bound out the door,
home's perfect crescendo,
sunlight filtering through a bottle of perfume.

Now
I strive to notice them all.

Boy on the bridge,
I will always wonder what was on your list
and why it wasn't enough.
For you, I promise to witness miracles.
        —*Tess Hinchman*

The class and I read "March 15" as a daily poem. We talked about our own lists— what we'll try to notice and appreciate about the everyday in honor of the boy on the bridge. Then other students wrote poems that channeled their incomprehension, grief, and gratitude for the little things. Each poet acknowledged the influence of their friend Tess Hinchman.

For the Boy on the Bridge
After Tess Hinchman

I didn't think about the little things:
late nights watching action-packed movies,
the soft pat of a soccer ball hitting my cleats,
a whistle of breeze sliding through the screen door,
my iPod at night, dimly lit, playing music under the covers,

the burst of mango as I slip a piece of gum in my mouth,
the popping of gravel under Mom's tires as we pull into the garage,
the rush of adrenaline and bright lights shining as I step on a stage,
the last *I love you* before my eyes close for the night.

Now
I notice them all.

If your life had continued,
what would be on your list?
It wasn't enough to find out?
That isn't what
we're here for?

         —Graydon Nuki

Just because test makers and bureaucrats make decisions about which genres to test, that doesn't mean these should be the only genres taught. Teachers need to make decisions, too. We can narrow our instruction to the version of writing—and reading—called for on standardized tests, or we can invite students to experience and embrace a range of age-appropriate forms and formats. Instead of teaching just a few things that a writer might do, we need to introduce many genres and help kids fulfill many purposes, as writers and as human beings.

A robust writing workshop encompasses genres to be tested and genres that will never be tested. The Common Core State Standards omit poetry from K–12 and narratives in high school. But poetry is an essential window on the craft of writing and the experience of being human, while the most important piece of writing any college-bound high school senior will compose is a story from his or her life. Exposure to and practice with diverse kinds of writing motivates students to write, teaches them there are many ways to write well, and gives them a healthy taste of what writing can do for them.

Thumbtacked over my desk at home is a quote I copied out from a novel I love, *Alone in the Classroom* by Elizabeth Hay: "A child lies like a grey pebble on the shore until a certain teacher picks him up and dips him in water, and suddenly you see all the colors and patterns in the dull stone, and it's marvelous for the stone and marvelous for the teacher" (2011).

Writing and reading workshop is this kind of liquid environment. We dip kids in and then revel in the colors and patterns that emerge when teachers steep students in diverse stories and forms of self-expression. The workshop respects writing, reading, teachers, and childhood by immersing every student in the real, marvelous thing.

Quotations to Inspire Writers, Readers, and Their Teachers

"Nulla d'es s'ne l'nea." ["Never a day without a line."]
—*Anonymous*

"The story of your life is not your life. It is your story."
—*John Barth*

"To learn about a tree, go to a tree."
—*Matsuo Bashō*

"The things you're looking for, Montag, are in the world, but the only way the average chap will see 99 percent of them is in a book."
—*Professor Faber in* Fahrenheit 451 *by Ray Bradbury*

"There is only one way to develop a sound taste in literature . . . read poetry."
—*Joseph Brodsky*

"Poetry is life distilled."
—*Gwendolyn Brooks*

"Most of the basic material a writer works with is acquired before the age of fifteen."
—*Willa Cather*

"Write what makes you different."
—*Sandra Cisneros*

"Poetry is elegant shorthand."
—*William Coles*

". . . all they want to do
is tie the poem to a chair with rope
and torture a confession out of it.
They begin beating it with a hose
to find out what it really means."
—*Billy Collins*

"The hardest battle is to be nobody but yourself in a world that is doing its best, night and day, to make you like everybody else."
—*E. E. Cummings*

"I might revise a page twenty times. . . . Good writing is rewriting. I am positive of this."

—*Roald Dahl*

"Poetry like bread is for everyone."

—*Roque Dalton*

"If I feel physically as if the top of my head were taken off, I know that is poetry."

—*Emily Dickinson*

"The truth dazzles gradually or else the world would be blind."

—*Emily Dickinson*

"My business is circumference."

—*Emily Dickinson*

"One sacred memory from childhood is perhaps the best education."

—*Feodor Dostoevsky*

"If there is no struggle there can be no progress."

—*Frederick Douglass*

"A thread runs through all things: all worlds are strung on it as beads: and men, and events, and life, come to us, only because of that thread."

—*Ralph Waldo Emerson*

"'Tis the good reader that makes the good book."

—*Ralph Waldo Emerson*

"I become a transparent eyeball."

—*Emerson, on the essayist's relationship with the world*

"Get it down. Take chances. It may be bad, but it's the only way you can do anything really good."

—*William Faulkner*

"The figure a poem makes. It begins in delight and ends in wisdom . . . it assumes direction with the first line laid down, it runs a course of lucky events, and ends in a clarification of life—not necessarily a great clarification, . . . but in a momentary stay against confusion."

—*Robert Frost*

"The best way out is always through."

—*Robert Frost*

"No tears in the writer, no tears in the reader."
—*Robert Frost*

"Poetry is a way of taking life by the throat."
—*Robert Frost*

"You must be the change you wish to see in the world."
—*Mahatma Gandhi*

"We look at life once, in childhood; the rest is memory."
—*Louise Glück*

"There is always one moment in childhood when a door opens and lets the future in."
—*Graham Greene*

"The new metaphor is a miracle, like the creation of life."
—*Donald Hall*

"Anything under the sun is beautiful if you have the vision—it is the seeing of the thing that makes it so."
—*Nathaniel Hawthorne*

"There were no books that showed what was really going on with teenagers. I wrote *The Outsiders* because I wanted to read it."
—*S. E. Hinton*

"A poem is language in orbit."
—*Seamus Heaney*

"The book which you read from a sense of duty, or because for any reason you must, does not commonly make friends with you."
—*William Dean Howells*

"Why memoir? It means the world becomes yours. If you don't do it, it drifts away and takes a whole piece of your self with it, like an amputation. To attack it and attack it and get it under control—it's like taking possession of your life."
—*Ted Hughes*

"Try to be one of the people on whom nothing is lost."
—*Henry James*

"The house of fiction has . . . not one window, but a million."
—*Henry James*

"A man ought to read just as inclination leads him, for what he reads as a task will do him little good."
—*Samuel Johnson*

"One can never be alone enough when one writes . . . there can never be enough silence around when one writes . . . even night is not night enough."
—*Franz Kafka*

"I know a poem is finished when I can't find another word to cut."
—*Bobbi Katz*

"I would define literature as memorable writing of any sort."
—*X. J. Kennedy*

"In the essay, a writer steps forward."
—*Tracy Kidder*

"The road to hell is paved with adverbs."
—*Stephen King*

"Fiction is truth's older sister."
—*Rudyard Kipling*

"The title and the first few lines of your poem represent the hand you extend in friendship toward your reader."
—*Ted Kooser*

"It matters where you put those little indents. They show connections and separations in the flow; they are structurally essential."
—*Ursula K. LeGuin, on paragraphs*

"I try to leave out the parts that people skip."
—*Elmore Leonard*

"My best friend is the man who'll get me a book I ain't read."
—*Abraham Lincoln*

"We are the ones we've been waiting for."
—*Audre Lord*

"Outside of a dog, a book is a man's best friend. Inside of a dog, it's too dark to read."
—*Groucho Marx*

"The days that make us happy make us wise."
—*John Masefield*

"A book is completed only when it is finished by a reader. This is the ultimate privilege of art. In fact, it's the intimate privilege of being alive. When telling stories we are engaged in a democracy like no other."

—*Colum McCann*

"The capacity to revise determines the true writer. Suspect the finished poem. Your evil twin wants your poem to be finished."

—*Wesley McNair*

". . . language is the house to run to,
in wild nights, chased by dogs and other sounds,
when you've been lost for a long time,
when you have no other place."

—*Anne Michaels*

"If I knew my own mind, I would not make essays. I would make decisions."

—*Michel de Montaigne*

"The compulsion to read and write . . . is a bit of mental wiring the species has selected over time in order, as the life span increases, to keep us interested in ourselves."

—*Lorrie Moore*

"When we try to pick out anything by itself, we find it hitched to everything else in the universe."

—*John Muir*

"Problems make good subjects."

—*Donald Murray*

"Readers read to satisfy their hunger for information—specific, accurate information that they can use."

—*Donald Murray*

"There's no [one] way to outline. . . . But you should find some way of preseeing what you may write. . . . Most of the time my drafts collapse unless I have outlines in my head or on paper."

—*Donald Murray*

"I *never* proceed without an opening that I think will produce a good piece of writing. That's the only never in my personal toolbox."

—*Donald Murray*

"The end [of an essay] must connect with the opening. What has been promised must have been delivered. Read the opening over to see what closing it implies."

—Donald Murray

"And it was at that age poetry arrived in search of me . . . I wheeled with the stars. My heart broke loose on the wind."

—Pablo Neruda

"Write what makes you happy."

—O. Henry

"Tell me, what is it you plan to do with your one wild and precious life?"

—Mary Oliver

"Imagination is better than a sharp instrument. To pay attention, this is our endless and proper work."

—Mary Oliver

"The most important point in the line is the end of the line."

—Mary Oliver, on line breaks in poetry

"I cannot say too many times how powerful the technique of line lengths and line breaks are. You cannot swing the lines around, or fling strong-sounding words, or scatter soft ones, to no purpose."

—Mary Oliver

"The main thing is to make rooms that are big enough to be useful, shapely enough to be attractive, and not so empty as to be disappointing."

—Ron Padgett, on stanzas

"Poetry is a rich, full-bodied whistle, cracked ice crunching in pails, the night that numbs the leaf, the duel of two nightingales, the sweet pea that has run wild, creation's tears in shoulder blades."

—Boris Pasternak

"Our reasons for reading what we do are as eccentric as our reasons for living as we do."

—Daniel Pennac

"I've never had time to read. But no one ever kept me from finishing a novel that I loved."

—Daniel Pennac

"To find ourselves spoken for in art gives dignity to our pain, our anger, our lust, our losses. We can hear what we hope for and what we most fear in the release of cadenced utterances. We have few rituals that function for us in the ordinary chaos of our lives."
—*Marge Piercy*

"True education flowers when delight falls in love with responsibility. If you love something, you want to look after it."
—*Philip Pullman*

"The moment of change is the only poem."
—*Adrienne Rich*

"Be patient toward all that is unsolved in your heart and try to love the questions themselves."
—*Rainer Maria Rilke*

"Breathe in experience, breath out poetry."
—*Muriel Rukeyser*

"Let yourself be drawn by the pull of what you love. It will not lead you astray."
—*Rumi*

"Writing stories has given me the power to change things I could not change as a child. I can make boys into doctors. I can make fathers stop drinking. I can make mothers stay."
—*Cynthia Rylant*

"The more that you read, the more things you'll know. The more that you read, the more places you'll grow."
—*Dr. Seuss*

"Unpredictability is not the exception in [English] spelling-sound correspondences. It is the rule."
—*Frank Smith*

"My proper education consisted of the liberty to read whatever I cared to. I read indiscriminately and all the time, with my eyes hanging out. . . ."
—*Dylan Thomas*

"Don't say the old lady screamed. Bring her on and let her scream."
—*Mark Twain*

"A memoir is how one remembers one's own life, while an autobiography is history, requiring research, dates, facts double-checked."
—*Gore Vidal*

"Poetry is especially an art of compression."
—*Robert Wallace*

"Reader and writer, we wish each other well. Don't we want and don't we understand the same thing? A story of beauty and passion, some fresh approximation of human truth?"
—*Eudora Welty*

"When a mosquito bites me—I scratch. When I write something, I guess I'm trying to get rid of the itchiness inside me."
—*E. B. White, on essays*

"Remember that paragraphing calls for a good eye as well as a logical mind. Enormous blocks of print look formidable to a reader. He has a certain reluctance to tackle them; he can lose his way in them."
—*E. B. White*

"Perception is the first act of the imagination."
—*William Carlos Williams*

"It is difficult
To get the news from poems
Yet men die miserably every day
For lack of what is found there"
—*William Carlos Williams*

"Say it, no ideas but in things."
—*William Carlos Williams*

"Literature is no one's private ground, literature is common ground . . . let us trespass freely and fearlessly and find our own way for ourselves."
—*Virginia Woolf*

"Fiction is like a spider's web, attached ever so lightly perhaps, but still attached to life at all four corners."
—*Virginia Woolf*

"People don't realize how a man's whole life can be changed by one book."
—*Malcolm X*

"Clutter is the disease of American writing. We are a society strangling in unnecessary words."
—*William Zinsser*

"Don't be kind of bold. Be bold."
—*William Zinsser*

"A succession of tiny paragraphs is as annoying as a paragraph that's too long."
—*William Zinsser*

"Good writing is lean and confident."
—*William Zinsser*

"Writing is a craft, not an art."
—*William Zinsser*

SAMPLE STUDENT WRITING RECORD

p.1

Nancie Atwe.
Center for Teaching and Learning

Pieces of Writing Finished by _Xander_ during _2012-13_

#	TITLE	GENRE	DATE COMPLETED
1	"Bittersweet"	Poem	9-16
2	"Home"	Poem	10-2
3	"October"	Collection of Haiku	10-4
4	"Xander"	Bio-poem	10-15
5	"Where I'm From"	Poem	10-19
6	"Child Fears	Collaborative Poem	10-20
7	"everyday"	Gift of Writing	11-4
8	"The Darkness"	Memoir	12-4
9	"Standardized"	Parody	12-4
10	"The Boy"	Gift of Writing	12-19
11	"Our Moment"	Gift of Writing	12-19
12	"Violence + Redemption: Afghanistan"	Book Review	1-18
13	"Loki"	Poem	1-22
14	"Our Sonnet"	Sonnet	2-2
15	"Now"	Poem	2-21
16	"Teens and Cell Phones: Needless or Necessary?"	Essay	3-16
17	"Tsunami Dreams"	Microfiction/Prose Poem	4-5
18	"What the Wind Knows"	Microfiction/ " "	4-11
19	"A Connection with the Land"	Advocacy Journalism	5-1

(over →)

SAMPLE STUDENT READING RECORD

Reading Record for _Gabrielle — 1st Trimester_

Nancie Atwell
Center for Teaching and Learning

#	TITLE	GENRE	AUTHOR	DATE FINISHED	DATE ABANDONED	RATING
1	Seasons of Ice	mystery	C. Plum-Ucci	9/10		9
2	The Great Wide Sea	adventure/survival	Herlong, M.H.	9/14		10
3	the Summer I turned pretty	CRF	Jenny Han	9/19		10
4	Never Let Me go	Dystopian Sci Fi	K. Ishiguro	9/25		9
5	Breaking Night	memoir	Liz Murray	9/27		9
6	Tips on Having a gay(ex)Boy..	CRF	C. Jones	9/28		10
7	The glass castle	Memoir	J. Walls	10/3		bella
	Ttyl	CRF journal	L. myracle		10/5	5
8	Upstate	CRF	K. Buchanan	10/10		bella
9	Charlie St Cloud	Supernatural	B. Sherwood	10/13		8
10	Twenty-Boy Summer	CRF	S. Ockler	10/16		10
11	Love and other Uses for Duct Tape	CRF	C. Jones	10/25		8
12	Eighth grade Bites	Humor	H. Brewer	10/27		9
13	Monsters of Men	Dystopian Sci Fi	P. ness	11/1		bella x10
14	Give a Boy a Gun	CRF	T. Strasser	11/3		8
	What Happened to Lani G.	mystery-mental	C. Plum-Ucci		11/4	6
15	The Game of Sunken Places	mystery-action	M.T. anderson	11/10		9
16	The maze Runner	Dys. Sci Fi	J. Dashner	11/14		10
17	The Diving Bell and the...	Memoir	J.D. Bavby	11/16		9
18	The Perks of Being a Wallflower	CRF	S. Chbosky	11/18		7+
19	Scarlet Letter	classic	Nathaniel Hawthorne	11/19		8
20	Be more Chill	CRF	Ned Vizzini	11/23		10
21	The Story of a girl	CRF	S. Zarr	11/26		9
22	Choosing a Religion	Humor	R.C. sproul	11/28		9

Individual Proofreading List for _____

1. _____

_____

2. _____

_____

3. _____

_____

4. _____

_____

5. _____

_____

6. _____

_____

7. _____

_____

8. _____

_____

9. _____

_____

10. _____

_____

11. _____

_____

12. _____

_____

EDITING CHECKSHEET

TO BE PAPER-CLIPPED TO THE TOP OF WRITING SUBMITTED FOR TEACHER EDITING

NAME _____

TITLE OF PIECE _____

DATE OF PIECE _____

CONVENTION	EDITED (✓)	TEACHER'S COMMENTS
		WORDS TO ADD TO MY SPELLING LIST

Peer Writing Conference Record

Writer's Name_____ Date _____

Responder _____ Topic and Genre _____

Writer, when you've identified something you want help with in a draft, consider who in your group might be most effective in supplying it.

- For example, are you looking for a response to your title, lead, conclusion, dialogue, descriptions of thoughts and feelings, descriptions of people in action or other visuals, theme or *so what?*, logic, structure, flow, information, specifics, verbs, narrative voice, verb tense, diction, sensory imagery, evidence, arguments, or use of such poetic techniques as line breaks, stanza breaks, compression, cadence, metaphor, simile, or personification?
- Next, given what you've learned about your classmates as writers, readers, and people, who might have expertise in this area? Approach a person who you think knows about

_____

and ask for a response to _____

_____

_____

Responder, when you agree to confer with a classmate, your job is to help the writer make decisions about his or her drafts and improve it. To do that, you'll need to:

- Ask questions to clarify what the writer wants help with, until you're sure you understand.
- Either read the draft, or listen and read along as the writer reads it to you. Then give the writer the help he or she asked for.
- In addition, if there are parts that confuse you, you don't understand, you'd like to know more about, or don't draw you into the writing and keep you there, ask the writer about them.
- Jot down your suggestions, reactions, and questions on the lines below, for the writer's reference.
- Ask the writer what he or she plans to do next.
- Give this record of the conference to the writer.

_____

_____

_____

_____

Writer, at the end of the conference, jot down your plans, so you don't forget them:

_____

_____

SPELLING STUDY FORM

Weekly Word Study

Name _____

Date _____

	COPY	REWRITE	REWRITE	REWRITE	SPELL	SPELL AGAIN OR ★
1.						
2.						
3.						
4.						
5.						

A THESAURUS FOR WRITERS WHO *WALK* AND *LOOK* TOO MUCH

**WALK IN A
LEISURELY FASHION**

saunter
stroll
meander
wander
amble
ramble
drift
mosey
cruise
straggle
traipse

**WALK WITH
GRACE/JOY**

dance
glide
float
sashay
whirl
waltz
skip

WALK WITH ENERGY

spring
flit
prance
bound
dash
dart
skip
tear
fly
race
sweep

WALK QUIETLY

pad
sneak
slink
tiptoe
slip
creep
scurry
skulk
prowl
steal
stalk
inch

WALK LOUDLY

clatter
crash
stomp
hurtle

WALK FAST

lope
gallop
jog
hike
bolt
sweep
scurry
tear
charge
swoop
hustle
fly
hurry
rush
barrel

race
hurtle
dash
scamper
scramble
zip
whiz
zoom
rip
trot
stampede
march
dash
scoot
dart
sprint
spring

WALK SLOWLY

inch
creep
crawl
stumble
lumber
waddle
wobble
bumble
trail
limp
hobble
lurch
plod
trudge
stagger
straggle
shuffle
slog

WALK PROUDLY

stride
swagger
parade
strut
swish

WALK IMPATIENTLY

pace
flounce

WALK AWAY

flee
troop
slip
escape
fly
steal
desert
bolt

WALK CAREFULLY

pad
creep
ease
inch
wend (one's way)
slip
tiptoe
feel (one's) way

WALK PURPOSEFULLY

aim
head
march
troop
tramp
make for
head for
stride
hike
trek

WALK INTO A SPACE

enter
barge
burst
dive
invade

WALK OUT OF A SPACE

emerge
explode
escape
abandon
exit

WALK UP

jump
zoom
rocket
vault
leap
ascend
climb
spring
clamber
charge
trip

WALK DOWN

descend
plunge
dive
plummet
tumble
trip
leap
charge
clamber

WALK ANGRILY

stalk
tramp
stomp

LOOK TOO MUCH

admire

attend

behold

check out

concentrate

contemplate

detect

discern

discover

examine

eye

find

gape

gawk

gaze

glance

glare

glimpse

glower

hunt

inspect

leer

locate

notice

observe

pay attention

peek

peep

peer

pore

regard

review

scan

scowl

scrutinize

search

see

snoop

spy

squint

stare

study

survey

view

watch

witness

Editing Symbols

Symbol	Its Meaning
⌗	Create a new paragraph here.
⟶	Combine these sentences as one paragraph.
a̲	Make this letter a capital.
A̸	Make this letter lower case.
⊙	Insert a period here.
(,)	Insert a comma here.
∧	Add a punctuation mark or word(s) here.
⌣	Close this gap: this is one word.
# / ∧	Add a space here.
⸺	Delete this.
/	In a poem, create a new line here.
=	In a poem, create a new stanza here.
∿∿∿	Rethink this word, phrase, or line: it's clunky.

Ways Student Writers Can Go Public

A sense of audience—knowing that someone beyond the teacher will read what students have written—is crucial to the success of a writing workshop. Publication takes many forms; it includes all the ways a writer might connect with a reader. Sometimes the writing comes first, and later on its author or I will recognize a publication possibility—for example, when a piece in a student's finished-writing folder matches the theme or genre of a new contest. Other times the goal of publication comes first: after learning about a new option, a writer will decide to pursue it. Either way, it's part of a workshop teacher's job to look for, create, and demonstrate opportunities for writers to be read and heard.

Publication in the workshop should be a given for everyone, never a reward bestowed on the "good" writers. If class or school magazines are juried, the kids who most need recognition will never be published, and the "good" writers will be published time and again.

1. Individual pieces of writing printed or photocopied and shared with friends and families. The result is instant publication.

2. Pieces of writing intended as gifts: poems, stories, memoirs, and letters. These can be handwritten on cards, posters, or bookmarks; mounted or matted; illustrated; printed in beautiful fonts on special paper; or rendered in calligraphy.

3. Submissions to class anthologies that address a theme or explore a genre. These are enjoyed in class readings, accompanied in my workshop by chai, decaf, and cocoa.

4. Submissions to a school literary magazine.

5. Submissions to an eighth-grade yearbook, which might include reminiscences, poetry, vital statistics, and a class will and prophecy.

6. Submissions to newspapers, including letters to the editor, editorials, feature articles, profiles, and poetry.

7. Submissions to print or online magazines that publish student writing. *Teen Ink* is my favorite.

8. Submissions to student writing contests—local, regional, state, and national. My favorites include River of Words (nature poetry, K–8, December 1 deadline), Letters About Literature (5–12, early January deadline), Poetry Society of Virginia (K–8, January 19 deadline), Norm Strung Writing Awards (6–12, outdoors-oriented poetry and prose, March 16 deadline), Sarah Mook Poetry Prize (K–8, March 31 deadline) and contests sponsored by *The New York Times* on their Learning Network for found poetry and editorial/essay writing. The website winningwriters.com provides a clearinghouse for contest opportunities.

9. Poems or songs copied onto oaktag charts to recite or sing at assemblies or morning meetings.

10. Submissions to a principal's newsletter: announcements, poetry, and guest editorials.

11. Posters—poetry, announcements, handbills, jokes, riddles, and advertisements—for classroom bulletin boards and school corridors.

12. Framed one-pagers: I purchase Plexiglas box frames for student writing and hang them along the wall outside my classroom. Students can pop out old work and pop in new in thirty seconds, and the display looks professional *and* satifies the state fire marshal.

13. Displays at public events, such as local fairs and festivals and open houses for parents.

14. Enactments and recitations of scripts and speeches, including skits and plays, readers' theatre performances, assembly presentations, and graduation speeches.

15. Petitions—to the principal, school board, board of selectmen, YMCA, governor, etc.

16. Correspondence—letters of inquiry, thank-you notes, complaints, postcards, fan letters, condolence notes, cover letters, Ted L. Nancy parody letters, messages in bottles, time-capsule lists, etc.

17. Blog entries (at CTL, book reviews for our blog You Gotta Read This).

NANCIE'S CURRICULUM CYCLE

My students are with me for two years in a combined grades 7 and 8. Every year I teach the essential principles of craft and conduct the major genre studies, but I make sure to vary my examples and models, so eighth graders can approach the lessons from fresh perspectives. Redundancy is a benefit in this case, as the older group reviews principles and conventions, revisits genres, and builds on their experiences from seventh grade.

The themed groups of poems I listed below are in *Naming the World: A Year of Poems and Lessons* (2006). Minilessons not included here appear in *Lessons That Change Writers* (2002).

YEAR ONE EMPHASES

First Trimester

Writing: rules, expectations, and routines of the workshop; organization of the writing–reading handbook; what writers do; genre study of free-verse poetry; the Rule of *So What?* or theme; the Rule of Thoughts and Feelings; how to edit; dashes vs. hyphens; writing off-the-page; the Rule of Write About *a* Pebble; a brief history of the English language; the spelling study process; peer writing conferences; genre study of memoirs; sensory verbs and how to use a thesaurus; personal survival spelling words; ideas for poems about the natural world/River of Words poetry competition; how to self-assess as a writer

Reading: rules, expectations, and routines of the workshop; booktalks; someday titles; how to read and unpack a poem as a critic; glossary of poetic terms; psycholinguistic reading theory; literary lexicon; letter-essays about books; readings of class poetry anthologies; read and unpack poetry about identity and cats and dogs, plus poems by Naomi Shihab Nye, Jim Harrison, and William Stafford; how to self-assess as a reader and critic

Second Trimester

Writing: the trouble with adverbs; genre study of some poetic forms (tritinas, sestinas, pantoums, villanelles, and abecedarias); holiday gifts of writing; genre study of reviews of books/films/TV shows; capitalization conventions; writing contests; techniques for proofreading spelling; madeleine poems; the origins of punctuation; common comma omissions; genre study of micro fiction; apostrophes on possessive nouns

Reading: read and unpack tritinas, sestinas, pantoums, villanelles, abecedarias; holiday gifts of writing; poems about growing up; madeleine poems; poetry by E. E. Cummings, Emily Dickinson, and Wallace Stevens; readings of class anthologies of memoirs, reviews, and micro fiction; participate in the national African American Read-In; unpack poems by Maya Angelou, Countee Cullen, Rita Dove, Nikki Giovanni, Marilyn Nelson, and Kevin Young

Third Trimester

Writing: haikus and senryus; genre study of essays; paragraphing; when to write numbers as words; spelling generalizations that work; Mother's Day gifts of writing; genre study of advocacy journalism; word-usage confusions; pronoun-case conventions; graduation speeches; Father's Day gifts of writing

Reading: read and unpack haikus and senryus; poems about games/sports, gender, and language play; and poetry by Ted Kooser (and Jim Harrison), Marge Piercy, and Billy Collins; reading of the class anthology of essays; how to read poems independently and present one to others; discussion of summer slide and selection of summer book loans; how and where to find good books after eighth grade

YEAR TWO EMPHASES

First Trimester

Writing: rules, expectations, and routines of the workshop; organization of the writing–reading handbook; genre study of free-verse poetry; the Rule of *So What?* or theme; the Rule of Thoughts and Feelings; how to edit; dashes vs. hyphens; writing off-the-page; the Rule of Write About *a* Pebble; spelling study process; poetry heart maps; figurative language/personification; where poems hide / "ideas in things;" genre study of homage and parody; River of Words nature poetry contest; how to self-assess as a writer

Reading: rules, expectations, and routines of the workshop; booktalks; someday titles; why we have reading workshop; how to read and unpack a poem as a critic; glossary of poetic terms; literary lexicon; National Banned Books Week; letter-essays about books; readings of class poetry anthologies; read and unpack poems that demonstrate what poetry can do, poems with sensory diction, poetic homages and parodies, poems about the natural world, and poems by William Carlos Williams, Mary Oliver, and Robert Frost; plus how to self-assess as a reader and critic

Second Trimester

Writing: genre study of memoirs; holiday gifts of writing; writing contests; Neruda's irregular odes; genre study of reviews of books/films/TV shows; comma usage; begin genre study of micro fiction

Reading: brief history of young adult literature; unpack poems with playful language, irregular odes by Pablo Neruda, antiwar poetry of World War I, World War II, Vietnam, and Iraq, and poems by Gwendolyn Brooks and Langston Hughes; participate in the national African American Read-In; participate in readings of class anthologies of memoirs and reviews

Third Trimester

Writing: continue genre study of micro fiction; uses of the colon and semicolon; comma splices; genre study of essays; paragraphing; when to write numbers as words; Mother's Day gifts of writing; genre study of profiles; the Elizabethan sonnet; how to use a rhyming dictionary; graduation speeches; Father's Day gifts of writing

Reading: read and unpack poems about reading and writing and social and political issues, plus poetry by Walt Whitman, Allen Ginsberg, Tony Hoagland, and Edwin Arlington Robinson; learn about Shakespeare as a playwright and poet and unpack a selection of the sonnets; learn how to read poems independently and prepare to present one; readings of class anthologies of micro fiction and essays; discussion of summer slide and the selection of summer book loans; how to find good books after eighth grade

SUBSTITUTE PLANS FOR
WRITING–READING WORKSHOP

You'll find the record-keeping forms for students' independent work as writers and readers on the clipboards I store on the top shelf of my bookcase, which is next to the rocking chair. Please trust the routines of the workshop and the kids. They know what to do. My students _____ and _____ have volunteered to be informants, if you get stuck or need clarification.

WRITING AND READING (8:50–10:15)

1. *Spelling:* If it's a Tuesday or Thursday, walk the inside of the circle of beanbags and ask kids to show you their *spelling studies.* On Tuesday you're checking to see that each student has printed five words in the first column on the form and that they're spelled correctly. On Thursday, check to see that each study form is completely filled out and that the words in the final column are spelled correctly. Students know that the next step is to test each other in pairs. If there's an odd number of kids, you quiz the one without a partner. I don't collect the tests or record the scores.

   If you're unsure of a word's spelling, ask the student to look it up in a dictionary or handheld spellchecker and show it to you. If anyone comes to class without his or her spelling homework, record the name(s) for me. That student won't be tested today.

2. *Daily Poetry Discussion:* The poem for today is _____ by _____ (from *Naming the World*). A class set of copies and my notes for teaching it are on the top shelf of my bookcase. Before class, please practice reading the poem a few times to yourself, so you can deliver it smoothly. Call on a range of volunteers in the discussion that follows, not just the first hands up.

3. *Status-of-the-Class (Writing):* Find the class clipboard, call the roll, and record on the grid who is working on what; use my previous notes as guidelines. Then send everyone off with the injunction: "Off you go—work hard, and make literature."

4. *Independent Writing Time:* Insist on silence. If necessary, remind kids that writing is thinking and writers need to be able to concentrate. Circulate among them, and whisper when you stop to talk with a writer.

   Say:

   > "How's it going?"
   > "Can I help you?"

If you feel comfortable responding to their writing, read it and say, as appropriate:

"Where are you going with this piece?"
"Tell me more about X."
"I don't understand Y."
"How did you feel or what did you think about X?"
"I'm confused about . . . ."
"What will you do next?"

5. *Reading Workshop:* At 9:45, ask students to come to a good stopping point in their writing, clean up, grab their books, and come back to the circle.

Books that individuals in the class wish to introduce to their peers are stacked on the bottom shelf of my bookcase, with students' names on cards in the books. Select two of these titles to be *booktalked*.

Afterward, announce: "It's time to segue into the reading zone." Locate the reading clipboard for this class, move among students as they read, and record their book titles and page numbers on the class reading record: again, use my previous notes as your guide. Please initial any titles that students return to the classroom library on their bookcards, which they'll give to you as you circulate among them.

Works Cited

Professional Works

Allington, Richard and Anne McGill-Franzen. 2013. *Summer Reading: Closing the Rich/Poor Achievement Gap*. New York: Teachers College Press.

Andrews, Richard, Carole Torgerson, Sue Beverton, Terry Locke, Graham Low, Alison Robinson, and Die Zhu. 2004. *The Effect of Grammar Teaching (Syntax) in English on 5 to 16 Year Olds' Accuracy and Quality in Written Composition: Review Summary*. York, UK: University of York.

Atwell, Nancie. 1987. *In the Middle: Writing, Reading, and Learning with Adolescents*, 1st ed. Portsmouth, NH: Heinemann.

———. 2002. *Lessons That Change Writers*. Portsmouth, NH: firsthand/Heinemann.

———. 2006. *Naming the World: A Year of Poems and Lessons*. Portsmouth, NH: firsthand/ Heinemann.

———. 2007. *The Reading Zone*. New York: Scholastic.

———. 2011a. *Reading in the Middle: Workshop Essentials* (DVD). Portsmouth, NH: Heinemann.

———. 2011b. *Writing in the Middle: Workshop Essentials* (DVD). Portsmouth, NH: Heinemann.

———. 2014. *Systems to Transform Your Classroom and School*. Portsmouth, NH: Heinemann.

Baldick, Chris. 2009. *The Oxford Dictionary of Literary Terms*. Oxford, UK: Oxford University Press.

Bartlett's Familiar Quotations, Seventeenth ed. 2004. Boston: Little, Brown & Co.

Beckson, Karl, and Arthur Ganz. 1989. *Literary Terms: A Dictionary*. New York: Farrar, Straus and Giroux.

Bianchi, Martha Gilbert Dickinson. 1924. *Life and Letters of Emily Dickinson*. Boston: Houghton Mifflin.

Bissex, Glenda. 1980. *GNYS AT WRK: A Child Learns to Write and Read*. Cambridge, MA: Harvard University Press.

Brooks, Gwendolyn. 1975. *Beckonings*. Detroit: Broadside Press.

Bruner, Jerome. 1986. *Actual Minds, Possible Worlds*. Cambridge, MA: Harvard University Press.

Cullinan, Bernice. 1998–2000. "Independent Reading and School Achievement." Washington, DC: Westat, Inc., and U.S. Department of Education.

Dacey, Philip. 1977. "Thumb" from *How I Escaped from the Labyrinth and Other Poems*. Pittsburgh: Carnegie-Mellon University Press.

Davies, Robertson. 1959. "Battle Cry for Book Lovers." *The Saturday Evening Post*. Expanded and reprinted in *A Voice from the Attic*, 1960. New York: Knopf.

DeMille, Ted. 2008. *Making Believe on Paper: Fiction Writing with Young Children*. Portsmouth, NH: Heinemann.

Eliot, T.S. 1920. *Sweeney Among the Nightingales*. New York: Knopf.

Fogarty, Mignon. 2008. *Grammar Girl's Quick and Dirty Tips for Better Writing*. New York: Holt.

Frost, Robert. 1939. Preface to the *Collected Poems*. New York: Henry Holt.

Gardner, Howard, and Katie Davis. 2013. *The App Generation*. New Haven, CT: Yale University Press.

Gladwell, Malcolm. 2008. *Outliers: The Story of Success*. Boston: Little, Brown & Co.

Graham, Steve, and Delores Perin. 2007. *Writing Next*. New York: Carnegie Corp.

Graves, Donald. 1975. "The Child, the Writing Process, and the Role of the Professional." In *The Writing Processes of Students*, edited by Walter Petty. Buffalo: State University of New York.

———. 1983. *Writing: Teachers and Children at Work*. Portsmouth, NH: Heinemann.

———. 1994. *A Fresh Look at Writing*. Portsmouth, NH: Heinemann.

———. 2003. *Writers and Children at Work*, 20th anniversary ed. Portsmouth, NH: Heinemann.

Greene, Graham. 1940. *The Power and the Glory*. London: Heinemann.

Harrison, Jim, and Ted Kooser. 2003. *Braided Creek: A Conversation in Poetry*. Townsend, WA: Copper Canyon Press.

Harvey, Stephanie, and Harvey Daniels. 2009. *Comprehension and Collaboration*. Portsmouth, NH: Heinemann.

Harvey, Stephanie, and Anne Goudvis. 2002. *Think Nonfiction! Modeling Reading and Research*. Portland, ME: Stenhouse.

Harwayne, Shelley. 1992. *Lasting Impressions: Weaving Literature into the Writing Workshop*. Portsmouth, NH: Heinemann.

Hay, Elizabeth. 2011. *Alone in the Classroom*. Toronto, Canada: McClelland & Stewart.

Heard, Georgia. 1999. *Awakening the Heart: Exploring Poetry in Elementary and Middle School*. Portsmouth, NH: Heinemann.

Heyns, Barbara. 1979. *Summer Learning and the Effects of Schooling*. New York: Academic Press.

James, Henry. 1934. *The Art of the Novel*. New York: Charles Scribner's Sons.

Janeczko, Paul. 2009. *A Kick in the Head: An Everyday Guide to Poetic Forms*. Somerville, MA: Candlewick.

Just, Marcel, and Patricia Carpenter. 1987. *The Psychology of Reading and Language Comprehension*. Newton, MA: Allyn & Bacon.

Kennedy, X. J. 1993. *An Introduction to Poetry*, 7th ed. Reading, MA: Addison-Wesley.

Lesesne, Teri. 2003. *Making the Match: The Right Book for the Right Reader at the Time, Grades 4–12*. Portland, ME: Stenhouse.

Macrorie, Ken. 1988. *The I-Search Paper*. Portsmouth, NH: Boynton/Cook.

Moffett, James, and Betty Jane Wagner. 1976. *Student-Centered Language Arts and Reading, K–13*, 2d ed. Boston: Houghton Mifflin.

Murphy, Bruce, ed. 1996. *Benét's Reader's Encyclopedia*, 4th ed. New York: HarperCollins.

Murray, Donald. 1982. *Learning by Teaching*. Portsmouth, NH: Boynton/Cook.

———. 1999. *Write to Learn*. Fort Worth, TX: Holt, Reinhart, and Winston.

———. 2003. *A Writer Teaches Writing*, rev. 2d ed. Belmont, CA: Wadsworth.

National Governors Association Center for Best Practices and Council of Chief State School Officers. 2010. *Common Core State Standards for English Language Arts and Literacy*. Washington, DC: NGA Center and CCSSO.

New Roget's Thesaurus. 1986. Revised ed. New York: Berkley Books.

Newkirk, Thomas. 2000. "Literacy and Loneliness." *Ohio Journal of the English Language Arts* Fall: 18–21.

Newkirk, Thomas, and Penny Kittle. 2013. *Children Want to Write*. Portsmouth, NH: Heinemann.

Oliver, Mary. 1994. *A Poetry Handbook*. New York: Harcourt Brace.

Padgett, Ron, ed. 1987. *The Teachers and Writers Handbook of Poetic Forms*. New York: Teachers & Writers.

Paterson, Katherine. 1981. *FLB Newsletter 3* (3). Chicago: Follett Library Book Company.

Pennac, Daniel. 1994. *Better Than Life*. Toronto, Ontario: CouchHouse Press.

Plimpton, George, ed. 1963. *Writers at Work: The Paris Review Interviews*. Second series. New York: Viking Press.

Rief, Linda. 1992. *Seeking Diversity: Language Arts with Adolescents*. Portsmouth, NH: Heinemann.

Rodale, J. I. 1986. *The Synonym Finder*. New York: Grand Central Publishing.

Romano, Tom. 1987. *Clearing the Way: Working with Teenage Writers*. Portsmouth, NH: Heinemann.

Rosenblatt, Louise. [1938] 1983. *Literature as Exploration*. New York: Noble and Noble.

———. 1980. "What Facts Does This Poem Teach You?" *Language Arts* 57: 386–94.

———. 1994. *The Reader, the Text, and the Poem: The Transactional Theory of the Literary Work*. Carbondale, IL: Southern Illinois University Press.

Scholastic. 2007. "Kids and Family Reading Report." Conducted by Yankelovich. Retrieved from www.scholastic.com/aboutscholastic/news/readingreport.htm.

Sebranek, Patrick, Dave Kemper, and Verne Meyer. 2001. *Writers Inc: A Student Handbook for Writing and Learning*. Burlington, WI: Write Source Educational Publishing House.

Sherwood, Martha. 1982. "Thunder" (excerpt). In *Knock at a Star: A Child's Introduction to Poetry* by X. J. Kennedy and Dorothy M. Kennedy. Boston: Little, Brown.

Sitton, Rebecca. 1996. *Spelling Sourcebook Reviews for High-Use Writing Words*. Spokane, WA: Egger Publishing.

Smith, Frank. 1997. *Reading Without Nonsense*, 3d ed. New York: Teachers College Press.

———. 1988. *Joining the Literacy Club*. Portsmouth, NH: Heinemann.

———. 2004. *Understanding Reading*, 6th ed. London, UK: Routledge.

Smith, Larry, and Rachel Fershleiser. 2009. *I Can't Keep My Own Secrets: Six-Word Memoirs by Teens Famous and Obscure*. New York: HarperCollins.

Staton, Jana. 1980. "Writing and Counseling: Using a Dialogue Journal." *Language Arts* 57: 514–18.

Stern, Jerome, ed. 1996. *Micro Fiction: An Anthology of Really Short Stories*. New York: W. W. Norton.

Stevens, Wallace. 1951. "The Noble Rider and the Sound of Words." In *The Necessary Angel: Essays on Reality and Imagination*. New York: Alfred A. Knopf.

Stewart, Martha. 1983. *Martha Stewart's Quick Cook*. New York: Clarkson Potter.

Strunk, William, Jr. and E. B. White. 1979. *The Elements of Style*, 3d ed. New York: Macmillan.

Truss, Lynne. 2006. *Eats, Shoots & Leaves*. New York: Gotham.

Turabian, Kate. 1976. *The Student's Guide for Writing College Papers*. Chicago: University of Chicago Press.

Vonnegut, Kurt. 1984. *Palm Sunday*. New York: Dell.

Vygotsky, L. S. 1962. *Thought and Language*. Cambridge, MA: MIT Press.

Wallace, Robert. 1996. *Writing Poems*, 4th ed. New York: HarperCollins.

Weaver, Constance. 1994. *Reading Process and Practice: From Socio-Psycholinguistics to Whole Language*, 2d ed. Portsmouth, NH: Heinemann.

———. 1996. *Teaching Grammar in Context*. Portsmouth, NH: Boynton/Cook.

White, E. B. 1977. *Essays of E. B. White*. New York: HarperCollins.

Whitman, Walt. 1991. *I Hear America Singing*. Illustrated by Robert Sabuda. New York: Philomel Books.

———. 2004. *When I Heard the Learn'd Astronomer*. Illustrated by Loren Lord. New York: Simon & Schuster Books for Young Readers.

Williams, William Carlos. 1963. *Paterson*, Book 1. New York: New Directions.

Woolf, Virginia. 1947. *The Moment and Other Essays*. New York: Harcourt Brace.

Young, Sue. 1997. *The Scholastic Rhyming Dictionary*. New York: Scholastic.

Zinsser, William. 2006. *On Writing Well: The Classic Guide to Writing Nonfiction*. New York: HarperCollins.

Literature Cited

Abbott, John. [1875] 2012. *The History of Maine*. London, UK: Forgotten Books.

Adiga, Aravind. 2008. *The White Tiger*. New York: Free Press.

Alexie, Sherman. 2009. *Absolutely True Story of a Part-Time Indian*. New York: Little, Brown Book for Young Readers.

Amis, Kingsley. [1954] 2000. *Lucky Jim*. New York: Penguin Modern Classics.

Anderson, M. T. 2008. *The Astonishing Life of Octavian Nothing; Traitor to the Nation, Volume I: The Pox Party*. Somerville, MA: Candlewick.

Andrews, Jesse. 2012. *Me, Earl, and the Dying Girl*. New York: Harry N. Abrams.

Atkinson, Kate. 1995. *Behind the Scenes at the Museum*. New York: Picador.

Atwood, Margaret. 1998. *The Handmaid's Tale*. New York: Anchor Books.

Austen, Jane. [1813] 1995. *Pride and Prejudice*. New York: Dover Thrift Editions.

Barker, Pat. [1991] 2013. *Regeneration* (Book 1 of Regeneration Trilogy). New York: Plume.

Bedard, Michael. 2007. *Emily*. New York: Doubleday Book for Young Readers.

Bradbury, Ray. [1953] 2012. *Fahrenheit 451*. New York: Simon & Schuster.

Brontë, Charlotte. [1847] 2006. *Jane Eyre*. New York: Penguin Classics.

Bulgakov, Mikhail. [1967] 1996. *The Master and Margarita*. New York: Vintage.

Burnett, Frances Hodgson. [1911] 2008. *The Secret Garden*. New York: Puffin.

Castañeda, Carlos. [1968] 2008. *The Teachings of Don Juan*, 40th anniversary ed. Berkeley: University of California Press.

Cleary, Beverly. [1959] 2007. *Jean and Johnny*. New York: HarperCollins.

Collins, Suzanne. 2010. *Mockingjay*. New York: Scholastic.

Coy, John. 2007. *Crackback*. New York: Scholastic.

Cunningham, Michael. 1998. *The Hours*. New York: Farrar, Straus and Giroux.

Daly, Maureen. [1942] 2010. *Seventeenth Summer*. New York: Simon Pulse.

Dessen, Sarah. 2004. *Dreamland*. New York: Speak/Penguin Books.

Donnelly, Jennifer. 2003. *A Northern Light*. Orlando, FL: Harcourt.

———. 2011. *Revolution*. New York: Ember/Random House Children's Books.

Eggers, Dave. 2007. *How the Water Feels to the Fishes*. San Francisco: McSweeney's.

Eliot, George. [1847] 2003. *Middlemarch*. New York: Penguin Classics.

Farmer, Nancy. 2004. *House of the Scorpion*. New York: Atheneum Books for Young Readers.

Fitzgerald, F. Scott. [1925] 2004. *The Great Gatsby*. New York: Scribner.

Flack, Sophie. 2011. *Bunheads*. New York: Poppy/Little, Brown.

Foer, Jonathan Safran. 2011. *Extremely Loud and Incredibly Close*. New York: Mariner Books.

Forster, E. M. [1910] 2002. *Howard's End*. New York: Dover Publications.

Fowles, John. [1969] 1998. *The French Lieutenant's Woman*. Boston: Back Bay Books.

Frank, Anne. [1947] 1993. *Diary of a Young Girl*. New York: Bantam.

Gaiman, Neil. 2003. *Neverwhere*. New York: William Morrow Paperbacks.

———. 2010. *The Graveyard Book*. New York: HarperCollins.

Golding, William. [1954] 1988. *Lord of the Flies*. New York: Perigee Books.

Graham, Robin L., with Derek L. T. Gill. [1972] 1991. *Dove*. New York: William Morrow Paperbacks.

Green. John. 2012. *The Fault in Our Stars*. New York: Dutton.

Handler, Daniel. 2013. *Why We Broke Up*. New York: Little, Brown.

Harrington, Laura. 2012. *Alice Bliss*. New York: Penguin Books.

Hautman, Pete. 2005. *Godless*. New York: Simon & Schuster Books for Young Readers.

Hawthorne, Nathaniel. [1850] 1994. *The Scarlet Letter*. New York: Dover.

Heller, Joseph. [1961] 2011. *Catch-22*, 50th anniversary ed. New York: Simon & Schuster.

Hemingway, Ernest. [1929] 1995. *A Farewell to Arms*. New York: Scribner.

———. [1952] 1995. *The Old Man and the Sea*. New York: Scribner.

———. [1926] 2006. *The Sun Also Rises*. New York: Scribner.

Herbach, Geoff. 2011. *Stupid Fast*. Naperville, IL: Sourcebooks Fire.

Heyerdahl, Thor. 1972. *Kon-Tiki*. New York: Rand McNally.

Hickam, Homer Jr. 2000. *Rocket Boys*. New York: Delta.

Hinton, S. E. [1967] 2012. *The Outsiders*. New York: Speak/Penguin.

Homer. 1990. *The Iliad*, translated by Robert Fagles. New York: Penguin Books.

Huxley, Aldous. [1932] 2005. *Brave New World*. New York: Harper Perennial Modern Library.

King, A. S. 2012. *Please Ignore Vera Dietz*. New York: Ember.

King, Stephen. 2010. *11/22/63*. New York: Scribners.

Kingsolver, Barbara. 2005. *The Poisonwood Bible*. New York: Harper Perennial Modern Classics.

Korman, Gordon. 2008. *Schooled*. New York: Disney–Hyperion.

Lee, Harper. [1960] 2010. *To Kill a Mockingbird*, 50th anniversary ed. New York: Harper.

Lockhart, E. 2009. *The Disreputable History of Frankie Landau-Banks*. New York: Disney–Hyperion.

Lore, Pittacus. 2011. *I Am Number Four*. New York: HarperCollins.

Machiavelli, Niccolò. [1532] 2003. *The Prince*. New York: Penguin Classics.

Martel, Yann. 2003. *Life of Pi*. New York: Mariner Books.

Martin, George R. R. 2005. *Feast of Crows* (Book 4 of Game of Thrones series). New York: Bantam.

McCarthy, Cormac. 2007. *No Country for Old Men*. New York: Vintage Books.

————. 2007. *The Road*. New York: Vintage Books.

McEwan, Ian. 2001. *Atonement*. New York: Anchor Books.

Meyer, Stephenie. 1990. Twilight series, 4–book boxed set. New York: Little, Brown & Co.

Moriarty, Jaclyn. 2005. *The Year of Secret Assignments*. New York: Scholastic.

Murray, Liz. 2011. *Breaking Night*. New York: Hyperion.

Myracle, Lauren. 2010. *Peace, Love, and Baby Ducks*. New York: Speak/Penguin.

Nancy, Ted L. 2004. *More Letters from a Nut*. London: Ebury Press.

Ness, Patrick. The Knife of Never Letting Go series. London: Walker Books.

Oliver, Lauren. 2011. *Before I Fall*. New York: HarperCollins.

Paterson, Katherine. 2006. *Bridge to Terabithia*. New York: HarperFestival.

Prose, Francine. 2004. *After*. New York: Harper Teen.

Proust, Marcel. [1913–1927] 1982. *Remembrance of Things Past*, 3 vols. New York: Vintage Books.

Remarque, Erich Maria. [1929] 1987. *All Quiet on the Western Front*. New York: Ballantine.

Robertson, Dougal. [1973] 1994. *Survive the Savage Sea*. Dobbs Ferry, NY: Sheridan House.

Roth, Veronica. 2012. *Divergent*. New York: Katherine Tegen Books/HarperCollins.

Rylant, Cynthia. 1993. *But I'll Be Back Again*. New York: HarperCollins.

Satrapi, Marjane. 2004. *Persepolis*. New York: Pantheon.

Smith, Betty. [1943] 2001. *A Tree Grows in Brooklyn*. New York: Harper Perennial Modern Classics.

Thoreau, Henry David. [1854] 1995. *Walden: Or, Life in the Woods*. New York: Dover Publications.

Trumbo, Dalton. [1939] 1984. *Johnny Got His Gun*. New York: Bantam.

Twain, Mark. [1885] 1994. *The Adventures of Huckleberry Finn*. Mineola, NY: Dover Publications.

Vidal, Gore. 1996. *Palimpsest*. New York: Penguin Books.

Vizzini, Ned. 2005. *Be More Chill*. New York: Disney–Hyperion.

————. 2006. *It's Kind of a Funny Story*. New York: Hyperion.

Walls, Jeannette. 2006. *The Glass Castle*. New York: Scribner.

Weisel, Elie. [1960] 2006. *Night,* rev. ed. New York: Hill and Wang.

Whaley, John Corey. 2012. *Where Things Come Back*. New York: Atheneum Books for Young Readers.

Wharton, Edith. [1920] 1997. *The Age of Innocence*. Ware, Hertfordshire, UK: Wordworth Editions.

Whitman, Walt. [1865] 2008. *Drum Taps*. Gloucester, Gloucestershire, UK: Dodo Press.

————. [1855] 2005. *Leaves of Grass*, 150th anniversary edition, ed. David S. Reynolds. New York: Oxford University Press.

Woolf, Virginia. [1927] 1989. *To the Lighthouse*. Orlando, FL: Harcourt.

Wright, Richard. [1944] 2007. *Black Boy*. New York: Harper Perennial Modern Library.

Young, Rusty. 2004. *Marching Powder*. New York: St. Martin's.

Zusak, Markus. 2006. *I Am the Messenger*. New York: Knopf Books for Young Readers.

————. 2007. *The Book Thief*. New York: Alfred A. Knopf.

Index

Dewey, Ben, 329

dialogue, 242–43, 280, 377, 422, 433–35, 444–46

Diary of a Young Girl, The (Frank), 272–74, 476

Dickinson, Emily, 195–97, 320, 559

digital technologies, 31–32, 37, 487

DiGiulian, Elizabeth, 479–80

dining room table talk, 18, 20–21, 98–99, 246

Disreputable History of Frankie Landau-Banks (Lockhart), 97

"DNA" (Genus), 485–86

"Do Not Go Gentle into That Good Night" (Thomas), 387

Doctors Without Borders (nonprofit organization), 530

Dodge, Marshall, 12

"Doing What It Shouldn't" (Moorhead), 498

"Don" (Elkins), 367–68

Donnelly, Jennifer, 274

DonorsChoose, 41, 531

Drum Taps (Whitman), 198

"Dulce et Decorum Est" (Owen), 580

Dybek, Stuart, 472

E

"Eagle, The" (Tennyson), 189

easel, in the workshop, 38–40, 309, 433

Eats, Shoots & Leaves (Truss), 163

"Ebony" (Brown), 345

ebooks, 31–32

"Eclipsed" (Shuster), 472

editing checksheet, 54, 144, 147, 595

editing symbols, 601

Edwards, Jack, 19

efferent mode of reading, 179

Eggers, Dave, 472, 479

"Eight O'Clock" (Housman), 189

Eliot, T. S., 354

Elizabethan sonnet, 390

Elkins, Morganne, 366–68, 412–13, 418–21

Elkins, Parker, 387–88, 478, 538–39

Emerson, Ralph Waldo, 165, 198

Emily (Bedard), 197

"Emily Dickinson and Elvis Presley in Heaven" (Ostrom), 197

"Emily Dickinson's Defunct" (Nelson), 197

"Emily Dickinson" (Pastan), 197

"Emily Dickinson's To-Do List" (Carlisle), 197

engagement and book choice, 21–23

"Enough" (Kelly), 351–52

Entertainment Weekly, 541

environment, classroom, 30–42

essay genre study

class magazine and reading, 528, 529

conclusions, 518, 520–21

criteria for an effective essay, 506–508

defining the problem, 511

Internet search terms, 514

kinds of information, 512–14

launch of, 505–506

leads, 514–17

organizing and planning, 517–18

process for writing, 511–12

sources of model essays, 505

thesis statements and questions, 511

topic generation and selection, 508–11

transitional words and phrases, 518, 519

evaluation

assessment procedure at CTL, 282–83

assigning grades, 308–11

minilesson about self-assessment, 295

portfolio contents checklist, 295–97

reading self-assessment, 290–94

reflect students' day-to-day activity, 282, 300–301

teacher goals for readers, 306–308

teacher goals for writers, 303–306

teacher progress reports, 301, 310

writing self-assessment, 284–90

"Evergreen, The" (Nuki), 398

expectations for reading workshop, 58

expectations for writing workshop, 50–52

"Express Your Inner Dog" (Kelly), 219–20, 221–22

"Extreme Writing Workshop" (student collaboration), 567–69

F

Fahrenheit 451 (Bradbury), 214–15

Fame Monster, The: Deluxe Edition (Lady Gaga), 227

Farmer, Nancy, 297

Farewell to Arms, A (Hemingway), 27